CW01666090

American Cryptology During the Cold War
1945-1989

The Complete Declassified Official Four-Volume History of the NSA

by Thomas R Johnson

Red and Black Publishers, Florida

First published 1995 by the Center for Cryptologic History, Washington DC

Contents

Book I: The Struggle for Centralization 1945-1960

Book II: Centralization Wins 1960-1972

Book III: Retrenchment and Reform, 1972-1980

Book IV: Cryptologic Rebirth 1981-1989

Note

Certain portions of this declassified document have been deleted before release for reasons of national security. These are marked with the notation [censored].

Book I: The Struggle for Centralization 1945-1960

Foreword

The Center for Cryptologic History (CCH) and its predecessors have published thirty-seven volumes—monographs, crisis studies, source documents, bibliographies—concerning the history of signals intelligence and information systems security, the yin and yang of modern cryptology. These publications have treated specific events, organizational issues, and technical developments in peace and war; most have been pioneering efforts, based on original documentation, and, in many cases, are the first history of their particular topic in any venue.

There has been a strong need, however, for a single work to undertake the full sweep of cryptologic history, providing a context into which the more specialized studies may be placed; Such a cryptologic Cook's tour should incorporate the military-political events of our time and the history of interaction between cryptologic organizations and other components of the intelligence community—access to SIGINT and INFOSEC is limited to "insiders," but it is clear that cryptologic operations do not occur in a vacuum.

Thomas R. Johnson's "American Cryptology during the Cold War, 1945-1989" meets these requirements admirably. Drawing on over a decade of study and reflection on cryptologic history, Dr. Johnson deals with three facets of cryptologic history: first he explains how cryptology responded to the landmark events and challenges of the post-World War II era. He next provides profound analysis of how events and personalities affected the development of cryptology institutionally and professionally. Finally, and even better, Dr. Johnson spins a fascinating tale of the success or failure of cryptologic operations in the various crises that have challenged the SIGINT system.

With Books One and Two of this projected four-book work now available, "American Cryptology during the Cold War" is "must reading" for the cryptologic professional. The narrative and analysis in these first two books are essential background for understanding how the cryptologic community progressed to its present configuration. This is the definitive work on American cryptology after World War II.

For readers who may wish to explore American cryptology prior to the modern period, I recommend as a companion piece to the present book, Dr. Ralph E. Weber's "Masked Dispatches: Cryptograms and Cryptology in American History, 1775-1900" (CCH, 1993). Two more useful books with background on pre-World War and World War II cryptology are Frederick D. Parker's "Pearl Harbor Revisited: United States Navy Communications Intelligence, 1924-1941 (CCH, 1994) and Thomas L. Burns's "The Origins of the National Security Agency, 1940-1952" (CCH, 1990).

David A. Hatch, Director
Center for Cryptologic History

Preface

What It Is and What It Is Not

This book is intended to be a general overview of U.S. government cryptology since the end of World War II. It is projected to be a four-book study carrying the story to the end of the Cold War, symbolized by the fall of the Berlin Wall.

I have attempted to include the entire effort, which includes the Service Cryptologic Agencies (as they were once called), as well as certain CIA programs. These organizations comprised almost the totality of the cryptologic efforts of the federal government, although other organizations (FBI is a good example) have occasionally dabbled in the discipline. Because it is comprehensive rather than strictly organizational, it contains information about the field sites, intermediate headquarters and the SCA headquarters themselves. It does not cover in detail the organizational aspects of the creation of the National Security Agency. That is covered in good detail in Thomas L. Burns's book, "The Origins of the National Security Agency: 1940-1952", published in 1990. Thus the coverage of events between 1945 and 1952 is sketchy and simply tries to fill in blanks in the record that the Burns book did not cover.

This is not a history of private or nongovernmental cryptology. Although it covers relationships with our Second and Third Party partners, it does not focus on that aspect either, except as it contributed to the development of our own effort. Our long-standing debt to the British cryptologic effort at GCHQ should not go unnoticed, however. It deserves a separate book.

If you are looking for a history of your specific organization, you will not find it. This is a history of events, not organizations. The importance of the cryptologic contribution to American security is so broad as to obscure individual organizations and, often, the specific people involved. In certain cases, however, I have identified major individual contributors to cryptologic history or those who were, by chance, thrown into momentous events.

Two overarching themes characterized American cryptology from the end of World War II to the end of the first Nixon administration: centralization and expansion. The SIGINT system underwent a period of almost unbroken expansion from 1945 to the American retreat from Southeast Asia. These themes dominate the first two books in the set.

The end of the Vietnam War and the era of the Watergate scandals that followed marked a watershed, and new themes of retrenchment and decentralization marked the period that followed. These will be the themes that open Book III.

Thomas R. Johnson

Chapter 1 Cryptologic Triumph and Reorganization, 1941-1949

"The combined U.S.-U.K. COMINT operation of World War II was perhaps the most successful large-scale intelligence operation in history." — [censored] CIA, 1971

World War II And The Intelligence Revolution

The Second World War began a true "revolution" in intelligence. The impact of intelligence on the strategy and tactics of the Allies (and to a somewhat lesser extent on the Germans and Japanese) was truly revolutionary, and it is just now coming to be recognized for what it was. Through the publication of books like Frederick Winterbotham's "The Ultra Secret" and John Masterman's "The Double Cross System" and by the massive declassfication of war records begun by the British and Americans in 1977, the true extent of this influence is now emerging.

No other intelligence source had the revolutionary impact of SIGINT. World War II was, in the words of historian Walter Laqueur, "a SIGINT war." The influence of SIGINT was so pervasive that it is now hard to imagine how we might have fought the war without it. Even prior to the direct engagement of American and British forces against the Germans and Japanese, two of their most complex ciphers were broken. The British effort at Bletchley Park first produced plaintext reports from the German ENIGMA system in September 1940, the same month that a small Army team under William F. Friedman broke the Japanese diplomatic cipher machine called PURPLE. By February of 1942 the Navy had broken the Japanese Fleet Operational Code, called JN25. In 1943 the Army broke the Water Transport Code, while in 1944 a lucky battlefield retrieval of cipher material allowed the Army to read the Japanese Army codes. When combined with successes in direction Finding, traffic analysis, and the exploitation of plaintext communications, SIGINT yielded a torrent of useful information.

British achievements have come in for the most scrutiny (and praise). We know that Churchill "revelled" in his ability to read Hitler's mail and spent hours pondering on Nazi strategy as revealed in the decrypted messages. The British set up a very efficient and secure system for disseminating SIGINT, the precursor of our SSO (Special Security Officer) system. Always wary of the "blabbermouth" Americans, they insisted that we adopt their system before they would share everything in the SIGINT larder with us. As the Combined Chiefs prepared for Overlord, they knew precisely how the Germans were reacting to the invasion plans and where they were positioning their units for the expected blow. Moreover, once the invasion was launched, they knew what the Germans were doing and were able to adjust accordingly. As Allied troops moved across France, they moved in sync with the gold mine of intelligence which detailed most of the important German military movements. Their intelligence officers must have looked like geniuses—they were able to predict German moves before they happened and could advise commanders how to react. If every dog has its day, this was the day of the G-2, the military intelligence officer. The product of breaking high-grade ciphers was called ULTRA, and it was so good that when it was not available, as it was not at the Battle of the Bulge, the G2 corps scarcely knew what to do. A few predicted the German offensive, but most did not. They were wedded to the SSO and the bonanza of information that he could provide.

The Pacific was the American theater, and the U.S. was as successful there as the British were in Europe. Navy cryptanalysts broke JN25 in time for Admiral Nimitz to use it in the Battle of Coral Sea in May of 1942. The success of strategic SIGINT was so important that Nimitz had become a permanent convert. When the cryptologists at Pearl Harbor came to Nimitz with information outlining a much bigger battle shaping up in the central Pacific, the admiral was quick to believe and quick to act. To his dying day he credited SIGINT with the key to the victory at Midway. This turned the war in the Pacific completely around and launched Nimitz on his Central Pacific campaign which took him to Okinawa. He considered SIGINT as an absolutely critical component, and he learned to use information from both the high-grade cipher traffic and the plaintext messages and operator chatter. Some of his subordinates were as successful as Nimitz in the use of this intelligence, some were not. But it is hard to argue with results.

SIGINT and MacArthur had a turbulent marriage. The commander in the Southwest Pacific had outstanding success in using SIGINT on some occasions, the most conspicuous success coming in his 1944 New Guinea campaign. There were also some failures resulting from several causes. His staff never came to trust SIGINT as did that of Nimitz. When they did use it, it was sometimes hard to get it melded into the battle plan, as MacArthur was a classical intuitive decision maker. Jurisdictional disputes between MacArthur and the War Department in Washington caused him to come to distrust this strange SSO lash-up which he could not control because it did not work for him.

In the battle for the sea lanes, SIGINT again played a decisive role. The Japanese merchant marine was devastated largely because its movements were being given away in the Water Transport Code. Sinking the defenseless and slow-moving merchant vessels was relatively easy when their movements were known beforehand. In the Atlantic, the U.S. and the British used decrypted ENIGMA messages to track German U-boats and to drive their wolf packs from the sea lanes. This was not quite as easy as going after merchantmen, and the marriage between SIGINT information and operational procedures to effect a kill represented a very high level of military and technological expertise. It may have been the most difficult and delicate use of SIGINT during the war.

One other wartime accomplishment would become significant in later years. In 1944 the British and Americans established a Target Intelligence Committee (TICOM) to interrogate captured German COMINT personnel. The major objective was COMSEC—to determine how well the German cryptologists had exploited Allied communications. The flip side of that effort was COMINT—to see how well the Germans were doing against other, and particularly Soviet, communications. TICOM was at Bletchley Park, headquarters for the British cryptologic service, Government Code and Cipher School (GC&CS). Six teams of American and British COMINTers were dispatched to the battlefields of the Continent. They sent their "take" to the Document Center at GC&CS. The original documents remained there while the microfilm copies were sent on to Washington. TICOM teams also captured equipment. One-of-a-kind equipment remained at GC&CS, while duplicates were sent to the United States.

The new system was so successful that teams were established in the Pacific, with the British taking the lead in Southeast Asia, the United States in the Central Pacific and Japan, and joint American and Australian teams in Rabaul and Borneo. Although TICOM was formally dissolved in November of 1945, American and British experts continued to exploit the material for years afterward, and TICOM was later re-created in the United States as TAREX (Target Exploitation), minus British participation.

If the strength of American SIGINT was in providing militarily useful information, its weakness was in its organization. The Army and Navy were at constant loggerheads over the control of cryptology, and at times the factional disputes were little short of catastrophic. British historian Ronald Lewin, a great admirer of American technical ingenuity which yielded the SIGINT bonanza, was frankly contemptuous of our inability to get along: "The old antagonism and suspicion between Army and Navy persisted in a manner that may at times seem infantile, until it be remembered that tribal loyalty, narrowness of vision, and sheer egocentricity can make even the most senior and hardened officers occasionally enter a second childhood."

Army and Navy cryptologic organizations had a long and inglorious history of failing to coordinate their efforts, dating back to the 1920s. In 1940, when the Army's success in breaking Japanese diplomatic cipher systems became known to the Navy, there ensued lengthy and difficult negotiations to determine how the effort was to be divided. They finally arrived at a Solomonic solution by which the Army processed Japanese diplomatic traffic originating (i.e., cipher date) on even days of the month while the Navy would process traffic from odd days. This resulted in a fair division politically, but from the standpoint of cryptanalytic continuity it was a horror. To make matters even worse, there was in those days no thought, no concept, of centralized and coordinated intelligence analysis. What little analysis and interpretation was done (and there was very little indeed) was accomplished by each service on the traffic which it had decrypted, leaving for each a checkerboard pattern of information in which every other day was left out. This almost inconceivable situation persisted until 1942, when diplomatic traffic was, by mutual agreement, left to the Army, while the Navy concentrated on Japanese naval material.

The disaster at Pearl Harbor resulted in a thoroughgoing Army internal investigation. Secretary of War Henry Stimson picked Yale lawyer Alfred McCormack to lead the way. McCormack discovered a scandalously incompetent Army G2 and a nonexistent SIGINT analysis and dissemination system. He set up a separate system called Special Branch, Military Intelligence Division, and was picked as the first deputy. (Colonel Carter W. Clarke became the first commander.) At the same time, the Army and Navy arrived at a joint modus operandi regarding the division of overall SIGINT responsibilities. Each service was to work what we now call "counterpart" targets. Since there was little in the way of Japanese Army traffic to work, the Army took on the task of diplomatic intercept. The third partner was the FBI, which shared with the Navy the task of working Western Hemisphere agent and clandestine traffic. These three were to be the only participants in SIGINT for the duration of the war. Roosevelt's directive of July 1942 specifically excluded the FCC (Federal Communications Commission), Office of Censorship, and the OSS (Office of Strategic Services) from SIGINT production.

At the same time a standing committee of Army, Navy, and FBI COMINT officials was established. It met only a few times and had little lasting impact on organizational matters. Meetings were frequently marred by vituperative arguments, especially between Navy and FBI, which were supposed to be sharing Western Hemisphere clandestine traffic. It was not cryptology's finest hour. Meanwhile, the COMINT activities of the FCC and Censorship Bureau continued virtually unabated. Only the OSS seems to have been temporarily frozen out of the COMINT community. Resurrected after the war as the CIA, it exacted revenge over a period of many years for having been excluded from wartime cryptology.

The Army and Navy cryptologic organizations, Signal Security Agency (SSA) and OP-20-G, respectively, found cooperation difficult. The Army was willing to share everything it had with the Navy, but OP-20-G would not reciprocate. What finally brought matters to a head was the breaking of the Japanese Army code in early 1944. This produced information vital to the Navy in the Southwest Pacific. SSA decided to withhold information from it until the Navy agreed to expand cooperation. The Navy quickly came around, and the result was a wartime agreement signed by Army Chief of Staff General George Catlett Marshall and Chief of Naval Operations Admiral Earnest J. King. Called the Marshall-King Agreement, it provided for the total exchange of COMINT materials (but at the Washington level only).

It quickly fell apart, and for a time this informal agreement seemed a dead letter. But the need to cooperate was by then so vital that the two services were driven to a more permanent solution. Thus was formed the Army-Navy Communications Intelligence Coordinating Committee (ANCICC) in April of 1944. The committee was to coordinate and settle "such controversial matters as can be resolved without reference to higher authority," a plain attempt to keep disagreements out of the offices of Marshall and King. Although the Navy was consistently the more parochial of the two services in COMINT matters, the "godfather" of this cooperation was almost certainly Joseph Wenger, a naval commander and career cryptologist within OP-20-G. Meanwhile, coordination under the terms of the Marshall-King Agreement continued its bumpy course, now underpinned by this policy committee.

In late 1944 the Navy (probably Wenger] once again suggested improving cooperation. This time they proposed creating a new board called the Army-Navy Communications Intelligence Board (ANCIB). Representation would be of a higher level—instead of the heads of the cryptologic organizations, the members were to be the heads of intelligence and communications for the two services. The board would be formally established (ANCICC was informal) and would be approved by Marshall and King. Although the Army initially answered "No," it later changed its mind, and ANCIB became official in March 1945. ANCICC became a working committee of ANCIB, insuring that the heads of COMINT organizations would continue to meet. To keep COMINT out of the JCS arena (in order to tighten security), ANCIB reported directly to the Chairman of the Joint Chiefs of Staff, rather than through the Joint Staff.

FBI was not invited to be a member of the board, a deliberate move which was occasioned by Navy-FBI friction over the control of clandestine intelligence. But in December 1945, the State Department was invited, and ANCIB became STANCIB. This recognized the existence of a small COMINT exploitation unit at State and implicitly acknowledged that State would have to be invited if ANCIB were to represent the United States in postwar COMINT negotiations with the British. In 1946 the board changed name once again, to USCIB (the United States Communications Intelligence Board), a lineal predecessor of today's National Foreign Intelligence Board. At virtually the same time, the newly created Central Intelligence Group, soon to change its name to CIA, accepted an invitation to join. Through all this, ANCICC changed to STANCICC and then to USCICC.

No matter what the name of the board, cooperation remained purely voluntary, and all decisions required unanimity. There was no higher authority imposing central control of COMINT. The British, who had a unified COMINT service under the Government Code and Cipher School (GCCS), were scandalized. During the war they were forced to deal separately with the three organizations with COMINT interests—the Army, Navy, and FBI. British officials regarded negotiations with the Americans as a little like dealing with the former colonies after the American Revolution—disorganized and frustrating at times, but they could still play one off against another to achieve their objectives.

The Way COMINT Was Organized At The End Of The War

The cryptologic system that emerged from World War II was profoundly and tenaciously decentralized. Instead of a central control (like NSA) and Service Cryptologic Elements (SCEs) as we know them, there were only the separate COMINT organizations of the Army, Navy, and FBI. Naval COMINT was under an organization called the Supplemental Radio Branch and designated OP-20-G, part of Naval Communications. There was a headquarters in Washington called CSAW (Communications Supplementary Activity, Washington) where centralized processing functions were performed, chiefly against the German naval ENIGMA problem. For the Pacific theater there were virtually independent processing centers: one in Hawaii, called FRUPAC (Fleet Radio Unit, Pacific); one at Melbourne, Australia, called FRUMEL (Fleet Radio Unit, Melbourne) and, late in the war, one on Guam, designated RAGFOR (Radio Analysis Group, Forward).

Naval COMINT had grown through the years, From its beginnings in 1924 with one officer, Laurance Safford, and a single civilian, Agnes Driscoll, OP-20-G had by 1941 increased to 730 bodies. During the war the number of intercept sites in the Pacific increased from four to eight, and the receivers allocated to Japanese intercept increased from 68 to 775. Shipborne collection began with one operator and one receiver in the Pacific in 1941, but by 1945 there were eight shipborne operator teams with 120 receivers. Yet in 1945 the entire system quickly collapsed. OP-20-G closed ten of its sixteen intercept and DF stations. When the war ended, the German cipher exploitation section went from over 2,000 to only 200.

Since its creation, OP-20-G headquarters had been in the Navy Building on Constitution Avenue in Washington. COMINT success required more people and more space to work the traffic, and the Navy began looking for a separate facility for its most secret activity. They found it in the fall of 1942, at a girl's school on Nebraska Avenue called the Mount Vernon Seminary for Women. The Navy bought it for about $1 million and began converting the ivy-covered red brick structure into a military facility. One of the first things they did was to build new barracks for the 4,000 WAVES (Women Accepted for Volunteer Emergency Service) who were brought in primarily to operate the "bombes" that deciphered ENIGMA messages from German submarines.

The Army, too, took over a girls' school. In 1942 Signal Intelligence Service (SIS) was, like OP-20-G, looking for a new and larger home. Then it found Arlington Hall, a junior college located in the rolling hills of suburban Arlington. The school was big on horses and equestrian pursuits but had always been short on cash. Its founder, a Dr. Martin, went bankrupt in 1929, and the school limped along on a hand-to-mouth existence until it was mercifully extinguished by the Army. Paying $650,000 for the property, SIS acquired it in June of 1942 and moved from the Munitions Building, which stood beside the Navy Building on Constitution Avenue.

Organizationally, SIS was similar to OP-20-G. Although it changed its name to Signal Security Agency (SSA) in 1943, it remained part of the Signal Corps. In September 1945 it was finally severed from Army communications, attaining status as an independent command called Army Security Agency (ASA), an implicit recognition of its contributions to winning the war. Elevated status gave it a two-star command billet and an independent position in the Army hierarchy, but it now took its operational direction from Army intelligence. This placed it back in roughly the same position that it had been when, in the 1920s, it had been named MI-8 and had been under G2.

For SIS, intercept work was more difficult than for OP-20-G because the Army lacked geographic access. During the early 1930s, SIS relied on the telegraph cable companies to provide it with message traffic. The earliest SIS efforts to develop intercept sites resulted in stations in Hawaii and Panama later in the decade, and by 1938 SIS had additional sites at the Presidio in San Francisco, Fort Sam Houston in Texas, and Fort Hughes in Manila. In 1942 SIS attempted to hear German transmissions from a new site (USM-1) at Vint Hill Farms in northern Virginia. By the end of the war, SSA had eleven intercept stations. The force at Arlington Hall numbered 7,848, of whom 5,661 were civilians.

To Army cryptology, as to the Navy, peace was devastating. Most of the work force at Arlington Hall left civilian government service, and within days the halls were almost empty. Intercept sites overseas were suddenly confronted with no Japanese or German intercept mission. One former soldier described the experience as being left stranded on Okinawa with no Japanese mission to copy and no instructions on a follow-on assignment. His unit eventually moved to Seoul, relocated to a former Japanese communications station, and there got a new mission—Soviet and Chinese Communist communications. European units tackled French and Greek missions, and, by mid-1946 nearly half the Army's end product was based on the intercept of French communications.

The late 1940s were a period of damaging retrenchment. The Army and Navy cryptologic organizations that began the Soviet mission had little experience, less money, and no expertise. Yet ASA was able to survive better than OP-20-G. The Army had relied historically on civilians, and many of the best, including William Friedman, Frank Rowlett, Abraham Sinkov, and Solomon Kullback, stayed on. Missing the excitement of wartime cryptology, others drifted back to Arlington Hall after brief, humdrum civilian careers. The Navy, which had relied on uniformed cryptologists, lost a far higher number to civilian life and found the transition to peacetime a difficult one. In 1947 ASA and OP-20-G were joined by yet a third cryptologic service, that of the newly created Air Force. The Army Air Corps had actually established its SIGINT service in the Pacific in 1944. The Air Force acquired an early reputation for parochialism and interservice rivalry. The feuding led Carter Clarke, then head of Special Branch of Militar lntelligence Service, to write in June 1944 that "the Air Force insists that these [censored] operate only for the Force and insists further that no personnel can be attached or detached therefrom; neither should the theaters give them any operational directives in the sense that we think of it." The first Air Force unit in the Pacific was the [censored] which began operations in 1944 in New Guinea.

When the independent Air Force was created in 1947, there was no direct reference to cryptologic activities, and for a time ASA continued to provide these to the nascent Air Force. Yet the Air Force was determined to establish its own capability. Certain Air Force generals were aware of the contributions of COMINT during the war. One in particular, Hoyt S. Vandenberg, who was later to become Air Force chief of staff, was convinced that the Air Force had to have its own cryptologic service. He saw how the British controlled cryptology in Europe and felt that it was essential to get this under American, and particularly Air Force, control.

In early 1948 the Air Force fashioned a transition agreement with ASA. The latter established an Air Force Security Group within its headquarters at Arlington Hall to oversee the transfer. Three [censored] and eight COMSEC units were turned over to the Air Force. The Air Force role was defined as mobile and tactical, and ASA continued to operate all fixed sites. A set number of ASA officers (thirty-two) became blue-suiters, and this group became the "founding fathers" of Air Force cryptology. Air Force cryptologists were to continue to train at ASA schools and were to contribute instructors and financial support as soon as the Air Force had a budget of its own. Significantly, the Air Force assumed all responsibility for "the investigation for intelligence purposes of all types of electronic emissions relating to radar, radio control of guided missiles and pilotless aircraft, proximity fuses, electronic navigation systems, infrared equipment and related subjects." In other words, the Air Force was to take the ELINT and electronic warfare missions, which were at the time too new to even have a name. Needing equipment but not yet having a budget, the Air Force arranged for the transfer of equipment from the Army, which turned out to be castoff receivers and antennas that ASA no longer wanted.

On 20 October 1948, the new Air Force cryptologic organization was officially established as the U.S. Air Force Security Service (USAFSS), still located at Arlington Hall. It was a major air command, responsible to neither intelligence nor communications. Thus from its earliest existence the Air Force accorded a loftier organizational position to its cryptologic service than did the other, more senior, services. And the Air Force did something else that was unprecedented. In May of 1949 it moved completely out of Washington. Security Service set up shop at Brooks Air Force Base outside of San Antonio, Texas. The move was calculated to remove USAFSS from geographical proximity to the central control authority for COMINT—at the time the Coordinator for Joint Operations, shortly to become the Armed Forces Security Agency. Thus USAFSS hoped to be insulated from any sort of outside control, which it regarded as bald interference in its affairs.

The CJO

The lack of central control for COMINT was the most pressing problem of the postwar years. Cooler heads recognized that the uncoordinated and fractionalized efforts that had existed since the 1920s simply had to be better controlled. They had already agreed on a committee system, at that time called STANCIB and STANCICC. The committees could and did arrive at policy decisions which, in the case of unanimity of the board, were binding on the services. What was still lacking, though, was an executive organization to carry out the routine business of central coordination.

In early 1946 the Navy proposed such an executive body. They called it the Coordinator for Joint Operations, and it was to work out routine intercept coverage and processing responsibilities between the services. The Navy got Army concurrence, and on 15 February STANCIB approved the proposal. The Coordinator for Joint Operations, or CJO, was born.

The CJO was to implement general policies on allocation of joint tasks as approved by STANCIB. It was to be assisted by three groups: the Joint Intercept Control Group (JICG), the Joint Processing Allocation Group (JPAG) and the Joint Liaison Group (JLG). The CJO agreement owed its existence to the two most influential sponsors, Joseph Wenger (who commanded OP-20-G) and Preston Corderman (chief, ASA) for the Army, and it was in those days referred to as the "Corderman-Wenger Agreement." But when the first CJO was appointed, it turned out to be Colonel Harold G. Hayes, a long-time Army COMINTer and the new chief of ASA.

The first task of the CJO was to allocate intercept tasks. This was not as easy as it appeared. Agreement was reached that counterpart targets were to be copied by the respective U.S. service cryptologic organization. All other targets, even those being intercepted entirely by a single service, were to be considered "joint." The CJO then reallocated the intercept responsibilities. This had the largest potential impact on the resources of the Navy, which during World War II, as previously discussed, completely gave up "joint" targets (with a few exceptions) to the Army.

Intercept allocations really got down to priorities. With limited resources (and 1946 resources were constrained), the key to obtaining copy was in the priority system. In September of that year USCICC decided to hold monthly meetings to consider priority problems. By this process a standing priority list, in rather general terms, was established. The CJO then made intercept assignments to positions in the field. When the CJO assigned a joint case to a position it controlled (i.e., one which had been turned over by one of the Service Cryptologic Agencies, as they were then called) there was no problem. But occasionally the CJO assigned a joint target to a service-protected position. This invariably met with resistance, and the CJO had no enforcement authority. The Service Cryptologic Agencies (SCAs), for their part, insured that counterpart positions were manned with the best operators, that they were never left uncovered, and that technical data were always up to date. In short, if a target had to be slighted, it was likely to be the joint target. The servicemen never forgot whom they worked for.

CJO also allocated processing tasks through the JPAG. Since people and equipment for processing were in very short supply, processing on each major target was to be done in only one place—either Arlington Hall or Nebraska Avenue—no matter which service collected the traffic. In those days communications systems were mutually exclusive rather than common and interlocking, and once traffic was intercepted by one service, it had to pass vertically through those communications channels all the way to Washington. This meant that there had to be communications between Nebraska Avenue and Arlington Hall so that the traffic could be exchanged, and under CJO a teleprinter link was set up. The services had a great deal of difficulty talking to each other (electrically, not to mention in person), and it was a real effort to establish common cryptographic gear for interoperability. In the late 1940s this process was just getting started.

Communications security policy was, if possible, even more difficult to meld into a cohesive system than was COMINT. Through the war each service handled its own COMSEC matters with little reference to joint policy. In the Army, ASA was responsible for both COMINT and COMSEC, a development substantially influenced by such technicians as Frank Rowlett and William Friedman. In the Navy, COMSEC had begun within Captain Laurence Safford's embrace, but it had eventually become part of a separate organization under Naval Communications, called OP-20-K.

After the war, COMSEC policy was allocated by an unregistered executive order to a Cryptographic Security Board consisting of the secretaries of state, war, and navy. This very high-level board quickly became moribund, and the real actor in COMSEC policy was the Joint Communications-Electronics Committee (JCEC) and its subordinate, the Joint Security and Cryptographic Panel. When COMINT was unified in 1949 under the Armed Forces Security Agency (AFSA), COMSEC was still decentralized.

The CJO was a compromise between those who wanted tight central control and those who wanted to continue a loose arrangement. It was voluntary, as had been all of its predecessors. It never resolved the conflict over joint targets, much to the dismay of the State Department, which was the principal customer for most of those targets. But the establishment of an executive organization was the first step in creating an organization to control COMINT. It didn't work, but it pointed the way toward the future.

The Cryptologic Allies

America's SIGINT relationship with Great Britain also dates to World War II. In July 1940, the British ambassador to Washington, Lord Lothian, proposed that the two nations exchange information on, among other things, technological secrets related to "submarine detection and radio traffic." This appears to have pertained generally to SIGINT, but the wording of the now famous Lothian Letter did not really say precisely what he (or Churchill) meant. It also appears that day-to-day intelligence cooperation predated the Lothian Letter, for in April of the same year President Roosevelt met Churchill's special envoy William Stephenson to discuss a plan for secret cooperation between the FBI and British secret intelligence. According to a fascinating account in the somewhat unreliable book by William Stevenson (unrelated to the wartime William Stephenson), it was at that meeting that Stephenson informed Roosevelt of British progress in breaking the German ENIGMA system. (This might have happened but was quite out of character for the security-conscious British.) This meeting did, in fact, lead to the establishment of the British Security Coordination (BSC) in Washington, with Stephenson in charge. During its early days this organization dealt primarily in HUMINT and counterintelligence.

The Lothian Letter was followed in August by a visit by Sir Henry Tizard, scientific advisor to the Royal Air Force (RAF). This inaugurated a series of technical discussions on a wide variety of subjects. Tizard, not a SIGINTer, was mainly interested in discussing radar and other such technical developments. At the same time, the United States sent to Britain a delegation consisting of Brigadier General George V. Strong (Chief of War Plans), Brigadier General Delos Emmons (United States Army Air Forces—USAAF), and Rear Admiral Robert Ghormley (Assistant Chief of Naval Operations). Though the discussions were to be general, it appears that Strong had, or thought he had, considerable latitude to discuss cryptologic intelligence. On 5 September he cabled Washington to propose a total exchange of information on SIGINT product and technical matters (i.e., cryptanalysis). Back in Washington there was a good bit of concern. The Navy said "No," while the Army vacillated. Their top cryptanalyst, William F. Friedman, was consulted, Friedman favored the exchange.

So initial hesitance was eventually converted to approval, and on the day after Christmas 1940, the Army decided once and for all to initiate a complete cryptologic exchange with the British. In February 1941, Captain Abraham Sinkov and Lieutenant Leo Rosen of the Armys SIGINT organization, along with Lieutenant Robert Weeks and Ensign Prescott Currier of the Navy, sailed to London. They brought with them a PURPLE Analog, a machine the Army was using to break the keys for the Japanese diplomatic cipher system. They had instructions to initiate a complete exchange of cryptanalytic and SIGINT information.

The British appear to have been flabbergasted. Never had they anticipated that the United States would simply walk in and plunk down their most secret cryptanalytic machine. This was, indeed, an intelligence exchange worth the money. But they were cautious. They did not tell the Army and Navy emissaries everything they were doing, and they did not show them the ENIGMA operation at first. Agreed upon in principal in 1940, the complete exchange of cryptologic information and techniques progressed slowly through the war. Once again the Navy, reluctant in the beginning, produced the more beneficial exchange. This was due largely to historical circumstances. The Army was still mobilizing and clearly would not see action in Europe until at least late 1942, if not later. But the Navy was already engaging German U-boats in the North Atlantic. They and the British had worked out a convoy system, and daily cooperation in intelligence was essential to avoiding wolf packs. Thus it was that Commander Roger Winn, who headed the Operational Intelligence Center in the Admiralty, convinced the U.S. Navy that it must have something similar. Prompted by Winn, the U.S. Navy established the mysterious organization called F-21 (Atlantic Section, Combat Intelligence Division, U.S. Fleet) and its still more mysterious submarine tracking room. The latter used all sources of intelligence, including U-boat positions obtained by ENIGMA decrypts, passed to them by the British.

The arrangement worked well at first, but in February 1942 the Germans introduced the four-rotor ENIGMA, and the British at Bletchley were unable to read it. The Americans were already suspicious because the British kept the cryptanalytic techniques so closely held. So in 1942 the Navy embarked on a project to break the ENIGMA themselves, in defiance of British protests. Colonel John Tiltman, a temporary GC&CS resident in Washington, finally convinced the British that the Navy would proceed with or without British help. In June 1942, after Tiltman's intervention, the Navy sent two expert cryptanalysts, Lieutenant R. B. Ely and Lieutenant Junior Grade Joseph Eachus, to Bletchley to learn all they could about ENIGMA processing. In September the Navy began a project to build a four-rotor ENIGMA processor (called a "bombe" by the British). When, in the summer of 1943, the Navy moved to its new headquarters on Nebraska Avenue, a major portion of the space was reserved for the bombes, which were being employed to break the keys on German submarine ENIGMA traffic. In the end, the two nations drove the U-boats from the North Atlantic, based in part on information provided by the bombe project.

Meanwhile, the Army was having its own problems on the SIGINT front. Increasingly suspicious of British reluctance to share cryptanalytic techniques, they retaliated by refusing to share information on voice ciphony equipment with Alan Turing. Since Turing was one of the top Bletchley scientists (and has been given credit for developing the first British bombe), this was a very serious breakdown in cooperation. It became the subject of a long series of exchanges between General George Marshall and Sir John Dill (chairman of the British Joint Chiefs of Staff], and at one point it seemed possible that the two sides might break COMINT relations. The dispute was resolved in 1943 when the British agreed to allow a total technical exchange. The agreement was hammered out during a series of sessions between Military Intelligence Service and Commander Sir Edward Travis, who headed GC&CS, during Travis's trip to Washington in May. The paper specified that the United States would be responsible for the COMINT problem in the Far East, while the British would worry about Europe. To implement this, it was agreed that the Americans would send a team of cryptologists to Bletchley to work side by side with the British in all aspects of COMINT, including cryptanalysis of the ENIGMA. That way the Americans would gain technical expertise on the system without mounting a competing cryptanalytic effort on the American side of the Atlantic.

To begin the new relationship, the Army sent a three-man team consisting of Colonel Alfred McCormack, William Friedman, and Lieutenant Colonel Telford Taylor to Bletchley. By mutual agreement, Taylor was left behind in London to serve as a liaison officer and to act as a funnel for British COMINT being sent to the War Department in Washington. Taylor's job was not easy, as there was a good deal of second-guessing the British forthrightness in the exchange. But as the war progressed it became smoother and eventually became a very open exchange of highly sensitive information.

With the Axis almost defeated, the thoughts of cryptologists in 1945 turned with increasing frequency to the Soviet Union. Both nations had maintained rudimentary efforts against the "Communist menace" since the 1920s, and they both kept small efforts even during the war. In June of 1945 ANCIB proposed to the British that they extend their wartime cooperation to the intercept and exploitation of their erstwhile but distrusted ally. They called the project BOURBON, and it was kept compartmented for the obvious reason that the Soviets were still officially on our side. The arrangement was largely informal and involved the exchange of liaison units on both sides of the Atlantic.

But in September, with the war officially over, the U.S. had a legal problem. Could it now continue to collaborate with its British allies? Clearly, the American cryptologists, good as they had become, still regarded GC&CS with a certain awe. In many cryptanalytic areas the British were still ahead of us, and their organization of the COMINT system was superb. And of course there was the problem of the Soviet Union. Already the wartime alliance had disintegrated. In September of 1945 both the Army and Navy suggested to President Truman that collaboration with the British continue for the present "in view of the disturbed conditions of the world and the necessity of keeping informed of the technical developments and possible hostile intentions of foreign nations. . . ." In reply, Truman signed a brief, single-sentence note sent to him by the Joint Chiefs of Staff: "The Secretary of War and the Secretary of the Navy are hereby authorized to direct the Chief of Staff, U.S. Army, Commander-in-Chief, U.S. Fleet, and Chief of Naval Operations to continue collaboration in the field of communication intelligence between the United States Army and Navy and the British, and to extend, modify, or discontinue this collaboration, as determined to be in the best interests of the United States."

Now that the American side was officially unleashed to collaborate with the British, it seemed necessary to write a bilateral agreement for the postwar years. After months of meetings and conferences, the two sides sat down in March 1946 to sign the British-U.S., or BRUSA, Agreement. The paper which charted the future course of both countries was only four pages long. (The policy conference at which it was signed was followed by a technical conference which wrote all the fine print appearing later as annexes and appendices.) [censored]

With the signing of the BRUSA Agreement, the BOURBON liaison offices on both sides of the Atlantic became representatives of STANCIB and LSIB, [censored] The BOURBON officer, Commander Grant Manson, was invested with the rather cumbersome title of U.S. Liaison Officer, London SIGINT Centre (LSIC, as GC&CS was then known)—or USLO LSIC. He reported to STANCIB through the deputy coordinator for Liaison, part of the new CJO structure. In early 1946 the British moved LSIC from its wartime location at Bletchley to Eastcote, outside London, and began using a new title, Government Communications Headquarters, or GCHQ. Space for Manson was provided at Eastcote. The BOURBON liaison office had maintained an office in London, and Manson had to cover two locations, in Eastcote and London. (This situation continues to this day, with NSA holding offices in both London and Cheltenham.) USLO never controlled the TICOM group, which also found quarters at Eastcote.

The British, meanwhile, had a more difficult problem. While the U.S. dealt with only one COMINT organization, GCHQ, the British had two—the Army at Arlington Hall Station and the Navy at Nebraska Avenue. Not wishing to choose, the British diplomatically located their liaison officer in the State Department building in downtown Washington. (They did, however, maintain a technical staff at Arlington Hall.) Their first liaison officer was Colonel Patrick Marr-Johnson, who had signed the BRUSA Agreement for the British side. When he retired in 1949, he was succeeded by Tiltman, who was already well known to the Americans and had served for a time as Travis's deputy at GC&CS. This began a practice, continued to this day, of assigning very senior cryptologic officials to the respective liaison offices, and the USLO eventually became SUSLO—Senior U.S. Liaison Officer.

And where were the British Dominions in all this? They were mentioned in the BRUSA Agreement, and it was agreed that they would not be termed Third Parties, but they were not direct and immediate partners in 1946. Arrangements that Great Britain might make with them would be communicated to STANCIB. STANCIB, in turn, would make no arrangement with a Dominion without coordination with LSIB. Thus the now-famous UKUSA Agreement was not that at all; at least to begin with. It was a BRUSA Agreement. How it became the UKUSA Agreement was a development that spanned another eight years.

Of the three dominions with which the Americans eventually associated, the relationship with Canada began first. Canadian-American SIGINT cooperation appears to have begun in 1940, in the form of service-to-service collaboration between the respective armies and navies. These decentralized arrangements were eventually overtaken by a centralized relationship centering on the Examination Unit of the National Research Council, established in 1941 as one of those clever cover terms denoting a Canadian SIGINT organization. Its purpose was to decode traffic to and from the Vichy delegation in Ottawa. This unit's control was gradually broadened until it was the dominant force in Canadian cryptology. (It was the linear predecessor of the postwar organization Communications Branch, National Research Council [CBNRC] and its successor, Communications Security Establishment [CSE].) By 1943 it had its own submarine tracking room and was receiving plots from the British based on ENIGMA decrypts. When the British began cooperating with the U.S. in 1941, they requested that the U.S. bring the Examination Unit into the scope of the cooperation.

But the Americans were leery. They knew that the Examination Unit had been established by Herbert O. Yardley, the renegade American cryptologist who had published cryptologic secrets in 1931 in "The American Black Chamber". The Signal Intelligence Service, which had been victimized by Yardley's revelations, informed the British that they were willing to cooperate only if Yardley were let go. The British, holding no brief for Yardley, had the Canadians get rid of him, and collaboration with the Americans flowered. By April of 1942 details of the Canadian-American cooperation were hammered out. Collaboration was particularly close in direction finding (DF) of German naval vessels.

[censored] But the United States was suspicious; Canada had just been through a major spy scandal, the Gouzenko affair (chapter 4), and USCIB wanted to go slow. Making matters worse was the head of the Canadian policy committee on COMINT, a rather prickly character [censored] refused for several years to adopt some of the security procedures which the United States and Great Britain had agreed upon at the BRUSA Conference. Moreover, while the United States wanted a formal document on COMINT cooperation, [censored] did not. After several years of very difficult negotiations, the two countries finally agreed to exchange letters between [censored] and USCIB chairman Major General C. P. Cabell. Thus [censored] won the battle of the legal documentation while the United States got its way on security procedures.

Furthest from the mainstream were the Australians. British-Australian COMINT collaboration appears to have begun in the late 1930s when a small Australian cryptographic organization under the Director of Naval Intelligence began working with the British Far Eastern Combined Bureau (FECB) in Singapore. In early 1940 an Australian naval commander named T.E. Nave set up the nucleus of an Australian SIGINT group in Melbourne, which was the origin of the modern Australian SIGINT organization. Its most important organization was the Central Bureau, set up in April 1942 as a combined Australian-American COMINT group. When the Americans departed in 1945, the Australian remnant of Central Bureau became Defence Signals Bureau (DSB).

The British were determined that DSB should enjoy the same status on BOURBON as the Canadian, and, immediately after the war, began including the Australians in their technical exchanges. But in 1947 this procedure became embroiled in a lengthy dispute over Australian security practices. The procedures in dispute were arcane, and the origins were almost as difficult to fathom, but both apparently originated with a spy scandal.

In 1947 SIS succeeded in decrypting some KGB messages which had been sent more than a year earlier and which contained certain classified British military estimates. The messages came from the Soviet embassy in Canberra, and it was immediately assumed that an Australian was passing classified information. The British, alerted by the Americans, sent Sir Percy

Sillitoe, chief of British Secret Service, to Australia to discuss this with the prime minister. Sir Percy was under instructions to conceal the origins of the information, and when the prime minister, a Laborite named Chifley, demanded proof, Sillitoe mumbled something rather lame about a possible mole. After considerable discussion, Chifley agreed to establish a new Australian security organization, called the Australian Security Intelligence Organization.

With the Australian security house supposedly in order, the British prime minister, Clement Attlee, intervened with President Truman to get a new hearing of the Australian matter. Attlee complained in a letter to Truman that: "The intermingling of American and British knowledgde in all these fields is so great that to be certain of denying American classified information to the Australians, we should have to deny them the greater part of our own reports. We should thus be placed in a disagreeable dilemma of having to choose between cutting off relations with the United States in defence questions or cutting off relations with Australia."

With matters at the crisis level, Attlee proposed to Truman that Sir Francis Shedden, the powerful and respected Australian defense minister, visit the United States to plead the case. Truman accepted, and Shedden visited Washington in April. But he was unable to sway USCIB, and the British were back to their dilemma—whether to choose the United States or the Commonwealth as allies. In 1949 the outcome was anything but certain.

Then one of those unexpected quirks of fate intervened which was to save the day: the Labor government under Chifley went down to defeat at the polls, and Robert Menzies formed a new Liberal-Country Party coalition in December. The conservative Menzies was able to successfully disassociate his government from the leftist elements of the Labor government. This was critical since the actual source of the leaks was known (through the VENONA project; see chapter 4) to be two leftists within the Australian diplomatic corps. With a Conservative government in power, USCIB authorized a limited resumption of cryptologic exchange with Australia. Full resumption of ties did not occur until 1953. The incident tarnished American-Australian intelligence cooperation for years and caused a serious rift with Britain which was made worse just a few years later with the Klaus Fuchs case and the Burgess and McClean defections. It also had a deleterious affect on early U.S SIGINT efforts against the People's Republic of China (PRC).

By 1953 relations had warmed to the point where Australia was reincorporated as a full COMINT partner. The foundations of the Australian participation in the UKUSA Agreement (the name BRUSA was changed at British request a year later) came at the Melbourne Tripartite Conference of September 1953. [censored]

New Zealand came in as a fifth partner, [censored] New Zealand had contributed mainly DF to the Allied cryptologic effort in World War II and had sent people to Australia to serve with the Commonwealth effort in Brisbane. [censored]

Chapter 2 AFSA and the Creation of NSA

The formation of AFSA resulted from both technical and budgetary causes. The technical concerns were first surfaced within the Army Security Agency (ASA) over the conclusions of a study on World War II German SIGINT done by the Target Intelligence Committee (TICOM—see chapter 1). TICOM had studied the German failure to crack high-grade Allied codes and ciphers and concluded that it resulted from a badly fragmented effort. The Germans mounted at least five different cryptanalytic efforts. Each competed for resources and attention, and each jealously guarded its resources and techniques from outside encroachment.

The result was failure. As Frank Rowlett, perhaps the leading ASA cryptanalyst in 1948, said, "they all skimmed the cream off and they did the easy ones and nobody, none of them, were [sic] ever able to concentrate on the more important and more secure systems and bring them under control."

The Stone Board

The disastrous results of German cryptologic competition spurred Rowlett and his associates to press for unification of the American effort. In 1948, under the direction of Brigadier General Carter Clarke, Rowlett chaired a committee to write a paper proposing cryptologic unification. The committee included some of the leading names in subsequent American cryptology, including Herbert Conley, Benson Buffham and Gordon Sommers. Rowlett's concerns were mainly technical. With so many good cryptanalysts leaving the services, there was a greater need than ever to concentrate resources. Fragmentation would guarantee the same fate that had met the Germans. This technical argument had been supported in 1946 by the results of the Congressional Pearl Harbor Committee, which, as part of its final report, recommended cryptologic unification.

Army secretary Kenneth Royall was persuaded to support unification, but at his level the concerns were mainly financial. Royall was concerned that the formation of the new U.S. Air Force Security Service (USAFSS or simply AFSS) would mean a smaller slice of the monetary pie for ASA. His report convinced Secretary of Defense James Forrestal, who in August of 1948 established a DoD-level committee to look into the matter of cryptologic unification. Although the committee contained members of the intelligence establishments of all three services, it became known as the

Stone Board, after its chairman, Rear Admiral Earl E. Stone, the director of Naval Communications.

The Stone Board was anything but harmonious. The Navy was dead set against unification, and Stone was the "chief arguer" (in his own words) against the concept. He got the Air Force behind him, and the result was a majority report arguing against the very concept it had been set up to consider. That report agreed to certain reforms in the current CJO (Chief of Joint Operations; see chapter 1) set-up, but refused to endorse any sort of thoroughgoing restructuring. The Army report favored cryptologic unification under a single agency, but it was only a minority report. The two documents were sent to Forrestal. Since the majority report favored a sit-tight approach, nothing happened, and the results of the Stone Board languished in a desk drawer until after the death of Forrestal in March of 1949.

It is important to understand what was going on at that time. The interservice rivalry which had characterized American conduct of World War II had led to calls for service unification. The first step toward a reform of the U.S. military structure was the National Security Act of 1947, which established the Secretary of Defense, the National Security Council, and the CIA. Although all three institutions have become very powerful, in the early years they were not, and gaining control of their respective domains was a process marked by fierce rivalry and bitter infighting.

The new secretary of defense, Louis P. Johnson, arrived at the Pentagon during the worst of these interservice clashes. Cryptologic unification was one of the most hotly contested issues. The protagonists did not leave him alone very long. Carter Clarke pushed Johnson hard on the issue. According to Clarke's own description, he approached one of Johnson's top aides, General Alfred Gruenther, to resurrect the Stone Board documents. Clarke argued that lack of unification was partly responsible for the failure at Pearl Harbor. Johnson, apparently impressed by this, called in General Joseph T. McNarney, a known supporter of unification. McNarney wrote a report which recommended creation of a central organization, called the Armed Forces Security Agency, but which retained the separate cryptologic organizations of the three services. The report was then discussed at a JCS meeting on 18 May 1949. At this meeting the Air Force chief of staff, General Hoyt S. Vandenberg, changed the Air Force vote to pro-unification. The minority had suddenly become the majority, and it was clear that unification was to be forced through. The Navy quickly reversed its vote, too, and the decision to create AFSA was unanimous.

Why did Vandenberg change the Air Force vote? He may have seen the creation of AFSA as an essential ingredient in better intelligence, but he may also have felt that he could keep the fledgling USAF Security Service effectively independent. Vandenberg's central concern in those days was to establish a strategic strike force (Strategic Air Command, or SAC) which would be supported by an all-Air Force intelligence center. He regarded

SIGINT as the key ingredient in such a creation and wanted to place a SIGINT analysis center within USAFSS which would be beyond the control of AFSA. It is possible that he changed the Air Force vote after assurances that USAFSS would be permitted to establish such a center. (This center, called the Air Force Special Communications Center, was actually created, and it resided at Kelly Air Force Base, home of USAFSS for many years.) The later creation of the [censored] a device to keep intercept facilities independent of AFSA, might also have been part of such a plan. Vandenberg's thinking was probably also influenced by log-rolling in other areas, and may have represented an attempt to obtain Army support for other Air Force programs by yielding on the cryptologic issue.

AFSA

And so the Armed Forces Security Agency was created on 20 May 1949. It was promulgated by JCS directive 2010. AFSA was thoroughly military, and, because it answered to the JCS, its central concerns were all military. Organizations outside the JCS got short shrift in the collection of intelligence. State Department and CIA were intensely unhappy with this development, but they lacked the power to wrench AFSA out of the military chain of command.

AFSA began life in borrowed quarters. Its people, just over 5,000 in the beginning, occupied spaces in Arlington Hall and the Naval Security Station on Nebraska Avenue, sharing space with the Army Security Agency and Naval Security Group from which the space was obtained. Admiral Stone decided that the Naval Security Station would be used by AFSA for COMSEC, while the COMINT mission would be done at Arlington Hall. This decision began a historic physical separation between SIGINT and COMSEC which has never been completely bridged, despite the later move to Fort Meade. It was logical, though. Naval Security Group (NSG; formerly OP-20-G) was strong in the COMSEC discipline. Moreover, the Naval Security Station (NSS) at Nebraska Avenue had only about one-fourth the space available that Arlington Hall did, and this disparity in size meant that NSS was about the right size for COMSEC, while the larger spaces at Arlington Hall would be ideal for COMINT. There was a certain amount of shuffling back and forth as COMINTers from NSS moved their desks to Arlington Hall and COMSEC people from Arlington Hall transferred to NSS. But when it was finished, all the COMSEC people were housed in almost 214,000 square feet of office space at NSS, while the COMINT operations were lodged in 360,000 square feet at Arlington Hall. Including administrative, storage and machine space, there were only 79 square feet per worker at the Hall, but about 98 square feet at NSS.

Workers often sat at tables rather than desks, in large warehouse-like rooms, cheek-by-jowl, as they worked complex code or callsign systems. Floors were tiled and the noise level was high. There was practically no air conditioning, and in the summertime it was common to close down for the day when the ratio of temperature to humidity got too high.

AFSA owned two other facilities. The cryptologic school, a rudimentary training ground used originally to keep newly hired workers busy before their clearances came through, reposed in a structure on U Street Northwest in the District of Columbia. The Agency also maintained a courier facility at National Airport, then called Congressional Airport.

The impact of AFSA on the services was immediate and severe. Besides turning over more than 600,000 square feet of space to the new organization, the Army and Navy had to donate about 80 percent of their existing Washington-area billets—79 percent for ASA and 86 percent for NSG. Although ASA kept many of its uniformed service people, its corps of over 2,500 civilian experts was turned over to AFSA virtually intact. This made the Service Cryptologic Agencies little more than collection organizations, with practically no central processing—all arms and legs, but no body. This revolution was accomplished virtually overnight with only minimal dissension and was AFSA's most noteworthy success.

The sole exception to this trend was USAFSS. The Air Force cryptologic agency practically seeeded, opening its first headquarters at Brooks AFB, Texas, 1,600 miles away from the menace of centralization. Even more startling, it was required to donate only thirty officers, twenty civilians, and eighty enlisted billets to AFSA. So when USAFSS opened its processing center, it had plenty of billets to do it with. If this was what Vandenberg had in mind, it was working.

AFSA organization reflected service competition. The director was to be chosen from among the three services on a rotating basis, and its first director was its most ardent opponent, Earl Stone. Assisting him were three deputy directors, one for each service. Below them were four major divisions, which have survived to this day—Operations, Research and Development, COMSEC, and Administration. The office designator system was numerical, so that Operations was AFSA 02: R&D was 03, COMSEC was 04, and Administration was 05. Each of the military deputy directors also had a sphere of influence. The Navy deputy director, Captain Joseph Wenger, controlled COMINT, while the Army deputy, Colonel Samuel Collins, supervised COMSEC, and the Air Force deputy, Colonel Roy Lynn, handled administrative matters.

The field collection effort consisted of the intercept sites which had survived the budget cuts after World War II. Army Security Agency had seven sites: Vint Hill, Virginia; Petaluma, California; [censored] Helemane, Hawaii; [censored] Fairbanks, Alaska; and Clark AFB in the Philippines. The Navy had twelve: [censored] Adak, Alaska; Dupont, South Carolina; [censored] Skaggs Island, California; Cheltenham, Maryland; [censored] The Air Force had ten mobile units, whose status and location were somewhat vague. Finally, ASA had six SHAMROCK units, whose task was to screen commercial cable messages turned over to ASA by the cable companies under an arrangement which had existed since World War II.

Field intercept was the rock that sank AFSA. In theory all the intercept positions were to be under AFSA control. In fact, some were not. Of the 763 intercept positions existing at the time AFSA was dissolved, 671, including all the Army positions, were under some form of AFSA control. Just over 100 were reserved by the Navy for fleet support and were thus completely beyond AFSA tasking authority. But even the positions under AFSA control could be tasked only by treading a complex paper mill by which tasking was routed through the SCAs, rather than being levied directly. This was true especially in the Navy and Air Force—the Army was more accommodating and permitted some form of direct tasking.

Completely beyond AFSA purview, however, were the mobile intercept stations. In theory, these were small mobile efforts for direct tactical support. But AFSS floated AFSA control by simply designating all their stations as "mobile." Thus even the most permanent and sedentary station was designated as a "radio group mobile, or a [censored]" beyond AFSA control. The Army and Navy quickly caught on and by 1952 ASA had seven mobile units, while the Navy had three.

AFSA's lack of tasking authority over Air Force positions was intolerable, and late in 1950 Major General C. P. Cabell, Air Force director of intelligence, and Rear Admiral Stone signed an agreement granting AFSA the authority to task automatic Morse and radioprinter positions, while USAFSS retained control over voice. The Morse positions were split 50/50. Still later, in 1951, this arrangement was changed when the new director of AFSA, Lieutenant General Canine, and Colonel Lynn of USAFSS signed an agreement dividing the Air Force positions down the middle, regardless of mode of intercept.

Meanwhile, USAFSS established its headquarters in San Antonio—first at Brooks AFB and later at nearby Kelly AFB, on a low rise west of the runway which is now known as Security Hill. Within its headquarters it proceeded to establish a stateside COMINT processing center, Air Force Special Communications Center (AFSCC). This was done despite direct orders by Canine that it not be established. AFSA also directed that USAFSS not establish third-echelon processing on the [censored] target, but USAFSS did it anyway. Air Force defiance fragmented the processing effort and had much to do with the demise of AFSA. Despite this, AFSCC continued to process on the [censored] target until the late 1960s, when it was finally turned into an electronic warfare center.

Service rivalry led to duplication. During the early days of the Korean War, for instance, both ASA and USAFSS covered the Soviet and Chinese air problems in the Korean area, and ASA did not discontinue its coverage until March of 1952, after many months of AFSA mediation. Likewise in the DF area, AFSA was unable to force a common DF net control for the Korean problem for more than a year. Ultimately the Navy kept its DF system separate. All three SCAs established second-echelon processing centers in the Pacific with or without AFSA blessing. Without firm control of SIGINT, there was simply no way to organize effectively. This lack of control attracted unfavorable reviews from the generals trying to fight the Korean War and played a part in the COMINT reorganization of 1952.

The final blow to AFSA was the development of a policy mechanism outside of AFSA itself. It was called the Armed Forces Security Advisory Committee (AFSAC), and it was created by the same JCS directive that established AFSA. The original plan was for an advisory committee composed of nine members—three from each service—chaired by the director of AFSA. But the JCS gradually changed AFSAC's charter from advisory to directive. Had AFSAC possessed a proper decision-making mechanism, the conversion of its role to that of direction might have worked after a fashion. But the rules required unanimity on all substantive matters. AFSAC was immediately immobilized by interservice disputes and was ineffective from the start. AFSA had become a body with no head.

One small success during these early years was the development of customer liaison organizations. By 1949 both the Army G2 and the Office of Naval Intelligence had established informal liaison offices with their cryptologic counterparts at Arlington Hall and NSS. When AFSA was established, these arrangements continued undisturbed. Both the Army and Navy groups developed a very close relationship with AFSA, and their people often worked in an intelligence production role. By the end of the Korean War, the Army organization, which called itself SRB (Special Research Branch), had some fifty people. Air Force Intelligence had a similar group, which was gradually subsumed by AFSS into a large organization of over sixty people performing both a customer (for Air Force Intelligence) and producer (for AFSS) role. Thus the Air Force group performed both as a producer and consumer, while the Army and Navy acted only as producers.

Both CIA and State maintained small offices within AFSA, under a USCIB edict of 1948. Although AFSA regulations permitted them to see semiprocessed intelligence, they never participated in the production process, niaintaining their offices for liaison purposes only. FBI's refusal to establish any office at all reflected J . Edgar Hoover's adamant opposition to COMINT centralization.

While COMINT was fractious, COMSEC was relatively serene. During World War II there had been a single authority for joint service communications matters, the U.S. Joint Communications Board, established in July of 1942. Its principal members were the chiefs of communications for the Army, Navy, and Air Force. In 1948 it gave way to a new organization, the Joint Communications Electronics Committee (JCEC), which reigned supreme in this area for many years thereafter. The JCEC was concerned with communications planning, standards, and interoperability, but its charter by implication gave it a determining voice in COMSEC policy as well.

When AFSA was created, JCEC effectively transferred central COMSEC functions to it. The charter did not extend to non-JCS organizations, but the State Department and other civilian agencies with communications security concerns had for years relied on the Army and Navy for COMSEC support, and this reliance was transferred to AFSA. AFSA began producing codes and ciphers for all the armed services and many of the non-DoD agencies. In addition, it undertook centralized COMSEC R&D functions, planning and programming, setting of security standards, and technical supervision of the communications security activities of the armed services. The SCAs retained many residual functions, such as distribution of AFSA-produced codes, security monitoring of transmissions, and the like.

While AFSA successfully controlled the highly technical function of COMSEC, it was never able to control COMINT. This lack of control made powerful enemies. The State Department was upset because, under AFSA, the number of positions allocated to [censored] actually declined in the three years of AFSA existence, from 64 to 51, and from almost 17 percent of the total to only 6.5 percent.

The Brownell Committee

The entire intelligence community was concerned over performance of the COMINT system in Korea. AFSA had not predicted the outbreak of war. A watch committee established under the wing of CIA in early 1950 listed Korea fifth on the list of world trouble spots, but this was not translated into action, and when the war began AFSA still had no positions allocated to Korean military. [censored]

AFSA had no more dangerous opponent than Walter Bedell Smith, director of Central Intelligence. In 1950 the wartime feud between the COMINT empire and Smith's HUMINT organization boiled over. On 10 December of that year Smith wrote a memorandum recommending that a committee be established to "survey" COMINT. Smith was "gravely concerned as to the security and effectiveness with which Communications Intelligence activities . . . are being conducted." He pointed to "the system of divided authorities and multiple responsibilities" which was endangering national security. The National Security Council in turn forwarded the recommendation to President Truman, who directed that a committee be formed.

The JCS could not take heart from the composition of the committee. Its chairman was George A. Brownell, a New York lawyer and layman in intelligence matters. The members were Charles Bohlen, a prominent State Department official; William H. Jackson, special assistant to the DCI; and Brigadier General John Magruder, special assistant to the secretary of defense. Thus the Joint Chiefs, who owned the COMINT organizations, had no one on the committee. It was composed of "enemies,"representatives from State and CIA—the two most vocal opponents of the existing system.

The Brownell Committee held fourteen days of formal sessions, which were backed up by many days of research and data-gathering. Its report was a scathing indictment of the old ways of doing business. Its bottom line stated bluntly that "[censored] The added difficulty of the problem under attack places a greater premium than ever on the quantity and quality of the physical and intellectual resources available, and on the efficiency and clarity of the organization charged with the task. While much has recently been done to provide adequate physical resources for the job, the Committee is convinced that the present organization of our COMINT activities seriously impedes the efficiency of the operation, and prevents us from attracting and retaining as much top quality scientific management manpower as this country ought to be investing in so important a field. It is highly significant to the Committee that the return of many of the best wartime COMINT brains to more attractive [censored]

The committee concluded that the creation of AFSA, coinciding as it had with the creation of USAFSS, had resulted in four COMINT agencies where there had formerly been two. It criticized AFSAC for obstructionism and requested that it be abolished. It attacked USAFSS as a virtually autonomous organization not operating under joint control at all.

The positive recommendations of the Brownell Committee are worth studying, because they encompass the present-day structure of SIGINT in the United States. AFSA should be greatly strengthened, especially in its ability to control tasking at SCA collection sites. AFSA or its successor should be removed from JCS control and should be placed under USCIB, whose membership should be revised, and whose procedures should be governed by a vote of four, rather than unanimity, as had been the case with AFSAC. AFSA should centralize and consolidate processing operations wherever possible to increase the resources brought to bear on intractable cryptanalytic problems. The director should be upgraded to three-star rank, and should be appointed by the president to a four-year term. He should have a civilian deputy. Civilian career development should be encouraged to a much greater extent than formerly.

The next several months were spent putting the Brownell report into directive language. The result was the Truman Memorandum, issued on 24 October 1952. This memo directed a complete restructuring of COMINT along the lines that Brownell recommended. It resolved an on-going dispute about how to change AFSA by abolishing it and creating in its place a new organization called NSA. Its director would work for the secretary of defense, who would become the "executive agent" for COMINT for the entire government. On the same date the National Security Council issued a revised NSCID 9, almost a verbatim quote of the Truman Memorandum. Both documents were classified Top Secret, thus hiding the official creation of NSA from the American public for many years.

All that remained was for the secretary of defense to issue a memorandum establishing the new agency. He did so on 4 November, the day that Dwight Eisenhower defeated Adlai Stevenson for the presidency. The creation of NSA was one of the last historical legacies of twenty years of Democratic governance.

The Truman Memorandum, on the advice of Lieutenant General Canine, had excluded COMSEC. Despite his belief that NSA should have both a COMINT and a COMSEC role, Canine recommended against mixing both in the same document. Lovett's memorandum on 4 November did mention that NSA would inherit the COMSEC functions formerly performed by AFSA. A memo in December spelled out those functions in more detail, and this marked NSA's first formal COMSEC charter.

Korea

"It has become apparent . . . that during the between-wars interim we have lost, through neglect, disinterest and possibly jealousy, much of the effectiveness in intelligence work that we acquired so painfully in World War II. Today, our intelligence operations in Korea have not yet approached the standards that we reached in the final year of the last war." General A. James Van Fleet, Commanding General 8th Army, June 1952

The Country

American intelligence interest and attention, so painfully refocused on the Soviet threat after World War II, were not to be rewarded. The next war occurred not in Europe, where allies and commitments were, but in Korea, a remote Asian peninsula whose name many Americans had never heard in 1950.

Korea had, throughout its recorded history, been a battleground between China, Japan, and Russia. Frequently invaded and occupied, its primary purpose seemed to be as a strategic buffer among three conflicting imperial ambitions. The most recent change of ownership had come after the Russo-Japanese War of 1904-05. Russia, the loser, was forced to cede its influence. Korea became forcibly Japanese.

The Allied powers recognized during World War II that Korea was one of those geopolitical oddities whose status had to be resolved. It obviously could not remain Japanese, and so at the Cairo Conference of 1943 Roosevelt endorsed a policy that would ensure a "free and independent Korea." At Yalta in April of 1945, the Big Three (the United States, the USSR, and Britain) agreed to an Allied trusteeship, to be administered by the three plus China.

Nothing further happened until the USSR declared war on Japan on 8 August 1945, simultaneously invading Manchuria and Korea. The sudden movement of Soviet troops onto the peninsula appeared to portend Soviet occupation, and MacArthur was directed to rush troops to the southern end of Korea. The United States proposed a division of military occupation on the 38th Parallel, splitting the peninsula roughly in half. Moscow unexpectedly agreed, and still more unexpectedly, complied.

American forces dwindled down to about 30,000 by 1948. In March of that year President Harry Truman, following the country's mood of dedicated military budget-cutting, decided that America would simply have to abandon Korea to the United Nations, to sink or swim on its own. He decided to end the American trusteeship and sponsor free elections. So in the spring of 1948 American forces marched out of Korea. The South boycotted the elections, which led to a new National Assembly and a government headed by Syngman Rhee, a seventy-three-year-old militant anti-Communist who had spent forty years in exile in the United States waiting for the liberation of his homeland. The North formed its own government, the Democratic People's Republic of Korea (DPRK), headed by a young thirty-six-year-old Communist named Kim Il-sung. The peninsula was divided at the waist.

The Asia Dilemma

In 1949 catastrophe struck in the Far East. The corrupt and despotic Chiang Kai-shek and his Nationalists were ousted by the Communist forces of Mao Tse-tung. As the Communists marched into Beijing, Chiang fled to the island of Formosa (Taiwan), some 100 miles off the coast, followed by as much of his army as could flee with him. By the end of the year, Mao was making confident proclamations about his intent to invade Formosa and drive Chiang and his army into the sea.

In Washington, the administration was convulsed over whether the United States should support Chiang and the Nationalists. In the end the anti-Chiang faction won, and Truman, on 5 Januaty 1950, issued a public statement that the United States had adopted a "hands off Formosa" policy. Ambiguity about which side of the line Korea stood on was resolved a week later when Secretary of State Dean Acheson, at a press conference, described an American sphere of interest in the Pacific that implicitly excluded Korea.

By June 1950 the United States had boxed itself into a very weak position in Korea. From a full army corps, it was reduced to 500-man Korean Military Aid Group (KMAG). The U.S. had left behind plans and equipment for a 50,000-man ROK (Republic of Korea) "constabulary" (rather than a real army) but devoid of heavy equipment, as the U.S. was afraid that the militant Rhee would use it to invade the North. Rhee drew up plans for a real army of 100,000, and he succeeded in extracting additional American commitments of weapons (but still no heavy, mobile offensive weapons). On the other side of the 38th Parallel stood a DPRK army and air force of about 135,000 men, equipped by the Soviets with much of the heavy equipment that the Americans had denied to Rhee.

American military forces, overall, in 1950 were in a weakened state. Defense budgets had continued to decline from their World War II peak, and the defense budget for 1950 was only $12.3 billion, with an authorized Army strength of 630,000 (but an actual strength of only 591,000). Of these, only 108,500 were in the Far East, almost all of them in Japan. In line with administration policy, the Pentagon had no plans to defend Korea and no one there to do it. The American contingency plan for the peninsula was basically to evacuate all dependents to Japan.

Parallel to the national lack of interest in Korea was AFSA's neglect of the problem. There were no documented high-priority national intelligence requirements on Korea, and the only requirement that related at all was couched in terms of keeping track of Soviet interest in the peninsula. At the time AFSA had "no person or group of persons working on a North Korean problem." During the previous year, SCA intercept sites had stumbled onto some [censored] North Korean messages which were originally collected as suspected [censored] When in May 1949 these messages were identified as North Korean, two intercept positions at [censored] and a tactical unit not under AFSA control, were tasked with follow-up copy. AFSA had no Korean linguists, no Korean dictionaries, no traffic analytic aids, and no Korean typewriters.

No one really expected an invasion in Korea. There was fragmentary HUMINT reporting, generally disbelieved by all, that there could be an invasion by North Korea in 1950. In March an Army organization called the Intelligence Indications Steering Committee cited the possibility of military activity in Korea sometime in 1950. But this was set against a general disbelief in the intelligence community that Korea presented a real problem.

After the war broke out, there was the usual scramble by intelligence agencies to find the indicators that had been missed. AFSA, for instance, discovered traffic indicating that there had been large shipments of medical supplies going from the USSR to Korea beginning in February. A Soviet naval DF net in the Vladivostok area had undergone a dramatic switch to South Korean DF tasks beginning in February. This did not quiet the critics.

The Invasion

About 0330 on Sunday morning, 25 June 1950, Captain Joseph Darrigo, a KMAG military advisor to the ROK posted near Kaesong, was jarred awake by the roar of artillery. Darrigo, the only American on the 38th Parallel, was in the middle of an invasion of North Korean ground forces into South Korea. He managed to make it to the ROK 1st Division headquarters at Munsan just ahead of the advancing North Korean forces, and he spread the alarm.

There appears to have been no tactical intelligence warning. A reporter in Seoul got word of an invasion and rushed to the American embassy for confirmation. At the same time that he got off a wire to New York, the American ambassador was cabling Washington. His cable had to be encrypted and decrypted, and it got there late. The Americans learned of the invasion from the reporter in Seoul.

ASA decided to support the fighting with a communications reconnaisance battalion at Army level and three battalions to serve each of the three corps. The 60th Signal Service Company at Fort Lewis,

Washington, appeared to be closest to being ready for deployment of any ASA tactical asset, so that organization was selected. But it took time to get ready, and in the meantime ASA Pacific (ASAPAC) in Hawaii rushed a signal collection unit to the Korean peninsula, arriving there on 18 September. The Fort Lewis unit did not arrive until 9 October.

Meanwhile, the Truman administration had decided to help the fledgling ROK army and got UN backing for the deployment of a multinational defensive force to Korea. Truman directed MacArthur to rush the 8th Army from Japan to Korea, and the first American troops reentered Korea by air on 1 July. But it took time to get enough troops into the country, and the DPRK army charged ahead, pushing ROK defensive units ahead of it pellmell. By mid-August, ROK defenders had been shoved into a perimeter around the port city of Pusan, the last remaining large city still under the control of the Rhee government. When the first ASA unit arrived in September, the ROK army, bolstered by newly arrived American divisions (the 24th Infantry, 25th Infantry and 1st Cavalry), was desperately hanging onto this slice of the Korean landmass, and the American and Korean defenders were in the middle of a fierce struggle to retain the town of Taegu.

ASA's primary concern was to get linguists. Perhaps the only two first-rate Army Korean linguists were Y.P. Kim and Richard Chun, who were both instructors at the Army Language School in Monterey in 1950. Chun had been cleared in World War II, but Kim had never been in the COMINT business. ASA needed linguists at Monterey to train what was expected to be a sudden flood of Korean language students, but they also needed someone in Korea who could translate Korean. ASA hesitated just a brief moment, and then Kim and Chun, neither as yet actually cleared for COMINT, were on their way to Korea to assist the newly arrived tactical COMINT unit. Until their clearances came through, they worked in a locked and guarded room every day. Intercepted messages were brought in periodically. They would translate the traffic and then pass it through a slot in the wall to the communications center.

The Air Force Security Service likewise had one unit in the Korean area in 1950—the 1st Radio Squadron Mobile (RSM) at Johnson Air Force Base outside Tokyo. This unit had been created in 1942, and it had supported 5th Air Force through MacArthur's Pacific campaign from New Guinea to Japan. In 1950 it was still engaged in support to 5th Air Force, but by then had changed its mission to [censored] In late June it scrambled to change over to Korean targets. It had no cryptanalytic capability, and so began with a traffic analytic attack against North Korean air targets. It likewise had no cleared Korean linguists, so it could do little against readable voice communications.

The Murray Mission

The Air Force Security Service actually beat ASA to Korea—their first representative, First Lieutenant Edward Murray, arrived in Taegu on 19

July. But Murray's mission quickly became entangled in one of the most bizzare incidents in the history of American cryptology.

When Murray arrived, 5th Air Force already had a COMINT service. The origins of that organization are very murky but appear to go back to the days after the end of World War II. At the time a civilian named Nichols, who also had a reserve commission as an Air Force major, headed the local Air Force Office of Special Investigations. Nichols, whose background and training in COMINT are completely unknown, decided that Korea needed a COMINT service. The South Korean government under Syngman Rhee did not appear interested, so Nichols proceeded on his own, seeking out the assistance of some Koreans with COMINT experience.

Among his recruits was one Cho Yong Il, who had come from North Korea, where he had been a radio operator and cryptanalyst with the North Korean Army. Joining Cho was Kim Se Won, a captain in the ROK navy. Kim had served as a COMINTer with the Japanese army in World War II and, owing to having been interned by the U.S. Army in Hawaii, spoke excellent English. Cho, Kim, and those who worked for them did intercept and translation work for Nichols; the source of funding has never been discovered. In 1949 Cho, with Nichols's assistance, obtained a commission in the Korean air force (ROKAF), and his group dual-hatted as a private group working for Nichols and as the ROKAF COMINT service. At about the same time the ROK navy set up Kim and some colleagues from the Nichols group as their COMINT service, so they, too, were dual-hatted.

When the ROK army retreated south in July of 1950, Nichols and his COMINT group retreated with them. As they fled south, fissures developed between Cho and Kim, and in late July or early August the Kim group seceded. Gho stayed with Nichols to supply COMINT to the Air Force, while Kim eventually hooked up with ASA units entering Korea. Nichols was reporting directly to 5th Air Force, which was releasing his reports into USAF intelligence channels at the noncodeword level.

Meanwhile, AFSS had sent Murray to Johnson Air Force Base to put together a direct support package. Murray assembled some vans and other equipment from 1st RSM, and on 15 July he flew to Korea to set up a mobile COMINT effort. AFSS was operating under a misty-eyed concept of COMINT as covert operations, and 1st RSM was directed to expunge its identifications from the equipment, and to insure that Murray could not be indentified as a COMINTer. The direct support went under the codename Project WILLY.

Murray's first concern on arriving in Korea was linguists. Fifth Air Force offered him eight of them, straight from the Nichols pool. The only problem was that Nichols still controlled them, and the upshot was that Nichols wound up with 1st RSM's equipment for use by his own operators. As for 5th Air Force, they were quite happy with the support they were getting from Nichols and informed Murray that he was no longer needed. First Lieutenant Murray returned to Japan on 1 August, having utterly failed to set up a Security Service unit in Korea and having lost his equipment to boot.

The breathless nature of Nichols's coup left USAFSS spinning. A severe jurisdictional battle ensued, encompassing command organizations in the United States, Japan, and Korea. Security Service appeared to carry the day, and Murray was ordered back to Korea on 12 August, armed with a letter of authority from General Banfill (Deputy for Intelligence, Far East Air Force). But the struggle was far from over. Nichols was still unwilling to relinquish control of his COMINT organization, and he had the backing of 5th Air Force. Nichols was a local asset under their complete control, was publishing COMINT without the restrictive codewords that limited dissemination, and already had the expertise that Murray lacked. On 17 August, 5th Air Force ordered Murray to catch the next plane out of Korea. AFSS was again out of the picture.

The Nichols effort was limited by its lack of national-level technical support from AFSA and USAFSS, and 5th Air Force eventually realized this. On 20 November, 5th Air Force reversed its earlier position and asked for the deployment of a radio squadron mobile to Korea to provide support. Cho's group became Detachment 3 of the 1st RSM, and Nichols disappeared from the scene.

Meanwhile, back in Tokyo 1st RSM was trying to mobilize an effort against the North Korean air force. When Murray returned to Japan the first time he carried with him some captured North Korean code books turned over to him by Nichols; lacking Korean translators, the unit came upon a Catholic priest named Father Harold Henry, who had spent a number of years in Korea as an Army chaplain. AFSS agreed to give him access to intercepted materials but did not agree to give him an SI clearance. He began applying the code books to the traffic, and he turned out to he a pretty good cryptanalyst, even though he was doing the work without benefit of formal clearance. Father Henry produced the first decrypts of enciphered North Korean air traffic.

Counterattack

While ASA and AFSS were having trouble getting organized tactically, AFSA pushed rapidly ahead. Despite an almost total lack of expertise and resources to work the unfamiliar Korean target, codebreakers in Washington succeeded in penetrating North Korean communications by late July. At the time, DPRK troops were being readied for their all-out assault on Taegu, which, if successful, might have caused the collapse of the Pusan perimeter and American defeat. Three divisions of Lieutenant General Walton Walker's 8th Army were on line with the remnants of five ROK divisions; opposing them were fourteen battle-tested DPRK infantry divisions. On 26 July AFSA decrypted a North Korean message which contained much of the battle plan for the assault on the 30th. The information reached Walker on the 29th, and he shifted his forces to meet the attack, thus saving Taegu and the Pusan perimeter. It was one of AFSA's most conspicuous successes.

On 15 September MacArthur launched the spectacular Inchon invasion, the second largest amphibious landing in history, near Seoul. North Korean troops suddenly had a large American force in the rear of their operations. On 19 September 8th Army began its breakout from the Pusan perimeter, and in a brief month they had pushed DPRK forces back north of Seoul. Syngman Rhee's government formally returned to the capital on 29 September. But the dynamic and committed Rhee wanted to push the fighting into North Korea, and on 30 September, ROK troops crossed the 38th Parallel. Washington viewed this development with anxiety. But MacArthur was confident that Chinese and Soviet forces would not intervene and, like Rhee, lobbied for authority to go all the way to the Yalu River. The CIA issued an assessment that MacArthur was right. The risks of invading North Korea appeared minimal, and in the end the Truman administration backed MacArthur. American forces crossed the 38th Parallel on 9 October, heading north.

China

The Chinese problem which MacArthur was so blithely underestimating had been building for years. The postwar COMINT effort against Chinese communications began officially in 1945 during the mission of General George Marshall to try to get Chiang Kai-shek and Mao Tse-tung to the bargaining table. Marshall, familiar with what COMINT had done during World War II, requested information from both Communist and Nationalist communications.

ASA mounted a small effort against both the Nationalists and Communists. [censored] ASA could still report that the two sides were far apart, and it was obvious from the COMINT traffic that they were determined to settle their differences on the battlefield. The Marshall mission was withdrawn in 1946, and in October of 1949 Mao triumphed.

Following the withdrawal of the Marshall mission, the COMINT mission against China suffered, as ASA employed all available resources against the Soviet target. [censored] ASA kept only a small section against Chinese civil communications [censored] Collection resources were concentrated at [censored] security problems.

When American and South Korean troops crossed the 38th Parallel, the Chinese had already decided to intervene in North Korea. The decision was taken at a meeting in Beijing from 3 to 7 October 1950. On the first day of the conference, Chinese foreign minister Chou En-Lai called Indian ambassador Panikkar to tell him of the decision, and Panikkar relayed this news to the West. But Indians were regarded as pathologically left-leaning, and Panikkar's communique was disbelieved. Chou's warning was followed up by Chinese radio broadcasts, but these, too, were disregarded.

Historian Clay Blair asserts that "when MacArthur returned to Tokyo from Wake Island [in mid-October] he had no inkling of the CCF armies gathering in North Korea." This was wrong. AFSA had clear and convincing evidence of the massing of Chinese troops north of the Yalu and had published it in product reports available to the JCS, the White House, and to MacArthur. As early as July, AFSA began noting references in Chinese civil communications to army units moving north. Rail hubs in central China were jammed with soldiers on their way to Manchuria. By September AFSA had identified six of the nine field armies that were later involved in the fighting in North Korea and had located them in Manchuria, near the Korean border. Ferries at Anshan (on the Yalu River) were being reserved for military use. Maps of Korea were being ordered in large quantities. On 7 November, in voice communications intercepted and published by the COMINT community [censored] stated, "We are already at war here."

That was not news to the ROK army. On 25 October a ROK division had been badly mauled by elements of the Chinese 40th Army, already reported by AFSA to be close to Korea. Five days later MacArthur's chief of staff, Lieutenant General Ned Almond, reported that he had seen Chinese POWs being held by a ROK unit. On the first of November, a Chinese force attacked a U.S. unit for the first time. But Charles Willoughby, MacArthur's G2, preferred to believe that these encounters represented isolated PRC volunteers rather than division-strength regular army units confronting UN troops.

AFSA reports continued to document the presence of major Chinese forces on the Yalu, but the reporting was subtle. AFSA was regarded as a collection and processing agency, not as a producer of intelligence. There were no dramatic wrap-ups, no peppery conclusions—just the facts, strung through a flood of intelligence reports. The COMINT community had almost the only hard information about the status of Chinese forces.

Intelligence agencies were beginning to pay attention. The Watch Committee of the JIIC, which began noting Chinese troop movements as early as June, concluded by September (probably on the basis of AFSA reporting) that these troops were moving north rather than to the coastal provinces near Formosa. By mid-October, influenced perhaps by MacArthur's opinions, the Watch Committee had concluded that, though there was convincing evidence that startling numbers of Chinese forces were in Manchuria, the time for intervention had passed—they assessed that the Chinese would not intervene. However, encounters with Chinese ground and air forces in late October and early November caused the committee to take another look. Admiral Arleigh Burke, who commanded naval forces in the region, was convinced that Chinese intervention was imminent and brought up the subject twice to Willoughby, who summoned his very large staff to try to dissuade Burke.

MacArthur continued to press ahead with offensive operations to reach the Yalu and get the boys home by Christmas. But on the snapping cold night of 25 November with trumpets braying, thousands of Chinese soldiers fell on unsuspecting units of the 8th Army. The American offensive turned quickly into a defensive, and a defense into a rout. The American and ROK armies were overwhelmed, and some units were virtually wiped out. Weeks later the front stabilized near Seoul, and the war settled down to grim trench warfare for almost three more years.

AFSS and ASA Operations

AFSS operations in Korea continued their harrowing path. The decision in November to send regular AFSS units occurred just prior to the Chinese invasion. Two locations were envisioned: one in Sinanju to intercept North Korean targets in the battle zone and a rear detachment in Pyongyang to intercept related Soviet and Chinese communications. But even as the two detachments were in the air on their way to Korea on 28 November, the Chinese had attacked, and Sinanju was not safe. The unit destined for Sinanju was diverted to Pyongyang, much further south, while the detachment commander was flown to Sinanju to assume command of the troops on the ground (the Cho detachment) and to get them to safety farther south. AFSS in Korea operated as Detachment Charlie of 1st RSM until 1951, when the 15th RSM was activated to control all AFSS Korean operations. The Cho group made it safely back to Allied lines, and by February of 1951 the front had stabilized just south of Seoul.

ASA tactical units dug in for the winter. ASA manual Morse intercept efforts in Korea were having very modest success. Most intercepted material was [censored] providing little of tactical value. But sometime in February reports began to filter to ASA that UN front line troops were hearing Chinese voice communications. ASAPAC (Advance) sent an investigating officer to IX Corps, and he reported that there was a good volume of spoken Chinese interceptable.

ASA already had some Chinese linguists, but what they needed to exploit this type of nonstereotyped communications was native linguists. An arrangement was made with a former Nationalist Chinese general working for the U.S. in Tokyo to begin hiring former Nationalist officers from Formosa. They were enticed to Korea by the promise of earning GS-6 pay as Department of the Army civilians, and they were to enjoy officer status while in Korea. Competition was keen, and by the summer of 1951, Chinese linguists were flocking to ASA units in Korea.

The linguists were formed into Low-Level Voice Intercept (LLVI) teams and were positioned as close to the front lines as possible. The effort was expanded to include Korean LLVI, although that part of the program got off to a slower start because of the difficulty of getting good linguists in a cleared status. Low-level voice quickly became the prime producer of COMINT in Korea, and the demand for LLVI teams overwhelmed ASA's ability to provide enough good linguists. The program expanded from one unit, to seven, to ten, and by the end of the war there were twenty-two LLVI teams, including two teams dedicated to tactical voice intercept.

In September of 1952 the 25th Infantry Division began picking up Chinese telephone communications from their tactical landline telephones. This was accidental, of course, and apparently originated from a sound detecting device normally used to indicate the approach of enemy troops. When the unit moved off line, they passed on the technique to the relieving 40th Infantry Division. The 40th improved the equipment but did no analysis. In November, an ASA liaision officer at division headquarters was notified, and ASA proceeded to develop the technique on other sectors, supporting it with LLVI teams consisting of either Korean or Chinese linguists, depending on which type of unit was on the other side of the line. The Americans had accidentally rediscovered a technique for gathering intelligence which had originally been developed during World War I and which had been a prime producer of tactical information. [censored]

These LLVI teams were quite small, consisting only of an ASA officer, a couple of enlisted men for analysis, and two or three native linguists. Their value to front-line commanders, however, far outran their cost, and LLVI was hailed as one of the most important producers of tactical intelligence during the war.

White Horse Mountain

As the conflict settled down to unremitting trench warfare, highlights were few, and peace talks gradually replaced warfare in American newspapers. But the front lines continued to shift imperceptibly as the two sides bludgeoned each other in a series of bloody encounters to take high ground. One of those, the battle for White Horse Mountain, illustrated the use of COMINT in a tactical situation.

The action was originally tipped off by [censored] a Chinese Communist military message that was in the hands of the tactical commander before the battle took place. ASA set up a special [censored] effort and tactical communications to report information that might bear on the battle. [censored]

True to the intelligence prediction, the Chinese launched a massive infantry assault on American and ROK troops at White Horse on 6 October and persisted until 15 October. Throughout the battle, LLVI teams kept the American commander informed of the position and activities of Chinese units. In a precursor to Vietnam, the American units were able to call artillery fire on Chinese positions on the basis of the LLVI-provided information. The Chinese suffered nearly 10,000 casualties out of some 23,000 committed to the battle.

AFSS Introduces Tactical Warning

Like ASA units, AFSS operations in Korea depended increasingly on intercept of low-level voice communications, using this for tactical warning.

The concept relied on the Joint Training Directive for Air-Ground Operations published in 1949, which stated that the primary purpose of radio squadrons mobile for tactical support was to collocate with the Tactical Air Control Center (TACC) so that direct tactical warning could be supplied. (This followed World War II COMINT doctrine used effectively by Lieutenant General Kenney at 5th Air Force.)

Because of the lack of linguists, AFSS was slow to set up this service in Korea. However, in the early spring of 1951 AFSS units began intercepting Soviet ground-controlled intercept (GCI) communications, and this spurred Far East Air Force (FEAF) into requesting AFSS tactical support. Fortunately, AFSS did have some Russian linguists, and eight of them were on their way to Korea in April to form the first linguist team. They originally set up a mobile intercept and processing hut at Pyongtaek in central Korea, and communicated with the TACC by landline. No one in the tactical air operation was cleared for COMINT, so it was disguised using a simple substitution code to identify enemy aircraft and ground checkpoints. Arrangements were made for the TACC controller to pass relevant COMINT, intermixed with radar plots, to fighter pilots. The operation was nicknamed "YOKE," and became highly successful because it significantly expanded the range of control of the TACC and improved the air controllers' ability to warn pilots of impending threats.

As the front advanced north of Seoul, so did the air control operations. In June of 1951, the entire air control operation moved forward to a hill four miles northeast of Kimpo Airport near Seoul. But in August hearability deteriorated, and the operation, including the TACC and Security Serice operations, migrated by LST to Pyong-Yong-Do island. Only six miles from enemy lines, "P-Y-Do" (as it was called) was in an ideal location. The site at Kimpo was kept open, and linguists were split between the two sites.

Soon AFSS was finding tactical voice communications in Chinese and Korean as well as Russian. Two more voice teams were established for the additional languages. The Korean voice team consisted of the Cho contingent of the Nichols group. The Chinese team set up shop on the campus of Chosen Christian College in Seoul (today, Yansei University). AFSS acquired its Chinese linguists in Korea basically the same way that ASA did—they hired foreign-born linguists. In this case, they did business with one General Hirota, a former chief of the Japanese army COMINT agency during World War ll. Hirota hired twelve Japanese linguists who were fluent in Chinese.

With so many languages involved, the tactical support operation was unusually complex. The AFSS facility at Kimpo correlated Chinese early warning voice, Chinese GCI voice, Soviet GCI voice, Chinese air defense Morse and Korean GCI voice. Each input was produced by a separate team, and each team was in a different location for security purposes.

In September of 1951 the P-Y-Do operation was closed down and moved back to Kimpo, and that fall all AFSS operations were consolidated at

Chosen Christian. This was the first time that all components of the operation were collocated, which made correlation of activity easier. According to one officer involved in the operation, "the present top-heavy success of the F-86s against MIG-15s dates almost from the day of the inception of the new integrated voice-CW-YOKE service."

In early 1952 much of the GCI traffic that AFSS had been intercepting began to dry up, and AFSS became convinced that it had gone to VHF. Moreover, about that time the Chinese stopped tracking Communist aircraft, and they tracked only "hostiles." These twin changes spelled potential disaster for AFSS tactical operations. From a practical standpoint, the lack of tracking would force AFSS to rely almost entirely on intercepting GCI communications. But since these communications were disappearing, probably to VHF, that source of information was also drying up. The changes also generated a security problem, since the positions of Communist aircraft had been disguised as radar plots when being passed to the TACC. If there were no more radar position reports, disguise of the origin of the information would be much more difficult.

These developments roughly coincided with the arrival of the first batch of school-trained American Chinese linguists, headed by Lieutenant Delmar "Del" Lang, in mid-1952. At the time the unit was located in Seoul, where VHF intercept was hardly possible, while the TACC had moved to Cho-Do Island, near the North Korean harbor of Wonsan. Information had to be relayed from the AFSS unit to Kimpo and from Kimpo to Cho-Do. Lang moved the operation to Cho-Do Island and collocated it with the TACC. Tests on Cho-Do in August of 1952 confirmed that both the Soviets and Chinese were now using VHF for their GCI control activities.

To solve the security problems and to make sure that the TACC controller got the best possible support, Lang positioned an AFSS linguist in the TACC in March of 1953, sitting next to the controller. The linguist had a field phone on his desk, the other end of which was attached to the output of a receiver at the Security Service intercept unit three-fourths of a mile away. In an era when no one knew much about TEMPEST (see chapter 5), such a wireline was regarded as secure simply because it was a landline.

Combined with improved hearability, the new lash-up at Cho-Do Island provided the best support that AFSS mustered during the entire war. In one day, which Lang described as the "great Korean turkey shoot," American F-86s downed fifteen MIGs without a loss, even though none of the MIGs was ever seen on radar. The information came, of course, from the COMINT operation at Cho-Do. A visiting ASA colonel commented that "it was just like shooting ducks in a rain barrel." It was a model for tactical COMINT operations and was resurrected by the same Del Lang years later in Vietnam. (See chapter 12.)

The Navy

Naval cryptology was a bit player in Korea. The DPRK had no blue-water navy, and it was so weak that the Inchon invasion went unopposed from the naval standpoint. The naval COMINT unit in the region was [censored] But [censored] was not concerned with the small collection of DPRK coastal patrol craft. The organization concentrated instead almost entirely on the Soviet navy in the Pacific, to determine what moves, if any, the Soviets would make toward the U.S. presence on the Korean peninsula.

The unit was housed in cramped quarters in a former Japanese artillery training school, entirely small and inadequate for the purpose. NSG found an old Japanese ammunition storage building about ten miles from [censored] Rehabilitation began in 1951, and in November 1952 [censored] moved to [censored] where it remained for many years.

Most of the NSG support to the war effort came from its afloat detachments. Originating out of Hawaii, detachments were placed aboard 7th Fleet vessels beginning in August 1951, and at the end of the war, 7th Fleet had three such units.

The AFSA Factor

On the home front, AFSA provided significant help to battlefield commanders. AFSA's quick work [censored] in time to turn the tide at Taegu appeared to portend the same kind of COMINT effectiveness that the U.S. had enjoyed during World War II. But it was not to be. [censored]

In November 1950, with Chinese Communist troops flooding into North Korea, AFSA turned its attention to Chinese communications. [censored]

In 1952 the painfully slow progress on traffic analysis of Chinese army nets finally began to bear fruit. There were indications through traffic analysis that the 46th Army was moving northward. The army eventually arrived in Manchuria and crossed the border into Korea. As it did so, AFSA began exploiting People's Volunteer Army (PVA) nets from a traffic analytic standpoint, and it achieved a level of competence on PVA nets that allowed extremely accurate order of battle determinations, unavailable through any other intelligence source. Through traffic analysis AFSA noted the build-up of PVA units on the eastern front, and this allowed 8th Army to reinforce its right side prior to a major PVA assault on 15 July 1953.

Relations with ROK COMSEC and COMINT

COMSEC assistance to ROK forces began almost as early as COMINT collaboration. In 1950 ASA was asked to furnish low-level cryptographic assistance for use by the ROK army. After conferring with AFSA, ASA shipped some strip ciphers and Playfair squares. It was soon found, however, that these very time-intensive systems would not be fast enough, and in 1953 ASA provided the first electromechanical cipher equipment, the BACCHUS system. Later in the year ASA also released the DIANA one-time-pad system.

Cryptologic cooperation with the ROK COMINT organizations continued throughout the war. USAFSS continued its relationship with the Cho group, while ASA continued to do business with the Kim group. In November 1951 ASAPAC proposed the consolidation of the two efforts, but AFSS firmly rejected the overture. This was probably based on Air Force fear that ASA would dominate the relationship and get back into the business of copying North Korean air targets, but this may also have been based on the very realistic appraisal that the animosity between Kim and Cho was unbridgeable.

The situation continued unchanged, and late the next year an official for the newly created NSA [censored]

By charter (NSCID 5), CIA had control of all foreign intelligence relationships. But the "battlefield marriage" between the American and South Korean COMINT organizations represented a significant exception to the general rule. Korea was JCS turf, and military commanders were cool to CIA participation in their arena.

[censored]

Korea—An Assessment

The Korean War occurred during a period of struggle inthe cryptologic domniunity. It began a year after the formation of AFSA and concluded after the AFSA ship had been finally scuttled in favor of a new vessel, the National Security Agency. The demands of war highlighted the fissures in the structure, and those fissures in turn made prosecution of the war more difficult. AFSA wrestled with the SCAs over control of intercept positions and targets throughout its existence, and many of those battles were related to the war effort. The Brownell Committee was convened in part because of complaints by organizations outside the Department of Defense over degraded cryptologic support resulting from the war. The committee stressed in its final report that the cryptologic community had been shown deficient in its effort during the war. NSA replaced AFSA partly because of what was happening (or not happening) in Korea.

But after forty years the picture does not look quite so bleak. Actually, AFSA and the SCAs provided good support to the war effort. Although AFSA (along with everyone else) was looking the other way when the war started, it did a remarkable about-face, and within a month it was producing large volumes of decrypted information from North Korean communications. Its accomplishments during the battle for the Pusan perimeter, [censored] and using the information to support tactical commanders, were considerable and important. The reporting program, although hampered by restrictions on AFSA's production of "intelligence" as opposed to "intelligence information," was farsighted and effective. AFSA, almost alone among intelligence agencies, foresaw the Chinese intervention. The development of Chinese and Korean order of battle owed much to AFSA's high-powered traffic analytic effort.

After a slow start occasioned by lack of mobility, tactical resources, linguists, and working aids, ASA and USAFSS put together highly credible battlefield COMINT organizations. ASA's LLVI program produced more valuable information for ground commanders than any other source. AFSS put together a system for warning fighter pilots, which was partly responsible for the much-ballyhooed kill ratio in that war. [censored]

AFSA's quick start was not sustained. Beginning in July of 1951, the North Koreans began a total changeover of their communications procedures [censored]

In the first month of the war, AFSA read more than one third of all North Korean cipher messages received, and by December AFSA was reading more than 90 percent. [censored] The new North Korean security measures were evidently inspired by the Soviet Union, whose communications had in 1948 undergone a similar transformation in the face of possible exploitation efforts. (See chapter 4.) It was accompanied by a decline in North Korean radio messages incident to the beginnings of static trench warfare roughly at the 38th Parallel, which gave the enemy a chance to divert radio communications to landline.

[censored]

Security was a problem in Korea, as it has been during all wars. Occasional press releases exposed COMINT support to battlefield commanders. The release of information about AFSS exploitation of GCI communications became so serious that in October 1951 Detachment 3 of 1st RSM took the extraordinary step of suspending operations for a few days until they got the attention of key officers in 5th Air Force. The employment of tactical GCI voice and tracking information in the air war caused AFSS to devise new measures to cover the information, and it set a precedent for use of similar information during the war in Vietnam.

When NSA was created in November 1952, immediate steps were taken to sort out the effort in Korea. NSA's recommendations amounted to a classic "lessons learned" about war. Most pressing was a program which would allow the use of indigenous personnel with native language capability. Almost as urgent was the need to sort out the tangled relationships with the various ROK COMINT efforts. It would also be necessary to increase NSA representation in the field and to expand existing field offices with technical experts assisting the SCAs. Finally there was a call to develop new special identification techniques that would allow NSA and the SCAs to track target transmitters [censored] NSA sponsored these themes for years, until they became tantamount to COMINT doctrine on warfighting.

One beneficial effect of the Korean conflict was to begin a rapid rise in cryptologic resources. In July 1950 USCIB recommended to the National Security Council that COMINT receive a hiring jolt. The NSC approved this on 27 July in a meeting attended by the president himself.

Korea was America's first stalemated war, and recriminations resounded for years later. But even an acerbic CIA critic of the cryptologic community had to admit that "COMINT remained the principal source of intelligence for threat until 27 July 1953, when the armistice was signed at Panmunjom."

Chapter 3 Cryptology under New Management

"There is something about cryptologic work that gets into the hide. . . ."
Ralph Canine, 1968

NSA began life under a pall. The Brownell Committee had declared its predecessor to have been a failure. Outside the cryptologic community ther was a common feeling that COMINT was broken and in serious need of repair. According to [censored] who was appointed by Allen Dulles to ride herd on the cryptologic effort, "The early 1950s were the dark ages for communications intelligence. Intelligence officers who had been accustomed to providing information not only on the capabilities but also on the intentions of the enemy during World War II were reduced to providing the government with estimates based on frail fragments of information rather than factual foreknowledge. [censored]"

The creation of NSA was an attempt to address the problems of cryptology as the Brownell Committee saw them. (As we saw in the section on Korea, that perception was not 100 percent accurate.) That is, it attempted to institute a firm control mechanism that would unify the system and create an organization which was, in and of itself, responsible for getting the job done. No longer would consumers have to go to four different organizations to get answers or to fix blame for the lack of answers. It did not give the organization resources, improve its personnel situation, or give it adequate working space.

When NSA began life, it simply inherited its resources from its predecessor. It got the AFSA billets and the people in them, the AFSA spaces at Arlington Hall, and the AFSA rooms at the Naval Security Station. And it inherited an idea, that unification worked better than division. The difficulty was in trying to implement the solutions that the Truman Memorandum imposed. AFSA, despite its failings, had been a step in the right direction. NSA now had to take the next step.

To the AFSA population, the name change must have seemed more for appearance than for any practical value. There was no immediate change in their condition. They stayed where they were—if they were COMINTers, they remained at Arlington Hall, and if they were COMSECers, they stayed at Nebraska Avenue. Lieutenant General Canine, who had replaced Admiral Stone as AFSA director, stayed on as director of NSA. When Canine first gathered the NSA work force together on 25 November 1952, he alluded to the conflicts which had preceded the establishment of NSA, but they must have seemed remote to those who listened. It looked like business as usual.

Canine and the New Organization

But it was not to be business as usual, largely because of the personality of the first director. Lieutenant General Ralph Canine, who dominated early NSA policies and stamped his character on the Agency, had been a line Army officer with no intelligence experience until he became deputy assistant chief of staff for army intelligence in 1949. Prior to that he had been an artillery officer, with wide experience in combat (both world wars, serving under Patton in World War II) as well as logistics. Although he brought no technical education to cryptology, he exerted his influence through a hands-on management style. He was forceful and determined and tenaciously enforced the Brownell recommendations on the reluctant SCAs. His whimsical personality produced legions of "Canine stories," which simply embellished his reputation as a maverick. Collins proclaimed him a "fortunate choice," and said that "he . . . raised the National Security Agency from a second-rate to a first-rate organization." Canine was no diplomat, and he might have failed had he come along ten years later. In 1952, however, he was the right man for the job.

One of the first things Canine did was to get rid of the triumvirate of service deputies who, under AFSA, had represented their own service interests rather than the interests of the central organization. He replaced them with a single vice-director, and named Joseph Wenger to fill the position. But Wenger was probably not very happy as the vice-director. By all contemporary accounts, Canine served as his own vice-director. He tended to make all key decisions himself. He had no patience with long vertical lines of control, and when he wanted an answer, he went directly to the person involved. He relied on his staff to keep others in the chain of command informed of his comings and goings but did not feel bound, himself, to use the chain. The system smacked of paternalism, and one of Canine's subordinates once said, "Whenever I see him nowadays, I expect him to pat me on the head."

Canine organized NSA rather like AFSA had been structured, with Production, COMSEC, and R&D being the major divisions. But he broke Administration into its component pieces (security, personnel, training, logistics, and plans and policy) and placed them on his "special staff," a classically army way of doing things. The office designation system was a trigraph, NSA followed by a dinome: for instance, NSA-02 was the Office of Operations.

In February 1953 Canine changed Operations to Production, or NSA-06. Production was structured much like a factory, in which the parts of the cryptologic process were organized functionally rather than geographically. The major divisions within Production were Collection (NSA-60), Analysis (NSA-70), Machine Processing (NSA-80), and Exploitation (NSA-90). Although NSA has since changed over to a more geographical approach, the original organization more closely corresponded to how cryptologists viewed their profession at the time—as part of a complex process suitable primarily for highly skilled factory technicians. What made cryptology different from other intelligence disciplines was both the intricate technical challenge and the assembly-line processing system. It also represented NSA's way of conceptualizing the process of intelligence—as underlying data revealed through mathematical attack rather than as cognitive insight arrived at through inspiration.

The Early Work Force

The Korean War had ushered in a period of explosive growth in the cryptologic population. This was followed by a long period of fairly steady personnel growth, as Table 1 shows.

Table 1

Cryptologic Population, 1949–1960[5]

Year	AFSA	NSA	Totals (includes SCAs)
Dec 1949	4,139		10,745
Dec 1952		8,760	33,010
Nov 1956		10,380	50,550
Nov 1960		12,120	72,560

The work force in 1952 was double what it had been under AFSA, but it was still smaller than either ASA or USAFSS and larger only than NSG.

[censored] The Hoover Commission, which was probably the most extensive investigation of the federal bureaucracy ever, estimated that cryptologic costs amounted to about half a billion dollars.

In the early days, the work force was about one-third military and two-thirds civilian. A snapshot of NSA's work force in 1956 (Table 2) showed most of the population working in Production.

Pay tables were not quite as generous in those days, as Table 3 clearly shows. A grade 5 employee (the most numerous group of NSA employees) started out making $3,410, which smacks of impoverishment. But with houses costing below $10,000, and frequently below $5,000, employees may have been just as well off in real terms then.

Table 2
NSA's Work Force by Organization, 1956

Element	
Production	
R&D	
COMSEC	
Communications	
Training	
Directorate, admin, overseas	
Totals	

Table 3
Pay grade allocations and salary (basic level) 1952 and 1993[8]

Grade	Salary 1952	1993	Grade Alloc 1952	1993
1	$2,500	$11,903	(0.2%)	(0%)
2	2,750	13,382	(0.7)	(0.07)
3	2,950	14,603	(6.5)	(0.5)
4	3,175	16,393	(13)	(0.7)
5	3,410	18,340	(26)	(1.9)
6	3,795	20,443	(7)	(1.6)
7	4,205	22,717	(18)	(4.9)
8	4,620	25,259	(1.5)	(1)
9	5,060	27,789	(12)	(6.8)
10	5,500	30,603	(0.5)	(0.2)
11	5,940	33,623	(7)	(12.1)
12	7,040	40,298	(4)	(22.1)
13	8,360	47,920	(2)	(26)
14	9,600	56,627	(0.8)	(11.5)
15	10,800	66,609	(0.6)	(6)
16	12,000	–	(.02)	
17	13,000	–	(.02)	(2)
18	14,800	–	(.02)	

Included in Table 3 are the grade allocations in 1952 compared with those in 1993. This is a striking illustration of grade creep—more of a gallop than a creep. In 1952 the average grade was 6.7, while in 1993 it was 11.7, a grade inflation averaging fully five General Schedule grades over a period of forty-one years. This followed the trends in the general federal work force: in 1952, the average grade was GS-5.5, while in 1993 it was GS-9.

The conditions under which NSA employees labored were not much different from the AFSA days. Offices were badly overcrowded, especially at Arlington Hall. In 1954 approximately 30 percent of the work force worked the evening shift to relieve overcrowding on days. Air conditioning in the Washington area was still virtually unknown, and the NSA hot weather policy permitted relief from work only when conditions became fairly unbearable, as the temperature versus humidity chart (Table 4) shows. On really hot days the man whirling the hygrometer was the most popular person at the station.

Table 4
NSA Employees Could be Released When

Temperature reached	And humidity reached
95	55
96	52
97	49
98	45
99	42
100	38

There was a view, widely held in 1952, that the expertise of the civilian work force had declined since 1945. This was to some extent true. Not only had ASA and NSG lost some of their best minds at the end of the war, but the structure of the central organization created built-in problems for the civilian promotion system. The Navy had always run its cryptologic service with military officers, while the Army, believing that military officers rotated too frequently, had let its civilian work force run the cryptologic effort. By 1949, when AFSA was formed, NSG had a number of very senior officers involved in the business, and many of those people transferred into AFSA. Admiral Stone placed them in the key leadership positions, and the Army civilians were often shunted aside. Moreover, Stone took no steps to create a senior civilian work force, and when he departed in favor of Canine, there were no civilians above grade 15.

In 1953 a committee chaired by H. P. Robertson of California Institute of Technology (more commonly referred to simply as Cal Tech) looked at NSA's future and concluded that there was no future if the Agency was unable to obtain and retain outstanding civilians in various technical fields. This, according to Robertson, would require the establishment of a cryptologic career management program within NSA, with regular progression through the grade ranks and supergrade promotions to the top performers. The Robertson Committee also concluded that the services would have to improve their own cryptologic career advancement programs to attract and retain good uniformed people to COMINT. Robertson noted the lack of such a program in the Army and the lack of a stateside rotational base. (At the time, fully 66 percent of all ASAers were overseas.)

Canine met this problem head-on. Soon after the Robertson Report was released, he directed the personnel office to begin working on a cryptologic career system, with technical specialties and a system of regular advancement. This work was well under way by early 1954 and eventually led to the structuring of the current cryptologic career program for civilians. Canine was credited personally with getting NSA's first three supergrades: William Friedman, Abraham Sinkov, and Solomon Kullback. (Frank Rowlett, hired in 1930 with Sinkov and Kullback, had joined CIA and so was not on the list.) Even more significant, in 1953 he obtained for NSA the authority to hire under the so-called Civil Service Rule Schedule A, which permitted NSA to hire without obtaining permission from the Civil Service Commission. Rather than having NSA applicants take the standard Civil Service test and then having a board interview the top three scorers, NSA devised its own peculiar aptitude tests, and hired without outside interference.

Under Canine, NSA moved in many directions at once to strengthen its civilian work force. The director got NSA a slot at the National War College in 1953, and Louis Tordella was the first appointment, Abraham Sinkov the second. The Training Division initiated a presupervisory training program, which was curtailed in 1955 in favor of an intern training program oriented more toward technical education. NSA began local recruiting in the Baltimore and Washington areas by 1954.

Fielding the Field Offices

Canine moved very aggressively to establish field offices. Under Stone, AFSA had had no field organization, and the censorial AFSAC appeared to guarantee continuation of the situation. But as soon as he became AFSA director, Canine made an end-run around AFSAC. On a trip to the Far East in September of 1951, he got the concurrence of the theater commander for an AFSA field office and returned to Washington with a fait accompli. Early objections by NSG were muffled when Canine named Captain Wesley A. ("Ham") Wright, one of the most senior naval cryptologists, to head the newly formed AFSA Far East office in Tokyo. By the time AFSAC got around to considering this surreptitious move in January of 1952, the office already existed (official date: 1 January 1952) with Wright and a staff of six. When AFSAC approved a formal charter, it stripped Wright of any direct control over SCA field operations, but Canine had the nucleus of a field organization and awaited only the creation of NSA to augment the authorities of the chief.

In Europe, Canine began by sending a top civilian, Hugh Erskine, on a survey trip, the result of which, as in the Far East, was theater command concurrence with an AFSA branch office. This time Canine submitted his plan to AFSAC before officially establishing the office. AFSAC approved, and Erskine began work formally on September 1952 in offices in the I.G. Farben building in Frankfurt. NSAEUR competed for a time with an office titled NSAUK (NSA United Kingdom), located in London, and the two shared responsibility for some of the continental COMINT functions—for instance [censored] This lasted until 1956, when NSAUK was abruptly disestablished.

When CINCEUR shifted to Paris in 1964, NSAEUR stayed in Frankfurt but finally shifted to Camp des Loges, outside Paris, in 1963. While the policy and liaison functions resided there,[censored]

Once NSA was officially established, Canine moved swiftly to create more field offices. NSA Alaska (NSAAL) was created in July 1953, NSAUK on 26 August 1953, and NSAPAC, established to advise CINCPAC, on 16 August 1954. He also created at home an office to monitor field operations.

Backed by the authority of NSCID 9 (the predecessor of the present-day NSCID 6), Canine imposed on the reluctant SCAs a group of field offices that had basically the same power as he himself within their geographic spheres. They had two functions—liaison with theater commanders and technical control of the theater COMINT system. Their main reason for existence was to impose order on the chaotic growth of the field sites, and they established large and active technical staffs which worked directly with the sites. NSA field offices could task SCA field sites directly (although they customarily did not do so). NSA's theater chiefs strove to create a cooperative atmosphere with the SCAs, but everyone involved recognized the implied threat that they represented as personal emissaries of the feared Canine. The SCA field chiefs fought this "encroachment" into their territory with every resource at their disposal.

During and after World War II, American military organization in the Atlantic and Pacific theaters contained inherent turf conflicts. In Europe, for instance, the main power resided with CINCEUR (originally in Frankfurt), but there was also a military organization in Great Britain that competed with it for power. In the Pacific the competition between CINC Far East (MacArthur) and CINCPAC (Nimitz) was even more stark. And so it was with NSA organizations. In Europe, the latent competition between the NSA offices in Great Britain and Germany was resolved in 1956, but in the Far East the competition between the offices in Tokyo and Hawaii continued for many years. [censored]

Civilians in the Trenches—the Civop Program

In the early 1950s NSA turned to the problem of field site collection. Military operator turnover was high, some years as high as 85 percent. The long-range expansion of intercept positions set by JCS during the Korean War appeared to be a dead letter unless a stable manpower pool could be established. NSA liked what it had seen of the GCHQ program of hiring civilian operators because of the exceptionally long retention rates and [censored] NSA was also aware that CIA was hiring civilian operators for [censored] Negotiations were begun with ASA, and in 1954 an agreement was hammered out which would start with a pool of one hundred civilian operators at four ASA field sites: [censored] NSA would recruit and train the operators, who would be under the control of the field site commander. For the initial group, rotation at all four bases was set at two years, and the grade ranges for the program were 5 through 11. The NSA planning group waxed a little poetic, formulating long-range plans for thousands of operators and an eventual NSA field site of its own.

The trial group was duly recruited, trained, and deployed. But even as things were moving ahead, the services' attitudes were beginning to cool. NSA promised to recruit only operators who had retired from service, but ASA and USAFSS foresaw keen competition for their first-term operators contemplating better salaries doing the same job for NSA. By 1957 the services had turned against the program, and it was quietly discontinued. It had long-lasting beneficial results, however. It yielded, in later years, a cadre of experienced civilian operators who performed well in crisis after crisis.

COMINT Reporting in Transition

The reporting legacy of World War II was translations. ASA and NSG issued thousands of translations per month, a reflection of the huge volume of readable traffic. Once the cryptanalyst had finished his or her job, and the translator had put the message into readable English, the verbatim transcript was released to either G2 or the theater commander (in the case of the Army) or Office of Naval Intelligence or the appropriate naval commander (in the case of the Navy). The mechanism for this was to hand the information in raw form to an intelligence analyst collocated with the cryptologic organization. Traffic analytic information was also passed in bulk to the appropriate intelligence organization, which would put it into readable intelligence. In other words, the COMINT factory simply passed raw information to the organization, which would itself put it in context.

The postwar cryptologic community continued to produce primarily translations, accompanied by all the COMINT technical information [censored] necessary for the service intelligence analyst to analyze it. NSA was not supposed to analyze. The information (it could not be dignified with the term "report") lacked a serialization resembling the modern system. [censored]

AFSA began to evolve a similar system. Releases tended more and more toward reporting rather than translations, [censored] Reports were more formal and had wider distribution. AFSA devised its own primitive serialization system; an example would be [censored] followed by a date. [censored] was the subject matter [censored] and 13-50 indicated this was the thirteenth report produced in 1950 by that section. But reports still contdued [censored] and other sorts of technical data later prohibited in COMINT reporting, and narrative portions were often very heavy on discussion of details of [censored] rather than on higher-level information like unit movements. The distribution was still very limited by modern standards. Collocated organizations (ASA, USAFSS, and NSG representatives, for example) decided who in their services should see the information and made further distribution from there.

Early NSA reporting was more formal still. [censored] Distribution was broader as NSA ceased to rely on the SCA and service intelligence collocated liaison offices to distribute further. Reports in 1953 still contained [censored] had finally been expunged. There was still much information [censored] but analytical conclusions were now separated into a "Comments" section at the end of the report. Later in 1953 NSA excluded "COMINT technical data" from product reports completely and formed an Operational Management Control Group to enforce discipline. Collateral information could be used when necessary.

The COMINT reporter was often bedeviled by the same problems then as today. Periodically NSA organizations would chastise reporters for overusing "possibly" and "probably." A 1953 memo found NSA reporting "generally so cluttered with qualifying expressions as to virtually preclude their use by a consumer."

[censored] The National Security Agency was a term shop.

In 1955 the Hoover Commission declared that NSA, while producing some very valuable information, was not an official member of the intelligence community. But the commission undercut this general statement by noting that the volume of COMINT was so huge that it could never all be turned over to consumers, and by the very act of selecting individual pieces for dissemination, NSA made analytic judgments about value and applicability.

This trend was to continue and intensify. Key NSA executives knew that the organization had to move away from translations and into true intelligence reporting. Various sources of COMINT had to be synthesized, and the results must be packaged into a meaningful explanation of the situation. If possible, the reporter should make comments as to meaning and, on occasion, should make conclusions based on COMINT. This was a higher level of analysis than the rest of the intelligence community foresaw for NSA, and it would get the organization into trouble with consumers who resented what they regarded as turf encroachment. But it was the wave of the future.

NSA Training—The Early Years

Training had been the "bastard child" of AFSA. Originally the training school had been a section of the personnel office, a way station for new and uncleared personnel. New recruits were given unclassified Army traffic analysis and communications manuals to read until their clearances came through. The training was good—many of the manuals were written by Friedman himself—but the way AFSA treated the problem was all wrong. The staff was miniscule, facilities practically nonexistent, and the function was almost totally ignored. The real training concept was on-the-job training in the duty section. Almost all operations training was conducted in Production, with little centralized control and practically no classroom instruction. There was a training staff that tried to coordinate all this, but it did not work in the same organization as the cryptologic school, which was still part of personnel.

When the Korean War began, the training school was still in languid decay, with one hundred uncleared recruits reading musty traffic analysis manuals in the training spaces at Nebraska Avenue, supervised by a staff of six people. By the end of the year all was chaos. There were 1,100 trainees jammed into the same spaces, still with a staff of 6. Canine was aware of the problem, and AFSA went to work to improve the situation. In April of 1951 the school was moved to larger quarters at 1436 U Street, N .W., designated Tempo R. In June 1954 the school moved to another World War II building—Tempo X—located on the north side of East Capitol Street, in the area that is now part of the RFK Stadium parking lot. When, in the mid-1950s, NSA moved to Fort Meade, the training school moved to a former hospital a couple of miles from the main NSA complex.

Canine later separated training from the Office of Personnel and elevated it to the level of Office of Training. Its chief was named commandant of the NSA School. Canine was also a proponent of management training, which was begun in 1952, and he placed the first NSA students in service war colleges in 1953.

AFSA also began paying more attention to formal classroom instruction. Instead of the "sit in the corner and read a book" approach, it began offering a selection of classroom traffic analysis, cryptanalysis, mathematics, language, and technical training. By 1952 the school was offering training (at some level, at least) in eighteen different languages. Secretaries got instruction in clerical and stenographic skills, and there was a four~week teletype operators course for those assigned to communications. There was also a one-week indoctrination course for all new hires, with follow-on instruction for certain specialties. By mid-1952 AFSA was also offering three levels of management training—junior (presupervisory), supervisor, and executive. Classes were very small, but at least a rudimentary program existed.

NSA also began using education as inducement. Begun under AFSA, the College Contract Program began with a contract with George Washington University and amounted to NSA payment of tuition to qualifiers. Classes were held at Arlington Hall, Nebraska Avenue in the District, and at Thomas Jefferson Junior High School in Virginia. There was also a program for graduate students and, for a select few, a fellowship program which offered full-time study away from NSA.

NSA's role in broader cryptologic training within the services was less certain. Both AFSA and NSA enjoyed a theoretical technical control of cryptologic standards, which included training, but AFSA never exercised its review function. An early AFSA proposal to create a consolidated cryptologic training school was scuttled by Brigadier General Roy Lynn, an AFSA deputy director, who was concerned about retaining USAF Security Service independence.

After 1952, things began to change as NSA became active in reviewing SCA cryptologic courses. The Agency was especially active in providing technical assistance for language training and at one time took responsibility for all language training beyond the basic level. It did not, however, try to take on COMSEC training, preferring to leave that to the SCAs.

Canine continued to strengthen the organizational position of the training function. As it migrated up from branch to division level, it took on added responsibilities and acquired more resources. The people who were involved in training in those early days were first rate—Lambros D. Callimahos (a close protégé of Friedman) and Navy captain Thomas "Tommy" Dyer (one of the Navy's great pioneers in codebreaking) were especially notable examples. William Friedman, who had personally built the Army's cryptanalytic system, spent much of his career as a teacher and authored many textbooks on cryptanalysis. With such talent and influence, it was only a matter of time before NSA's training system became a model.

Setting Up Security

Security was one area with which Canine had experience, and he tackled it very early. Under AFSA, perimeter guards at Arlington Hall and Nebraska Avenue had been uncleared. Interior guard duty was pulled on a rotating basis by reluctant uniformed cryptologists, each division taking its turn for a month at a time. Canine eliminated the interior guard duty in early 1952 by bringing in cleared, uniformed security police. Later he decided to add some prestige to the NSA guard force and convinced the Navy to give up a detachment of Marine guards to begin guarding the new temporary NSA facilities at Fort Meade in 1955. Normally reserved for embassy duty, the Marine guard detachment became a fixture and source of pride at NSA for many years.

Given the size of the cryptologic complex in Washington, some sort of universal personnel identification system became necessary. The Army appears to have begun using personnel badges during World War II. Their badges in those days were round metal tabs with a picture overlayed with plastic—fully cleared people had red badges, opposite the system of today. After a costly experiment with glass badges, AFSA settled on a plastic badge. Color coding identified organization, with seven colors total. In 1956 the organizational affiliation began to fade as NSA reduced the number of colors for cleared people to four and began using green badges for fully cleared employees. Metal badges returned in 1959 and were standard until the late 1970s. NSA employees found them ideal for scraping ice off windshields.

Along with a badge system, NSA began restricting area access. By 1953 the security division had devised three work area designations: restricted, secure, and exclusion. The "red seal" and "blue seal" tabs used for so many years to designate compartmented areas did not, however, come into use until NSA moved to its new quarters at Fort Meade in 1957.

NSA's controversial experiment in polygraph screening was rooted in the Korean War. As new employees flooded into the training school at Nebraska Avenue, the security system was overwhelmed with clearance requirements. Then, as now, employees were cleared through a combination of the National Agency Check and background investigations, conducted by the services. By December 1950 the system was so inundated that 39 percent of AFSA employees were uncleared. NSA security people began casting about for a quick way to process clearances and fastened their attention on the polygraph, long used by law enforcement agencies in criminal investigations. Although polygraphs were not admissable in court, AFSA discovered that CIA had begun using them for people being indoctrinated for COMINT as early as 1948 and only two months earlier, had broadened testing to include the entire CIA work force. Studies showed it to be a more reliable indicator of loyalty than the background investigation, and it was proposed that the polygraph be tried as a way to get an "interim" clearance. Canine approved a trial program in January 1951, but implementation was tricky. AFSA had to buy the equipment, recruit polygraph examiners from the police departments and private detective agencies around the country, build soundproof rooms for the interviews, and become experienced in interpreting results in this new and experimental area of loyalty verification.

The new polygraph procedures began on a trial basis at the U Street location in May of 1951. Soon examiners were working from seven in the morning to eleven at night. By the end of September, they had cleared the backlog and went back to regular hours. AFSA had suddenly acquired hundreds of employees with something called a "temporary" clearance, who still required completion of the background investigation to become "permanent." But in the helter-skelter time of war, no one paid the slightest attention to the difference, and on the day NSA was created a large portion of the work force worked with a temporary clearance. This situation would come back to haunt NSA in 1960 when Martin and Mitchell fled to Moscow and NSA's clearance practices were called into question.

In the rush to clear people, there was considerable breakage. Examiners were used to dealing with criminal investigations, and some of them had trouble making the transition. Hostile questions elicited emotional responses, and the rate of unresolved interviews approached 25 percent. The incredibly long hours added to the stress, and by the end of the first summer it was hard to tell who was more stressed, the examiners or the examinees. But after a very bumpy start, things smoothed out, and the security organization claimed to have cleared up lingering administrative problems by 1953.

When first begun, the polygraph was "voluntary," but Canine declared that if an applicant did not volunteer, the application went no further. The fiction of optional polygraphs continued until 6 December 1953, after that historic date all applicants were polygraphed. But there were always exceptions to the general rule that all employees were polygraphed. No requirement was established to include existing employees in the system, and the military, amid much controversy, refused to allow its people to be polygraphed.

The modern (and usually functional, if somewhat cranky) classified waste disposal system of the 1990s was a good deal less high-tech in 1952. Early destruction at both Arlington Hall and Nebraska Avenue was by incineration. Burnbags were stapled shut, as they are today, were marked with the originators' organization, and were placed in central collection locations. Once picked up, they were pitched into the fire by a military detail, and destruction was certified by a commissioned officer.

In late 1951 AFSA, determined to modernize the procedure, ordered two Somat machines, which AFSA officials had seen in operation at CIA. The machines operated much like the present destruction facility but on a much smaller scale. There was a whirling tub resembling a cement mixer, into which the burnbags were thrown. The door was then closed, water was injected, and the tub churned. But the early models did not work very well, and the whole process was as dirty as a paper mill. NSA later returned to the old standby incinerator until something better could be devised.

NSA And The U.S. Intelligence System

NSA and its director were coping with the problems—technical, organizational, and fiscal—in establishing a truly global SIGINT system, which at one and the same time would serve national and parochial interests. This required a strong central institution and considerable adjustment of the old ways of doing business. When Canine tried to make the adjustments, he ran into opposition from every direction. His attempts to impose uniformity were opposed by the SCAs, while his SIGINT turf was simultaneously being invaded by the CIA.

Consumer Groups Come to NSA

The modern method of marketing SIGINT is primarily through Cryptologic Support Groups (CSGs) accredited to consumer organizations. Many NSAers are surprised that it was not always such. But in fact, the system began exactly opposite. In the beginning, consumers established liaison detachments (sometimes referred to as "beachheads") within NSA. Indeed, NSCID 9 codified what already existed in AFSA when it stated that "the Director shall make provision for participation by representatives of each of the departments and agencies eligible to receive COMINT products in those offices of NSA where priorities of intercept and processing are finally planned." The motivating force appears to have been to give customers a voice in setting COMINT collection and reporting priorities. But the customers did not limit themselves to expressing requirements. All of them sifted COMINT information and interpreted the meaning back to their parent organizations. Some of them actually produced their own report series and distributed them to their home offices.

In the beginning, many of these organizations were quite large and robust: in 1954 both Army and Office of Naval Intelligence had fifty-two analysts at NSA, CIA had [censored] and State had four. Air Force Security Service, however, had by far the largest, a total of eighty-one analysts working in an outfit called AFSSOP (Air Force Security Service Office of Production), which produced COMINT summaries digested from the mass of technical information available only at NSA headquarters.

NSA did not like the system, and over the years it made moves to cut off the flow of technical information that kept the consumer groups alive. These attempts were initially unsuccessful, but the beachheads gradually became smaller and finally faded out of existence, victims of an aggressive NSA external reporting program that made them unnecessary. By the end of the 1950s they were gone, except for liaison detachments that had no production or interpretive responsibilities.

The Struggle for Technical Control

NSCID 9 gave NSA "operational and technical control" of all U.S. COMINT operations. This revolutionary authority proved to be the glue that knit the COMINT community together.

Those who have lived within a unified system all their working lives cannot appreciate the technical problems that confronted NSA in November 1952. For instance, among the British, Army, and Navy, there were in the 1940s seven different naming conventions for Soviet codes and ciphers.

The Navy began the Second World War using [censored]

The British began with [censored]

The Army began with [censored]

The Navy copied Soviet intercept [censored] while the Army used an [censored]

The British were copying things [censored]

Each organization had its own traffic formats. When the traffic came into NSA, it all had to be hand-massaged to make it suitable for any sort of processing A coordinated attack on high-grade systems would be too time-intensive without standardization. Someone had to dictate formats.

The impetus behind standardization was processing. Raw traffic and digested extracts (called TECSUMs, or technical summaries) cascaded into NSA headquarters in unmanageable volumes. An NSA Technical Management Board created soon after NSA itself was established concluded that collection, and thus collection equipment, would have to be homogenized to permit NSA to process the traffic.

The original vehicle for securing compliance was a program of NSA circulars. They covered procedures for intercept, traffic forwarding, end product reporting, and services and facilities. In addition, NSA published Unit Operations Orders describing in general terms the mission of each unit authorized to produce COMINT. These publications, when taken together, constituted the NSA Field Operating Manual, a device borrowed directly from Army usage. Canine regarded them as directive, and he tenaciously enforced compliance, but the SCAs resisted. They initially regarded NSA directives as voluntary suggestions.

By 1956 the SCA units were having trouble distinguishing operating policy from technical guidance, which had over the preceding four years become hopelessly scrambled between the two categories of documents. So NSA created a new system that looked a lot less like an Army directive, called MUSCO (Manual of U.S. COMINT Operations). Within two years ELINT had been added to the national cryptologic mission, and MUSCO was changed again, to MUSSO (Manual of U.S. SIGINT operations). On those occasions when a consumer needed to know how SIGINT was produced or what NSA's operating policy was, a special series of MUSSO documents called INFOCONS was issued.

In April 1954, Canine unceremoniously yanked control of field site placement away from the SCAs. Henceforth, the establishment of field sites would be done only with the permission of the director. Even site surveys had to be coordinated with NSA first. Canine relented to the extent of allowing SCAs to place small (less than ten-position) sites during peacetime without his direct "chop." The important message, however, was that DIRNSA had now delegated this authority, implying rather directly that what he delegated he could rescind.

And while he was at it, the director pushed the concept, completely foreign to the SCAs, of cross-servicing, whereby targets would be collected by the most technically capable intercept site regardless of service affiliation. During the Korean War, for instance, ASA sites collected a good deal of North Korean air force communications under the cross-servicing concept (and to the loudly voiced complaints of USAFSS).

NSCID 9 gave the director untrammeled authority over COMINT direct support resources. A theater commander could request such support, but it was entirely up to DIRNSA whether the request was honored or not. Canines directive on control of direct support assets narrowly defined the conditions under which the director would delegate control. When and if he did, it would normally be to the SCA chief, not an "unlettered" field commander. There were no provisions for appeal should DIRNSA deny the request. This provision of DIRNSA's authority stood basically unchallenged through the 1950s, a time when there was very little direct tactical support to be done, anyway. It did not become an issue until the advent of the war in Vietnam.

Having destroyed the prerogatives of the armed services, Canine barely a month later released control of two ASA tactical units, [censored] to the commanding general of ASA. He made it plain, however, that these units were being released solely at his sufferance and pointedly reserved the right to task them temporarily or withdraw them completely for national tasking, at any time.

In 1955, Canine decreed that new types of field site equipment would henceforth require NSA coordination. In a letter to the three SCA chiefs, he stated that NSA would establish standards for facilities and equipment, manning and staffing factors, site surveys, and operational procedures. NSA set up a large and aggressive R&D program to work out equipment and facility standards. The people and equipment for this effort had been inherited from ASA and NSG, though in San Antonio AFSS clung to its own R&D organization and was more independent in this respect than the other two services.

The Decentralization Plan

While Canine moved to secure unchallenged authority over COMINT, he began, almost simultaneously, a parallel and apparently opposite program called "decentralization." The objective of the program was to improve the speed of delivery of COMINT information to consumers. [censored] The issue had been pushed hard by General Hoyt Vandenberg when he had been Chief of Staff of the Air Force. Vandenberg had wanted to make COMINT the basis for an independent Air Force intelligence component to back up the strategic force. Security Service and Air Force intelligence officials insisted on direct support and, in a series of conferences with NSA in the summer and fall of 1953, hammered out an agreement which resulted in NSA turning on a flow of high-precedence reports to both commands. This first included reporting from NSA but soon devolved on both field units and AFSCC. By 1964 NSA had reluctantly delegated analysis and reporting on the [censored] problem to AFSCC and it became the key player in COMINT warning to Air Force commands, a virtual third echelon competitor to NSA.

When the decentralization plan was officially launched in August 1954, it looked like planned engine thrust reversal. Under it, NSA assigned specific COMINT problems to specified field sites. The criteria for assignment were perishabilty, collectability, and [censored]

Relations with the SCAs

By the mid-1950s Canine basically had what he wanted—unrestrained authority over the entire Defense COMINT system (with a single exception which will be discussed below). But it had not been a cost-free victory. Relations with all three SCAs were strained to a greater or lesser degree.

The relationship with ASA was probably the best. ASA and NSA came to agreement on key issues such as decentralization and release of operational control to direct support resources somewhat earlier than the other two services. ASA was of a mind to play the centralization game with NSA "straight up" and gained considerable good will as a result, occasional complaints from ASA field offices about "meddling" by NSA field offices notwithstanding.

[censored]

Regarding naval COMINT, Canine and the Navy were speaking a different language. That they did not get into as many battles as NSA and the Air Force one can probably ascribe to the fact that most of the time they were simply speaking past each other.

Canine thought that Navy COMINT was organized like Army and Air Force COMINT, but this was not the case. The Navy had no integral cryptologic command akin to ASA or AFSS. Navy COMINT came under naval communications (OP-20), and fixed field sites were generally assigned to naval communications organizations for administrative and organizational matters. Naval afloat detachments were instruments of the fleet commander, not NSG. Certain central functions were performed at Nebraska Avenue by Naval Security Group, but it did not have the same authorities as its counterparts at Arlington Hall and Kelly AFB. In 1955, a frustrated Captain Jack Holtwick penned a lengthy memo bemoaning the difficulty that Canine was having with naval COMINT:

"For more than ten years, people . . . have been talking about something which has never really existed as an entity, namely the Navy Cryptologic Agency. . . . These organizations [speaking of all Navy COMINT organizations] were an entity only insofar as they were engaged in the same trade and mutually complemented one another in it. They have never had a legal cryptologic organizational head, let alone a functional commander. Their lowest common superior was and is the Chief of Naval Operations. . . ."

[censored]

By 1956, however, Canine apparently understood enough of Navy COMINT organization to object to its entire philosophy. He took aim at the subordination of detachment commanders to naval communications: "This is an unsatisfactory arrangement; there is always a conflict of basic interests in the direction of the units. The superior officers in the chain of command . . . are primarily concerned with general service communications; they are generally inexperienced in COMINT functions. . . ." He related the submersion of Navy COMINT to Navy communications with SCA position totals, in that from 1953 to 1956 NSG grew by only 7 percent, while ASA expanded by 380 percent and AFSS by 410 percent. This, he contended, resulted from deficient naval COMINT organization.

In contrast to NSG, AFSS growth was breathtaking. From a tiny cadre of 156 people in 1948, AFSS grew to 23,128 people by the end of 1960. The command had over 1,000 positions, a budget of more than $26 million, and it had surged ahead of both ASA and NSG on all counts in only twelve years.

NSA's relations with AFSS, however, were the worst of the three. Although COMSEC relations were smooth, COMINT was not. Under the hollow gaze of AFSA, AFSS had virtually seceded from the COMINT community, carrying its entire field site list with it. It had called the field sites [censored] so as to exempt them from AFSA tasking. (Major General John Morrison [USAF], a former NSA assistant director for production, once said that [censored] with very isolated exceptions, were about as [censored] as the Eifel Tower.") Canine's dicta on operational and technical control were intended largely to corral the errant AFSS resources. This was effective but did not make AFSS very happy.

The biggest row of the decade was over the Air Force Special Communications Center (AFSCC). Officially created in July 1953 as the 6901st Special Communications Center, AFSCC was intended as a third echelon processing center to satisfy Air Force desires for an indigenous Air Force COMINT center. The organization picked up such miscellaneous functions as the SSO system and the USAFSS training school but was intended all along as an analytical center and began functioning as one from its very first day of existence. Canine had said "No" to the Air Force plan but lost the battle. In January 1954 he gave up and, under the aegis of the decentralization plan, AFSCC acquired the mission of processing and reporting on the [censored] To this nucleus was added, over the years, virtually the entire [censored] as well as, beginning in 1961, the [censored] Relationships continued to deteriorate, and by the end of his term as DIRNSA, it was rumored that Canine was barely on speaking terms with the AFSS commander, Major General Hunt Bassett.

[censored]

The SCAs Create Second Echelons

The decentralization plan spawned a second concept, [censored] frequently wound up controlling related intercept positions at smaller units. The arrangement amounted to a de facto layering system in which large units controlled operations at smaller units, and in some cases the smaller units were officially subordinated to the larger ones. The intermediate tier came to be known as "second-echelon," while NSA (and in the Air Force, AFSCC) operations were called "third echelon."

[censored]

All three services created administrative units to supervise theater intercept sites, and to serve a liaison function with the supported commander(s). However, they all showed a disinclination to combine operational and administrative functions in the same organization, believing those to be separate tasks.

Watching the Watchers

DIRNSA's supervisor was not really the secretary of defense, despite what the Truman Memorandum said. In 1953 the secretary of defense assigned that job to General Graves B. Erskine, a Marine Corps four-star who was already assigned to his staff as head of the Office of Special Operations. Erskine monitored the CIA budget, which was hidden in the DoD budget, and after July 1953 he also monitored NSA. His deputy, Air Force colonel Edward Lansdale, later became famous as the author of covert actions projects in both the Philippines and Vietnam.

The monitoring that Erskine did was rather loose. He always retained professional cryptologists on his staff to work the details of cryptologic money, and under such a system, oversight was not detailed. Occasionally a big-ticket item would come up, like LIGHTNING, and Erskine's office would become involved. But Congress had not yet instituted an effective review of the intelligence agencies (and did not until the mid-1970s), and CIA did not yet have the authority to ride herd on the finances of the DoD intelligence organizations. So by the standards of later days, no one was really paying much attention to the intricacies of NSA's money.

NSA And CIA—The Early Years

"Will you please have the proper instructions issued discontinuing the cryptanalytical units in the offices of the Director of Censorship, the Federal Communications Commission and the Strategic Services. If you are aware of any other agencies having services of this character, will you please have them discontinued also." —Franklin D. Roosevelt, Memorandum for Director of Budget, 8 July 1942

The origins of CIA were rooted in World War II. Roosevelt, under the pressure of wartime exigency, created an espionage agency in 1942; called the Office of Strategic Services (OSS), under New York lawyer and World War I battlefield hero (winner of the Medal of Honor in France) William Donovan. Donovan's agency both collected and produced intelligence and mounted covert operations around the world. It was a mission that CIA was to inherit several years later.

NSA's difficulties with CIA stemmed from decisions made in the 1940s, almost all of them bad. JCS, which owned most of America's intelligence assets, opposed OSS from the beginning and did everything in its power to deny to OSS the resources to do its job. The Joint Chiefs failed to keep OSS out of the HUMINT business, but in one area they succeeded almost totally: COMINT was denied.

Roosevelt's order (above) resulted in the closure of a small OSS COMINT organization. Even worse, it was used by the JCS to deny to OSS access to ULTRA. Thus OSS reporting was crippled from the beginning. It had access to agent reports, photoreconaissance, POW and defector reports—everything, in short, but the most useful and reliable information. If World War II was, as has been claimed, a COMINT war, OSS remained on the intelligence sidelines.

And it rankled. OSS seniors who later served in the higher ranks of CIA never accepted the JCS policy. The British intelligence services, which dealt closely with OSS, were appalled. Their own intelligence community was unified, and HUMINT was routinely integrated with COMINT in highly specialized offices, in order to reap full value from both. (For instance, Ian Fleming, a British naval officer and later author of some note, was responsible for the integration of Bletchley-produced ULTRA with the Navy's HUMINT and special operations.) JCS had used security as justification for the denial of ULTRA to OSS, but the British were at least as security conscious as the Americans, and they seemed able to get COMINT of the highest sensitivity to those in the HUMINT business who needed it. The outright denial of ULTRA to OSS just did not make sense.

Truman discontinued OSS immediately after the end of the war, partly to rid himself of Donovan, who was not in favor with the president. But within six months Truman once again had himself an intelligence organization, called the Central Intelligence Group. CIG was bedeviled by the same problems that submerged AFSA—lack of its own budget and personnel resources (people were loaned in from other intelligence organizations), absence of a congressional mandate, and lack of firm direction from the top. But the idea was the same as that of AFSA—to establish central control of U.S. intelligence operations. When CIA was created in 1947, succeeding CIG, it got its congressional mandate, its budget, and its own personnel. It still lacked firm leadership, but that was remedied in 1950 with the appointment of General Walter Bedell Smith as DUI. Smith had been Eisenhower's chief of staff in Europe, and he knew how to run a tight ship. Tussling with "Beetle" Smith was like landing in a cactus patch.

In the early days the only high-level COMINT available to CIG was a copy of the MAGIC Summary put out by the Army, which was available in the Pentagon. In the very early days, only fifty people in CIG had a COMINT clearance. But in June of 1946 Hoyt Vandenberg became DCI. Vandenberg was fresh from a tour as chairman of USCIB and knew the value of COMINT. In December he created an organization within CIG, called the Advisory Council, to deal with what he hoped would be aflood of COMINT reports.

For a while there were few reports to disseminate. Requests for access to COMINT reports were generally denied. But in early 1947, two CIG organizations began to get involved with COMINT operations. The first was OSO (Office of Special Operations, the clandestine organization), which in March proposed to the Army and the Navy that they begin a Joint Counter-intelligence Center (JCIC), using COMINT as the basic source of information. The services received this enthusiastically, and JCIC was established at Nebraska Avenue, with the understanding that it would eventually move to CIG. (It moved to CIA in 1949.)

At about the same time, Colonel Robert Schukraft, chief of the Communications Division at CIG, was establishing a relationship with ASA.

Schukraft had been a key figure in wartime Army COMINT and knew many of the people involved in the COMINT business. He began a relationship with Frank Rowlett at ASA [censored]

The operational aspects of these budding relationships eventually came under the aegis of OSO, and specifically one William ("Bill") Harvey, a former FBI agent who became legendary for his clandestine operations. Under Harvey, who took over in 1950, COMINT operational matters became centralized [censored]

Meanwhile, CIA requests for COMINT reports were still being routinely turned down. But the [censored] contributed to breaking the logjam, and ever larger volumes of COMINT report series were forwarded to CIA. Once at CIA, the material was subdivided according to subject matter and farmed out to analysts through the auspices of the Advisory Council. CIA was determined to base reporting on all-source information, rather than to strictly segregate COMINT from all other sources. Of necessity, then, the number of CIA COMINT clearances rose rapidly, until by 1970 most intelligence analysts were cleared for the source. CIA policy stood in contrast to that of the Pentagon, which generally chose to compartment COMINT and to deal with two separate handling systems—COMINT and all other sources.

[censored]

When AFSA was created, CIA made a pitch for a more active role in COMINT. Then-DCI Roscoe Hillenkoetter proposed that he should be given the chairmanship of USCIB, but this was quickly overruled. CIA [censored] but was being told in unmistakable fashion that they would remain on the sidelines when it came to the policy aspects of COMINT. That was still the domain of the JCS.

CIA remained a major critic of COMINT throughout the AFSA period, and Hillenkoetter's successor, Walter Bedell Smith, played an important role in getting the president to appoint the Brownell Committee. CIA was determined to get a bigger stake in the game.

Smith got much of what he wanted from Brownell. He was made chairman of USCIB and, as such, could play a large role in COMINT policy. The results of the Brownell Report also gave CIA the chance to lean on the new NSA to get its own requirements satisfied. No longer would the civilians have to take a perpetual backseat to military requirements.

CIA Enters the COMINT Business

In the beginning, CIA probably did not intend to build its own cryptologic organization. Two very senior NSA officials, Louis Tordella and [censored] both closely involved in the NSA-CIA relationship, categorically deny that this was the intent. [censored] himself described his first interview with Allen Dulles when he transferred from NSA to CIA: "I mean Dulles put it flatly, we were not going into competition with NSA. We've got enough to do in CIA and we're not going to fragmentize [sic] our efforts by going over there and starting a . . . COMINT organization. . . ." But CIA needed certain information, and as long as cryptology remained the province of the Department of Defense, he felt it could not get its requirements satisfied. Smith decided to change things.

The CIA Act of 1949 gave the espionage agency the authority to expend what were called discretionary funds". [censored] for which the director would not have to answer to Congress in any detail. According to Tordella, the DCI first used these moneys [censored]

To a great extent this developed out of on-going CIA operations. [censored]

[censored]

[censored]

CIA And Cryptographic Materials

[censored]

The [censored] Business

In no area did NSA and CIA clash more frequently and with as much vigor as in [censored] matters. There, NSCID 5 was in direct conflict with the BRUSA Agreement. The former gave CIA control of foreign intelligence relationships, while the latter required [censored] one of the half-dozen most important cryptologists in America; had had a choppy relationship with General Canine. [censored] felt that his own temperament was too methodical for the hip-shooting Canine, and the two were not getting along when Canine, in a mood to reorganize, decreed that all his seniors would rotate jobs in order to infuse the organization with new ideas. [censored] who had been working COMINT, was ordered to COMSEC. [censored]

[censored] was joined by a small but experienced group of NSAers, including [censored] whose province was COMINT matters. [censored] who was well aware of the benefits of continued collaboration with the [censored] partners, brought some order into CIA's COMINT matters.

[censored]

[censored]

The Third Parties in the Early Years

[censored]

[censored] On its side, however, NSA also made mistakes. The most serious was in denying technical help to some of the more advanced Third parties. This unyielding position often reduced CIA equities in other areas and damaged NSA's relationship with its senior intelligence partner.

CIA In The NSA Trenches

The most direct CIA involvement in NSA was a CIA-controlled analysis division which existed for the better part of six years. This strasnge story began with the explosion of an atomic bomb.

When, in September of 1949, the Soviet exploded their first nuclear device, the erie light from the explosion silhouetted a US intelligence system in disarray. It had been CIA's job to follow Soviet nuclear technology, but JCS intelligence organizations gave CIA only lukewarm cooperation. The result was a National Intelligence Estimate (NIE), issued earlier in the yar, featuring a wide variety of estimates of Soviet acquisition of efective nuclear technology, none of them even close to being accurate. [censored]

[censored]

As AFSA-246 became NSA-75, CIA turned more and more to direct action. In 1963, Canine and Leftus Becker, CIA's deputy director for intelligence, inked an agreement that turned management of the division over to CIA. It was captained by a CIA person, kept its own database, did itsown reporting, and even forwarded raw COMINT to CIA headquarters for further analysis.

[censored]

[censored]

In 1948 CIA, in cooperation with a Department of State organization called OPC (Office of Policy Coordination), began beaming propaganda (some would say "news") broadcasts toward the Soviet Bloc. The operation was called Voice of America, and it lived a long and healthy life during the Cold War. Predictably, however, as soon as the VOA stations went on the air, the Communist nations at which they were targeted began jamming the broadcasts. Thus ensued, in February of 1948, yet another area of intense competition between CIA and the cryptologic community.

Tackling the problem of jamminig would involve radio monitoring. CIA took on the job in 1949 and immediately began preparing a plan to identify and locate the jammers and devise a solution. In June 1950 an ad hoc group of the IAC (Intelligence Advisory Committee chaired by the DCI) approved a preliminary monitoring plan, called [censored]

Just how Admiral Stone of AFSA found out about it is not known, but it was hard to keep secrets at the IAC level. In any case, Stone contacted the Department of State (at the time OPC was still officially part of State rather than CIA) in July of 1950 to let them know that he regarded this as an AFSA responsibility under NSCID 9. Hillenkoetter justified CIA activity to AFSAC as being performed under the section of the National Security Act that permitted CIA to perform "such additional services of common concern as the National Security Council determines can be more efficiently accomplished centrally. . . ." This was a weak reed, and Hillenkoetter made his case even less plausible by stating that monitoring facilities so established could be used for other purposes in time of war. Such a direct challenge to AFSA authority in COMINT brought a predictable AFSAC response, and in November USCIB took up the issue. USCIB concluded in November that [censored] was a COMINT mission and should be headed by AFSA. A USCIB study costed the problem at $5 million and 355 people. But when the matter went before the National Security Council in early 1951,

CIA won. The NSC directed that CIA be the focal point for a multi-agency attack on the jamming problem.

AFSA wrote a supporting plan but continued to insist that it be given the mission. When Canine became director, he took forceful exception to CIA encroachment in the [censored] situaton. But Canine was handicapped by limited resources. [censored] was going to be expensive, and when the SCAs were polled, they offered only part-time DF facilities. NSA did not have the money to create a separate system just to monitor jamming, and the military services contended that they could not provide the communications to interlock a monitoring system anyway. So in February 1952 President Truman approved a plan for CIA to proceed on its own.

[censored]

Just what was [censored] anyway? Jammers actually produced noncommunications signals, and the Army contended that they were ELINT, not COMINT. The entire subject of ELINT was in chaos at the time, and [censored] simply contributed to the disorder. The services also saw electronic warfare applications, and they wanted their own people in the projected NSA-controlled [censored] sites to send EW-related information to their parent services. NSA feared this approach because it would spread COMINT-related information outside codeword channels, and the services might turn the information into EW (electronic warfare) projects that would block COMINT hearability. This prompted NSA to appoint a committee to study the matter of jamming versus COMINT requirements. The confusion in definitions foreshadowed more serious divisions during the Vietnam era.

[censored] This was a direct invasion of NSA's turf.

In the mid-1950s, as [censored] continued along an inconclusive course, various schemes emerged for the eventual institutionalization of [censored] Most had as their central assumption that CIA would not continue in charge, and some placed NSA in control. The services wanted the mission but did not want to budget for it. One proposed plan would even have given the mission to the Federal Communications Commission. In late 1955, the secretary of defense put the matter to rest by decreeing that it was an ELINT mission and made the Air Force executive agent. The Air Force had only recently become executive agent for ELINT, and it had a central ELINT processing center. Since no resources were allocated to do [censored] it became subsumed in the overall service ELINT mission.

So in the end a separate monitoring system was not built. The jamming mission was handled as a corollary mission by the three SCAs, and when, in 1958, control of ELINT went to NSA, the threat posed by [censored] vanished.

[censored]

[censored]

In April 1956, after heavy rains caused interruptions in communications service in the East Zone, East German maintenance workers discovered the taps and unearthed the entire operation. In the space of a few hours, [censored] was shut down, and the acting commandant of the Soviet Berlin Garrison held a press conference on the site of the "capitalist warmongers' expensive subterranean listening post." Now that the whole world knew about [censored] CIA could not continue [censored] for security reasons. After April 1955, CIA sent an enormous volume of unprocessed channel hours [censored]

[censored]

Years later the "accidental" discovery of [censored] came under serious question. In 1961 George Blake, a British MI-6 official who had been involved with the planning of [censored] was identified as a Soviet mole by a Polish defector and was subsequently arrested and jailed. In 1970 Blake, who had escaped from a British jail and fled to Moscow, bragged to the press that he had betrayed the Berlin Tunnel operation. It was also suspected that he had blown the whistle on the [censored] operation, too.

Bitterness between NSA and CIA lasted for years. Canine was understandably upset when he found that he had been bypassed and left in the dark. DCI Allen Dulles once mused that [censored]

NSA and CIA continued to clash over a variety of issues as long as Dulles and Canine were the respective helmsmen. Yet the warfare was oddly out of place in Dulles's office According to historian Thomas Powers, Dulles "never attempted to exercise [authority over the Defense Department intelligence components], partly in the interest of maintaining bureaucratic peace with the military, and partly because he just did not care."

Dulles was interested in HUMINT and covert operations, not technical intelligence. Richard Bissell, who headed the CIA's operations organization in the late 1950s, once said that "Dulles was always being encouraged by successive Presidents to exercise more direction of the whole intelligence community. And Allen always resisted that. . . . He always wanted to run his Agency and exercise a direct, unambiguous control..."

[censored]

According to senior NSA officials of the time, the era of CIA's SIGINT system was already beginning to fade. They had neither the time nor the money to pursue a big SIGINT system and a big HUMINT/covert actions system simultaneously, and so SIGINT was sacrificed.

General John Samford, who replaced Canine in 1956, moved to heal the breach with Dulles and the CIA. Samford was a consummate diplomat, and he probably gained more by soft-soaping the downtown intelligence people than Canine could have done through head-on collisions.

NSA's Other Competitors

The growing size and importance of COMINT made it inevitable that the cryptologic organizations of the armed services would have other competitors from time to time. During World War II there had been several.

The Federal Communications Commission had a long history of communications monitoring to secure compliance with federal radio regulations. During the early part of World War II, the FCC published a series of magazine articles plugging their successful efforts at finding Axis agent communications. The Army and Navy cryptologists did not appreciate this glare of publicity on their secret profession, and they sought to get Roosevelt to close down FCC operations. Roosevelt's order of 1942 (cited at the beginning of this chapter) was meant to apply to the FCC and other competitors of the Army and Navy, but there is evidence that the FCC continued a small intercept effort into the postwar period. At some undefined point in the 1950s, the effort was probably shut down.

The FBI represented a far stronger and potentially more dangerous foe. But J. Edgar Hoover's interests were more limited, and throughout his life the FBI displayed a certain ambivalence toward involvement in COMINT. During World War II the FBI was one of the three organizations given a COMINT role. Namely, they were responsible for monitoring of the communications of Axis agents in Latin America. This apparently simple division of effort placed the FBI in almost constant conflict with OP-20-G, which had a very similar mission. By all accounts, the FBI had a small but competent intercept and cryptanalytic section of indeterminate size. But COMINT had nothing to do with Hoover's main thrust as FBI director, and after the war the FBI COMINT effort was reduced. When FBI joined STANCIB in 1947 (which then became USCIB), Rear Admiral Thomas Inglis, the chairman of USCIB, offered COMINT resources to monitor agent communications and do the cryptanalysis. Hoover accepted, mainly because this would allow him to divert FBI resources to other matters. In 1947 FBI withdrew from USCIB, allegedly because of declining budget to do COMINT tasks.

[censored] Even more important was the AFSA-FBI liaison which led ultimately to the arrest of the atomic spies.

ELINT and NSA

ELINT as an intelligence discipline probably began during the Battle of Britain. The intercept of noncommunications signals was first attempted by one R. V. Jones, who successfully collected mysterious German navigational signals used by the Luftwaffe to steer their bombers to targets over Britain. Jones employed electronic countermeasures to divert the bombers and cause many of the bombs to fall off target. It was one of Churchill's top secrets of the war.

The British understood the close relationship between ELINT and COMINT, and they centralized both under GCHQ. But when they tried to deal with the United States, they found American ELINT to be frustratingly decentralized. It wasn't just that they had to deal directly with the SCAs rather than AFSA and NSA, they found that even within the individual services there was no focal point.

The SCAs did much of the ELINT collection for their respective services. Each one had a network of ELINT collection sites, often collocated with

COMINT sites. But the tactical commanders also had their own ELINT assets, often airborne (and shipborne, in the case of the Navy). Once collected, the intercepted tapes were forwarded to processing centers in the theater and on to the United States. Some of the processing centers were joint-service operations, while some were single-service.

By 1953 the Army and Navy had established a consolidated ELINT processing center called ANEEG (Army-Navy Electronic Evaluation Group) collocated with NSG at Nebraska Avenue. The Air Force did not participate, preferring to keep a separate processing facility at AFSS headquarters, under the auspices of the Air Force Technical Intelligence Center (ATIC) at Wright-Patterson Air Force Base near Dayton, Ohio. NSA was not involved in this tangled web.

In 1953 the Robertson Committee reported to Canine on the profoundly disorganized nature of American ELINT and concluded that as a source of warning information, this intelligence discipline was in danger of becoming irrelevant. The committee recommended that a focal point be found.

CIA, too, was unhappy with the way ELINT was being managed and in the same year conducted an internal study that indicted the Defense Department for mismanagement of ELINT. CIA pointed out that there was no central authority, no coordination of ELINT activities, and no central processing. The study opted to place central control in USCIB, but one option which the drafters seriously considered was to give NSA the job.

There being no focus in U.S. intelligence for ELINT, CIA began to take on this task also. In 1954, the deputy director, General C.P. Cabell (USAF), appointed an ELINT czar by giving H. Marshall Chadwell, the assistant director for scientific intelligence, an additional hat for ELINT. [censored]

When he received the Robertson study in November of 1953, General Erskine in the office of the secretary of defense called in Canine and requested an NSA response. On returning to Arlington Hall, Canine found his agency badly divided over what to do. The eminent logic of combining ELINT and COMINT was sometimes obscured by the evident difficulty of getting the services to heel to central authority and the dismal prospect of ever getting a charter as clear and unequivocal as NSCID 9. If COMINT, with NSCID 9 conveying absolute authority, was proving so difficult to manage, what of ELINT?

Despite this, the allure of finally getting the two pieces of the electronics puzzle together proved too strong. Under Canine's direction, NSA's Office of Plans and Policy produced a draft report which placed operational and technical control of ELINT with DIRNSA. The battle was joined.

When the issue went to USCIB, the JCS predictably defended decentralization. Over the ensuing two years, piles of studies were completed, and hundreds of options were tossed about. The services never relented in their opposition to any sort of restriction on the latitude of the tactical commanders to collect, process, and report ELINT. All concerned recognized that there should be some sort of overall coordinating mechanism and that the government must set up a central processing facility at which all the players would be represented, including non-DoD organizations (i.e., CIA). NSA appeared to be the only organization that felt that NSA should be in charge.

The "ELINT Problem" was temporarily resolved in May of 1955 with the publication of NSCID 17. This document gave ELINT policy to USCIB and directed that a centralized ELINT processing center be set up (the National Technical Processing Center, or NTPC). However, it still allowed for separate management of DoD and CIA ELINT activities. The Air Force was given executive responsibilities for both ELINT and monitoring of jamming signals [censored] Neither NSCID 17 nor the DoD implementing directive resolved the issue of where NTPC was to be located. After months of discussion, the services decided to keep it at Nebraska Avenue, where ANEEG was already located.

NTPC was comprised initially of approximately one hundred people from the three services and CIA-NSA was not even represented. Most of the billets came from ANEEG, and the SCAs exercised a predominant influence since they provided most of the expertise. CIA, however, sent a very strong delegation. An ELINT requirements group was established in 1956, comprising representatives from the services plus CIA, and later in the year a committee on [censored] was created. This was the first NTPC organization that had any sort of NSA representation.

In 1956 NTPC was given the additional mission of processing telemetry from Soviet missiles. This problem was to grow and multiply almost geometrically as the Soviet missile problem became a national preoccupation. Sitting between COMINT and ELINT, telemetry would soon become another area of controversy between NSA and its competitors.

NSCID 17 was remarkable for what it did not do. It did not establish operational control in one organization. Nor did it rein in the propensities of the armed services to fund separate ELINT assets for nearly every operational command. It did not unify the technical aspects of the business. Instead, it consigned management to a committee which was already deeply fractured on other issues (such as the dispute between NSA and CIA over control of COMINT). It did not resolve anything at all, but it merely perpetuated an existing condition.

Building The Overt Collection Systems

Few cryptologic field sites survived World War II. By 1947, the two services were operating [censored] The Army maintained large fixed field sites, but very few of them. The Navy tended toward small sites, many with only a DF mission, scattered throughout the world to maintain a DF baseline.

Even more striking was the geographic pattern. The United States had but one cryptologic organization on the continent of Europe. [censored] sites were in the U.S. Of the rest, the Army collection site in [censored] had existed since the early days of World War II. The other overseas sites were in [censored] and they copied primarily [censored] targets. The Navy's overseas sites were all in the [censored]

This soon changed. The Cold War, the Communist takeover in Czechoslovakia in 1948, the Communist victory in China in 1949, and the unpleasantness in Korea, combined to force a revolution in America's cryptologic posture. The somnolent late 1940s became the go-go 1950s. Cryptologic planning was stirred to a white heat, and the collection system fairly exploded. By 1960 American's cryptologic collection system [censored] had basically been built.

Three things typified this system:

1. The target was the Soviet Union. China, Korea, and the East European satellites were simply corollary targets. [censored]

2. Containment of Communist expansion was the objective. The collection system became geographically arrayed to resemble Lenin's predicted "capitalistic encirclement," a figurative string of pearls beginning in [censored] And despite this seemingly heedless expansion, NSA was barely able to keep up with customer requirements.

3. This was the Golden Age of HF. Long-haul HF systems dominated the world communications networks. Above-HF transmissions did exist, but in HF's Golden Age, most of the truly important messages seemed eventually to find some mode of HF expression. Propagation vagaries demanded that collection sites be placed in a wide variety of locations. But in theory, if one established enough sites and built [censored]

Expansion proceeded on two fronts. The first was ELINT, which was chaos reborn. The services embarked on a period of virtually uncontrolled site-building. ELINT was above HF so sites tended to be located in great profusion [censored] In this field each SCA had been given primary collection job by its respective service, and each moved quickly to establish sites. In many, if not most, instances ELINT preceded COMINT, and again in most cases ELINT sites already existed where COMINT sites were later added. [censored] Added to this was a burgeoning airborne collection system, fielded by USAFSS. NSA played no role in ELINT, either in collection or processing.

When it came to COMINT, though, NSA employed its guiding hand. Even before NSA was created, AFSA had a master plan for the establishment of SCA intercept sites which [censored] This plan was passed on to NSA which refined it. NSA worked very closely with each SCA to determine collection requirements and determine the best candidate locations. In the early 1950s NSA asserted control over site surveys, without which no collection site could be established. NSA balanced customer requirements against existing overt [censored] sites, documented hearability, and Second and Third Party contributions. If the project did not make sense, DIRNSA could be counted on to oppose it.

[censored]

[censored]

[censored]

Berlin was in an entirely different situation. Its status as a four-power occupied city meant that Soviets could walk relatively freely even in the American Sector. Stalin's attempt to squeeze the Westerners out of Berlin (resulting in the Berlin Airlift) in 1948 placed the city in a uniquely precarious position. In such circumstances the first COMINT intercept organization, a detachment of the ASA site [censored] arrived in a covert status and stayed only a few weeks in 1951.But ASA covert detachments kept appearing in Berlin, and in the following year the command established a permanent unit there, and the troops moved from tents to covered buildings.

In 1953 the Army G-2 concluded that the results had been paltry and recommended the site be closed, a strange finding given the later reputation of Berlin as a SIGINT bonanza. Fortunately, no one listened to the G-2, and ASA continued to occupy a variety of locations [censored] AFSS followed ASA into Berlin in 1954, beginning a presence in the city that would last until alter the fall of the Berlin Wall.

Berlin became a SIGINT gold mine, a window into the heart of the Communist Bloc military system. In the mid-1950s the collection sites began to report the existence of VHF communications, and NSA moved in to investigate. An NSA technician [censored] discovered that Berlin was crisscrossed with above-HF communications that the West had never before intercepted, including Soviet high-capacity multichannel and microwave transmissions. The discovery was to have a profound influence on the development of the SIGINT collection system.

[censored]

[censored]

[censored]

The Far North

All three services established collection sites in Alaska. The Navy site at Adak dated back to World War II, and the Air Force and Army soon followed. The USAFSS site grew out of the [censored] a World War II Army Air Corps asset. Security Service established its first collection site [censored] The Army site was established near Fairbanks (1950). But AFSS soon eclipsed ASA in resources, as the [censored] proved to be very lucrative and the predominant one in Alaska. [censored] eventually grew to become one of the major Security Service sites, while the ASA site closed in 1959.

[censored]

What It Was Like

Military units tend to form around existing support organizations. Army units cluster at Army posts, Air Force organizations locate at existing Air Force bases, Navy units form at Navy bases. Cryptologic units, however, must go where they can hear targets. Where there is an existing military base, so much the better. But if there is none, one must be built specifically for the collection organization. This condition was especially true in the 1950s, when collection was done primarily to satisfy national strategic requirements rather than to support tactical commanders. In such a situation, it was not necessary for cryptologic organizations to stay with a supported commander. They could, and often did, go off on their own.

Geographically, collection sites were scattered. They tended to be small, isolated, and largely self-sufficient. Running a site required a very high level of independence and self-reliance. Even when collocated on a major military installation, the SIGINT unit was not part of the command structure. The post or base commander was generally not SI cleared and treated the cryptologic unit somewhat like a leper. Under such conditions, support was difficult to obtain.

In the late 1950s, Air Force Security Service under Major General Gordon Blake decided to solve its logistics problems itself. With the blessings of the Air Force, AFSS began managing bases at which its unit represented the major activity. Begun in July of 1958, the program eventually resulted in USAFSS's taking over [censored] as well as their training base, Goodfellow AFB, Texas. The huge 466L building program (see chapter 8) may have been a factor, but Blake himself claimed that troop support was the driving force behind this program. It changed USAFSS into a large-scale landowner, and it was not copied by either ASA or NSG.

Climate could be an enemy. Air Force and Army sites at place [censored] would frequently be snowed in much of the winter. Roads [censored] were often impassable. Some sites could be supplied only by helicopter. In the tropics, the lack of air conditioning at places like Clark made work almost unbearable.

Even when the weather cooperated, conditions in places like [censored] were primitive. Army troops arriving [censored] lived in pup tents for months. There was initially no airstrip, and visitors to the site had a two-day drive from [censored] over almost nonexistent roads.

Living conditions presented further challenges. A former resident of [censored] a relatively "plush" location [censored] describes the site in fairly realistic terms: "The station itself was a loose cluster of small, dusty buildings perched on the cliff above the village [censored] The age old strategic value of the place was shown by the fact that our work went on in the shadow of a ruined [censored] castle. Water had to be hauled a mile from a spring. The site produced its own elecricity with diesel generators, as the local power could not be relied on. There were no barracks, personnel lived in apartments [censored] and commuted by bus and boat [censored] to the site. Since the ferry did not run after dark, the eve and mid shifts had to report at 1600 and the off-duty watch slept in bunks in a quonset hut."

In the early days, intercept sites took on all manner of configuration, from squad tents to quonsets to clapboard "hootches" in Southeast Asia.

(The term "hootch" derived from the Japanese word "uchi," meaning "home," and migrated from the postwar occupation forces to the jungles of Southeast Asia.) But they gradually assumed a classic appearance as systems were standardized and permanent structures built. Most permanent sites were windowless blockhouses surrounded by high chain link fences with a single guarded aperture.

[censored] and the base commander sometimes economized on space by building the golf course in the antenna field.

[censored]

The intercept area was generally divided into smaller rooms. Manual Morse, radioprinter, and voice modes usually had separate rooms, and at larger sites the Morse mission was frequently subdivided into rooms by target. Operators in the early days often [censored]

[censored]

[censored]

All services showed an interest in DF as a SIGINT technique, but the Navy was far ahead of the other two. The Navy had begun experimenting with VDF as a navigational aid as early as 1906, and until the mid-1930s DF was developed for its short-range navigational value. But by 1935 OP-20-G had got hold of DF for intelligence purposes, and it gradually turned the Navy's primary interest toward strategic and tactical intelligence applications. By 1941 the Navy operated twenty-two strategic DF stations, organized into Atlantic, West Coast, Mid-Pacific, and Asiatic nets. In addition, the Navy had found that the British had invented effective shipboard DF systems (something the U.S. Navy had yet to accomplish) and began buying these systems from the British.

[censored]

SIGINT Goes Airborne

Even by the end of World War II, the HF spectrum was becoming very crowded, and the Germans were beginning to experiment with VHF communications. Both the British and Americans flew airborne intercept missions against VHF targets during the latter stages of the war.

Eighth Air Force, concerned about the possibility of a German march into the VHF spectrum, began to install recorders and receivers set to pretuned frequencies on some of their strategic aircraft [censored] This they referred to as their "airborne Y Service." General "Hap" Arnold of the Army Air Force directed a crash program to develop a dedicated airborne reconnaissance program, replete with special schools, dedicated aircraft (a modified B-24) and designated equipment. The AAF called the program "Ferret," and in early 1943 sent the first B-24s to Adak in the Aleutians. In March of 1943 a Ferret aircraft flying out of Adak obtained what was probably the first airbome intercept of a Japanese radar emission.

Spurred by the fortuitous capture of a Japanese radar on Guadalcanal in 1942, the Navy put together a seat-of-the-pants ELINT collection effort in the

Pacific. The program did not have dedicated aircraft or specific units; the people involved just loaded their intercept gear on any airframe that happened to be flying in the right area. The effort paid off in June 1943, when Navy airborne intercept operators collected their first Japanese radar emission. Despite this success, however, the Navy realized that this approach was too haphazard, and in late 1943 a special reconnaissance unit was formed for the Southwest Pacific Theater. This very early effort eventually became the VQ-1 squadron.

Following the war, the Air Force continued aerial reconnaissance against the [censored] By 1947 the Army Air Force already had a rather elaborate postwar Ferret program in both the Far East and Europe. The AAF requested ASA assistance in placing COMINT intercept aboard, but at the time ASA displayed little interest.

BLUE SKY

Postwar COMINT airborne collection, however, developed from the Korean War rather than from the Soviet threat. In 1952 Air Force Security Service became concerned about reports that North Korean pilots were using the VHF spectrum for GCI communications. As their intercept of HF GCI communications was beginning to dry up, this seemed plausible and led to the establishment of a survey site on Cho Do Island. Cho Do definitely proved the existence of VHF GCI communications, and this finding boosted an embryonic program to build a COMINT collection aircraft using an RB-29 as the platform.

But the people in the Far East were not willing to wait for a long-range fix. The commander of [censored] working with Far East Air Force, initiated an in-theater effort which they called Project BLUE SKY. The idea was to seize whatever platform was available—this proved to be a C-47. It was modified by the addition of collection equipment and antennas formed up into a single intercept position and was launched into a series of trial orbits. Although there was plenty of VHF to be had, the orbit, because of requirements to be able to communicate with the ground station, was far from ideal, and the initial trials were only moderately successful. The Air Force adjusted the orbit, but results were still mixed because the wire recorder produced scratchy, almost unintelligible voices.

After the armistice in 1958, coverage requirements became even more pressing, and an additional VHF position was added. Results were better, but aircraft maintenance problems, equipment failures and lack of qualified transcribers on the ground prevented the program from fully realizing its potential. By 1958, however, BLUE SKY had expanded by the addition of three more C-47s, and the program continued until 1962, when all C-47s were replaced by USAFSS RC-130s.

Peripheral Reconnaissance

The reconnaissance program of which BLUE SKY was a part came to consist of a bewildering variety of programs operated by [censored] American military services. Most of the missions were peripheral to the Soviet Bloc nations, and to those missions some rather strict rules applied. But some parts of the program apparently dealt with deliberate overflights. In the very early days, the penetration missions in Eastern Europe were for the purpose of unloading tons of propaganda leaflets. As time went on, however, CIA radio broadcasts substituted for more intrusive measures, and the overflights turned toward intelligence collection. The best known of the latter were the U-2 overflights which originated in the mid-1950s. Even when actual penetrations went out of favor, SAC continued to fly "exciter flights" along the periphery, nudging the boundaries of the Soviet air defense system to actually stimulate reactions and get them to turn on their equipment.

By the early 1950s the Soviet Union had built a capable air defense system. It was deficient in high-altitude aerial intercept capability, but the Soviets had an outstanding radar detection system, beginning originally with American lend-lease equipment. And as American [censored] aircraft began playing with the borders, the Soviets began coming up after them.

The ensuing twenty years were marked by repeated border incidents, both aerial and naval. A study by NSA in 1986 documented 126 incidents, 81 of them occurring during the 1950s. The peak year, 1952, was marked by nineteen incidents, including the downing of an RB-29 in the Sea of Japan on 13 June, the first SIGINT aircraft shot down during the Cold War (and the first loss of life by USAFSS intercept operators).

The Soviets and their allies became hypersensitive to peripheral reconnaissance, and on occasion they acted "trigger-happy." In some cases, such as the shootdown of a USAF photo mapping mission north of Japan in 1954, Soviet radars showed the American aircraft in Soviet territory. In other cases, especially in the Berlin air corridors, Soviet pilots showed a predisposition to fire at an Allied aircraft no matter which side of the border it was on. Some missions were shot down; others were simply fired on or harassed by "buzzing."

Although there is no direct evidence for it, it appears very likely that the pattern of peripheral reconnaissance employed by the U.S. and its allies exacerbated an already touchy situation and led to more incidents. As Table 6 shows [censored] of the incidents were clearly aerial reconnaissance [censored] and of the [censored] reconnaissance incidents, [censored] Reconnaissance CPAs (closest point of approach) were frequently within a few miles of the twelve-mile limit and often paralleled the border at that distance for many miles. To the Soviets, this must have appeared as a taunt. The SAC exciter flights were the most provocative by far. This was made worse by the inherent inaccuracy of radar, which sometimes placed the Allied reconnaissaince aircraft closer to the Soviet border than the aircraft's navigator believed to be the case. Into this volatile mix came the Soviet bloc fighter pilot, who had no way of knowing exactly where he was relative to the international boundary.

Table 6

Summary of Incidents by Type, 1949–1985

Type	Number
Non-SIGINT aerial reconnaissance	22
Other military	56
Commercial/private air	18
Military ship	3
Commercial ship (*Mayaguez*)	1

The number and pattern of peripheral reconnaissance flights over the years, and the nationalist sensitivities of the Communist nations, produced a lively time. Some of the shootdowns became international incidents which heightened the Cold War tensions and seriously affected international diplomacy.

All three services developed their own aerial reconnaissance programs, each using different types of aircraft. Of the three, USAFSS had the largest program. Security Service began laying plans as early as 1948, but it was not given the go-ahead from USAF until August 1950. Originally USAFSS hoped to use the C-47 as an airframe, and it actually tested that aircraft and a C-54. USAFSS decided on the RB-50, a modification of the B-29, as its long-range airframe, but none was available, and in the early 1950s the command used an RB-29 as an interim measure. The single RB-29 went operational in the Pacific in 1954, flying out of [censored] but this was never more than an experiment. AFSS finally ended up with a group of ten RB-50s in 1956, and by the fall of 1957 all ten were distributed—five to Asia and five to Europe. The program was a joint effort between AFSS and the theater commanders, who operated the front end of the planes. In the early years of the program, only the back-end crew was COMINT cleared. All positions were under local control, and tasking was done by USAFSS with little or no NSA input.

The Navy program developed from the early VQ-1 and VQ-2 sqdadrons originally established in World War II. VQ-1 was originally based at Sangley Point Naval Station in the Philippines, flying P4M Mercators, P2V Neptunes, and A3D Skywarriors. In 1955 the [censored] In Europe the SIGINT reconnaissance mission, VQ-2, evolved out of a World War II naval unit at Port Lyautey, Morocco. [censored]

The SAC Ferret program continued in the postwar years with only minimal involvement by the cryptologic community. [censored] By late summer of 1951, both AFSS and AFSA had become interested in the program, and by September the plans were expanded to include [censored]

The Origins of Advisory Warning

The AFSS unit at [censored] by now renamed [censored] realized that they held in their hands information that could save an aircraft from being shot down. [censored] In early 1952 [censored] worked out a plan to warn aircraft in imminent danger, by passing coded warning to the Air Control and Warning (AC&W) sites [censored] They wrote down their plan into a document which they called Project BITTERSWEET and sent it to USAFSS for approval. In May 1952 AFSS approved the plan for temporary implementation, [censored] details of the new warning procedure were still being worked out when, on 13 June, an RB-29 SIGINT collection flight was shot down over the Sea of Japan. The two AFSS operators who were killed might have been saved had a system been in place; the event added a real sense of urgency to this, the earliest advisory warning plan in American SIGINT history.

At this point BITTERSWEET got bogged down in the tangled thicket of COMINT classifications. The problem revolved around the possible [censored] USCIB approved the USAFSS advisory warning plan for the Far East, but LSIB was reluctant to go along except in a war zone (i.e., Korea).

It appears that at least one version of the plan was given interim approval by USCIB, and a former USAFSS operator claims that it was actually implemented in the early 1950s for at least one mission. Various modifications were introduced to make it more palatable, such as the use of bogus messages disguised as warning messages by AC&W units.

In 1956 President Eisenhower, concerned over the number of incidents and loss of reconnaissance aircraft, directed that positive action be taken to remedy the situation. The only change that resulted was the implementation of a Navy warning program in the Far East, which contained certain safeguards, chief among these being the initiation of "blind" (unacknowledged) broadcasts. Through the summer of 1958, there existed no universal advisory warning program.

The RC-130 Shootdown

The RB-50 program lasted only a few years. The aircraft were old and difficult to maintain and had room for only five positions. The success of AFSS collection against the growing VHF problem led to a new program on the heels of RB-50s, in which the new McDonnell-Douglas C-130 would be converted to a collection platform. The C-130 had room for [censored] positions, could fly longer and higher, and, being new, had few maintenance problems. AFSS planned for a fleet of [censored] in each theater, to begin in 1958. The first [censored] went to Europe, and in September AFSS, in association with USAFE, began to fly trial reconnaissance missions in [censored] areas.

Then disaster struck. On 2 September 1958 an RC-130 on its initial flight out of Adana strayed over the border and was shot down. Two pairs of MIG-15s (or 17s; there was not enough evidence to determine which) attacked the reconnaissance aircraft in waves in a well-coordinated operation which left no room for doubt that their intent was destruction. The voice tapes were as dramatic as they were damning.

The Soviets said nothing, so the State Department on 6 September sent a note to the Soviet government requesting information on an unarmed C-130 carrying a crew of seventeen which had disappeared during a flight from Adana to Trabzon, Turkey. Finally, on the 12th the Soviet embassy in Washington replied that the missing transport had crashed in Soviet Armenia, killing six crew members, but that Moscow had provided no information about an additional group of eleven. An exchange of diplomatic notes over the next ten days shed no further light on the missing eleven bodies, so on 21 September the State Department admitted that they knew the aircraft had been shot down and appealed for information on the rest of the crew on humanitarian grounds. The Soviets replied that they considered the flight to have been an intentional violation of their borders but made no reference to the involvement of fighter aircraft or a shootdown.

PBS [pilot billet suffix]: CONVERSATION

"582: The target is a large one. . . . Roger

201 to 218: Attack! Attack! 218, attack.

201: I am attacking the target

201: Target speed is 3000, I am flying with it. It is turning toward the fence [i.e., border].

201: The target is banking. . . . It is going toward the fence. Attack!

218: Yes, yes, I am attacking.

[missing]: The target is burning. . . .

[missing]: The tail assembly is falling off the target.

[missing]: Look at him, he will not get away, he is already falling.

[missing]: Yes, he is falling. I will finish him off on the run.

[missing]: The target has lost control, it is going down."

A crew of seventeen men, including eleven USAFSS airmen and a front-end crew of six, was lost.

In October the Soviets produced the bodies of the six members of the front-end crew, but the bodies of the eleven USAFSS airmen were never turned over; and this strange circumstance produced a spate of conspiracy theories regarding the possible capture and long-term incarceration, not to mention forceable interrogation, of the COMINT crew. The evidence of the voice tapes makes it quite clear that no one could have escaped the fiery crash in a mountainous region of the Caucasus, but what happened to the bodies remains a mystery to this day.

In November, after more than two months of Soviet "stonewalling," Deputy Under Secretary of State Robert Murphy summoned Soviet ambassador Mikhail Menshikov to his office, told him he had the voice tapes of the shootdown, and said he would play them immediately. Menshikov declared that he was not a technician and walked out of the office. In January of the following year, Vice President Nixon and Secretary of State Dulles protested the Soviet attitude on the shootdown to First Deputy Chairman of the Council of Ministers Anastas Mikoyan, but their representations were again brushed aside. Out of patience, the administration on 5 February released copies of the tape to the *New York Times*, which published them on page one. This deliberate leak of COMINT had already been placed before USCIB, which had concurred, as had the British.

The downing of the RC-130 had immediate and serious consequences. USAFE grounded the entire RC-130 fleet, and Headquarters USAF requested a complete review of the ACRP program worldwide. USAFSS produced statistics designed to prove the effectiveness of the program when compared with ground collection sites, and by mid-October the flight ban had been lifted. As part of its review, USAFSS also investigated the possibility that the aircraft was meaconed (intentionally lured over the border) by Soviet navigational facilities. This possibility added to the conspiracy theories surrounding the fate of the RC-130, but it was largely contradicted by the internal evidence of the study which showed that three navigational beacons in the area, two of them in the Soviet Union, were all operating on virtually the same frequency. Thus, the aircraft very likely homed on the wrong beacon and pulled itself off course. Although President Eisenhower himself believed it to have been a deliberate meaconing incident, it was more likely a navigational error on the part of the SAC crew.

Advisory Warning Is Implemented

The downing of the RC-130 decided the advisory warning issue. USAFSS gave its units immediate authorization to man the heretofore unmanned manual Morse position aboard the RC-130s for internal advisory warning. And the long-stalled plans for the provision of warning [censored] got untracked. By 1961 USAFSS and SAC had implemented a limited advisory warning program, [censored] applying to their own reconnaissance aircraft. In 1963 this was merged into a national program encompassing all peripheral reconnaissance aircraft, a JCS plan named WHITE WOLF.

[censored]

The construction of the super-sites in the 1950s resulted in an intercept system that was increasingly effective in its ability [censored] By 1960, USAFSS demonstrated a high level of competence to [censored] during the U-2 shootdown. But since [censored] communications in the 1950s [censored]

The RB-47 Shootdown

As time went on, progressively fewer reconnaissance aircraft were shot down, but those that were took on a heightened diplomatic importance. Surely the most significant was the 1 May 1960 shootdown of the U-2 piloted by CIA's Francis Gary Powers. (This shootdown will be treated in detail in a separate section.) Second only to that, however, was the shootdown of an RB-47 ELINT mission over the Barents Sea on 1 July 1960. The aircraft took off from [censored] and proceeded on its charted course in the Barents, until it was intercepted by a covey of Soviet fighters. As the aircraft paralleled the Murmansk coast, two Kilp'Yavr fighters intercepted it, and at least one fired a burst, destroying two of the four engines. As the pilot fought to control the seriously damaged aircraft, [censored] After a twenty-minute struggle, the plane crashed in the icy waters of the Barents off the coast of Ostrov Kolguev. Two of the crew were picked out of the waters alive by a Soviet trawler, but the other four died.

Coming as it did only two months after the U-2 incident, it presented Soviet premier Nikita Khrushchev with another opportunity to heat up the Cold War. After waiting a few days to see what the Eisenhower administration would say, the Soviet leader went on the attack, revealing that thev had shot down the plane and were holding the two survivors in Lubyanka Prison. [censored]

In the Oval Office, Eisenhower worried about the diplomatic and political implications of peripheral reconnaissance and asked his military advisors if it was worth it. General Nathan Twining of the Air Force delivered a ringing defense of the program, and he convinced Eisenhower to keep the airplanes flying. But the president directed that the Air Force find faster reconnaissance aircraft so that the Soviets would have a more difficult time shooting them down. The quest for a better aircraft eventually led to the SR-71 program.

During the Oval Office review of the peripheral reconnaissance program, the Air Force revealed the extent of the program in 1960. [censored] SAC had two strategic reconnaissance wings flying worldwide missions, [censored] In Europe the COMINT aircraft (mostly RC-130s) were operated by USAFE, which seemed to be getting all the newest and best aircraft and collection gear, in line with Eisenhower's expressed desire to [censored] (The promised nine RC-130s had evidently not yet arrived.) The Navy had a naval air squadron at [censored] equipped with smaller naval patrol craft. [censored] and the Marines operated an airborne collection unit from [censored] A special naval unit operating from [censored]

As for the fate of the RB-47 flyers, Khrushchev kept them in Lubyanka until after the change of administration and then returned them as a cynical olive branch to the newly elected President Kennedy a few days after his inauguration. Kennedy met the released flyers at Andrews Air Force Base and, to flaunt his Cold War sympathies; had them to the White House for coffee. If Khrushchev hoped to use the reconnaissance program to curry favor, he failed. Kennedy was even more fervently anti-Communist than Eisenhower.

Chapter 4 The Soviet Problem

The Early Days

"From Stettin in the Baltic to Trieste in the Adriatic, an iron curtain has descended across the Continent. Behind that line lie all the capitals of the ancient states of centrel and eastern Europe . . . all these famous cities lie in what I might call the Soviet sphere, and all are subject, in one form or another, not only to Soviet influence but to a very high and in some cases increasing measure of control from Moscow." —Winston Churchill, 6 March 1946

The end of World War II did not result in a large number of unemployed cryptologists. That it did not was due almost entirely to the advent of the Cold War and an increasing concern with what came to be called the Soviet Bloc. (In the 1950s, believing in a world-wide Communist conspiracy, Americans called it the Sino-Soviet Bloc.)

Wartime cooperation with the Soviet Union began to break down in early 1945. Through a series of late-war conferences among the Allies, it became clear to the West that the Soviet Union did not intend to retreat from Eastern Europe at the end of the war. An increasingly frustrated Roosevelt administration became less and less constrained about public references to the rift with Stalin, but Roosevelt himself remained convinced up to his death in April 1945 that the rift could be healed by diplomacy. His successor, Harry Truman, did not share this optimism.

The administration moved to check Soviet expansionism abroad. As a result of strong pressure, Stalin removed Soviet troops from Iran later in the year. Meanwhile, Greece was faced with a USSR-inspired internal Communist threat, while neighbor Turkey faced an external threat by Soviet divisions massed on its borders. Truman again faced down Stalin, announcing the Truman Doctrine, a promise to come to the aid of countries in that area faced with Communist subversion or external threats. Administration policy toward the USSR hardened with the publication, in the magazine *Foreign Affairs,* of an article by George Kennan, late deputy chief of mission in Moscow, postulating the Cold War doctrine which became known as "containment."

The next year a democratically elected government in Czechoslovakia fell to a Communist coup, and the new government became an effective satellite of the USSR. Meanwhile, Soviet troops remained in Poland and East Germany, while Communist governments took over in Hungary and the Balkans. In June 1948 Stalin tried to cut Berlin off from the West, and Truman initiated the Berlin Airlift to resupply the city. The Truman administration also saw the Korean War as the first move in a Soviet-inspired military offensive.

The Advent of BOURBON

American cryptology had dabbled with the Soviet problem over the years, with indifferent success. Yardley, in his book *The American Black Chamber,* claimed to have broken Soviet diplomatic codes. The truth is that, though Yardley's MI-8 worked Soviet diplomatic traffic, only a single instance of success was ever recorded, and in that case the transposition being attacked was based on the German language.

Friedman's Signal Intelligence Service obtained MI-8's traffic upon MI-3's demise in 1929 and made a brief, unsuccessful attempt to solve the codes. Then in 1931 a Soviet espionage front posing as a trading company called AMTORG came under the glare of Representative Hamilton Fish of New York, who subpoened some 3,000 AMTORG cables from the cable companies in New York. Fish turned them over to OP-20-G, which, having at the time only two cryptanalysts (Safford and Wenger), failed to solve them. The cables were then transferred to SIS, which also blunted its spear. This was virtually the only attempt at Soviet diplomatic traffic by the services during the 1930s, and Friedman's people doubted that any Soviet codes could be solved.

They were, in fact, wrong. [censored] attack on Soviet military systems throughout the 1930s. The primary target was COMINTERN (Communist International) traffic, [censored] But when, in June of 1941, Hitler's army invaded Russia, the British allowed the Soviet problem to wither. GCCS made a brief attempt to turn the USSR into a COMINT Third Party, and even established an intercept site in Russia near Murmansk in 1941. The dialogue came to a quick halt when the Soviets began inquiring into British success against ENIGMA. In 1942, the Radio Security Service and the London Metropolitan Police discovered an extensive Soviet illicit network in Great Britain, and Stewart Menzies, head of British intelligence, directed that work be renewed against Soviet communications, especially KGB, GRU, and COMINTERN nets likely to carry information of counterintelligence value.

In the United States, SIS was collecting a small amount of Soviet traffic on a casual basis as early as 1942. On 1 February 1943 the Army opened up a two-person Soviet section. The inspiration for this effort was the Army's successful attack on Japanese diplomatic communications, in which the Japanese discussed their efforts against Soviet systems. The Japanese material gave SIS some handholds into Soviet systems. OP-20-G came in later, opening both intercept and cryptanalytic study in July 1943. Because the USSR was a wartime ally, the effort was rigidly compartmented and known to only a few. In August 1943 the Army and Navy cryptologists began cooperating on the new Soviet problem and, during 1943 and 1944, cooperatively worked a number of Soviet cryptographic systems.

Meantime, the Navy, in order to collect Soviet naval traffic, had opened up an intercept effort at Bainbridge Island in Washington State. Tightly controlled, it was headed by Louis Tordella, later the deputy director of NSA.

By the end of the war, both cryptologic organizations were mounting extensive efforts against Soviet communications, despite the official designation of the USSR as an ally. OP-20-G, concentrating on Soviet naval communications in the Pacific from Skaggs Island and Bainbridge, employed 192 people, while ASA had almost 100. They had both been surreptitiously training Russian linguists for a year.

But the effort was charged with political implications. Roosevelt was trying to maintain the fragile alliance with the USSR, and was being challenged on the left by Henry Wallace, a potential political rival who felt the administration was anti-Soviet.

In this atmosphere Brigadier General Carter Clarke of the Army G-2 paid a visit to Preston Corderman (chief, SIS) and Frank Rowlett several months before the end of the war. Clarke said that he had received informal instructions—allegedly from the White House—to cease any effort against the Soviet problem. It appeared that someone in the White House had gotten word of the compartmented Soviet problem and had concluded that it did not accord with the current diplomatic situation. (It was discovered years later that the White House staff was in fact infiltrated by a single Communist or "fellow traveler," who may have been in a position to know about the Army program.) Clarke did not desire that the program be closed, and in fact SIS (soon to be renamed ASA) received a steady increase in resources for the program.

In June 1945, with the war coming to an end, the Navy proposed formal collaboration with the Army on the Soviet problem, which was then referred to as the RATTAN project. The Army wanted a more integrated effort, but they eventually agreed to organize under the more decentralized Navy scheme.

At the same time, ANCIB proposed to LSIB that their cooperation against Germany, Italy, and Japan now be extended to include the USSR. The Americans proposed that the cooperation be fully as close as it had been during the war. This included sharing all details, including the status and method of cryptanalytic attack, and the exchange of raw traffic and code/cipher recoveries. The British agreed, and in August the two sides arrived at an unwritten agreement predicated on an understanding arrived at in June between Rear Admiral Hewlett Thebaud, chairman of ANCIB, and [censored] for LSIB. This historic agreement extended bilateral cooperation into the Cold War and established the basis for what became known as the BRUSA Agreement. The two sides agreed to call the new project BOURBON.

During the mid-1940s the two sides mounted a relentless attack on the wartime generation of Soviet ciphers. The British provided much of the cryptanalytic expertise, the Americans most of the processing capability.

They used whatever material they could get their hands on, including information on the Japanese cryptanalytic attack. TICOM debriefings of German cryptologists also gave the two partners useful information about Soviet systems.

[censored]

VENONA

Alone and compartrnented, the effort against Soviet diplomatic traffic had continued throughout World War II. In the long run this tightly held problem would have the greatest impact on American history in the postwar period and would become the most widely known. It was called VENONA. In the early years of the war, the Army received incidental Soviet diplomatic traffic, most of it through its arrangements with the cable companies, which carried a large bulk of common-user communications. Since New York was the terminal for the transatlantic cable, Soviet diplomatic traffic was routed through that city. The Army arranged with the cable companies to get copies of most of the cables that the Soviets were sending, both to and from Washington and, more important, to and from AMTORG. Much of this traffic was believed to be KGB-related.

In 1943, ASA had mounted a secret effort to attack these communications, but they looked impossible. They were produced from cudebooks enciphered by means of one-time additive tables. Assuming no re-use, there was no point in continuing. But ASA was not assuming anything, and Lieutenant Richard T. Hallock of ASA directed that his small section machine punch and process the beginnings and endings of some 5,000 messages to test for depths. In October 1943, ASA found the first indication that the additive pads may have been used more than once, a find which was to change the history of the postwar world.

Hallock and his small band of cryptanalysts had found what is called "manufacturer's re-use" caused by the first German invasion of the Soviet Union in 1941. The KGB's additive pad generating facility produced two sets of some pads, presumably because of the pressures associated with the rapid German advance toward Moscow. These were disseminated to widely separated KGB organizations, which were unaware that they had duplicate pads. ASA never found depths of more than two, and at that depth, decryption was only theoretically possible but practically a back-breaking job, assuming one ever got hold of the depths themselves.

Months went by, but finally ASA cryptanalysts, in November of 1944, were rewarded with their first depth. This was followed by others, and it appeared that they might be able to eventually break some traffic. But the job still looked gargantuan.

While one section worked on identifying depths, another worked on the underlying codebooks that were slowly emerging from under the additive key. This effort was led by a reclusive linguist and bookbreaker named Meredith Gardner. A Texan originally, Gardner had obtained a Master of

Arts in German from the University of Texas and had been a Ph.D. candidate at the University of Wisconsin before going to work teaching at the University of Akron. He had joined SIS in 1942, and although he began in the German section, he quickly switched to Japanese, where he proved his linguistic gifts by picking up this extremely difficult language in just three months. At the end of the war, he switched again, this time to the Soviet problem and spent his first several months learning Russian. In December 1946, he had only recently emerged from language school when he made a major break into a KGB message, decrypting and translating a digraphic sequence of a 1944 message from New York to Moscow sending English text. Gardner found that the KGB used the code values for "spell" and "end spell" anytime they needed to encrypt a foreign word or other term that did not appear in the codebook. It was these two values that yielded many of the early breaks.

In December 1946, Gardner broke a portion of a KGB message that listed American scientists working on the atomic bomb. This message turned heads. Why would the KGB be interested in such information? ASA immediately turned the translation over to the Army G-2, and Carter Clarke had General Omar Bradley, the Army chief of staff, briefed on the message. G-2 expressed a continuing interest in any messages that contained like information.

Through the war ASA had proceeded virtually unaided, but after World War II several outside factors speeded the tortuously slow process of additive key diagnosis and recovery and bookbreaking. The first was the defection of a Soviet GRU cipher clerk, Igor Gouzenko, from the Soviet embassy in Ottawa, in September 1945. The case caused a sensation because Gouzenko indicated the existence of a possible Soviet effort against the American atomic research effort.

Because Gouzenko worked with communications, Frank Rowlett of ASA was invited to interrogate him. During his sessions Rowlett learned much about the way the KGB codebooks were put together and how the additives were used. This information cut time off ASA's cryptanalysis effort.

A second outside source of information was a 1944 FBI burglary of AMTORG, during which the agents carried off stacks of unenciphered messages with their cipher text equivalents. In 1948 the FBI turned over this bonanza to Gardner, who began comparing the traffic against transmitted messages. In this way he could identify some of the code group meanings because he had both plain and cipher texts.

A third outside source was called "Stella Polaris," a Byzantine story which began in the early days of World War II. When, in June 1941, Germany invaded the USSR, the Finns went to war against the Soviets, siding with Germany against their mortal enemy. On 22 June a Finnish unit, presumably security police, entered the Soviet consulate in the Finnish town of Petsamo, near the Russo-Finnish border. Here they found the Soviet communications people frantically destroying cryptographic material. Some of it was burned beyond use, but certain of the codebooks were recovered more or less intact. These codebooks were property of the First Chief Directorate of the KGB—they were, in fact, the same codebooks which, in the mid-1940s, Meredith Gardner was working on.

The charred codebook fragments were turned over to the Finnish COMINT service, headed by one Colonel Hallamaa. By 1944 the war was not going well for Germany, and Hallamaa became concerned about an impending Soviet invasion of his homeland. He arranged to smuggle the contents of the Finnish COMINT archives, including the Petsamo trove, to Sweden, where photocopies were made. Copies of the Petsamo materials wound up in the hands of the Swedish, German, and Japanese COMINT organizations. Along with the documents went Hallamaa and the entire Finnish COMINT service.

At some point information got out to the newspapers, and the fact that Finnish intelligence people were working hand in glove with the Swedes became public knowledge. Knowing that the KGB was almost certainly after him, Hallamaa and most of his people fled to France, where, after the war, they worked nominally with the French intelligence people, but were actually controlled, according to some sources, by the British. So it was that the British got their own copies of the Petsamo codebooks. At the same time (1945) an OSS representative began working with Hallamaa, and the OSS, too, received its own copies (although not, perhaps, a complete set).

The code-books eventually made their way to ASA and AFSA. Since by this time a number of intelligence services had copies, which source did AFSA get? In the days after the war, a TICOM team obtained a copy from the Germans, and it was this set that first made it all the way to Meredith Gardner's office. Shortly thereafter AFSA began obtaining Petsamo materials from the British under the codename Source 267 and may, at some point, have received copies from OSS/CIG, but these were no more than duplicates of materials they already had.

The Stella Polaris find did not break the KGB codes. They were fragmentary and pertained only to one version, [censored] But they did shorten the time involved in the laborious bookbreaking process by providing Gardner with "models" of Soviet codes on which to base his own recoveries.

After reading some of Gardner's earlier translations showing the scope of KGB operations in the United States, Carter Clarke, the Army G-2, called on the FBI for help. His first contact was in July 1947; it was with Wesley Reynolds, the FBI liaison with Army G-2. Reynolds had joined the FBI in New York in 1941 after several years of law practice with his father and older brother. He had begun liaison work with G-2 in 1942, and ten years later jumped ship to NSA, where he became NSA's first professional chief of security.

Reynolds concluded that VENONA could turn out to be a full-time job, and he appealed to Mickey Ladd, head of the FBI counterintelligence operations, for a dedicated agent. Ladd assigned one Robert Lamphere, who, like Reynolds, had joined the bureau in 1941. Lamphere had worked virtually his entire career in counterintelligence, mostly in New York. He knew the territory, but he did not yet know ASA and Meredith Gardner.

What ensued was one of the most remarkable partnerships in intelligence history. The shy, brilliant Gardner, speaker of half a dozen languages, brought to the relationship his ability to break codebooks and produce translations of extremely difficult material. Lamphere brought his detailed knowledge of KGB operations and personalities, along with his contacts within the counterintelligence community. Together they worked over the fragmentary texts of old KGB messages.

One of the first products of this marriage of convenience came in 1948. It was a decrypt of a message sent in 1944, in which the KGB reported on the recruiting efforts of an unnamed spy. Using the counterintelligence file, Lamphere identified two possible candidates: [censored] an employee of the Navy Ordnance Department, and [censored] an engineer working on airborne radar for Western Electric. Both had been under FBI suspicion for possible Communist liaisons. Neither was ever brought to trial, but it was the first fruit of the Gardner-Lamphere relationship.

The next lead was a 1948 translation of a verbatim quote on the progress on the Manhattan Project given by one Klaus Fuchs, a respected British atomic scientist, also sent in 1944. The information became urgent when, in September of 1949, the USSR exploded its first atomic bomb. It became clear through the COMINT information provided by Gardner where the scientific information for the USSR's atomic bomb project was coming from. Fuchs was arrested in late 1949, confessed, and was convicted of espionage. Just as important, he led the FBI to a contact in America, Harry Gold, and Gold, in turn, led to the unravelling of an entire network of spies at work for the USSR.

As the atomic spy network was undone in 1950 and 1951, Lamphere played the information now pouring in through counterintelligence work and confessions against the AFSA KGB decrypts. Most important for Lamphere's subsequent work was an agent covername, ANTENNA/LIBERAL, whose true identity, Julius Rosenberg of New York City, was fully confirmed in June of 1950, based on a series of cascading confessions coming from the network originally unearthed during the Fuchs interrogations earlier in the year. (Gardner later contended that the original tentative identification of Rosenberg was actually done by G-2 before Lamphere became involved).

One of the most sensational spy trials was that of Alger Hiss, a top State Department official who had traveled with Roosevelt to Yalta in 1945. Fingered originally by a KGB defector, Walter Krivitsky, in 1941, Hiss was publicly named in 1947 as a spy by two reformed Communists, Elizabeth

Bentley and Whittaker Chambers, before the House Un-American Activities Committee. He was never taken to court for spying, but in January 1950 he was convicted of perjury for lying about his associations with Chambers, and he served a prison term. Although the evidence in court was all assembled from testimony and confessions, along with some circumstantial evidence produced by Chambers, VENONA traffic from the 1945 period contained possible confirmatory evidence that Hiss was probably a GRU asset. The covername ALES was identified in the March 1945 traffic as an individual who flew to Moscow after the Yalta Conference. Hiss was identified as the probable culprit based on the fact that there were only four other possibilities, including the secretary of state himself. The VENONA traffic refers to an individual who could fit the description of Hiss, which could confirm that Hiss was indeed a spy.

The most famous spy of all was Kim Philby, the British MI-6 liaison officer assigned to work with the Americans on the VENONA project. VENONA also became the lever which pried open the Philby spy ring, and Philby watched it all unfold. He kept to himself until, in early 1951, the FBI went after one HOMER, the covername of a KGB agent identified originally in VENONA traffic. HOMER, the FBI suspected, was actually one Donald Maclean, a first secretary of the British embassy who, as part of his duties, was in charge of the coderoom in Washington. As such, he had passed the text of certain Churchill-Roosevelt messages to Moscow, and these appeared in decrypted VENONA traffic. Because of his position as liaison with the Americans on VENONA, Philby knew the axe was about to fall, and he warned Maclean of impending exposure. Maclean fled to Moscow with a fellow spy, Guy Burgess, who had been posted to Washington with Maclean. Brought under suspicion by Hoover's FBI, Philby resigned his post and in 1963 fled to Moscow himself.

All the readable VENONA messages which supplied information about U.S. spies were transmitted by 1946 or earlier. Most of the decrypted traffic came from ASA's 1944-45 files and was not decrypted until the late 1940s and early 1950s. But exploitation efforts continued for years and were not finally closed down until 1980. By then, the traffic being worked was thirty-five years old. The reason for this long delay was simple. VENONA translations were incredibly difficult, each one requiring approximately one man-year of work.

The VENONA material played a key, although by no means exclusive, role in catching the atomic spies and the Philby ring. Most of the evidence came from meticulous counterintelligence work by the FBI, not from COMINT. VENONA frequently confirmed what the FBI had suspected, but it never had to be used in court. All the prosecutions stood solely on evidence gained from other sources. What, then, was its historical importance?

First, VENONA provided the prod. Early VENONA decrypts revealed the scope and direction of KGB operations. It confirmed that fragmentary information provided by people like Krivitsky and Gouzenko, and public allegations by Elizabeth Bentley and Whittaker Chambers, was precisely on target and had to be pursued. With VENONA in hand, Lamphere got his marching orders.

Second, it was the evidence that led to the arrest and confession of Klaus Fuchs, the first atomic spy unmasked. Subsequent actions were taken based on an unravelling skein of evidence provided by the conspirators themselves. One arrest led to a confession, another arrest, and still another confession. The investigation proceeded in whirlwind fashion, gaining momentum as it roared around every corner. At that point VENONA simply confirmed and solidified what the FBI had learned from its sources.

Third, it began the exposure of the Philby spy ring, surely Britain's most infamous confrontation with traitors. Although the FBI was already onto Maclean, it might never have proceeded further but for the bits of information that VENONA was unearthing. At the very least, the ring would have operated months, if not years, longer before being unmasked.

The guilt or innocence of Alger Hiss, the decision to execute the Rosenbergs, the culpability of the Philby ring, the very existence of the atomic spy ring and what J. Edgar Hoover called the "Crime of the Century" quickly acquired stark political overtones. They got all mixed up in McCarthyism, and in the 1960s the New Left took up the mantle in behalf of Hiss, the Rosenbergs, and a wide variety of others who, justly or unjustly, had been hauled before the House Un-American Activities Committee and the McCarthy hearings. In the early 1970s a National Committee to Re-Open the Rosenberg Case took up the cudgels in behalf of the executed couple. Believing that the documents would prove them right, they used the Freedom of Information Act to pry off the lid of the FBI investigation and began publishing articles purporting to show how the FBI materials proved that Hiss and the Rosenbergs were innocent. Then in 1983 two former true believers, Ronald Radosh and Joyce Milton, published a book entitled *The Rosenberg File,* which showed that a dispassionate examination of the documents proved just the opposite.

What had they got hold of? It was FBI papers based on the VENONA translations. Unknown to NSA, the FBI had released them through the FOIA process (a release which led to a change in the way such FOIA requests are handled).

Not many people still believe in the innocence of the Rosenbergs. Even those who hold firm to the belief that McCarthy's methods were wrong (and that encompasses most Americans) understand that the KGB had done some serious spying. McCarthy so sensationalized and distorted the anti-Communist campaign in the 1950s that an entire era came into disrepute. The historical importance of VENONA is that this entire episode in American history was not dismissed as a figment of someone's imagination. No matter how lurid and disreputable portions of the anti-Communist campaign became, the spy network can no longer be regarded as a fairy tale.

As for its long-term significance for cryptology, NSA learned several important lessons. First, the difficulty of an effort is not an automatic disqualifier. VENONA was one of the most intensely difficult projects that American cryptology has ever undertaken. The cryptanalytic effort was gargantuan. But the results would rock the foundations of post-war America.

Second, it illustrated the absolute essentiality of cross-fertilization. COMINT without counterintelligence was just as unthinkable as counterintelligence without COMINT. Yet if the effort had been undertaken during World War II, with the intense competition between the military services and the FBI, it might have fallen on the rocks of secrecy, and the atomic spies might never have been uncovered.

"Black Friday"

[censored]

[censored] (AFSA had not yet been created, and there was no mechanism to resolve interservice security squabbles and investigate [censored]

But if one went looking for spies, there was no end of possibilities. The most obvious suspects were those three miscreants, Philby, Burgess, and Mclean,who were in a position to know the general outlines of the American [censored] attack on Soviet systems, even though they were unacquainted with the technical details.

But a very likely contributor was one of America's own. William Weisband, who had been working in ASA for the duration of the war and into the late 1940s, was later discovered to have been a KGB agent. Weisband, whose story will be covered in more detail in chapter 7, almost certainly provided information critical to the Soviet COMSEC effort. He was the U.S. cryptologic effort's first traitor.

ASA and AFSA Turn to Radioprinter

As the [censored] problem became more difficult, ASA turned gradually to a new source of Soviet traffic. Through [censored] interrogations and later contacts with foreign COMINT specialists, ASA had become aware that the Soviets had begun using radioprinter, [censored] ASA had very little intercept capability for such a sophisticated system, and early intercepts were copied onto undulator tape, whose readout was laborious and time-consuming.

Confronting the same problem, NSG and ASA received a postwar allocation of something over $200,000 to design and build intercept equipment. Working in the basement of Arlington Hall under the cafeteria, they beganbuilding [censored] positions whose output was punched paper-tape onto which was alsoprinted the Cyrillic characters, a big improvement over-undulator tape. (Printers were then viewed as too expensive and their output too bulky.)

[censored]

The outputs were huge, and ASA and NSG were quickly flooded with Russian language material. NSAers Jacob Gurin and [censored] who headed up the transcription effort, began hiring Russian linguists from a former OSS organization that had been transferred to the State Department. They also began scouring college campuses for linguists and set up language training at civilian universities.

[censored] Printer seemed to be the wave of the future.

The Soviet Strategic Threat

[censored]

The United States emerged from World War II with a lock on nuclear weapons technology and strategic delivery systems. The Soviet Union represented a threat only from the standpoint of a land war on the Eurasian landmass.

This enviable pinnacle of security did not last very long. On 3 September 1949, an Air Force weather reconnaissance aircraft detected an unusually high concentration of radioactivity over the North Pacific east of the Kamchatka Peninsula. The Soviets had exploded a nuclear device. The timing was a shock. The intelligence community had adjudged the Soviet program still several years away from actually exploding a device.

The arms race was on, and America's lead in nuclear technology seemed to be disappearing. The U.S. exploded its first hydrogen bomb in 1952; the Soviets followed a year later, another surprise to the intelligence community.

In 1953 American military attachés in Moscow observed Soviet strategic bombers in apparent series production. If true, this would give the Soviets a delivery capability for their newly acquired atomic weapons. Stuart Symington, senator from Missouri and former secretary of the air force, fastened on this information to propound the famous "bomber gap" thesis. This information was later proved wrong by early U-2 photoreconnaissance flights, but the public perception profoundly altered intelligence priorities and led to an almost paranoid focus on Soviet strategic systems.

In 1956 Symington originated the "missile gap" controversy which was to influence the presidential election of 1960. Symington was apparently being fed data from Air Force sources that SAC believed the Soviets might have slipped ahead of the United States in the development of strategic missile delivery systems. The launch of Sputnik in 1957 appeared to confirm Symington's contentions, and every failure of a U.S.-developed launch system over the next several years just drove another nail in the lid. The concentration of intelligence energies on the Soviet advanced weapons problem became fierce.

How It Began

The Soviet missile program had originated in 1945 when a covey of German missile scientists fell conveniently into Soviet hands. Working at Peenemunde on the North Sea coast, this group had developed the V1 and V2 missiles, the latter a true ballistic missile capable of distances in excess of 200 miles. The captured scientists were hustled off to a research institute in Bleicherode, East Germany, and then in 1946, amid great secrecy, were transferred to the Soviet Union itself. They were first set up in a new Scientific Research Institute 88 at Kaliningrad on the Baltic Sea. Their first test center, established in 1947, was at a remote desert site called Kapustin Yar, some 100 miles east of Stalingrad.

The Germans labored in Kaliningrad, Kapustin Yar and other locations until 1950 or 1951. By that time the Soviets had themselves the rudiments of a missile program. They had succeeded in replicating the V2 and a primitive indigenous missile, called the R-10, had been designed with German help. At that point the Soviets returned the Germans to their homeland, where they brought the CIA up to date on the Soviet program. None of the first Soviet rockets, designated R10-15, ever amounted to more than "designer toys," but the most advanced, the R-15, was designed for a nuclear payload and was to have a range of 3,700 statute miles.

Reports of Soviet missile development reached the Oval Office, and the president demanded more information. But there were precious few assets to be had. In the latter days of Stalin's reign, the Iron Curtain completely closed off the Soviet Union from CIA HUMINT penetration—they had no secret agents in the USSR. There was no photography, the U-2 still being several years away. Virtually the only asset available was SIGINT.

[censored] In 1954 the German scientists who had worked on the project told American intelligence about a system of communications between the missile and its ground station, a derivative of a system the Germans had developed at Peenemunde in World War II. It was a 16-channel PPM system operating in the 60 MHz range that the Germans called MESSINA. The U.S. intelligence community called it "telemetry."

[censored]

The American Response

[censored]

In 1957 the Soviets opened a new range at Tyura Tam, some 700 miles east of Kapustin Yar. [censored] that this would be the site for the Soviets' first ICBM launches, and a CIA-driven search through U-2 photography in the summer of 1957 [censored] confirmed this. [censored]

[censored] Moreover [censored] became more and more a cue card for U-2 missions. When U-2 pilot Frances Gary Powers was shot down in 1960 he was on a dangerous cross-Soviet mission searching for evidence of a new missile test site [censored] which had been recently identified [censored] as being possibly missile associated.

[censored] this discovery led to the elevation of the problem to division level. By 1958 it had become the Advanced Weaponry and Astronautics Division [censored] which concentrated NSA's resources into a single organization. It came to be referred to as "SMAC" (Soviet Missile and Astronautics Center). [censored] SMAC established a new operator-to-operator communications system which became known as the [censored] Joseph Burke, now regarded as the "father of SMAC," is believed to have originated this system.

To orchestrate the system, SMAC established an all-night watch, virtually eliminating the call-in system for this critical project. SMAC was one of the organizations that eventually got NSA out of the eight-hour-per-day mode, and it pioneered in the development of tip-off systems and quick reaction capabilities. In both concept and technology, it long preceded NSOC.

NSA had numerous competitors in the missile arena. The Air Force had launched a small detachment of ATIC (Air Technical Intelligence Center at Wright-Patterson Air Force Base, Ohio) in San Antonio. Collocated with Air Force Security Service, SMTIG (Soviet Missile Technical Intelligence Group) consisted of a cross-section of the Air Force intelligence disciplines, but it was dominated by SIGINT people. Its analysis directly overlapped much of what NSA was doing. In addition, CIA was well along on its missile analysis effort and included SIGINT as well as other intelligence disciplines in its program.

The Soviet Atomic Bomb Project

While the Soviets were developing delivery systems, Stalin directed that the development of the nuclear weapons themselves be given the highest priority. Working with information provided by the atomic spies in the West, and with captured German nuclear physicists, the Soviets raced to get the bomb. Their first test site was constructed at Semipalatinsk (now referred to as "Semey"), a remote Siberian location, and for some years the Soviets used that site exclusively. The Semipalatinsk monopoly on nuclear tests was finally broken in 1955 with the explosion of an underwater device in the sea off Novaya Zemlya, a large Arctic island northeast of the Kola Peninsula.

As with the missile development program, so it was with nuelear weapons [censored]

The American system for monitoring nuclear tests consisted of a complex of seismic and infrared sensors positioned around the world. The entire system depended, [censored]

The bomber and missile gap controversies in the late 1950s triggered a search for an operational Soviet strategic nuclear delivery organization. With the launch of Sputnik in October 1957, this became a white-hot priority, [censored] The Soviets did not yet have a nuclear delivery organization, all the information from Senator Symington notwithstanding. In January 1960 the USSR publicly announced the formation of a new Strategic Rocket Forces (SRF) command, [censored]

In 1960, DCI Allen Dulles directed that the chairman of the Guided Missile and Astronautics Intelligence Committee (GMAIC) organize a study group to completely evaluate the Air Force contention that there was a missile gap. Using [censored] photographic evidence collected from the U-2, the committee concluded that only the test site at [censored] was capable of launching a missile. This contradicted the latest national intelligence estimate, which postulated that there would be thirty-five operational launchers by mid-1960. Dulles then directed that a permanent Deployment Working Group be established to comb all the evidence thoroughly.

The crash of the U-2 piloted by Francis Gary Powers on 1 May temporarily ended overhead photography as a source of intelligence, and the committee had to proceed from [censored] Using old photographs and up-to-the-minute [censored] the group finally concluded that only Tyura Tam and possibly one to three other operational launchers existed, including Verkhnyaya Salda and Yur'ya. Plesetsk was still assessed as unfinished. [censored]

The paranoia of the 1950s receded to be replaced by the optimism and military force projection policies of the 1960s. By the time Kennedy became president, Dulles had proved that the Soviets still presented no real strategic nuclear threat, although clearly that threat was on the horizon. During the dark days of the 1950s, though, when no one really knew what went on behind the Iron Curtain, [censored] It was President Eisenhower's hole card.

The Chinese Threat

Compared with the Soviet Union, China could hardly be considered a strategic threat. But Stalin and Mao appeared to be on friendly terms. China had intervened in Korea, and many Americans (including some in the intelligence business) believed in an overarching Communist conspiracy—the Sino-Soviet Bloc. If Stalin had the bomb, could Mao be far behind?

American suspicions of a close Sino-Soviet relationship were confirmed through COMINT by the exploitation of COMINTERN communications. This traffic showed a long-standing liaison between the COMINTERN and Mao's forces, going back to the 1930s. When, in the late 1940s, ASA first began exploiting Soviet plain-language printer, analysts discovered that the Soviets were sending World War II lend-lease equipment to Mao, who was then attempting to overthrow Chiang Kai-shek. Clearly, the USSR was the major arms supplier for the Chinese armies, and the Soviets had nuclear weapons.

During the 1954 Quemoy and Matsu crisis, Secretary of State John Foster Dulles pledged American arms in defense of Formosa. The pledge was repeated during the 1958 renewal of the offshore islands imbroglio, but Dulles persuaded Chiang to renounce the use of force against the PRC, and the islands never again caused a confrontation between the U.S. and China.

Meanwhile, however, U.S. intelligence poured ever-increasirig resources into the China problem.

In many ways, China resembled the USSR. [censored] resources to go against the second-most-serious threat were scarce. [censored] The Chinese program was delayed for several years by the Sino-Soviet rift, [censored] China's strategic defense system did not make rapid progress until the 1960s.

The Early Days of Overhead

The early days of the new Eisenhower administration represented the blackest period for U.S. intelligence on Soviet forces and strategic capabilities. [censored] If the United States could not penetrate the Iron Curtain [censored] they would have to do it from the air.

Attempts had already been made. In the late 1940s the CIA had tried to float high altitude balloons over the USSR, equipped with cameras and recorders. This so-called [censored] program failed dismally. The few balloons that floated all the way from [censored] to [censored] yielded little useful information.

More determined were deliberate overflights of Soviet soil. SAC had a highly compartmented (and still obscure) overflight program, carrying a variety of sensors. This dangerous approach to intelligence collection was augmented by the RAF, which mounted occasional overflights. But their participation was limited and ended after one famous incident in 1953. At American behest, RAF aircraft overflew Kapustin Yar, [censored] They came back with their planes shot full of holes and allegedly told the Americans that if they wanted that sort of thing done, they could jolly well do it themselves. [censored]

A series of ground-breaking studies in the early 1950s urged Eisenhower to plunge into advanced technological alternatives. One of the most attractive proposals was suggested by the Surprise Attack Panel, a committee set up under Dr. James R. Killian, president of MIT. Dr. Edwin Land, a member of the panel and inventor of the Polaroid camera, suggested that a camera could be devised which could take pictures from very high altitudes, if the Air Force could build an airplane from which to mount such a camera. In November 1954, Allen Dulles got [censored] to build some thirty new aircraft which had been designed for just such a purpose by Kelly Johnson, the top designer at Lockheed. They were called U-2"s.

There was at the time no guarantee that the U-2 was the answer. In fact the Eisenhower administration continued to play with the balloon option. Project [censored] consisted of more than 500 balloons which were floated across the USSR from Europe to Asia in early 1956. [censored] and some of them may have [censored] But[censored] was no more successful than [censored] and of the 500, only forty-four were ever recovered after their long ride from west to east.

The U-2 project was a very risky gambit by an administration desperate to find out what was happening in the Soviet Union. Advanced equipment was placed aboard an aircraft easily picked out on radar, and defensible only because of its operational altitude. If the Soviets ever got a weapon that would shoot that high, the U-2 could be a sitting duck.

This was undoubtedly in Eisenhower's mind when in 1955 he broached the Open Skies proposal to Khrushchev. The U-2 had not yet been launched, but when it was, it would be a target.

From the time of the first U-2 overflight on 7 April 1956, to the shootdown of Francis Gary Powers on 1 May 1960, the Eisenhower administration launched twenty-four missions. The objective was photography, and the targets related to Soviet strategic systems. The aircraft also carried an [censored] package, but this was probably used for internal defense (presumably to warn the aircraft of the presence of unfriendly threats) and to target the cameras. [censored] in special rooms—only a few individuals at each site were cleared. [censored]

[censored]

Prior to the Powers flight, NSA began to note increased [censored] Henry Fenech, the NSA official in charge of the operation, stated that a mission just prior to the infamous May Day flight was chased by a Soviet interceptor aircraft all the way to Afghanistan. It was obvious to Fenech that the Soviets were loading up. Powers took off on 1 May 1960.{censored] Back at NSA, Fenech reported to CIA that the aircraft had probably been lost to unexplained causes. It was the first loss of a U-2. [censored]

CIA was desperate to know what had really happened to the aircraft, and in early 1962 General C. P. Cabell, deputy director of the CIA, decided to trade Soviet spy Rudolph Abel for Powers. In March 1962, only a month after the return of Powers, CIA called a board of inquiry, and into the middle of it marched Fenech, accompanied by NSA Director Laurence Frost, Deputy Director Louis Tordella, and Assistant Director for Production Oliver Kirby [censored]

Both the Soviets and Powers said that the plane had been shot down at high altitude with an SA-2, [censored] Fenech told CIA that it appeared Powers had begun a descent well before the SA-2 hit. Had he gone to sleep? Was it inattention or hypoxia? Did he flame out and search for a lower altitude to restart his engines? All Fenech knew was that [censored] Fenech did not believe what Powers had told CIA. The CIA crowd was not amused, and Fenech underwent a long and hostile grilling by the board.

[censored]

What really happened? We will probably never know. Powers died in a helicopter crash in 1977, so no more information is available from him. But the leaned so heavily on was suspect. [censored] Moreover, the Soviet officer who was in charge of the SAM battery that supposedly shot Powers down stated after the end of the Cold War that the air-defense operators were so shocked at the shootdown that they didn't believe it, and for twenty minutes or so they continued to reflect the aircraft on its presumed track to cover up their befuddlement. If the Soviet defenders did not know for sure what had happened, and if they covered up information so as not to look bad up the line, the chance at ever arriving at the truth looks very dim indeed. The theory that he was downed by an SA-2 at very high altitude (68,000 feet) appears more plausible today than it did in 1960.

[censored]

The Attack On Soviet Cipher Systems

[censored]—Baker Report, 1958

When it was created, AFSA inherited a Soviet problem that was in miserable shape. [censored]

There were only two bright spots. The first was unenciphered radioprinter, which carried valuable [censored] information. These links had not yet begun to go to cipher. [censored]

Even the darkest days, however, had their rays of hope. Howard Engstrom, a World War II cryptologist now in the civilian computer business, suggested in 1950 that AFSA might make progress by establishing a research institute comprising eminent civilian scientists to attack the problem, very much in the pattern of Los Alamos of the Manhattan Project. Then, two years later, AFSA's Scientific Communications Adviser Group (SCAG, a predecessor of NSASAB), chaired by Engstrom, [censored] given sufficient resources and a strong research and development effort. The need for a skilled civilian work force or the employment of an outside research institute was essential. AFSA did not have a strong enough civilian work force, and the Brownell Committee made this point forcefully that same year.

[censored]

[censored]

As NSA struggled with the [censored] problem, two camps formed concerning the prospects for success. The first group felt that the effort was hopeless and should not be funded. The 1957 Baker Panel leaned toward this viewpoint. The committee recommended that an effort be kept alive [censored] but it was pessimistic about long-range chances for success.

A second group felt that the United States would never know whether it would be possible or not because of inadequacies at NSA. The organization was too skewed towards military manning, was not hiring the right kinds of civilians, and did not have an adequate budget. [censored] This opinion was well entrenched at CIA and was led by former NSAer Frank Rowlett. A variant on this inteipretation was offered by the Baker Panel, which suggested that the internal NSA structure could not cope with the complexities of high-grade systems. That job should be given entirely to a Los Alamos-style civilian research institute.

But within NSA itself there was a strong undercurrent of disagreement with both camps. Representative of this view was the report of a committee chaired in 1956 by captain Jack Holtwick. Holtwick felt that a concentrated attack would yield enough [censored] alone to justify the effort, and he recommended a massive computer attack. Such a super-high-speed computer would cost in the neighborhood of $5 million per year, a considerable sum in those days. [censored] NSA would need [censored] and would probably have to have some of the work done at a private research organization (the Los Alamos option again). [censored]

[censored]

Tracking Submarines—The Story Of Burst Transmissions

Late in World War II, German scientists had once again come up with a serious threat to Allied cryptologic efforts. This time, they had devised a way to compact lengthy manual Morse messages into messages lasting only a few seconds. When played at normal speed, a message sounded like a burst of noise in the receiver. The Germans called it KURIER and intended it to be on submarines, agents (spies), and eventually aircraft for low-probability-of-intercept communications. Early models were deployed before war's end, and GCCS intercepted transmissions on at least one occasion. Fortunately, however, KURIER was still in the experimental stage.

When the war ended, a German submarine surrendered in Argentina, the nearest landfall. Aboard the sub was a German scientist with extensive engineering notes and knowledge of the system, and he was willing to talk to the Americans about it. Even luckier, the British captured an actual KURIER system, and both the British and Americans experimented with it, primarily for the purpose of building burst systems for their own submarines.

Unfortunately, the Soviets also captured German scientists working on KURIER, and the TICOM teams discovered this during their debriefing sessions. At the time, the Navy [censored]

[censored]

[censored]

Chapter 5 Building the Internal Mechanism

Cryptology Is Automated—The Story Of Early Computerization

"The trouble with machines is people." —Edward R. Murrow, 1952

Antecedents

Modern cryptanalysis, with its emphasis on the manipulation of large amounts of data, was one of the earliest government enterprises to acquire the new office automation equipment being produced by a small company called International Business Machines (IBM). In 1931, 0P-20-G obtained some of the new IBM machines and quickly employed them in the cryptanalytic process to sort large amounts of data and determine likes and unlikes. In 1935 Signal Intelligence Service (SIS) acquired the same type of equipment for the same purpose. By World War II "EAM" (electronic accounting machine) equipment had become commonplace in COMINT processing, and it contributed mightily to codebreaking, especially in the Pacific Theater. By the end of the war, OP-20-G and SIS combined were using more than 700 IBM-type machines.

Of the two, the Navy seemed to be further along. During the 1930s and into the early war years, OP-20-G had attempted a partnership with Vannevar Bush, the renowned MIT (Massachusetts Institute of Technology) scientist, to build a faster comparator for analytic (read cryptanalytic) use. This rather bumpy relationship had so far yielded a number of notable technological and administrative failures when, in 1943, OP-20-G became a partner with GCCS in running attacks against the four-rotor German naval ENIGMA. They ultimately decided on a huge, clunky mechanical marvel which has been dubbed the "American bombe." A technological dinosaur when compared to the devices Bush was experimenting with, the bombe at least worked and was used in the last two and a half years of the war to break German naval ENIGMA keys. The Navy development and contract monitoring operation was called the Naval Computing Machine Laboratory (NCML); it was located on the grounds of National Cash Register in Dayton, Ohio, the prime production contractor.

Although a very fast comparator, the bombe was not a true computer. It did not have a stored digital program which could be modified. But even as the Navy designed and built the bombes, the British were moving ahead into the era of true computers. To attack systems even more complex than ENIGMA, GCCS was developing a computer which employed an electronically generated key that was compared with the German cipher text. Although it did not have a true internally stored program, the settings were operator-adjustable according to how close he or she thought they were to a cryptanalytic solution. They called it Colossus. Some contend that it was the world's first true computer, although Colossus must compete for that honor with ENIAC, which was being developed at the University of Pennsylvania's Moore School of Electronics to generate complex artillery ballistics tables for the Army. Either Colossus, designed for cryptologic use, or ENIAC, for ballistics, probably deserves the title of the world's first computer.

Postwar Developments

OP-20-G could see the technological possibilities in the bombe, and it was decided even before the war ended that the effort should continue. But National Cash Register had no intention of continuing the association. They wanted to return to making cash registers. So at the end of the war, NCML was physically evicted, along with the remainder of its undelivered bombes, and the project came to a halt.

OP-20-G needed a prime contractor with which to work. Months before the war ended, Howard Engstrom, a key figure on the bombe project, decided to start a new company specifically to do business with OP-20-G. At war's end, he left the Navy and took with him the best and brightest technicians at NCML. They set up a new company called Electronic Research Associates (ERA), under the wing of an already established firm called Northwestern Aeronautical Corporation in St. Paul, Minnesota. The Navy made no specific promises regarding contracts for the fledgling company, but none were needed. Engstrom and associates had a corner on the technological expertise that OP-20-G required, and contracts flowed almost immediately.

The relationship between ERA and the Navy was emblematic of the way relationships had developed between the cryptologists and private industry. During the war OP-20-G had developed a close relationship with IBM, Eastman Kodak, and National Cash Register. SIS had a similar kind of relationship with Bell Laboratories and Teletype Corporation. Those businesses kept a stable of cleared people who could do jobs quickly and quietly for the cryptologists. In the COMINT and COMSEC businesses, it did not pay to advertise.

Both the bombe and ENIAC had been developed through classified wartime military contracts. Thus computing in the United States began in the rarified atmosphere of tight security. Though the cryptanalytic aspects were not publicized, the Army relationship with the Moore School became a matter of public knowledge in 1946 when the inventors of ENIAC, John Mauchly and J. Prosper Eckert, gave a series of lectures on electronic computers. As the two men left the Moore School to establish a computer manufacturing company, they dispersed their knowledge nationwide in what became known as the Moore School Lectures. Many felt that this lecture series launched the computer industry in the United States.

Howard Engstrom had found out about the Moore School lectures, and he suggested that the Navy send a cryptologist to observe. Thus, when the lectures began, sitting in the back of the room was Lieutenant Commander James T. Pendergrass, a Navy mathematician employed at Nebraska Avenue. Pendergrass delivered a report to the Navy on the Moore lectures which focused attention on the emerging new computer technology. This resulted in negotiations with ERA which led to the construction of the Atlas machine.

Like the bombe before it, the first generation of postwar cryptologic computers produced highly specialized machines, called in those days "rapid analytic machines" (RAMs). Each machine was constructed for a different purpose and attacked a different cryptanalytic machine or problem. Programs were particular rather than general, and inputs and outputs were of specialized design. A list of AFSA machines, both present and projected, in 1952 contained sixty RAMs, as opposed to only eight that had more flexible objectives. An example of a RAM was [censored] which was developed by ERA to attack [censored]

Even in those early days computer companies were willing to take on difficult developmental tasks. For instance, operating under a 1947 contract, ERA developed the world's first magnetic drum storage system as part of a RAM project called GOLDBERG. A successor project, called ATLAS (also built by ERA) applied the drum storage technology to a more general purpose cryptanalytic processor. ATLAS was ERA's first major computer development, and it led to the company's first commercial product, the ERA 1101, produced after the company had become merged with Remington-Rand-Univac to form the first major American computer company.

While NSG forged ahead, ASA was trying to catch up. In ASA, the role played by Engstrom, Tordella, and Pendergrass was at first taken on single-handedly by Samuel Snyder, one of Friedman's most talented prewar cryptanalysts.

Snyder's 1947 paper "Proposed Long-Range Cryptanalytic Machines Program for Literal Systems" played a seminal role in ASA's first postwar venture into the new technology. In it, Snyder proposed that ASA develop its own analytic computer based on extensive research into existing technology. Snyder himself did most of this early research, drawing at first on information provided by Pendergrass and Howard Campaigne of NSG. He made pilgrimages to the fountainheads of computer research: Aberdeen Proving Grounds to see ENIAC, Bell Labs to see its Relay Computer, IBM to see the IBM Selective Sequence Calculator, and MIT to see its Differential Analyzer. He attended a lecture series at the National Bureau of Standards (NBS) which concentrated on Univac products (Univac had been formed in 1946 by Mauchly and Eckert), Raytheon computers, and the Ace Computer (one of the earliest British entries into the commercial computer field). Snyder suggested that ASA team up with NBS, which already had some expertise in the field, and he proposed that ASA form a committee to guide the effort.

ASA decided to go ahead with development of a general-purpose analytic computer called ABNER. Working through NBS, ASA arranged for subcontracts on mercury delay memory and for magnetic tape drives from Technitrol and Raytheon, respectively. Snyder contended that ABNER 1, which was released for use in 1952, was the first machine that placed primary emphasis on nonarithmetic operations. Although it played a role in the development of later computers for cryptologic applications, one expert in the field called ABNER "barely functional." This was an appellation that could have applied to many of the early experiments in machine-age cryptology.

The early cryptologlc computers were troglodytic. They were physically programmed in binary instructions input via paper tape. They used octal numbers and words twenty-four bits long. There was no "computer language" as such. Memories were tiny by today's standards—the drum memory for ATLAS, for instance, held only 16,000 words. There being no more advanced technology available, vacuum tubes were used for relays, despite the obvious disadvantages this created in terms of heat buildup and tube replacement. Early computers were usually "down" more often than they were "up." When they were "up," though, they provided answers faster than anything imaginable.

Vacuum tubes were on the way out, to be replaced by transistors, developed at Bell Labs in the 1940s by future Nobel prize winner William Shockley and others. NSA scientists were among the first to apply the new transistor technology to computers, and in the mid-1950s it developed an in-house computer called SOLO, the world's first computer to be entirely transistorized. SOLO was subsequently marketed commercially by the contractor, Phileo, as the Transac S-1000.

Other innovations were on the way. In the mid-1950s NSA began making the transition from centralized computer operations to remote job access systems. The first remote job access computer, ROGUE (for Remotely Operated General Use Equipment), used hardware called Alwac IIIE developed by a small firm called Logistics Research, Incorporated. ROGUE had three remote terminals connected to a small central processor.

RAMs like ROGUE were good for specific jobs, but cryptologists recognized very early that they would require more generalized systems to process very large volumes of data. A study in the mid-1950s depicted just how much material must be massaged. Raw traffic arrived in courier shipments every day at the rate of thirty-seven tons per month. An additional thirty million groups of traffic arrived (in Tecsumized form) via teletype. Traffic from some entities (particularly the mechanization-resistant manual Morse intercept) received less than 50 percent detailed processing—the rest was held in case it was needed.

As early as 1946, NSG began the search for a computer that could hold very large volumes of data. Studies of mass data handling methods led to a contract between the Navy and Raytheon in 1951 to develop and produce a machine called NOMAD that would be physically and financially the largest cryptologic machine yet. But the NOMAD contract went badly off schedule from the first, and the contract was killed in June 1954.

The best general-purpose computer in the early days was an IBM product, the 701, designed in partnership with NSA. NSA leaned toward magnetic tape rather than disks, and the 701 had the first truly functional tape drives controlled by vacuum columns.

The 701 was followed by the IBM 705, which became the mainstay for general-purpose computing. Coming on line in the mid-1950s, the 705 was a nonfixed-word-length machine. It had the best sorter around, an assembler (called a "transembler") that mimicked punched card machines. The 705 had a major impact on data processing, and it made it possible to begin processing massive volumes of data rolling in from the rapidly expanding network of collection sites around the world.

Parallel to the general-purpose processors was a line of special-purpose scientific machines. Notable was the IBM 704, which had a 36-bit word, punched card input, and tape drives for storage.

Cryptology still needed a general-purpose system. A committee, formed to review the demise of NOMAD, specified the requirement for a system that could be of use to both traffic analysts and cryptanalysts. For the traffic analyst, it would have to have large storage, have a file capability for collateral information, and be capable of sorting quickly. For the cryptanalist it should be able to tackle [censored] To achieve the requisite flexibility, the system would require a general purpose mainframe with special-purpose peripherals. The project was called FARMER.

At the time, IBM was working on a project to extend the performance of its latest product, the 704, by a factor of 100. They called it STRETCH. IBM approached both NSA and the Atomic Energy Commission (AEC), the two government agencies that it felt would have the most use for such a system. AEC agreed to proceed, but NSA ultimately decided that it wanted something specifically optimized for cryptologic applications. However, IBM was on the right track, NSA concluded, and awarded Big Blue contracts for research in high-speed memory (SILO) and to design a general processing system for Agency use (PLANTATION, later called RANCHO). The entire project was eventually folded into a gigantic effort to develop a large-scalel computer. It was called HARVEST.

The most difficult part of the project turned out to be designing the magnetic tape drives. Under a project called TRACTOR, IBM developed new tape drives and a unique automatic cartridge loading system having 100 times the speed of the IBM Type 721 tape drives then in use. Each of the three TRACTOR units managed two tape drives, and it automatically retrieved and hung data tapes in a robotic environment that was the wonder of the U.S. government. It made for great theater and was on the mandatory show-and-tell tour for years.

HARVEST worked after a fashion and remained the Agency's central processor from the time it went on line in 1962 until it was finally retired in 1976, a phenomenal life span for any computer system. But those who had to make it work remember it as balky, difficult to program, and not performing anywhere near the specifications that had been set for the system. It was a transitional machine.

NSA's most lasting contribution to computer history was undoubtedly Project LIGHTNING. LIGHTNING resulted from NSA's reaction to outside criticism that it could not break [censored] systems and to proposals that this part of COMINT be transferred to an outside research organization. Pricked by the criticism, Canine initiated an all-out attack [censored] As part of the project, Canine proposed that NSA develop a computer that would advance the state of technology by three orders of magnitude. He decreed that the goal was a "1,000 megahertz machine," and at a USCIB meeting in August of 1956 he requested $25 million seed money. The sum angered the Defense Department and placed NSA's budget in jeopardy. In order to get it approved, General Samford took his case directly to President Eisenhower and his top scientists, Vannevar Bush and Jerome Wiesner. Eisenhower came down hard in favor, and he authorized the use of his name to push the project ahead.

Three major contractors participated—IBM, RCA, and Sperry Rand Univac—but Ohio State University, Kansas University, Philco, and MIT also performed lesser roles. LIGHTNING never resulted in a computer, but the research teams turned up information that drove the next generation of commercial machines. Among the most significant findings were in the field of cryogenics. IBM's Dudley Buck developed the cryotron, and through his research IBM proved the now-obvious axiom that the lower the temperature, the faster the computer. Sperry Rand Univac concentrated on thin magnetic field devices and, through these early experiments in chip technology, found that computer speed would increase when components were subminiaturized in order to place them closer together. RCA concentrated on applications of the tunnel diode, one of the fastest switching devices known.

As the 1950s wore on, cryptologists broadened computer applications to include far more than just cryptanalysis. NSA first used computers to generate COMSEC material in 1959, when the COMSEC organization began employing the Univac File Computer for that purpose. And for the processing of intercepted traffic for traffic analytic applications, the IBM 700-series computers continued to be the mainstay.

[censored] For scanning in the field, CDC (Control Data Corporation, the successor to ERA) developed the concept of key word search under a project called FADE-IN. Text scanning in the field was not implemented until the early 1960s. SOAPFLAKES was believed to be the first key word scan system at NSA.

Most of these processes were off-line. Intercepted traffic in Tecsumized or diarized form spilled off the communications lines in paper tape form and was carted off to another area of the building to be input to processing computers. But it was not the wave of the future. SMAC first began experimenting with the use of a computer to directly receive inputted messages from the field, and so avoid the paper tape step. This effort used Univac 494s and was in a very early stage of development as the 1950s came to a close.

NSA Communications In The Pre-Criticomm Era

"Equipment is obsolescent, insufficient in number and inadequate for the purpose. . . . Such essentials to operations as, for example, a place to put live traffic and operators' logs, are neglected in the installation and are provided, if at all, as an afterthought when operations begin. . . . Homemade bins in the aisles, traffic piled on the floor or clipped to overhead wires like clothes on a line, logsheets resting on machines, et cetera, are the inevitable result." —1955 study of the COMINT communications system

Rapid communications is the lifeblood of SIGINT. Cryptologists have grown so accustomed to virtually instantaneous access to remote corners of the globe that they could not operate any other way. But in the early days, they operated in a decidedly different mode.

AFSA, when created, had no indigenous communications at all. Instead, the organization depended entirely on communications paths and facilities provided by the services. COMINT passed from collection sites to Washington on armed service communications. It was encrypted off-line at the field site, then was passed to a local communications center manned by non-SI indoctrinated people, who put it on common user circuits for transmission. If the traffic originated at a Navy site, it was put onto naval communications; if it was an Army site, it went via Army communications; and so forth. The traffic was long, vertical umbilical, service-unique and electrically sealed until it reached Washington, where the information could then be passed to other services or to AFSA.

The message went via HF single sideband, passing through up to six relay centers before finally arriving at either Arlington Hall or Naval Security Station. It might have to be reencrypted up to five times, and the process required from twenty-four to forty-eight hours to send a routine message to the capital. Because of the many relays and inherent degradation of HF channels, up to 30 percent arrived undecipherable and had to be retransmitted. Messages required several hours for decryption, and the handling time for each message, including marking and routing to the intended recipient, took several more hours. The ASA communications center at Arlington Hall, for instance, was taking approximately four days (on top of the one to two days of transmission time) to deliver a routine message. The fastest possible handling time on the most critical information was not less than five to six hours from time of intercept, according to information furnished to the Robertson Committee in 1953.

When AFSA came into existence, the communications system on which it relied was reported to be "in a deplorable and deteriorating state." Arthur Enderlin, one of AFSA's top communications people, conducted a study detailing the decrepit conditions and sent it to Admiral Stone. A disbelieving Stone decreed a full-blown study, which just confirmed Enderlin's contentions.

Nothing was done under Stone. But when Canine arrived, plans were immediately laid by Enderlin's successor, Lieutenant Colonel William B. Campbell, for a separate AFSA communications center to process traffic destined for AFSA organizations. In July 1952, the new communications handling facility opened in B Building at Arlington Hall, using Teletype Corporation Model-19s. This was a good first step, and it reduced the message handling time for routine messages to three hours, while cutting the message backlog to almost nothing.

Another Canine push was for secure telephone communications. The NSA gray phone system, formally known as NSA/CSS Secure Telephone System (NSTS), began in AFSA's waning days with a total of 200 lines, 100 each for Nebraska Avenue and Arlington Hall. AFSA took possession of two-thirds of the telephone instruments, while the collocated SCAs got one-third. A month later (September) a new microwave system became operational between the two locations, ushering in an era of high-reliability, high-fidelity communications. At the time, the system required an operator to connect the two parties, just like commercial telephone circuits of the era. The following April NSA issued its first consolidated telephone directory.

AFSA began broadening its secure communications contacts with its customers. The Zone of Interior Connectivity (ZICON) net, originated in the early 1950s, consisted of landline communications paths between AFSA and its principal customers: the three services, State, and CIA. Later, the National Intelligence Indications Center in the Pentagon was added, as well as SAC and CONAD (Strategic Air Command and Continental Air Defense Command) for the Air Force.

The COMINT Comnet

By 1952 it was already clear that the growing volume of cryptologic communications would not permit newly established NSA to pursue the old way of doing business. Already, the daily group count was considerable and would grow in the ensuing years, as the following table shows.

Table I
Total Mean Daily Average Group Count at NSA[34]

Year	Count
1952	648,000
1953	1,247,117
1954	1,322,552
1955	1,320,073
1956	1,227,158
1957	1,424,351
1958	1,729,430
1959	2,059,763
1960	2,615,377
1961	3,896,211
1962	4,306,910
1963	5,089,777
1964	6,134,601

Spurred by the studies by Enderlin and Campbell, and by the insistence of Canine, NSA devised a plan to establish a worldwide cryptologic communications system. Initially, NSA would establish a network of dedicated channels on the service communications systems, manned only by SI-cleared people to eliminate the multiple encryption-decryption exercises.

But the ultimate plan was to establish a separate system, called the COMINT Comnet. The dedicated circuits would gradually be internetted into a series of relay stations, manned only by SI-cleared people. Initially there were to be six of these relay centers, but the number would expand along with the system of field sites that they serviced. [censored] Intercept sites would feed into the relay centers, which would bulk-forward traffic (primarily intercepted material) back to NSA.

The relay centers would operate initially using torn-tape relays, but would eventually transition to automated relay systems, thus significantly reducing handling time. Once in the system, a message would never have to be reencrypted. When it reached NSA, it would be distributed internally using facsimile equipment. In 1953 Canine announced to a field site commanders' conference that the ultimate objective was to be able to return priority traffic through the communications system within five to ten minutes, while routine traffic would flow through in no more than an hour.

Canine was able to obtain, in short order, direct communications circuits to Stateside users, GCHQ and CBNRC (as the Canadian cryptologic organization was then called). By the end of 1952 NSA had nine such circuits and plans for six more in the near future. These on-line circuits formed the basis for the COMINT Comnet.

But the rest of the plan depended on service cooperation, and that was a different matter. Planning for the COMINT Comnet was entrusted to the Joint Communications Electronics Committee, a joint JCS-level planning body whose chairman, Admiral John Redman, had been a prominent member of the Navy cryptologic team during World War II. But Redman was also a dedicated Navy man, and he viewed the proposed Comnet as cutting down on the channel capacity available for other, uniquely service, uses. Under such auspices the plan for a Comnet did not have a bright future.

A steering committee called CENSA (Communications-Electronics—National Security Agency) decreed that each service would fund its own portion of the Comnet. And there was where the rocks were. The services had other funding priorities, and moneys never seemed to be available for the Comnet. Every year NSA communications planners enthusiastically charged up the hill, only to be beaten back again.

By the mid-1950s, the system was only partially funded, and so far no one had agreed on an automated switch for the new relay centers. The centers that existed were entirely manual operations, in which traffic from an incoming circuit generated a perforated tape on the Mod-19. When the reperforator finished chattering, a communications center operator coiled up the tape and carried it across the room to an outgoing circuit for onward relay to the next center. Coiled tapes sat in boxes behind teletypewriters, awaiting transmission. Communication centers were chaotic, operators were overworked, and twelve-hour shifts were standard.

Meanwhile, NSA did what it could to improve the operation. The greatest technical innovation of the 1950s was the introduction of the Burroughs-produced KW-26 on-line encryption device. The KW-26 was a marvel of its day. [censored] It almost doubled transmission speed. Serial #1 of the KW-26 was placed in operation at the new NSA communications center at Fort Meade in 1957. The last of these devices was not pulled off the line until 1988. In the ensuing thirty-one years it became the mainstay of cryptologic communications around the world, the most secure and reliable on-line encryption device the United States had ever fielded.

The new communications center at Fort Meade was planned to overcome the inherited inadequacies of the facilities at Arlington Hall and Nebraska Avenue. Canine had wanted NSA Fort Meade to start life with KW-26s, but the acquisition plan ran behind schedule, and the new communications center on the 2-E corridor began with a hodge-podge of equipment.

But on one thing Canine was insistent—he would not move to Fort Meade without a secure ("gray") phone system. The secure phone system had expanded rapidly, and by 1956 it linked NSA with most important Washington-area customers. In 1957 work began on the microwave tower on Fort Meade that was needed to carry the gray phone system to Washington. The Chesapeake and Potomac Telephone Company provided the path, while Motorola provided the radio equipment for the link. Although Canine never actually moved to Fort Meade (he retired with his office still at Arlington Hall), his successor, General Samford, had a gray phone on his desk, courtesy of his predecessor.

Meanwhile, the early flirtation with facsimile equipment for internal distribution had turned out badly. Fax, as it was called, could not handle the mountainous volumes of traffic flooding into NSA every day. So in 1954 the Agency decided on distributed teletypes. Teletype Corporation equipment was ordered, and equipments were parcelled out through the Production working spaces. A new communications router would be assigned to all incoming traffic. It would be called the DDI (Delivery Distribution Indicator) and would have a very long and prosperous life.

In the fall of 1957, Sputnik went up, and the White House wanted all military and warning communications systems brought up to par. At the time, the COMINT Comnet was still in a state of partial being. NSA had managed to purloin some dedicated channels, and the cryptologic community operated a few relay centers around the world. But the system needed to be consolidated. More, it needed updated equipment, especially automated relays to get rid of torn tape relay arrangements. Moneys for these improvements had managed to find their way into military budgets throughout the 1950s, but they always seemed to disappear into the outyears as the services took care of more pressing requirements. All involved had grown cynical, and the budget for FY59 was not even covered with the fig leaf of outyear moneys. It contained nothing at all for the COMINT Comnet, and this was how the Eisenhower administration found it in early 1958.

Securing American Communications

"It become apparent to me early in my work in the Signal Intelligence Service that it was more important to secure our own messages than to read the communications of others. . . . I think it is imperative that our history show the importance of our communications security effort as compared with intelligence production." —Frank B. Rowlett

The COMINT Comnet would be no good if it were not secure. The business of securing American communications had always been integrated with the task of breaking the communications of other countries. Thus from the earliest days the cryptologic coin had two sides: COMINT and COMSEC. During World War II, Signal Intelligence Service had a COMSEC arm, and it produced COMSEC equipment and materials for the Army around the world. In the Navy the integration was more tenuous and the COMSEC mission more diffuse, but closely allied offices of OP-20 were involved in both functions. When the Air Force was created, it gave COMSEC responsibilities to USAFSS. Thus the uniquely complementary aspects of COMINT and COMSEC were recognized from the first. They were never, as they were in Germany, divided among various organizations. Although the two were, as World War II naval cryptologist Joseph Eachus once said, "natural enemies," the dependence of one on the other was firmly established.

The Era of the Wired Rotor

Since the Revolutionary War, the U.S. government had been using manual (mostly paper-based) code systems for communications security. With the advent of radio in the early part of the twentieth century, communications security became even more important. At the time, only manual codes and ciphers were available. Encrypting and decrypting was a laborious process which slowed down communications and limited the amount of information that could be sent from place to place.

Paper codes were archaic solutions to modern communications requirements. After World War I, inventors around the world worked on the problem, and almost simultaneously three or four of them came up with the same solution—a mechanical device consisting of rotors which moved to a different position each time a letter was depressed on a keyboard. In the United States, the inventor of the hour was an eccentric Californian named Edward Hebern. Hebern tried to sell his device to the Army and Navy, but they found it to be both inherently insecure and mechanically unsound. Because of this and patent and contractual difficulties, the relationship with Hebern was terminated.

This did not mean, however, that the services ceased work on rotor machines. Paralleling their competitors in the other industrialized nations, they made the wired rotor the basis for most COMSEC devices used during World War II. The most secure machine in the war, the SIGABA, was a wired rotor machine designed more or less jointly by the Army and Navy in the late 1930s. The SIGABA was large, heavy, and required a good deal of electricity. Some 11,000 were produced during the war. To communicate with the British, SIS devised a modified SIGABA called the CCM (Combined Cipher Machine), and the British used a very similar device on their end called Typex. CCM continued in use long after the end of the war and was not replaced until 1958, when the KL-7 was introduced for NATO use.

For tactical use, the Army used a modified Hagelin machine called M-209. It was small and light, and being completely mechanical, it required no electricity, which made it ideal for foxhole use. But it was difficult and time-consuming to set up properly. (Nonetheless, it continued in use into the early 1960s.) Smith-Corona produced it in huge quantities for $64 a copy—one former NSA official estimated that some 125,000 devices were built before it went out of production.

The wartime machines were, with two exceptions, off-line devices. One typed the plain text of the message on a keyboard, and the machine produced cipher text on (usually) a sticky-backed tape which could be glued on a paper and taken to the communications operator for transmission.

To handle the increasing volumes of messages, what was needed was a machine that could convert plain to cipher text on-line. SIS devised a solution early in the war. Called SIGCUM (Converter M228), it was not as secure cryptographically as SIGABA, and a new key setting was required for every message. As a result SIGCUM was used in only limited numbers.

A different sort of on-line machine was the SIGTOT, which used a one-time tape. One-time tape machines became known generically as Python systems because of the huge coils of cipher tape that they required. Python systems were used until the early 1960s, but they were cumbersome because of the enormous quantities of tape that had to be generated, handled, and fed through the TD (transmitter-distributor). They were not the long-term answer.

The Early Years of Secure Speech

Voice was far more difficult to secure. Systems devised in the early days of World War II were cryptographically vulnerable, and better security was needed. Bell Labs built a more sophisticated system during the war to carry high-level transatlantic phone calls. Called SIGSALY, it was a true archetype. SIGSALY consisted of forty-five racks of equipment, weighed thirty tons, occupied an entire room, required thirteen technicians to operate, sucked up 35 kilowatts of power, carried only one voice channel, and cost $1 million per copy. But given the cryptanalytic sophistication at the time, it was secure. At that price, the government ordered only twelve systems and installed them in the key capitals of the Western world, including Washington, London, and Melbourne. Churchill used it a few times, and, apocryphally, Roosevelt also tried it out once. He allegedly gave up on it, unhappy with the speech quality. The United States entered the postwar era needing a much smaller and less costly secure voice system.

Organizing for COMSEC in the Postwar World

The SCAs slipped into the postwar period with their COMSEC authorities virtually unchanged. The newly renamed ASA was responsible for all Army COMSEC tasks. COMSEC functions were part of the same organization, and personnel rotated between COMINT and COMSEC jobs.

The Navy COMSEC functions were still less monolithic than those of the Army, and the tasks of engineering development, COMSEC research, production of keying material, and building COMSEC machines were spread out across several organizations. COMSEC functions involved the Bureau of Ships, Deputy Chief of Naval Communications for Administration, Deputy Chief of Naval Communications Supplementary Activities (CSA, i.e., NSG), and the Naval Code and Signal Laboratory. It was a complex bureaucracy, but the link-up with the COMINT and COMSEC organizations within CSA seemed to keep naval COMSEC moving in the same direction.

The newly created Air Force did not at first have a centralized COMSEC organization, and for the first year or two of its existence it was serviced by ASA. But when USAFSS was created in 1948, the Air Force assigned its centralized COMSEC functions to the new cryptologic organization.

The three service efforts were rather loosely coordinated by the Joint Communications-Electronics Committee. When one service developed and procured a COMSEC device with broad applicability, it took care of the requirements of the other services, a seat-of-the-pants approach to centralization which worked as long as everyone agreed on the program. So when AFSA was created in 1949, all three SCAs were doing their own COMSEC.

Almost unnoticed at its creation, AFSA was anointed with centralized COMSEC responsibilities. Naval Security Station at Nebraska Avenue became the locus for COMSEC activities. Army colonel Samuel P. Collins and civilian Abraham Sinkov headed AFSA's COMSEC organization. Centralized COMSEC functions were placid by comparison with COMINT, and contributed little if anything to the demise of the organization. When AFSA collapsed, it was because of turmoil in COMINT, not COMSEC.

When in October 1952 President Harry Truman established NSA, he also signed a memorandum creating a centralized COMSEC function. The memo declared that COMSEC (like COMINT) was a national responsibility, and it set up the secretary of defense and the secretary of state as a special committee of the National Security Council for COMSEC. It also directed that a new central board be established, to be called the United States Communications Security Board (USCSB) to serve as an interdepartmental source of COMSEC policy.

But his memo did not actually establish the board, and a year dragged by before USCSB received a charter. In the interim, Ralph Canine moved into the breach and acted as the central COMSEC authority for the United States. The COMSEC function at Nebraska Avenue continued as before while NSA waited for an official COMSEC structure to be set in place.

The long delay in establishing an official COMSEC charter, NSC 168, was due to disagreements over wording and authorities for NSA. Canine objected to the lack of specific centralized authorities for NSA, and to a provision which placed DIRNSA under the JCS for COMSEC. He was successful in getting the offending sentence removed and in strengthening his other authorities. In October 1953, NSC 168 was published, and USCSB was officially launched.

Besides DIRNSA, USCSB comprised representatives from State, Defense, Treasury, FBI, the three services, CIA, AEC, and Justice. At the first meeting, the board began an unstated but unswerving policy of always electing the Defense representative as the chairman. This was normally the top scientific and technical official, and in the 1960s Harold Brown, Eugene Fubini, Finn Larsen, and Gardiner L. Tucker, all deputy secretaries of defense for research and engineering, successively chaired USCSB.

NSC 168 did not give Canine the whip hand for COMSEC that NSCID 9 did for COMINT. The COMSEC process was very different, and it was never amenable to the rigid structure and centralized control that applied to COMINT. Centralized authority was couched in terms of cajolery rather than direction. NSA had specific technical authorities to prescribe cryptoprinciples and cryptosecurity rules. But organizational authorities such as budget, research and development, cryptosecurity monitoring, program review and the like were expressed in less authoritarian terms such as "develop," "plan," "prepare," "formulate," and "insure." The services retained much of their COMSEC functions and structure (generally resident within the SCAs). If a technical standard were violated, pulling the offender back into line was to be done through the parent service. NSA could not force a service to employ cryptosecurity on a given link; it could only point out the consequences of noncompliance. Canine did not have central budgetary authority over COMSEC, and he could not force a service to allocate money to COMSEC.

However, if a service decided to encrypt communications, NSA ruled the technical specifications with an iron hand. It produced all the keys, wrote the procedures, governed all compromise reporting and evaluation, established key supercession requirements, and so forth. In this respect its COMSEC authority approximated its hold over COMINT.

Unlike USCIB (later USIB), USCSB did not become a strong and vital organization. During the 1950s it held only a single meeting per year. In 1960 it met four times to solve the problem of release of crypto equipment to NATO (a difficult issue which is covered on the following page) and to deal with the problem of communications security. After that it did not meet again for eight years. It named only one standing committee, the Special Committee on Compromising Emanations (SCOCE)—TEMPEST. NSA acted as its secretariat and effectively did all the work.

Far more than just prescribing COMSEC policies, NSA became deeply involved in the design and production process. The Agency generated keying material using a wide variety of techniques. NSA also designed COMSEC machines and simply turned the production process over to a contractor after all the designs were completed. The contractor in those days was little more than an assembly organization. All the interesting work was done in-house. This would change in the 1980s under Walter Deeley's "New Way of Doing Busines."

AFSAM-7

In the early 1950s AFSA, and later NSA, pushed ahead [censored] to develop their first central, multiservice encryption device, the AFSAM-7, later the KL-7. Although the Army wanted a [censored] rotor and the Navy only a [censored] rotor, Canine decreed uniformity, and NSA adopted the Army's [censored] rotor as the standard. The KL-7 proved immensely popular, and some 20,000 were produced at the very reasonable cost of $1,200 a piece. Weighing only thirty pounds, it could run off either AC or DC power (including a jeep battery).

The Navy strongly resisted the AFSAM-7/KL-7 development. After rejecting several modifications designed to satisfy their requirements, they adopted a modified device called a KL-47. The KL-47 was to have along and interesting history. The Navy endedup using it extensively aboard ship. [censored]

When the AFSAM-7 was still new, the JCS proposed giving it to NATO countries. This got NSA into a very murky area. Defense and State had for years been concerned about the security of U.S. defense information on NATO communications. [censored]

Several different systems, including Typex and M-209, were loaned for NATO use, but none of them solved the problem of availability and security. Then in 1953 the JCS proposed the brand-new AFSAM-7, the best off-line system the US had. State and CIA both opposed the decision, but after several years of acrimonious disagreement, USCIB approved the AFSAM-7 for transfer to NATO. NSA voted with the majority, [censored]

The Push for On-line Encipherment

The conversion of record communications to on-line encipherment was probably the most significant COMSEC development of the postwar era. In the space of a few years NSA led the U.S. government into the era of secure circuitry.

After the war, the cryptologic community began the search for a reliable and efficient on-line device. For a time it appeared that one-time tapes were the answer. The British developed the 5UCO or the Secretape, which achieved limited use during the early 1950s. But tape production and handling were still a nightmare, and the volume of communications required in the 1950s dictated another solution.

Circuit speeds were beginning to exceed the capability of mechanical rotors to keep up. What was needed was an electronic key generator. The solution was the NSA-developed KW-26, the first on-line electronic key generator to come into wide use in the United States. First fielded in 1957, the KW-26 remained the mainstay of U.S. enciphered text communications for thirty years. According to a former NSA COMSEC official, the KW-26 made the Agency's COMSEC reputation.

The KW-26, because it was electronic rather than electromechanical, had no moving parts, and its speed was limited only by the speed of the associated teletypewriters, which at that time was up to 100 words per minute. Built during the transition from tubes to transistors, the KW-26 had a little of both. It had a simple-to-set key system using cards manufactured at NSA. When an operator pulled the card out of the machine, a knife sliced it in half so that it could not be reused. Its chief disadvantage was that it could be used only for point-to-point circuits, which dictated that a huge number of machines be manufactured. At one time the NSA communications center alone had 336 of them.

The point-to-point modus limited the KW-26's utility in the Navy. Naval communications were marked by wide-area fleet broadcasts to large numbers of ships afloat. Naval vessels needed the capability to tune into a broadcast at any time during the day or night and just receive traffic—transmitting messages was a much smaller communications function. To solve this problem, NSA designed the KW-37, a crypto device that permitted a ship's communications operator to tune into the fleet broadcast using a cryptographic catch-up function.

The next on-line crypto device to be widely adopted was the KG-13. Unlike the KW-26, it was a general-purpose key generator, which meant that it could be used for more than just teletypewriter security. Fully transistorized, it was smaller and lighter and was suitable for a wide variety of uses. It could encrypt voice with the HY-2 vocoder, became the backbone of the Autosevocomm voice encryption system in the 1960s.

From SIGSALY to Modern Voice Encryption

As soon as the war was over, the paleolithic SIGSALY was scrapped. Surely the U.S. could find something smaller, lighter and cheaper. In the late 1940s AFSA developed a voice encryption device called the AFSAY-816, which was used to encrypt the new secure voice system between Arlington Hall and Nebraska Avenue. Using a primitive vacuum tube key generation and pulse-code modulation, it produced good voice quality. The drawback was that it needed a 50 KHz carrier.

When computers came into general use in cryptology, NSA judged that the AFSAY-816 was cryptologically suspect and replaced it with the KY-11, [censored] The KY-11, however, had the same drawbacks as the earlier AFSAY-816. It was a large system and was kept in the communications center. It sucked up huge swatches of bandwidth, making it appropriate for the microwave systems in the Washington area, but hardly anywhere else.

Because it required communications center security, the KY-11 was not suitable for general executive level use in Washington. To remedy the problems of size, weight, and security protection, NSA developed the KY-1. It was packaged in a single cabinet about half as high as an ordinary safe and was secured with a three-position combination lock. It was distributed to very high-level users like the secretary of defense, secretary of state, DCI and others. It was the first voice security system installed in private residences, and one of the early models was placed in Eisenhower's farm in Gettysburg.

To use it must have been mildly frustrating, as it was a half-duplex, push-to-talk system. Voice quality was high, but at a familiar cost—it required wideband voice circuitry. By the mid-1960s, it had been replaced by the KY-3.

NSA's first entry in the narrowband sweepstakes was the KO-6, a multipurpose equipment which could encrypt speech signals as well as others. It could compress and digitize speech into a narrowband transmission system, but only at considerable cost. The KO-6 weighed a ton, required three kilowatts of power, and, according to one NSA expert, "provided almost intelligible narrowband secure voice." As a result, it was seldom used in the voice mode.

TEMPEST

During World War II, Bell Laboratories, under contract to develop various devices for the Signal Corps, was working on a one-time tape mixing device called a 131-B2. Engineers in the lab noticed that every time the device stepped, a spike would appear on an oscilloscope in another part of the lab. [censored]

Bell Labs reported this to the Signal Corps but the report attracted little attention. So the Bell engineers mounted an intercept effort, copying and reading plain text from the Army Signal Corps communications [censored]

This time the Signal Corps took notice and asked Bell Labs what could be done. The Bell engineers found that the problem was caused by [censored] The resulting signal could emanate through the [censored] They suggested that the problem could be corrected by shielding the keying devices, by filtering the power lines, or by masking. They built a modified mixer using both shielding and filtering. But the Signal Corps refused to buy it because it virtually encapsulated the machine, making it difficult to work on and was subject to heat buildup. Instead, they sent a message to the field urging commanders to control [censored] their communication centers to prevent hostile signal monitoring.

The Germans knew about this problem and understood the potential for obtaining plain text from close-in ranges. The USSR, which was using the technique by the 1950s, very likely learned it from captured Gernians. There is evidence that other Allied governments knew about it, too. Despite this, the Americans forgot what they had learned during the war. For all practical purposes, it was rediscovered by a CIA technician in 1951, while working on the very same 131-B2 mixers. CIA notified AFSA of its findings, and AFSA set to work on the problem. Designing countermeasures required time, however, and while equipment was being developed, AFSA issued instructions to the field requiring that all COMINT activities control a zone 200 feet in all directions of the communications center. As an alternative, a commander could require that at least ten teleprinters chatter away simultaneously, the idea being that this would introduce masking.

At this point, the newly established NSA decided to test all its equipment. The result— everything radiated. Whether it was mixers, keying devices, crypto equipment, EAM machinery, or typewriters, it sent out a signal [censored] Plain text was being broadcast through [censored] the electromagnetic environment was full of it.

Thus was the TEMPEST industry spawned. NSA initiated a joint project with the SCAs, which in the early years discovered problems much more rapidly than it could design solutions. In 1955 the problem of electromagnetic emanations was [censored] Moreover, there was hard evidence that in this one area the Soviets were far ahead of the U.S. technoloigically and that America's East Bloc embassies were all being penetrated. It was a Frankenstein House of Horrors.

The first big breakthrough was by Naval Research Labs, which redesigned the offending 131-B2 mixer and called it the NRL Mixer. NRL used a technique called low-level keying, in which the power was lowered to such an extent that a signal previously [censored] The KW-26 contained this circuitry, as did every crypto device after that. As long as the communications center used the device at the suppressed keying mode rather than at full power (an unwarranted assumption), it was reasonably well protected.

By 1958 NSA was ready with the first generally applicable TEMPEST standards, which were published under JCS authority. According to the new guidelines, Department of Defense organizations could not use equipment that would radiate farther than the zone of control, [censored] NSA published NAG-1, a TEMPEST bible that established TEMPEST measurement techniques and standards. The new rules did not, however, say anything about when the guidelines had to be met, nor did JCS budget money to fix the problem. Funds had to come from the individual commands and had to compete with all other funding priorities. Recognizing that the problem was far from fixed, USCSB in 1960 established its first and only subcommittee, the Special Committee on Compromising Emanations. But many years would pass before TEMPEST standards reached general acceptance.

Chapter 6 Cryptology at Mid-Decade

The Early Assessments

"It has become exceedingly difficult to obtain significant information from covert operations inside Russia. The security zones at the border, the general restrictions on the interior, the thousands of security police, and the innumerable informers among the population are brutally effective in limiting infiltration, exfiltration, and usefulness of agents. Therefore, we must more and more depend on science and technology to assist and to complement the best efforts of classical intelligence." —The Killian Board, 1955

The Eisenhower administration's intelligence focus was not on traditional espionage—it was on technical intelligence, whence, Eisenhower knew through personal experience during World War II, he could obtain vast quantities of information. His concern over the apparent breakdown in COMINT during the Korean War caused him to refocus again and again on NSA. Reports about NSA's performance began to flow back to him almost from the moment the Agency was created. The reports are important today because they indicate the direction that cryptology was to travel in subsequent years.

The Robertson Committee

The first reports on NSA were a product of President Eisenhower's concern with Soviet [censored] capabilities. In the summer of 1953, the National Security Council began examining America's strategic vulnerabilities, and, with it, the intelligence system that must provide the warning. But Canine adamantly opposed granting clearances to the members of the panel, and USCIB backed him. Instead, Canine esteblished a largely in-house examination of COMINT, chaired by Dr. H. Robertson of California Institute of Technology, a member of Canine's advisory panel, the NSA Scientific Advisory Board (NSASAB). Four of the seven members were from NSASAB, and the remaining two were from the Office of the Secretary of Defense.

Robertson reported during the dark days after "Black Friday," when Soviet [censored] was still an unrevealed mystery. [censored] The immediate result of this was the intercept, in 1954, [censored] This opened up a new world [censored] The committee also recognized the indivisability of COMINT and ELINT and stressed the effort to fuse both sources into a single report.

But Robertson made plain that NSA must be in the game for the long pull. The long pull was Soviet [censored] and he urged an all-out attack on the new [censored] systems introduced in the early 1950s. His committee recommended the development and deployment of new intercept [censored] equipment.

The Hoover Commission

The Hoover Commission was a far larger effort. Established by Eisenhower in 1954 and chaired by former president Herbert Hoover, it was at the time the most thorough reexamination of the federal government ever attempted. Hoover subcommittees delved into every cranny of the bureaucracy seeking improvements and economies. One such subcommittee was a task force chaired by General Mark Clark to investigate intelligence activities. The committee looked closely at NSA.

The thrust of the Hoover Commission set the mold for all subsequent panels. Responding to the entreaties of Canine, it recommended increased authority for NSA in virtually every area of its operation. NSA should have the authority to prescribe equipment standards; it should prescribe all intercept and processing standards; it should inspect service cryptologic training and direct modifications as necessary. There was almost no area in which it did not feel that NSA should be further empowered.

What the panel did for NSA it also recommended for the SCAs. They should have more authority within their respective services, and each should be at the level of a major command. At the time only USAFSS was at that level, although ASA was granted major command status before the report was published. This left only NSG at a lower level within its service. It noted that "largely because of its status as a major command, the AFSS has developed a dynamic and promising program for recruiting, developing and holding on to technically qualified military career personnel." The committee noted the dismal record of the three services in assigning people to cryptologic posts, and it recommended that security strictures be changed to permit military personnel offices to understand the importance of the jobs.

More controversial was the panel's recommendation that NSA acquire additional authority over ELINT. Canine, who saw himself teetering over the black hole of interservice fighting, opposed this. He was having enough trouble unifying COMINT, without trying to swallow ELINT whole. USCIB noted that NSCID 17 had just been issued, and it urged that this new approach be tried before considering further integration of ELINT. (The impact of NSCID 17 will be discussed in chapter 7.)

Clark and his committee proposed an all-out attack on Soviet high-grade ciphers, equivalent, in their words, to the Manhattan Project. It would require the best minds in the country, equipped with the finest resources money could buy, but it would be worth it if even a portion of the Soviet [censored] systems were unlocked. Canine hailed the potential resource augmentation with glee, but cautioned against a total commitment before NSA had thoroughly analyzed the prospects for successs. USCIB supported him.

Cryptologic personnel requirements weighed heavily on the committee. Clark urged an improved grade structure, including the addition of supergrades, higher pay for consultants, improved assignment of service officer personnel, better perquisites for NSA people assigned overseas (to be the equivalent of those received by CIA), and NSA exemption from the Classification Act. To improve the revolving door nature of military intercept operators (few of whom stayed in the service past their initial enlistment), Clark urged the assignment of civilians to intercept positions overseas.

Clark and his committee were concerned about two other potential problems. The first was the state of COMINT requirements, which were expressed in a document called the Master Requirements List. This, they said, was about the size of the Washington phone directory, and about as specific. And since customers wanted COMINT to tell them everything, without narrowing the target further, NSA simply specified its own requirements. This had been going on so long that there was danger that the cryptologic commhnity would become completely isolated from its customers and insensitive to them.

What was occurring in requirements, they felt, was also true in security. COMINT security had become so tight that cryptologists were isolated from their customers. In time of war there was real danger that essential information would not get to the battlefield because of clearance restrictions. Thus the system would defeat itself and become a vestigial appendage. It was a debate that would rage for years within the intelligence community.

The Killian Board

Eisenhower's preoccupation with the Soviet nuclear threat spawned a number of committees to look at American vulnerability. By far the most important of those was the Scientific Advisory Committee, commonly known as the Killian Board. In July of 1954 Eisenhower asked Dr. James R. Killian of MIT to head a study of the country's capability to warn of surprise attack. Killian named a panel of the elite from academia, the scientific community, and the military.

The committee quickly came to the conclusion that spying on the Soviet Union in the classical sense (agents and that sort of thing) was not the answer. The Soviet Bloc was too hard to penetrate. Warning, if it were to come in time, would have to come from technical intelligence like COMINT, ELINT, and photography. This recommendation was to begin a revolution in the way the government thought about, organized, and used intelligence. From that time on, technical intelligence became the "answer" to the problem of strategic warning. It would remain so for the duration of the Cold War.

As part of the Killian Board, the Land Panel was to achieve a measure of renown. Chaired by the farsighted Edwin Land, inventor of the Polaroid camera, the panel was to concern itself with the development of new reconnaissance programs. The Land Panel came to have a profound influence on the future of overhead photography, the U-2 program, and intelligence collection satellites. It was this group that first envisioned COMINT and ELINT intercept packages aboard orbiting satellites.

Land believed that science made anything possible. [censored]

The Jackson Report

The most personal and confidential report on NSA was by William H. Jackson. One of the original members of the Brownell Committee, Jackson was appointed by Eisenhower to monitor NSA's progress and to make periodic progress reports through Sherman Adams, Eisenhower's chief of staff. In meetings with Jackson, the president expressed his personal concern that NSA should be effective, and Jackson kept him apprised of what still needed to be done.

Jackson insisted that NSA needed a strong research and development organization, and he regarded the appointment of a director of research in 1956 as a significant step forward. A more difficult matter was the naming of a chief civilian deputy. Canine insisted on running his own show and did not want, and refused to appoint, a civilian deputy. Only when Samford came aboard in 1956 and quickly named a civilian, Joseph Ream, as deputy was Jackson satisfied on this point.

Yet a third organizational problem was the matter of a point of contact for COMINT within DoD. Brownell had envisioned that COMINT matters would be handled at least as high as the assistant secretary level. This high-level attention had not occurred, and Jackson reported in 1956 that the nominal point of contact, General Graves B. Erskine, head of the Office of Special Operations, normally turned COMINT over to a lower-ranking staffer. In Jackson's view, this level of concern was wholly inadequate to the task at hand.

The objective of all this organizational to-ing and fro-ing was to put NSA in position to mount a full-scale attack [censored] "Only after such an attack has been made," Jackson noted, "can we determine safely, in the event of failure, that the effort is hopeless and the annual expenditure of forty odd millions can be saved."

NSA was clearly still on probation. It was a probationary period that would not end with a bang but would slowly fade away. The corner was not turned during either the Eisenhower or Kennedy administration. NSA did not come off probation until the presidency of Lyndon Baines Johnson.

1956

[censored]

Certain years mark watersheds in cryptologic history. Nineteen fifty-six was such a year. Twin crises, Suez and Hungary, came virtually together in time to pressure a new NSA-managed COMINT system that had never been stressed in such a way. The conjunction of crises, rolled into a COMINT alert called Yankee, resulted in short and long term changes to the system. It was a year for crytologists to remember.

Suez

Suez was a significant benchmark in the postwar American involvement in the Middle East. It also represented the greatest crisis in the post-World War II Western Alliance.

The creation of Israel in 1947 had been accompanied by war, dislocation, and bitterness. In 1952 the Egyptian government had been captured by hard-line pan-Arab, anti-Israeli nationalist military officers headed by Gamal Abdel Nasser. When Nasser officially took over the government in 1954, he set a course which resulted in a distinct tilt toward the East. When, in 1956, the Western nations hedged on earlier commitments to fund a Nile dam at Aswan, Nasser courted the [censored]

In the spring of the year, as the situation in the Middle East darkened,[censored]

[censored] But the transition was only in its early stages when, on 29 October, the Israeli army struck Egypt in the Sinai.

Secretary of State John Foster Dulles expressed shock and outrage. The outrage was real—the shock was made up. His own brother, CIA chief Allen Dulles, had sent him two national intelligence estimates earlier in the fall which predicted the invasion. [censored] Dulles was furious.

[censored] Timely reporting over a period of months could have left no doubt within the administration that Soviet diplomacy consisted of posturing. They were not going to go down to the Middle East to bail out anyone. Forces just weren't moving. The Soviets had their hands quite full with Hungary, whose crisis had flopped down directly on top of Suez.

[censored] But they in no way approximated what was happening at the ministerial level. [censored] Such a strong alliance could not be torn asunder by Suez. As Peter Wright said in his book Spycatcher, "Only GCHQ, which had a formal charter of cooperation with its American counterpart, the National Security Agency (NSA), under terms of the 1948 UKUSA agreement, remained relatively immune to the turbulent currents which battered the previously intimate wartime Anglo-American intelligence relationship."

Hungary

For the Soviets, the real problem in 1956 was the East Bloc. Domestic Hungarian unrest culminated in a revolution that Soviet troops put down violently in November of 1956.

The Hungarian revolution was a surprise to the intelligence community. But as events gathered speed, the Soviet reaction was not. [censored] provided fairly complete indicators concerning Soviet military unit movements throughout the crisis. As Soviet forces moved into Hungary and concentrated on Budapest in the waning days of October, [censored] tracked and identified the participants. [censored] there was very little else available to the White House about the unfolding Soviet reaction.

The National Security Agency did not specifically predict that Soviet forces would become involved—prediction was not its role. There was enough [censored] to lead one to that conclusion prior to the 4 November Soviet takeover of the capital. But no one drew the strings into a bundle. It was all a hodgepodge of [censored] poorly understood by customers. [censored] It was an opportunity lost. [censored]

The Yankee Alert

Suez occurred on 29 October; Hungary broke on 4 November. [censored]

Nineteen fifty-six was a bad time for NSA to get involved in crisis. The organization was in the middle of its move from downtown Washington to Fort Meade. Some analytical branches were in newly established quarters at Fort Meade, while others had remained behind at Arlington Hall. Communications between the two geographical areas were temporary, and much of the routme traffic was being couriered four times a day from Washington. [censored]

Having no NSOC, NSA had to take extraordinary steps to deal with the crisis. [censored]

NSA technical support to the field was slow in coming. [censored]

Lebanon, 1958

The Eisenhower administration was pulled into the Middle East quite by accident in 1956. But the president quickly yanked U.S. foreign policy into line with the new situation. In January 1957, in a State of the Union address focusing on the Middle East, he proclaimed what became known as the Eisenhower Doctrine: the United States would use its armed forces to help any country requesting assistance in maintaining its independence "against overt armed aggression from any nation controlled by International

Communism." Just two short years later, he employed the new doctrine in its first test. The occasion was Lebanon.

Nasser had continued to extend his pan-Arabism, and he was the idol of the Middle East. In January 1958 he announced the formation of the United Arab Republic, an amalgam of Egypt and Syria, with Egypt clearly the dominant partner. The new UAR then launched a propaganda assault on the more conservative regimes in Lebanon, Jordan, Iraq, and Saudi Arabia. An arms race involving the U.S., Britain, France, and the USSR produced a Middle East that was "armed and dangerous."

On 14 July pro-Nasser forces overthrew the Iraqi monarchy and assassinated the royal family. Camille Chamoun, who headed the pro-Western government of Lebanon, believed that he was next and hurriedly requested American assistance. Eisenhower believed that Nasserists were about to take over the oil supply and decided, on the spur of the moment, and after consulting with virtually no one, to come to Chamoun's assistance. He ordered the Sixth Fleet to the Eastern Mediterranean and instructed the chairman of the JCS, General Twining, to put Marines ashore in Beirut the next day. Harold MacMillan, the British prime minister, requested that it be a joint operation, but Eisenhower wanted a unilateral action, and he suggested that British paratroops be deployed to Jordan rather than Lebanon.

[censored]

1956 in History

By the end of 1958, the United States was firmly in the Middle East, [censored] By the time of the 1967 Arab-Israeli War, [censored] The problem proved difficult to address because of the wild mood swings between somnolence and war in the Middle East. But the cryptologic community eventually had a core of expertise and resources [censored]

The Hungarian crisis marked the dawning of a new capability. [censored]

Unfortunately, such sophisticated analysis, available in later decades, simply did not exist in 1956. [censored] It was an art form that had to be learned.

As for crisis response, all was chaos. The cryptologic community proved incapable of marshalling its forces in a flexible fashion to deal with developing trouble spots. The events of the year did not demonstrate success—they simply provided a case study to learn from.

The Reorganization

Ralph Canine departed NSA on 23 November 1956. But before he did, he hired the management firm of McKinsey and Company to look at NSA's organization from top to bottom. The McKinsey study resulted in a thorough revamping of the way NSA functions that still had repercussions through the 1980s.

Canine was concerned with primarily two questions: would operations function more effectively on a functional or geographic organization, and to what extent should staff functions be centralized?

McKinsey introduced a modified geographical concept. Organization for COMINT would be along target (i.e., country or geographical lines, but within that scheme, specific processes like cryptanalysis, [censored] and resource tasking, would often appear in separate organizations. The new scheme brought with it a greater focus on targets, but retained many aspects of the factory-like origins of the business.

When the team presented its findings to Canine only a few days before his retirement, it showed him a new organizational concept. Gone was the old numerical organizational system, replaced by pronounceable syllabic office designators. Thus DDO became PROD, and within PROD were four major offices:

GENS—[censored

ADVA—[censored]

ACOM—[censored]

ALLO—[censored]

The principle of pronounceable syllables was carried through the Agency. For instance, MATH was the Mathematical Research Division within R&D; RADE was the Radio Equipment Division; STED was the Communications Seciirity Division; PERS was personnel; MPRO (pronounced em-pro) was machine processing; SEC was security, etc. It was a profoundly rational way to designate offices, but it did not do a very good job of obscuring office functions from an inquiring public. Ultimately, that was to spell the end of the pronounceability craze, although the basic organizational scheme would continue to the end of the Cold War.

As to the second question, relating to centralization of staff functions, McKinsey came down heavily on the side of decentralization. The firm viewed the director as being far too involved in day-to-day management of Production and only distantly concerned with the easier-to-manage COMSEC and R&D organizations. To correct this, McKinsey recommended that a virtually independent Production function be created. All ancillary functions would be gathered up under PROD, [censored] and even some logistics functions. It was a powerhouse organization.

The director's staff was reduced in proportion to the matters transferred to PROD. Gone were such offices as Headquarters Commandant and Adjutant General, Army-type organizations whose very meaning is obscure today. To manage a potentially unwieldy Production organization, McKinsey created the staff system that carried through the Cold War: the 02, 03, 04, etc way of staff organization.

By far the biggest organization in the Agency was GENS. Out of just over [censored] people assigned to PROD, almost [censored] called GENS home. The GENS organizational system, as modified by a 1957 re-reorganization, created a [censored] organizational scheme that retained its character for more than thirty years. GENS-1 [censored] GENS-2 [censored] GENS-3 [censored] GENS-4 [censored] GENS-5 [censored] and GENS-6 [censored]

McKinsey was concerned about COMSEC. Once the move to Fort Meade took place, it would be physically divorced from the rest of NSA. To accomodate this, the firm recommended special decentralization authority for COMSEC, including certain aspects of physical security, supply, and engineering.

The R&D organization, said McKinsey, should stick solely to research and development. Development of off-the-shelf equipment applications, local component fabrication, equipment repair, or anything that involved known or proven technologies, should come under some other organization—most notably, PROD. Regarding the fielding of COMSEC equipments, unless it involved pure research, it was not properly an R&D function, McKinsey said, and should be resubordinated to COMSEC. This was an issue, however, that would be replayed many times during the Cold War,

The Move

"It is desired that you take immediate action to recommend for my approval a suitable location for the Armed Forces Security Agency within a 25-mile radius of Washington . . . the new site survey should be carried out as a matter of high priority. . . ." —William C. Foster, Deputy Secretary of Defense, 1951

When AFSA was created in 1949, it was without its own facilities. The new organization was forced to borrow space at Arlington Hall and Naval Security Station (NSS).

In an appendix to the document that created AFSA, the JCS directed that AFSA prepare a plan consolidating COMINT and COMSEC into a single facility. After studying the problem, AFSA concluded that the two could not be consolidated into their existing buildings at Arlington Hall and Nebraska Avenue. In its September 1949 report to the JCS, AFSAC pointed out that the buildings in use at Arlington Hall were temporary structures designed for wartime use.

In the autumn of 1949, with the explosion of the Soviet nuclear device, atomic hysteria was sweeping Washington. To its original charge, the JCS added one other—that a standby location be procured which was outside the Washington area to minimize the possibility that American cryptologic capabilities be destroyed on the first day of a war.

Commander Arthur Enderlin, whom Admiral Stone had appointed to chair the study committee, was adamantly opposed to a standby location. He and his committee considered it a waste of money and refused to recommend an alternate site. The JCS demanded a recommendation, but

Enderlin refused. Stone reiterated the order—Enderlin remained unmoved. Stone fired Enderlin and in his place appointed Captain Thomas Dyer, one of the leading cryptanalysts of World War II. Dyer was a known advocate of the alternate location concept.

But then Dyer turned the solution on its head. He recommended that the alternate become primary—this would effectively move the cryptologic headquarters out of Washington. Dyer carried the day, and his committee began to look at possible relocation sites in the spring of 1950. The selection criteria were developed over a period of months, but generally focused on the following requirements:

a. Be within twenty-five miles of a city of at least 200,000
b. Have work space totalling at least 700,000 square feet
c. Possess a "reasonably equable climate"
d. Be suitable for complete physical isolation by fences and the like
e. Be accessible to mainline air, rail, and highways
f. Not be less than twenty miles from the Atlantic Ocean
g. Possess dependable and secure water and electric power sources
h. Be accessible to commercial and military communications

The basic ground rule was that the location selected had to be on an existing military base. The move was to be completed by July 1955. One option the board looked at was to select a site that already possessed a building—like a hermit crab, AFSA could simply crawl in after modifying the shell. Locations in Kansas City, Tulsa, and St. Louis were considered. Another option was to construct a new building on a military installation. The board looked at Fort Knox, Kentucky; Fort Benjamin Harrison, near Indianapolis; Fort Meade, halfway between Baltimore and Washington; Brooks Air Force Base, near San Antonio, Texas; and Rocky Mountain Arsenal, near Denver.

Then in early 1951 the board sent AFSAC two recommendations—if the existing structure criterion were used, Kansas City should be the choice, and if a new building were wanted, Fort Knox was the way to go. This produced great controversy in AFSAC. Some pressed for an existing structure, maintaining that the lower cost and quick availability would help meet the July 1955 deadline. Others opposed moving into someone else's offices—that had been tried at Arlington Hall and Nebraska Avenue and had not worked. The Air Force pressed for Fort Knox, contending that it was less vulnerable to a Soviet nuclear strike. Stone and Major General Canine (who would soon become director of AFSA) both opted for Fort Meade. But in the end AFSAC voted for Fort Knox. The JCS approved the Fort Knox option in April, but only after another heated argument about the advisability of moving to a relatively isolated location. Many, including Stone and Canine, were concerned about the critical lack of housing in the Fort Knox environs, and some wondered if their civilians would accept the choice.

While orders were being cut and contract proposals were being written for the Fort Knox construction, AFSAC members argued vehemently over the functions to be moved. Dyer was the author of a plan to split COMINT into two parts—three-fourths of it would move to Kentucky, while some residual functions would stay in Washington, along with most of COMSEC and some liaison offices. He was opposed by Admiral Joseph Wenger, who felt that splitting COMINT would be disastrous. Ultimately, Wenger won, and it was decided to leave COMSEC in Washington, while all of COMINT would move to Fort Knox and Arlington Hall would be closed.

The board knew Fort Knox to be objectionable to some of the civilian employees because of its distance from Washington. The lack of housing was worrisome, as was the rigid segregation practiced in Kentucky in 1951. But AFSA pressed ahead with the selection anyway, until a startling thing happened: Someone decided to ask the civilians what they thought.

No one knows now who originated the civilian opinion survey, but by May of 1951 it was being circulated at Arlington Hall and Nebraska Avenue. The results were a show-stopper. Most of the civilians planned to resign rather than go to Fort Knox. Without them, AFSA would find it difficult to operate. The problem had to be fixed.

The matter came to a head in October of 1951. Deputy Secretary of Defense William C. Foster told Canine, the new director of AFSA, that he had a problem. AFSA's civilians were not in favor of the move to Fort Knox, and neither were AFSA's two most important non-DoD customers, the State Department and CIA. Canine went directly to see General of the Armies Omar Bradley, the Army chief of staff. Bradley told him to meet with the JCS. At the JCS meeting in early December the Fort Knox move was cancelled, and Canine was directed to appoint another site selection board.

Canine's new selection board, still chaired by Dyer, but including some civilians, held hurried meetings in January and February of 1952. The new site had to be between five and twenty-five miles from the center of Washington. This placed it within the postulated blast zone of then-existing Soviet atomic weapons and thus violated a JCS stipulation that the new AFSA site had to be at least twenty-five miles from the Washington Monument. But Soviet atomic weapons were progressing all the time, and the twenty-five mile limit no longer made sense anyway. The JCS could have either atomic invulnerability or a skilled civilian work force, but apparently it could not have both.

The board looked at several sites in suburban Virginia, including Fort Belvoir, some land along the George Washington Parkway inhabited by the Bureau of Roads (later to become famous as the site of the new CIA headquarters building), and Fort Hunt. In Maryland, it considered several sites within the Beltsville Agricultural Research Center, White Oak (site of the Naval Ordnance Laboratory), Andrews Air Force Base, and Fort Meade. Of those, Fort Meade was the only one on the original list. It was twenty-two miles from the Monument, the furthest removed of any site considered the second time around. Despite the distance from Washington, transportation difficulties would be solved by a new parkway then under construction between Washington and Baltimore. There was plenty of vacant land on Fort Meade for construction of headquarters and life support buildings. It was the obvious choice, and on 5 February it became official. (Considering that Canine said he had already selected Fort Meade himself, and had informed Lovett of that, the proceedings of the board may well have been window dressing.)

Fort Meade, named for the Civil War victor at Gettysburg, inhabited a thickly wooded 13,500 acre tract precisely halfway between Baltimore and Washington. Originating as Camp Meade during World War I, it had been a training facility during both World Wars I and II. During World War II some 3.5 million men passed through on their way to Europe and at the peak of the war 70,000 people inhabited the post. After the war it became a headquarters, first for the 2nd Army and later (in 1966) for the 1st U.S. Army.

When Canine first looked at it, Fort Meade consisted of hundreds and hundreds of temporary wooden structures being used as barracks, offices and training facilities, with only a few permanent brick buildings. The corner of the post that NSA proposed to use was uninhabited, but was near a major intersection—the new Baltimore-Washington Parkway and Maryland Route 32.

The new building would be U-shaped with double cross-members, designated the center and west corridors. Entry would be in the middle of the west corridor, the portion of the building facing Route 32. At 1.4 million square feet, it would be the third largest government building in Washington, smaller only than the Pentagon and the new State Department building. But it was designed for the AFSA population in 1951, and it did not take into consideration the growth that took place up to mid-decade, which left the new building critically short of space. The only solution was to leave someone behind, and that "someone" became the COMSEC organization, which remained at Nebraska Avenue until another building was completed in 1968.

In 1954 a contract was awarded to two co-prime contractors, Charles H. Tompkins Company of Washington, D.C., and the J.A. Jones Company of Charlotte, North Carolina. The contract price was $19,944,452. Groundbreaking occurred on 19 July 1954. When the building was completed, the total cost turned out to be $35 million, an overrun of almost 100 percent.

A few miscellaneous facts wowed the local community. It had the longest unobstructed corridor in the country, 980 feet long (center corridor). At its birth it had a German-made pneumatic tube system that could carry papers at twenty-five feet per second and could handle 800 tubes per hour. The cafeteria could seat 1,400, and the auditorium (later dedicated to William Friedman), 500. As its new occupant, NSA would become the largest employer in Anne Arundel County. It was a far cry indeed from the quaint but antiquated Arlington Hall, the stately Naval Security Station, and the Firetrap A and B buildings at Arlington Hall.

NSA handled the move in stages. There was an "interim move," which put parts of NSA's operation into temporary quarters on Fort Meade. This had the advantage of moving the operation gradually so that large parts of it were not shut down for any period of time. The new operations building would not be ready for occupancy until 1957, and so the interim move also had the advantage of placing cryptologists at the new location in advance of the July 1955 deadline.

It began with an interim move to four brick barracks constructed for NSA use in 1954 just behind the proposed site for the main complex. The first to arrive, in November of 1954, was a contingent of 149 Marine guards to provide security. The other 2,000 plus people taking part in the interim move included virtually the entire population of GENS, plus enough communicators, personnel, and logistics people to keep them going. Heat for the operation was provided by an old steam engine which was brought in on the old Baltimore, Washington and Annapolis tracks, and was installed in a small copse of trees, which still exists, between the present OPS2A and the barracks area. (In fact, the original barracks themselves, now converted to living quarters, also still exist.)

GENS and its support staff became an outpost, connected to the main headquarters by inadequate electrical communications. Most classified material was couriered back and forth four times a day—the electrical circuits were reserved for only the most critical and time-sensitive information.

To NSA's military population, the move to Fort Meade was a matter of routine. The military moved frequently, and the relatively cloistered atmosphere of a rural Army post was closer to the normal state of affairs. Family housing was of the two-story brick variety, constructed under the Wherry Housing Act. More would be needed, and over 2,500 new Wherry units were planned to accommodate the increased military population occasioned by NSA's move.

For civilians, however, it was an entirely different matter. The move to Fort Meade was initially contemplated nervously by a standoffish civilian population. Most lived in Virginia and Washington and faced a long commute over narrow and traffic-clogged roads through the heart of a major metropolitan area. There was no beltway to take traffic around Washington—the trip north would have to be via Georgia Avenue, Colesville Road, New Hampshire Avenue and other city streets. The only plus to this situation was the brand new Baltimore-Washington Parkway, whose projected completion date was January 1965. That would take care of the drive north from Anacostia and would mark a very significant reduction in the driving time.

For those who did not own cars (a significant number in the early 1950s), there was public transportation. Although the old Baltimore, Washington and Annapolis Railroad, which had a spur that ran across the street from the planned NSA facility, had closed its passenger service in

1935, the Baltimore and Ohio Railroad still operated commuter train service from Washington's Union Station to Laurel. For $1.82 per day, one could travel round trip to Laurel and back in thirty-six minutes aboard one of the two trains operating each morning and afternoon. Once in Laurel, the commuter could take the railroad-operated shuttle bus to Fort Meade for an additional round trip fare of 50¢; it required twenty-three minutes each way.

Unfortunately, the train and bus schedules did not match very well, and there was no bus service at all for a commuter catching the late train. For the early train, the total one-way commuting time from Union Station to NSA was one hour and twenty-three minutes, not including the time required to get from one's residence to Union Station. Both Greyhound and Trailways offered bus service from downtown Washington to Laurel in just thirty-seven minutes, and at 99¢ per round trip, it was a bargain. But neither service brought passengers to Laurel in time to catch the shuttle to Fort Meade, so commuters would be left high and dry in Laurel. For urbanites used to a short commute to Arlington Hall, this was not a happy prospect.

For most, this meant picking up the family and moving to the Maryland suburbs. To help with the move, NSA created the Meademobile, a trailer parked between A and B Buildings at Arlington Hall. The Meademobile carried information about Fort Meade and surroundings, including real estate ads, school and church information, and locations of shopping areas. On Saturdays NSA ran a special bus to Fort Meade so that employees could look over the area. For those who were still unsure, NSA announced that a move to Fort Meade would be regarded as a PCS, and the government would pay to move household effects. For many, that was the decider.

The closest community of any size was Laurel. Housing prices in Laurel ranged from $8,990 for two bedroom homes to $10,990 for three bedroom homes with basements. There was also a supply of apartments which could be had for rents ranging from $79.50 to $112.50 per month. In the other direction was the waterside community of Severna Park, whose houses ranged in price from $6,000 to $16,000. Waterfront lots could also be purchased in the subdivision of Ben Oaks, but the lots alone sometimes ran as high as a finished house in other areas. A little farther afield was Glen Burnie, where housing prices ranged from $5,995 to over $10,000. South was the planned community of Greenbelt, in the Washington suburbs. This was originally built with government subsidies, and a house there could be had for as low as $4,700. Single bedroom apartments rented for $51 and up. Columbia had not been built yet.

Whatever NSA did to entice civilians out to Fort Meade, it worked. Early estimates of civilian attrition by a panicky personnel office had ranged as high as 30 percent, but the actual attrition rate was less than two percentage points higher than would normally have been expected had there been no move at all. By anyone's standards (except for the COMSEC population left behind at Nebraska Avenue), the move was a success.

Chapter 7 The Eisenhower Reforms

The Post-Crisis Centralization Of The SIGINT System

Following the mid-decade crises of Hungary, Suez, and Sputnik, President Eisenhower instigated a thorough reexamination of the intelligence system. For NSA, this meant sweeping changes and new challenges.

Criticomm

The long-stalled COMINT Comnet proposal was not jarred loose until the Sputnik crisis of 1957. Sputnik came as a complete surprise to the Eisenhower administration. Following as it did after Suez, Hungary, and Lebanon, it caused Eisenhower to focus hard on intelligence warning issues. Part of the administration's concern was for timely warning, and that meant timely communications. The Critical Communications Committee (CCC), which had representatives from various governmental organizations (including NSA), proposed communications criteria which clearly would require a totally new system.

The committee defined critical information (they called it "Critic" information, the first time the term came into use) as that information "indicating a situation or pertaining to a situation which affects the security or interests of the United States to such an extent that it may require the immediate attention of the president and other members of the NSC." The CCC then stipulated that such Critic information should get to the president within ten minutes of recognition that it meets Critic criteria.

It sounded like pie in the sky. No communications system then in existence could come close to meeting a ten-minute deadline. (Ten hours was more like it.)

When USCIB began looking at various proposals, the system that most closely resembled what the CCC wanted was the COMINT Comnet, which was still a mythic concept. Negotiations between NSA and the services had broken down, and the Air Force had even de-funded a previously agreed-to plan to open the first relay station at Chicksands. The second Robertson Committee strongly supported the establishment of the Comnet as a high-priority requirement, but noted that the CCC was already working in that direction anyway.

In July 1958, the JCS approved a plan for a new Criticomm system. It involved establishing a network of automated relays worldwide, building on the rudimentary COMINT circuitry that NSA and the services had put together. The pattern the JCS used was the fledgling COMINT Comnet, and the expertise came from NSA. The new program was promulgated by the DCI as DCID 1/8, "Handling of Critical Communications."

The DCID jumped the gun a little; Eisenhower had not yet been briefed. In August of 1958 General Samford, who had been in the traces for two years, and Louis Tordella, who had been NSA's deputy director for only a few days, were summoned to the White House to brief the NSC on the proposal. Tordella, who did the briefing, sold the program by stressing that at least 90 percent of the expected Critics would come from COMINT and that the COMINT Comnet proposal would enfold fully 200 out of the 245 potential entry points for critical information. The draft directive, NSCID 7, was already written and ready to go. All they needed was Ike's go-ahead. After Tordella had finished talking, the president turned to Donald Quarles, his deputy secretary of defense, and asked, "Don, can we do it?" Quarles said, "Yes, I think we can." "Let's do it," was all the president said, and it was done.

The new NSCID made the secretary of defense the executive agent, and it decreed that the system would consist of the existing COMINT communications system augmented and modified as necessary. The DCI would establish Critic criteria. NSA was not mentioned, but it was hardly necessary. The JCS had already named NSA to manage the system. It was to be completed by 1961.

No one was really sure how NSA would magically produce a system that could meet the ten-minute timeliness goal. COMINT communications at the time were a lash-up of NSA and service communications. Communication centers were basically "torn-tape" relays, and there was no hope of getting anything to the White Hohse in that sort of time frame. NSA had been working on an automated switching device for several years, but had not yet come up with a switch that was acceptable to all parties. In this atmosphere someone would have to improvise.

NSA's communicators, headed by Arthur Enderlin, Max Davidson, and [censored] began tinkering with off-the-shelf commercial hardware that would permit a Critic to steam through the system untouched by human hands. A key element in their search was the shunt box, a device invented by Teletype Corporation that could recognize a unique combination of letters (for instance, ZZZ) and open up circuitry all the way to Washington. Nothing else would flow in that path until the "express train" had passed through.

Back in Washington, NSA had created a system of direct communications, called ZICON, with its Washington-level customers. This communications group was expanded to include all organizations on distributions for the initial Critic. This included, in the early days, the White House and members of USIB (less FBI and AEC). Later, SAC (Strategic Air Command), ADC (Air Defense Command), TAC (Tactical Air Command), and STRICOM (Strike Command) were added and still later, the other Unified and Specified Commands.

The advent of the KW-26 cryptoequipment was critical to the functioning of the new system. With it, the system speeded up to 100 words per minute, and messages zipped through at almost twice the previous speed.

Criticomm needed relay centers, and in 1959 NSA directed that the Army operate centers in Europe, Eritrea, the Philippines, Okinawa, and Japan. The Navy would do the job in Hawaii, while the Air Force would take on the same responsibilities in England, Turkey, and Alaska. NSA would operate the central hub at Fort Meade. At the same time the TCOM organization, which had so recently been subordinated to Prod, was once again made independent, in recognition of its new standing.

Through these and other hasty improvements to the system, NSA was able to report a dramatic improvement in handling time. In the early days of the program, Critics averaged one and one-half hours to reach the White House. Two years later, the time had been reduced to a mean elapsed time of ten minutes. Criticomm was still operated with jury-rigged equipment, but already the timeliness goal of having all Critics to the White House in ten minutes was within sight.

The Baker Panel

In 1957, two high-level committees were taking independent and simultaneous looks at NSA. Both were to have a long-range impact on American cryptology.

The Baker Panel was appointed by President Eisenhower to recommend to him whether or not there was a [censored] Chaired by William O. Baker, vice-president for research at Bell Laboratories, the committee quickly strayed from its intended charter. Baker wanted to look at everything, and his examination became the most intensive look at the cryptologic process ever performed by an outside organization.

When Baker delivered his report to Eisenhower in February 1958, he began by answering the question directly put to him by the president: "No national strategy should be based on the hope or expectation that we will [censored] Even with the greatest optimism, it is clear that no substantial [censored]

But this, said Baker, was not the whole story. Cryptology was a tremendously valuable asset to the nation, one which was producing most of the fast and reliable intelligence then available. It was doing it, [censored] by putting together all the [censored] disciplines, [censored] The cryptologic system was capable of squeezing out of the ether a veritable cornucopia of information, if it were properly managed and funded. And this, said Baker, was the focus of his recommendations.

In order to properly employ the cryptologic system, NSA needed to focus on the important things. [censored] had monopolized the talents of too many smart people. They should be spread throughout the organization, [censored] This meant, in many cases, reallocating resources to ALLO and ACOM or to different divisions [censored] What they had learned working [censored] could now be employed against other [censored]

NSA should forget about developing a general purpose computer and go for more RAMs. Baker was not impressed with Project LIGHTNING; he wanted smaller but more cost-effective efforts

The Agency was receiving stupendous volumes of intercepted material, a product of the rapid expansion of overseas collection sites. Computers should be employed in processing this take, so that analysts could be free from manually logging [censored] Machines should also be employed at collection sites to reduce the pile of material that had to be forwarded. This, to Baker, was the next great field of computer applications at NSA.

Echoing the recommendations of the Hoover Commission, Baker felt that pure cryptanalytic research should be removed outside NSA, to a Los Alamos-style institute. This would isolate pure research from a production organization and reduce the temptation to employ the best minds in the day-to-day tasks of getting out the news.

As for the cryptologic system in general, it should be further centralized under NSA. Only by centralization could anyone integrate all the pieces of the puzzle and move the organizations involved in the same direction. Baker took dead aim at the AFSS processing center in San Antonio (AFSCC), which he singled out as an unwarranted duplicative processing facility. In fact, the entire collection and processing system should be overhauled under NSA's direction. Some field processing should be transferred to NSA, and the Agency should direct the services to close down redundant collection. NSA should centralize theater processing centers under its own jurisdiction. Better communications and machine processing systems could speed the flow of intercepted materials through those centers, and information would be distributed more quickly to customers. Moneys saved from the rationalization of the entire process could be applied to other parts of the system.

Certain specific field operations should be improved under NSA leadership. For instance, analog signals should be converted to digital form for processing; the technology was already available. NSA should develop improved intercept and recording equipment and make them standard throughout the cryptologic system. Punched paper tape, used universally throughout the system, should be phased out in favor of magnetic tape.

Finally, the two related disciplines of COMINT and ELINT should be combined under NSA direction. This was the ultimate rationalization of the system and was, according Baker, long overdue. This generated controversy even at the White House. Deputy Secretary of Defense Donald Quarles said that ELINT had only recently been centralized under the Air Force, and he appealed for time to make it work. But Quarles was losing; was the clear consensus of the meeting with Eisenhower that ELINT would ultimately be placed under NSA.

Baker's recommendation regarding a Los Alamos-style research institute met substantial skepticism. Some (like CIA) felt that it wasn't necessary. Edward Lansdale, deputy assistant to the secretary of defense for special operations, pointed out that success on high-level systems often stemmed from working medium-grade codes from the same country. Physically and organizationally separating cryptanalysts working those systems from those working high-grade systems would be technically unsound. Moreover, NSA would likely face severe morale problems if part of its mission were to migrate to a separate research institute led by higher-paid private consultants.

[censored]

But the proposal that generated the most heat (although not the most light) was the ELINT proposal. The Air Force and Navy adamantly opposed it; CIA was standoffish. Even the director of NSA did not want the job unless he got with it a substantial grant of authority. The Navy called the treatment of ELINT "superficial"; the report suffered "from a lack of balance." USCIB was not sure what to do, and it played for time by establishing a task force to study the issue.

[censored]

The Reuben Robertson Report

The second look at NSA stemmed from budgetary pressures. Eisenhower had for years been in a running battle with the Democratic-controlled Congress over the defense budget, and in 1957 Secretary of Defense Charles Wilson was looking for excess money anywhere he could find it. It occurred to him that he might find it in NSA's budget, and in January of 1957 he directed Deputy Secretary of Defense Reuben Robertson (a different Robertson than the H. P. Robertson who had chaired a committee in 1953) to establish an ad hoc committee to look at the COMINT and COMSEC budgets. He told Robertson that his objective would be to hold cryptology under [censored] per year. Robertson chose to chair the committee himself, and on it he placed a number of under secretaries and assistant secretaries. It was very high-powered indeed.

Robertson zeroed in on the [censored] bottom line but couldn't find it. The cryptologic budgeting process, spread across the Defense Department, was a mess. He finally concluded that what the department really spent on cryptology was closer to [censored] and he determined to try to hold that bottom line. But he found even that goal hard to reach. The reason was that cryptology was having an unexpectedly high payoff. Robertson found that much of what the United States knew [censored] came from COMINT. He tried to effect economies, but it was unrealistic to attempt any rigid focus on [censored]

When the committee first began, it took a very close look at collection. This, it figured, was where most duplication occurred. It recommended that total collection sites be reduced [censored] The economies thus effected would result in a net increase in total numbers of positions; the new positions would be financed by the station closures. This would scuttle plans for a continued major expansion of collection resources but would not really diminish the size of the system.

What the committee came to understand, in the end, was that a apparent duplication of targets and positions was usually not actual duplication. [censored] Only [censored] cases were being copied on more than 1 position, and in most cases there was sound rationale for the duplication. What had appeared so simple at Wilson's level did not look at all simple up close.

Instead, the committee worked on station consolidations. Virtually collocated Army, Navy, and Air Force stations [censored] should be combined, with AFSS hosting. A similar situation [censored] should be resolved in the same way, with the Army as host, and [censored] with the Navy as host. [censored] They noted with approval Air Force plans to close [censored] and centralize the resources [censored] They especially liked [censored] as collection real estate and recommended that the AFSS site at [censored] be enlarged. But most of these consolidations were already in the planning stages—Robertson simply gave them a shove.

The lasting contribution of the Robertson committee was in the budgetary mechanism itself. Robertson was a big advocate of centralization, and he wanted increased NSA control over the process. But he was frustrated by the difficulty of determining what the actual cryptologic dollar figure was. He dealt with cryptologic budgets from all three services, as well as NSA (and to a lesser extent CIA). He believed that this should all rationalized somehow. So he recommended that all cryptologic budgeting be centralized under DIRNSA. It would be called the Consolidated Cryptologic Program (CCP). The recommendation was acted on almost immediately, and fiscal year 1959 was set for the implementation target date.

The Marriage of ELINT and NSA

When a matter gets to the Oval Office, it can no longer be ignored. The marriage (some say an unhappy marriage) of NSA and ELINT began at last following the recommendations of Baker to President Eisenhower. This forced a reluctant and disunited USCIB to further consider what it had already considered many times. USCIB appointed a special study group under [censored] the CIA representative. So as to leave no doubt about which direction the decision was to go, Louis Tordella of NSA was made the deputy chairman.

Overriding strenuous objections by the Air Force, [censored] opted for a consolidated ELINT system under NSA. His report to USCIB in June of 1958 recommended that the NSC "appointthe secretary of defense as the executive agent of the government for ELINT and assign the Director, National Security Agency, the authority and responsibility for providing an effective, unified organization to control and direct the ELINT intercept, processing, and reporting activities of the United States Government." A new directive, NSCID 6, would replace NSCID 9 and would encompass both COMINT and ELINT.

NSCID 6 appeared to give NSA the cryptologic authorities it had been asking for. When the secretary of defense published the DoD implementing directives for COMINT and ELINT, however. they came out very differently. The COMINT directive gave DIRNSA operational and technical control of all U.S. COMINT operations except for a very restricted list of SIGINT-related operations not directly related to intelligence gathering (such as search and rescue and various electronic warfare operations). The ELINT directive, however, reserved this right to the secretary of defense himself. Only he had the authority to "determine the ELINT activities which are essential to provide support to commanders who plan and conduct military operations, and which must be directly assigned by the secretary of defense to provide an integral ELINT capability. . . . "

The services interpreted this to mean almost any type of ELINT collection or processing operation. General Samford told his immediate boss, General Erskine, that he assumed that the only ELINT collection that he actually controlled now was that being done by the SGAs. His assumption was correct.

At first NSA did not know quite how to organize the new mission. The key issue revolved around the competing desires to combine ELINT and COMINT on the one hand and to maintain a separate identity for the new discipline on the other. But ELINT arrived with old baggage—the central processing center, NTPC—and so the forces advocating a separate identity won a partial victory. After some indecision, it was decided to graft it onto an existing organization, and ELINT first landed in the Office of Collection within PROD. The name of the office was changed to COSA (Collection and Signals Analysis). It was a temporary way station on the way to its own home, W Group, established in 1968.

NTPC thus became the first clearly identifiable ELINT asset at NSA. When NSCID 6 was promulgated, it was decided to transfer the entire resources of the organization—the people, the equipment, the files—to NSA. This amounted to something over [censored] people, split rather evenly among the 3 services and [censored] and the equipment for third-echelon processing.

Along with ELINT came signal search. CIA and NSA had competed for the mission of spectrum search and signal cataloguing since 1953, but in the long run the CIA effort was unsupportable. The basic CIA SIGINT effort was too small to give it an adequate technical base for the search mission, and, anyway, it was as clearly a cryptologic mission as could well be imagined. NSCID 6 was the last straw, and in the summer of 1959 CIA gave up its effort. COSA, which under its previous incarnations had always had a signal search organization, lost a competitor (without, in this case, picking up assets).

Telemetry was another new arrival. Telemetry had always been handled as ELINT. The services, heavily reinforced by private contractors like HRB-Singer, General Electric, Jet Propulsion Laboratories, and Lockheed, all had telemetry collection and analysis efforts. Beyond that, CIA had an effort of its own, emphasizing (as did its ELINT mission) the cutting edge of technology. Third-echelon telemetry analysis had been concentrated at NTPC, but contractors still performed the major share of fine-grain analysis.

There was considerable discussion over the nature of telemetry. Was it really COMINT, as NSA contended, or really ELINT? Melville Boucher, an NSA telemetry analyst, once said that "telemetry has always been a gray area surrounded by fuzz seen through a thick mist." The answer would determine how telemetry reports would be handled—spread far and wide as straight-secret ELINT reports or bottled up by COMINT codewords. In the summer of 1959, coincident with the transfer of ELINT assets to NSA, the ELINT committee of USIB (renamed from USCIB by the publication of NSCID 6) decided, rather predictably, that telemetry was really ELINT and that it would go forth without hampering codewords. But that did not change its resubordination. The telemetry mission migrated to NSA where it eventually became TELINT and later FISINT.

Since NSA had no telemetry analysts, it would need help. ASA came first, agreeing to transfer its telemetry assets, including its contracts with JPL and HRB-Singer, to NSA. NSA established its first telemetry analysis effort under Joseph Burke, who became known as the father of NSA telemetry.

The transition from Air Force to NSA telemetry was more difficult. The Air Force retained a residual telemetry effort and resisted turning over its telemetry mission to NSA for months. In the end they did so only through the considerable persuasive powers of General Samford.

Once NSA took over telemetry, it found out just how chaotic the situation was. Each organization involved had its own equipment and used its own set of collection and processing standards. Telemetry tapes arrived at NSA in a hodgepodge of formats, and at first it was difficult to simply collect information on the formats involved. To bring order to the chaos, Louis Tordella, in the spring of 1960, created [censored] it became a clearinghouse for technical information, and it marked NSA's first big initiative in consolidating the effort.

NSCID 6 did not solve the problems that had plagued ELINT. Within two years, the President's Foreign Intelligence Advisory Board (PFIAB) was already complaining that NSA had been given too meagre a grant of power. It did eventually result in standardized technical rules and procedures, and in that sense the ELINT experiment of 1958 became a success. In the area of command and control, however, it was a dismal failure.

The Kirkpatrick Committee

The tireless process of reviewing intelligence functions continued to the end of the Eisenhower administration. The last player in the game was the Kirkpatrick Committee. Chaired by Lyman Kirkpatrick of CIA, its purpose was to assess all defense intelligence programs, including SIGINT (a term that came into the language after NSCID 6 was inked).

Kirkpatrick, like the CIA whence he came, was distressed at the uncoordinated and duplicative nature of defense intelligence. Centralization was the only way to rationalize the system, and in SIGINT that meant more power to NSA. ELINT was out of control (an old refrain), and the decentralizing tendencies of the Unified and Specified Commands had to be thwarted. Moreover, COMINT and ELINT had not been fused, as Baker had envisioned. This was due in some degree to classification differences and the tendency of COMINT people to shield their information from many of the people who really needed it.

Two of Kirkpatrick's recommendations would have a long-range impact on intelligence. First, he recommended that an "intelligence community staff" be established, responsive to the DCI. Second, and much more specifically germane to the SIGINT world, he called for a broader use of COMINT. The committee viewed the SSO system as having devolved into an obstructionist group that held information too closely and kept key players out of the inner circle. According to Kirkpatrick, the SSO system shduld "be staffed by personnel of rank commensurate with a courier function" and "avoid placing their own interpretation on material transmitted by the Special Security Officer System."

If true, the charges indicted a system which had been quite dynamic during World War II. The Kirkpatrick report marked the beginning of the end of that era of dynamism. He offered no prescription for the problem of interpreting SIGINT. But the very next year NSA came up with the solution with the creation of a fledgling Cryptologic Support Group (CSG) system.

NSA Centralizes the Field System

Cryptologic centralization was having a profound effect on the field system. Some of this proceeded from the new authorities that NSA was gaining and from the new responsibilities that it was undertaking.

Much of it, however, emanated from a different source. In 1958 Eisenhower had succeeded in getting a sweeping Defense Reorganization Act through Congress. It took the JCS out of the direct chain of command and made them advisors and planners. Within the command structure, it created the Unified and Specified Commands. This marked a sea change in the way America did its fighting. Henceforth, wars would always be fought with combined commands, with component service forces integrated under a single military boss, the commander of the relevant unified command.

Overseas, this reorganization demanded major changes in the way cryptology was organized. Now it was more important to render cryptologic support to the unified commander. The SCA theater headquarters, representing as they did only the cryptologic assets of a single service, were incapable of doing it. Only the NSA field organization could.

The first theater to change was Europe. NSAEUR, which had been established in Frankfurt, had exercised only a technical support role within the cryptologic community. But as early as 1955, an experienced NSAEUR analyst was sent to join the CINCEUR staff at Camp des Loges, outside Paris. [censored]

In that year, NSAEUR, over the strenuous objections of ASAEUR, gave its small staff at Camp des Loges augmented authority to represent the cryptologic community to CINCEUR. The new functions involved theater-wide planning and representation, and they marked the first time that the field offices had strayed far beyond technical functions. NSAEUR continued to augment the staff in Paris and in 1963 moved its office there, leaving behind in Frankfurt the technical support staff to deal with internal cryptologic issues. Included in the 1963 move was a new organization, NSA Europe Intelligence Support Section (NSAEUR/ISS), an element that had been set up to interpret SIGINT product. It was the first Cryptologic Support Group (CSG.)

AFSS and the Development of Second-Echelon Reporting

A parallel development produced profound changes in theater reporting. Ultimately, it was to lead to the revolution in SIGINT reporting which resulted in the creation of the National SIGINT Operations Center (NSOC). It started with the [censored]

AFSS understood at its birth that airplanes move faster than almost anything and that to conduct a COMINT support function for the Air Force, it would have to create an extremely rapid reporting system. At first this led to negotiations with Canine over field site reporting authorities. But AFSS had bigger plans. Keeping track [censored] would involve networking all its theater collection sites, and this would require the creation of a theater-level center. [censored] The plans for this were on the drawing board even before the demise of AFSA.

NSA and AFSS went back and forth during the early 1950s over what organization should handle this responsibility and where it should be located. By 1955, however, they had resolved their differences. [censored]

The [censored] as it was called, would have considerable power. It would "direct the intercept and analysis of foreign communications" and would "exercise routine operational control . . . of all COMINT, ELINT, and [censored] matters..." It would collect traffic forwarded from field sites under its control and would forward raw and semiprocessed traffic back to the States. It also had its own independent reporting authority.

This was not unique. ASAEUR exercised similar responsibilities at its processing center in [censored] differed by the way that it evolved. A key figure in the evolution of [censored] was a young Air Force captain named Benjamin Ardisana.

Ardisena had begun his service career in the Army Signal Corps during World War II. He had entered the cryptologic business in 1952, and after a series of assignments with AFSS units in the Far East, where he had shown an exceptional talent for innovation and initiative, he arrived in [censored] in July 1952.

Less than a year later (May 1959) Ardisana set up the first European field Opscomm circuit, between [censored] to coordinate the [censored] between the two organizations. (Some claim that this was the first Opscomm in the community; the strength of that claim rests on the date that SMAC first set one up, a date which is less well documented.) At the same time, Ardisana established an around-the-clock surveillance and warning center to watch the [censored] as it was being reported from subordinate sites.

[censored]

All this emanated from four massive stone buildings left over from World War II. The reporting operation was on the fourth floor of one of them, under the very eaves of the building, in a room filled with up to twenty-six Opscomm machines (Teletype Mod 19s and 28s) all clattering away together. [censored]

The Struggle for Control in the Pacific

The Pacific theater was very different from Europe, and it developed in a very different way. Unimaginably huge and far-flung, it was made to order for fragmentation. In World War II it suffered from two different and competing commands employing different lines of attack—MacArthur in the southwest and Nimitz in Hawaii. Supporting each was a separate and unique cryptologic system. When, in 1945, the two commanders went into garrison, their cryptologic organizations followed them.

In Japan, MacArthur's cryptologists centered on Tokyo. NSA Far East (NSAFE), the cryptologic flagship in the Pacific, eventually came to be located on Pershing Heights in downtown Tokyo. ASAPAC and 6920th SG, the ASA and AFSS senior representatives in theater, were also posted to the Tokyo environs. Among them they controlled most of the Army and Air Force cryptologic assets in the theater.

Supporting Nimitz was NSAPAC. But the offices in Hawaii were just that—offices without dynamic functions. NSAFE had garnered all NSA's technical expertise in the theater. This was an accident of history, which resulted from the collapse of the Civop program in the mid-1950s. The program had been roundly disliked by the SCAs, but it did provide highly skilled civilian talent that they found most useful. Thus an organization which became known as PACEXFAC (Pacific Experimental Facility) developed as part of the NSAFE staff in Tokyo, and it absorbed most of the billets. Like NSAEUR Office Germany in Frankfurt, PACEXFAC was the cryptologic troubleshooter for the Pacific. It reinforced the real utility of the Tokyo office.

In 1957, Samford decided to rename the offices, but he kept the pecking order the same. NSAFE was renamed NSAPAC, but the office in Hawaii was called NSAPAC (Rear), as if it were a skiff being towed by a battleship. It was a name that grated.

This was how NSA was organized in the Pacific when the Unified and Specified Commands were created in 1958. Under the new scheme, CINCPAC in Hawaii was clearly the senior commander in the theater. When Samford's immediate superior, General Erskine, came through on a trip the following year, however, he was surprised to see that NSA had not changed to conform to the realities of the new military command structure. NSAPAC (Rear) was still in Hawaii, and its chief was the deputy to NSAPAC in Tokyo. He returned to Washington complaining that NSA had it all wrong in the Pacific.

This unusual organizational scheme bumped along until a new director, Admiral Frost, toured the Pacific in the spring of 1962. Frost talked it over with the current CINCPAC, Admiral Harry Felt. When he returned to NSA, he decreed that NSAPAC would henceforth be located in Hawaii to support CINCPAC [censored]

[censored]

Samford Joins the Agency

The Canine era came to an end on 23 November 1956. His replacement was Lieutenant General John A. "Sammy" Samford. As mellow as Canine was forthright, Samford came to NSA to smooth ruffled feathers and give the Agency some room to breathe. Canine's five years (including one year as director of AFSA) had been a hectic time.

Samford was actually better prepared for the job than Canine had been. He came to NSA from the Pentagon, where he had been chief of Air Force intelligence, and served a grooming period of six months as Canine's vice-director. When he became DIRNSA, he already knew the players.

His style was fluid—Samford was as smooth as silk. A CIA official described him as "more of a pedant than a pilot, more of a philosopher than a fighter, ... a man who understood and loved the SIGINT business." He set out to calm the waters between CIA and NSA, and when he left the job in 1960, the two organizations were back on speaking terms. His relations with USAFSS, contentious under Canine, settled back down. Samford had developed a close personal relationship with Gordon Blake, who became commander of USAFSS in 1957, based on old school ties established when they had both been cadets at West Point. They both knew that the independence of AFSCC would have to end, but with as little bloodshed as possible.

In order to enshrine the new era of good feelings, Samford initiated a novel experiment in 1958, in which the chief of the Soviet Navy shop (GENS-2), a Navy captain, would actually work for the director of naval security, while continuing to respond to DIRNSA on operational matters. The next year he extended this unique arrangement to the Air Force and Army, resubordinating the chiefs of GENS-1 and GENS-3 to their parent SCA commanders. The idea was to give each SCA a stake in NSA, but it did not last long. Seeing that it had failed to sublimate service factionalism (and even in some cases making it worse), Frost scuttled the system in 1962.

Samford also moved quickly to resolve a longstanding dispute between Canine and Deputy Secretary of Defense Reuben Robertson. The 1956 McKinsey Study recommended that NSA be run more on private business principles. To instill a sense of corporate management, the director should appoint a civilian deputy from the business community. But Canine, having called in the McKinsey group, rejected the recommendation. Instead, he continued with his system of elevating one of his service deputies to a position called the vice-directorship, and he continued to act as his own de facto deputy. The dispute between Canine, who opted strongly for military management, and Robertson, who demanded a business approach, grew acrimonious and soured Canine's last months in office.

Samford found, on being elevated to the directorship, that Robertson already had someone in mind. That someone was Joseph H. Ream, a top CBS executive. So, only some two months into office, Samford named Ream to the new job of deputy director, just to give the idea a whirl.

It soon whirled into oblivion. Ream had no SIGINT background, and the learning curve was too steep. He had serious family problems that required extended trips to Florida and that cut into his learning time. His lack of technical qualifications for the job simply could not overcome his well-documented managerial skills. Further, he found it hard to deal with an entrenched bureaucracy that viewed him as an outsider. Ream quit in frustration only six months into the job. It was the last time anyone succcessfully imposed a nongovernment outsider on NSA's top-level management structure.

In his place, Samford hired Howard Engstrom. Engstrom's impact on cryptology had already been considerable. He was brought into the Navy from the Yale math department during World War II. He quickly became influential in the development of computers for cryptologic work, and when the war ended, he left the Navy to form Electronic Research Associates (ERA), where he was the guiding genius in the effort to develop computers for NSG, AFSA, and later NSA. In the mid-50s he left Remington Rand (which had swallowed ERA), where he was a vice-president, to join NSA's R&D organization. When he arrived at NSA, Samford elevated Engstrom to the position of associate director, which gave him and his R&D organization special status and was designed to answer DoD-level concerns that NSA was not doing enough in research and development. When Ream quit, Samford moved Engstrom to the post. But he remained only a year, and in August of 1958 NSA experienced yet another change in the revolving door position of deputy director.

The Tordella Era Begins

In late July of 1958, Samford summoned Louis Tordella, NSA's influential representative at Office of Special Operations (OSO), to his office to talk. Tordella remembers a short chat about inconsequential matters, following which Samford asked Tordella what a deputy director should be. Tordella told the director that the deputy should be his "alter ego." That sounded good to Samford, and he offered Tordella the job on the spot. It was the last time any director would have to do that for sixteen years. The revolving door shut with a bang behind the lanky form of Louis Tordella.

Like Engstrom, Tordella had been plucked from a college math department for Navy service in World War II. Originally a Hoosier, he had gone to school in Illinois. OP-20-G's Laurence Safford found him on the campus of Chicago's Loyola University through his unique program of recruiting academics with an expressed interest in cryptology. And also like Engstrom, he was, in 1958, already a cryptologic legend. Tordella had pioneered in so many areas of Navy cryptology that he was close to being a universal man, like the Army's Frank Rowlett. He joined NSA when it opened its doors and served in numerous key positions which permitted him to push his favorite projects, especially the application of computers to cryptanalysis. Tordella had been NSA's representative on numerous high-level committees. This, and his tour in the Pentagon, had given him the opportunity to get acquainted with just about everyone who counted, and when Samford proposed his name to Deputy Secretary of Defense Donald Quarles (who had replaced Reuben Robertson) in 1958, he got no opposition.

Tordella did indeed become the director's alter ego. Staying through the tenure of seven directors, he was the details man, the continuity. To many inside and outside the Agency, Louis Tordella was NSA.

Public Law 86-36

In 1959 Congress passed Public Law (PL) 86-36, which contained provisions permitting NSA to separate its personnel system from the regular Civil Service system, a permission which CIA had had since its inception. The problem that NSA had faced was that it had never been created by statute (only by executive order, the now-famous Truman Memorandum). There was thus no law which could keep NSA's personnel system apart from that of the rest of the federal government. Civil Service regulations straight-jacketed NSA procedures, and classification hampered NSA adherence to procedures which were intended for a completely open system. To eliminate the dilemma, PL 86-36 exempted NSA from the laws relating to the classification and grading of civilian positions from disclosing any information regarding the number of employees, the names, titles, or job descriptions. Public Law 86-36 was to have a major impact on NSA policies in both the personnel and security areas.

NSA And The American Public—The Issue Of Legality

"No person not being authorized by the sender shall intercept any communication and divulge or publish the existence, contents, substance, purport, effect, or meaning of such intercepted communication to any person. . . ." —Federal Communications Act of 1934

Cryptologic activities, which in the United States began during the early years of World War I, occupied an uncertain place in government. Early American cryptologists worked without the knowledge of the American public. They even worked without knowing if what they were doing was legal or not. It was an odd and unsettling position to be in.

Early statutes affecting cryptology were devised by Congress to protect radio, a new invention which required protection. Thus it was that a series of acts, beginning with one in 1912, was passed to protect information in radio messages from being passed to a third party to be used for commercial gain. This appeared to have a benign effect on cryptologic activities in the Army and Navy until 1927, when a revised statute stated that "no person not being authorized by the sender shall intercept any message and divulge or publish the contents, substance, purport, effect, or meaning of such intercepted message to any person. . . ." The aim of the legislation was the same as that of earlier statutes—to protect the information "unless legally required to do so by a court of competent jurisdiction or other competent authority. . . ." Other competent authority could be the president or someone in the Army or Navy chain of command. But as the word "intercept" had crept into the statute, for the cryptologists who secretly plied their trade, this was unnerving news. It implied that what they were doing might be illegal. Further, it had the effect of shutting off liaison with the telegraph cable companies, who had in the early years supplied most of the material that the Army worked on. (But by the late 1920s the Army, like the Navy before it, was beginning to set up its own intercept stations.)

Meanwhile, the American public was blissfully unaware of any cryptologic activity at all—unaware, that is, until the publication of Yardley's *The American Black Chamber* in 1931. Worse, Yardley was hard at work on a sequel, to be called "Japanese Diplomatic Secrets." It was never published—it became, in fact, the first publication ever suppressed in the United States on the grounds of national security. To prevent any other revelations, Congress in 1933 hurried through a bill that prohibited all government employees from revealing their knowledge of American codes "or any matter which was obtained while in the process of transmission between any foreign government and its diplomatic mission in the United States." The penalty would be a $10,000 fine or ten years imprisonment, considered to be a heavy enough hammer in those days. This appeared to be a backhanded way of authorizing other black chambers. If such activity were illegal, then why protect its activities from disclosure?

This step forward was followed immediately by disappointment. When the Federal Communications Act was passed the following year, it contained the same clause regarding "intercept." There was a good deal of discussion about this within SIS and OP-20-G. Legal minds pointed out that the statute prohibited intercept "and divulging" of such communications. If it had said "or divulging," it would clearly have singled out the process of intercept as illegal. But the intercept activity would not be illegal unless it were accompanied by "divulging," which, once again, referred to use of the information for commercial gain. And the so-called Yardley Act the year before seemed to imply legality. But there was a lingering suspicion that they might someday be prosecuted for what they were doing on the basis of Section 605 of the Federal Communications Act of 1934. The penalties were exactly the same as they were under the Yardley Act.

Following the 1945 Pearl Harbor hearings, which amounted to the second public revelation of cryptologic activities, there were loud demands for legislation protecting this vital activity. Within the Army and Navy themselves, lawyers drafted protective statutes, and the Truman administration moved toward the introduction of legislation. Finally, in 1949 a draft was ready, and it was steered through the Senate by Lyndon Baines Johnson, a young senator from Texas. In 1950 the bill became law: Title 18, U.S.C. 798.

The United States already had legislation. But the Espionage Act of 1917 required proof that the person revealing the secret information intended to injure the United States. The courts had required a high standard of proof, including the direct involvement of agents of a wartime enemy, in order to secure a conviction. What if no enemy agents were involved? Or what if the agents were from a "friendly" country? Or what if the person simply gave the information to a reporter who published it?

Title 18 took care of all that. It made it a crime to divulge information relating to various aspects of cryptologic activities to an unauthorized person "or uses in any manner prejudicial to the safety or interest of the United States or for the benefit of any foreign government. . . ." It cast a very broad net, was almost totally inclusive, and was legally enforceable even in the absence of intent to injure. It could thus deter, or be used against, well-meaning but misguided idealists.

Just as important, it implicitly authorized COMINT activities by acknowledging that they were going on and by protecting their secrecy by law. Here was an implicit voiding of Section 605 of the Federal Communications Act of 1934 and earlier statutes as they related to cryptology.

This was followed two years later by the Truman Memorandum creating NSA and describing its responsibilities. Here was the "lawful authority," even though classified, so needed in the years prior to the war. As the years rolled on and Congress appropriated money for NSA's activities, the legal status of the business became less and less debatable. The 1959 anonymity statute (Public Law 86-36) for the first time named NSA in legislation. Finally, in 1968 the Omnibus Crime Control and Safe Streets Act specifically overruled Section 605 of the Federal Communications Act of 1934. Cryptology had made the journey from a secret black chamber to an officially authorized and avowed government activity.

Public Revelations And Cryptologic Secrecy

"[It is] of the essence of a secret service that it must be secret, and if you once began disclosure, it is perfectly obvious that there is no longer any secret service and that you must do without it." —Austen Chamberlain, British foreign secretary in the 1920s

Following Yardley, COMINT went underground. The Black Chamber had already been destroyed by Secretary of War Stimson in 1929 (through the device of pulling State Department funding). Its successor, Friedman's SIS, was so small (he started with a staff of six) as to be effectively invisible. The Navy had an effort of comparable size, and the entire enterprise proceeded reasonably secure from the eyes of the public.

Beginning in 1939, a series of magazine and newspaper articles trumpeted the success of the federal government in breaking up German espionage rings. Some of the articles referenced German codes and discussed U.S. intercept activities. SIS and OP-20-G officials were livid—someone was calling attention to COMINT activities in such a way that the Germans could be alerted and might take countermeasures.

The "someone" turned out to be the Federal Communications Commission (FCC). FCC revelations to the press, designed to boost its stock with the public, were at least partly responsible for the War Department's securing Roosevelt's order in 1942 directing that such activities be discontinued in all but the Army, Navy, and FBI. Despite the order, the FCC continued its radio monitoring and codebreaking activities throughout the war and even accompanied this with leaks to the press boasting of its COMINT effectiveness.

Potentially more damaging was an article in the *Chicago Tribune* immediately after the Battle of Midway alleging that the U.S. had had advance knowledge of Japanese plans. The article was bylined by Stanley Johnston, a reporter who had been with the Pacific Fleet during the battle of Coral Sea. The next month columnist and broadcaster Walter Winchell stated that this knowledge had come from the breaking of Japanese naval codes. The Navy demanded that Johnson be indicted, and the case went to a federal grand jury in Chicago in August. No indictment resulted, a blessing for an over-eager Navy legal department that would have had to reveal far more damaging information in court to secure a conviction. The glare of national publicity was mercifully diverted, but in August, far ahead of schedule, the Japanese Navy changed all its codes. (There was never any direct evidence, however, that the Japanese read the *Tribune* or changed their codes in response.)

Classifying Cryptologic Information

Service cryptologists were almost instinctively aware of the extreme sensitivity of their work. They began in such small organizations, though, that the process itself was easy to protect. Once they developed information that needed to go to someone, they generally distributed it on a by-name basis to those few Army, Navy, and State Department people who had an absolute need to know. Information was often taken in locked containers, and a courier stood by while the official involved read and initialed the paper.

As for a formal classification, they had to use what was available. Existing service regulations at the beginning of World War II contained only two classifications: Secret and Confidential. Another quasi-classification, called Restricted (an earlier version of For Official Use Only, or FOUO), was reserved primarily for information relating to military hardware.

Their British allies had three classifications. Above Secret they added the term Most Secret. In 1944 the Army adopted the British three-tiered system, but called the highest category "Top" Secret. COMINT, being among the most sensitive items on the menu, was classified Top Secret.

When the Army obtained an agreement with GCCS in 1943, the Americans had to agree to attach a security caveat associated with COMINT. The most sensitive information (which at the time included ENIGMA and MAGIC decrypts) was now handled under a special codeword called ULTRA. Information derived from traffic analysis, DF, and plain text received codeword protection, but different codewords were used to denote lesser sensitivity—THUMB and PEARL were two which appeared during World War II. After the war the system devolved into two codeword categories: Top Secret Codeword, and everything else. That which related to COMINT but was not derived directly from communications intercepts began to receive the stamp Handle Via COMINT Channels Only (HVCCO).

Within cryptology, there were certain projects that received much more limited distributions. BOURBON, the early Soviet problem, was a good example, and VENONA got even more limited handling still. This system of ad hoc compartmentations continued into the early 1960s, when it was augmented by a more formal compartmentation system which was applied to SIGINT product reports. The most sensitive category was Gamma, [censored] A lesser category, called Delta, was often used to protect [censored]

Despite the strict secrecy applied to the trade, the number of people indoctrinated for COMINT rose steadily as its utility came to be recognized. By 1955 the number of COMINT clearances within the federal government (and to contractors) had grown to over 31,000, and the Hoover Commission expressed concern about the spread of highly sensitive information to such a large group. Of these [censored] This was a far cry from the six people that Friedman hired to carry on the Army's COMINT business in 1929 or the two people (Laurence Safford and Agnes Driscoll) who began Navy COMINT in the 1920s.

Pulling on the other end of the rope were the people who advocated an even broader dissemination of COMINT. In 1960 Lyman Kirkpatrick (who headed the Kirkpatrick Committee) took the Defense Department to task for over-strict rules regarding intelligence. (And by intelligence, he was clearly referring to COMINT.) Kirkpatrick wrote: "Entirely apart from the well-known tendency throughout the intelligence community to over- classify, the special handling required for a very significant portion of intelligence information has at times deprived key personnel of information vital to the successful discharge of their responsibilities."

The tug of war between the advocates of secrecy and dissemination was never-ending. Nor could the conflict be resolved. As SIGINT became more successful, it became an inevitable victim of its own success. Utility meant dissemination, and dissemination meant risk.

Breaches In The Dike—The Security Cases

The first significant breaches of the security system came from within rather than from without. The first two were quiet, and while they both involved significant compromise, their very obscurity minimized the damage. Neither became a cause célébre, although one of them became public. The third, however, did major damage primarily because it became a public case.

L' Affaire Weisband

The first case did the most real damage. But it was so successfully hushed that only a few insiders knew that it had occurred. It involved an AFSA analyst named William Weisband.

Weisband was an immigrant. Born in Alexandria, Egypt, in 1908, he had entered the United States in either 1926 or 1929. (The record on this point is obscure.) He became a citizen in 1938 and, while living in New York City, was inducted into the Army. Weisband went into the Signal Corps, and he first began working with ASA in 1943, where he became a favorite of Colonel Harold Hayes (who headed the Army's cryptologic activities in the Mediterranean). As an accomplished linguist, he was an ASA natural and received a transfer from North Africa to Arlington Hall in 1944. The end of the war found him still working there, and he hired on as a civilian. ASA needed all the help it could get in 1945, and getting a linguist like Weisband was a good day's work.

Unfortunately for ASA, Weisband was a Communist and suspected of being a spy. He had handled other agents passing defense information to the Soviets even before he entered the Army. He apparently gave up handling agents once he entered the service, but after he arrived at Arlington Hall he probably resumed his old avocation.

At the Hall he had a reputation as a stroller. He wandered around, chatting and picking up bits of gossip. He was also adept at getting himself on distribution for documents that did not directly concern the work of his section. Highly gregarious, Weisband had a wide circle of friends, and he entertained some of the top officers and civilians in ASA. His postwar wedding party was talked about as a who's who of Army cryptology.

Although Weisband had been on an FBI list of suspected Communists since 1948, he was first tagged as a possible spy through the VENONA project. In 1949 a Soviet agent identified in VENONA traffic led the FBI to another agent, who led them to another, who finally implicated Weisband as a "handler." The FBI began piecing together information on this new identity and was aghast to learn in 1950 that Weisband was employed at Arlington Hall, the very place whence the VENONA decrypts were coming. In April 1950 Wesley Reynolds of the FBI went to Carter Clarke, commanding general of ASA, to report the news. Clarke told Reynolds that Weisband had transferred to AFSA. They went to Admiral Stone.

At the time, Weisband was working as a section chief on the Soviet problem. Co-workers had already reported him as a possible security risk, and he had been removed from access to some of the more sensitive projects while security looked into it. He was immediately suspended and interrogated. He denied everything. But the walls were falling in on him even as he spoke. In August, as the subject of an unrelated investigation, he appeared before a federal grand jury in Los Angeles investigating west Coast Communism. Ordered to return for further testimony, he did not comply, was arrested and was convicted of contempt, for which he served a year in a federal prison.

He never returned to AFSA, and in 1951 he was mustered out of federal employment by a loyalty-security board in San Francisco, which, not surprisingly, found that removal from federal employment was in the best interest of national security. He remained in the Washington area, working as a car dealer and apartment manager, and died in 1967 in Fairfax. He never admitted anything.

The FBI never found out what, if anything, Weisband passed to the Soviets. But his close involvement with the Soviet problem argued suggested some of the tightening up of Soviet communications was a result of Weisband's activities. Many AFSA employees believed, rightly or wrongly, that he was single-handedly responsible for "Black Friday." His case instilled a certain paranoia within the profession, and accounted to some degree for NSA's extremely close guarding of COMINT.

The Petersen Case

The second security breach involved an NSA analyst named Joseph Sydney Petersen, Jr. Petersen had served with ASA in the South Pacific in World War II and had formed a close liaison with Dutch cryptologists with whom the United States was exchanging information. After the war this liaison came to an end, but Petersen decided on his own to become a one-man Third Party office to the Dutch intelligence service. He collected documents at his home and periodically passed them on to Dutch intelligence people from the embassy. This apparently went on for several years.

Petersen's espionage might never have come to light had it not been for an unrelated naval security case involving an officer who had been separated from the service for [censored] He implicated Petersen as a [censored] and an investigation was launched. But when NSA learned that Petersen had close friends at the Dutch embassy, the investigators forgot about the [censored] charge and called in the FBI. In September 1953 the FBI began questioning Petersen, and he began revealing his story. A search of his apartment uncovered a large number of classified documents, and the FBI reckoned that it had enough to prosecute.

The joint NSA-FBI team consulted with Canine in his quarters. The options were to try to prosecute or to be satisfied with a simple resignation on his part. This would be the first prosecution under Title 18, and a hearing in open court might bring to light information that would be more damaging than just giving Petersen his walking papers. But Canine decided to go for prosecution, and he later overrode objections by USCIB that the resulting publicity would seriously damage NSA.

When Petersen's lawyer found out that the government had opted for prosecution, he began negotiatinga plea bargain. On the day the trial was to begin, he told the judge that Petersen was pleading guilty to a violation of Title 18. Petersen fully cooperated with the FBI and in return was sentenced to seven years in prison. He was paroled after four years.

The Petersen case was similar to that of a much more notorious case years later, the espionage of Jonathan Jay Pollard. He passed cryptologic documents to an ally who he felt had been left in the lurch. Along with technical information regarding the establishment of cryptanalysis courses, Petersen also informed the Dutch [censored] When the FBI searched his house, they found cryptologic documents dealing with several COMINT targets, among them Korea and Communist China. The NSA damage assessment found that the number of documents passed to the Dutch was "very large."

When Petersen was indicted, the Associated Press ran a dispatch which was printed in many newspapers across the country. It was the first time the new agency had ever fallen under the klieg lights. The dispatch described NSA as "essentially a radio monitoring service. It has a network of radio receiving stations and other equipment, some of which are based overseas. It listens in on the world's radio traffic, both conventional messages and coded material . . . secrecy even tighter than that shrouding the Central Intelligence Agency surrounds the National Security Agency. It is not listed by name either in the Washington directory or in the Pentagon phone directory."

A number of other details about NSA appeared to bring about a focus on the Agency's anonymity. NSA's obscurity had been so perfect that Richard Russell, the chairman of the Senate Armed Services Committee, once asked, "What does the NSA do?" The job description appearing in the U.S. Government Organization Manual was a marvel of obfuscation: "The National Security Agency performs highly specialized technical and co-ordinating functions related to the national security." The Petersen case was the first to pry open the lid of anonymity.

Martin and Mitchell

On 1 August 1960, a small story appeared in the local Washington newspapers. Two Department of Defense employees of the National Security Agency had failed to return from vacation and were still missing.

The story did not stay small very long. NSA's reputation for secrecy guaranteed that any news would be big news, and by the next day it was on the front page. On 5 August the Department of Defense issued a brief statement that it was now known that the two employees, Bernon F. Mitchell and William Martin, had flown to Mexico City and thence to Cuba. It was assumed that they were behind the Iron Curtain.

But the most shattering blow came on 7 September. Listeners to Radio Moscow tuned in on one of the most remarkable press conferences of the century. Now in Moscow, Martin and Mitchell were introduced by the Soviet announcer and proceeded to tell their story in exquisite detail. They related how they had become analysts at NSA, full of confidence in the integrity of their government. They described how the U.S. government was intercepting and breaking communications of its allies (Turkey was named specifically), about intentional violations of Soviet airspace to collect intelligence, about alleged American plans for a nuclear first strike, and how NSA was trying to exploit Soviet communications. They exposed NSA's organization (PROD does this and ADVA does that, etc.). They described the arrangements between NSA, GCHQ, and Canada. They spent a good deal of time on the RC-130 shootdown in 1958. It was marvelous theater for Khrushchev, who had launched a diplomatic and press offensive against the United States in May following the U-2 shootdown.

Martin and Mitchell were young mathematicians. Both had gone into NSG and had been assigned together at [censored] Mitchell, who was from California originally, was quite bright and had been something of a prodigy in high school. But he was extremely immature socially and had a great deal of difficulty adjusting. While he was at [censored] Martin was his only close friend. Martin was from Columbus, Georgia. He, too, had been labeled as very bright and, compared with Mitchell, was more gregarious. Certain questions about their psychological health came up on the polygraph and background investigation but were not regarded as serious impediments to employment. Once out of the Navy, both pursued college degrees in mathematics, and upon graduation both were approached for employment by NSA. They entered on duty as GS-7s in 1957.

In 1959 Martin was sent to the University of Illinois for graduate study. While there he established Communist associations, and in his private conversations became more and more critical of the U.S. government. (He expressed special distaste for the U-2 overflights and other reconnaissance activities, and this was reflected in the statements of both men to the press in Moscow.)

At the time, Mitchell was having his own problems and finally sought psychiatric advice. The private psychiatrist concluded that Mitchell was in all probability a homosexual with serious personality disorders. But the psychiatrist felt that this sexual orientation was not the root of his problems. More serious was his poor relationship with his own family.

It has been alleged that in 1959, in violation of standing rules for government employees, Martin and Mitchell visited Cuba. Despite this, there was no evidence that they actually established an espionage relationship with any Communist country prior to the defection.

In June of 1960, just after Martin returned from Illinois, they both applied for annual leave. They stated that they were going to visit family on the West Coast. Instead, they departed for Mexico City and from there flew to Cuba. Apparently they proceeded from there via Soviet trawler to the Soviet Union.

Back at the office, no one thought to question their absence until they were a week overdue. When their supervisor failed to reach them either in their Laurel apartments or at their families' homes, the FBI was called in, and there began an intensive investigation. The security people concluded that the defections were impulsive and self-initiated.

There was no evidence that they carried off any documents, which argued for the theory that they made their decision after going on leave. Still, the route they took required considerable planning, and they left a defection note in a safe deposit box in a Laurel bank, to which they referred during the Radio Moscow broadcast. So the whole idea had been evidently a long time abuilding.

The defection precipitated a storm of criticism of NSA. The secretary of defense initiated an investigation of NSA security practices. Not to be outdone, the House Un-American Activities Committee, chaired by Representative Francis E. Walter of Pennsylvania, launched its own investigation. Finally, President Eisenhower directed that the FBI initiate an investigation to determine if there were any more potential Martins and Mitchells in the ranks at NSA.

All three investigations lambasted the current practice at NSA of granting interim security clearances upon successful completion of the polygraph. Canine had authorized this procedure as an emergency measure during the Korean War, and it had come into routine use. After Martin and Mitchell the practice was terminated, and every employee had to have a complete background check in addition to the polygraph before performing any sort of classified work at NSA.

The Walter Committee investigation was exhaustive. It spanned thirteen months, took two thousand man-hours, covered fifteen states, and resulted in sixteen separate hearings. Thirty-four present or former NSA employees testified in closed session. NSA and the Department of Defense began by opposing committee access to NSA records, but eventually a compromise was worked out, and NSA and the committee finished on reasonably good terms. Still, the Agency could not keep the process from being sensationalized, and it was stung by a charge by Walter that NSA was a "nest of sexual deviates".

The legislative result of the Martin and Mitchell affair was a law which set up the legislative authority for NSA's security system. Among other things, it established that employment at NSA was appropriate only when it was "clearly consistent with the national security." It required a full field investigation prior to employment (i.e., no interim clearances) and gave the secretary of defense additional authority to fire NSA employees "when such action is deemed necessary in the interest of the United States..."

In addition, the committee made certain recommendations concerning NSA's administrative practices—for instance, making professional psychological and psychiatric services available in assessing applicants and employees who revealed instability. But almost all the committee's recommendations had already been implemented, and in its final report the committee gave NSA credit for this. The most far-reaching of the changes related to the termination of the procedure of granting routine interim clearances, and the institution of the so-called three-hour rule, which required that employees three hours overdue for work would be reported to the security office. These and a long list of other changes became a permanent part of NSA's way of doing business.

[censored]

As the Walter Committee proceeded, the FBI investigation was winding down. An intensive screening of on-board employees had turned up a small number of people whose sexual conduct, in light of the sexual mores of the time, might be questioned, and of these some twenty-six had been terminated. The proceedings were not all that a civil libertarian might have wanted, but they calmed the waters long enough for NSA to begin functioning again.

The damage to NSA's public image was so severe that it overshadowed the cryptologic damage that had been done. Because it appeared that the two defectors had not carried away documents and that they had not had a previous relationship with the Soviets, just what the Soviets did know as a result was speculative. Martin and Mitchell had known about [censored] the Soviet problem, but they were in a position to give away information [censored] on certain Soviet cipher systems, especially a system called [censored] NSA employees blamed Martin and Mitchell. But no one ever had proof. And unlike Weisband, their defection was not coincident with any sort of "Black Friday." This, the most famous (or infamous) of NSA's security cases, was not the most damaging.

Book II: Centralization Wins 1960-1972

Chapter 8 The Kennedy Years

The New Administration

"In the long history of the world, only a few generations have been granted the role of defending freedom in its hour of maximum danger. I do not shrink from this responsiblity—I welcome it. I do not believe that any of us would exchange places with any other people or any other generation. The energy, the faith, the devotion which we bring to this endeavor will light our country and all who serve it—and the glow from that fire can truly light the world." —John F. Kennedy, Inaugural Address, 20 January 1961

John Kennedy came to the White House with an abiding interest in foreign affairs and defense policy. His politics, forged during formative years of the Cold War, were hard-line anti-Communist and anti-Soviet. But unlike Eisenhower, whose instinctive conservatism drove him toward small government and small defense budgets, Kennedy wanted a liberal remake of the world. Under the driving and optimistic Kennedy, it seemed that anything was possible and that John Fitzgerald Kennedy could make it happen.

Kennedy knew little about intelligence when he arrived at the White House. He needed an interpreter but avoided the existing channels (DCI, secretaries of state and defense). Instead, he came to rely on an official on his White House staff who held the title of national security advisor. His choice for this relatively little-known office was McGeorge Bundy. Previous occupants of the position had been relatively obscure, but Bundy and his successors, Walt Rostow and Henry Kissinger, were to become household names. Power had shifted to the White House staff.

McNamara at Defense

For many years, the office of the secretary of defense had been weak and understaffed. The first secretary of defense had an office but little else.

James Forrestal had no legal deputy, no staff, a miniscule budget, and no tools to curtail the interservice feuding which had erupted after the war. In 1949 President Harry Truman got a reluctant Congress to create a Department of Defense, with a staff and a budget to go with the solitary office of secretary. The Defense Reorganization Act of 1958 accorded the secretary more staff and more power. Subsequent secretaries (the despondent Forrestal having committed suicide) battled the three warring services through the Eisenhower years, and each was driven nearly to distraction.

No one quite anticipated someone like Robert McNamara when the Defense Department was established. He had come over from industry. Brilliant and driven, he had become CEO of Ford Motor Company at the age of forty-four. McNamara was a Republican and had been so far from Kennedy's inner circle that the two had never met. He brought with him new techniques for managing large organizations. He was a centralizer par excellence, and he ruthlessly beat back internal opposition. McNamara resembled less a secretary than a cyclone.

The new secretary brought with him a management team headed by Charles Hitch of Remington Rand. Hitch had had a hand in inventing a new discipline called Operations Research. Essentially, OR, as it was called, tried to quantify the basis for all managerial decisions. Using scientific methods, he would reduce all the variables of a decision to a mathematical quantity and choose the most attractive. Hitch institutionalized the PPBS (planning, programming and budgeting system), a seven-year planning cycle which is still in use. As DoD comptroller, he scrutinized every element of the defense budget. The largest intelligence package was the newly created CCP, and Hitch and friends examined it rather thoughtfully every year.

Kennedy was not happy with the doctrine of massive retaliation. He was an activist, and MC 14/2 (the document that codified massive retaliation in 1956) was essentially a defensive strategy. Instead, he opted for Maxwell Taylor's strategy of flexible response, which required conventional and unconventional forces to meet tactical threats. Finally codified in MC 14/3 in 1967, flexible response in fact dominated the strategy of both Kennedy and Johnson throughout the decade.

NSA and the Cryptologic System at the Beginning of a New Decade

Flexible response caught off guard an unsuspecting SIGINT system that had been optimized over an eight-year period to warn of, and support, total nuclear war. Not enough attention had been paid to SIGINT, not enough resources had been allocated. Servicemen had flocked to large fixed sites and had learned how to work strategic SIGINT problems. The weaknesses of the existing SIGINT system had been exposed [censored] and the services were working on solutions. But no one was really ready for the decade of crisis and war that was to follow.

This became a decade of SIGINT centralization. Just as the McNamara Defense Department strove to tighten the reins, so NSA, bolstered by repeated recommendations by high-level boards, commissions, and committees, drew SIGINT control back to Fort Meade. True, there were countervailing forces, most notedly tactical commanders in Vietnam, who strove for a decentralized system. But at decade's end, the SIGINT system was far more tightly knit than it had been ten years earlier. Former deputy director Robert Drake once jokingly formulated a law that said, "Centralization is always bad, except at my level." NSA employed Drake's Law to centralize its own system, but at the same time fought a spirited rear guard defense against McNamara's people at DoD. Centralization was fine, unless it meant giving up any powers to the Office of the Secretary of Defense (OSD). Thus NSA tried to stave off the intrusions of Hitch's budgeteers. Succeeding directors fought the authority of the newly created Defense Communications Agency. The creation of the Defense Intelligence Agency (DIA), too, represented a threat that NSA constantly crossed swords with. And NSA rejected the idea (pushed by Kennedy's PFIAB) that the DCI spend more time coordinating the entire intelligence effort, including the intelligence components of the Department of Defense. CIA was still regarded as a threat.

Even to defense intelligence specialists, NSA was still an obscure agency in 1960. It entered the decade known primarily as a communications research organization which played with expensive toys and produced huge volumes of highly classified translations in a fairly leisurely time frame. Analysts still worked basically an eight-to-five schedule, and shift operations, when mounted, were highly unusual and tailored for specific crises.

But pressure was mounting to change things. SIGINT had proved to be of great utility on a widening variety of targets. It had become the most prolific producer of strategic warning information, and President Eisenhower had demanded that such information get to him faster. Kennedy was an activist president, who demanded even quicker and more accurate responses. He prodded the system, and NSA responded. By the end of the decade, NSA's world would change.

Enter the New Director

Vice Admiral Laurence H. Frost, who arrived at the end of the Eisenhower administration in 1960, was better prepared for the job than any other previous director. He had had three prior tours in intelligence, including a two-year tour as Canine's chief of staff, and he had been director of Naval Intelligence. In addition, he had achieved distinction as a ship driver in two wars. The Army and Air Force had had their turns as DIRNSA—now it was the Navy's turn.

Frost contributed to SIGINT centralization by revoking the independence of the Soviet Navy problem at NSA. A compromise device instituted by Samford to bring the SCAs more fully into the NSA system, it had resulted in divided loyalties and jurisdictional disputes. In March of 1962 Frost resubordinated the chief of the Soviet navy problem to DIRNSA, removing him from the Navy chain of command where he had been directly subordinate to the director of the Naval Security Group. The independence of the Soviet ground and air problems lasted not much longer than that. But Frost himself lasted only two years in the job, and aside from that organizational change, left behind no distinctive legacy (for reasons which will be made clear later).

People, Money, and Organization

By the time Kennedy arrived in the White House, cryptology had become the elephant in the intelligence closet. McGeorge Bundy discovered that of the 101,900 Americans engaged in intelligence work, 59,000 were cryptologists of one stripe or another (58 percent). Of those, about half worked in the Continental United States, while the other half plied their trade overseas at collection and processing sites. NSA had 10,200 assigned (17 percent of the total) but only 300 overseas billets. The field sites were still the domain of the SCAs. At NSA, the military filled 25 percent of the billets.

Of the three services, NSG was still the smallest, with 6,900. AFSS, with 21,200, and ASA, with 20,400, dwarfed the Navy in size, although NSG made up in quality what it lacked in quantity. Cryptologic manpower was projected to grow through the decade until it would hit a peak of 93,067 in fiscal year 1969.

Within NSA's Production organization, fully 50 percent worked the Soviet problem. Another 8.4 percent worked in Acom (Asian Communist) while 7.6 percent were in Allo (all others, i.e., Third World). The remaining 35 percent was allocated to centralized technical or staff functions such as machine processing and collection support (including ELINT).

NSA's complex at Fort Meade underwent a building boom in the 1960s. Ground was broken for the nine-story headquarters building, and it was occupied in 1963. (General Canine attended the ceremony, and his wife cut the ribbon.) The new COMSEC building was dedicated in November 1968, and the quarters on Nebraska Avenue were finally given back to NSG. In the same year, owing to a moratorium on military construction, NSA began to lease three newly constructed "tech park" type buildings at Friendship Airport (which later changed its name to Baltimore-Washington International, or simply BWI). The complex was called Friendship Annex and came to be abbreviated as FANX. In 1961 NSA acquired the buildings that had housed the old Fort Meade post hospital and moved the training school from downtown Washington. The training component, newly renamed the National Cryptologic School, was one of the first occupants of the Friendship complex, gladly abandoning the antiquated hospital structure.

A New Reorganization

Following the Martin and Mitchell defection in 1960, the director established a management board to review NSA's organization. It was the first comprehensive review since the McKinsey study in 1956. This time, instead of an outside management team, Admiral Frost used home-grown talent. The board was chaired by Frank Bowlett (who had rejoined NSA during the Samford administration), Oliver Kirby from Prod, Brigadier General George M. Higginson, Maurice Klein (the head of personnel), and Dr. William Wray, with Dr. Milton Iredell as recorder.

Its report, handed to Frost in July 1961, amounted to a reversal of the McKinsey approach. What was needed was not decentralization (a key element of the McKinsey report) but centralization. The director's staff had grown too small, and too many functions had been farmed to Prod. "The Board found no effective mechanism within the existing organization to exercise the strong centralized control of national policy, planning, and programming functions, which appears essential to insure concentration on and responsiveness to the Director's national responsibilities." Thus it created a policy staff to manage Second and Third Party affairs, to do central budgeting for the CCP and to effect systems planning and evaluation. It was similar in approach to that being used by McNamara's people in OSD (although probably no one at NSA would admit it).

The naming conventions for office designations was also tossed out the window. Martin and Mitchell had, at their press conference, reeled off a long list of NSA organizations, and it would be necessary to change to a new system. Out were the pronounceable syllables, in was the obfuscating alphanumeric system. Key components were to be designated by a single letter (R for R&D, P for Production, etc.), and subordinate elements would carry trailing numbers.

PROD itself consisted of three key components:

A. the Soviet problem;

B. everything else, including former ACOM and ALLO;

C. technical functions such as machine processing, central reference, and the former office of collection (including, for the time, ELINT processing).

Included on a central PROD staff would be a permanent watch office and an office of cryptologic research (an early version of P1). The board also recommended that the arrangement come to an end whereby the chiefs of the Soviet naval, ground, and air problems were subordinated to their SCA chiefs. Frost (as noted above) acted on this the next year.

The board recommended that R&D be strengthened to handle increased responsibilities. (This was in accord with, and partly in response to, DoD-level recommendations that NSA take a more active hand in the development of cryptologic equipment across the board). The R&D organization should assume policy direction on major new projects such as the Air Force [censored] collection system and the Space Collection (Spacol) systems. The COMSEC R&D function, which historically shuttled between COMSEC and R&D, returned to the research organization.

Finally, the board took another swipe at the continuing lack of a career civilian cryptologic service. This had been a big issue during the Canine years, and fragments of the system had been put in place. But a systematic professionalization system, with categories and criteria, had never been implemented. Under Samford the proposals had languished, and now another board made another recommendation. It was a continuing irritant.

Changing the Field Organization

While Europe remained stable, cryptologic organization in the Pacific was changing. The switch of NSAPAC from Tokyo to Honolulu, already mentioned, occurred under Frost in 1962. In the same year ASA and USAFSS moved their own regional headquarters to Hawaii to be in synch with military organization in the theater. This was also a time when second-echelon processing in the Pacific finally came together in [censored] In the fall of 1961 a new processing organization, [censored] opened its doors.

The first commander was an army colonel, Kenneth Rice of ASA, but there was also a large contingent of NSA civilians working [censored] As time went on, it acquired processing responsibilities for North Vietnamese air, air defense, General Directorate of Rear Services (GDRS), and shipping.

Bucking the trend toward centralization, AFSCC remained operating in San Antonio. NSA wanted to move it to Fort Meade but did not have the space. This problem would not be solved until the Friendship complex was leased in 1968. Meanwhile, AFSCC continued to work the third echelon aspects of the Soviet air problem, and it even acquired the [censored] problem under an agreement negotiated with ACOM early in the decade.

In the meantime, NSA continued to set its own targeting priorities. Systems were devised throughout the 1950s and 1960s to allow for the expression of customer requirements, but none really had any teeth, and they were so general ("copy and report the world") that NSA was forced to prioritize for itself.

The best indication of where NSA's priorities lay was the Agency's input to the new PPBS system in 1961. NSA thought that exploiting [censored] was Job One, followed in order by [censored] It is fair to note that the Soviet problem encompassed four of the seven and that [censored] was not among the listed requirements. This omission would not last long.

The Cryptologic Map In The Mid-1960s

By the time NSA was eight years old, the cryptologic map had exploded. NSA and the SCAs were in seventeen countries plus the Continental United States, Alaska, Hawaii, and [censored] The three SCAs had major field sites in thirteen locations, and NSA had a theater headquarters in Frankfurt. [censored]

[censored]

[censored]
[censored]

Back Home

In the Continental US, ASA maintained major collection sites on both coasts, at Vint Hill Farmws in Virginia and Two Rock Ranch at Petaluma, California. [censored]

[censored]

New Collection Systems

All three services modernized their field site equipment to equip the new sites being built around the world. But during the 1950s no SCA was as aggressive as AFSS. The 1950s marked the birth of a major new HF and VHF collection system. [censored]

[censored]

Beginning the systems R&D work in 1956, NSG fielded its first [censored]

Among the three SCAs, Air Force Security Service began life in the worst shape from an equipment standpoint because it simply inherited cast-off ASA equipment. But the Air Force emphasis on building its own, completely independent and self-sufficient SIGINT system resulted in very large amounts of money being poured into the USAFSS coffers. It also resulted in an AFSS R&D organization that was larger and better funded than the other two SCAs. In the early 1950s, AFSS set to work designing a new collection system from the ground up.

The proposal went forward as a package under Gordon Blake, the new USAFSS commander, in March of 1957. It was called [censored] and included three components:

a. [censored] a VHF system, optimized for ELINT collection and first-echelon processing.

[censored]

b. [censored] the HF system, optimized for COMINT. The distinctive antenna was called FLR-9, but the package included more than just that.

c. [censored] a VHF airborne system. It never got past the prototype stage.

In addition, the [censored] came to include computers for second-echelon processing. It was a complete field system, minus the buildings. Sylvania won the contract to build the systems.

[censored]

The above-HF portion of the system, called [censored] was to be optimized for ELINT collection and first-echelon processing [censored] At a projected cost of [censored] a copy, [censored] was hideously expensive. It was also fraught with technical risks which ultimately jeopardized the entire project.

NSA Gets Involved

NSA watched from the sidelines in the mid-1950s as NSG and AFSS independently designed and fielded separate collection and DF systems. The Agency urged, with no result, that the two services compromise their differing requirements and develop a single system good for both tasks. Then in 1957 NSA became directly involved when it was asked by the Air Force to review the AFSS [censored] proposal. The level of involvement increased in 1958 when NSCID 6 gave the Agency a more explicit role in guiding and coordinating service cryptologic R&D.

NSA opposed the way AFSS was proceeding with the project. Apart from the lack of agreement between AFSS and NSG on harmonized development, NSA was concerned that:

a. The project, especially the [censored] was far too expensive;

b. Major components were overdesigned (again [censored] was the culprit);

c. AFSS was proceeding with a generalized requirement, while NSA believed that AFSS should proceed with a "special purpose" approach, and that this would reduce costs;

d. Sylvania, selected as the prime contractor for the FLR-9, lacked experience in several important areas;

e. AFSS had planned no test models of either system but had designated the initial sites [censored] for the FLR-9) as "prototype sites." Nonetheless, AFSS planned to contract for the follow-on sites before knowing how things were working out at the prototypes.

In 1960 NSA took its concerns about the [censored] system to DDR&E and convinced him to freeze money for out-year funding. At this point the [censored] prototype design was thoroughly reworked by NSA and AFSS, and many of the [censored] "frills" were eliminated before the [censored] system was built. So extensive were the changes that the system was retitled and became known as FLR-12. The prototype sites were retrofitted to the new FLR-12 design.

Security Service planned originally for [censored] FLR-9 sites: [censored] As a result of experience with the prototype systems ad NSA participation in the later R&D stages, the follow-on sites eliminated some of the features, such as automated DF flashing, that had made the earlier sites so expensive. [censored]

Alone among SCAs, ASA showed little initial interest in CDAAs. But by 1960 the command was looking more closely at the future of the FLR-9 and was attending joint-service planning meetings at NSA. Soon thereafter ASA decided that its newly planned intercept site at [censored] would be a CDAA based on the Air Force's FLR-9 design. They named the project [censored] and the new site [censored] [censored] was opened in 1965. When ASA began planning consolidation of its three largest [censored] sites [censored] into a single supersite, the FLR-9 was again the option selected.

By coming into the game late, ASA avoided the substantial development costs that AFSS had incurred. They simply bought "off-the-shelf" designs.

[censored]

The Airborne System

USAFSS remained the biggest user of airborne collection platforms. Called the Airborne Communications Reconaissance Program (ACRP), the program then consisted of a fleet of [censored] RC-130s. [censored]

In the late 1950s Security Service began working on a new program that would bring the RC-135 airframe into the ACRP program. It was developed from the KC-135 tanker used throughout SAC. Owing to the fuel capacity, the aircraft could routinely fly in excess of sixteen hours (the RC-130 was generally limited to an eight-hour mission) at altitudes topping 40,000 feet. USAFSS initially funded [censored] airframes, packing [censored] intercept positions into its innards. The flying partner was SAC, rather than a theater component command, and [censored] positions were converted to ELINT, to be manned by SAC electronic warfare officers. The program was called [censored] and it began flying out of Eielson AFB, Alaska, in early 1963. The RC-135 became the Cadillac of airborne collectors and eventually took over the entire job from the RC-130s.

In the 1960s SAC continued its own SIGINT airborne collection program. The SAC program [censored] initially used RB-47s with a limimted ELINT capability. Later the program [censored] converted to RC-135s with ELINT collection being the objective. COMINT positions on board (manned by USAFSS operators, and [censored] served for advisory warning.

As for the Navy, it continued to rely on its fleet of seven EC-121s, although a newer and better aircraft, the P3 Orion, was first delivered in 1962. It would eventually replace the slower 121s, whose vulnerability was convincingly demonstrated when the North Koreans shot onw down in 1969. The Navy program also retained its specific fleet-support role, and it was always regarded as something of a maverick by NSA because its tasking was entirely a Navy matter.

[censored]

The airborne reconnaissance program occupied the thoughts of President Kennedy in the early days of his administration. He had learned that Krushchev was planning to turn over the surviving RB-47 pilots (shot down in the White Sea in July 1960) as a kind of diplomatic peace offering to the incoming administration. But nothing had been done to avoid future incidents, and Kennedy was anxious to insure that Khrushchev not be able to again hold captured fliers as diplomatic pawns. The White House demanded action.

At the time, six advisory warning programs were in existence in various theaters, all with different criteria and warning methods. Some airborne programs (the Navy being the most prominent example) still flew without any warning capability at all. In 1961 the Pentagon took two actions to try to establish a program that would satisfy the White House. First, it created the Joint Reconnaissance Center, which would be responsible for coordinating and approving all peripheral reconnaissance worldwide. Second, it directed that a USAFSS advisory warning plan be modified and adopted worldwide.

The USAFSS program, which had originated in the Far East in the early 1950s, had received NSA blessing in 1961. The chief impediment to its adoption worldwide was lack of agreement on a standard communications system. The Pentagon finally settled on the SAC single sideband communications system, which was a worldwide HF system accessible to all parties. The Navy held out until 1962, but finally agreed to the standard plan, and the new advisory system, called White Wolf, was adopted the following year.

The shootdowns dropped to almost zero—the only notable exception was the 1969 shootdown of a Navy [censored] mission along the coast of Korea, an incident that precipitated the creation of NSOC. The danger of peripheral SIGINT airborne reconnaissance missions becoming diplomatic contests dropped almost out of sight, and a long-standing source of diplomatic embarrassment simply went away.

The TRS Program

The Soviet SIGINT trawler program has been of such long standing and so visible that it is often forgotten that the United States, too, at one time had its own SIGINT trawlers. It was called the Technical Research Ship (TRS) program.

[censored] was the beginning. NSA had no collection in [censored] 1956, and land-based sites being so difficult to acquire, it requested that NSG look into the possibility of building a floating collection site [censored] The Navy thought that the need could best be satisfied by taking some World War II Liberty ships (essentially, freight-haulers) out of mothballs and converting them to SIGINT use. The Bureau of Ships estimated that it could be done for about $4.5 million per ship and would require eleven to twelve months.

Defense budgets were slim in the late 1950s, and the first money was not in the budget until fiscal year 1960. The first ship selected, the USS *Oxford*, put to sea in 1961. She could do eleven knots [censored] Not much was happening [censored] at the time, so the *Oxford's* first cruise was set for [censored] later in the year. Instead, in November it was diverted to the [censored] Already, the TRS program, only one ship large, was showing how flexible it could be.

Enthusiasm over the potential of such floating collection sites led NSA to cut corners in order to get a second ship on line quickly. In early 1961 the Agency, beset with insistent collection requests by the DCI, found that the Military Sea Transport Service (MSTS) had a smaller, slower vessel that could be converted in fairly short order for only $2.5 million. Despite being smaller, the *Valdez* [censored]

There developed from this decision two sorts of TRSs. The first, of the *Oxford* class, was a wholly Navy-owned and manned ship, larger and faster by a few knots. The second, owned by the MSTS, was a coastal type vessel with a civilian crew to go along with the NSG people in the SIGINT compartment. The Navy ships were designated USS vessels, and by mid-decade the navy component of the TRS fleet consisted of five ships: the *Oxford, Georgetown, Jamestown, Belmont,* and *Liberty*. The smaller maritime vessels were designated USNS and consisted of only two ships: the *Valdez* and *Muller*. In 1968 a third was added to this list: USS *Pueblo*.

As for intercept positions the ships did not vary much. The *Oxford* class typically carried, when fully outfitted [censored] while the *Valdez* class had [censored] Where they differed was in speed and general seaworthiness. Clearly, the *Valdez* class represented a less capable, but cheaper, option.

One variant of this program was established specifically to monitor [censored] In late 1961 there arose an urgent requirement to monitor a [censored] An MSTS charter vessel, the *Robinson,* was hastily converted in only a few days and sailed from New York in January 1962. Its SIGINT manning was unique for a vessel—it was a combination of NSG and ASA operators in a partnership similar to the [censored] program [censored] at the time. In February the *Robinson* relieved the *Valdez,* which had been pressed into emergency service [censored]

In May 1963 there was another urgent collection requirement. The *Robinson* was headed for port after a long cruise, and so JCS arranged for NSA to use an [censored] USAFSS provided an equipped van and ASA furnished ELINT operators for the cruise. [censored] stayed on station through July when the *Robinson* returned. So began a collection progam that was to result in the [censored] vessel which became an important [censored] collector in later years.

The Cuban Missile Crisis

"We were eyeball to eyeball, and I think the other fellow just blinked."
—Dean Rusk, 28 October 1962

About the greatest crisis of the Cold War, three things can be said that concern cryptologists:

1. It was very definitely not precipitated by SIGINT warning. It was, and always has been, regarded as a crisis initiated by photographic intelligence, and there is nothing in the historical record to alter this statement. It marked the most significant failure of SIGINT to warn national leaders since World War II.

2. SIGINT played a very significant role in the unfolding crisis, a role which subsequent publicity and declassification of documents have not fully revealed.

3. It marked a watershed, like the 1956 event, in the way cryptologists do business.

The Cuban situation began on its own. Years of poverty and political repression on the island ended in a young revolutionary, Fidel Castro, marching into Havana in January of 1959. But hopes that it would develop into a pluralistic, liberal-style government were quickly dashed, as Castro put in place more and more institutional trappings of a solid Communist dictatorship. Experts eventually conceded that he had probably not been driven into the arms of the Communists by American hostility, but had planned it all along. Diplomatic contacts with the USSR had begun almost immediately, with the arrival of Soviet foreign minister Anastas Mikoyan in February of 1960 to open a Soviet trade exposition. Formal diplomatic ties were established in May.

The SIGINT Effort

[censored]

SIGINT also tracked burgeoning trade between Cuba and the Soviet Bloc. Although cargo manifests were rather vague, it was becoming clear through SIGINT (as with a variety of other intelligence sources) that much of the trade was military. In July 1960 the first substantial military aid arrived in Havana, and it included Czech small arms and ammunition and five MI-4 helicopters. Soon thereafter Cuban pilots were noted in SIGINT training in Czechslovakia, originally on piston-engine fighter trainers.

[censored]

By the Bay of Pigs failure of April 1961, NSA's level of effort had increased [censored] people but was still not a large-scale effort. At that point the Kennedy administration began directing a major concentration of intelligence assets against Cuba, and SIGINT resources increased rapidly. A year late [censored] people were involved, and by October 1962 [censored] were allocated to the Cuban problem.

The Berlin Wall

Although it began as a uniquely Caribbean phenomenon, Cuba quickly became a part of the international struggle between the U.S. and the Soviet Union. It came to be a pawn in the Cold War, a piece of Communist real estate located within the American sphere of geographic influence. On the other side was Berlin, Western-owned property clearly located within Khrushchev's zone of control. Khrushchev understood the relationship between the two territories and exploited them adroitly.

Berlin as a crisis first erupted in 1948 when Stalin cut off land access to the city. The resultant Berlin Airlift lasted for just over a year and marked a significant test of American resolve. It remained a potential sore spot, and in 1958 Khrushchev announced that in 1959, lacking an overall settlement of the Berlin problem, he would give control of East Berlin to East Germany. Although the Eisenhower administration managed to talk the problem nearly away, it was clearly only a temporary respite. In 1961 Khrushchev again increased pressure on the city, and it seemed that Berlin, rather than Cuba, would be the flashpoint for war.

At midnight on 11 or 12 August 1961, heavy trucks and troop carriers rumbled to the demarcation line between East and West Berlin. Construction crews jumped out and, under the guard of East German soldiers, began flattening a thin strip of land and stringing barbed wire in the middle of the zone. The Berlin Wall, soon to become a high concrete and cement block barrier, was begun.

Kennedy was vacationing in his yacht off Hyannis Port, and he was not notified until noon on the 13th. He was reportedly furious, and he summoned CIA director McCone to examine the intelligence failure. CIA, in sifting through everything that had been available, did find one significant bit of information, [censored] and the Watch Committee assessment had stated that this might be the first step in a plan to close the border. McCone could come up with with no other predictive information: the Berlin Wall was still regarded as an intelligence failure, despite the xistence of [censored]

Kennedy denounced the Berlin Wall, and American-Soviet relations worsened. On 1 September the Soviets ran their first nuclear test since 1958, breaking an informal moratorium that had been in place since the middle of Eisenhower's second term.

But the one bright spot was in comparative strategic strength. The so-called Missile Gap, which had loomed so large in 1960, had become a proven chimera. In September 1961 Lyman Lemnitzer, the chairman of the JCS, briefed Kennedy that the US enjoyed a 7 to 1 advantage in strategic nuclear delivery capability. The Soviets still had only ten to twenty-five operational ICBMs, and Kennedy could launch more than 1,000 delivery systems carrying 1,685 nuclear warheads, compared with 253 for the Soviets.

The Buildup to Crisis

In late 1961, as a result of the Kennedy administration's continuing concern with Cuba, the intelligence community was directed to increase its efforts against the island. NSA instituted a rapid buildup of the problem, almost certainly in response to this edict.

NSA's initial plan was forwarded to McNamara in November. It included manning additional positions [censored] bringing TRS resources into the picture, and instituting a new program for translating Cuban communications. This and an augmented plan presented in February of 1962 were pushed rapidly ahead.

Given the go-ahead, NSA assembled cryptologic resources with remarkable speed. The most significant addition was the *Oxford*. This first TRS had been launched in 1961, and the early plans were for an African coastal cruise. But NSA diverted the vessel to [censored] Cuba. [censored]

The *Oxford* conducted a [censored] off the coast of Cuba in December 1961, and it soon began forwarding [censored] intercept to NSA.

The linguist project, called [censored] (because it occupied quarters in the old Fort Meade Post hospital) employed native Spanish speakers in a semicleared status until their expedited clearances came through. [censored]

All of this was accompanied by explosive growth of NSA's Cuban shop. At the time the Cuban problem was worked in an organization called B1, whose chief, Juanita Moody, had arrived from the Soviet problem in July 1961. Moody would become a central figure in NSA's Cuban response effort, presiding over an effort that went from [censored] analysts in April 1961 to [censored] people on October 1962.

[censored]

The SIGINT Contribution

The first important SIGINT contribution to the Cuban problem was the reporting of Cuban commercial ties with the Soviet Bloc in mid-1961. [censored] Soviet communications revealed very large cargo shipments, but the cargo manifests were conspicuously missing, and this, in and of itself, was an indicator of sensitive military cargo. SIGINT, photography, and HUMINT all combined to form a very accurate mosaic of the increasingly close commercial and arms ties. The U.S. government was kept fully informed of these developments through intelligence sources.

The Cuban military problem also began to take on distinctive East Bloc overtones. Intercepts of Czechoslovak communications showed, as early as the fall of 1961, that Cuban pilots were training in East Bloc fighters. [censored] It came as no surprise, then, that photography began showing various MIG fighters and IL-28 bombers in Cuba in mid-1962.

In June 1961 the first ELINT intercepts from Cuba showed that they had Soviet radars, and before the end of the year there were both early warning and AAA fire control varieties. By May of 1962 Cuban air force communications reports [censored] Just a month later NSA reported intercept [censored] in Cuba, definitely indicating the presence of MIG fighters on the island. Soviet controllers were being heard on [censored] frequencies in heavily accented Spanish, instructing Cuban pilots and controllers in operational procedures.

The Soviets became progressively more active, both in numbers and in degree of control over the Cuban air defense system. USAFSS [censored] intercepted the first Cuban grid tracking on 9 October; it employed the classic grid system used by the Soviet air defense system. After 27 October (the date the U-2 piloted by Rudolph Anderson was shot down), the Soviets virtually took over the air defense system, and Cubans, who had been in the center of things from the beginning, moved to the sidelines.

[censored] In September NSA confirmed operation of a SPOON REST radar, often associated with the SA-2 system. At least one site appeared to be nearing operation.

The Crisis

The crisis itself did not begin with the 14 October U-2 flight that found the missile construction sites, nor with the 22 October presidential broadcast announcing that fact to the world. It had been building all summer, and each escalation of Soviet assistance to Cuba brought the White House more directly into the picture. The president was deeply concerned about Soviet military assistance, and the reports he was getting (primarily CIA HUMINT sources) indicated that the technicians accompanying the military equipment were really Soviet troops disguised as civilians.

The confirmed arrival and operation of SA-2s brought the crisis to a new level. CIA director McCone contended that the only purpose he could see for such a modern defensive armament would be to protect something of very high value, and that something, he felt, would be offensive missiles. So from August on, the intelligence community focused quite specifically on that possibility.

To try to head off a crisis, Khrushchev on 4 September dispatched Anatoly Dobrynin, the USSR's ambassador in Washington, to the Oval Office to reassure Kennedy that offensive missiles were not in Cuba. On the basis of this reassurance, Kennedy authorized Pierre Salinger, his press secretary, to announce the arrival of the SAMs, but to stress that they were not offensive in nature. But, Salinger added, the gravest consequences would result from the introduction of offensive missiles. On 11 September the Soviet newspaper Tass buttressed Krushchev's confidential communique on 4 September with a public announcement that the weapons in Cuba were defensive.

On 31 August politics intruded. Senator Kenneth Keating of New York, a Republican, reported in the Senate chamber that he had evidence that there were 1,200 Soviet troops in Cuba, and "concave metal structures supported by tubing" that appeared to be for rocket installation. To this day no one knows where Keating got his information, but CIA had at the time a profusion of unsubstantiated HUMINT reports dealing with such possibilities from their HUMINT interrogation center at Opa Locka, Florida.

The overt result of Keating's charges was political. The congressional elections were due in November, and Kennedy obviously wanted to hang on to as many Democratic seats as possible. He was keeping his hands off Cuba with Soviet assurances that no such missiles existed there, but the clamor for action on both sides of the congressional aisle was considerable. Any revelation that affected the equation could become politically explosive and might alter the balance of seats during the election. In this atmosphere the White House became extremely sensitive to any intelligence that might bear on offensive arms in Cuba.

Meanwhile, on 7 September Kennedy was confronted with a new crisis. Major General Marshall "Pat" Carter, the deputy DCI (who would, three years later, become DIRNSA) showed the president U-2 photographs of a surface-to-surface missile complex under construction at the Cuban coastal town of Banes. The installation was for a short-range naval coastal defense missile, and Ray Cline, CIA's director of intelligence, speculated that it might be for the purpose of insuring that the *Oxford* stay well offshore. But in view of Keating's recent charges, any surface-to-surface missile might be misconstrued as offensive (as Kennedy at first did), and such information had to be held very closely. So Kennedy directed that any indication, however tenuous, of the introduction of Soviet offensive forces in Cuba, be kept tightly compartmented. Huntington Sheldon, the assistant deputy secretary for intelligence (and CIA's top liaison on SIGINT matters) designed a compartmentation system, which was subsequently approved by USIB.

The result of this decision was an overly tight compertmentation at NSA. Information on the subject was extremely limited in distribution, and SIGINT reporting on the subject was to be specially flagged "Funnel." This was on top of an already rigid compartmentation system for U-2 photography, so secret that even Juanita Moody, the chief of B1, and her chief of staff, Harry Daniels, were not brought into the picture (although Moody was told about the impending 14 October overflight by William Wray of NSA the morning that it happened). During the crisis SIGINT analysts were forced to work in a vacuum. (However, some of the A Group analysts on the Soviet problem knew about the photography program).

SIGINT was coming up dry. Intensive effort by both B1 and A6 analysts revealed no indication whatsoever that the Soviets were bringing in offensive missiles. But unknown to NSA, CIA, or the White House, the materials for the missile sites were already in Cuba. Since the end of the Cold War, top Soviet officials have revealed that the decision to place offensive missiles in Cuba was taken in May, and this was followed immediately by the preparation and shipment of site construction materials. The first materials arrived in Cuba in mid-August, followed, the first week of September, by large pieces of equipment for the MRBM sites. The Soviets assessed that October would be the month of maximum vulnerability—site construction would be visible from the U-2, but the missiles would not be ready to fire, and Cuba would thus still be vulnerable to U.S. military action.

NSA did not have the information, but neither did anyone else. The matter of the Soviets introducing offensive missiles in Cuba was considered by the intelligence community no fewer than four times in the first nine months of 1962, and each time the assessment was negative. On 19 September, during the middle of the building crisis, National Intelligence Estimate 85-3-62 assessed that such activity "would be incompatible with Soviet practice to date and with Soviet policy as we presently estimate it. It would indicate a far greater willingness to increase the level of risk in U.S.-Soviet relations than the USSR has displayed thus far. . . ." John McCone was out of town at the time, but indicated that he did not concur with the assessment of his own estimates shop.

In early October CIA got photos of crates on board Soviet ships bound for Cuba, which probably contained IL-28 light bombers. These were clearly offensive (if a bit deficient in real offensive punch), and Kennedy directed that the information be suppressed. McCone "stated that this was extremely dangerous," but he was overruled. He and Kennedy then agreed that such information be disseminated to the principals of USIB (which included NSA's director, Lieutenant General Blake), who would in turn restrict it "to their personal offices.

Since the first of August, CIA had mounted seven U-2 flights over Cuba, and it would have flown more but for Secretary of State Dean Rusk's constant protests that overflights were diplomatically risky. (Those protests were given additional weight when, on 8 September, a U-2 on loan to the Chinese Nationalist government on a special CIA program was shot down over western China.) Those that were flown carefully skirted Cuba's periphery, darting briefly into Cuban airspace for a quick overhead photo. Much of the island was thus going unphotographed.

McCone persisted and finally got authorization for overflight of an area west of Havana which, according to some fairly coherent HUMINT reports, was undergoing construction for what looked like missiles. Bad weather forced several postponements, but the flight finally took off on 14 October and flew directly over the suspect area. The National Photographic Interpretation Center (NPIC) got a look at the pictures the afternoon of 15 October, and the CIA analyst, Victor DiRenzo, found what looked like six SS-4 MRBMs at a construction site. Looking at the photos on a light table in the Steuart Building in downtown Washington, NPIC's director, Arthur Lundahl, turned to the photo interpreters huddled around the light table and said, "We are sitting on the biggest story of our time."

It was seven days before the president would go before the world and announce the presence of the missiles and impose a naval quarantine around Cuba. Back at NSA, it was a frantic seven days. The Soviet and Cuban shops concentrated their resources on communications that bore on the problem. The A Group element that was working the Cuban air defense system (controlled by theSoviets) physically moved into B1 spaces to facilitate interworking. A and B issued independent product reports, but they also issued periodic combined wrap-ups in order to tell a coherent story. Upwards of [censored] A Group analysts and linguists joined the new combined outfit.

NSA needed a command center for the crisis. As it happened, A05, headed by Colonel [censored] USAF and NSA civilian [censored] had recently taken over a small room across the hall from the A Group front office to receive and display compartmented information like photography (TK). During the crisis this became the new command center. [censored] hurriedly outfitted the room with telephones and employed A Group analysts to begin publishing a new product, the [censored] a daily electrical report detailing the status of [censored] The director, Gordon Blake, kept the

Oxford on station throughout the crisis, and AFSS upped its ACRP flights off Cuba [censored] Blake directed that ASA get its SIGINTers [censored] as soon as possible and that the shipment of new equipments to the existing SCA intercept sites [censored] be speeded up.

The most valuable intercept came from [censored] There being no processing capability in the field, all this was shipped back to NSA; there the [censored] Throughout the crisis new and better equipments were added to the mix for faster and more complete processing.

The Soviets and Cubans had their own separate communications systems on the island. As the Soviets set up military operations (SAM sites, naval surface missile batteries, air defense networks, etc.), they maintained separate communications, supplying to NSA strong evidence that they were not integrated with the Cuban armed forces. NSA intercepted no cross-net communications. There must have been points at which th two sides talked—for instance, in Havana there was a command center housing both Soviets and Cubans, and it was served by communications of both countries. But there were no instances in which Soviets were intercepted talking to Cubans on the same communications facility. NSA concluded that the Soviets controlled all their own facilities, including their SAM and air defense systems, and this conclusion was accepted at the national level.

The [censored] intercepts provided a wealth of command and control information, and when married with photography, supplied a good picture of what was happening in Cuba. [censored]

Once Kennedy went on television (22 October), Soviet communications in Cuba lit up. A new air defense-associated net went on the air immediately. (This was what prompted the A Group processing element to physically move into space in B1.) [censored]

The crisis continued to deepen over the next two days. Soviet merchant ships steamed toward Havana, heedless to the looming catastrophe. But early on 23 October the Navy [censored] intercepted a broadcast from Moscow to all ships headed for Cuba to stand by for an extremely urgent cipher message. The message came throuh an hour later, and the intelligence community waited tensely for the reaction. [censored]

Late the same day NSG direction finding indicated that some of the Soviet merchant vessels heading for Cuba had stopped dead in the water, while others appeared to be turning around. At this point, according to CIA's Dino Brugioni, the Office of Naval Intelligence (ONI) felt that this information had to be verified before it was reported. John McCone was awakened in the middle of the night and informed that the Navy had unconfirmed information, but this was not passed to the White House or the secretary of defense until around noon of the following day, once ONI had "confirmed" the information. When he found out, McNamara was furious, and he subjected Admiral Anderson, the Chief of Naval Operations, to an abusive tirade. So many years have passed that it is impossible to determine why the Navy held up information that seemed critical to the president's decisions.

On 27 October the crisis reached its climax. At that point, Soviet ships had turned away from Cuba, a clear indicator that Khrushchev was wavering. But so far the two nations had not resolved anything. That day a U-2 piloted by Air Force major Rudolf Anderson (SAC had taken over U-2 flights from CIA on 12 October) was shot down, and NSA reported that an SA-2 from the area around the naval base at Banes had been responsible. Based on COMINT intercepts, the U.S. believed that the SA-2 sites were manned and controlled by Soviets. The shootdown of Anderson was a wide departure from the caution the Soviets had so far shown. Was it a major escalation?

The shootdown of Anderson precipitated an ultimatum. In a meeting with Dobrynin that day, Kennedy told him that the United States would attack the missile sites in Cuba by Tuesday morning unless there was firm evidence that the missile sites were being dismantled. That gave the Soviet Union only forty-eight hours to resolve the crisis before air attack, which would be followed by a fullscale invasion. Khrushchev caved in, and he sent a frantic telegram to Kennedy that very night promising to remove the missiles.

The Aftermath

NSA learned two years later that Cubans might have been in control of the site that fired at Anderson. In digging through the intercepts, NSA analyst [censored] pieced together some fragmentary SAM-associated [censored] communications from the Banes area, and discovered that the Soviets at one of the SAM sites were talking about a firefight at one of the other sites on 26 October possibly involving invading Cuban military forces. Soviet security forces at neighboring SAM sites had been summoned, and it appeared to [censored] that the fight was over by the morning of 27 October when Anderson's U-2 was shot down. But he could not be absolutely sure that the Soviets were back in control, and the possibility remained that Cubans had actually "pulled the trigger." This story created a sensation when, in 1987, investigative journalist Seymour Hersh published an account of the incident, as related to him from an unnamed analyst from an "intelligence agency." Internal evidence from Hersh's article points away from any NSA analyst as a source of the information. [censored]

The Hersh story appeared in conjunction with a series of conferences on the Cuban Missile Crisis, which came to include Soviet as well as American participants. During a conference in Havana in January 1992, a Soviet general claimed that the Soviet commander on the island, one Issa Pliyev, had been given authority to launch nuclear missiles if Cuba were attacked. If true, this would have brought the world much closer to nuclear war than anyone suspected at the time. Robert McNamara, who had been secretary of defense at the time, uncritically accepted the Soviets story, as did most other observers at the conference. The issue was sensationalized in the press.

It made good press, but it was not true. A search of declassified Soviet documents relating to the crisis showed that precisely contradictory orders were issued to Pliyev. (Even the general who made the statements, Anatoli Gribkov, eventually backed away from his earlier assertions.) All evidence now supports NSA's long-held contention that Soviet forces were subject to monolithic central control and that local commanders, particularly in situations involving nuclear weapons, were strictly controlled through central release authority similar to that in the U.S. armed forces.

The U-2 flights over Cuba had not been receiving advisory warning support from the cryptologic community. It occurred in that interregnum between the JCS decision to impose a standard, worldwide warning system and the actual publication and implementation of the resulting White Wolf plan. After the Anderson shootdown, Juanita Moody and Harry Daniels directed the hurried implementation of a warning system for the Caribbean area, and it was subsumed the next year under the White Wolf program. The shootdown undoubtedly increased pressure for the system that soon emerged.

One of NSA's major jobs during the crisis was watching Soviet force readiness. On 11 September the Soviets suddenly went into their highest readiness stage since the beginning of the Cold War. Although the units at highest readiness were generally defense-related, the alert included some unprecedented activity among offensive forces, too. [censored] The alert may have been called because Moscow suspected that Kennedy had found out about the missiles. [censored]

The 11 September alert was cancelled ten days later, but on 15 October Soviet forces went into a preliminary, perhaps precautionary, stage of alert. [censored] Once again, this readiness was likely due to Khrushchev's supposition that the U.S. had discovered a missile site. (He knew the White House would find out; the only question was when).

Following Kennedy's Oval Office speech on 22 October, Soviet forces again went into an extraordinarily high state of alert, similar to the September event. This time, however, with nuclear war threatening, defensive forces were primary. Offensive forces avoided assuming the highest readiness stage, as if to insure that Kennedy understood that the USSR would not launch first. Long-range aviation units continued normal training, although some precautionary steps were taken, such as insuring that the Arctic staging bases could be used. (Bombers were not deployed to the Arctic.) PVO (air defense) units went into the highest state of alert everobserved, as did Soviet tactical air forces.

Although Soviet offensive missiles and IL-28 bombers were pulled out of Cuba following the end of the crisis, a Soviet garrison force remaned. [censored] The air defense system which the Soviets had imported to the island was slowly turned over to the Cubans, although during the crisis the

Cubans had had no say whatever in its operation (which might in turn have led to the 26 October attack at Banes.) [censored] Cuba remained a bastion of Soviet influence and military force presence until the collapse of the Soviet Union itself.

As for the cryptologic community, temporary sites became permanent. [censored] It was a permanent diversion of SIGINT assets, contributing to the overall SIGINT force buildup during the decade.

SIGINT warning, so highly touted during the Eisenhower administration, failed in Cuba. Although SIGINT detected some of the troops and equipment as they were moving, the key elements of the movement that would have given the Kennedy administration decisive information about offensive capabilities did not come from SIGINT. In a 1963 post-mortem, the National Indications Center faulted the entire intelligence system for failure to detect those key elements. Soviet communications security was almost perfect.

Although SIGINT failed in its job to warn, it was an integral link in the chain of intelligence that supported the administration during the crucial days of decision-making. It gave the United States its most timely and specific information about the movement of troops and supplies to Cuba. It provided the only information about force command and control—absolutely critical in making decisions about Soviet involvement. It gave the White House the only timely information that it had about Soviet reaction and military force alert posture. And it provided most of the hard information about the air defense system, should the invasion (set for 30 October) proceed as planned.

The response to the crisis at NSA was more coherent and orderly than in 1956. The six-hour SIGINT wrapups, including both Soviet and Cuban activities, were the first such attempt by NSA. Agency reporting gave a better overall picture to customers than it had in earlier crises.

Within the intelligence community, the crisis precipitated a debate about NSA wrap-up reporting. Roundly criticized in the fall of 1962 for exceeding its supposed reporting charter, NSA defended itself in USIB circles by pointing out that no other agency was performing the essential function of summarizing developments as seen through SIGINT. In the months following the crisis an unrepentant NSA began putting out a daily wrap-up of SIGINT events, called the SIGINT Summary. The name was customarily abbreviated to the term "Sigsum," but many just called it the "Green Hornet" (because it was distributed under a cover of dark green paper). It survives today as the SIGINT Digest.

Chapter 9 The Post-Cuban Missile Crisis Reforms

"The CCP review process has, in the judgment of NSA officials, become a vehicle for various OSD and outside DoD elements to manipulate resources assigned to the Director, NSA and a forum for the encouragement of opponents of a centralized SIGINT structure. . . ." —NSA internal memorandum, 1967

Intelligence reform did not, of course, begin after the Cuban Missile Crisis—significant soul-searching had begun after the Bay of Pigs. But the events of 1962 made the matter more imminent. Kennedy demanded a responsive intelligence system to get him information when he needed it. The emphasis was on speed.

At CIA, the Bay of Pigs ended the intelligence careers of both DCI Allen Dulle and Richard Bissell, who had supervised the invasion attempt. Owing perhaps to the rather small SIGINT involvement, it did not end careers at NSA, but it definitely hastened the pace of centralization.

PFIAB, which had been told to get the intelligence house in order by a disturbed president, reported in June of 1962. Its SIGINT emphasis was on further centralization of the system under NSA. PFIAB wanted NSA to corral fugitive SIGINT efforts and to exercise strong central management over those it already headed. Noting that ELlNT centralization directed in the 1958 NSCID 6 had been a failure, it suggested ways that NSA could gain control of the process. It specifically wanted a National ELINT Plan with stern NSA management of resources under the plan.

In 1964 it reported on progress over the two-year period. The board was intensely unhappy about ELINT, which remained frustratingly decentralized. As for internal NSA management, PFIAB made several technical recommendations for strengthening the research and development process, for rationalizing SIGINT requirements, and for establishing an operations research discipline at NSA similar to that which existed at the DoD level. PFIAB especially wanted NSA to expand its influence over the cryptologic research and development process then performed by the services. The SIGINT effort was expensive, and PFIAB felt that a stronger NSA could reduce duplication and bring down the cost.

Studies of the cryptologic system in the 1960s by the PFIAB, by DOD-level committees, and by the Bureau of the Budget all came down heavily on a more centralized process. The emphasis was always on doing more with less, but in fact, cryptologic budgets increased steadily during the decade. What happened in practice was that NSA did more with more.

The National Security Agency was only too happy to oblige. Beginning in the early 1960s, NSA management began working on a plan to centralize cryptologic operations in the United States. Field operations would be reduced, especially at the theater level; SCA processing centers would be phased out; and, using the new digital data links sprouting up in the DoD communications system, data would be brought back to the States for processing. Using the PFIAB's recommendations as a hammer, NSA could achieve a degree of centralization dreamed of, but never achieved, in earlier years.

The Dilemma of Centralization

Whenever there is a major foreign policy crisis, the response of an administration is usually to tighten up. The Kennedy administration responded to the Bay of Pigs and the Cuban Missile Crisis with a series of actions which resulted in an ever-tighter centralization of the intelligence mechanism. The effect on the SIGINT system was to further centralize a process which had been on a course toward centralization ever since World War II.

But centralization meant the same both upwards and downwards. As NSA further strengthened its hold on the cryptologic system, McNamara got a firmer grip on the Defense Department, including NSA. The Agency had never had to answer in detail to anyone about its program—certainly Graves B. Erskine's miniscule staff in OSO could not police a system composed of tens of thousands of cryptologists working in over twenty countries, with a budget of hundreds of millions of dollars. But McNamara did away with OSO in 1961, and in its place he put the director of defense research and engineering (DDR&E), Dr. John Foster, in charge of cryptologic matters. (The post of DDR&E had been created by the Defense Reorganization Act of 1958, as a response to the Sputnik crisis.) Foster in turn delegated the job to his deputy, John Rubel. The reform measure was accomplished without even contacting Admiral Frost at NSA.

McNamara brought with him a team of "whiz kids" and a whole new management superstructure. Instead of dealing with just Graves B. Erskine or just John Foster or just John Rubel, Frost suddenly found himself talking to all sorts of subalterns like an assistant secretary for comptroller, an assistant secretary for management, an assistant secretary for international security affairs, ad infinitum. Each one felt he owned a piece of NSA. None was experienced in cryptology, and few managed to attain any appreciation for the arcane business of breaking and protecting codes: and the flip side of the coin was increasing OSD control over NSA. McNamara's staff bore down hard on the Agency's programs, placing each one under a microscope. As the CCP made its annual pilgrimage through the OSD machinery, increasing numbers of officials came to question cryptologic programs. NSA's existence became a constant battle to educate the legion of noncryptologists on McNamara's staff.

Cost control was a dramatic example of the dilemma that successive directors of NSA had always found themselves in. Late in the 1950s the Eisenhower administration introduced the concept of centralized cryptologic budgeting, in which the SCAs would send their annual budget recommendations to NSA, which would consolidate the inputs, add its own, and produce what came to be known as the CCP. This changed NSA's role from that of coordinator to centralizer. The SCAs were now beholden to

NSA for their very livelihood. When the Agency looked down its nose at a major SCA procurement, as it had with the Air F'orce's 466L program, that program was in trouble. The new COP was not fully implemented until fiscal year 1961, but in the two years in which it was being phased in it had already changed the landscape significantly.

McNamara arrived with a new cost management system called the Planning, Programming, and Budgeting System (PPBS). There were, under PPBS, nine major military programs. Cryptology, which began in Program Seven (general support), was soon switched to Program Three, general-purpose forces, where it stayed. Within each program there were five cost categories: R&D, procurement, personnel, O&M (operations and maintenance), and military construction. The cryptologic budget itself was in turn divided into fifty-six cost categories, called subelements. All cryptologic expenditures, both for NSA and the SCAs, had to fit into one of the fifty-six.

This new process gave NSA substantial power. The subelements were managed at NSA, and the SCA budgets had to be structured and submitted to the subelement managers for their review. After DDR&E and the secretary of defense approved it, the plan became the approved cryptologic force level. NSA could then change the mission of each cryptologic component, right down to the collection site, to fit the program. The entire process resembled a gigantic funnel, in which the most significant narrowing took place at NSA. It effectively ended SCA independence.

NSA's influence came to extend even to the equipment on collection positions. In a spate of technical control never before achieved, NSA wrote a document (TECHINS 1037) which dictated what equipment must be on each position to make it conform to the program. It was up to the SCAs to get their positions in line with the edict.

Most directly involved were Jack O'Gara, who managed the cryptologic program at the OSD level, and Dr. Eugene Fubini, who became deputy director for research and engineering under McNamara. O'Gara had a cryptologic background, but Fubini was a scientist. For the first time, the director's cryptologic staff found itself arguing individual line items at the OSD level with people who wanted to know why it was necessary to have more than one position targetted on the North Vietnamese Navy or why two positions at different locations remained targeted on the same case notation. NSA was forced to provide proprietary personnel and facilities information to GSA (General Services Administration) and the Bureau of the Budget, and the Agency frequently discovered that outside organizations were auditing NSA's operations without its concurrence; or even, in some cases, its knowledge. In 1967, Director Marshall Carter charged that ". . . the CCP review exercise became a means for various DoD elements to manipulate resources assigned to the Director, NSA . . . an undesirable feature of this Office of the Assistant Secretary of Defense for Administration (OASD[A]) review is that these officials are not SIGINT-oriented and they frequently make unrealistic comparisons of agency positions to those in the Defense Agencies." Each director in the 1960s, from Frost to Blake to Carter, claimed that McNamara's OSD staff was micromanaging NSA.

Everywhere NSA turned, there were new restrictions on its independence. Allen Dulles's replacement as DCI, John McCone, did not share Dulles's aversion for centralized management of intelligence resources. McCone moved aggressively to place the extensive Defense Department intelligence assets under CIA's general coordination. His newly created National Intelligence Programs Evaluation (NIPE) office was an early attempt to establish an intelligence community staff; it gave the DCI a way to inventory and evaluate all intelligence programs. He never achieved control of DoD intelligence budgets, but under him CIA was clearly headed in that direction.

A New Director

The hard-driving McCone was partly responsible for the relief of Admiral Frost as director. Frost was not a driver. His soft-spoken manner and laid-back style were not for McCone. He did not have Canine's "presence," and at USIB meetings would speak in a voice so low that he could scarcely be heard. One very senior NSA official who worked directly for Frost said, "He was a professional SIGINTer, he knew about SIGINT, but somehow or other he did not project that he was a knowledgeable, dynamic leader for the SIGINT effort." Nor did he fare well with McNamara and his staff. People like McNamara and Fubini expected clipped, precise answers to specific questions, and when they did not get them, began to look elsewhere for a director. Frost was relieved on 30 June 1962, more than a year before his term was up, was reduced in rank by one star, and was placed in charge of the Potomac River Naval Command. Such was the ignominy that Robert McNamara could visit on someone in his personal doghouse.

Frost's relief, Lieutenant General Gordon Blake (USAF), had shuttled between air operations (he was a command pilot) and communications assignments his entire career. His only intelligence assignment had been as commander of the Air Force Security Service from 1957 to 1959, but that had at least given him an introduction into the field which Canine, for one, had lacked. Blake, like Samford, was exceptionally good at personal relations and was very highly regarded in Washington. He had been in the job only three months when Cuba erupted, and he established high marks in the White House during the crisis. It has been said that no one disliked Gordon Blake, but even as smooth an operator as he still acknowledged difficulty getting along with McNamara's staff.

NSA's Community Relationships

USIB, which in 1958 had become preeminent in intelligence affairs with the disappearance of the Intelligence Advisory Committee, became honeycombed with committees in the 1960s. Instead of dealing solely with

COMINT, as had USCIB, it dealt with general intelligence matters, and it assigned SIGINT to the dual COMINT and ELINT committees. By the time Kennedy took office, USIB already had twenty-six committees, and most of the work was done there rather than in a committee of the whole.

In 1962 John McCone combined the COMINT and ELINT committees into a new SIGINT committee and chose John Samford to head the new panel. Samford was an ideal choice; he lent prestige to the committee—never before had such a senior person been chosen to head a USIB committee. Samford spent a lot of time trying to rationalize SIGINT requirements, and it was he who first proposed that COMINT requirements be related to CCP line items. His overhaul of the antiquated requirements system in place paved the way for a new system introduced in the mid-1960s, the Intelligence Guidance for COMINT Programing. Throughout this period the day-to-day influence of USIB became more pervasive, and it operated as yet another check on NSA's independent authority.

The dark days of the Canine-Dulles feud were over, but that by no means ended the problems between the two agencies. CIA still had intercept operations spread throughout the world, and by 1970 it was reputed to have[censored]

In 1966 Huntington Sheldon of CIA studied CIA SIGINT operations to determine the proper size and to allocate funds. He found that CIA had [censored] people doing SIGINT with a budget of [censored] The result, which ecame known as the Sausage Study, was the first to document the truly significant CIA stake in SIGINT.

In 1961 a new compctitor arose. The Defense Intelligence Agency (DIA) was created to centralize defense intelligence matters. DIA began life with a headquarters in the Pentagon but with subordinate offices scattered all over Washington. Arlington Hall's A and B buildings housed much of the effort.

The fragmented physical situation in which DIA found itself came to symbolize its participation in the intelligence business. DIA had stepped into a department whose intelligence was fragmented and decentralized and whose intelligence programs were managed under feudal baronies with great power and internal cohesion. None was more powerful than NSA. DIA began churning out intelligence reports and estimates in competition with the existing organizations. But ultimately the organization had to carve out its own unique turf, and one of the first areas it chose to invade was the private game preserve of SIGINT. In 1963 DIA proposed that it, rather than NSA, should run the COMINT dissemination system. The next year it wrote a draft directive which would have the director of DIA become the principal advisor to the secretary of defense "concerning the security, use, and dissemination of COMINT." DIA would take over the SSO system, including the communications apparatus. McNamara accepted the proposal, and the SSO systems of the SCAs were turned over to DIA in 1965.

The post-World War II SSO systems managed by the SCAs had long since become more administrative than substantive, and by the time DIA got hold of them, they were serving as little more than communications and security managers. In their place, NSA was in the process of establishing a network of SIGINT representatives. This network consisted of two components. The first was the official representation system, which NSA managed at Unified and Specified levels, and the SCAs represented SIGINT to the component commands. This system took some working out, and resulted, especially in the early (post- 1958) years, in turf battles between the SCAs and NSA.

The second type of organization was the CSG. This was where the interpretive function was performed, and it closely resembled the functions performed by the World War II SSO network, minus most of its dissemination control (i.e., housekeeping) features.

DIA's demarche into the SSO field accelerated the creation of CSOs. The first CSO, called NSAEUR/ISS, had been around since the late 1950s, and it served as a model for others. In 1964 Brigadier General John Morrison, NSA's representative in Hawaii, heard about NSAEUR/ISS and journeyed to Paris to see how it worked. He liked what he saw and created what he called the NSAPAC NOG (NSA Pacific Operations Group). The idea of having CSGs spread quickly and was incorporated into JCS Memo 506-67, which became the bible for SIGINT support to military organizations. By 1974 there were eight CSGs, with two additional CSGs in the process of being formed.

CSGs became effective because of the access they had to the SIGINT system. To a great extent they depended on the growing network of Opscomms to get them that access. Every CSG began life with an Opscomm circuit to NSA. With it, the CSG could get quick and accurate information to the supported commander.

ELINT (Again)

While COMINT was coming under increasingly centralized control, ELINT was still fragmented. A study commissioned by McNamara in 1961 concluded that little real control over ELINT had been instituted in the three years since NSA had been given the charter. Theater commanders were still running their own ELINT operations, and in many cases they were proliferating processing centers without coordination or control. Their Third Party ELINT relationships continued unabated, and their collection assets were pumping low-quality and often inaccurate ELINT into the processing system, unaffected by any sort of quality control.

The study group concluded that there should be a strict apportioning of ELINT assets between the U&S commands and NSA, and that the Agency should institute stringent technical controls over all DoD assets. NSA should take control of all Third Party ELINT arrangements. Theater-level ELINT processing centers should not be established willy-nilly, but should conform to some overall plan. That plan should be coordinated by NSA, which would accept inputs from the military commands and crank out the final product. It would be called the National ELINT Plan (NEP). But the bottom line was that it would have no teeth. Coordination, not direction, would be the modus operandi.

A National ELINT Plan finally emerged in 1966, after several years of bureaucratic struggle and false starts. It marked the first real attempt to organize and control ELINT, but since it was not directive, it had only a minimal impact on the actual course of DoD ELINT.

Meanwhile, NSA and DIA tried to negotiate a system of ELINT tasking which would conform to DIA's new charter to centralize all DoD intelligence requirements. They worked out a complex system in which all parties to the National ELINT Plan (including CIA) would forward ELINT requirements to DIA for registry. NSA would maintain a complete list of all ELINT collection assets (including those that the Agency did not control) and would assess the capability of relevant assets to satisfy each requirement (called a SICR, Specific Intelligence Collection Requirement). NSA would then return the requirement to DIA, which would task the appropriate U&S command, while NSA would task assets under its own control.

Attempts to rationalize theater-level ELINT processing centers were only semi-successful. Proposals for NSA control were opposed by theater commanders and thus went unimplemented. The best NSA could achieve was to appoint a technical assistant to the director of the theater processing center [censored]

Successive directors felt that the job of managing ELINT was simply too much for NSA. General Blake felt that "a National ELINT Plan [was] neither desirable nor practical." Given the job of writing the plan, General Carter found that NSA was not set up internally to manage such an effort, and he had to create an ad hoc group, which he called Dagger, to write it. Looking back in later years, Carter called the NEP "unworkable." Difficult relationships with the Unified and Specified commands, disputes over ownership with DIA and CIA, and internal dissension over how the effort should be organized within NSA all contributed to the sense of frustration.

News from the ELINT front continued to be gloomy throughout the decade. In 1964 PFIAB launched a rocket at theater ELINT centers: "Meanwhile new centers from ELINT analysis are being established without coordination, terms of reference, or technical guidance from our proven competency in established programs." CIA, which had retained a tenacious hold on telemetry, opened a new telemetry center called FMSAC (pronounced "Foomsack": Foreign Missile and Space Analysis Center), which became, as was intended, a direct competitor with NSA's efforts. ELINT requirements were in a chaotic state, and local commanders were constantly confusing the situation with overlapping demands.

The 1968 Eaton Committee found that the NEP was a marginally effective document negotiated to compromise among various competing power centers. NSA had never been given tasking authority over many ELINT collectors—SAC airborne assets came immediately to mind. There was no central budget review process for ELINT and no way to deconflict competing assets. There was no effective quality control, resulting in parametric garbage cluttering disparate databases managed by widely separate organizations that did not talk to each other. Despite the 1961 recommendation that NSA should take over Third Party ELINT, nothing of the kind had taken place, and those relationships were still being managed by CIA and the theater-level component commands, as well as by NSA. No wonder NSA directors were so ambivalent about the task which NSA had shouldered for ten years running.

DEFSMAC

Occasionally the demands of centralization resulted in measurable steps forward, relatively unaffected by bureaucratic rivalries. The 1964 creation of the Defense Special Missile and Astronautics Center (DEFSMAC) was such a moment.

[censored]

A41 had two round-the-clock operations centers. The A41 Operations Center (Opconcen), located next to the A41 offices on the third floor of the operations building, was the nerve center. It had Opscomms to the primary warning sites and had established a tip-off system so that warning information [censored] could be flashed back to A41. That organization, in turn, alerted [censored] that were standing by. By 1962 the Opconcen had six opscomms to collection sites. It was further linked by Opscomms to customers. [censored] and the Washington-area organizations.

Downstairs in the computer complex was the Sigtrack center. [censored] The Sigtrack center was in close touch with the Opconcen, but, although there were plans to consolidate the effort, they were still physically separate.

When the consolidated facility, the Space and Missile Analysis Center (SMAC), was created in January 1963, it had Opscomms to sixteen facilities, plus the customers. Several different organizations had mounted twenty-four-hour operations, but SMAC and NORAD were far and away the major players—others simply fed off the information generated through the air defense and SIGINT warning systems.

The disorganization in the missile warning business led, in 1963, to a full DoD-level review. The team surveyed the entire problem, talked with every organization involved, and made field trips to warning facilities like SMAC and NORAD (in Cheyenne Mountain, outside Colorado Springs), They found that NSA had the only coherent, centralized program, and, at the suggestion of A4, they took SMAC as the organizational model for a new, combined facilty.

It would be called DEFSMAC, would be located at NSA, and would be jointly staffed by NSA and DIA people. The chief and deputy chief would be selected jointly by DIRNSA and the director of DIA. Because most inputs were SIGINT-based, NSA possessed virtually the sum total of technical expertise. DIA was charged with integration, reviews, and nontechnical analysis of findings. DEFSMAC would have the same inputs, through the same Opscomm net, that SMAC had had. But because its official charter was established at the Department of Defense level, it carried with it far more authority than had SMAC. DEFSMAC had tasking and technical control of all DoD intelligence collection activities directed against foreign missile and space activities. It provided technical support, including tip-offs, to all DoD missile and space intelligence collection activities. The only exception to its virtual blanket authority was that it could not launch airborne collection platforms on its own—that required a JCS go-ahead.

At its creation in 1964, DEFSMAC had [censored] NSA billets, to twenty-three for DIA. Its first director (and all thereafter) was an NSA official, Charles Tevis, while the deputy was a DIA official.

The Advent of the Command Center

Present-day NSOC and the plethora of round-the-clock watch operations that Agency workers know evolved slowly over a long period of time. The key date in its evolution was October 1962—the Cuban Missile Crisis. But the development began years before that.

AFSA had had a shift operation, established originally to monitor developments [censored] during the Korean War. It was part of AFSA-25, the organization that dealt with customers, and, within that organization, the publications and distribution branch. Manned originally by a staff of two junior officers and several analysts and enlisted communicators per shift, it scanned outgoing messages for release and maintained a liaison group to answer requests for information. After NSA was created, it became known as the Prod Watch Office, or PWO, but proposals to give it executive powers were scotched whenever they came up. In 1954 it became responsible for the director's daily intelligence briefing, and when the Critic program was created in 1958, the PWO insured that all Critics had the correct external and internal addressees. But when real horsepower was needed, the PWO called in day workers.

The COMSEC organization also had a watch office, charged specifically with responding to reports of compromise. Although small, it did a good job of quick response, and over the years kept potential compromises from becoming major hemorrhages.

Through a succession of reorganizations, the PWO became the PIWO (PROD Intelligence Watch Office), and more civilians were added. In 1962, the last year of its life, the PIWO consisted of [censored] people, ten of whom were civilians. But its functions still remained procedural rather than substantive. NSA's method of handling round-the-clock responsibilities bespoke the way that the organization viewed itself. NSA thought of itself as a long-term reporting shop, a concept which had become completely outmoded by the Soviet strategic threat [censored]

The vision of NSA as Sleepy Hollow ended abruptly in October 1962. The new director, Gordon Blake, realized that he did not have a command post, and his assistant director for operations, Major General John Davis, created one during the middle of the crisis. The chief of the new shift operation was known as the SNOO (Senior NSA Operations Officer, and he had [censored] analysts on duty. The original command post was located close to the PIWO and the communications center and had telephone connectivity to both.

After the dust settled, General Davis decided that he could not continue to operate on an ad hoc basis, and early in 1963 the Command Center was made permanent. With eight bays of space and $50,000, the reporting staff was headed by [censored] and [censored] fashioned a command post look-alike, with situation maps, multicolored telephones, and pony circuits from the communications center. (This came to include a KY-3, which permitted secure voice contact with the White House, CIA, DIA, and several other Washington consumers.) The PIWO was wiped out and the bodies transferred to the Command Center.

Although the Command Center became a nerve center of sorts, it never became what its creators had hoped. To begin with, the SNOO did not represent the director; he only represented the assistant director for production. Executive decisions above Production required that other deputy directors be called in. Second, even within PROD the Command Center was to some degree emasculated. This owed to the refusal of the analytic groups to contribute skilled analysts. The Command Center wound up with a personnel cadre, but the real power remained within the analytic groups themselves, each of which, over a period of years, established various watch operations. These "puddles" (as they were called] tended to arise during crises and simply continue. Thus it was that the B Watch Office was set up in 1965, when Vietnam heated up, and the B1 Watch was established as a result of the *Pueblo* capture. G Group established no permanent watch but continued to call analysts to duty during crises.

Regulations governing the Command Center carefully circumscribed the authorities of the SNOO who, after all, was only a grade 13 or 14. He monitored the Critic program, and could change distribution, but he could not change the text or issue a new report. He could not call a SIGINT readiness, did not have direct connectivity to field sites, and could not modify field site collection instructions. A and B Groups had "coordinators" in the Command Center, but whenever a problem arose, either referred the matter to one of the "puddles" or called someone in.

Centralization of Theater Processing

As the Vietnam War heated up, Robert McNamara began looking for money. He put considerable pressure on all DoD elements to become more efficient. In the early 1960s Gordon Blake was under considerable pressure from McNamara's staff. According to them, the SIGINT system was too big, too costly, too spread-out, and inefficiently organized. If McNamara needed money, they thought they could sweat some of it out of the SIGINT budget.

And anyway, they believed that centralization was inherently good as well as cost-effective. McNamara's point man in this effort was Dr. Eugene Fubini.

In 1964 Blake was directed to take a close look at theater processing. Fubini believed that there were too many theater processing nodes, [censored] and so NSA turned its attention to the [censored] theater. Studies in that year turned up quite a complex of centers [censored]

The Air Force had centralized SIGINT processing [censored] which by 1964 had become a complex of over [censored] people, IBM 1401 processors, and Opscomm connectivity [censored] The reporting operation alone was the busiest and largest reporting center ever put together up to that time. It was the hub for timely reporting [censored] an absolutely irreplaceable asset. [censored]

The Army operation [censored] had a very different focus. Its COMINT Processing Center (CPC) concentrated on preliminary processing of the increasing volumes of [censored] ASA refused to join [censored] and it maintained its own development effort in [censored]

[censored]

In July 1964, under continuing pressure from Fubini, Blake named Benson Buffham to chair an ad hoc committee to produce an austere SIGINT posture [censored] This group wrestled with the problem of the competing power centers [censored] and it finally came down on the side of [censored] But the committee went much further. It decided that ultimately much of what was going on [censored] would be done at Fort Meade.

The interim [censored] architecture would close [censored] and create two separate but closely related organizations [censored] The first, [censored] would take over theater processing operations [censored] The second, called [censored] would take over the timely reporting functions then exercised at [censored] Manning for the new facilities would come directly from the hides of ASA and AFSS, with a significant NSA admixture.

The panel was looking at far more than reorganizing theater assets, however. It began to consider a longer-range plan of closing theater operations and moving them to Fort Meade. NSA would establish a high speed (2400 baud, high speed for the mid-60s) data link from [censored] to Fort Meade [censored] was clearly a way station on a much longer journey.

The plan to close theater functions also included [censored] NSA decided to establish a world-wide printer steering group at Fort Meade. Called the COC (Collection Operations Center) it functioned muchlike [censored] interacting with field sites through a network of Opscomms. When opened officially in 1969, COC began using a new reporting system, called [censored] The basis of [censored] reporting was a short, preformatted report resembling a [censored] The reports were formatted for computer input and formed a database on all printer intercept worldwide. COC adjusted collection of [censored] inks based on the [censored] reporting and daily contact with cryptanalysts in A5, the office of [censored] It was not officially phased out until 1993.

Back in A Group, the planning committee came up with two schemes: Plan A and Plan B. Plan A assumed that processing functions would be moved to Fort Meade but that basic timely reporting would remain in the theater, at [censored] and [censored] Plan B assumed that these centers would eventually be closed and the functions moved to Fort Meade. General Carter favored Plan A, but his staff favored Plan B. Ultimately, the reluctant director was persuaded to sign Plan B, and the residual organizations in [censored] were doomed.

The adoption of Plan B required drastic changes in A3, the analytic organization responsible for the Soviet problem. A3 was basically a term reporting organization, but under the new scheme it would have to split into two camps, the term shop (A7, material older than seventy-two hours) and the current shop (A8, material not yet seventy-two hours old). The current shop, A8, would have to pick up responsibility for a number of daily summary reports produced [censored] More significant, it would have to create a shift effort to monitor timely reports like spot reports and Critics. It would interact closely with the [censored] which would retain some of [censored] reporting functions. The [censored] would be an emasculated [censored] retaining substantial authority for coordinating timely reporting on U.S. reconnaissance flights, but without the reporting or collection management authority that [censored] had exercised. A3 would pick up some [censored] billets in order to mount the required reporting effort.

CSOC

The A7/A8 split was the genesis of a new organization, called the Current SIGINT Operations Center. CSOC, as it was usually referred to, was formed by Walter Deeley of A05 from a group of A Group analysts and reporters who had been in proximity to, but not an integral part of, the Command Center. Deeley believed that, by integrating processing computers with communications systems, he could create an analytic and reporting center in which all activity was electronic. He later popularized this as his "paperless environment", a concept that was adopted when NSOC was created.

Deeley planned to reterminate the [censored] reports from [censored] to CSOC but instead of the reports being dumped onto a Teletype Corporation printer, they would appear on computer screens, where analysts could manipulate them. A communications interface computer would be required to receive the incoming [censored] reports, sort them according to type of activity, and route the sorted reports to analysts who were trained to watch different types of activity. CSOC would have the same reporting and collection management authorities that [censored] had. Deeley wanted a new name for the tip-off reports, and he came up with the name KLIEGLIGHT, which would be used into the 1990s. The computer Deeley selected was a Univac product, which was the best machine at the time for communications interface. The TIDE software system, which managed the KLIEGLIGHT database and routed reports throughout CSOC, was written for the Univac computer. A8 was established officially in June of 1961.

CSOC guaranteed that [censored] would die. It was put into operation a year prior to [censored] and by the time [censored] was ready to assume reporting responsibilities, CSOC had already proved it could do them. Real authority thus bypassed [censored] and went directly back to Fort Meade.

Moreover, CSOC proved the feasibility of a global SIGINT view. Now there was a reporting center that had inputs from all SIGINT sources on the Soviet problem. Army, Navy, and Air Force data flowed into the new center, and CSOC could see the interrelationships between activities in differing Soviet military forces and theaters of operation. The idea that SIGINT might get a handle on Soviet force posture by such an across-the-board look took hold, and A8 analysts William Black, [censored] and others begun looking at activity level indicators from various areas of the [censored] problem.

Just as [censored] was in its death throes, [censored] was under threat. The high-speed data link, called the DLT-5, permitted SIGINT to flow back to Fort Meade at the then-incredible rate of 2400 bauds per second. Cecil Phillips, who was placed in charge of processing operations in C5, was told to try to duplicate, as near as possible, the operations then existing at [censored] Phillips even used the same computer, an IBM 1401, to receive the data and format them for follow-on processing on the IBM 7010, which was an upgraded version of the 1410 used at [censored] Originally he used the same software package in use [censored] As long as the DLT-5 was operating, [censored] was superfluous. NSA had succeeded in duplicating the field processing center.

SIGINT at the White House

All presidents since Pearl Harbor had a mechanism for timely notification of crises. In the 1950s intelligence warning was funneled through CIA, which was responsible for alerting the president through his military advisor. The Army ran the White House communications center, which in turn served the military advisor. This placed CIA in the position of deciding what the president saw and when he saw it. By the time of Kennedy's inauguration, the alerting mechanism in the White House had come to be called the White House Situation Room. It was basically a communications handler—no substantive analysis was performed in the "Sit Room."

Following the Bay of Pigs incident, Kennedy decided to put some teeth into the Situation Room [censored] CIA was brought in to create a truly round-the-clock intelligence center. The Situation Room began taking a more active hand in crisis alerting and in keeping the president informed. It was basically an arm of the CIA, however.

All SIGINT product of interest to the president and the National Security Council staff passed through CIA, which forwarded key items after it had taken off the NSA header. SIGINT reports arrived in fairly significant volumes, but NSA was not directly involved. It produced only "information," not "intelligence." Some of the products got to the White House because they related to impending or ongoing crises. Other reports were forwarded simply because the intercepted messages mentioned political figures by name.

During the Cuban Missile Crisis, the "White House" (presumably National Security Advisor McGeorge Bundy) was unhappy with the delay experienced in getting certain SIGINT reports. The incident involving McNamara and the DF of Soviet merchant ships was emblematic of the problem. But CIA remained the chokepoint as long as Kennedy lived.

Things began changing under President Johnson. In late 1965, [censored] began meeting with Deputy Director Louis Tordella and Chief of Policy John Connelly, along with representatives from CIA and State. The president wanted direct distribution of certain SIGINT, and he wanted it immediately. CIA and State protested that NSA did not produce "intelligence" and that it should not send things directly to the White House. [censored] was adamant—they could protest all they wanted, but the president had already decided. A direct circuit to NSA was already being installed, and [censored] and Tordella had developed a procedure to courier especially sensitive material to the Situation Room.

The White House wanted direct distribution for Critics. Moreover, it wanted to see product reports that quoted or named White House people, including the president, his key advisors, and cabinet secretatries. (This was the material that Tordella was having couriered to the White House.) The White House concern may have been spurred by SIGINT product reports detailing [censored] Placing the White House on direct distribution for these reports, and cutting off other addresses from normal distribution, [censored]

It is difficult to know what John Kennedy thought about SIGINT, if he ever thought about it at all. His national security advisor McGeorge Bundy seems to have used it as part of a larger intelligence mosaic, and he acceded to the CIA method of organizing intelligence, in that it came to him only after it had been massaged. Bundy appeared to violate this scheme near the end of his stay at the White House by demanding direct infusion of SIGINT. This was partly to keep a better handle on late-breaking events, but it was also to [censored]

But Kennedy was assassinated in November of 1963, and the new president, Lyndon Johnson, replaced Bundy with Walter Rostow in 1966. Rostow had worked in England during World War II to plan the strategic bombing campaign. He learned not to accept filtered intelligence and worked directly with SIGINT every day.

Lyndon Johnson was the most avid consumer of intelligence ever to occupy the White House. He consumed it voraciously, chewing through stupendous piles of intelligence reports every day. Johnson did not like to be briefed—as former DCI Richard Helms once said, "President Johnson, when he had something on his mind, simply wasn't listening to what one had to say to him. . . . But when he read he read carefully, and he hoisted aboard what he read." Johnson insisted on direct information. He had a great variety of direct information feeds, including a three-screen television set for all three networks, tickers, and other devices to stay on top of things.

In series of crises (and his administration seemed to be one long series of crises) he would sidle down to the Sit Room and pore through the intelligence reports. If a key military operation was about to be launched in Vietnam, he might stay nearly all night, so that he could get the latest information, or he might come in early the next morning to read the latest news. He resembled no one so much as Abraham Lincoln in the telegraph office waiting for the news of battle to come off the wire. Even when he vanished to the Oval Office during the day, he would often call the Sit Room to receive updates, and he knew many of the officers by their first names. He was totally absorbed in military operations and intelligence reports.

Under Rostow, the trickle of direct SIGINT reporting into the Sit Room widened to a freshet, then a flood. SIGINT reporting on Vietnam was highly regarded in the White House. Sometimes it was used to cross-check other sources, other times as a stand-alone source. During the secret negotiations with the North (which occurred more or less continuously through three adminstrations) SIGINT was a highly prized source of information [censored]

The main target remained the Soviet Union, [censored] The Agency processed the material ahead of everything else and sent it dirctly to the White House. Rostow got the information raw, analyzed some of the data himself or employed members of his staff to do it, and sent the conclusions to the president. [censored]

Having an avid SIGINT consumer in the White House had its drawbacks. David McManis, who replaced Edward Fitzgerald as the NSA representative to the Sit Room, remembers having to explain the nuances of SIGINT reporting to White House staffers all up and down the line. During the height of the war in Vietnam, the National Security Council staff wanted an accurate count of North Vietnamese infiltration into the South, and they buried McManis under a snowstorm of questions about infiltration groups appearing in SIGINT (the only high-validity source on infiltration). To some, he had to explain that there was no turnstile for infiltration groups heading south, but this just got into SIGINT intricacies that the questioners were not prepared to handle. McManis summoned battalions of NSA briefers to the White House to explain trail group accountability in SIGINT.

The White House insistence on raw, unevaluated SIGINT created other problems. Johnson wanted to be kept in touch with every crisis, and he once told [censored] that he wanted to be called on every Critic, not realizing how many there were. SIGINT Critics on [censored] were fairly commonplace, and [censored] wisely decided not to call the president on them, lacking other indicators.

Most of the SIGINT reports flooding into the Situation Room were relatively low-level reports and translations, with very little analysis and even fewer assessments. Assessing things was still not NSA's job. This situation kept the volume of reports up, but there was little analytic glue to fit the disparate pieces together. It was critical that someone be available to interpret and assess the SIGINT. Thus McManis found himself spending long hours in the White House. Moreover, NSA began contributing other Situation Room staff members on a permanent basis, the better to minimize the misuse of SIGINT. (The arrangement continues to this day.)

Very few people outside NSA liked the new, elevated status that SIGINT was getting. But it was a logical progression of events. Presidents wanted to know, and to know quickly. They tended to be impatient with bureaucracy, and when they found a spigot of critical warning information, they turned it on, no matter whose feelings got bruised. When Nixon entered the White House, his Situation Room chief was an NSA official, and a major portion of the inputs to the White House was coming from the SIGINT system. Whatever anyone else in government might think of SIGINT, the White House was known to view it as the fastest and the most unimpeachable source. Through this reputation, the position of NSA grew, until it was virtually coequal with CIA and had for exceeded the other intelligence assets of the Defense Department.

Carter Takes Command

Gordon Blake retired in 1965. He was replaced by Marshall Sylvester Carter, the deputy director of CIA, on 1 June 1966. Carter, a crusty Army general in the mold of Ralph Canine, presided over the stormiest period of NSA's history.

"Pat" Carter (the name he went by was bequeathed him by a Japanese maid when the Carter family lived in Hawaii) was from a military family, his father rising to the rank of brigadier general. As a result, his growing up was itinerant, and he set his sights on a military career early. He took a traditional path up the chain, graduating from West Point in 1931 and going into the artillery branch (specializing in defensive artillery). During World War II Carter caught General Marshall's eye, and from then on he was a George Marshall protege, serving Marshall in various executive capacities when he was chairman of the JCS, representing Truman in China, and secretary of state. After Marshall retired, Carter held a variety of positions in combat units and also served a tour as chief of staff of NORAD.

In his NORAD job he had a fairly detailed involvement with various intelligence sources, including SIGINT, but had never had a job directly in intelligence until 1962, when President Kennedy nominated him to become deputy DCI. Carter came upon the position in the wake of the Bay of Pigs fiasco. There had been quite a shakeup at CIA, and one of those to lose his job was Air Force general C. P. Cabell, the deputy director. Carter survived his trial by fire, the Cuban Missile Crisis, in good shape, and was generally regarded to have had a successful tour at CIA.

He provided a human face to the Directorate, which was headed by the austere and remote John McCone. He became known as an inveterate prankster and became popular with the work force while handling day-to-day business for McCone, whose ties were to the Kennedy family rather than to the bureaucracy. One "Pat Carter story" that CIA employees loved to tell was about the door between McCone's office and Carter's. McCone was not close to anyone at CIA, and, as if to make the point, one day he had the door between his office and Carter's walled over. Carter placed a false hand at the edge of the new wall, as if a door had shut on it, and enjoyed a good laugh at McCone's expense. John McCone was apparently not even aware of the hand.

Marshall Carter became DIRNSA almost by accident. When McCone left CIA in 1965, President Johnson appointed Admiral Raborn to replace him. By law, CIA could not be headed by two military officers, so Carter was out of a job. He put his problem to General Johnson, the Army chief of staff. A few days later he got a call from the deputy secretary of defense, Cyrus Vance. Gordon Blake had decided to retire, and Vance wanted to know if Carter wanted the job. It took him only a few seconds to make the decision. He had been a deputy or chief of staff virtually his entire career—as DIRNSA, he would finally run his own show.

Carter knew a lot about NSA and had a high regard for the Agency. But he felt that NSA needed to be more forceful about its conclusions, more aggressive about carving out a place for itself at the intelligence table. He made it his business to make NSA more aggressive. The days of reticence and retirement under Samford, Frost, and Blake were over. Carter fell on a startled national defense community like a bobcat on the back of a moose.

He began with a symbolic assertion of NSA's independence. He directed that the NSA seal, which had its Defense Department affiliation prominently displayed, be changed to a new seal which referred only to the United States of America. Carter seriously considered the possibility of requesting that NSA be removed from the Defense Department and set up as an independent executive agency along the lines of CIA. He often referred to the fact that NSA was for him, as it had been for all previous directors, a final stop in a long military career. He was not up for promotion, and he did not care whose toes he stepped on.

Even when he was deputy DCI, Carter did not get along with Eugene Fubini. He made his acceptance of the NSA job conditional on an assertion from Vance (which he got) that he would report directly to Vance, rather than through Fubini at DDR&E. He did not hide his disdain for the brilliant and opinionated Fubini, once calling him "a radar technician beyond his competence." But since DDR&E continued to exercise a major influence over NSA's programs, it did not matter much whether Fubini was in Carter's direct line of supervision or not. The two battled almost daily until Carter's retirement in 1969, to the ultimate detriment of NSA's programs.

Carter's abysmal relationship with Fubini and the OSD staff was more than matched by his almost disastrous relations with the armed services. The assertive Carter was ever on the lookout for service encroachments on NSA's prerogatives, and he found them daily. The military were, he felt, constantly building up their intelligence staffs, adding more analytic capability than they needed, especially in the SIGINT field, and doing more interpretation of NSA's information than they were qualified to do (especially at DIA). He felt that they were engaged in a continuing effort to redefine SIGINT as "electronic warfare," the better to take it out of codeword channels and build up their own tactical SIGINT capabilities outside of DIRNSA control.

The services, for their part, complained about perceived lack of NSA response to their needs in Vietnam. SIGINT was too compartmented, NSA refused to clear field commanders for the information they so badly needed, NSA was overprotective of its resources and too quick to fence off new capabilities under codewords and compartments. A battle royal erupted during Carter's regime over the handling of SIGINT and the provision of SIGINT support in Southeast Asia. It poisoned the atmosphere and led to a confrontational relationship between NSA and the military it was sworn to support. When Carter retired in 1969, NSA's relationship with the JCS was at an all-time low. Successive directors were so instructed by the experience that they never allowed relations to return to that level.

To the SIGINT community, however, Carter was a champion. Like Canine, he elevated the status and pay scale of the work force, obtaining more supergrade billets and a generally higher average grade. Displaying his vaunted independence of action, he went directly to Senator Sam Ervin to get the billets and to make sure that the new billet allocation was designated specifically for NSA so that OSD could not co-opt some of them (as he suspected Deputy Secretary of Defense Cyrus Vance of planning). After years of struggle at the OSD level, NSA under Carter got the authorization to begin a career cryptologic service, separate and apart from the systems of any other agency.

At the same time, Carter began the civilian intern program, starting with a small number of recent college graduates entering the NSA work force. In 1969 he extended it to the on-board population. He fended off proposals that NSA's cryptologic work force join a DIA-sponsored intelligence community career development program, carrying with it the clear implication that there should be transferability between the general intelligence field and cryptology.

Internally, Carter wanted a strong central staff, and he created an executive secretariat to manage his staff and its acyivities. This reflected his Army background and his experience as staff chief for General Marshall. He strengthened the training school by upgrading its staff to assistant directorhip and calling it the National Cryptologic School. Frank Rowlett was its first chief, bestowing a status and prestige which it had never had before. Carter was an Anglophile, and worked hard to maintain the strong ties with GCHQ that had developed over the years.

Under Carter the centralization of SIGINT moved quickly ahead. A Group implemented Plan B and closed the theater processing centers. [censored] opened only in 1961, was made in 1965. [censored] was a victim of improved communications programs, especially the move to [censored] under the AG-22/STRAWHAT program. At first, arrangements were made for the AG-22 traffic to be routed through [censored] where data of interest were stripped off for computer processing. But like [censored] could do nothing that could not be done at Fort Meade, and the center at [censored] was doomed. As in [censored] the theater military commanders fought the closure of [censored] energetically, but to no avail.

It was also during Carter's tenure that AFSCC was finally closed. Though closure plans originated as early as the AFSA period, AFSCC was even stronger and more important when Carter arrived than when Canine became the director. But Carter signed a new closure plan in 1967 and made it stick. NSA had begun quietly transferring functions from AFSCC to Fort Meade in 1966, and after the closure plan this accelerated. First to go was the [censored] followed by larger efforts like the [censored] AFSCC officially went out of the COMINT processing business on 30 June 1969. [censored] were transferred to NSA [censored] were eliminated, and [censored] remained in San Antonio, where they merged into a new organization called Air Force Electronics Warfare Center, which analyzed the effectiveness of military-wide electronics warfare efforts, based primarily on SIGINT inputs.

NSA would have closed AFSOC earlier if space could have been found, but the Agency was always chronically short of space. The dedication of the new nine-story headquarters building in 1963 just barely caught up with an expanding population, and there was still no room for the Center. The key event was the lease of the Friendship (FANX) complex. NSA moved into the first building, FANX I, in the fall of 1967, and as new buildings were completed, it occupied those also until by the fall of 1970 the Agency was the tenant in FANX I, II, and III. (NSA was the first and only resident of all the FANX and Airport Square buildings that it leased except for FANX I, whose lease has been given up.) It was not cheap — Carter once stated for the record that for four years worth of rent, NSA could have built its own buildings. But military construction money was carefully controlled by Congress.

Mechanization Of The SIGINT Process

"You people are doing a tremendous job producing history. You are not producing intelligence." —Juanita Moody to the B1 workforce, 1961

SIGINT had a reputation for being laborious and expensive. Intercept operations tended to be labor-intensive, while processing was equipment-intensive. Of all Department of Defense organizations, the SCAs were the most far-flung, draining the federal government of foreign currency in the attempt to maintain small sites in remote areas difficult and expensive to supply. Robert McNamara had a war to fight, and he exerted intense pressure on the SIGINT system to economize. This manifested itself in pressure to reduce the number of people involved in the system front end, both through field site mechanization, and through the transfer of operations back to the Continental United States.

Along with the economic pressures came demands to speed up the system. Eisenhower's concerns over war warning information, far from disappearing after his administration ended, intensified under Kennedy. The Bay of Pigs and Cuban Missile Crisis instilled a sense of hurry-up.

The twin demands of economy and speed pushed the cryptologic community into a thorough remodeling of SIGINT. The result was the fashioning of a new system, drastically different from the one which had emerged from World War II and had stood relatively intact through the 1950s.

It had been the dream of cryptologists for years to modernize and automate manual Morse intercept, the largest part of the front end. A first try at it was during World War II, when OP-20-G attempted to produce a punched paper tape from a manual typewriter, thus readying the intercept for introduction into a follow-on processor without further manipulation. The results of the experiment are lost. It was the last attempt at that sort of thing for at least ten years.

In 1957 NSA began toying with the idea of copying Morse on a special typewriter that would do more than just copy alphanumeric characters. The Agency modified a Remington-Rand Synchro-tape typewriter by adding special keys at the top of the keyboard that designated tags, indicating such things as callsigns and frequencies. The project was called SPIT (Special Intercept Typewriter).

While technicians modernized the intercept operation, NSA began looking at processing techniques. Since the dawn of America's SIGINT system, intercept sites had forwarded raw traffic to Washington for processing. While raw traffic went by courier and took weeks to arrive, traffic extracts, often called TECSUMS (technical summaries) were prepared at the field site from the raw traffic and were forwarded electrically so that Washington had at least a summary of significant intercepted material. Prior to the late 1950s the TECSUMS went by formal message, but with the advent of Opscomms, more and more TECSUMS were put on Opscomm circuits.

At the time, NSA technicians and analysts were engaged in a philosophical debate about mechanization. Should traffic be brought back in bulk to NSA, where machines could prepare it for computer processing, or should the mechanization occur in the field, closer to the front end of the process? In the end the front-enders won, and NSA began designing equipments that would mechanize the intercept operation.

[censored]

The experiment with the SPIT typewriter spawned a new project, called [censored] or the AFSAV 311D. The [censored] equipment consisted of a modified Remington-Rand typewriter similar to the SPIT model, with special keys referring to such traffic components as callsigns and to traffic externals like start-of-message, end-of-message, and case notation. These features would speed the intercept process by relieving the operator from having to type them manually. But [censored] added a new feature similar to the World War II experiment—the output was both page copy and a seven-level paper tape. The beauty of this modification was that the tape could be transmitted just like an outgoing message, and it could be input to a computer at the other end, providing that it was compatible with both.

[censored] quickly became the focus of the Joint Mechanization Group (JMG). This ad hoc committee was the brainchild of Frank Raven and Juanita Moody. Raven, one of the leading cryptanalysts to emerge from the Navy in 1945, was at the time chief of GENS, while Moody was a division chief within ADVA. They were intrigued by the possibility of automating the front end of the system and pushed [censored] as a possible answer. Moody named her deputy, Cecil Phillips, to head the JMG. A field test performed at ASA's [censored] site in 1960 proved the intercept portion of the concept.

The next logical step would be to input intercepted traffic produced on an [censored] position into a computer and do some processing on it. Frank Pinkston, a USAFSS staff officer, heard about the [censored] machines, which at the time (1961) were lying idle, and asked if Security Service could run its own test. The Air Force liked the idea because it would facilitate the rapid transmission and processing of highly perishable air-related traffic. Pinkston designed a test in which [censored] positions would be located at the AFSS site [censored] would produce communications-formatted tapes, and would forward the tapes via Opscomm to [censored] where they would be fed into the IBM 1401, which would produce an automated TECSUM. The JMG got a Bogart programmer to design the software, and in September 1961 AFSS ran a successful test. (Bogart was one of NSA's RAM systems.)

The project then languished, primarily because every field site would need a 1401. The 1401 was at the time part of AFSS's [censored] system, which was under intense fire from NSA because of its complexity and expense. But interest never vanished. ASA had emnarked on its own project, called [censored] which was soon subsumed under the auspices of the JMG. Meanwhile [censored] proclaimed the concept revolutionary and proposed that it be broken down into component portions and implemented gradually. Rather than locate computers at each field site, [censored] proposed that traffic be forwarded to central locations. This concept would reduce the number of computers required (computers were still regarded as exotic and outlandishly expensive), but it would also overload the communications system. Thereby hung the dilemma.

AG-22

While the policy people thrashed out the dilemma, the technical people continued working on improvements to the device. The Remington-Rand equipment was judged not sturdy enough and was replaced by a Teletype Model 35, extensively modified by the addition of the special tagging keys. The Agency named the device the AG-22 and changed the output to an eight-level tape. NSA also standardized the tagging and traffic formatting requirements into a new TECHINS (T-5004),so that Morse traffic intercepted anywhere would look just like any other Morse traffic. Computer formatting requirements were beginning to drive the SIGINT system.

Changing the Communications System

The communications system that AG-22 tapes were preparing to assault had become creaky and outmoded, and it was incapable of handling the new requirements. [censored]

After the creation of Criticomm, NSA continued to try to develop a high-speed switch that would improve reliability and reduce handling time. At first, technical hurdles delayed adoption of a new switch. But in 1962 a new, bureaucratic obstacle appeared with the creation of the Defense Communications Agency (DCA). Such an agency was a logical outgrowth of McNamara's centralization strategy, but it confused the Criticomm situation. DCA took over the job of searching for a new switch, regardless of the feeling at NSA that this would slow the development process. There is little doubt that the project was further delayed by hard feelings between the two agencies.

In the mid-1960s, DCA decided on a new satellite communications system called Defense Special Security Communications System (DSSCS), and it decreed that the new Criticomm switch would have to be compatible with the rest of the system. The fact that operators in general service (Genser) communications centers were not SI-cleared created more policy problems, and the search for a switch slipped further.

Then in 1964 the picture was further clouded when DIA got approval to manage the SSO system. Part of the package was the creation of a separate communications system for the distribution of COMINT, called Spintcomm. This introduced new bureaucratic conflicts over who would be the ultimate manager of the composite Criticomm/Spintcomm system, and the edict that established Spintcomm further confused the picture by assigning significant responsibilities to all three participating agencies (NSA, DIA, and DCA). Gordon Blake strongly protested DIA management of the system, but he was overruled at the OSD level. This set off new turf battles and further complicated the technical design of a switch that would have to handle all communications requirements.

Meantime, more and more traffic flooded the system, largely because of the Vietnam War, and message throughput actually declined from year to year, while errors increased. To stave off disaster, NSA took various halfway measures. Much traffic was diverted to the expanding Opscomm systems, and Criticomm was reserved mainly for formal messages. The Agency also designed terminal equipment which would speed and improve handling of traffic within the Criticomm centers.

One such solution was the BIX (Binary Information Exchange), a high-speed local message switch which could operate at various speeds to handle traffic from many different inputs. NSA awarded the contract to ITT, which delivered the first BIX in 1961. The principal improvement was in data storage (the BIX used magnetic tape to store large amounts of data) and in improved throughput (BIX could handle 100,000 words per minute). As an automatic switch, however, it failed, and messages still had to be processed manually.

At the same time, the COMSEC organization was working on crypto that would handle the new circuit speeds. The KG-13, which could encrypt circuits up to 2400 bauds per second (the speed of the DLT-5 from Frankfurt) went on line in 1965.

STRAWHAT

NSA planned to install AG-22s [censored] but the Opscomm system would not be able to handle the volume. Originally designed for analyst-to-analyst conversations. Opscomms were, by the mid-1960s, becoming overloaded with new TECSUM and [censored] forwarding requirements. They were slow of foot, either 60 or 100 words per minute, and barely able to handle current requirements. If AG-22 data were diverted to Opscomm, it would expand the circuit requirements geometrically. Lacking a revamped Criticomm system, the solution lay in a separate, high-speed data system specifically for AG-22 formatted tapes. In 1967 NSA came up with the answer—the Agency called it STRAWHAT.

STRAWHAT was a 9600-baud data link system from field sites to processing centers. A time division multiplex system capable of up to eight-level forwarding, its equipment could be patched directly from the circuit terminal to a computer, bypassing the person in the communications center. The first circuit became operational in December 1968, and NSA planned to wire up more stations with STRAWHAT circuits beginning in 1969. By mid-1970, the entire SIGINT system would have at least an interim STRAWHAT capability.

The Computer Industry at NSA

By the mid-1960s mainframe computers had taken over much of the manual processing at NSA. Although the dual tracks of scientific versus general-purpose processors were continuing, increasingly the Agency was focusing on the latter. It had to do so in order to handle the TECSUM data flowing into Fort Meade via the burgeoning Opscomm network. At that time, the computer of choice for this operation was the IBM 7010, an advanced model of the IBM 1410. IBM machines almost totally dominated the general purpose processing job, and the collection of 7010s was simply called "the IBM complex."

IBM was not the only company doing business with NSA. In 1963 the first mini-computer, the PDP-1, was delivered to the Agency. That, and its successor, the PDP-10, were used for a wide variety of special-purpose processing jobs. That same year, NSA purchased the Univac 490, which had a capability of handling thirty remote stations simultaneously. The stations were equipped with both paper tape and Teletype Model 35 input devices. The software, called RYE, was developed at NSA and was ideal for handling simultaneous inputs from the remote stations. It was made to order for processing from communications terminals, and thus it fitted NSA's emerging needs for handling Tecsumized inputs from field sites, as well as a variety of other small-job applications.

By 1963 NSA's computer collection was by far the largest in the country and probably the world. The value of its computers topped [censored] which was greater than the Census Bureau, the Baltimore headquarters of the Social Security Administration, and all the field offices of the Internal Revenue Service put together. By 1968 General Carter could boast that NSA had over 100 computers occupying almost 5 acres of floor space.

NSA continued to do pioneering work in partnership with the commercial computer industry. One such innovation was the so-called Josephson Junction technology. This was a very-low-temperature phenomenon in which "switching an electron tunneling junction between two states is accomplished by means of a magnetic field." Discovered in the mid-1960s, the potential for speeding up computer processing was so attractive that NSA funded about one-third of the IBM research on the Josephson Junction technology. Unfortunately, it didn't work, and IBM ultimately gave up on the Josephson Junction. The project illustrated both the need for research in advanced technologies and the risks involved.

NSA also pioneered in techniques for mass storage. One such experiment was called TABLON, developed in concert with IBM and Ampex in the 1960s. TABLON used a photodigital process developed at IBM and a tape storage system developed by Ampex. The storage systems were internetted by means of two PDP-10s. The philosophy was to have a central data storage system that could be used by the entire agency. But TABLON had serious technical problems. Ampex was unable to develop a tape drive that met system specifications, and too much software was required to run the PDP-10-based star network. Ultimately TABLON was overtaken by new disk storage technology.

NSA programmers were in the forefront of special computer language development. Agency programmers created special languages for HARVEST (called Beta), for the IBM 1401 (called PAL) and punched card emulation language (Transembler) for the IBM 705. Still, the Agency was losing its edge in pioneering work, as the commercial world forged ahead with new innovations that owed less and less to the inspirations that had stemmed from cryptologic applications. It was an inevitable process.

IATS

The new AG-22/STRAWHAT marriage, innovative though it was, had some problems that could only be called "logistical." A large field site, with row on row of manual Morse positions, could produce a considerable amount of eight-level tape in a day. The process of accounting for, and carting to the communications center, long coils of tape cascading off collection positions was time-consuming, and an analyst (who had now become a communications tape handler rather than a SIGINT analyst) could literally become buried in tape before the end of the shift.

In the mid-1960s K Group (the PROD organization responsible for interfacing NSA with the field sites) began working on a system for accepting manual Morse data directly onto a magnetic tape. After experimenting with several different computers, it settled on the Honeywell 316, which could accept data from 128 different sources simultaneously. (Thus, a field site would have to have more than 128 Morse positions before it required more than one 316.) Honeywell, which sold the 316 at a very competitive $12,500, agreed to loan one to NSA, and a test was run at Vint Hill in Virginia. The test system worked, and the Agency, which called the new system IATS (Improved AG-22 Terminal System), got [censored] in 1968 to install Honeywells at all AG-22 field sites. The AG-22 positions were wired to the on-site Honeywells, which packed the intercept files onto a magnetic tape. Periodically (usually every six hours) the tape was transmitted on a high-speed data link to NSA.

At this point NSA embarked on a major software development effort to handle the expected influx of IATS data. Cecil Phillips gave the job to John W. Saadi, who was a team chief in Phillips's C Group. Saadi, writing in assembly language, created a series of processes (called [censored] resident on a Univac 494, which accepted the data from the communications system. The 494 built batch files and passed them to the IBM 360 through a shared disk arrangement. This was a ground-breaking task because IBM machines were notoriously difficult to interface with the machines of any other company.

The IBM 360, the first third-generation machine, was introduced at NSA in the late 1960s to replace the 7010s. [censored] Each production organization wrote applications programs for the 360 complex, so that its data, handed to the 360s from [censored] would be processed and ready for the analyst. The complex did its heaviest work at night, so that the output would be ready for the analysts in the morning.

Now that raw intercept files were available on computer, each production element developed databases. Some of the work in this area, especially that done by A Group to create a relational database for the Soviet problem, was on the leading edge of technology.

The Communications Solutions

The impasse that had been created between NSA, DIA, and DCA lasted through the end of the Carter regime. By 1968 DCA had still failed to produce an adequate communications switch, and Carter felt that DCA failed to understand SIGINT (despite the fact that the director of DCA, Lieutenant General Richard Klocko, had been one of the founding fathers of the Air Force Security Service). But the next year brought a new director, Vice Admiral Noel Gayler, and a new approach to the logjam. Gayler moved quickly to iron out differences, and in August of 1969 he signed an agreement with Klocko covering management of the communications systems that supported SIGINT.

The agreement was a carefully crafted compromise. DCA would manage the entire system, based on technical specifications submitted by NSA. DOA could satisfy communications requirements using any type of circuitry, as long as NSA technical specifications were adhered to. The next month DCA cancelled the automatic switch contract with ITT. Shortly thereafter, OSD decided that the new DCA communications system, called Autodin, would be used for SIGINT traffic. This decision would result in NSA relinquishing a proprietary net that it had controlled since its birth. Some were not happy, but Gayler held to the compromise package, and an era of relative good feeling resulted between Gayler and Klocko.

Lacking a DCA automatic switch, NSA developed its own in-house version and hatched plans to use it in its own communications center at Fort Meade. The Agency decided to scrap the Teletypewriter Distributions System in use since the new building had opened in 1957 and replace it with a new communication center based on the new switches. It was to be called IDDF (Internal Data Distribution Facility], and it opened its doors in early 1972 on the third floor of the Ops-1 building. The year before, NSA introduced optical character readers in the message processing facility, an innovation which led to the elimination of the time-consuming step of teletype operators hand-poking every outgoing message. Called AMPS (Automatic Message Processing System), its rigid formatting requirements and special IBM Selectric typewriter balls were at first hard for secretaries to get used to, but a godsend to the communications center.

Automating the Collection Process

New methods of forwarding data to NSA did not change the basic process of signal collection. Most of an operator's time was still spent searching for target signals. But with the new digital technology and smaller on-site computers, it should theoretically be possible to acquire certain signals automatically. In the early 1960s, R&D began working on the development process. The early development work was done in 1963/1964 under a project called [censored]

The production model of [censored] was a more sophisticated system, which had an automated digital front end connected to several back-end manual Morse collection positions. [censored]

Digital computer-based collection systems eventually became the rule rather than the exception. Some, like the IRON HORSE system used in Vietnam, automated the collection of manual Morse signals. But Morse transmissions had a huge variety of formats, and the length of the mark or space varied depending on the sending operator. Computer-based collection was far more adaptable to baud-based signals. An early success in this area was [censored] The on-site computer (a CP 818) [censored] demodulated the signal, then scanned the plaintext transmissions for key words. The system would alarm on recognition of high-interest text, and the operators would react with special peocessing and forwarding routines. It replaced the "ancient" CXOF equipment which had been the equipment of choice [censored] since the late 1940s. [censored] with its stable frequencies, plain text, and bauded structure, was especially suitable to automation, and NSA collection and processing systems for that effort became among the most automated in the business.

In the 1960s NSA automated the collection of a very wide variety of signals. [censored] The Agency employed a bewildering variety of minicomputers for these specialized jobs, sometimes buying commercial computers from outfits such as Honeywell and DEC, sometimes building its own computers in-house.

Bauded Signals [censored]

In the late 1950s NSA was struggling to cope with the increasing use of bauded systems for record traffic. The trend toward the bauded world resulted partly from increasing traffic flow, which required faster circuit speeds that radioprinter made possible; it also had a corollary benefit of making [censored] possible. The field sites were collecting ever higher volumes of printer messages, most of which languised in NSA'swarehouses on magnetic tape, waiting to be converted and processed [censored] By the early 1960s the volumeof unprocessed magnetic tape was becoming difficult to manage technically and wasembarrassing politically.

R&D's first approach wasto build a general-purpose digitizer and diarizer for bauded signals. Project [censored] which originated between 1956 and 1958, at first targetted the online [censored] was only part of the problem, and R&D, working with A Group, began working toward the on-line digitization and diarization of the entire bauded signals problem. An ad hoc committee was established in 1959 to study the problem, and R&D began designing equipment to digitize printer signals onto magnetic tape at the collection position. [censored] consisted of a numberof special-purpose components [censored] which were designed to digitize, diarize and format onto magnetic tape. It resulted in two parallel avenues, [censored]

While R&D experimented with general-purpose processors, DDO was becoming overwhelmed by magnetic tape. During July 1961 NSA received 17,000 reels of magnetic tape, all of which required signal conversion prior to processing. In fiscal year 1961 the Agency needed over [censored] just to convert bauded signals for further processing.

To stem the tide, Operations initiated a QRC (Quick Reaction Capability) project called [censored] which quickly changed its name to [censored] and the various spin-offs of the [censored] project were in full swing (and in direct competition with each other) when, in 1962, DDO initiated a crash requirement [censored] to collect the burgeoning [censored] signals. The urgency of the requirement vaulted it ahead of everything else. The new project, [censored] would eventually result in the conversion of [censored] to a standard position. The new positions would intercept, digitize, and record [censored] Everything would be processed at NSA in a standard format, thus simplifying the job of the processing organization and the task of designing processes.

[censored] The Attack Continues

[censored]

[censored]

COMSEC at Mid-decade

In the 1960s the KW-26, the equipment of choice for securing long-haul point-to-point record traffic circuits, dominated American COMSEC. But American involvement in Vietnam led to a new set of tactical encryption requirements. Typical of the new COMSEC demands was the need to encrypt record traffic on low-level tactical nets in a combat environment. The KW-26 was ill-suited for this application, and to meet the demand, NSA developed the KW-7 to secure terminals which received traffic from multiple transmitters. This equipment added a unique indicator for each message, so that stations in a multiple-station net could correspond using a single crypto device.

The Development of American Secure Voice

The big news in COMSEC in the 1960s, however, was secure voice. U.S. government users would use the telephone for classified talk, and the only solution was to provide them with a secure handset. Secure voice requirements spanned a broad swath from high-level point-to-point conversations to tactical military applications in the jungles of Southeast Asia. Well aware of the vulnerabilities of voice, NSA approached secure voice cautiously, and for many years secure voice capabilities lagged behind record traffic.

For strategic systems, NSA developed two devices in the 1960s. The KY-9 was a narrow-band digital system using a vocoder, and it was the first speech system to use transistors. The advantage of the KY-9 was that it could be used on a standard Bell System 3 kHz-per-channel telephone system without modification. The disadvantages were many, however. It was big and heavy, encased in a safe that had to be unlocked every morning before the system could be activated. It was also expensive (over $40,000 per copy) and was a true "Donald Duck" system which required the users to speak slowly to be understood. Only about 260 sets were deployed, all to high-level users, mostly Air Force.

Far more significant was the KY-3, developed about the same time. Built by Bell Labs under contract, it too was housed in a safe. It, was big, klunky, and looked a lot like the KY-9, but without many of the drawbacks. The KY-3 was a broadband digital system, so voice quality was better, and it was not a push-to-talk system. But what brought it into wide use was its employment in the Autosevocom network.

Autosevocom was a secure voice network designed by NSA. Local networks consisted of KY-3s, whose individual voice conversations were first decrypted, then reduced to narrow-band signals and digitized in the HY-2 vocoder, and finally re-encrypted for transmission using a KG-13. The Autosevocom system achieved wide acceptance, and some 2,700 KY-3s were sold to users world-wide, including the White House, the Joint Chiefs of Staff, and the Strategic Air Command.

As Vietnam heated up, NSA's attention turned increasingly to tactical voice encryption. An early entry into the tactical arena was a set of systems called PARKHILL. An analog system, it was acknowledged to be vulnerable to exploitation and was not authorized for conversations above the Confidential level. Knowledgeable COMSEC people called it [censored] But it was better than nothing, and NSA assumed that the Soviets, if they were to exploit it at all, would have to devote inordinate resources.

For digital encryption, the Agency first turned to the KY-8, whose development had begun in the late 1950s. The Air Force tested the KY-8 in its F-100 series jet fighters, but found it heavy and cumbersome to key. (As former COMSEC official David Boak once said, the Air Force would accept a device "only if it had no weight, occupied no space, was free, and added lift to the aircraft") More to the point, if the KY-8 were to stay, the fire control radar would have to go. The Air Force opted for the fire control radar, and American aircraft in Vietnam remained without voice encryption.

The Army and Marine Corps, however, found that they could use the KY-8 in jeeps, and some 6,900 devices were eventually deployed. Meanwhile, NSA embarked on a whirlwind project to provide a KY-8 type of device, absent the bulk and weight. The result was two new tactical voice encryption systems, the KY-28 and KY-38. The former was developed for aircraft, while the latter was employed in man-pack radio systems. Weight in both was reduced by the use of integrated circuits. The three devices (KY-

8, 28, and 38) were referred to as the NESTOR family. By the end of the decade, there were 27,000 NESTOR equipments in the U.S. inventory.

The next generation of voice encryption systems was called [censored] consisting of VINSON (KY-57/58) and BANCROFT (KY-67), they were smaller, lighter, and consumed less power than the earlier NESTOR sytems. They also employed updated keying systems and could actually be rekeyed from an aircraft, permitting the control station to remotely change the keys on a net in case a station were overrun by the enemy. BANCROFT was the first-ever combination radio and encryption device in a single unit. VINSON and BANCROFT were not introduced until the early 1970s.

TEMPEST

TEMPEST standards had been set forth in the late 1950s in a document called NAG-1. Like other COMSEC policy documents, however, this one was advisory. What was needed was a directive policy and enforcement procedures. NSA spent the decade of the 1960s working on that aspect of TEMPEST.

In September 1960 NSA briefed the USCSB on existing American TEMPEST vulnerabilities. It shocked USCSB into action, and at a meeting in October the board agreed on a crash program and established its first and only subcommittee, SCOCE (Sub-Committee on Compromising Emanations). The first item on SCOCE's agenda was a request from USIB to evaluate the Flexowriter, which was being considered for almost universal adoption within the intelligence community as a computer input-output device.

The Flexowriter, SCOCE found, was the strongest radiator ever tested, hardly a recommendation for its adoption within the intelligence community. With the proper equipment, an enemy listening service could read plain text as far as 3,200 feet. The subcommittee posted a series of recommendations that became known as the "Flexowriter policy," including recommendations that it not be used overseas at all, that in the U.S. it not be used for classifications higher than Confidential (and then only if the using organization controlled a space 400 feet in circumference), and that the Navy be tasked with a long-range technical fix. At the same time, SCOCE published two lists: one containing equipment that could not be used at all with classified information, and one listing equipments that could be used only on an interim basis.

USCSB took the issue to McNamara, who became an ally. In December 1964 he signed a directive imposing the policy DoD-wide. The reaction was consternation. Without waivers, some agencies would have to virtually close down. All would have to buy new equipment, that expense coming directly out of their O&M moneys. In many cases the cost of equipment would double—in some cases no fix at all could be designed, and the equipment would have to be scrapped or sold. The result was that many went straight for the waivers, and in the face of imminent operational shutdown, got them. Even most SIGINT sites had to operate under waivers for years as agencies scrambled to comply.

Geographical Retreat

[censored]

The conventional collection system reached its point of maximum expansion in the early 1960s. Then, like a star imploding, it began to shrink. The shrinkage was basically a product of two problems, one internal and one external.

The internal cause was money. The Vietnam War, and President Johnson's domestic initiatives like the War on Poverty, began to squeeze the cryptologic budget (not to mention other DoD programs). By 1963 a serious international balance of payments problem had already developed, and the far-flung conventional SIGINT collection system became a prime target for reduction. Directed to study the problem, NSASAB concluded in 1963 that technology to remote collection sites back to the U.S. did not yet exist, except for the technique of recording signals on wideband tape and transporting the tapes back to the CONUS for transcription. Since this did not in most cases meet timeliness requirements, overseas reductions would mean real reductions in SIGINT collection capability.

The second problem was developing Third World nationalism. Many of the countries which hosted SIGINT collection sites were moving toward more independent foreign policies, and foreign troops on their soil did not play well in domestic politics. As the Vietnam War wore on, there was, in addition, a sense of diminishing American power in the world, and a feeling that it was better to move into a neutral camp, rather than to lean on weakening American military protection. These trends often manifested themselves in a demand that the Americans somehow "pay" for their rental of foreign space.

[censored]

[censored]

[censored]

Airborne Collection

The success of the [censored] USAFSS use of RC-135s to collect COMINT; [censored] prompted AFSS to ask for more RC-135s. After a lengthy struggle, six aircraft were added to the program, and all were initially ticketed for [censored] collection program hard pressed to satisfy collection requirements [censored] The addition of the far more capable RC-135s pushed the RC-130 program farther down the priority list, and all eventually became strictly theater assets before they were phased out of the inventory in the early 1970s. It also meant that the airborne collection program would inevitably take on a stronger global connotation, with home basing at [censored] and much less of a theater presence.

As collection requirements multiplied, so did AFSS airborne programs. Many responded to the need to collect against [censored] and they were usually joint SAC-USAFSS operations. During the late 1960s, airborne operations were pulled in different directions by conflicting requirements in [censored] For several years airborne SIGINT assets of the Air Force and Navy were frantically juggled to keep up with requirements.

Many of the RC-130s were ultimately replaced by "mini-manned" U-2s. Receiver front ends were placed on a pallet that was loaded on board, and the aircraft served as a high-altitude intercept station, downlinking intercepted RF to operators on the ground.

These programs were preceded, however, by an experiment using drones. Begun in [censored] 1971, the drone program (under a variety of names) never worked. The drones were vulnerable to antiaircraft fire, and it eventually became too expensive to keep replacing them.

[censored]

The Wood Study

Budgetary pressures and the rise of nationalism in the Third World led to a series of high-level basing studies in the mid-to late 1960s. Aside from the NSA study that led to the closure of [censored] the most significant was the so-called Wood Study, named after General Robert J. Wood, called out of retirement in 1968 to chair a Senior Interdepartmental Group (SIG) looking at the worldwide intelligence posture. The objective was to save money; the target was SIGINT.

Wood felt that much of the expense of SIGINT was with the front end—the overseas bases. He put forth a litany of ways that SIGINT could be done more cheaply, which would be repeated by future study groups. NSA should pour money into advanced technologies (such as satellites and remoting) that would reduce force posture overseas. It should place more reliance on Third Parties. It should develop transportable SIGINT assets. It should rely more on technical research ships (despite the relatively recent destruction of the *Liberty* and the capture of the *Pueblo*). And it should be much more aggressive about consolidating overseas field sites.

There were very cogent reasons why SIGINT sites were spread so widely throughout the world; they related to propagation phenomena and a perceived need to diversify intercept in case of attack. But these objections were drowned by the need to economize. The Wood Study increased pressure to "do something" about the huge number of sites, and the first move was to further reduce assets [censored] Thus the decision was made (it had been impending for several years) to close the three Army sites [censored]

One interesting spin-off of the Wood Study was an assessment of political vulnerability in countries housing U.S. SIGINT operations. The chart rates postulated tenure (as measured by the Wood Study) and actual withdrawal dates:

[chart censored]

To a SIGINTer used to an expanding SIGINT system, 1968 must have seemed like a shrinking world. General Carter, protesting late-decade cutbacks, protested "a pattern of subtractions from U.S. cryptologic strength." He fought reductions like a tiger. But the twin pressures of paying for Vietnam and reducing the balance of payments deficit combined to trim the SIGINT posture no matter whar Carter said. Thus base consolidations [censored] tightened up the SIGINT waistline. The pressure for this was budgetary, and it came from the top.

Viewed from the standpoint of international geopolitics, however, the picture was a little different. Of the ten countries (above) that the U.S. abandoned from an overt SIGINT collection standpoint, nationalist pressures were the clear culprit in seven cases and were at least partly responsible in two others. Thus, SIGINT reductions came from internal budgetary causes, while outright abandonment of a country resulted almost inevitably from nationalist sensitivity. SIGINT sites were generally acceptable as long as they were invisible to the local population. Thus the U.S. was forced to close its site [censored] The lesson was clear, and it became a factor in the new remoting technology that was, even in 1968, picking up steam in NSA.

[censored]

Manning the front end of the SIGINT system with civilians had long been an NSA goal. In the 1950s NSA sent integrees to SCA sites, but the numbers were never large, and as the decade wore on, the SCAs tended to get tougher on the idea of NSA invading their turf. [censored] However, civilianization took on a life of its own, chiefly because of the afbantages that could accrue.

The most significant advantage was expertise. The SCAs had trouble training collectors [censored] Moreover, NSA could sometimes provide linguistic talent that was hard to come by in the military world.

A second advantage was retainability. Military retention rates, low in the 1950s, dropped even lower during the Vietnam war. NSA wanted to [censored] employ civilian collectors and analysts at the front-end of their system for many years. The Americans could not match the expertise found at [censored]

The 1958 Robertson Committee initially considered a system of NSA-only collection sites, but withdrew the recommendation from the final report in the face of determined SCA hostility. Instead, the report recommended increasing NSA civilian presence in hard-to-find skills and establishing roving teams of experts to help out with special field site problems. But even that proved difficult to implement, and civilianization appeared to be a dying concept.

This turf fight between NSA and the SCAs stopped civilianization cold until 1965, when a new factor appeared. The factor was Vietnam.

By 1965 the drain on military manpower wasbecoming severe.In August, the Defense Department canvassed all its activities looking for jobs that civilians could do so that the military people in them could go to the war zone. The most severe pressure was in the Army, and Army stations were threatened with the most serious manpower cutbacks to support the war. Faced with rows of potentially unmanned positions, NSA proposed that it be authorized to coordinate a program of civilianization within the cryptologic community. After a heated internal debate at NSA regarding civilianization at [censored]

[censored]

Naval SIGINT Ships

The signal success of the *Oxford* [censored] during the Cuban Missile Crisis resulted in a boom in the Technical Research Ship (TRS) program. NSA's long-term TRS program include [censored] Military Sea Transport Service (MSTS) charters and five of the larger *Oxford*-class Liberty ships. The Navy had an even more grandiose plan to build a TRS fleet from the keel up, at a cost of $35 million per vessel. They would have a cruising speed of at least twenty knots. But despite the giddy success of the *Oxford*, the numbers did not add up. For instance, it cost $13.5 million to convert a Liberty ship into an *Oxford*-class vessel, but only $3.3 million to redo a *Valdez*-class MSTS ship. DoD was strapped for cash for the Vietnam buildup, and this kind of floating SIGINT platform, logical in theory, fell victim to the budget axe.

Failing in the big plan, the Navy opted for a far cheaper option. The idea was to convert some trawler-type vessels at very minor cost and outfit them for general intelligence collection, including (but not limited to) SIGINT. Their primary purpose would be naval direct support, with a secondary national tasking mission from NSA. They would call the vessels AGER (Auxiliary General Environmental Research).

NSA opposed the program from the beginning. Some Agency seniors believed that it was an end run around NSA's authority to control SIGINT. Nonetheless, the Navy converted the first AGER in 1965, calling it the USS *Banner* (AGER-1). The long-range program was to have twelve such vessels. When, in late 1965, the Navy went forward with a request to convert two more *Banner*-class trawlers, NSA opposed it, and Cyrus Vance, the deputy secretary of defense, sent the proposal back to the cryptologic community to resolve the conflict.

NSA and the Navy fashioned a compromise in which the vessels would sail sometimes on solely direct support missions, sometimes on hybrid national tasking and direct support orders. It would be a wholly Navy owned, manned, and protected program. The ships were smaller and less capable than the *Oxford*- or *Valdez*-class vessels, and as for speed, could not even make ten knots. They would be almost defenseless, but up to that time SIGINT ships had never been bothered by hostile forces. The *Pueblo*, which put out on its first operational voyage in December 1967, was an AGER-type trawler.

TRS communications were, in the early years, bothered by crowding of the HF spectrum. To solve this problem, the *Oxford,* in February of 1964, demonstrated for the first time the feasibility of bouncing microwave signals off the moon from a ship at sea. This technique had been used first in 1959 between two stationary locations, Hawaii and Washington, but the technical problems involved in doing it from the deck of a pitching ship were daunting. Although the problem was considered essentially insoluble, Commander William Carlin White of NSG managed to get the Naval Research Laboratory interested, and White, NRL, and NSA, all working together, gathered the equipment for a test. When the *Oxford* successfully communicated with the NSG site at [censored] a new era of naval communications was under way. Soon CNO-approved installation of this new gear (called TRSSCOM, or TRS Special Communication System) was programmed for the *Belmont* and *Liberty,* and plans were made to convert all TRSs to the so-called Moon Shot system.

TRSs became very popular substitutes for dry land SIGINT real estate. With nationalism on the rise and the United States experiencing declining popularity in the Third World, it was often the only platform available. A TRS was sent to [censored] TRSs were thrown into the Vietnam conflict, essentially as augmentation for existing fixed sites. An Oxford-class vessel, the *Liberty,* was deployed to the Mediterranean during the 1967 Arab-Israeli War. [censored]

In the flush of enthusiasm, the latent problems in the program remained hidden. Program flexibility led to scattershot deployments to areas where the technical database was nonexistent. Vessels were put against targets with exotic language requirements that the Navy could not meet. SIGINT crew training and expertise levels appeared to many NSAers to be declining the face of so many short-fuse deployments to strange places. Command and control became convoluted, especially in war zones like Vietnam or the [censored] and at times it appeared that no one really knew who had control of TRSs in certain areas. Occasionally a TRS would wind up doing non-SIGINT work like hoisting refugees aboard—this happened during the Cuban Missile Crisis, and was ordered, but not done, during [censored] Further, TRSs had to compete, in essence, with even more rapid AFSS airborne assets. Often the airborne fleet won out because it could get there faster, and AFSS had better trained operators and linguists.

Finally, and fatally, floating SIGINT platforms proved to be not as secure as had been expected. The *Liberty* incident in 1967 shocked a cryptologic community that had always assumed that American SIGINT platforms would be accorded the same courtesies that the U.S. gave to the Soviet SIGINT trawlers. The incident was repeated (with variants) the very next year when North Korea captured the *Pueblo.* NSA support for the program was already crumbling because of the dispute over the control of AGERs. With the *Pueblo*, it completely died.

The program was good in theory, and if the execution had been better, TRSs might still be around. It is still a good idea today, but the *Pueblo* incident probably killed it forever.

The End of HF?

The decade of the 1960s inexorably led NSA into above-HF signals, more and more difficult to intercept, more and more exotic to process once intercepted. Fixation on the the [censored] problem marked one very difficult and expensive avenue, which would require complex intercept and processing gear and unconventional collection locations or platforms. The trend toward above-HF communications, especially [censored] radio relay, and communications satellites, marked another knotty problem for the cryptologic community.

[censored]

Still, all long-range forecasts agreed [censored] NSA had been worrying about this problem for some years, and the Agency was in the process, in the late 1960s, of designing and fielding systems that would accommodate the expected surge in above HF communications.

[censored]

[censored]

[censored]

Overhead

Since the science fiction writings of Arthur C. Clarke in the 1930s and 1940s, it had been an American dream to place a reconnaissance satellite in orbit around the earth. At the end of World War II, General Curtis LeMay, then deputy chief of staff for Research and Development for the Army Air Corps, commissioned the Rand Corporation to do a study on the feasibility of just such a project. The Rand study, dubbed Project FEEDBACK, proceeded in secret for eight years. It was finally turned over to the Air Force in 1954, coincident with the Eisenhower administration's thorough examination of the strategic warning dilemma under the Killian Board.

The Technological Capabilities Panel (TCP) on the Killian Board recommended that Eisenhower proceed with the highly compartmented U-2 project being developed by Lockheed. In addition, the Intelligence Committee of the TCP, chaired by renowned optics scientist Edwin Land, recommended that the United States begin to develop reconnaissance satellites. This also got Eisenhower's approval, and it proceeded along a parallel track.

The Air Force immediately began developing an intelligence satellite program. The prime objective was photoreconnaissance, but the initial operational requirement, published in 1955, also contained provisions for an ELINT package.

From the beginning, the program was beset by competing jurisdictions and security concerns. The Air Force, the Navy, and CIA (the latter by virtue of its domination of the U-2 program) all designed entries into this new intelligence sweepstakes. The prize for the most successful system was money and people, both on a very large scale. Overhead reconnaissance loomed as the biggest potential spender in the intelligence system.

Once the Soviets launched Sputnik in 1957, American attention focused on a competitor. Although the main objective would be reconnaissance, it would have been imprudent to be up front with this. So in 1958 Eisenhower decided that the Americans would publicize their satellite program as a purely peaceful program, with scientific objectives. The first program, called Discoverer, was pushed ahead as an overt "white" program. Reconnaissance would be a "black," covert program, with classified payloads attached initially to the Discoverer vehicles.

The way Eisenhower created it, the new overhead program had a divided jurisdiction. The Air Force was to build and launch satellites, while CIA was to process the photography. The first processing center was actually set up by CIA to process photos from the U-2. Called NPIC (National Photographic Interpretation Center), it was established in the old Steuart Motor Car Building at 5th and K St., N.W., in downtown Washington. The CIA's Richard Bissell was in charge of the program, and Arthur Lundahl headed NPIC.

Meanwhile, the Air Force had set up operations on the West Coast. In October 1955, the Air Force moved its satellite development project from Wright-Patterson AFB in Ohio to Inglewood, California, locus of their ballistic missile development. This was done in order to insure that both programs remained in synch and that they would not compete for boosters. To control satellite operations, the Air Force chose to collocate with its prime contractor in California.

The Air Force ELINT Programs

The first SIGINT packages were a product of SAC's desire to support the SIOP, or Single Integrated Operational Plan, the plan for nuclar warwith the Soviet Union.[censored] At the time (the mid-1950s), ELINT was blissfully fragmented, and NSA was a COMINT agency. SAC proceeded with its program unchallenged.

While all this was going on, [censored] working in CIA's Office of ELINT, became concerned that the ELINT payloads might not be ready for the first launch of a photoreconnaissance satellite. [censored] concluded that a small, interim, piggyback payload could be designed and ready for the first launch. Its only mission would be to detect threat radars. The interim program was called [censored] and it became an end unto itself.

Discoverer experienced all sorts of disasters, as payload after payload plunged into the ocean, was fired into an unrecoverable orbit, or just exploded on launch. But when the first photoreconnaissance payload

(Discoverer XIII) actually achieved its mission and was snagged on reentry by elated Navy frogmen in August of 1960, [censored]

Program Management

[censored] remained an Air Force program, and SAC did the early signals processing. But in 1961 McNamara appointed Eugene Fubini to look into the proper relationships in the SIGINT satellite program. The Fubini committee concluded that the SIGINT satellites had to be a partnership. The satellite payloads and their booster systems remained an Air Force and NRO concern, but processing and reporting became an NSA responsibility. This decision led to a series of fragmented agreements between NSA, on the one hand, and the various satellite operators on the other, regarding the precise terms of NSA's participation in each program.

One beneficial result of the Fubini study was the signing, in September 1961, of a formal agreement between NSA and SAC regarding the processing of ELINT from the Air Force program. Essentially, they agreed that a certain amount of parallel processing would be done—NSA to benefit the intelligence community, SAC to support the SIOP.

In 1961, just before leaving office, Eisenhower set up a special compartmentation for overhead reconnaissance. Called Talent-Keyhole, or TK for short, it covered both the on-going U-2 program and the nascent satellites. CIA, which exercised general supervision of the programs [censored] TK billets, of which NSA would have exactly [censored] The Byeman compartment was set up two years later to handle technical aspects of the satellite programs.

The next year the two main players in the satellite reconnaissance game managed an accommodation. The CIA and Air Force agreed that a new multiagency program would be established, called the NRP (National Reconnaissance Program). The CIA component of the NRP would be headed by Richard Bissell, who had managed the U-2 program from its infancy. The Air Force component would be housed in a new organization directly responsible to the secretary, called SAFSS (Secretary of the Air Force Space Systems), with Joseph Charyk as its head. The same directive established a joint agency, the National Reconnaissance Office, or NRO.

NSA was still a minor player. It had very few cleared people, and its only responsibility was to process and report ELINT data. Even though NSCID 6 gave it significant responsibilities in both ELINT and COMINT, NSA had no official role in the tasking of reconnaissance satellites.

Satellite tasking was then handled by COMOR (Committee on Overhead Reconnaissance), a USIB subcommittee. COMOR was concerned at first only with PHOTINT, but as the ELINT packages broadened in function from purely a vulnerability assessment to wider intelligence applications, ELINT tasking came to be done by the SIGINT Working Group (SWG) of COMOR.

SWG tasking tended to be very specific, and mission ground stations found it almost unworkable. NSA was used to having USIB set general collection priorities, which the NSA tasking messages would flesh out. One of the problems that bedeviled the overhead program for years was the lack of sufficiently flexible tasking documents.

In 1962, reacting to this situation, NRO set up a Satellite Operations Center (SOC) in the Pentagon. NSA predictably saw this as another intrusion into its authority to task SIGINT collectors, and it soon was sending representatives to the SOC to represent its interests.

Tasking continued to be handled by COMOR until Huntington Sheldon of CIA became chairman of the SIGINT Committee in 1967. Sheldon lobbied USIB to split apart SIGINT and PHOTINT satellite tasking and succeeded in getting COMOR divided into two pieces. A new USIB committee, COMIREX (Committee on Imagery Requirements and Exploitation) tasked satellites, while another committee, SORS (SIGINT Overhead Reconnaissance Subcommittee) tasked the ELINT and COMINT payloads.

The Advent of Overhead COMINT

Although satellites were originally the domain of PHOTINT and ELINT, NSA was studying possible COMINT applications. A 1959 study by NSA analyst [censored] concluded that it would be feasible to collect COMINT signals from the ELINT packages aboard Air Force satellites.

Beginning in the early 1960s, COMINT-targeted payloads piggybacked on the [censored] systems [censored]

The [censored] Payloads

In the early [sencored] days engineers designed a specialized payload that would do ionospheric mapping [censored] They realized during the development phase that the payload could be injected into an orbit different from the mother payload. Since the objective was independent of satellite electronic defense, there was no special reason for it to stay with the main payload. This led to the development of a separate program [censored]

[censored]

Program C

The Navy's share of the satellite pie was called Program C. (Program A was Air Force and Program B was CIA.) But, though it was last in the alphabet, it had the first successful launch of an ELINT payload on 22 June 1960. Moreover, the Navy designed a unique program that outlasted all the others.

The program was actually conceived early in 1958 by Naval Research Laboratory engineers. They designed a program to receive [censored] and transmit this intercept in real time to Navy ground sites [censored] These ground sites were self-contained units called ESV huts, mounted on vans that could be moved around quickly. The huts would be located primarily at

NSG field sites, but because of geography it might be necessary to use sites owned by other organizations. Most sites acted as "dumb" terminals, receiving and recording the signals. Recordings were shipped to NSA for analysis.

This early program, which was solely under the auspices of the Navy, was called [censored] and was referred to in unclassified terms as GRAB. It was the first to document the extremely rich radar signals environment in the Soviet Union. But to some extent it was a targetting anomaly. The Navy was collecting signals of interest to all services and the CIA, but the program was not doing ocean surveillance. In 1962 the program was subsumed within the overall satellite collection system as Program C, and it was renamed POPPY.

In 1966 [censored] showed considerable progress toward site construction [censored] This became a matter of grave concern to the President's Scientific Advisory Committee, and a study group was appointed. If [censored] were not the highest priority target up to that point, the committee made them such. A series of [censored] payloads was developed and launched rapid-fire to respond to the concern.

Program C was also affected. [censored]

[censored]

As for the control issue, that was solved [censored] by moving tasking control to NSA. [censored] NSA set up a new facility called SSSC (SIGINT Satellite System Control) to provide technical support and tasking guidance to the program. Some non-NSA USIB members were less than pleased because SSSC amounted to a de facto delegation of tasking control to NSA. The direction was irreversible, however, and by 1972, representatives from the SOC in the Pentagon had moved to SSSC.

The program was not popular downtown, and it came under repeated attack. When this happened, Admiral Gayler himself indicated that he wanted to attend the NRP Executive Committee meetings to defend the program. At his very first meeting, Gayler went on the attack, not just defending the money that had been put into the system to date, but demanding more money to launch more satellites and to buy more processing equipment. [censored]

RAINFALL

The RUNWAY program was encountering such ferocious opposition in Washington partly because CIA already had a competitor. The CIA project had been initiated by Albert "Bud" Wheelon, who had come to CIA during the early years of the Kennedy administration. A brilliant and aggressive administrator, as well as a top-notch scientist, Wheelon had been newly installed as John McCone's director of science and technology when he read about the Syncom II geosynchronous satellite. [censored]

The project was fraught with tremendous risk. [censored] The Department of Defense, wanting CIA out of the satellite business anyway, opposed it from the beginning.

CIA cleared no one at NSA. Thus, CIA knew about NSA's nascent plans [censored] This situation changed in the late summer of 1965, because General Marshall Carter migrated from the position of deputy DCI to director of NSA. When he arrived, he arranged to clear a handful of NSA people and sent them to CIA to learn [censored]

The road proved rocky in the extreme. CIA wanted no NSA partipation at all, and in the early months did a great deal to shut NSA out. But a breakthrough of sorts occurred in December of 1965, when [censored] To clear the air. Through these high-level contacts, the two organixations began joint planning.

NSA immediately suggested that COMINT become an ancillary mission. After a period of hesitation, CIA accepted the proposal and gave NSA the job of collecting what COMINT they could from a bird whose job was TELINT, not COMINT. Through the Director's Advisory Group for ELINT and Reconnaissance (DAGER), headed by Charles Tevis, NSA negotiated the details of their participation [censored] NSA got a COMINT processing subsystem and an ELINT subsystem [censored] and when the money for those systems was cut from the budget, NSA allocated CCP funds. DAGER was also instrumental [censored]

[censored] Eventually NSA provided all the COMINT staff and about half of the TELINT crew.

SIGINT satellites were the wave of the future, and they offered breathtaking new opportunities [censored] But it also offered a significant new battleground for the control of intelligence resources. CIA-Air Force conflicts over the control of imagery became well known to the American public through the publication of such books as William Burrows's *Deep Black*. Far more obscure, but just as fierce, was the competition between NSA and others (especially CIA) over the ownership and control of SIGINT payloads. It eventually settled down to a series of compromises based on the areas of respective technical competence. But the early years, when these compromises were still in the future, were not easy.

[censored]
[censored]

Germany

[censored]

Basically the BND, like almost all West German governmental organizations, was penetrated and publicized. The problems began in 1952, when a leftist journalist named Sefton Delmer published a highly critical article in the *London Daily Mail* entitled "Hitler's General Now Spies for Dollars." Delmer appeared to get much of his material from one Otto John, who had headed the West German equivalent of the FBI until his defection to East Germany. John was, in 1952, engaged in a bitter bureaucratic struggle with Gehlen over the control of intelligence.

Things just went from bad to worse. In 1953 one Hans Joachim Geyer, a member of the Gehlen organization, fled to East Germany with the names of Gehlen agents. Within hours more than 300 Gehlen agents had been rounded up, and East Germany exposed the "spy ring" in a resonating press conference. Geyer had been passing classified documents to the KGB for several years, although it appears that he was not involved in SIGINT.

But the coup de grace was not administered until 1961, with the exposure of Heinz Felfe. A rising star in the BND, Felfe had worked for the KGB since the early 1950s and had passed thousands of documents. He worked in counterintelligenee, not SIGINT, but his access was very wide, and nothing in the BND was really safe. The exposure of Felfe in November 1961 led to a prolonged and highly public spy scandal, during which it was revealed that the BND had been thoroughly compromised by the East Bloc. At the same time Gehlen himself was involved in a public row with Franz Josef Strauss, the minister of defense. His inflexibility in dealing with outsiders, and his lack of appetite to rid the BND of East Bloc agents, ended his effectiveness. Gehlen continued to head BND until 1968, but withdrew more and more from active management.

[censored]

[censored]

Chapter 10 SIGINT in Crisis, 1967-1969

After the relatively placid decade of the 1950s, the 1960s produced a series of international paroxysms unmatched in post-World War II history. Although cryptology was involved in virtually all the events, four crises in late decade had particular impact on the cryptologic business. The Arab-Israeli War of 1967 was a defining moment in cryptologic contributions to the intelligence picture. The Soviet invasion of Czechoslovakia in August 1968, and the accompanying crisis concerning Romania, helped shape SIGINT production and reporting in later years. The other two events, the capture of the Pueblo in 1968 and the shootdown of the naval EC-121 in 1969, were uniquely cryptologic in their origins and implications, and they changed the way NSA and the cryptologic community have done business from that day to this.

SIGINT And The Second Arab-Israeli War

[censored]

On the Arab side, the late 1950s marked the height of pan-Arab sentiment. In 1958 Egypt's Nasser had convinced Syria to join Egypt in forming the United Arab Republic (UAR). But the idea never worked. Syrians chafed under heavy-handed Egyptian bureaucratic regimentation. In 1961 Nasser, believing that state socialism was the only true path, nationalized virtually all manufacturing, banking, and utilities. He also reduced to 100 acres the amount of land that a farmer could own, and he put a ceiling on the amount of money that a citizen could earn. This was too much for the Syrians, and two months later a military coup in Damascus ended the Syrian involvement in the union. Nasser, hoping that another Arab state would take Syria's place, obstinately kept the name (UAR), but none did.

Three years later a new transnational organization emerged. The Palestine Liberation Organization (PLO) was formally established at a conference in Jerusalem in 1964 with Ahmed Shukeiri as its head. It formed a conventional army composed of Palestinians and their Arab sympathizers throughout the Middle East. The real power, however, developed around a guerrilla movement called al-Fatah, headed by Yasir Arafat.

A low-intensity Fatah-Israeli conflict developed almost immediately. It was punctuated by cross-border raids and terrorist bombings, and each incident led to reprisals which created the foundation for the next incident. At the same time, the ambitious Nasser was becoming enmeshed in a civil war in Yemen in which the other proxy was Saudi Arabia. This created strains in the Arab world and accentuated the division between the so-called Nasserists and the more conservative Arab governments like Saudi Arabia and the Arabian desert sheikdoms.

By early 1967 the Middle East was clearly about to boil over. Terrorism was at a high level, and Nasser seemed spoiling for a fight. Then on 14 May [censored] Three days later, on 17 May, Nasser demanded the withdrawal of UN forces from Gaza, and UN troops immediately began evacuating what was obviously to become a war zone. On 23 May Nasser took the warlike step of blockading the Straits of Tiran, and he announced that Israeli commercial shipping, whether in Israeli or foreign bottoms, would be stopped.

The Cryptologic Posture

[censored]

[censored]

Prior to Nasser's eviction of UN forces from Sinai, there was no consensus in the U.S. on the likelihood of war. A National Intelligence Estimate published in April assessed that there was no near-term likelihood of war in the region. In May, State/INR assessed Egyptian military activities as defensive. Thomas Hughes, the top State Department intelligence analyst, based much of his estimate [censored] Walter Rostow, President Johnson's national security adviser, was hopeful that things could still be resolved by negotiation, and he noted that the Soviet Union did not seem to want to get directly involved.

[censored] NSA expanded the alert to include the entire Middle East. This was quickly elevated to a SIGINT Readiness Bravo when Nasser closed the Straits of Tiran on 23 May. A Bravo was as high as the SIGINT readiness system could proceed short of war. By the accounts of all involved, it was no longer a question of if; but when.

[censored]

To further bolster collection in the eastern Mediterranean, NSA decided on 23 May (the day Nasser blockaded the Gulf of Aqaba) to deploy a TRS. [censored] and realizing that even combined Air Force and Navy airborne collection could not produce round-the-clock coverage, NSA diverted the USS *Liberty* to an eastern Mediterranean cruise. The *Liberty* was selected because of its superior cruising speed (18 knots, best of all the TRSs), its multichannel collection suite, and its availability. (It had just begun a cruise and was fitted out for an extended voyage.)

[censored] The intelligence community had other sources of information, but none was as timely or authoritative during an expanding crisis such as existed in May of 1967. In many ways the war preparations of 1967 resembled Japanese war preparations in 1941, [censored]

The entire Middle East was on the brink when, at 0745 Middle Eastern time on 5 June, Israel launched a preemptive strike on Egyptian air forces. In what became one of the classic offensive attacks in the annals of warfare, the Israelis destroyed virtually the entire UAR air force on the ground. Within a few hours, 309 out of 340 combat aircraft were in smoking ruins, including all 30 of its long-range TU-16 bombers. Unaware of how bad things were, Syria and Jordan jumped into the fray by launching attacks on Israel. But they were too late. No longer having to worry about the Egyptian air force, the Jewish state turned its attention to Syrian and Jordanian forces on its borders and to the Egyptian divisions massed in the Sinai. Having no protection in a desert environment, the ground forces were exposed and largely destroyed in three days. In all, 417 Arab aircraft were destroyed, 398 on the ground; only 26 Israeli aircraft were lost.

The White House first learned of the war from press sources. [censored] The Arabs and Israelis were making charges and countercharges, and the president wanted to know who fired the first shots. [censored]

Amid the conflagration in the desert, the Johnson Administration keptits eyes on the Soviet Union. What would the Soviets do? [censored]

To White House analysts, it appeared that the Soviets were willing to fully support Arab governments with equipment but were not willing to send troops. The Arab governments misread the Soviet attitude, [censored] Once the war began, the Egyptians and Syrians expected intervention—what they got was an emergency shipment of equipment to replace that which the Israelis had destroyed. [censored]

[censored]

On 6 June, the Egyptians and Syrians claimed that U.S. and British forces had provided air cover for the attacking Israelis. This sensational charge, repeated and believed throughout the Arab world, was apparently intended to provoke Soviet intervention, an event that could have produced a dangerous American-Soviet confrontation. But Kosygin rejected the claim outright. [censored] Nasser was furious, but he did not succeed in egging the USSR closer to involvement. That same day, Kosygin contacted Washington on the hotline and pledged to work toward peace. As the succeeding days unfolded and Israel pressed toward the Suez Canal, Kosygin's talks with the Johnson administration over the hotline became more testy, but direct negotiations played a key role in American and Soviet abilities to avoid military involvement.

Fighting finally terminated on the tenth. [censored]

The 1967 war was the closest that the United States and the Soviet Union came to war between the Cuban Missile Crisis and the end of the Cold War. [censored]

The Attack on the *Liberty*

The *Liberty,* NSA's choice as the TRS deployment to the Middle East, was a reconditioned World War II Victory ship, converted to an AGTR in 1964. The vessel already had five cruises under its belt. It had 20 intercept positions, 6 officers, a SIGINT crew of 125 and an overall complement of 172 men. With TRSSCOM, ship-to-shore radiotelephone circuits, and two receive terminals for fleet broadcasts, the *Liberty* was one of the best equipped ships in the TRS inventory. The Navy approved NSA's request, and the *Liberty,* off the west coast of Africa, steamed for Rota, where it took aboard an additional 9 linguists, including 3 NSA civilians, and more keying material for its communications circuits. On the second of June, it set off for the eastern Mediterranean.

The *Liberty's* sailing order specified that it was to stay at least 12.5 miles off the coast of the UAR and 6.5 miles from Israel. When war broke out on 5 June, the Sixth Fleet, to which the *Liberty* had been temporarily attached, was directed to remain at least 100 miles off the coasts of Lebanon, Syria, Israel, and the UAR, but the *Liberty's* instructions were not changed. When it arrived in its operating area late on 7 June, Captain McGonagle, the vessel's commander, still had written instructions that brought the *Liberty* close into the coast.

Nasser's charge on 6 June that the U.S. and Britain were providing air cover for the Israelis, and the possibility that the Soviets might intervene, brought new orders to the Sixth Fleet to stand off at least 200 miles from the eastern Mediterranean littoral. The next day the JCS decided to pull the *Liberty,* the only U.S. naval vessel still in the far eastern Mediterranean, back to at least 20 nautical miles from the UAR and 15 from Israel. Later that day JCS changed again, this time to 100 nautical miles from both countries.

The first JCS message never reached the *Liberty*—an Army communications center misrouted it to a naval communications station in the Pacific. When, an hour later, the Joint Reconnaissance Center of the JCS decided to pull the *Liberty* back to 100 nautical miles, a series of communications fiascos occurred which stretched on into the night. Message misroutings, delays occasioned by the press of other business, refusals by the Navy to transmit based on a verbal order, all combined to delay the message receipt until after the attack. It was a repeat of the warning message to Pearl Harbor on 7 December 1941, and there was blame aplenty.

The *Liberty* was reconnoitered by several unidentified aircraft during the morning hours of 8 June. That afternoon it was about twenty-five nautical miles north of the Egyptian city of Al Arish when, at about 1400 local, two French-built Israeli Dassault fighters veered toward the ship and began strafmg it with cannon and rockets. The attack put some 821 rounds into the hull and superstructure, wounded McGonagle, and killed 8 crew members. The *Liberty* managed to get off a desperate message to Sixth Fleet before the power to the radio equipment went out, and Admiral Martin, the Sixth Fleet commander, launched 4 armed A-4 Skyhawks for air cover. Since his flagship was 450 nautical miles away from the *Liberty*, however, the aircraft did not arrive before 3 Israeli torpedo boats launched 2 torpedoes at about 1430. The torpedoes tore through the SIGINT spaces, killing 25 men and putting a hole in the hull 39 feet across. As the crew of the *Liberty* scrambled to keep the vessel afloat, one more crewmember was killed by machine-gun fire from 1 of the torpedo boats.

Once the torpedo boats departed, McGonagle directed his vessel to Malta. Sixth Fleet escorts reached the *Liberty* sixteen hours after the attack and trailed the vessel, picking up classified and cryptographic keying material escaping from the hole in the hull. The *Liberty* limped into Malta on 14 June after a heroic struggle to stay afloat that eventually earned McGonagle the Medal of Honor. In all, thirty-four crew members were killed, including one NSA civilian Arabic linguist, Allen Blue. The men lost their lives in a war in which the U.S. was not a combatant because of errors in a military communications system that, by 1967, could no longer do the job.

At NSA, word of the attack reached Director Marshall Carter at 0915 Washington time. The telephone began ringing almost at once, as word of the attack spread through Washington. While Carter was directing intercept coverage reallocation, Secretary of Defense McNamara called him (at 1015) to ask for details on the vessel and the voyage so that he could make a statement to the press. Deputy Director Louis Tordella took charge of devising a cover story. Carter diverted many of the queries to NSG. At one point during the day the director got a call from the Joint Reconnaissance Center suggesting that the vessel be sunk. Carter replied that this was the worst thing they could do—heaps of classified documents and equipment would end up in shallow water. He was right, and McGonagle's heroic piloting of his vessel to moorage in Malta saved what could have become a much worse situation.

Lyndon Johnson got word at 0949. At the time the U.S. still did not know the identity of the attackers, but the White House soon found out through a Defense Attache Office message from Tel Aviv that the Israeli navy had admitted the error. This presented the president with a very touchy dilemma. Because of Arab charges that the U.S. had assisted the Israelis, the Sixth Fleet was standing far away from the conflict in the central Mediterranean. Yet here, unannounced, was an American naval vessel only a few miles off the coast of Israel, in the middle of a war zone. Johnson's first concern was about Soviet reaction. He had Walt Rostow send a message to Kosygin stating that the Israelis had apparently fired on a U.S. ship in error and that the Sixth Fleet was sending ships and planes to investigate (he repeated it twice). Kosygin replied that he had passed the message to Nasser.

Meantime, the Pentagon had released a statement about the attack, indicating that the *Liberty's* mission was to "assure communications between U.S. Government posts in the Middle East and to assist in relaying information concerning the evacuation of American dependents and other American citizens from countries in the Middle East." This was the cover story that NSA had devised under hurried circumstances. It didn't work, but like the U-2 incident in 1960, no cover story would have worked in the situation. The press very quickly sniffed out the truth, which was attributed to an anonymous military officer that the *Liberty* was a "spy ship." According to this source, "Russia does the same thing. We moved in close to monitor the communications of both Egypt and Israel. We have to. We must be informed of what's going on in a matter of minutes." The assertion was denied by official sources, but the true mission of the *Liberty* was never in doubt again. (The vessel did not, in fact, have an Israeli mission, because linguists were too scarce.)

How did the the incident happen? Was it a deliberate attack by Israel, as has been alleged countless times by many people? (Even General Carter believed it to have been deliberate.) If it was an accident, how could the Israelis have possibly misidentified the ship? The *Liberty* was flying an American flag, was clearly marked on the hull "AGTR-5," and when the first flag was shot down by the attacking fighters, McGonagle hoisted the largest flag he had aboard, a holiday ensign seven by thirteen feet. This enormous flag was flying above the *Liberty* when the torpedo boats executed their attack.

The idea that the attack was deliberate turned out to be wrong. Although there was no SIGINT bearing directly on the attack, there was a [censored] report shortly after the incident dealing with the aftermath. It reported air/ground conversations between a ground controller at Hatsor and two Israeli helicopters which reconnoitered the *Liberty* as it was turning toward Malta. Hatsor first identified the vessel as Egyptian; but later became unsure, and requested that the helicopter crews "verify the first man that you [bring up] as to what nationality he is." A few minutes later Hatsor instructed: "Pay attention: if they speak [B-val Arabic] and are Egyptians take them to Al Arish. If they speak English and are not Egyptians, take them to Lydda . . . the first thing is for you to clarify what nationality they are." Two minutes later Hatsor asked, "Did it clearly signal an American flag?" And a minute later, "Requesting that you make another pass and check again whether it is really an American flag."

One can imagine the panic at Israeli naval headquarters at the time. They had apparently attacked a vessel of their closest ally.

Based on this report, Rostow told Johnson that the Israelis appeared to be confused about the nationality of the vessel, and he suggested that there might have been some breakdown within the Israeli military which resulted in the attack.

The official Israeli court of inquiry concluded on 21 July that it had in fact been an identification error. When the *Liberty* was first discovered by an Israeli spotter plane on the morning of the eighth, it was unidentified but possibly hostile, and a red marker was placed on the map in the naval war room. Later in the morning, the identification was tentatively changed to friendly (American), and a green marker replaced the red one. But the Israeli navy then went a period of time without a location, and someone, instead of retaining the green marker with a question mark, pulled it off the map entirely.

The shift changed at 1100 Israeli time, and the new shift knew nothing about the American vessel, which was no longer designated on the map. What they did know was that Israeli army units in the Sinai coastal town of Al Arish were reporting artillery bombardment from an unknown source. (It later turned out to be the explosion of an ammunition dump.) The Israelis began searching the sea for a possible hostile ship, and they found the *Liberty*. The crew of the vessel that did the identification claimed that its radar showed the ship to be heading at twenty-eight knots toward Suez (an impossible speed for the *Liberty*—an error by the radar operator), and Israeli naval control ordered an air attack. Two Mirage fighters on their way home from an air patrol over the Suez Canal were diverted to the spot where the supposed hostile was. After a quick pass, the pilots claimed that the ship was not displaying a flag (another error) and were ordered to execute an attack.

The torpedo boats arrived in the area at 1418. A low-flying aircraft had just radioed to its controller that he had seen a marking "CPR-5" on the hull. The naval controller told the torpedo boats to attempt a better identification, but the captain of one of the boats claimed that when he requested identification, the ship requested him to identify himself first. Based on identification aids available on board, it appeared to him to be the Egyptian supply vessel *El-Kasir*, and with this information in hand Israeli naval control again ordered an attack. After the first torpedo hit the boat, the markings "CTR-5" were observed on the hull. Control immediately terminated the attack, just before the torpedo boats were about to launch additional torpedoes that would have sunk the Liberty. An Israeli helicopter flying over the ship after the attack finally noticed an American flag, and the Israeli navy realized what it had done.

An Israeli court of inquiry, whose findings were kept secret at the time (but which were uncovered and published by two Israeli journalists in 1984), condemned the confusion, incompetence, and interservice rivalry that contributed to the attack. There was no finding of a deliberate attack, but there was plenty of blame for all the Israelis associated with the incident.

The Johnson administration was properly outraged. The State Department, in a scathing statement highly unusual for diplomats, called the attack "quite literally incomprehensible. As a minimum, the attack must be condemned as an act of military recklessness reflecting wanton disregard for human life." But Clark Clifford, who was appointed by the president to render a final judgment, called it an identification error. Clifford relied heavily on COMINT reports showing Israeli confusion about the identification; these would have been difficult to fake. Going into it with a preconceived notion that the Israelis must have known, he concluded that what was involved was "a flagrant act of gross negligence . . . " rather than a deliberate act."

This did not, of course, quiet the press. Journalists, both reputable and disreputable, supported the "deliberate attack" theory, and the legend arose, without basis in fact, that the Israelis wanted to blind American SIGINT sensors to their communications, both to keep them from finding out that Israel actually started the war and to keep secret a plan to launch an attack on Syria. (As was stated already, the vessel was not targeting Israeli communications and had no Hebrew linguists on board.) All these charges were repeated and embellished by James M. Ennes, a lieutenant aboard the Liberty who published a book on the subject in 1980. Most of the crew still believes that the attack was deliberate.

Many of the journalists properly questioned the position of the vessel at the time. Clifford, too, made a special point of this. The *Liberty* was clearly not where it should have been. The original plan was formulated before war broke out. Once the eastern Mediterranean became a battleground, it was decided to hold the *Liberty* out of the area, but the messages never reached McGonagle. The U.S. communications system was approaching breakdown; war sufficed to push it over the edge.

The crew, on the other hand, performed magnificently, and they and their vessel deserved better. NSA wanted to refurbish the ship and use it again, but the price tag of over $10 million was too high. The *Liberty* was decommissioned a year after the attack, and in 1973 it was cut up for scrap in Baltimore's Curtis Bay Shipyard. An abashed Israeli government paid $13 million in compensation for the loss of life and damage to the vessel.

The attack on the *Liberty* should not be viewed as a bizarre, or even an especially unusual, identification error. Even in peacetime such errors are made all too frequently—the Soviet shootdown of KAL 007 and the American shootdown of an Iranian airliner are good examples. When a country is at war, the possibility of error is compounded by haste and fear. Losses to friendly fire always represent a substantial percentage of the casualties. And the Israeli agreement to compensate should not be taken as proof of guilty knowledge, but rather as an attempt to retain the friendship of a benefactor wronged.

The *Pueblo*

"Any way you look at it this incident is a loser. We cannot come out even. We must cut our losses." —Clark Clifford, 29 January 1968

Nineteen sixty-eight was a bad year for the United States. It started with the Tet offensive in Vietnam and saw the assassinations of Robert Kennedy and Martin Luther King and the Soviet invasion of Czechoslovakia. As disaster piled on disaster, the only people truly happy were the media.

The very first disaster, however, was, for American cryptology, the worst. On 23 January North Korea captured a small SIGINT trawler from the TRS program called the *Pueblo*. It was everyone's worst nightmare, surpassing in damage anything that had ever happened to the cryptologic community.

Set-up

After a long lull following the Korean armistice, North Korea had become more aggressive. A clarion call of sorts sounded from the convention of the Korean Worker's Party in Pyongyang in October 1966, at which Kim Il-sung announced a campaign of hostile acts aimed at the "liberation" of South Korea and unification of South and North. This was followed by a dramatic rise in North Korean infiltration, terrorist incidents, and firefights along the demilitarized zone (DMZ). Between 1966 and 1967 incidents increased tenfold. On 21 January 1968 a group of thirty-one North Korean infiltrators attacked the South Korean presidential palace in hopes of assassinating President Park Chung-hee. This infamous Blue House incident raised tensions along the DMZ to their highest point since the armistice.

Into this not very auspicious situation intruded the latest in a series of TRS vessels. The *Pueblo* was first constructed in 1944 as an Army freight and supply vessel, and it was used to haul materials to South Pacific islands during the latter days of World War II. Decommissioned in 1954, it had sat in mothballs at Clatskanie, Oregon.

In 1966 the *Pueblo* rejoined the Navy, this time as a TRS. It was recommissioned at the Puget Sound Naval Shipyard in Bremerton, Washington, and became the smallest version of the SIGINT ship, an AGER.

The *Pueblo* carried just six positions and could make twelve to thirteen knots at top speed. Its new captain, Lieutenant Commander Lloyd M. Bucher, reported to take command in January 1967, while it was still undergoing refitting.

The captain and his crew were mismatched from the start. Bucher resented being jerked out of submarines to the surface navy. He knew nothing of electronic espionage and apparently learned little in his courtesy stop at NSA. His autobiographical account of the visit revealed considerable distaste for the mission and the people involved in it. Once on board, he found it difficult to get along with his executive officer, Lieutenant Edward Murphy. Moreover, he resented the operational control that Lieutenant Stephen Harris, the NSG-provided chief of the cryptologic spaces, had. To Bucher, not being in full control of his ship was intolerable.

The cryptologic crew was ill prepared for duty. Harris had a good background, including Russian language training and assignment on several NSG afloat detachments. But only two enlisted members had ever been to sea. The two Marine linguists who put aboard at were very green at Korean, and during the capture they could not understand the North Korean voice transmissions discussing the impending fate of their vessel. NSG had placed a vessel in harm's way without an advisory warning capability.

The way the AGER program was set up, NSA had little influence on the mission. The Navy tasked the vessels, and NSA provided technical support and suggested secondary tasking. Risk assessment for the voyage flowed through Navy channels up to DIA, which rendered the final judgment. By 1968 there were literally hundreds of missions worldwide every month, and there is no evidence that anyone put much thought into the *Pueblo's* first mission. The Navy assessed the risk as minimal, and DIA rubber-stamped it. The mission raised a few eyebrows at the 303 Committee (the organization that reviewed the monthly reconnaissance schedule), but the risk was not changed and the mission profile was not modified. Since the risk assessment process occurred over the year-end holidays, it probably received less scrutiny than was normal.

In fact, it should have raised some eyebrows. The North Koreans had of late shown unusual sensitivity to coastal vessels. Just twelve days before they took the *Pueblo*, the small North Korean navy had chased 300 ROK fishing boats south of the Northern Limit Line (NLL—a geographical extension of the 38th Parallel into the Sea of Japan), capturing two and capsizing a third. On the 20th North Korea summed up its grievances about coastal vessels to the UN Command, claiming that the other side was dispatching "spy boats disguised as fishing boats and villainous spies together with fleets of South Korean fishing boats."

Even prior to this, however, NSA had dispatched a message to the Joint Reconnaissance Center discussing the recent increased North Korean sensitivity in relation to the upcoming voyage of the *Pueblo*. JRC simply sent the message to CINCPAC, which paid no mind.

On 16 January, after putting out from Sasebo six days earlier, the *Pueblo* arrived at the northernmost point of its mission area and began slowly working its way south toward the port city of Wonsan. It had firm instructions to stay at least thirteen nautical miles off the coast, and there is no evidence to suggest that this order was ever violated. The crew was not having a happy trip, though. The seas had been rough almost every day since they had departed from San Diego in November, and the mission, which consisted of some very basic SIGINT sampling, had been dull and unproductive in the extreme.

Capture

On the 20th, and again on the 22d, the *Pueblo* saw North Korean vessels that were close enough to note its position. Bucher was sure that he had been identified and broke mandatory radio silence to report this. At about noon on the 23d, a subchaser pulled up, and after requesting that the *Pueblo* identify itself, the subchaser reported back to his controller. Clearly, the North Koreans were by then certain that it was a surveillance ship of some kind, and after some minutes, during which time it was possible that Wonsan control radioed instructions, the subchaser requested the *Pueblo* to heave to. The *Pueblo* turned to flee, and the subchaser gave chase, joined by three torpedo boats.

The *Pueblo* radio room sent news of the incident to Kami Seya at Flash precedence. The *Pueblo* and the pursuing torpedo boats continued to play a game of tag, and for a time Bucher was successful in evading capture. But finally the subchaser got between the *Pueblo* and open ocean and opened fire. Almost simultaneously the torpedo boats opened up, and at this point Bucher very tardily ordered emergency destruction to begin. (One of the NCOs in the cryptologic spaces had already disobeyed an earlier Bucher order and had begun destroying things.) Finally Warrant Officer Lacy overrode a Bucher order and directed the ship to stop dead. The chase was over.

As the *Pueblo* limped slowly toward Wonsan, escorted by the North Korean vessels, the crew was below decks desperately trying to get rid of all the classified material. It was a futile effort. This ship had far more classified materialthan it should have had, and it was not equipped to destroy in an emergency even that which it was authorized. Lack of adequate equipment, confined spaces which prevented use of the most effective destruction techniques, and an inexperienced crew that had never practiced emergency destruction aboard the *Pueblo* combined to virtually nullify their efforts. When the ship was finally boarded, most of the material was still lying on the deck.

The boarding took place at 1445, almost three hours after the first North Korean vessel had been sighted. One crew member had been killed during a volley, and several, including Bucher, had been wounded. The radioman had succeeded in apprising Kami Seya of their predicament, and he kept the station updated until he had to go off the air to destroy crypto material. The *Pueblo* reached Wonsan at about 1900, after the harbor lights were already winking in the stillness. The crew was offloaded and placed in a captivity that would last almost a year.

Aftermath

In Kami Seya, things were anything but still. The unit had been on the line with the *Pueblo* for the better part of three hours, and it was frantically passing reports to Commander, Naval Forces Japan. But the initial reports failed to generate the appropriate concern there. Not until after hearing the phrase "we are being boarded" did the organization get itself mobilized. Mobilization, however, proved difficult. The quickest remedy would have been a flight of 5th Air Force fighters. But owing to the low risk assessment, no fighters were on alert, and it would have taken two to three hours to ready something. Adding flight time from Okinawa (where the aircraft were based), they could not have reached Wonsan before dark. Fifth Air Force F-4s in Korea were on SIOP alert and could not be rearmed in time. The carrier *Enterprise* was steaming south in the Sea of Japan on its way to Subic Bay when it got the distress call. But the *Enterprise* F-4s were armed with air-to-air missiles, and the time required to rearm and fly to Wonsan was too much. The *Enterprise* turned around and steamed toward Korea to rendezvous with other vessels headed for the same place, but none of them would be there in time. No help was available, and the U.S. military had to sit and watch.

The middle of the day in Japan was the middle of the night in Washington. Critic reports began at NSA and the White House at about midnight. The senior operations officer called in Major General John Morrison, the assistant director for production, who hurried in to look at the traffic. Morrison called General Carter, who began directing the NSA response.

At the White House, Walt Rostow, the national security advisor, came in first. After hasty calls to NSA and Hawaii to get more information, Rostow notified the president early in the morning.

Carter mobilized every SIGINT resource he could get his hands on, and assembled every scrap of paper that pertained. He called an Alpha Alert [censored] So within the cryptologic community, everyone was scrambling. But to the rest of the world Carter put up a stone wall. It was a Navy mission, and he directed that most of the questions be diverted to naval authorities and the Joint Chiefs of Staff. Rather than spread his cryptologic authority to encompass the *Pueblo,* Carter found it useful in this case to put the pressure on the Navy.

Now that the damage had been done, Carter wanted to assess what the damage was. Regarding COMINT, NSA's initial assessment was equivocal. Assuming that most COMINT documents had been destroyed before capture, NSA focused on the information that the crew might reveal under interrogation. It was potentially serious, but as yet unknowable. Regarding the COMSEC loss, however, NSA's conclusions, expressed initially only a day after the loss, were unmistakable: "The probable compromise of four major U.S. COMSEC equipments, including three of our modern electronic crypto-equipments, is a major intelligence coup without parallel in modern history." This was right on target as far as was known then, but the full extent of the loss was not known until the mid-1980s, as will be discussed below.

At the White House, the *Pueblo* capture was one of those transcending crises that occupied the president. Before the end of the month, Lyndon Johnson had participated in at least thirteen full-dress meetings on the subject, and Robert McNamara, Clark Clifford (McNamara's designated replacement; 23 January was his first day on the job), Secretary of State Dean Rusk, and Earl Wheeler (chairman of the JCS) were all fully engaged until 30 January at which time the Tet Offensive cornered their attention.

The first meeting was the Tuesday lunch on 23 January. Discussions focused on where the *Pueblo* was when captured and what the United States could do about it. lnasmuch as it was too late to take the ship back, the group ran through several warlike options such as capturing a North Korean ship, hitting the North Koreans with US forces, and augmenting U.S. forces in the Korean area. At this meeting the president articulated a feeling that came to dominate his thoughts—that the Soviet Union might be behind this and that it could be a "second front" designed to distract the U.S. from South Vietnam. There was no evidence to support this, just speculation.

Later that day Johnson phoned the Soviet Union on the hotline to complain about it. He demanded Soviet intercession with North Korea, to which the Soviets replied that it was not their problem. Proof of Soviet involvement was lacking then and is still lacking today.

Twenty-four January was the day which shaped the administration's response. In a series of marathon meetings which had come to define the White House in crisis, the "kitchen cabinet":

1. dealt with the problem of the ship's position. Not all the SIGINT evidence was in yet, but there was enough to show that the North Koreans themselves knew the *Pueblo* was outside their territorial limits. [censored] The president decided to go on the air to reveal this information and to bring the evidence to the United Nations;

2. determined, without evidence, that the capture was somehow related to Vietnam. All in attendance agreed that the Soviets must have known about it in advance. (Later that day CIA registered the only dissent);

3. tentatively decided to move additional military aircraft into Korea, as well as station the *Enterprise* task force off the coast; decided to activate selected military reserve units for the crisis.

That same day FBIS intercepted a Korean Central News Agency broadcast purporting to contain a "confession" by Bucher alleging, among other things, that the *Pueblo* had made a "criminal intrusion" into North

Korean territorial waters. That very afternoon the Pentagon issued a rebuttal, stating that "the *Pueblo's* position as determined by the radar track of the North Koreans themselves . . . " put the ship outside North Korean waters. [censored]

Simultaneously, the administration was working on a presentation to the UN, to be made by Ambassador Arthur Goldberg. As nothing appeared sufficient to head off this even more explicit release of SIGINT, Carter sent a team to New York to work with Goldberg and his staff on the statement. By cooperating closely, NSA had an opportunity to read Goldberg's statement before he went before the Security Council on the 26th.

Goldberg presented both North Korean voice and manual Morse [censored] to prove that the *Pueblo* was in international waters and that the North Koreans had known it at the time. [censored]

Over the next several days, the White House continued to wrestle with all the ramifications of the *Pueblo* incident. One of the most difficult problems was that of protection of reconnaissance vehicles. The group concluded that it was impractical, given the number of such missions every year. The TRS *Banner* was sent to Korea as part of the *Enterprise* task force, and when it patrolled the North Korean coast, it was under heavy escort. But this was more a matter of showing resolve than of collecting intelligence, and the president recognized that it would be impossible to provide this sort of service to every ship and airplane engaged in peripheral reconnaissance. In an interview given to Hugh Sidey of *Time* magazine and Jack Homer of the *Washington Star* on 26 January Johnson made this point: "The Soviet Union and the United States have many such ships at sea and conduct literally thousands of flights to collect intelligence by aircraft. Neither currently provide [sic] protection. If they did so, they would require navies and air forces enormously greater than their present forces."

During the various interviews and press conferences, the Johnson administration made a fairly clean breast of the peripheral reconnaissance program. During a meeting with the National Alliance of Businessmen on the 27th, Clark Clifford explained that the United States had both SIGINT and photographic satellites in orbit, and the photo satellites "can see a tennis ball on a tennis court." Regarding SIGINT collectors such as the *Pueblo*, he said, "We have communication ships and very sophisticated electronic equipment to intercept their communications. The Soviets have a number of ships. And so do we . . . The public has a bad idea about spying. However, we must do it."

The North Koreans continued to make propaganda hay. Several members of the *Pueblo* crew were forced to make "confessions" similar to Bucher's which laid out the SIGINT effort against North Korea and specifically implicated NSA in the effort. SIGINT tasking documents were displayed on North Korean television, complete with the then-current SIGINT codewords, Trine and Savin. (This resulted in another codeword change, and the codewords adopted in 1968 have been used ever since.) In the end, there was little left to publicize that the North Koreans had not already displayed to a curious world.

The *Pueblo* incident also became stage to one of the biggest battles ever between NSA and the JCS. As a result of a number of developments in Southeast Asia, NSA and JCS staffers had crafted a compromise on the provision of SIGINT support to field commanders. Called MJCS 506-67, it set out new ground rules for deployment and operational control of tactical SIGINT units. When it was decided, in the middle of the Pueblo crisis, to deploy an AFSS Emergency Reaction Unit to South Korea, the JCS thought that operational control would automatically transfer to Fifth Air Force. Not so, said Carter. These resources simply augmented existing AFSS assets and were in a direct service, not a direct support, role. Therefore, operational control would continue with NSA. The JCS viewed this as a betrayal of the compromise reached in negotiating the new document, and they ultimately prevailed. Operational control passed to Fifth Air Force on 19 February.

Assessments

Before the administration became caught up in a response to the Tet offensive in Vietnam, Johnson appointed a committee headed by George Ball to investigate the *Pueblo* incident. Ball and his committee concluded on 7 February that;

1. the *Pueblo* had indeed been in international waters;

2. the mission had been a necessary one;

3. there had been no way of predicting the outcome, which might have been a spur-of-the-moment decision by the North Koreans. "It was assumed on the principle of mutual tolerance that, so long as we paralleled the Soviet practice, our vessels would remain relatively free from danger. . . ";

4. such missions should be continued, albeit with improved protection. Off the North Korean coast it would be necessary to provide escort vessels within a reasonable distance—aircraft on strip alert somewhere was not sufficient. Moreover, the design, armament, and equipment of the AGER-class vessels should be improved, and adequate destruction devices should be available. The rules of engagement should not bind the skipper to radio silence nor prohibit the use of defensive weapons until defense was impossible.

In February Congress got involved. At least three different sets of inquiries were performed, including one by William Fulbright in the Senate Foreign Relations Committee. (Fulbright was acquiring an insatiable appetite for matters cryptologic, as would be revealed at the hearings on the Tonkin Gulf Resolution in August.)

But by far the most intrusive was a subcommittee of the House Armed Services Committee, chaired by Otis Pike. On 10 March General Carter testified at length about the *Pueblo* in executive session. Two days later Pike released some of Carter's information at a press conference, and Carter was furious. He had cultivated good relations with Congress and had occasionally provided sensitive information to members of certain Committees when he thought it necessary. Pike's release set a very bad precedent and may have influenced NSA's response to that same congressman's far more extensive investigation of the intelligence community in 1975—the so-called Pike Committee investigation. (At that time someone on the committee leaked the final committee report to the press, even though the House had voted to suppress it because it contained classified information, specifically cryptologic.)

Assessments within NSA began almost immediately. Once the Agency had made its initial damage assessment (see above), Carter appointed a committee to do a more complete job. Through the spring and summer, the assessment became more refined, but a full accounting would have to await crew debriefing. To this end the United States put on all the diplomatic pressure it could to secure the crew's release. In the end, however, the government had to sign a phony "confession" and apology at Panmunjom in order to get the crew back. They walked across the bridge at the truce village to freedom on 23 December, just in time for Christmas.

The complete mishandling of the crew debriefing was emblematic of the entire *Pueblo* incident. Viewing it as an internal matter, the Navy kept NSA uninformed of arrangements for the debriefing and insisted that NSG represent the cryptologic community. NSA viewed the assessment of cryptologic damage as their business, and finally got the Joint Chiefs to intercede with the Navy so that NSA could take its proper role.

The debriefing process itself was typified by heavy friction between NSA's team and the Navy authorities on the scene. The Navy even refused to allow NSA's team chief, [censored] to communicate with Carter except through him, and [censored] had to resort to extraordinary methods to get his cables back to the Agency. [censored] reported that ". . . we are encumbered by a totally uneducated admiral who has neither the rudimentary knowledge of SIGINT, or for that matter, general intelligence, and who is in the position to edit our reports to the intelligence community." In response, Carter sent a bubbly message to Admiral Moorer, the CNO, complimenting the effectiveness of the debriefing team and the support received in San Diego (the debriefing site). Passed on to the Navy in San Diego, this message opened doors for [censored] Sometimes the heavy-handed approach was not the smart way to go.

[censored]

NSA had always designed crypto devices under the assumption that the enemy would eventually capture the machine. In order to read any communications, it would also be necessary to get the keying material. This, said NSA, was the salvation of the *Pueblo* story. Assuming that the North Koreans turned over the material to the Soviets, they could be in position to read traffic through several crypto periods in late 1967 and early 1968, but nothing more. This was bad enough, but NSA's design principles had staved off further disaster.

[censored]

It was a bad situation made worse by negligence. The crew was poorly trained, and its linguists could not even render advisory support to protect the vessel from capture. The Navy loaded it down with far too much classified material and equipment, some of it even beyond the clearance level of those aboard. The crew never practiced emergency destruction, which was next to impossible anyway given the inadequate destruction systems then available on board. There was evidence of poor coordination between captain and cryptologic crew.

Following the capture, the Navy and NSA engaged in an unseemly jurisdictional battle over the debriefing process. On the Navy side, there was a lack of understanding of NSA's role.

Self-defense was only one of the problems besetting the TRS program. All the vessels had been recommissioned; most of them dated from World War II. They were becoming expensive to operate, and 1968 was to be the year in which NSA hoped to obtain money to refurbish and continue the program. Even while the *Pueblo* was being captured, NSA was working on an internal study of the future of the AGER portion of the TRS system. NSA felt that little was wrong with the AGERs that could not be fixed by a little redefinition of command, relationships. But the Navy, strapped for cash to continue its presence in Southeast Asia, as well as elsewhere in the world, favored diverting the money to combat vessels.

[censored] But the Navy noted the difficulty and expense of protection. After a limbo period, during which each budget decision went against TRS, Deputy Secretary of Defense David Packard cancelled the program in October 1969. The last of the ships, the *Belmont,* was decommissioned just three months later. Surely the *Pueblo* and *Liberty* incidents were on his mind to the end.

Czechoslovakia

"As the U.S. tried to figure out whether or not the Soviets would invade Czechoslovakia in 1968, these [SIGINT] reports quite simply muddied the water and [challenged] even the most experienced all-source analysts searching for meaning and patterns in a mountain of material. The conversations reported were relevant. There were just too many." —Angelo Codevilla, *Informing Statecraft: Intelligence for a New Century*

The Soviet invasion of Czechoslovakia in August 1968 stands in history as one of the masterstrokes of the assertion of imperial control. It was masterful because of its speed, its surprise, and its brute force. It was hidden as part of a series of military exercises which, like a tornado out of control, turned suddenly and savagely to stamp out a generation of new political leaders. And it allegedly took the West entirely by surprise.

Viewed from a distance and as a whole, this analysis generally holds up. But viewed from up close, the generalizations begin to break down. They are simplistic and not entirely accurate. The reality is more complex.

The Prague Spring

It began in October 1967. The old Communist order under Antonin Novotny was beginning to crumble. At home he had overcentralized the economic system, and in foreign policy his support of the Arab cause during the 1967 war grated on younger and more liberal colleagues. And he had dealt not very skillfully with the subsurface conflict between the Czechs and Slovaks. For all these sins Novotny confronted considerable unrest.

Internal dissent erupted on the night of 31 October when a routine protest of the lack of electricity for their dormitories by students from the Technical College overflowed in a melee between students and police. The pot continued to bubble during November and December [censored]

Novotny desperately clung to his position as first secretary of the Czechoslovak Communist Party until 4 January when the party leadership banded together to vote him out. In his place they installed an obscure Slovak nationalist, Alexander Dubcek, first secretary of the Slovak Communist Party. Dubcek was known as a good Communist, and at first the Soviet leadership seemed to regard it as a routine and perhaps overdue unhorsing of a used-up Communist functionary. But Dubcek turned out to be anything but a routine Communist. Under his leadership, the Czechoslovak government quickly turned to market reforms and political liberalization which included press freedom and budding capitalism. Newspaper reporters began calling it the "Prague Spring". [censored]

On 4 May according to press reports, Dubcek and his principal lieutenants made a hurried trip to Moscow. It was in fact a showdown with the Soviet Communist Party over the Prague Spring reforms and the general direction of Czech communism. The official communique spoke of a "comradely atmosphere," which one writer said "is Communist shorthand for cold disagreement." This was followed by a series of secret meetings in the Kremlin, almost certainly on the Czech "crisis." [censored] But CIA, wading through the huge volume of reports, assessed the readiness as being related to a field exercise. This calmed the White House somewhat, and Walt Rostow told the president that Warsaw Pact forces did not appear ready to invade. In fact, it was very difficult to determine what the Soviets would do. [censored]

This menacing troop buildup continued through the month, until there were some nine line divisions and three army headquarters just to the north and east of Czechoslovakia. [censored] (But the press also tracked the troop movements.) The situation in Czechoslovakia was tense; many believed that the Warsaw Pact would invade immediately.

On 24 May a joint communique was released announcing that Warsaw Pact exercises would take place in Poland and Czechoslovakia in June. [censored]

The exercise, called Sumava, played out from 18 to 30 June. Its scenario involved a three-prong invasion of Czechoslovakia, with Czech forces representing NATO as the sole defenders. Invading forces were Soviet, Polish, East German, and Hungarian, and the exercise served as a dress rehearsal for the real invasion in August. At the termination, Warsaw Pact forces did not return to their bases—they ominously stayed in place until mid-July.

Meanwhile, Dubcek and the Czech leaders played a dangerous game with the Kremlin. Dubcek refused to retreat from liberalization measures and declined to attend a 14 July meeting at the Kremlin to discuss the situation. The meeting was held without him. With Soviet troops still on Czech soil, it took a great deal of courage not to back down.

On 23 July the Soviets announced yet another large-scale exercise, to be held along the Czech border and in western Russia, Byelorussia, and Latvia. The announced purpose was to work out rear services procedures. On 30 July they announced that the exercise would extended into Poland and East Germany. It did not include Czech troops.

On 1 August Dubcek and his lieutenants attended an unprecedented face-to-face meeting with Soviet Communist Party secretary Leonid Brezhnev and the Politburo leaders in the Slovakian town of Cierna nad Tisou. The proceedings are thought to have been acrimonious, but Dubcek did emerge from it with a "Declaration of Bratislava," a general statement of socialist principles which papered over the disagreements and preserved a measure of public agreement.

[censored]

On 20 July the control authority moved to Legnica, in Poland, and stayed there through the invasion preparations. During the last week of July, GSFG and NGF (Northern Group of Forces) units moved to new positions closer to Czechoslovakia. [censored]

On 10 August Moscow announced the beginning of a communications exercise. [censored]

On 18 August, the same date that the command post exercise concluded, [censored]

[censored]

[censored] As luck would have it, though, NSA's David McMani, the deputy chief of the Situation Room, was looking at the indicators and had established an easy dialogue with Walt Rostow, the national security adviser. He and Rostow privately agreed that an invasion was likely, although they did not have enough information to predict the date.

On 19 August McManis noted to Rostow that the invasion they both thought would happen appeared to be immment [censored] The next day would be time for Johnson's Tuesday Lunch with his key national security advisors. At the lunch, Rostow broached the subject of Czechoslovakia; it appeared to him that something was about to happen. In his planning notes for the president, Rostow noted: "You may wish to encourage the group to speculate about basic Soviet strategy in U.S.-Soviet relations at this stage, including the relationship to possible moves against Czechoslovakia. . . ." [censored] According to Rostow "We judged the Central Committee meeting as ominous, not hopeful," at the Tuesday Lunch. Richard Helms (DCI at the time) felt that the Soviets had decided to move.

Later that day, Anatoly Dobrynin, the Soviet ambassador to the U.S., called to say he would like to see the president that evening. The timing was almost unprecedented—the president knew immediately that the subject must be Czechoslovakia, and it must mean invasion.

At about midnight, 20 August, Warsaw Pact forces, poised on the border, rumbled across. Some fifteen to sixteen Soviet divisions, augmented (for public relations purposes, no doubt) by three Polish divisions and smaller numbers of Hungarians and Bulgarians, attacked in three major spearheads. The largest contingent raced in from the north, along the East German border, toward the key cities of Prague and Pilzen, while smaller groups came in from the Soviet Union (Carpathian Military District) and north from Hungary. At the same time, airborne forces launched from bases in the Soviet Union (primarily Vitebsk and Panevezhis) to key nodes in Czechoslovakia.

[censored] It was sudden, massive, and effective. They rolled over the almost defenseless Czech forces virtually unopposed.

Once in Prague, Soviet troops arrested Dubcek and his liberal supporters in the National Assembly. There was little resistance from the population, but the invaders, who had been told to expect a jubilant reception, were taken aback by the deep hostility of the Czech citizenry.

[censored] No Soviet forces went on alert, and later postmortems called into question the validity of using alert status as an indicator of hostilities. It was of a pattern with the tactical situation, which was evidently designed to be disguised as exercise activity.

[censored] The alert was probably precautionary—since the end of the Cold War the deputy commander of the Warsaw Pact invasion forces has written that the Soviets were confident NATO would not interfere, and they did not feel extreme measures were necessary.

[censored]

Following the invasion, a great national debate ensued about the Czech "surprise." Journalists were unanimous in condemning the failure of intelligence to warn. *U.S. News and World Report* reported that Johnson learned of the invasion from Dobrynin. Tad Szulc, in his history of Czechoslovakia since World War II, said that intelligence abounded, but "the recipients of all this intelligence input seemed unable or unwilling to interpret it adequately," and he noted that NATO did not go on alert all summer. Historian Walter Laqueur wrote that the West learned about the invasion from a radio broadcast in Prague. He claimed that "technical intelligence [censored] had the information, but did not get it to decision makers in time."

They were all right, and they were all wrong. As with all intelligence analysis, success or failure depended on how you defined the two terms.

Strategic warning was impeccable. [censored] when 20 August came, and Pact forces were poised on the border, the United States knew it.

One modern-day analyst has proposed that had DIA possessed the warning indicator system in 1968 that it later developed, it would almost certainly have published a warning report by 19 August. The case for this is good—Warsaw Pact force posture, reported [censored] was clearly at the highest level ever achieved; higher even than in May and July of the same year. The failure to publish a specific warning report was due to the fact that the system for doing it had not yet evolved.

The president knew as much as was knowable by the afternoon of 20 August and was not, contrary to press reports, surprised by what Dobrynin had to tell him. What good would it have done to alert NATO forces? NATO could do nothing anyway. Better to stay cool and look surprised.

[censored]

Romania—The Invasion That Never Happened

On the last two days of August, [censored] reports began to arrive at the White House concerning a possible Soviet move into Romania to bring the errant Communist regime of Ceaucescu back into line. [censored]

As it happened, the White House had been concerned about this possibility as early as the 23rd. Romania had pursued an independent foreign policy since 1964, and during the Czech crisis had pointedly supported Dubcek (alone within the Soviet Bloc). Soviet troop movements in areas peripheral to Romania could be interpreted as threatening to that country, too. [censored] Just to be on the safe side, however, President Johnson issued a public warning to the USSR on the first week of September. Romanian diplomats thanked the president for his support, and the crisis seemed to subside.[censored]

[censored] Romania was the invasion that did not happen [censored]

The Shootdown Of The EC-121

The SIGINT crises of the decade came to a tragic end in 1969. The North Korean shootdown of a Navy EC-121, with the loss of all thirty-one men aboard, was one of those transcending events that precipitated drastic changes in the crisis structure at NSA Headquarters. The effects are still felt today.

North Korea and the Aerial Reconnaissance Program

By taking the *Pueblo* in January 1968, Kim Il-sung's North Korea had once more branded itself as an international outlaw. As the United States redoubled its efforts to protect its peripheral reconnaissance missions, North Korea continued its pattern of infiltration and subversion. In November 1968, a group of 120 well-armed commando infiltrators landed by sea on the east coast of South Korea and infiltrated villages in the area. It required 40,000 ROK militia and police nearly 2 months and the loss of 63 lives to clean out the group.

The situation on the ground was not necessarily mirrored in the air. Over the years there had been five incidents involving North Korean and American aircraft. Only two, involving RB-47 aircraft in 1955 and 1964, affected the peripheral reconnaissance program. In neither case was the aircraft shot down, so in reality North Korea had never shot down a reconnaissance mission, although they had tried twice. Considering the unsettled situation around the DMZ, and the hostility demonstrated by the Soviets and Chinese to this sort of electronic spying, this was not considered to be a very high number of incidents.

To see Soviet fighters in reaction to a peripheral reconnaissance mission was normal; often the Soviets would send fighters out in relays to pace the aircraft, staying between it and the Soviet coastline. By the mid-1960s, however, JRC had decided that the Asian Communist nations fell into a different category. When one of them launched a fighter in reaction, which was rare, they meant business. Because of this, two new conditions had been inserted into the White Wolf plan. Condition 3, which would be called any time a hostile fighter was seen headed over water within 100 nautical miles of the mission, required a heightened state of alert aboard the aircraft and diversion to a fallback orbit farther off the coast. If the fighter came within 50 nautical miles, this would be changed to Condition 5, which required an automatic abort. Since the institution of these new conditions, the U.S. had lost no missions to the PRC, North Korea, or North Vietnam.

[censored]

The week before the mission, General Charles Bonesteel, commander of U.S. Forces in Korea, warned of unusually vehement language and surly protests by the North Koreans at Panmunjom. The warning was sent to the VQ-1 squadron, which was advised to be extra cautious. But the North Koreans appeared to suffer through profound mood swings at the Armistice Commission meetings, and neither Seventh Fleet nor CINCPAC changed the risk category of 3 (hostile action unlikely). Conditions 3 and 5 appeared to cover any potential problems, anyway.

Despite the relative venerability of the White Wolf warning program and its apparent good effect (there had been very few incidents since it had been instituted in the early 1960s), VQ-1 aircraft were only loosely cobbled to the system. According to a senior NSA official involved with White Wolf, the Navy was an "unenthusiastic" player in White Wolf. Unlike the Air Force reconnaissance aircraft, the EC-121 had no secure method of contact with the ground. For warning, they relied on SAC HF broadcasts labeled "Sky King," which could not be acknowledged. Thus the ground station personnel issuing a condition did not know if a transmission had been received, or what the situation was aboard the aircraft. Moreover, the key Navy units involved in the mission (including [censored] were not on distribution for reports issued by AFSS sites watching the mission.

The Mission

The doomed aircraft departed [censored] at 0700L with a double load of thirty-one crew members—the excess members were in training status. It was to fly across the Sea of Japan to a point off the northern coast of North Korea, do two and a half orbits, an land at Osan Air Force Base in Korea. [censored]

[censored]

At about 1330, as the mission was nearing the topmost portion of its last orbit, two North Korean MIG-21s scrambled from the training school at Hoemun. The fighters had been there for about two weeks—it was unprecedented for MIG-21s to be at Hoemun, and their purpose there was never explained. As was customary, Osan waited for a second plot before issuing a Condition 3. They did not get one for eight minutes, at which time the fighters were reflected at about fifty-five nautical miles from the mission and closing fast. One of them peeled off to make a defensive patrol, but the other bore on straight for the mission. At 1340 Osan issued a Condition 5, as the second MIG-21 was by this time reflected as well under fifty nautical miles from the mission. Only four minutes later [censored] the two aircraft merging. The shootdown probably came at 1347, while the mission was about eighty nautical miles from the coast. The tracks separated at 1349, [censored] The MIG-21 was headed home by that time.

[censored] The North Korean reaction was virtually unprecedented [censored] They were in close touch with 314 Air Division in Korea, and at 1345, two minutes prior to the shootdown, Brigadier General Arthur Holderness, 314 AD commander, directed that F-102s be launched in case of trouble. But, incredibly (considering the *Pueblo* incident the previous year), the Navy had not requested strip alerts, so no fighters were actually airborne until shortly after the hour. [censored] The feeling was that the aircraft must have "hit the deck" to evade the MIG-21.

At the same time, Kami Seya was completely in the dark. The were making communications checks, but they were getting nothing in reply. [censored] The VQ-1 squadron was monitoring the SAC HF broadcasts, so they knew something was amiss, and they were making repeated calls to the air control facility at Fuchu asking for information.

Finally, at 1444, almost an hour after the shootdown [censored] issued a Critic. Still, no one knew for sure what had happened until FBIS monitored a 1600 North Korean broadcast claiming to have shot down a "spy plane." By then the aircraft was half an hour overdue at Osan.

Fifth Air Force aircraft swarmed to the spot, but debris was not spotted until the next day by a naval P-3. Eventually two bodies were recovered, along with some debris. Although Soviet vessels participated in the search and rescue (SAR) operations, compromise of classified material was never a significant issue, as it had been with the *Pueblo*.

While [censored] was trying to figure out if they had a shootdown or not, the Current SIGINT Operations Center at NSA had called Major General John Morrison, the assistant director for production. Morrison began coordinating the NSA response, but found it almost impossible. A Group had a crisis response center (the CSOC) with analysts and reporters [censored] But B Group had nothing equivalent to it, and analysts had to be called to duty in the middle of the night. By 0330 Local, CSOC had fashioned a follow-up to the Critic, [censored] Morrison wore out his shoes walking between the A and B Group areas to try to get a coordinated response. The follow-up finally went out at 0500, but not before a thoroughly frustrated Morrison had vowed to consolidate his crisis and warning facilities into a single organization.

The Crisis

NSA's disorganized response was reflected at the White House. At the Situation Room, David McManis was trying to piece together the details, and he was on the phone with several different NSA divisions. He finally found it necessary to drive to NSA and get together the materials that he would need to brief the president.

The shootdown plunged the new Nixon administration into its first international crisis. During the campaign Nixon had criticized the Johnson administration's handling of the Pueblo capture, and he had vowed to demonstrate that the Republicans were made of sterner stuff. Henry Kissinger, the new national security advisor, prepared a list of options which included a B-52 strike (according to journalist Seymour Hersh), and bellicosity nearly carried the day. But in the end the solid opposition of the secretaries of state and defense (Rogers and Laird) and the DCI (Helms) won out.

Instead, the administration launched a diplomatic offensive. The cornerstone of this offensive was a presidential press conference on 18 April. There, Nixon, using data supplied by NSA, stated that intercepts of Soviet and North Korean radar reflections proved that the aircraft had been in international waters. [censored]

The administration decided ultimately on a military show of force in the Sea of Japan, a move almost identical to that which Johnson had made in January 1968. A massive flotilla was assembled under the name Task Force 71. It included three carrier groups and 250 aircraft, [censored] On 24 April AFSS flew a special RC-130 mission off the North Korean coast, heavily defended by American military might. By then, however [censored] North Korea had crawled back into its leathery shell and was no longer an immediate threat. Moreover, there was no evidence that the Soviets or Chinese Communists were in any way involved in the incident.

A *Washington Post* story on 17 April called into question the value of the peripheral reconnaissance program. It was a good question, and it got a thorough airing in the Pike Subcommittee, which was still investigating the *Pueblo* capture. House Armed Services Committee chairman Mendel Rivers simply added the EC-12 shootdown to the list of things that Pike was tasked to look into.

While General Carroll of DIA came out four-square in favor of tho reconnaissance program, John Morrison was not so categorical. Morrison, an Air Force general, could see the value of the Air Force program, which appeared to him to be better managed, used more capable aircraft, participated more fully in PARPRO (the Peacetime Aerial Reconnaissance Program)—and were, hence, safer—and were more fully under national control. The Navy program, Morrison thought, suffered from a lack of all these attributes. NSA was getting only minimal value and had no control at all. Morrison stood his ground before Carroll and the Navy on the issue. He commissioned an internal NSA study of the situation, which basically backed his gut feeling. It was the second serious run-in between NSA and the Navy on peripheral reconnaissance.

The *Post* reporter, who seemed to have impeccable sources, also cited the extended delay in reporting the incident from the field. General Wheeler (chairman of the JCS) also raised questions, and NSA was called to answer. An internal investigation completely exonerated [censored] focusing on its performance of advisory warning functions (on which it did a credible job) rather than on the delay in issuing the Critic. This approach seemed to quiet external criticism, but any good field reporter knew that the Critic should have been issued as soon as there was any considerable doubt as to the fate of the mission. The investigation begged the real question.

The Pike Committee expressed disquiet about the real value of such airborne reconnaissance in view of the cost in dollars and lives over the years. Some of the committee's concern may have stemmed from NSA's unwillingness to defend the Navy's programs. Pike recommended that the full Armed Services Committee take a more active role in monitoring the programs.

The committee was also very critical of interservice disconnnects. The members cited failure of the VQ-1 squadron [censored] to receive any information from the Air Force about the mission until they received the Critic, and they noted that this time delay contributed to delays in launching the search and rescue effort. They were incredulous over the failure of the Navy to ask the Air Force for fighter strip alerts, especially so soon after the *Pueblo* incident.

The rivalry between the Navy and NSA was not defused until General Carter stepped down as director. The new director, Admiral Noel Gayler, had the contacts within the Navy to build bridges, and as the new director he took NSA's case directly to Admiral John Hyland, CINCPACFLT commander. Gayler wanted closer NSA involvement with Navy SIGINT reconnaissance, and the authority to task missions. He eventually got part of what he wanted [censored]

The 1960s absolutely overflowed with SIGINT crises. After the Arab-Israeli War of 1967 and the *Pueblo* capture of 1968, John Morrison proposed to General Carter that NSA establish a single national SIGINT watch center. The proposal was still hanging fire four months later when the EC-121 went down. Morrison pressed Carter for a decision, and on 17 July 1969 he got one. In the twilight of his term, Carter concurred with the establishment of a National SIGINT Operations Center (NSOC). Morrison himself was charged with putting it together.

As for the EC-121s, their time was almost over. A Navy Board of Inquiry, looking at the shootdown, noted the cumbrous nature of the aircraft (maximum speed 220 knots) and low headroom (maximum altitude 10-20,000 feet), and the board recommended that something better be procured. The replacement was the EP-3E Orion, which gradually took over all EC-121 orbits. The EC-121s were moved back to safer orbits until they could be mercifully retired.

Was the shootdown a deliberate act? Conspiracy theories usually require wild flights of imagination, but in this case it was the only explanation that made sense. Like the *Pueblo* capture, it seemed to follow no known North Korean procedure, and it did not appear to have simply been a routine operation gone haywire. Instead, it appeared to be a carefully preplanned event, from the placing of two MIG-21s at a training base that had never seen them before, to the flight pattern of the aircraft that allowed for little misinterpretation of intent. The shootdown happened to occur on Kim Il-sung's birthday, which led to speculation that it was a planned birthday present. Of course, the North Koreans had to hope that the JRC reconnaissance schedule conformed with Kim's birthday, which makes this part of the theory rather tenuous.

It was likely just another of North Korea's xenophobic strikes. This time a U.S. reconnaissance aircraft was in the way.

Security And The Work Force In The 1960s

Success on the cryptologic front did not translate into the security field. A succession of security problems in the early 1960s, begun in the summer of 1960 with the infamous Martin and Mitchell defection, rocked the NSA community. For the first four years of the decade, it must have seemed like the sky was falling.

Dunlap

The House Un-American Activities Committee investigation into the Martin and Mitchell affair ended in 1962 when a final report was issued. Legislation to give the director additional powers to dismiss personnel, which resulted from the committee recommendations, was still dragging through Congress when in July 1963 an Army sergeant named Jack Dunlap committed suicide. A month later his wife showed up at NSA with a pile of classified documents which, NSA's security organization discovered, Dunlap had been selling to the KGB.

Sergeant First Class Jack E. Dunlap had first come to NSA as the driver for Major General Garrison B. Coverdale, the chief of staff, in 1958. Dunlap had up to that time served a rather uneventful career in the Army, which included service in Korea as an infantryman. While overseas he had worked as a technician and messenger for ASA, which got him closer to the security business. But Dunlap was afflicted with serious character flaws. He liked money, lots of it, and when he had it, he spent it on yachts, fast cars, and fater women. Once at NSA, he discovered how to get it. Sometime in May or June 1960, Dunlap walked into the Soviet embassy in downtown Washington and offered to sell classified documents. He claimed he could get his hands on them.

Dunlap smuggled classified documents out of NSA literally under his shirt. He did not work in a technical area, had no knowledge of cryptology, and probably did not steal documents in any organized fashion. But he knew that the documents were worth money. He was in and about Coverdale's office and just scooped up whatever became available. The FBI and NSA security people were never able to determine with any certainty just what Dunlap had sold.

Twice the Army alerted Dunlap for overseas assignments. This represented a serious threat to his lifestyle, which by that time included two Cadillacs, a Jaguar, a thirty-foot yacht, a world-class hydroplane, and a blonde mistress. The first time, Dunlap evaded the assignment by pleading a bad back. The second time, he informed the Army that he intended to resign, and he applied for a civilian position at NSA.

He did not get very far. His initial polygraph turned up evidence of petty thievery, immoral living, and living beyond his means, and his second try did not go any better. NSA initiated an investigation and withdrew his access to classified material. The investigation began in May, and the FBI interrogated him on 17 July. Apparently convinced that he was about to be exposed, Dunlap committed suicide six days later by inhaling carbon monoxide. Later in the summer his wife turned up with the classified documents that were still in the Dunlap residence.

The Dunlap affair brought further unfavorable publicity to NSA, but it did represent a success of sorts. Had the polygraph not been in place, Dunlap might have have been hired in some capacity and would have continued his espionage. The incident renewed discussions about requiring military assignees at NSA to take the polygraph, but the armed services staunchly opposed it, and successive directors (Blake and Carter) made little headway. The custom of excluding the military from the polygraph did not finally end until 1985.

Much criticism attended the revelation of Dunlap's lifestyle, which had gone unreported by coworkers. Further, the affair spotlighted the ease with which employees could spirit classified documents out of the Agency. The impact was the initiation of exhaustive exit inspections, which continued for thirty years (until 1993), and a continuing focus on employee lifestyle, a point that was hammered home to NSA employees again and again during security awareness sessions. Although Dunlap is deceased, his ghost has lived ever after in the halls of Fort Meade.

Hamilton

The same day that Dunlap committed suicide, the Soviet newspaper *Izvestia* published an article about NSA attributed to one Victor Norris Hamilton, a former NSA analyst. The third security crisis of the young decade had burst on the Agency.

Hamilton, whose family name was originally "Hindali," was Lebanese by birth. He met and married an American working for Point Four (a foreign aid program) in Libya in 1953, and emigrated with her to the United States. Hamilton's fluency in Arabic attracted the attention of NSA, and he was recruited for employment in 1957.

He remained at NSA for only two years. In early 1959 Hamilton began evidencing psychological problems, and he was sent to the medical staff for an evaluation. He was diagnosed as paranoid schizophrenic, but refused hospitalization, and he was medically terminated in June. He visited Morocco briefly but returned dissatisfied. He applied for employment at CIA, but there was no billet available for him. NSA tried to get him committed for psychiatric evaluation, working through his wife, but this failed. In 1960 he wrote a letter to the House Armed Services Committee claiming that an agent had offered him money to do business with the Soviet Union. The matter was turned over to the FBI, which tried unsuccessfully to interview him. He worked briefly as a teacher in Iraq but was discharged, and he dropped out of sight from May 1961 until the *Izvestia* article appeared.

[censored]

Hamilton brought more opprobrium to a besieged NSA security organization. Yet in his case, as in Dunlap's, it could be argued that the system worked. His initial hiring was, in retrospect, inopportune, but the internal screening system weeded him out before he progressed into more responsible positions. [censored]

In March of 1974 the State Department reported to NSA that Hamilton was being detained in a Soviet psychiatric hospital. A Jewish emigré made a positive identification of Hamilton based on a photograph, and NSA closed the case in June.

The Hamilton and Dunlap cases heightened the sense of urgency in Congress about NSA personnel policies. When in 1964 Congress enacted PL 88-290, giving the director more authority to hire and fire NSA people, the legislation owed much to the three security cases that immediately preceded it.

David Kahn and *The Codebreakers*

The wave of publicity surrounding the Martin and Mitchell case interested a *Newsday* reporter named David Kahn. Kahn already had an active lifelong interest in cryptology sparked by his youthful reading of Fletcher Pratt's book *Secret and Urgent*. Subsequent to the Martin and Mitchell expose, he wrote an article for the *New York Times Magazine* on the influence of cryptology on current events, and this spawned a publishing contract with MacMillan. *The Codebreakers,* a monumental work on the history of cryptology, was published in 1967 to a good deal of fanfare. It was, and has remained, the definitive work on the subject in the open press.

The publication was not a welcome development at Fort Meade. When NSA learned of the forthcoming book, it obtained a copy of the manuscript from the publisher. Without a reasonable hope of cooperation from either Kahn or MacMillan, the Agency reviewed the manuscript and marked a few passages for modification or deletion. To NSA's surprise, Kahn, then in Paris, reviewed the changes and agreed with virtually all of them. The material NSA wanted removed related to [censored] and was not central to Kahn's thesis.

Although Kahn was reasonably cooperative, many other journalists were not. [censored] as the interest of the American public in NSA increased. Beginning as early as 1961 for instance, the *New York Times* quoted the presidential press secretary about the launch of Soviet manned space vehicles which referenced "listening posts" in the Middle East intercepting traffic between the launch site and downrange tracking stations. The next year *Newsweek* published references to satellite intercept of Soviet microwave transmissions. In 1966 the *New York Times* published a series of articles on SIGINT collection at the U.S. embassy in Moscow and on satellite intercept of Politburo-level limousine car phones. A year earlier a press photo of McGeorge Bundy with President Johnson contained a copy of the CIA Daily Bulletin with a clearly visible "Top Secret Dinar" (the then-current Category III COMINT codeword) stamp affixed. This produced numerous press references to a "codeword so secret the very existence is classified." All the reporters seemed to know that the codeword referred to SIGINT, even at that relatively early date. The anonymity that NSA had enjoyed in the 1950s was slowly disintegrating.

Cryptology is Legalized

The legal existence of a COMINT effort, tendered precarious by the Federal Communications Act of 1934, was finally established in 1968. The Omnibus Crime Control and Safe Streets Act of 1968 dealt specifically with the issue. While prohibiting all wiretapping and electronic surveillance by persons other than law enforcement authorities (and even then under restriction), it stated that: "Nothing contained in this chapter or in section 605 of the Communications Act of 1934 . . . shall limit the constitutional power of the President to take such measures as he deems necessary to . . .

obtain foreign intelligence information deemed essential to the security of the United States. . . ." It did so just in time; the Watergate period and the attendant Church and Pike Committee hearings called into question all that was illegal about espionage, and much that was legal, too. The 1968 legislation provided a much-needed defense for NSA and the cryptologic community.

American Cryptology At The End Of The Decade

"It is important that you recognize the systematic character of the cryptologic enterprise; that its integrity must be maintained because the challenge with which it is confronted cannot be met if that system is debilitated, fragmented, or destroyed." —General Marshall S. Carter on the occasion of his retirement, 1 August 1969

By the end of the 1960s, cryptology had become big business. SIGINT product reports had become common paperwork in the White House and at every level down from that. NSA sent representatives to nineteen organizations, ranging from enormous military commands like CINCPAC to [censored] A study of strategic warning done in 1967 called COMINT "the workhorse of warning intelligence; no other source can match its continuity, timeliness, and span of coverage."

The cryptologic community was at its height in terms of personnel numbers. NSA employed about 18,000 people [censored] percent of them military), while the SCAs had [censored] The total, about [censored] men and women, was a strength that had never been reached before and has not been attained since.

Relationships with the Military

Paradoxically, the relationship between NSA and the military commands had never been at such a low ebb. Strains in tailoring SIGINT support had developed during the Vietnam War. A series of situation-specific compromises had papered over the differences, while leaving the underlying issues unresolved.

At mid-war, 1966 and 1967, NSA and the JCS had tried to hack out a comprehensive agreement concerning the use and control of SIGINT resources. The resulting document, called MJCS 506-67, left DIRNSA in overall control of all SIGINT assets but provided that under certain circumstances certain types of assets would be delegated to the tactical commander. The memo carefully defined the procedures for doing this, and for the first time the role of the cryptologic support group was defined and standardized.

The trick was in universal interpretation and smooth implementation. The first try, during the Pueblo situation, collapsed in howling controversy, and it colored relationships for several years to come. Although the agreement was employed more successfully in later years, difficulties persisted.

In 1967, the same year that MJCS 506-67 was published, the Army convened a board under Brigadier General Harris W. Hollis to "examine cryptologic and related activities." At the root of this study were deep-seated differences between NSA and the Army over the management of cryptologic assets. The Hollis Board recommended a series of steps which would have both pulled ASA resources away from DIRNSA control on the one hand, and on the other, given ASA a more favored seat at the cryptologic table.

Hollis made a pitch to transfer ASA direct support resources from the CCP to the Army general-purpose program. This proposed move would have fragmented cryptologic resources while divorcing the Army from the CCP system. NSA opposed it, while recognizing the tendency to fully fund big-site resources and programs at the expense of tactical assets. Hollis also recommended that ASA be given operational control of tactical SIGINT resources at all times—the Army deferred this.

Distressed at the increasing concentration of resources at Fort Meade, the Hollis Board made a number of proposals that would have strengthened in-theater ASA processing. This move to improve SCA theater assets ammounted to an attempt to halt the tide. The waves of cryptologic centralization continued to wash inexorably over the valiant Hollis Board, and nothing came of the attempt.

Finally, Hollis proposed that the Army become more involved in centralized cryptologic activities, by taking a role in futuristic projects like [censored] and by increasing its manning at Fort Meade. While pointing out that ASA had already been given a piece of [censored] (a logistics piece, but nonetheless a piece), NSA noted deepening trends in the opposite direction. Army policy led in the direction of diversification, especially at the officer level, rather than toward the cryptologic specialization that was required for greater ASA participation in the centralized cryptologic system. It was an ominous trend which led ASA in a tactical direction and which eventually caused it to virtually abdicate its unique SIGINT expertise, established so laboriously by Friedman and others in the 1930s.

The debate over SIGINT control intensified in 1969 when JCS promulgated a new policy document for electronic warfare, called MOP-95. Electronic warfare (EW) had always been outside the purview of SIGINT, but MOP-95 broadened the definition of EW to include a new category called Electronic Warfare Support Measures. The new category sounded just like SIGINT, but without the codewords or centralized control. General Carter attacked the new JCS document, to no avail. The armed services continued to develop EW capabilities, in league with the SCAs, which were happy to participate in a new effort divorced from NSA control.

During the summer of 1969, as General Carter's term as director wound toward its end, the Joint Chiefs were considering a direct assault on NSCID

6. The objective was to expand JCS authority over cryptologic assets, at the expense of DIRNSA. Carter found out about the draft, and in a phone call to General Wheeler (chairman of the JCS) he called it an "absolute monstrosity." The revision of NSCID 6 was going through coordination when it was halted by Admiral Johnson, director of the Joint Staff, to await the appearance of Admiral Gayler at Fort Meade.

Marshall Carter Retires

Weary of conflict with the services and debilitated by medical problems, General Carter retired in August of 1969. But before he did so he loosed one final blast. In a letter to Secretary of Defense Melvin Laird the day before his retirement ceremony, he characterized the state of cryptologic management as "diluted": "Despite the vigor, ingenuity, enterprise, and growing competence of the national eryptoiogic establishment which emerged almost seventeen years ago, subsequent administrative and organizational arrangements . . . have diluted the original concept and clouded the original goals. More and more common tasks have been assigned outside the cryptologic community, with a corresponding loss of efficiency and economy."

He excoriated the legal hairsplitting that had been employed to shave cryptologic resources from the central system, to call a duck something other than a duck in order to free it from NSA's control. He was pessimistic about the future.

Carter was asked to hold invitations to his retirement ceremony at the Pentagon to 150. He invited only 3 people and zipped through the ceremony in ten minutes. The Pentagon was as happy to see the last of Marshall Carter as Carter was to leave the wars.

Gayler Takes the Helm

With Carter on the way out, the Department of Defense decided to experiment with a new kind of director. Instead of appointing an intelligence specialist on his final military assignment, DoD nominated an admiral with an operational background and ambitions to go higher.

Noel Gayler was untainted by the intelligence business. The son of a Navy captain, he had gone into naval aviation soon after his graduation from Annapolis in 1936. Gayler had served as a flyer in the Pacific in World War II, following which he had had many years of both operational and staff experience with the line Navy. He had been only the third naval officer ever to fly a jet aircraft, and when he was nominated to fill Carter's job, he still held the record for the longest flight from an aircraft carrier. He was a known protégé of Elmo Zumwalt, the new and reformist CNO.

Gayler was the most unusual director in NSA's history from many aspects. Personally, he was dynamic, mercurial, and high-strung. Gordon Summers, a senior civilian at USAFSS, described Gayler's management style as all Navy: "Gayler came from a Navy background, and his perception of command and control was the captain on the bridge of the ship with a speaker tube down to the boiler room yelling orders to throw more coal on the fire, and everybody down to the lowest level threw more coal on the fire."

His impatience with briefers was legendary, and he was known to throw things when especially agitated. He seemed to strike out in all different directions at once, and he moved with dizzying speed from one topic to another. Short, stocky and athletic, he resembled a fireplug in constant motion.

Gayler was put in the job to repair the damaged NSA-JCS relationship. He understood that he was to open up channels of communication, that he was to talk to the operational officials on the Joint Staff and get things moving again. One of his first moves was to create a permanent NSA representative to the Pentagon, accredited to the JCS, the military departments, and the office of the secretary of defense.

He was immediately confronted with the JCS staff papers, forwarded to him by Vice Admiral Johnson. The papers were more than just critical—they amounted to an indictment. In his reply to Johnson, he said that the basic directives (i.e., NSCID 6) seemed to be sound and that "any difficulties have been occasioned by the attitudes of personnel involved" (a clear reference to his predecessor and his antagonists). He believed that he could patch things up through personal diplomacy, and he began calling people at the Pentagon. Within weeks he had defused the situation.

Although he did put NSA back on speaking terms with the military, it is hard to see how he accomplished it. His personal relationship with most of the Joint Chiefs was cold to the point of hostility. But Gayler was politically astute, and he moved easily in Washington's power elite despite his mannerisms. When he departed, he was rewarded with the plum assignment of CINCPAC and got his fourth star; the first NSA director ever so elevated.

The Eaton Committee

By 1967 the SIGINT budget passed $1 billion, and manpower stood at nearly 100,000. Officials at the Bureau of the Budget were already taking a close look at the CCP when General Carter sent over his CCP proposal for FY69, which added another $200 million to an already high figure. The CCP monitor, William Mitchell, went through the roof. He took the Carter budget to Charles Schultz, director of the Bureau of the Budget, and convinced Schultz that cryptology had to be "investigated." Schultz, who had worked in ASA earlier in his life and probably thought he had special insight, sent an unstaffed memo to the president proposing a national-level cryptologic review.

Richard Helms, the DCI, found out about this invasion of his turf, and he called White House staffer Bromley Smith. Walter Rostow and Clark Clifford put a stop to the Schultz memo, but this did not solve the cryptologic budget problem. Ultimately Robert McNamara, whose empire included NSA, convinced the president that Helms himself should be charged with the job. The DCI was to appoint a high-level committee to investigate cryptology. The objective was to reduce the CCP, and it was to be a review to end all reviews.

Helms appointed a very high-powered group. Lawyer Frederick Eaton was chair, and the members were General Lauris Norstad (former SACEUR), Ambassador Livingston Merchant, and Dr. Eugene Fubini, the DDR&E and long-time nemesis of Marshall Carter. A more influential foursome could hardly have been found for the job.

The Eaton Committee suffered from the hostility of almost every organization with any stake in the problem. Helms himself had been cool to the idea when it was first proposed. Regarding NSA and SIGINT satellites, for instance, he stated that NSA's relationship with the NRO was a matter for him and McNamara to sort out, and it should not be discussed by a committee. He opposed any investigation of Third Party matters as intruding onto CIA turf. He demanded that the committee not interfere with CIA's independent SIGINT effort: "Relations between NSA and CIA on [censored] activities have been the subject of exhaustive discussion and review and present working arrangements appear to me to be satisfactory."

Helms suggested that the committee occupy itself with considerations of ELINT management and reduction or consolidation of SIGINT field sites in vulnerable overseas areas. But DIA and the services opposed any look at ELINT, and NSA viewed the idea of reducing field sites with suspicion.

The appointment of Fubini to the committee was, to Carter, the last straw. He determined to have nothing to do with the effort, and his appointees to the committee staff (Walter Deeley and Gerald Burke) defended NSA interests at every turn. The investigative effort was so fragmented by staff bickering and external hostility that Eaton was able to accomplish little. It was hardly a review to end all reviews.

The conclusions of the Eaton Committee, especially in the area of COMINT, tended to support NSA objectives. Eaton was a centralizer, and he proposed that NSA obtain more control over the cryptologic process. In his view, parts of the SCA staffs should be integrated with the director's staff. The committee recognized the central dilemma of resource control which was bedeviling SIGINT, and it viewed askance service attempts to flake off various parts of the process through inventive definitions of EW and increased control of cryptologic field sites. Service complaints about lack of SIGINT support should not be used as a lever to fragment the cryptologic effort: "The tendency on the part of the military, unilaterally, to remove essential resources, both men and equipment, from the approved Consolidated Cryptologic Program is detrimental to the entire effort and should be resisted."

Regarding ELINT, however, the panel proceeded in the opposite direction. Stating that "over the past ten years, it has become apparent that the decision to place ELINT as a whole within the COMINT structure has not proved workable," the committee recommended that ELINT remain decentralized. NSA's proper role was to exert technical control, to collect and process signals of national strategic importance [censored] and to maintain a central database for the intelligence committee.

On overseas basing, the committee simply repeated shopworn platitudes about the need to reduce bases without hurting the effort. Eaton and company seemed to understand that overseas real estate must sometimes be retained in a less-than-productive status to preserve options against future targets. The Eaton members also felt that the SIGINT targets would increasingly become high-tech problems which required huge amounts of money [censored] and the overhead SIGINT satellite program. The committee cautioned against rushing in too fast, but recognized that increasing amounts of money would have to be funneled into those efforts at the expense of conventional collection.

On the critical issue of assessing the effort against [censored] the committee admitted that it had not been able to gather enough information to make a recommendation. There were telltale signs that NSA had decided not to unburden itself of its most closely guarded secrets to a group which it did not trust and that Eaton recognized a stone wall when he saw one.

The only Eaton recommendation that had any long-range impact on intelligence was one which strayed beyond the borders of cryptology. The committee recommended that the DCI exert stronger direction over the overall intelligence program by creating a National Intelligence Resources Board (NIRB). This emphasis on centralized direction harmonized with the philosophical bent of the committee, and at CIA it fell on fertile ground.

The Eachus Committee

Following the failure of the Eaton Committee to resolve the central problem of the worth of the effort against Soviet cipher systems, the NIRB prepared to take on the problem. But in the fall of 1968, before the NIRB could get moving, NSA itself established a panel for the [censored] effort. The Eachus Committee was headed by Dr. Joseph Eachus of MIT, a former Navy cryptanalyst during World War II and one of the leading civilian authorities on the Soviet cipher system problem. Eachus was known to NSA and was a trusted friend. Carter placed his bets on a friendly assessment.

In contrast to the Eaton fiasco, NSA revealed all to Eachus. The Eachus report was the most thorough assessment of the NSA position on Soviet enciphered systems ever done.

[censored]

Although Deputy Director Louis Tordella tried to justify the expense [censored] Eachus's role was to validate the effort and urge that it be pursued with increased intensity.

German World War II Enigma code machine

Bombe machine used to help break the Enigma code

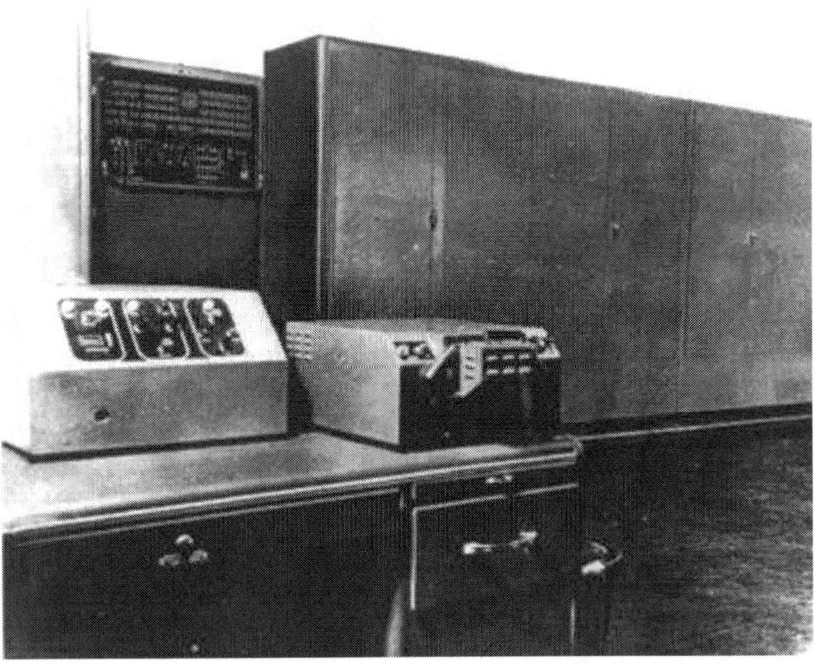

UNIVAC 1101 computer used for cryptologic work

U-2 spy plane

Cuban Missile Crisis, 1962

USS Liberty, 1967

USS Pueblo, 1968

Iranian troops confront protesters, 1979

Soviets in Afghanistan

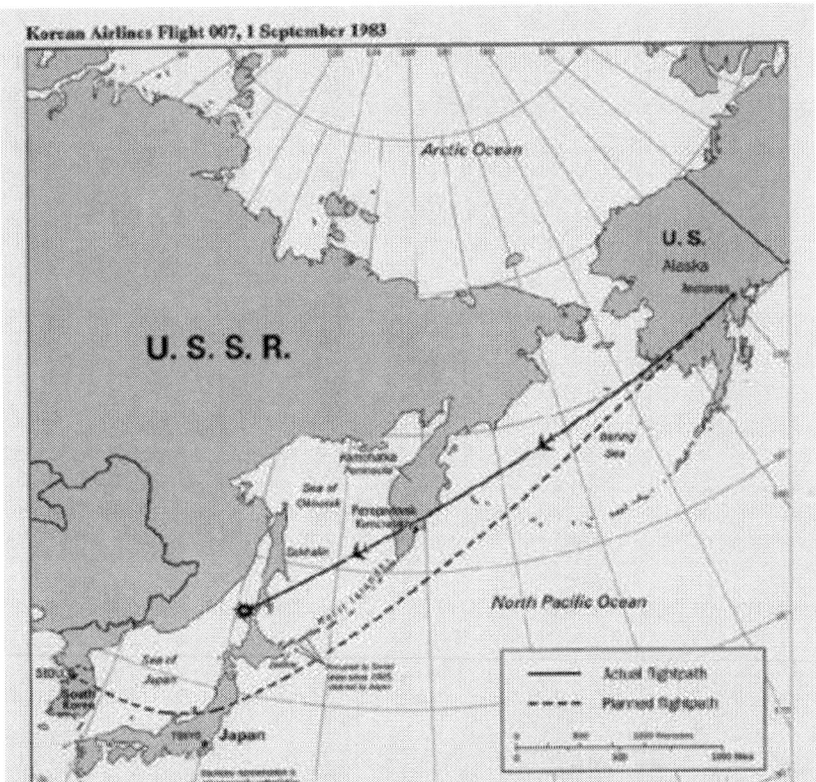

Flight path of Korean Air Lines Flight 007

The Creation of NSOC

Although the EC-121 shootdown pushed the NSOC cart over the crest of the hill, more than three years were to elapse before an organization actually took shape. NSOC's creation was delayed so long because of internal bureaucratic wrangling and logistics problems.

The first problem was space. Initial planning assumed that NSOC would physically move into spaces contiguous to CSOC, but it became clear fairly early that such a large organization would require its own spaces. Room could be made when the communications center (Tcom) moved to a new location on the third floor of Ops 1, but NSOC would have to wait for Tcom to move out. The second-floor spaces were to be available in 1971, but the calendar for the Tcom move kept slipping, and ultimately the area was not freed up until a year later. Meantime, the formation of NSOC was on hold.

The second problem revolved around what NSOC was to look like. In his initial NSOC concept paper, Major General John Morrison (the ADDO) deseribed NSOC as a center that "would provide NSA with a single facility from which to conduct the production and dissemination of current SIGINT information." It would track ongoing events, but it would also produce reports and direct activities. It would comprise A Group's CSOC, B and C Group's crisis centers, elements of K1 associated with tasking mobile SIGINT elements, P04 elements involved in reconnsissance missions, and the Command Center. Shift operations would be headed by the SNOO (Senior NSA Operations Officer). Manning would come from CSOC's [censored] workers, [censored] people from P04, [censored] from the Command Center, and unspecified numbers from B, G, and W Groups. Its communications would be primarily via Opscomms [censored] of them, a huge number at the time). Morrison named Air Force colonel [censored] to head the planning effort. [censored] fresh from Europe, knew exactly how the operation at [censored] functioned, and could get his hands on the people who had made it successful.

The operating concept that Morrison envisioned was basically CSOC with other Agency elements grafted on. At the time CSOC controlled [censored] reporting. It could direct reporting and could issue its own reports (although as time went on that function became almost the exclusive domain of the day shop). The day effort put out periodic summaries and wrap-ups, while events more than seventy-two hours old were turned over to A7, the term analysis shop. CSOC still lived in the days of the Teletype Model 28 Opscomm terminal, and analysts got their traffic delivered in paper copy from the Opscomms that resided in a separate room. Even so, things moved very fast in CSOC—it was closer to near-real-time than any other organization in the Agency. Morrison clearly modeled NSOC after CSOC.

And that was where the trouble began. CSOC might have been ahead of the competition, but it just wasn't the model that non-A Group organizations wanted to use. Morrison's concept paper raised a storm of controversy. Frank Raven, chief of G Group, agreed to place a desk in NSOC, but insisted that G Group operations were much too diverse to be amenable to centralization, and the G Group desk would be a watch desk only, with no production functions attached. [censored] of B Group took basically the same tack, and he agreed to relocate certain B functions only to lessen the physical distance between B Group and other Agency elements. W Group agreed to establish a desk in the new organization but its focus was still in DEFSMAC, and the NSOC effort was perfunctory. [censored] responding for K1, adamantly opposed absorption of any portion of the K1 mission (managing mobile collectors) by NSOC.

Morrison forged ahead anyway. In 1972 he appointed a planning group dominated by people with A Group experience, and he named a full-time NSOC staff headed by Richard "Dick" Lord, the former head of CSOC. Although key members of B and G Groups assisted Lord, the organization kept the A Group flavor. NSOC was being called "A Group and the Dwarfs".

The new NSOC edict was finally fashioned in the summer of 1972. By charter, NSOC was to "act as an authoritative and responsive interface on current SIGINT product and service both between SIGINT users and producers and between various producer organizations." It would also function as the NSA command center, and the senior officer, now called the SOO (Senior Operations Officer) would have true command responsibilities for the entire SIGINT system. In that capacity he or she represented the director.

Operationally, it resembled CSOC and its predecessor, the Air Force center at [censored] It monitored ongoing events and could take a variety of actions, including redirecting coverage and steering field reporting. Its original charter included the authority to do its own independent reporting, but this function was never exercised. NSOC did not become another [censored] except in the area of reconnaissance reaction reporting. But it did become the focal point for the release of all Agency electrical product reports. Finally, it did the daily director's brief and supervised the worldwide CSG system.

The NSOC that went operational in December 1972 (though the official ribbon-cutting did not occur till the following February) was in a state of technological transition. During the CSOC days, Walter Deeley, who had been Colone; [censored] deputy in A8 (CSOC), had been working toward what he called the "paperless environment." He planned to electrically connect the field Opscomms with a computer so that KLIEGLIGHTS could be processed and distributed automatically to CSOC floor analysts. A revolutionary concept at the time, Deeley pushed it with a dedicated singlemindedness. A Group selected the Univac 494 as the mainframe because of its communications handling capabilities. Software to manage the KLIEGLIGHT system was called TIDE. The concept was in only a partial state of existence when NSOC was created, but it soon became the dominant concept within NSA. It made near-real-time truly feasible.

SIGINT in the Nixon White House

The decade closed with a new president, Richard Nixon. It also opened with a new chief of the White House Situation Room. When [censored] of CIA departed the Situation Room at the end of the Johnson administration, General Alexander Haig was appointed to the job. But Haig was clearly destined for greater things, and soon NSA's David McManis was given the job.

The national security apparatus under the new administration was enmeshed in a rather strange structure. Henry Kissinger, a Harvard history professor, became the national security advisor, but he came to exercise power far beyond that. Kissinger was in effect Nixon's secretary of state (shoving aside the supine William Rogers), a DCI (moving into the turf of Richard Helms, whom Nixon distrusted) and still later, a de facto chief of staff for a president besieged by scandal and crime.

Like Walt Rostow in the Johnson administration, Kissinger became the funnel for intelligence to the president. When someone had to be called in, McManis phoned Kissinger, who lived only a short distance from the White House in Rock Creek Park. He was, according to all contemporary accounts, a brilliant man, but not as experienced in SIGINT matters as Rostow had been. Moreover, he was inclined to shield the president from the details of intelligence, where Rostow shared all. Thus when SIGINT did get to the Oval Office, it was generally subsumed into a mishmash of sources and not separated out and highlighted as it had been under Johnson. Nixon did not himself get involved in the details of intelligence, leaving those details to Kissinger.

To some extent this was an inevitable development. Johnson's handling of SIGINT had been unique, and it was not to be repeated. Journalists like Seymour Hersh have claimed, on what appears to have been good authority, that intelligence, and especially SIGINT, was being misused for political purposes. This has been confirmed to some degree by SIGINTers who had contact with the White House. It fell into a pattern that was to emerge during the second Nixon term—the Watergate pattern. It was not good for SIGINT, and it was deadly for the presidency.

Chapter 11 NSA in Vietnam: Building the Effort—The Early Years

"Cochinchina is burning, the French and British are finished here, and we ought to clear out of Southeast Asia." —Lt Col Peter A. Dewey (OSS) writing from Saigon, 1945

Much has been said about the American decision to become involved in Southeast Asia. The decision to intervene was hotly debated and controversial from the first. Intervention resulted ultimately in the nation's most humiliating military debacle (although by no means its first defeat). So many things went wrong that the failures obscured the successes, but successes there were. From both the military and the cryptologic standpoint, it was a learning experience.

Vietnam—The Country

Actually, three countries were involved: Laos, Cambodia, and Vietnam. (Vietnam's political geography is complex, involving as it does three separate areas: Cochinchina (presently known as Cochin China) in the south, Annam in the center, and Tonkin in the north.) But Laos was landlocked and primitive—it hardly counted—and Cambodia was little more than a "Sideshow to War" (to use British writer William Shawcross's phrase). Vietnam became the main show, the country where American lives and national prestige were put on the line.

Vietnam (meaning, literally, "South Viet") had been settled by a Sino-Tibetan group called the Viet, who had been pushed by Mongolian population pressures farther and farther south. They finally wound up in the Red River valley, a broad and fertile plain suitable for wet rice cultivation. As they migrated ever farther south, however, they were hemmed in by mountains, which cascaded, like boiling water, into the South China Sea. The Viets picked their way along the coast, inhabiting isolated valleys, until they finally arrived at the broad Mekong delta. There were no mountains on the delta, and they quickly converted it to rice-growing. As a result, Vietnam became long and thin in the center, averaging no more than fifty miles wide along the Central Highlands, with two large plains attached to each end. It has been compared in shape to a pole across the back of a farmer, with a basket of rice on each end.

Vietnam was a meeting place of disparate cultures—primarily Indian and Chinese. The Vietnamese warred fiercely with the armies of their neighbors, and they acquired a reputation for recalcitrance and military prowess. Chinese sovereignty over the region, strong during the Han dynasty (about a century before Christ), was reduced over time to a more or less nominal one. This was the situation when the French arrived in the mid-nineteenth century. France established a tenuous hold on the country—solid in Cochinchina, less sure in Annam, very loose in Tonkin.

The French overwhelmed the Vietnamese with technology but had little chance to stay permanently. After all, the Chinese, who lived next door, had never completely subjugated the restive Vietnamese. French efforts were, in the long run, doomed by distance and the stubbornness of the Vietnamese.

French colonial rule came to an effective end during World War II. The Japanese retained a French colonial government, but it was only a puppet, and in 1945, faced with defeat, the Japanese extinguished even this shred of French dignity. The Japanese defeat left Vietnam without a government.

What emerged was a government of sorts, efiective only in the Red River Valley to the north, under a communist named Ho Chi Minh. The remnants of the Japanese war machine transferred formal power to Ho's organization, the Vietminh, on 18 August. On 2 September Ho declared the independence of Vietnam. The United States, mostly through OSS, maintained distant contact with the Vietminh during the war. The opportunistic Ho, apparently hoping for substantial American aid, even adopted phraseology from the American Declaration of Independence when he declared Vietnam a sovereign country.

Occupied with larger matters, Allied leaders were not exactly consumed with worry over Vietnam. Roosevelt believed that colonial rule was finished everywhere, and that included Southeast Asia. But what to do with the former French properties was a more difficult question. He toyed with the idea of giving it back to the French under a trusteeship arrangement with independence guaranteed at a future date. He also offered it to Chiang Kai-shek, who did not want it. (He had enough trouble at home.) FDR died without resolving the issue, and Harry Truman had it on his plate.

At the State Department, a stealthy battle was going on between the Asianists, who were promoting independence for all Asian countries, and the Europeanists, who did not want a dispute over the colonies to jeopardize postwar relations with Britain and France. The Europeanists won, and the United States informed France in May 1945 that the U.S. recognized French claims to Indochina. It was decided that British forces would occupy the south of Vietnam, while Chinese forces under Chiang would occupy the north, until France could get some forces together to reoccupy its former colonies.

French troops eventually regained a tenuous hold over much of Vietnam, especially the southern portion. Meanwhile, negotiations continued with Ho, who, it will be remembered, had already proclaimed independence and had effectively occupied much of the north. But negotiations broke down in 1946, and outright warfare began. This period of conflict culminated in the French defeat at Dien Bien Phu in 1954.

Having successfully ejected this latest occupying power from Vietnam, all that remained for the Vietnamese was to formalize a separation. Divorce court was held in Geneva. It resulted in an independent and neutralist Cambodia and Laos and in a Vietnam divided at the waist. The part north of the 17th parallel, effectively controlled by the Communist forces under Ho, would become the Democratic Republic of Vietnam, while the portion below the 17th parallel would establish its own government. At some point the two would theoretically meet to hold elections of national reconciliation and reunite into a single nation.

The United States had by this time become deeply involved in Vietnam's troubles. American aid to the French mounted each year, and by the fall of Dian Bien Phu it came to about 80 percent of French expenditures for the conflict. There were behind-the-scenes talks of American air strikes to bolster the French position at the base, but at the last minute Eisenhower decided not to go ahead. At the peace conference, the Americans, frightened of communist encroachment, did everything they could to hem in Ho's government.

The Americans Enter the Fray

Once the war was over, the United States elfectively assumed responsibility for the mess. When Ngo Dinh Diem, the new president in the south, refused to go ahead with elections for fear of losing them, he had full American support. By early 1956 the U.S. had assumed responsibility for arming and training Diem's army. According to historian George Herring, "The United States inherited from France an army of more than 250,000 men, poorly organized, trained, and equipped, lacking in national spirit, suffering from low morale, and deficient in officers and trained specialists."

A military assistance group in Saigon steadily expanded in surreptitious ways beyond the Geneva-imposed limit of 342 people, until it reached almost 700.

[censored]

Laos and the Beginnings of Direct American Involvement

When Kennedy arrived in the White House, Laos, rather than Vietnam, seemed like the crisis to watch. The 1954 Geneva settlement had initiated a period of tenuous teetering between pro-Western and pro-communist sympathies, with a neutralist group holding the balance of power. Eisenhower had tried to keep a pro-American party in power through lavish subsidies, but in 1960 a series of coups pushed the government first toward the East, then the West. [censored] The outgoing Eisenhower administration succeeded in convincing Kennedy that American interest demanded a favorable outcome.

Wanting to appear firm, Kennedy had 500 Marines airlifted to the Thai side of the Mekong, which formed the border with Laos, while the carrier *Midway* moved into the Gulf of Siam.

But the Bay of Pigs fiasco brought Kennedy up short. If American military power could not secure a favorable outcome 90 miles from its shores, what might happen in an obscure, landlocked Asian nation more than 12,000 miles from Washington? The Pentagon estimated that at least 300,000 troops would be needed to maintain the pro-Western government So in late April Kennedy opted for a negotiated settlement and agreed to U.S. participation in yet another Geneva conference. A precarious coalition government emerged from the Geneva talks, but none of the three major factions was happy and within a year the cease-fire was violated by the Pathet Lao. Once again Kennedy mounted a show of force, dispatching 5,000 Marines and infantrymen and two air squadrons to Thailand. Again a coalition government was formed, but its long-term chances for success were not bright.

[censored]

The 1954 Geneva accords made it extraordinarily difficult to operate in South Vietnam. The Military Advisory Assistance Group (MAAG) staff was already bloated and obviously in violation of the agreements. [censored] Thailand was the obvious choice. But the Thai, with a long tradition of independence (alone in Southeast Asia, they had never been a European colony), were skittish, and negotiations dragged on inconclusively for years. Then the Laotian crisis served to pry open a crack in the door to 'I'hailand, [censored]

[censored] In 1965 ASA began building a major intercept site at Udorn, a Thai town in the far north, near the Mekong River. Called Ramasun Station, it became the location for an FLR-9 antenna, and at the height of the Vietnam War, it housed over 1,000 ASA and AFSS cryptologists.

Hanoi Decides to Intervene in the South

In 1954 Hanoi had decided to work on the infrastructure in the north and to put off attempted unification to a later date. But by 1959 the leadership decided that it must expand in the south or else its southern cadres would wither and die. In the spring of 1959, the leadership authorized resumption of armed struggle in the south, a decision that was ratified by a Party meeting in September 1960.

At approximately the same time, Hanoi created a new group, MR 559 (so-named because it was created in May 1959), within the General Directorate of Rear Services (GDRS), to control infiltration into the south. Beginning with only 500 people, it eventually expanded into a network of 40,000-50,000 military and civilian workers. It was organized into sixteen units called Binh Trams, battalion-size units in geographical areas, each controlling the infiltration network through its region. This evolved into the Ho Chi Minh Trail, which provided the wherewithal for revolution and invasion.

[censored]

NSA Expands Cryptologic Involvement

The nascent Kennedy administration adopted an initially cautious line toward Vietnam. The U.S. government had troops in the South, but they were still called "advisers" and the numbers were limited. At the time the only SIGINT involvement was the [censored] relationship with the South Vietnamese SIGINT service. There were no American cryptologists in the country, [censored]

But as the number of American "advisers" expanded, so did the cryptologic presence. In early 1961 the chief of the MAAG in Saigon advised Maxwell Taylor (chairman of the JCS) during one of his trips through Saigon that the ARVN (Army of the Republic of Vietnam) had no SIGINT capability. This touched off a debate back in the United States about the advisability of expanding in Vietnam.

At NSA, Admiral Frost directed a complete evaluation of SIGINT in Southeast Asia, and from that came a new plan to expand the ctyptologic presence. Essentially, two plans were written. The first was called SABERTOOTH, and it involved noncodeword assistance to the SIGINT services of [censored] Vietnam. [censored] The second, called WHITEBIRCH, would involve the establishment of a mobile ASA intercept unit with Morse, voice, and HFDF positions. NSA was skeptical of the voice positions because ASA had few qualified Vietnamese linguists, but the Agency approved the plan despite the reservations.

The new NSA plan also envisioned a beefed-up collection posture. In addition to expanding the cryptologic presence in [censored] ASA would introduce people directly into Vietnam for the first time. The burden of field processing would fall most heavily on the sites in the Philippines. It also called for an "Evaluation Center" in Saigon to integrate SIGINT with other intelligence for the chief of the MAAG. When General Paul Harkins showed up in February 1962 to become the first COMUSMAGV (Commandér, U.S. Military Assistance Command Vietnam), this became the Current Intelligence and Planning Branch, J2, and was housed in the MACV building, originally located in downtown Saigon.

Before Harkins arrived, NSA interests had been served by a TDY arrangenient. In April 1962, however, the first permanent NSA representative, [censored] was on board. His arrival was accompanied by vigorous protests by the Army. Secretary of the Army Zuckert sent a scorching letter to Assistant Secretary of Defense John Rubel protesting the assignment. "This action," he said, "would result in removing these SIGINT resources from the control of military commanders in the area. . . . Generally, responsiveness to intelligence requirements of CINCPAC and COMUSMACV would be dependent upon the decisions of a national level agency, far removed from their areas of responsibility. . . ." He proposed that all SIGINT assets in the area be placed under the operational control of MACV. It was the opening shot of a war within a war, the struggle to control SIGINT assets in Southeast Asia.

[censored]

The second step was to approve an Army COMINT unit in Vietnam in support of counterinsurgency planning. The National Security Council then required that the results obtained by that unit be shared with the South Vietnamese to the extent needed to launch rapid attacks on the Viet Cong.

The Buildup of Cryptologic Assets

The first ASA troops began arriving in May 1961. They were under cover, wore civilian clothes, and were prohibited from carrying military identification cards. They found spaces in an RVN AF hangar on Tan Son Nhut Air Base and lived downtown at the Majestic Hotel. Working areas were set up inside the hangar by piling boxes of C-rations seven feet high to make rooms. A few of the officers had desks, but the analysts worked at tables constructed of plywood and scrap lumber. Since there were few chairs, the tables were hoisted four feet off the ground so analysts could stand. Needless to say, there was no air conditioning, and the troops sweltered in the tropical heat.

The unit was called the 3rd Radio Research Unit (3rd RRU). Operationally it was called USM-9J, subordinate to USM-9 in the Philippines. The original processing mission consisted mainly of traffic collected by the South Vietnamese SIGINT service, which was at the time composed of only about 100 officers and men. They had two collection sites, at Saigon and Da Nang, and soon established a third site at Can Tho in the Delta. They were operating with equipment left over by the French or provided by CIA. Among the assets that they had inherited from the French were three DF stations and all the equipment, which happened to be of World War II vintage. In 1961 CIA gave them six AN/PRD-1 mobile HFDF sets. When 3rd RRU began processing, the main input was the DF bearings from the South Vietnamese.

Meanwhile, ASA advisors conducted classes in DF, traffic analysis, and intercept for the Vietnamese under the SABERTOOTH program. They were supposed to hold the classification to noncodeword, but the line between SIGINT and non-SIGINT was very shaky, and it was crossed regularly.

The focus of the operation, though, was DF. ASA set up an HFDF net, called WHITEBIRCH. Because of availability, the AN/TRD-4 was the equipment of choice. Three sets were mounted in vans and positioned at Nha Trang, Can Tho, and Bien Hoa, with control in Saigon. The Third/RRU was also receiving bearings from an ASA site in [censored] sites in Vietnam, and the [censored] ARVN operated its own three stations at Pleiku, Da Nang, and Ban Me Thuot, and the results were supposed to provide direct support to the South Vietnamese Army.

The WHITEBIRCH net was a failure. It had the lowest fix rate in the Pacific, and it was constantly short of manpower. This dismal state of affairs was due primarily to the circumstances surrounding its mission. In the dense and humid tropical jungles, the ground wave faded to imperceptibility in only a few miles. The sky wave came down at such a steep angle that the existing DF equipment (the ancient TRD-4s) could not cope with it. Moreover, the skip zone between ground and sky waves was almost ninety miles, meaning that most of the ASA sites were located in a skip zone. When inadequate maintenance and unreliable communications were added to the woes of WHITEBIRCH, it was clear that the system would not do the job.

Frustrated, ASA turned to the mobile PRD-1s now owned by the ARVN. These were effective, but only if the DF set was within five to fifteen miles of its target. To be that close to a VC transmitter was often a dangerous proposition, but they tried it anyway. On 31 December 1961, they found out how dangerous it was. An ARVN DF operation returning to Saigon from the DF site at Ha Tien (on the southern coast) was ambushed by VC. Nine ARVN soldiers were killed, along with Sp4 James T. Davis, the ASA adviser. Davis was later called by President Johnson the first American soldier to die in Vietnam. The 3rd RRU compound was named Davis Station, thus adding to the immortality of the unfortunate Davis. ASA had come to a full stop on the DF problem, and until they solved it, the amount of direct SIGINT assistance that they could provide to the ARVN forces was limited.

The next group of SIGINTers to arrive in Vietnam were the Marines, who sent a training detachment from Fleet Marine Force in Hawaii. They originally set up next to the ARVN SIGINT operation in Pleiku, and as such were completely cut off from direct contact with other U.S. SIGINT units. This proved unsatisfactory, even for training.

In 1962, the cryptologic community decided to move its main base of operation to Phu Bai. A large ASA site was constructed, and it became the center of SIGINT operations for Vietnam. The Marines decided to move in with ASA, but the Air Force Security Service was more standoffish. Da Nang was the center of air operations, and AFSS located its principal site there to support the Seventh Air Force.

At the time, the Vietnamese problem was entirel manual Morse. Rumors of VC voice swirled about, and in February 1963 the [censored] intercepted some voice traffic emanating from a low-level [censored] VHF net in Vietnam. ASA tried but, right up until the Tonkin Gulf incident of 1964, had not intercepted any.

As cryptologic resources expanded, the question of operational control occupied increasing attention both in Saigon and in Washington. The Army continued to insist that MACV should control all cryptologic resources in theater. During Admiral Frost's tenure as DIRNSA, a compromise of sorts was worked out. When the first ASA resources arrived in country, Admiral Frost delegated operational control to ASA and recognized the further delegation of control to the commander of the MAAG (later MACV). This gave MACV a handhold but kept the strings ultimately tied to DIRNSA.

In 1963 General Wheeler (chairman of the Joint Chiefs) negotiated directly with General Blake. They arrived at a new compromise whereby NSA would continue to control major, fixed sites like Phu Bai, while operational control of ASA's direct support units (DSUs) would be delegated to ASA, and thence to the supported Army commander. This was actually more restrictive than the original decision, and it was made more onerous by the edict that when MACV wanted additional units under its control it would have to submit the request through the lengthy and cumbersome chain of command which ran through Hawaii.

DF Goes Airborne

The ambush of Davis and the ARVN DF team in December 1961 brought about a scramble for a better system. The safest thing would be to put the mobile DF sets on airplanes. This technique had been tried as early as World War I, and the French had employed ARDF aircraft in their struggle with the Vietminh, with good results. But the technical barriers were serious. The problem was in the interference of ground and sky waves. Aircraft were up high enough to receive both, and the accuracy of the bearing was degraded because, while the on-board system tried to read the direction of the signal from the ground wave, the aircraft itself acted as a huge antenna for the sky wave, which arrived from a different direction.

An ASA engineer, Herbert S. Hovey Jr., went to work on the problem and was joined by a team from the Army's laboratory at Ft. Monmouth, New Jersey. Knowing of the French ARDF effort but not knowing what technique they used, Hovey experimented with different techniques and various aircraft. He tried rotary-wing options, but found that the rotor blades created too much turbulence. Hovey finally settled on the U-6A, a single-engine fixed-wing aircraft widely available in Vietnam. Instead of using the almost universal (in DF arrangements) loop antenna, he used antennas fixed on the leading edge of each wing, about forty feet apart, with the receiver in the center. This turned the aircraft itself into a large HF antenna. The aircraft had to be pointed directly at the signal, thus creating an aural null on the pilot's gyrocompass. To create the aural null, the pilot fishtailed the aircraft back and forth, going into and out of the maximum signal strength. He would then fly at the signal from three different angles, the three lines of bearing thus constituting a fix. This peculiar flying technique solved the problem.

ASA sent the first DF-equipped U-6 to Vietnam in March 1962. It was an instant success. In May 1962 the ARVN successfully struck a VC unit based on ARDF fixes. In December of that year, when an ASA ARDF fix located a VC radio transmitter in the northern Delta, American advisers under General Harkins used the intelligence to plan an assault on what they thought would be a communist unit of no more than 120 men. The ARVN 7th Infantry Division was employed in the action and swooped into the area by helicopter early on the morning of 3 January 1963. Instead, they ran into a unit of more than three times that many, which stood and fought. The resulting battle of Ap Bac was a turning point in the war for both the VC (which found that it could confront and defeat a main ARVN force) and for the Americans, who concluded that they would have to become more directly involved. The battle was initiated based on an ARDF fix.

The value of ARDF was quickly recognized. It became the most important advance in the employment of SIGINT for tactical applications in the war and the principal targetting tool for MACV. NSA boxed up this valuable technique within its own sphere of control by declaring that the ARDF aircraft were simply outstations of the WHITEBIRCH net, which was already a CCP resource. ARDF was to become the battleground on which the JCS and NSA fought for ultimate control of SIGINT in Southeast Asia. It was easily the most divisive issue in the entire intelligence community.

Into the Mire

"The troops will march in; the bands will play; the crowds will cheer; . . . and in four days everyone will have forgotten. Then we will be told we have to send in more troops. It's like taking a drink. The effect wears off, and you have to take another." —John F. Kennedy, 1961

While all this was going on, the Kennedy administration was assessing its chances in Southeast Asia. The first thing Kennedy did was to gather information, using the time-honored technique of a fact-finding team. In the spring of 1961 he sent Walt Rostow and his personal military advisor, Maxwell Taylor, to Saigon. They came back very pessimistic. The Diem regime was crumbling and would require a large infusion of American troops and material. They recommended that some 8,000 American "advisers" be sent to Vietnam under the cloak of providing "flood relief." Averell Harriman, the long-time advisor to Democratic presidents, and Chester Bowles, a senior diplomat, both doubted that the corrupt and repressive Diem regime could be adequately shored up, and he urged Kennedy to call a new Geneva conference and negotiate a settlement. But Kennedy had just emerged from the disgraceful Bay of Pigs incident and was in no mood to be perceived by either the Soviets or the American public as a "negotiator."

But he also rejected the Taylor-Rostow proposal as transparent. Instead, he compromised, increasing the size of the aid mission but failing to increase it enough to make a big difference. All the while he was disturbed by the narrowness and inflexibility of the Diem regime. To have a happy ending in Vietnam, it would be necessary to obtain a more reasonable and competent government.

[censored] the Crisis in Third Party Relations

[censored]

USIB decided to back away from SIGINT collaboration with the ARVN, and USM-626 (the former USM-9J in Saigon) was instructed to stop providing certain technical data. At the same time, NSA made plans to move most SIGINT operations to Phu Bai and to make it a U.S.-only site.

The USIB decision, prompted by NSA, created an uproar in the field. Harkins protested and was backed up by Huntington Sheldon, the CIA official who watched over SIGINT for the intelligence community. Moreover, General Khanh, the RVNAF chief of staff, refused to authorize a solely American operation at Phu Bai, thus holding the super-SIGINT site at Phu Bai hostage to a continued close SIGINT relationship. In the end, Khanh, Harkins, and Sheldon won. Admiral Frost issued a revised and liberalized interpretation of the USIB edict, and the Americans exited the controversy with as much grace as possible.

The Diem Coup

Riven by internal dissent, the Diem regime was tottering by 1963. The regime was controlled by Diem and his corrupt family, and no reform appeared possible. The last straw was a Buddhist revolt against the strongly Catholic Diem regime. The uprising began in May 1963 and became marked by self-immolations by Buddhist monks. When confronted by such opposition, no regime could last.

Even Diem know it and began exploring a negotiated settlement with the north. To the Kennedy administration, this looked like a way out. The JCS prepared a plan for a phased military withdrawal beginning later in 1963. The first 1,000 troops were actually withdrawn before the plan came to a halt.

But negotiations were never begun. In early November the generals in Saigon rose against Diem, with the knowledge, if not the active connivance, of the American embassy. Diem and his brother Nhu were captured and, in a twist which was not in the original script, executed, apparently on the orders of General "Big" Minh. Minh took over the government, beginning a series of revolving door regimes, each weaker and less popular than the previous one. The JCS withdrawal plans were shelved. Later in the month Kennedy was dead, and a new president had to look again at the morass in Vietnam.

The Cryptologic Expansion of 1964

With withdrawal plans on hold, the new DIRNSA, General Blake, directed a relook at the American cryptologic posture in Southeast Asia. Blake decided to accept Phu Bai as the super-site for Vietnam, with major resource additions there and at other sites in the Philippines and Vietnam. Collection from Thailand would also increase, and Udorn was selected as the Thailand super-site. In early summer, with Maxwell Taylor (the new ambassador in Saigon) lining up behind it, Blake took the plan to Fubini. They agreed that most resources for the new effort would be transferred from existing SIGINT problems [censored] except for some assets already targeted on Southeast Asia that would be moved to the mainland [censored]

SIGINT resources would also be needed for a major new operation, under the general rubric of OPLAN (Operation Plan) 34-A. This was a JCS plan to support South Vietnamese infiltration and unconventional warfare operations. The SIGINT support for OPLAN 34A, called KIT KAT, would come mainly from vans flown in [censored] and the Philippines and located at Phu Bai. A new SIGINT Support Group in Saigon would provide MACV with direct support to OPLAN 34A.

Communications still represented a sore point. SIGINT exited Vietnam through an Army communications center in Saigon that was known for its cramped quarters and ancient equipment. Worse, it was an HF shot to the Philippines, and in the heavy tropical atmosphere HF was even less reliable than usual. Reliability ranged from 30-75 percent, an unacceptable figure.

DCA came up with a solution. A submarine cable was installed between Nha Trang and the Philippines, and by the mid-60s all cryptologic communications were being routed through the cable (dubbed "Wetwash"). Circuit reliability leaped upward.

This development had a major impact on SIGINT operations in Vietnam. The submarine cable could take higher circuit speeds, and it was possible to ship much more SIGINT back and forth. This led to the feasibility of sending encrypted traffic back to a central processing center—at first in the Pacific (Clark AB and [censored] and later all the way back to NSA. It changed the way SIGINT was done in the theater, but it also increased the suspicion of tactical commanders who preferred to rely on their own people from ASA rather than on some unseen computer far away.

AFSS Comes to Vietnam

The Air Force Security Service did not actually start its Southeast Asian operations in Vietnam. Like the Army, it arrived in Thailand in early 1961 to provide SIGINT support for the Laotian crisis. [censored] The processing was done on the ground in spaces occupied by the tiny AFSS intercept unit that had been there since the summer of 1960. Spaces were so cramped that at one point a Russian linguist wound up transcribing his intercepted tapes in the shower room. But like the Laotian crisis itself, the SIGINT support operation lost steam, and by spring NSA had cancelled the deployment.

Vietnam was a ground war, and the U.S. Air Force did not get involved a big way until 1964. The Air Force did, however, set up a tactical air control system beginning in January 1962. The unit was located atop Monkey Mountain near Da Nang, which would give American radars the longest possible reach.

Along with the Air Force contingent of 350 people came an AFSS CCU (COMINT Contingency Unit), consisting of two H-1 vans airlifted from Clark Air Base and a mobile AFSSO, also in a van. A smaller intercept and SSO effort was located at Tan Son Nhut, but the hearability was bad, and the intercept unit was soon relocated to Da Nang. The next year AFSS reorganized its Southeast Asian assets, designating Tan Son Nhut as the headquarters, with subordinates at Da Nang [censored]

Da Nang remained the only AFSS unit of any size in the war zone. By 1964 USAFSS had two Da Nang sites, one atop Monkey Mountain and one at the air base below. Security Service successfully resisted an NSA master plan to move the unit to Phu Bai, arguing that hearability was better at Da Nang and that they should be closer to the supported commander.

In March of the same year, the ACRP returned to Southeast Asia. It arrived on the heels of reports that PRC-North Vietnamese military relations were becoming closer. [censored] NSA initiated ACRP collection to follow this activity, and a new program called QUEEN BEE CHARLIE, [censored] began flying missions out of [censored] In July a follow-on operation, QUEEN BEE DELTA, consisting of two RC-130s, began flying missions over

Thailand every other day. Initially processing was done at [censored] but plans were being drawn up to transfer the entire effort to Da Nang. That same year, the Navy began flying EC-121 and EA3B collectors in the Gulf of Tonkin.

Air Force ARDF trailed ASA into Southeast Asia. In 1962 AFSS tried out HFDF programs using two different platforms, a B-26 and a C-47. The ARDF effort had the strong personal support of General LeMay, then the Air Force chief of staff. From the beginning, however, the program was engulfed in controversy.

The first problem was control. The Air Force wanted the ARDF program to be purely tactical, unattached to NSA, operating in a noncodeword environment. NSA, however, insisted that it come under the direct control of USM-626, as outstations of the WHITEBIRCH net. The program was thus placed under double ignominy—within the cryptologic system and under the thumb of the Army.

Moreover, the Air Force insistence that it be noncodeword resulted in non-SI-indoctrinated people being assigned to it. USM-626 was at first prohibited from passing technical data to support the AFSS effort. This was soon straightened out, and all the Air Force people were SI cleared, but it was a bad start for a program.

Finally, the system did not work. It used larger aircraft but did not do well against low-power signals. The Air Force Security Service left the theater to do more research.

The next year AFSS was back, this time with a second ARDF system produced under a Navy contract and installed on an Air Force plane under Project HAWKEYE. It was more sophisticated than the Army system, using computers and larger, more capable aircraft. But it, too, did not work, and at the end of the year ASA continued to have the only effective ARDF system in Southeast Asia.

The small AFSS effort in Vietnam betokened the lack of an air war. They were not engaged in war—they were just waiting in case an air war happened. They hadn't long to wait.

The Crisis In The Gulf

"Well, I am the guy who rose from the ashes, and twenty years later telling you I saw it, and there were no doubts." —Adm. James B. Stockdale, Navy pilot, concerning 4 August attack

In the many years of conflict in Vietnam, no single incident stands out as more controversial than the 4 August 1964 incident in the Gulf of Tonkin. In it, two American destroyers patrolling in international waters were supposedly shot at by North Vietnamese gunboats. In retaliation, an angry president launched the first air raids on the North, and a few days later Congress passed the Tonkin Gulf Resolution, giving Lyndon Johnson a free hand to deal with North Vietnam in whatever manner he felt best suited the situation. For America, it was the beginning of an apparently irrevocable descent into the maelstrom.

The Desoto Patrols

The attack on the destroyers originated with the Desoto patrols. These were begun in 1962 as patrolling operations along the Chinese coast. There were three objectives: intelligence collection, realistic training, and assertion of freedom of the seas. Naval Security Group detachments on board pursued the collection of [censored] ELINT and naval COMINT. However, to naval authorities the mission of freedom of the seas clearly stood first, and training second; intelligence was the third priority. By December, the patrols had been extended to the coasts of Korea and North Vietnam. The rationale was to support special operations under OPLAN 34A.

OPLAN 34A stemmed from CIA covert operations which had been going on since the early 1960s under various names. Most of these involved the nighttime coastal insertion of ARVN commando forces, whose mission was sabotage. By early 1964 the Army had taken over most of the operations, under OPLAN 34A. The Desoto patrols were extended to North Vietnam primarily to provide SIGINT support to the commando raids. In addition to NSG afloat detachments on board Desoto craft, the Army was tasked with SIGINT support from positions at Phu Bai.

The operations got off to a very bumpy start in February 1964, but they eventually smoothed out. Although there was considerable behind-the-curtains controversy about their effectiveness, the raids were having at least harassment value by July 1964. The tiny North Vietnamese navy was beginning to pay them close attention.

North Vietnam could mount only a modest defensive threat. Their first-line combatants were twenty-four Swatow motor gunboats acquired from the Chinese over a period of years. More threatening, however, were twelve Soviet-built motor torpedo boats delivered to Haiphong in late 1961, capable of fifty-two-knot speeds. These, in addition to a few minesweepers, subchaser and district patrol craft, represented the North Vietnamese navy.

The 2 August *Maddox* Patrol

The increasing harassment value of OPLAN 34A was certain to make the North Vietnamese more belligerent. On 1 August NSA went on record as warning the Navy that their own Desoto patrols might be in danger of attack. A day earlier, the destroyer *Maddox* had begun a patrol in the Gulf of Tonkin.

On 2 August the North Vietnamese decided to attack the *Maddox*. During the morning hours, two SIGINT units, a Navy intercept unit in the Philippines (USN-27) and a Marine detachment collocated with ASA at Phu Bai (USN-414T), reported that North Vietnam's naval headquarters had directed preparations for attack. This series of reports was flashed to

Captain Herrick, the task force commander on board the *Maddox*, as the morning wore on. The information was sufficiently unsettling that Herrick questioned the day's patrol, considering it to be an "unacceptable risk."

Just after noon, USN-27 intercepted a message from one of the coastal control authority at Port Wallut to one of the Swatows: "Use high speed to go together with the enemy following to launch torpedoes." USN-27 issued a Critic on this inflammatory declaration, and Herrick had it in hand almost an hour before the attack was launched. It was preceded and followed by other North Vietnamese messages leaving no doubt that they were headed for a major engagement. It could, of course, have referred to the 34A operations that had been going on earlier, but Herrick knew nothing of those operations. He had to assume that the North Vietnamese meant him—and he was right.

At about 1600 local, three PT boats launched a high-speed attack on the *Maddox*. Herrick replied with surface fire, and within half an hour the torpedo boats withdrew. About that time air cover showed up, commanded by Admiral (then Commander) Stockdale from the carrier *Ticonderoga*. Stockdale's crew shot up the fleeing torpedo boats, sinking one and putting another out of action.

Meanwhile, the two SIGINT stations continued to monitor North Vietnamese communications, keeping Herrick informed of what was happening on the other side. The patrol made for the mouth of the Gulf and withdrew. Back at Fort Meade, NSA declared a SIGINT Readiness Bravo.

There was no doubt of the attack. Not only was it launched in broad daylight, but it was preceded and followed by communications (intercepted by the Navy and Marines) making the entire attack procedure and objectives crystal clear. SIGINT gave impeccable warning, and Herrick came to rely on it almost implicitly.

The Johnson administration chose not to reply militarily to the attack. But at the White House the mood was grim, and there was a feeling that they could not let another such attack pass unnoticed.

The 4 August Patrol

After assessing the 2 August attack, the administration decided to keep the *Maddox* in the Gulf at least through the 7th to assert freedom of the seas and to add a second destroyer, the *Turner Joy*, which had been part of the *Ticonderoga* task force. With two vessels, Herrick headed back to the Gulf on the 3rd.

After spending the day near the coast of North Vietnam, Herrick withdrew both vessels to the central Gulf of Tonkin for the night. Through intercepts of Vietnamese radar transmissions, he knew that he was being silently shadowed by at least one North Vietnamese PT boat. Moreover, this tended to be confirmed by reporting from San Miguel that one of the Swatows involved in the previous day's activity (T-142) had been ordered by a naval authority to "shadow closely." During the night a 34A task force shelled a radar station and a security post, fleeing to Da Nang at daylight.

Herrick believed his vessels were in imminent danger, but the next morning he was nonetheless ordered back to the area of the previous two days' patrol. The *Maddox* and *Turner Joy* loitered in the general area where the 2 August attack had taken place. At about 1700 they turned back toward the central Gulf to spend the night.

At about the same time that Herrick was ordering his two-vessel task force back to the central Gulf, the Marine detachment at Phu Bai issued a Critic on an intercepted message from Haiphong ordering three of the boats involved in the 2 August attack to make ready for military operations that night. To Herrick this was very ominous, since he had been shadowed by a North Vietnamese vessel or vessels the night before. Based on this and follow-up messages from Phu Bai, he sent a message stating that he believed that the Vietnamese were preparing to attack.

At 2041, the *Maddox* appeared to pick up radar contacts on North Vietnamese PT boats. For the next four hours, the *Maddox* and *Turner Joy* zigzagged through the central Gulf, apparently pursued and attacked by unknown and unseen vessels. The crews of the two vessels claimed to have had radar and sonar contacts, torpedo wakes, gun flashes, and searchlights, and fired repeatedly at whatever seemed to be attacking them. When air cover showed up from the *Ticonderoga* task force (led by Stockdale), the pilots could not see any boats, but it was an unusually murky night with very low overcast and poor visibility.

After the engagement, San Miguel reported that T-142 claimed to have shot down two "enemy planes" and that "We sacrificed two comrades but are brave and recognize our obligations."

Back in Washington, the events in the Gulf grabbed everyone's attention. The initial indication that something was afoot was the Critic and follow-up from Phu Bai. These were called over to DIA from NSA just after 8 A.M. By 0900 copies of the reports were distributed to McNamara and Wheeler, and McNamara called the president at 0912. This kicked off a long train of actions that spanned the entire day.

Thus forewarned, the president had no trouble believing that an attack had actually taken place once he received the first news at 1100. McNamara convened a meeting to discuss possible retaliation. At a lunch with Rusk, McNamara, Vance, McGeorge Bundy, and John McCone, Johnson authorized an aerial strike on North Vietnamese targets. But soon thereafter, the White House was looking at a message from Herrick casting doubts about the attack. Adverse weather conditions and "overeager sonarmen" may have accounted for many of the alleged contacts. Based on this, Admiral Sharp in Hawaii (CINCPAC) phoned McNamara to recommend that the air strike be delayed until they received more definitive information. At that time a retaliatory air strike, scheduled for 0700 Vietnam time, was only three hours away.

Soon after, Sharp received the new information about the supposed shooting down of enemy aircraft and the sacrifice of two vessels. Sharp, Admiral Moorer (CNO), and Johnson all became convinced that an attack had taken place, and Johnson authorized Pierce Arrow (the bombing attack on North Vietnam) to proceed. It was delayed almost three hours, though, and came very close to preceding Johnson's televised address to the nation announcing the Gulf incident and the American response.

The sequence of events at the White House was driven largely by SIGINT. The reliance on SIGINT even went to the extent of overruling the commander on the scene. It was obvious to the president and his advisors that there really had been an attack—they had the North Vietnamese messages to prove it.

But to the analysts working the problem at NSA, things did not appear to be so obvious. The preplanning messages could, after all, have been referring to reactions to the Desoto patrols. Or the entire series of messages might have been old traffic referring to the attack on the 2nd. NSA sent out frantic requests to the units involved (Phu Bai and San Miguel) to forward their raw traffic. NSA also requested verification from SIGINT intercept operators on the *Maddox* and *Turner Joy*. The ships' operators had nothing—their intercept capability (all VHF voice) was completely blocked by the ships' radios during the period of the incident. As for the mainland intercept, it took hours to obtain, and the first NSA follow-up was issued without the benefit of the messages intercepted in the field.

The first NSA report indicated that the vessels supposedly planning for operations on the night of the 4th apparently did not participate in the events regarding the *Maddox* and *Turner Joy*. A subsequent wrap-up on 6 August homed in on the 2 August attack (easy to substantiate), conveniently avoiding the direct issue regarding the 4 August incident.

The NSA analyst who looked at the traffic believed that the whole thing was a mistake. The messages almost certainly referred to other activity—the 2 August attack and the Desoto patrols. The White House had started a war on the basis of unconfirmed (and later-to-be-determined probably invalid) information.

There had been no dissembling in the White House. The messages looked valid, and Lyndon Johnson had come to be a believer in SIGINT. When he ordered the attacks, he was sure he was right. He wasn't, and it was not until NSA analysts laboriously pieced together the SIGINT information over a period of days that it became obvious how big a mistake had been made. The Johnson administration defended its actions in public for years, but the reality eventually sank in. Even the president was heard to say in later years, "Hell, those dumb stupid sailors were just shooting at flying fish."

Some months previously, William Bundy (deputy secretary of defense) concluded that Johnson would need some sort of congressional endorsement for the expanding American role in Vietnam. He felt that a declaration of war was too blunt an instrument, and its chances in Congress were slim. What was needed, he believed, was a joint resolution, similar to that which Congress had given to Eisenhower during the Quemoy and Matsu crisis in 1955. Bundy drafted a resolution that gave the president the right to commit forces to the defense of any nation in Southeast Asia menaced by communism.

The resolution was ready by June 1964, and the Pentagon had already identified some ninety-four targets in North Vietnam, in case the president should direct military retaliation. Everything was ready but was put on hold. Some sort of provocation would be needed. The Tonkin Gulf crisis was just such a provocation. The administration hustled the resolution through Congress with only two dissenting votes. It was shepherded through the Senate by the chairman of the Foreign Relations Committee, William Fulbright.

The Tonkin Gulf Resolution did not become a political issue until three years had passed. In July 1967, with antiwar passions heating, a reporter for the *Arkansas Gazette* quoted a former radarman on the *Maddox* as saying that North Vietnamese vessels had not been in the Gulf that night and that he believed his radar contacts had actually been reflections of the *Turner Joy*. This article came to Fulbright's attention. This appeared to wipe out the rationale for the resolution, and Fulbright, who was being gradually converted to the antiwar cause, felt that he had been hoodwinked, perhaps deliberately, by the White House in 1964. He began gathering the relevant material, including SIGINT reports obtained from the Department of Defense. When he felt he had enough, he convened a hearing on the Gulf crisis.

The hearings, held in February 1968, made the Gulf of Tonkin Resolution infamous and converted it into a weapon in the hands of the antiwar activists. During the proceedings, Fulbright managed to cast considerable doubt that the 4 August attack ever took place. Inconclusive radar and sonar hits, mysterious weather conditions, the lack of a single verifiable ship sighting—all were used to beat down the Johnson administration's contention that the retaliatory action and the resolution itself were justified.

But the central contention of the hearings became the SIGINT. When Fulbright brought McNamara to the stand, the secretary of defense kept referring to "intelligence reports of a highly classified and unimpeachable nature. . ." He meant, of course, the SIGINT reports that, first, indicated that the Swatows should prepare for nighttime operations, and, second, contained the after-action reports alleging that aircraft were shot down and the loss of the two boats. The committee kept pressing McNamara and eventually dragged out of him virtually the full texts of the messages involved. McNamara resisted, but it was very hard to defend his actions without resorting again and again to his most convincing pieces ofevidence.

These public disclosures damaged the SIGINT source—all the messages had been from decrypted North Vietnamese naval codes which were still in use in 1968. But it did not sell the case to the disbelieving committee, despite McNamara's contention that "No one within the Department of Defense has reviewed all of this information without arriving at the unqualified conclusion that a determined attack was made on the *Maddox* and *Turner Joy* in the Tonkin Gulf on the night of 4 August 1964."

In fact, not all DoD people were sold on this contention. NSA, for one, had failed to fully support the administration's position. It had confirmed the 2 August attack but had never confirmed the 4 August engagement. The Agency had concluded that the two Swatows instructed to make ready for action that night had never participated in the action with the *Maddox* and *Turner Joy*. The after-action reports could have referred to the 2 August engagement.

But it didn't really matter. The administration had decided that expansion of American involvement in Vietnam would be necessary. Had the 4 August incident not occurred, something else would have. Another expansion of the war occurredthe following February, following the mortaring of an American installation at Pleiku. McGeorge Bundy said at the time, "Pleikus are like street cars. If you miss one, another will come along." He could have been talking about the Gulf of Tonkin crisis.

Chapter 12 From Tonkin to Tet—The Heart of the War

The President Expands The War

Retaliation during the Gulf of Tonkin crisis was a one-shot affair, but it indicated that the administration was edging toward more active involvement. It did not, of course, dissuade the North Vietnamese. In November the Viet Cong (VC) mortared the air base at Bien Hoa, only two days before the U.S. elections. Johnson regarded this as a bald affront. Then, on Christmas Eve, they bombed an American officers' billet in downtown Saigon in broad daylight, killing two and wounding sixty-three. This further hardened American attitudes and made direct intervention the following year more likely.

Late in 1964, SIGINT began noting a strange communications pattern for the North Vietnamese 325th Infantry Division. The division headquarters at Dong Hoi opened communications with entities that controlled the infiltration routes into South Vietnam. Sometime thereafter, SIGINT (together with ARDF fixes) showed the 325th moving south, first into Quang Tri Province (just below the DMZ) and later all the way to the Central Highlands. It was the first move of a regular NVA division into the South, and it pointed to a new and considerably more dangerous phase of the war.

No longer were the ARVN facing an insurgent Viet Cong movement—they were up against North Vietnamese regulars. The 325th was in South Vietnam to prepare for the rainy season offensive, and it would create a bloody hell for the unlucky ARVN units in its path.

The president now knew what the American people did not—that North Vietnamese regulars were in the South. All that remained was for another provocation to take place. He had not long to wait. On 6 February 1965, the Viet Cong rocketed the American and South Vietnamese facilities at Pleiku, killing 8 Americans and wounding 108, bringing newspaper headlines and extensive television coverage. At the time, press coverage had the effect of pushing the administration into retaliation. (A few years later it would have the opposite effect.) Twelve hours later American A-4 Skyhawks and F-8 Crusaders were launched from the 7th Fleet against Dong Hoi (whence the 325th and other units had staged on their way south).

Twenty-one days later President Johnson institutionalized the pattern of isolated retaliation by starting daily bombings of the North and the Ho Chi Minh Trail in Laos. The operation, called Rolling Thunder, was planned to last eight weeks, but in April Earl Wheeler, JCS chairman, informed the president that it had had no effect at all on the North. So Johnson directed that it continue until it had an effect.

The attack on Pleiku almost shouted out the vulnerability of American troops and equipment. With the initiation of Rolling Thunder, U.S. aircraft were at Da Nang almost constantly, and they required protection. The U.S. commander, General William C. Westmoreland, asked Johnson for a defensive force, and the president obliged. On 8 March the first Marines splashed ashore at Da Nang, beginning the American deployment of ground combat troops to the theater.

The commitment of ground forces, once begun, became an inexorable upward spiral. In May, Westmoreland asked for a total of 185,000 by the end of the year, and 100,000 in 1966. Johnson sent Secretary of Defense McNamara to Saigon to find out what was happening. The secretary returned with a gloomy assessment—Westmoreland was actually understating the need, and the U.S. would need an additional 200,000 in 1966.

Operation Starlight and the Ia Drang Campaign

SIGINT was still small-time in Vietnam, but it was growing. In August 1965, with new American troops swarming ashore almost every day, ASA SIGINT and ARDF located a new enemy communications terminal near the Marine base at Chu Lai. In Saigon, the NSA representative [censored] took the item to Brigadier General Joseph A. McChristian, the J2, who passed it to Lieutenant General Lewis Walt, who commanded the Marines in Vietnam. Walt discussed it directly with his SIGINT people at Phu Bai and became convinced of its validity. He began planning a major entrapping operation. The VC forces, who had hoped to surprise the Marines, became themselves surprised and overcome in the operation, called Starlight. Starlight was a turning point in the direct employment of SIGINT and ARDF in operational planning.

Ia Drang, the first significant campaign by a large force of NVA regulars, began as an attempt by the NVA 325th Division to cut Vietnam in half in the Central Highlands. In the process, the 325th attacked a Special Forces camp at Plei Me, about twenty-five miles south of Pleiku. ARVN forces attempted to rescue the troops trapped inside but were ambushed by two NVA regiments of the 325th, the 32nd, and 33rd, with heavy casualties.

Following the engagement, the NVA retreated up the Ia Drang Valley, with the First Cavalry (Airmobile) in pursuit. Owing to the recent success in Starlight, the American forces had five ARDF aircraft in support. Moreover, for the first time the ARDF crew had the capability to pass fixes directly to the ASA Direct Support Unit (DSU) supporting the ground forces. ARDF fixes followed the 325th elements retreating up the valley until they were cornered at the Chu Pong Massif. The 1st Cavalry, employing helicopters in pursuit for the first time, and supported by B-52 air strikes, devastated the NVA. The two regiments suffered up to 60 percent casualties and were no longer an effective fighting force. The remnants retreated into Cambodia. During the action, the 33rd was so concerned about the Americans appearing to know their location that they concluded that they had spies in their ranks.

The SIGINT Deployment

To support American ground forces, ASA built Phu Bai into the largest ASA field site in the world, almost 100 positions. Together with the 3rd RRU in Saigon and the 9th in the Philippines, ASA had substantial fixed site assets.

The fixed sites were augmented by SIGINT tactical assets. ASA tactical units began to arrive with each incoming Army organization. Each unit normally had five manual Morse positions along with short-range DF and VHF intercept equipment.

NSA's concept of direct support was that, since the problem was centrally controlled from Hanoi, the SIGINT effort should remain centralized. NSA continued to exercise overall control from Fort Meade. In Vietnam, collection management authority (CMA) was divided into three areas, roughly corresponding to the division of American forces. USM-626 at Tan Son Nhut was CMA for the southern part of the country, USM-808 at Phu Bai for the northern portion, and USM-604 at Pleiku for the central area.

Following its relocation to Phu Bai, the Marine SIGINT detachment became the DSU in support of the III MAF (Marine Amphibious Force) in the north. Eventually the Marines established DSUs like the Army and wound up with the same sort of a decentralized SIGINT support arrangement, with small detachments composed of only a few positions each collocating with combat units. Lacking their own ARDF assets, the Marines received ASA ARDF support.

Air Force Security Service SIGINT collection from Vietnam itself was more limited. The unit at De Nang expanded quickly once Rolling Thunder began, but it never equalled the huge ASA contingent. This was not true, however, of the ACRP effort. USAFSS had a contingent of four RC-130s at Da Nang which expanded to six in 1967, by the device of raiding airborne assets in Europe [censored]

Beginning in 1967, a new ACRP program began flying in Southeast Asia. This program consisted of the far larger and more capable RC-135s belonging to a new unit at [censored] With SAC front-end crews and USAFSS collectors, the RC-135s flew very long (often in excess of seventeen-hour) missions into the Gulf of Tonkin. The RC-130s continued to fly out of Da Nang until the end of the year, when the [censored] unit took over the entire mission.

Operational control arrangements continued to cause friction. NSA opposed fragmentation, while the Army insisted that field commanders should directly control all cryptologic assets supporting them. This became a critical issue when Army units began independent operations.

In mid-1965 a new arrangement was hammered out between Rear Admiral Schulz of NSA and Brigadier General Eddy, deputy commander of ASA. Under this Schulz-Eddy agreement, when DSUs were in active support of an ongoing tactical operation the field commander would control them. When they were back in garrison, control would revert to ASA's designated field site (either Saigon, Pleiku, or Phu Bai). NSA continued to control all fixed field sites, to the loud disapproval of MACV.

The second control issue to arise in 1965 concerned the air problem. Brigadier General Rocle "Rocky" Triantafellu, the deputy chief of staff for intelligence at 7th Air Force, proposed that an organization be established in Saigon which would produce a daily recap of the status of North Vietnamese air and air defense systems. But what Triantafellu wanted and what NSA was prepared to deliver were very different. Triantafellu had in mind an Air Force Security Service organization, all blue-suiters working for 7th Air Force. NSA countered by proposing an NSA unit, manned only partly by uniformed Air Force people. This nasty scrap continued until NSA won in March 1966. The resulting organization, called the SIGINT Support Group (SSG), consisted primarily of Air Force people, but was under NRV control.

The very next year, MACV itself got into a struggle with NSA over the positioning of cryptologic assets. In this case, MACV requested that a SIGINT processing center be established in Vietnam, to bring processing closer to the fighting. By 1967, however, MACV was swimming against the tide. NSA had moved processing back to [censored] Fort Meade and was not about to change directions. SIGINT centralization was "in," and MACV did not get its processing center.

ARDF and the Two-Front War

In the beginning, ARDF was the exclusive domain of the Army. Starlight and the Ia Drang campaign had demonstrated the benefits of close ARDF support, and ASA expanded its assets rapidly. By the end of the year, there were four aviation companies in Saigon, Da Nang, Nha Trang, and Can Tho. The first two supported I FFV (First Field Force Vietnam) in the north, while the second supported II FFV. ARDF had clearly become a coveted asset.

In 1966 the ARDF picture became suddenly complicated. The Air Force deployed a new ARDF program, called PHYLLIS ANN. The Air Force considered ARDF to be an EW asset, and even in the test phase in 1962 had refused to submit to any sort of central control from the SIGINT system. The Air Force eventually conceded to bring its ARDF testing under cryptologic control, with USAFSS back-end operators and ASA technical support. (At the time, an ASA unit, USM-626 at Tan Son Nhut, was the tasking and technical support authority for Vietnam, and this made the pill doubly bitter.) But since the equipment was unsatisfactory technically, the issue of command and control became moot with the departure of the test aircraft.

PHYLLIS ANN was different. The equipment, mounted in C-47s, was good—just as accurate as the ASA systems, but because of technical factors, the C-47s (now called EC-47s) could shoot more DF shots in an hour than the Army aircraft. The Air Force Security Service activated the 6994th SS on 15 April 1966, at Tan Son Nhut, to man the ARDF positions. Soon they had detachments at Da Nang, Nha Trang, and Pleiku. A total of forty-seven EC-47s were deployed to the theater.

When PHYLLIS ANN aircraft arrived in theater, the issue of control and tasking of ARDF assets erupted into a three-cornered donnybrook. Seventh Air Force continued to regard them as EW assets and demanded complete tasking control. Westmoreland was equally insistent that all ARDF assets should be tasked centrally (i.e., by MACV). NSA was willing to see central tasking in theater, but insisted that ARDF was a cryptologic asset whose ultimate owner was itself. In the Agency's opinion, it had simply delegated temporary operational control to the commanding general of ASA in 1961.

By June of 1966, MACV had won the fight for in-theater control. EC-47s would be tasked by a central ARDF tasking center called the ACC(ARDF Coordination Center), collocated with Westmoreland's J2 in Saigon. Seventh Air Force continued the struggle throughout the war, but it could not get support from even PACAF (Pacific Air Force) for its position.

The struggle for control went all the way to the deputy secretary of defense. In 1966, Cyrus Vance ruled that ARDF was an EW asset and would be controlled by Westmoreland through his J2. The victory was only temporary, however. Two years later, Deputy Secretary Paul Nitze reversed Vance, holding that ARDF was actually a cryptologic technique and that it would be placed in the CCP. In the meantime, the ARDF controversy had spawned a compromise document, MJCS 506-67, an effort to cut the SIGINT Gordian knot.

Search and Destroy

Westmoreland's strategy was to get American troops out of a defensive posture and out into the countryside on search and destroy missions. This placed a premium on unit mobility. The SIGINT support for these sweep operations consisted basically of ASA tactical units with small numbers of Morse positions, supplemented by low-level voice and short-range DF. To this mix was added the ARDF fixes flashed from aircraft to the ASA units on the ground and intercept from major SIGINT stations like Pleiku and Phu Bai. This pattem, initiated in 1965 during the Ia Drang campaign, became the dominant system in 1966 and 1967, during the height of tactical operations.

ASA tactical SIGINT units provided direct support for a bewildering number of military operations during 1966. They came in all flavors: Masher/White Wing, Paul Revere, Nathan Hale, John Paul Jones, Geronimo, Attleboro, and many more. One was like the next.

An example was Paul Revere II, an operation in the Central Highlands in July and August. SIGINT support consisted largely of ARDF fixes from aircraft that were, for the first time, allocated, based, and flown in a direct reporting, close support role from the command post of the supported commander. The historical debate over the effectiveness of Westmoreland's strategy should not obscure the significant contributions of SIGINT. Some of the tactical operations were initiated based on SIGINT information, and most were prosecuted using updated SIGINT.

A second type was the riverine operation. Used primarily in the Mekong Delta and other low, marshy areas of the country, it was basically a waterborne search and destroy mission. But the difficult terrain, and lack of large-unit VC operations, made riverine operations frustrating and largely ineffective. This went as well for the SIGINT support. Working with the Navy and Marines, ASA would deploy low-level voice intercept (LLVI) and short-range direction finding (SRDF) teams on boats. Because of a lack of good linguists, the LLVI teams were generally ineffective. The SRDF operations proved to be no more successful on water than on dry land. Bearings were divergent and frequently produced no intersection at all.

Army Security Agency was willing to go wherever it was necessary to collect and support. Sometimes units would be choppered to the tops of mountains. One such operation placed an intercept team on top of Black Widow Mountain, an aptly named peak in a remote corner of Tay Ninh Province at the Cambodian border. This was VC territory, and it turned out to be one of ASA's most dangerous operations. As if enemy operations were not enough, the weather was atrocious - winds as high as eighty knots, heavy rain, low ceilings (which prevented helicopters from landing most of the time), and high humidity that would destroy intercept equipment in short order. But after only a four-day test cut short by hostile fire, NSA concluded that it was the only way to get Cambodian [censored] VHF air/ground communications aside from leaving a TRS in the South China Sea. Since TRSs were on the way out, Black Widow Mountain was on the way in. So in May 1968 the ASA team was back, this time supposedly permanently.

The second time around the team lasted two weeks. At that point, a VC attack killed one ASA operator and wounded another, and caused numerous casualties to the collocated Special Forces unit. The operation was withdrawn by helicopter at the first break in the weather.

However, the value of operations like Black Widow Mountain spawned an effort to locate intercept equipment on mountain tops and to remote the signal to a safer location. That way, only the equipment would be exposed. The effort, called EXPLORER, was developed at NSA in only three months, with [censored] Donald Oliver, and [censored] being the key players. The first EXPLORER operation lasted for almost a year before it was destroyed. But during its lifespan, it was highly effective. In ideal conditions ASA could intercept the traffic from the EXPLORER system, forward it to NSA for decryption, and have the decrypted text back in country in some four hours.

Another successful technique was wiretap. NSA developed various wiretap systems but they were uniformly dangerous to install. American or ARVN soldiers had to penetrate VC territory (especially risky in Laos, where most of the landlines were), find the landline, attach the tap to the line, and get out of the way. The VC would periodically sweep the line, and early wiretap systems required the Americans or ARVN to stay in the vicinity and, when a sweep came by, hurriedly detach the tap and get back into the bush. Later versions did not require a stay-behind person. Some taps looked like Vietnamese insulators and thus would not be viewed as possible taps. Still later, the U.S. developed poles that could be dropped by helicopter into the jungle near a landline.

Predictions

The highest intelligence art form is prediction. One of the most intensive activities in the war was the attempt to predict VC and NVA offensives—when, where, and how many.

[censored]

But in 1964, concurrent with increased NVA involvement in the south, ASA began to intercept Morse communications pertaining to VC military operations. As the Morse nets expanded, NSA began to recover the VC/NVA military structure through traffic analysis. The Agency identified the formation of five new organizations: MR TTH (Military Region Tri-Thien-Hue), NVA 3rd Division, B3 Front, Headquarters Southern Subregion, and VC 9th Division. The Binh Gia campaign at the end of 1964 showed the first extensive use of Morse to set up and coordinate a local campaign.

From then on, through painstaking traffic analysis and DF, the cryptologic community was able to discover communications patterns that indicated attacks. By 1967 it had become an art form, and many NSA seniors contend that past a point (probably in 1965 or 1966), the SIGINT system predicted every major VC or NVA offensive. This included date, point of attack, and units involved.

Indicators varied from battle to battle but almost always included the activation of a "watch net," contingency communications which indicated that the headquarters would soon deploy to a different location. Concurrently, a forward element would be activated, and would establish communications with the headquarters, which, until it moved, would become the rear element. It became important to locate the forward element and to track the movement of the headquarters. At a point in the operation, it would disappear from communications. When it reappeared, it would be in the area of the battle, and it would then be critical to locate it, usually through ARDF.

Other indicators would usually be present, including the use of unusual cipher systems, changes in message volume, the appearance of operational planning messages [censored] indications of increased intelligence collection, and heightened logistics activity. Plain text and the decryption of low-level ciphers were important, but most of the work was done solely through a combination of ARDF and traffic analysis. Greatly aiding this effort was the fact that the VC and NVA used the [censored] throughout the war. The U.S. had the book completely recovered and used this to identify the units involved.

Infiltration

A second resounding SIGINT success was in tracking North Vietnamese infiltration on the Ho Chi Minh Trail. Until the fall of 1967, this was done through a combination of photography, SIGINT (primarily traffic analysis), prisoner interrogations, and the like. It was a complex problem, which admitted of no easy answers. The U.S. did not, in fact, have a good handle on infiltration.

Then, in October 1967 RC-130 intercept operators began picking up L-VHF voice [censored] passing logistics information. The messages emanated from Vinh, a key logistics center on the Trail, just above the DMZ. Most of the messages pertained to [censored] which NSA decided must represent groups of infiltrators on the Trail.

NSA eventually broke out the entire Trail group system and was able to determine with fair accuracy virtually every group moving onto the Trail, where it was headed, and when it would probably arrive. Some of the groups proved to be specialists like medics, while others were simply combat soldiers, augmentees for an offensive or replacements for casualties. Late in the war, infiltration numbers were assigned to integral units rather than individuals. The surprising bonanza came to be called the "Vinh Window."

The Vinh Window was very big news. MACV now knew where the biggest strategic push would come based on projected augmentees to a given frontal area or military region. The White House thought it had unlocked the key to the magic door. David McManis, NSA's representative to the White House Situation Room, spent much of his time explaining the intricacies of trail groups. CIA cast aside much of its methodology of determining infiltration numbers and simply accepted the SIGINT numbers as virtually the final answer.

In Asia, the ACRP program was swept up in a tidal wave of requirements relating to the Vinh Window. The RC-135 unit which had only recently formed [censored] was pressed into premature service. The RC-130 program, which was eliminated in favor of the RC-135s by the end of the year, was replaced in the fall of 1968 by a new program called COMFY LEVI. RC-130s with roll-on SIGINT suites for the back end. The Air Force Security Service received authority to transcribe the most critical tapes in the aircraft and downlink the information to the Security Service unit at Da Nang in midflight. Untranscribed voice tapes began to pile up [censored] as demands overwhelmed resources.

The significance of the Vinh Window could not be overemphasized. Every intelligence agency adopted its own interpretation of the figures, and infiltration estimates varied to some degree depending on what agency one listened to. CIA's counts were probably the most accurate, but were not the only ones reaching the White House. The National Indications Center, in a 1968 study of the phenomenon, stated that ". . . the SIGINT material which is now available is not only of value for estimating the strengths of Communist forces in South Vietnam, but also is a significant factor in assessing their future plans and intentions.

The Dancers

The cryptologic community in Southeast Asia had been overwhelmed with Vietnamese voice long before the Vinh Window. The problem began in late 1964, when the first voice intercepts began to flood the SIGINT system. What had been entirely a Morse problem suddenly had a new dimension to it.

The services had very few Vietnamese linguists, and those they had were little better than school trained. In 1964 USAFSS requested authority to establish native-born South Vietnamese as linguists to transcribe voice tapes to be collected at Da Nang in support of 34A operations. After studying the problem, NSA concurred with a Vietnamese transcription operation, but established it, not at Da Nang, but in Saigon. The DANCER project (as it was called) was established in January 1965, using 3rd RRU SABERTOOTH spaces, with three South Vietnamese linguists.

By May 1965, USAFSS was processing Vietnamese voice off [censored] nets being collected by the ACRP program at Da Nang. The program in Saigon was not productive, partly because ASA could hear no Vietnamese voice from that location. Since Da Nang was the ground processing point for ACRP intercept, it was decided to move the DANCER program north—ultimately it wound up at both Da Nang and Phu Bai (selected because NSA believed [censored] communications could be heard from that location). DANCER recruits came from the SABERTOOTH program and were vetted by [censored] South Vietnamese SIGINT organization.

Originally employed to transcribe voice tapes, DANCERs eventually became qualified in a wide variety of skills. They proved to be skilled at various traffic analytic recoveries, and they were soon an absolutely essential asset to any SIGINT operation in South Vietnam. By 1966, ASA units were intercepting LLVI communications and needed DANCERs to go to the field with them. This effort became Project SHORTHAND. Because the U.S. had run through the supply of linguists available from the South Vietnamese SIGINT Service, ASA, under SHORTHAND, obtained authority to recruit from other sources within the South Vietnamese government.

The SIGINT Role in the American War

During the period of maximum American involvement on the ground, SIGINT developed from an arcane art form to a day-to-day bulletin on enemy dispositions. Most commanders interviewed after the fact estimated that SIGINT comprised anywhere from 40 to 90 percent of their intelligence, depending on the availability of POWS. Every sizeable unit deployment had its ASA Direct Support Unit (DSU), which gave it access to ARDF and a pipeline into the national SIGINT system. Many commanders used the information for daily battle planning.

A properly employed DSU thus became an essential resource. But it had warts. As in Korea, the LLVI effort was sometimes fruitless because of the difficulty of getting good linguistic support; an insufficiently trained linguist was sometimes worse than no linguist at all. South Vietnamese linguists under the DANCER and SHORTHAND programs were spread very thin and were often not available.

Moreover, short-range DF proved a dubious asset, especially in the Delta, where there were fewer targets. To the extent that DF was successful, it was generally ARDF.

ARDF sometimes overwhelmed other intelligence sources. Tactical commanders used it for daily targetting, and it became the primary source for targetting information in the entire war. Used effectively, it was irreplaceable. But sometimes a commander would blast a patch of jungle just because a transmitter had been heard there. The VC and NVA eventually became skilled at remoting their transmitters, just because of such American tendencies. There was still no substitute for understanding the source.

And much of the difficulty that the SIGINTers found themselves in stemmed from an unappreciative audience. Very few commanders had any training in SIGINT. In the 1950s it had been kept closeted, a strategic resource suitable only for following such esoteric problems as [censored]

Now that it was "coming out of the closet," a generation of officers received OJT under fire.

Some did well; some not so well. For every example of the proper use of tactical SIGINT, there was the opposite instance, where the source was either not believed or not used properly. No intelligence source was so technically complex or so difficult for the layman to understand. The lessons from the "American War" (1964-1968) were still being absorbed more than twenty years later.

The Air War

The air war began with the daily bombing of the North in March 1965. Like the ground war, the air war was a messy business organizationally. It involved three different air elements.

Seventh Air Force was the largest component. It had six tactical fighter wings and a tactical reconnaissance wing spread around Southeast Asia. Headquartered at Tan Son Nhut, 7th AF had a Control and Reporting Post on a hilltop called Monkey Mountain, near Da Nang. This was where command and control of tactical missions were executed, and this was where Air Force Security Service chose to set up shop.

In the Gulf was Task Force 77, a carrier task force belonging to 7th Fleet. The Navy launched Rolling Thunder missions from the carrier decks, and it had its own control authority, called Red Crown.

The First Marine Air Wing, under III MAF, operated out of airfields in northern South Vietnam. Although used almost exclusively for close air support in South Vietnam, they also flew some missions over the North.

Finally there was SAC. The Strategic Air Command launched B-52 strikes over both North and South Vietnam, flying out of Andersen Air Force Base, Guam; U-Tapao, Thailand; and Kadena, Okinawa.

In response, the North Vietnamese, with a third-rate air force and practically no technological sophistication, had fashioned a competent if not overwhelming defense. Proceeding from the visual observer stage in the late 1950s, North Vietnam had introduced Soviet radar systems, and by the mid-1960s it had some 150 radar sites and 40 radar reporting stations. The North Vietnamese navy also had radar sites along the coast, primarily to keep track of enemy ships. They had a small group of MIG-17s and MIG-21s which they carefully husbanded. They also introduced hundreds of AAA sites across the country and in late 1965 began installing SA-2 sites. American air strikes by no means went unimpeded.

[censored]

Fashioning the SIGINT Warning System—HAMMOCK

Following the Gulf of Tonkin crisis, 7th AF (then called 2nd Air Division) requested SIGINT support for air missions north of the DMZ. Security Service began planning an expansion of its unit at Da Nang (6924th SS, or USA-32) to provide some sort of Tactical Report (TACREP) service.

What developed initially was a system called HAMMOCK, which became operational in December 1965. HAMMOCK consisted of five manual Morse intercept positions at USA-32, copying North Vietnamese air defense communications which reflected MIG activity. USA-32 could pass warning information to 7th AF when, and only when, the tracking fell within the theoretical range of Americen radar. (There did not actually have to be a radar located at the hypothetical point; the postulated existence of such a radar was enough.) The information was supposed to be validated at the Tactical Air Control Center (TACC) at Tan Son Nhut, which would convert the SIGINT plot to a geographical coordinate and then send it on to the Control and Reporting Post (CRP) at Monkey Mountain. The CRP could warn the aircraft in jeopardy and would also pass the information via KW-26 secured circuit to Red Crown in the Gulf.

If communications were down, USA-32 could go directly to a Security Service detachment at the CRP, where the information was converted from the grid system and passed to an uncleared CRP controller. This was much faster, but everyone was nervous about security because there were so many uncleared people in the facility.

Needless to say, this convoluted system was less than satisfactory. It relied, in the first instance, on manual Morse tracking passed within the North Vietnamese air defense system, which introduced a delay of several minutes. It was burdened by so many communications relays and authorization authorities that it had little chance to get anywhere in time. HAMMOCK plots generally reached someone who could warn a fighter pilot anywhere from twelve to thirty minutes after the fact. The average time of receipt to Red Crown was nineteen minutes. The Navy was profoundly unimpressed and chose to rely on its on-board cryptologic detachments. The Navy operators had little experience with North Vietnamese air defense systems, but at least they could warn within a few minutes of real time.

Despite this, HAMMOCK was better than nothing. On 27 April 1966, the U.S. got its first confirmed MIG shootdown based on warning information provided by HAMMOCK. But the requirement to check everything with the TACC in Tan Son Nhut got the Air Force Security Service in the middle of a jurisdictional dispute between 7th AF and its subordinate CRP on Monkey Mountain. It was not the right way to run a war.

The ultimate answer was not manual Morse tracking, anyway—it was intercept of VHF air/ground communications by the RC-130 QUEEN BEE DELTA aircraft flying in the Gulf of Tonkin. The ACRP often had the information that pilots needed to avoid being shot down, or to do some shooting down themselves. Security restrictions, however, prevented its use.

The cropper came in April 1965, when two F-105s were shot down by MIGs. The orbiting ACRP had had information that would have been useful, and it was obviously imperative that a system be devised to incorporate their intelligence.

Pacific Security Region (the region headquarters for the Air Force Security Service) had devised a brevity code that could be used by the ACRP back-end crew to warn pilots in imminent danger, but it did not withstand COMSEC scrutiny. The only solution appeared to be a secure link between the ACRP and USA-32. A device called a URC-53 already existed. Priority was so high that the installation and use of the URC-53 at Da Nang was approved the same day it was requested, and the circuit was installed and operational within a month.

But this was still not fast enough. General Moore, commander of 7th AF, proposed putting his own controllers on the QUEEN BEE aircraft, clearing them, and having them pass MIG alerts directly to Rolling Thunder aircraft, using the callsign of another aircraft in the Gulf (COLLEGE EYE, an EC-121) as cover. Reversing the normal procedure, Morse tracking would be passed uplink from Da Nang to the ACRP, where it would be integrated with the voice data. Moore's weapons controllers were flown to Bangkok (whence QUEEN BEE flights then originated), and three days later the ACRP issued its first MIG alert.

Then Moore tried to get control of the ACRPs themselves. He felt this was necessary to insure that there was always an ACRP aloft during Rolling Thunder missions. Here Moore ran into a buzzsaw. The aircraft he wanted control of were national assets. NSA successfully opposed 7th AF on this issue. Even PACAF refused to back 7th AF, stating at one point that there had never been an instance when the ACRP had failed to respond to a 7th AF request.

The autumn of 1965 brought a new threat—the appearance of SA-2 surface-to-air missiles (SAMs) in North Vietnam. The North Vietnamese began employing SAMs against high-flying, nonmaneuverable targets like B-52s, while using AAA for the lower-flying Rolling Thunder aircraft. To counter SAMs, 7th AF introduced a procedure in which SAM activations acquired by the ACRP aircraft (now renamed SILVER DAWN) would be passed to 7th AF (through USA-32), which would direct Iron Hand (SAM suppression missions) against the offending SAM.

At this point Security Service ran into an Air Force mind-set regarding the use of intelligence that proved to be destructive of its own interests. Air Force doctrine was to launch suppression only if the SAM site had been documented by photography, and 7th AF refused to launch Iron Hand in cases where this had not been done.

The Border Violation Incident

On 8 May 1966, a flight of RB-66s escorted by F4Cs strayed over the border into Communist China and was attacked by four MIG-17s. One of the MIGS was shot down in the engagement, which occasioned an impassioned diplomatic protest from the PRC. The communists released photos of the downed MIG well north of the international barrier.

The off-course Americans should have been warned. [censored] None, unfortunately, reached the American pilots. The Navy EC-121 that was supposed to act as a communications relay had aborted, and the warnings from Monkey Mountain went off into the ether.

This incident led to a full-scale Pentagon investigation of command and control procedures in Southeast Asia. The "Pearl Harbor question" kept coming up—why, if SIGINT was available, wasn't it used? The proceedings, headed by Marine brigadier general Robert G. Owens Jr. were marred by mutual recriminations between the SIGINTers, who were sure of their facts, and the operations people, who were determined to defend their pilots. [censored] This claim was rejected by the full panel. In the end, Secretery of Defense McNamara reported to the president that "this account, derived from communications intelligence, is unequivocal. A thorough review of [censored] North Vietnamese messages reveals no significant discrepencies ... I am convinced that our aircraft penetrated Chinese airspace before they were attacked by the MIGs."

The Owens report laid bare the inadequacies of command and control and the disjointed way that SIGINT was introduced into the operational system. Owens demanded, and got, a thorough reorganization of the system in Vietnam. Authority to control operations was summarily removed from 7th AF in Saigon and placed where it should have been all along, on Monkey Mountain. The Tactical Air Control Center (TACC) at Tan Son Nhut was cloned on the mountain and called TACC/NS (North Sector). The control facility on the mountain was upgraded from a CRP to a CRC (Control and Reporting Center) and was given two subordinate CRPs at Udorn and [censored]

The Owens report also recommended that 7th AF have operational control over the ACRPs. This occasioned another huge fracas between the Air Force and NSA. The Agency won again, partly because it could certify that the ACRPs were already as responsive to 7th AF as they would be under that organization's direct control.

During the Owens deliberations, it became clear that factors other than operational control affected ACRP capabilities. The biggest problem was fighter CAP (Combat Air Patrol). Many ACRP missions were scrubbed because of lack of fighter CAP, or had to abort in midmission because the fighters went home early. Following the Owens report, JCS approved unescorted missions in the gulf at night (because of known North Vietnamese reluctance to fly at night). As time went on, the rules were relaxed even more.

The reforms permitted SIGINT to focus its input at one geographical point—Monkey Mountain. This shortened the chain of organizations through which a warning had to pass and simplified the task of the SIGINTers in Southeast Asia. It did not, however, provide a direct link-up between SIGINT and the operations people. That necessary step would not come for another five years.

IRON HORSE

In 1967 the SIGINT system improved the speed of its support to air operations by a quantum leap. The creaky manual system, HAMMOCK, was replaced by IRON HORSE, a flashy new automated system which could deliver information in seconds rather than minutes. Designed by NSA, IRON HORSE simply linked the electronic output of an AG-22 intercept position, through a computer, to a radar scope. Instead of using a plot-tell system for calling aircraft positions to the TACC or CRC, the computer would convert the grid plot to a geographical coordinate and display it on a radar scope. An Air Force Security Service analyst carefully selected the plots that were sent to 7th AF. Those that were passed went into the BUIC II air defense computer at TACC/NS and were integrated with radar plots from the U.S. system. Plots from SIGINT that went to the CRC, Task Force 77, and the Marines had a unique signature that identified them as not derived from American radar. USAFSS put a team of SIGINT experts in the collocated TACC and called it the Support Coordination Advisory Team (SCAT)—in effect, a CSG to help 7th AF interpret the data. SCAT integrated manual Morse data as well as VHF reflections from the ACRP, the Navy's EC-121, and a variety of other sensors.

IRON HORSE decreased throughput time from twelve to thirty minutes to anywhere from eight seconds to three minutes. It was state-of-the-art and about as fast as Morse tracking could be displayed.

BIG LOOK

The introduction of SAMs into Vietnam complicated the air warning picture. Special airborne warning systems to detect the SAM-associated Fan Song radars were thwarted when the North Vietnamese introduced the tactic of putting the Fan Songs on lower power except when they went into a track and destroy mode. Navy engineers devised a counter for this, a system that could intercept and DF very low power signals. They mounted these systems on EC-121 airframes allocated to VQ-1 for fleet support. The ELINT crews came from the home squadron [censored] while the four voice intercept operators were supplied by USN-27 at San Miguel, Philippines.

BIG LOOK was supplemented by WEE LOOK, an EA-3B fleet support aircraft outfitted with ELINT positions. WEE LOOK was also used for threat emitter warning. Although the EA-3B was designed to operate from carriers, WEE LOOK did not because of aircraft weight. Like BIG LOOK, it launched from land bases.

Weather and SAR Warnings

One obscure but vital SIGINT contribution was weather. Early in the war, 7th AF flew weather reconnaissance missions prior to operational launches, but it was an Operational Security (OPSEC) nightmare. Weather reconnaissance was the surest indicator that the North Vietnamese could have that a strike was imminent.

In 1965 NRV proposed to 7th AF that USA-32 at Da Nang begin furnishing "special weather" information intercepted on North Vietnamese nets. Da Nang initiated a two-week test and within a month had become the sole source of COMINT-derived weather information on North Vietnam. Special weather was relayed to Task Force 77 as well as 7th AF, and an Air Force historian, with pardonable exaggeration, called this perhaps the "premier contribution" of SIGINT in Southeast Asia.

When the Air Force and Navy began losing pilots over Vietnam, SIGINT was once more called in. A special program was designed for reporting indications (through VC or NVA communications) of downed pilot locations and capture attempts. The reports, called SONGBIRDS, were actually TACREPs, which went out at the noncodeword level to a wide group of organizations. Security Service averaged about ten SONGBIRD reports per month. There was very little feedback on SONGBIRD effectiveness, although one historian estimated that, because of the time required to translate the Vietnamese voice transmissions, most SONGBIRDs did not arrive in time.

PURPLE DRAGON

"President Johnson . . . expressed concerns over the number of aircraft being lost on Rolling Thunder missions. Between January and September 1966, a total of 228 fixed-wing combat and support aircraft had been lost during missions against North Vietnam. The question in Washington was, did the enemy have prior warning of U.S. raids against North Vietnam? . . . The answer was yes, they did." —Stephen J. Kelley in PURPLE DRAGON: The Origin and Development of the United States OPSEC Program

On Christmas Day 1969, a team of the First Infantry Division, on a sweep in Binh Duong Province near Saigon (part of Operation Touchdown), stumbled on an NVA COMINT unit. They captured twelve of the eighteen people assigned along with some 2,000 documents and the unit's intercept equipment. It was the COMINT "find" of the war.

NSA sent in a TAREX team to evaluate what the soldiers had found. The result confirmed an earlier, and generally ignored, Agency assessment that the NVA employed 4,000 to 5,000 COMINTers and that this was their chief source of intelligence. Their intercept effort was targetted at ARVN and American communications, from which they could do fairly sophisticated traffic analysis, DF, and even some cryptanalysis. Brevity codes were especially vulnerable. But their main target was unenciphered tactical voice, and the easiest pickings were from the U.S. Air Force.

It was obvious from studying the Touchdown material that NVA COMINTers were a source, probably the source, of predictive information on SAC Arc Light (B-52) strikes. But the Defense Department knew that already.

The story had begun in 1965. NSA had uncovered a communications net supporting Chinese forces in Vietnam. [censored] analysts noticed that some of the messages contained an unusual Morse character—a barred echo. They remembered that [censored] used this character to flag uncommonly urgent messages. On a hunch, the division chief, [censored] suggested that they might compare barred echo messages with Rolling Thunder operations. The result was a direct hit. The barred echo message appeared almost every time a Rolling Thunder mission was flown over the northeast quadrant of North Vietnam. The PRC appeared to be obtaining predictive alerts on 80-90 percent of the missions in the northeast quadrant.

At about the same time, NSA found that ground control stations [censored] were alerting air defense forcees [censored] as much as twenty-four hours in advance of SAC photo drone missions, called (at the time) Blue Springs. As a result, approximately 70 percent of the drones were being lost to hostile fire. A check of existing traffic showed that [censored] had been issuing alerts on SAC reconnaissance missions as early as mid-1965, and on Arc Light strikes, by late 1965.

NSA released its report in May 1966. The effect was immediate and dramatic. Within days, NSA analysts found themselves standing in the Pentagon briefing four-star generals. In August, after pulling together the full story (including indications of foreknowledge of SAC operations), General Marshall Carter briefed the JCS and, later in the month, the PFIAB.

As a result, DIA was tasked to find the problems and correct them. The director, General Carroll, named Rear Admiral Donald M. (Mac) Showers to head the effort. Showers put together an inter-agency committee which included NSA, the JCS staff, and the SCAs. The group was divided into two subcommittees, counterintelligence and communications security.

The counterintelligence group quickly concluded that the problem was enemy infiltration, but they could come up with no good way to stem the outflow of information. The COMSEC committee concluded that communications were the problem and that they were probably closer to the truth. But in addition, the COMSEC group came up with a methodology for investigating the problem and plugging the holes.

The COMSEC committee adopted a multidisciplinary methodology for looking at the problem in which all facets, including communications, would be studied. NSA had been working on the methodology for several years, and the Navy had already tried it with some success in surveying maritime operations in the Gulf of Tonkin (called Market Time).

The committee also borrowed from a COMSEC study of Arc Light operations done in 1965, called the Guam Area Study. Although the Guam study looked at the communications of all three services, it concluded that most of the insecurities came from SAC communications. Traffic analysis of encrypted messages yielded much pre-operations information, including probable launch times. They also discovered voluminous plaintext voice by logistics people an hour before the launch. Finally, they found that prestrike weather flights twenty hours before launch were dead giveaways (as they had been in World War II). In July 1966, Admiral Sharp (CINCPAC) ordered a broader COMSEC study of the problem, encompassing operations throughout the Pacific.

The PURPLE DRAGON Task Force

The CINCPAC and DIA studies joined in September. Sharp agreed to adopt the broader DIA multidisciplinary approach, and he named his J3 to head the effort. The new study, called PURPLE DRAGON, would encompass Rolling Thunder, Arc Light, and Blue Springs. Teams of experts would be dispatched throughout the theater. They would first interview all people involved in the three operations. They would then observe the operations, following that up with observations of support activities, including logistics and intelligence. They would build a database for their information and would build three profiles: operations, communications, and counterintelligence. An NSA person, Robert Fisher, served on the CINCPAC PURPLE DRAGON staff, and there was heavy infusion from the SCAs, primarily for COMSEC monitoring.

The first PURPLE DRAGON study concluded in April 1967. It had a big impact on operations in Southeast Asia, none more significant than Blue Springs. They discovered that the major leak was the encrypted single sideband messages from Bien Hoa to Da Nang prior to every mission. Using traffic analysis of that link alone, the team was able to predict eighteen of the twenty-four missions. As an almost direct result of introducing communications security on the link, drone recovery increased from 35 percent to 70 percent by November 1977.

Arc Light was much more complex and harder to solve. One of the main culprits proved to be the information fed to the Manila and Saigon air control centers. This information was released all over Southeast Asia as NOTAMs (Notice to Airmen) giving flight routes, altitude reservations, and the estimated time of arrival at Point Juliette, the aerial refueling spot, hours in advance of the mission. SAC tightened up by curtailing much of the information in the NOTAMs and by delaying that which was passed until a time closer to takeoff.

MACV had been passing warnings to villagers in the targetted area. This procedure was modified by simply declaring certain areas as free fire zones and discontinuing the advance notification program.

Of the three, Rolling Thunder was the most difficult to plug. PURPLE DRAGON investigators found that many of the enemy's sources of warning consisted of tactical information obtained after the planes were launched. They determined that between 80 and 90 percent of the missions were being alerted, with an average warning time of thirty minutes for Navy missions off the carriers and forty-five minutes for Air Force missions from airfields in South Vietnam. EB-66s accompanied many of the missions (those expecting hostile fire in particular), and those aircraft used distinctive callsigns. Rolling Thunder frag (read "operations") orders were distributed to 120 different organizations, and those in turn often issued information that could be tied to the takeoff of bombing missions. MACV cut down on the number of organizations getting gratuitous copies of the operations orders, and the Air Force changed callsigns for some of their operations.

Much of what needed to be done simply could not be because of outside factors. MACV never did alter stereotyped operations (such as takeoff times, refueling points, and ingress routes) sufficiently to confuse the North Vietnamese. Tanker operations remained highly stereotyped throughout the war and in fact represented the most vulnerable aspect of Rolling Thunder.

The Permanent Staff

Following the initial blush of success, Admiral Sharp made a permanent place on his staff for the PURPLE DRAGON operation. He placed it in the J3 (operations) directorate, and NSA assigned a permanent representative (once again, Robert Fisher).

There was obviously a need to educate people about the concept and about the methodology and specific information that PURPLE DRAGON uncovered. This generated the first worldwide OPSEC conference, hosted by DIA at Arlington Hall Station in May 1968. Following the conference, General Wheeler directed that all Unified and Specified commands establish OPSEC organizations. He also created an OPSEC organization on the Joint Staff. Meanwhile, OPSEC conferences continued annually and helped to focus activity for the U&S commands. Cryptology continued to be a major player, and in 1988 NSA was given the job of worldwide OPSEC training under the newly published NSDD (National Security Decision Directive) 298.

The OPSEC concept in use in the defense department of the 1990s was largely an outgrowth of the PURPLE DRAGON study. It was a significant factor in prosecuting the air war in Vietnam, although neither it, nor anything else the United States tried in Vietnam, was a panacea. The CINCPAC OPSEC team would periodically resurvey operations in Southeast Asia, and they found that, as the U.S. tightened up procedures, the North Vietnamese would find another leak, and their warning time would float back up to where it had been. Like cryptology in general, OPSEC proved to be a constant struggle to stay ahead.

Chapter 13 The Withdrawal

The Tet Offensive

"Americans do not like long, inconclusive wars—and this is going to be a long, inconclusive war. Thus we are sure to win in the end." —Pham Van Dong, North Vietnam's chief negotiator at the Paris peace talks

In Vietnamese history there are many Tets. Like the American Christmas, the lunar New Year holiday is celebrated every year—one of the big events in the timeless cycle of Southeast Asian civilization.

In American history there is only one Tet. It has become a synonym for defeat and withdrawal, the beginning of the great unraveling of American power in the region. Like many symbols, the characterization is desperately inaccurate in the military and cryptologic senses, but generally true from the political perspective. That is why Tet 1968 symbolizes the deep fissures about Vietnam within American society.

The Planning

It has become generally recognized that the communist strategy in Tet was to mount a sudden, massive assault, forcing the Americans to recognize the instability of their alliance with the South Vietnamese government and to realize the difficulty of ejecting the communists from their own country. It was to drive home to the Americans the long-range impossibility of surmounting a determined adversary on his own soil. Some say that it was a one-shot affair, but the weight of evidence is against it. Although the North Vietnamese leaders did call for a popular uprising against the Thieu government, there was no sense that, if it failed, they had come to the end. They would simply continue the struggle. Just as there would be lunar new years into the trackless future, there would be other times and other Tets.

The tactic of Tet was to divert American attention to border areas, while building for a major assault on the urban population. To do this, the North Vietnamese would have to mount a major dry season offensive. By attacking in outlying provinces, Giap, the Vietnamese general, sought to make them magnets for American units, then hit the unguarded cities. He aimed for surprise, but he was confronted with the extreme difficulty of readying so many people for such a herculean task without alerting the enemy.

The Beginnings

The winter-spring offensive began, it is now believed, in September 1967 with a surprise attack on a small Marine fire base located on a barren hill south of the DMZ near the town of Con Thien. Westmoreland was delighted that the North Vietnamese appeared at last to be mounting major unit-level assaults. To defend Con Thien, he called in B-52 strikes, artillery, tactical air bombardment—anything at hand. Con Thien held.

The next attack was planned for Dak To, a provincial town northwest of Pleiku in the Central Highlands. But this time it was not a surprise. On 20 October the ASA station at Pleiku picked up indications that the B3 Front had sent a detached element toward Dak To, and two other NVA divisional organizations appeared to be concentrating in the Dak To area. Three days later [censored] referred to "combat reconnaissance", an almost certain indicator of offensive action. Dak To was immediately reinforced. Aerial bombing in the area of an ARDF fix brought secondary explosions, and

American units air-assaulted a hill near the town, encountering heavy enemy resistance. The resulting battle was one of the biggest of the war. It came to involve nine American battalions, an airborne brigade, and over 2,000 air sorties. Roughly 1,600 NVAA troops were killed by ground action, and 500 more by aerial bombardment.

SIGINT picked up other indicators of major developments. In Nam Bo, the southern part of the country, changes to signal plans, accompanied by military reorganizations, long-distance unit moves, and the use of tactical signal plans appeared to presage some larger, undefined development.

The SIGINT indicators were accompanied by similar indications in captured documents and rallier interrogations. Something was afoot, and U.S. military authorities in Saigon had divined it by early January 1968. On the 7th, Westmoreland cabled the White House that "We think that the enemy made a major decision in September 1967 to launch an all-out effort to alter the course of the war . . . the Winter-Spring campaign which began in late October is offensive in nature and exhibits a disregard for casualties heretofore unseen. It calls for continuous military offensives by large and small units, and concurrent political efforts to stir up popular revolt against the GVN [Government of South Vietnam]."

But then, in one of the most infamous miscalculations in American military history, Westmoreland focused his attention on the border areas. There, he believed, was where the major blow would fall, with attacks in the cities serving primarily as a diversion to military assaults on the exposed periphery.

His assessment was supported by SIGINT indicators of a major buildup in the Central Highlands (witness the assault on Dak To and the significant NVA concentrations still in that area) and far to the north, in Quang Tri Province. One of his area commanders, General Fredrick Weyand, did predict on 10 January that the main assault would come in the urban areas. Weyand was in charge of III CTZ (III Corp Tactical Zone); which included Saigon, so his warnings seemed to have something to do with his own responsibilities. Westmoreland did not disagree with him; indeed, he made major changes in his defensive and offensive deployments to support Weyand's defense of the Saigon area. Still, Westmoreland continued to be concerned primarily about the north and west.

Khe Sanh

The largest diversion was at Khe Sanh. Located on the Khe Sanh Plateau in Quang Tri, the northernmost province of South Vietnam, Khe Sanh was a key point if one were to defend the area immediately south of the DMZ. Located astride major transportation links in the interior, some distance from the coast, it bore a superficial resemblance to Dien Bien Phu.

Beginning in November 1967, SIGINT began tracking the concentration of NVA units in the Khe Sanh area. Two divisions began moving from the North into South Vietnam, the first time two NVA divisions had ever moved simultaneously. This caught everyone's attention and clearly pointed to Khe Sanh as the major battleground for the upcoming offensive. Everyone believed it, most of all Westmoreland. He began building up forces at Khe Sanh in anticipation. Westmoreland believed that Khe Sanh was to be the Dien Bien Phu of the American war, but this time the result would be reversed.

The assault on Khe Sanh began on 21 January and did not end until April. It was defended by the Marines, assisted by a small Marine SIGINT detachment ranging from fourteen to twenty-four men. The Marine detachment had HF Morse, LLVI, short-range direction finding (SRDF), and access to the entire SIGINT system. This included ARDF support from the Air Force (EC-47s from two different programs) and links to the NSG detachment at Da Nang. Technical support was provided from USM-808 at Pleiku, which was collection management authority for the northern area. In addition, the ARVN had a small SIGINT detachment at Khe Sanh which was duplicating what the Marines were doing. When this was discovered, the American and ARVN SIGINT units were physically combined, and the ARVN were employed as linguists to transcribe tapes.

The amalgamation was successful, and Khe Sanh became one of the greatest SIGINT success stories ever. The ground unit intercepted NVA artillery firing orders in time for the Marines to get under cover. They also collected ground assault orders, and one participant estimated that SIGINT predicted some 90 percent of all ground assaults during the siege.

Hovering ARDF aircraft passed fixes on NVA units, and artillery fire from Khe Sanh was mostly directed from this source. Under good conditions, the elapsed time between obtaining a fix and "shells-in-the-air" was about ten minutes. At one point ARDF located Hanoi's forward command element for the Khe Sanh action, and tactical air strikes virtually obliterated it. COMINT was either the sole source of targetting information (30 percent of the time) or was married with other sources to produce what 7th AF intelligence chief, Major General George Keegan, characterized as the "best target database in the history [of the war]."

Khe Sanh cost the North Vietnamese about 10,000 killed, as opposed to 500 Marines dead. The level of effort at Khe Sanh, the time period it encompassed, and the casualties the North Vietnamese were willing to endure indicate that it was a military objective that stood on its own. Otherwise, Giap would have broken off the encounter far earlier.

NSA and the Impending Storm

By mid-January, NSA analysts were becoming concerned by NVA communications trends. This agitation began to show up in items in the Southeast Asia SIGINT Summary. One after another, the indications of a major assault bobbed to the surface. Never before had the indicators been so ubiquitous and unmistakable. A storm was about to break over South Vietnam.

Then on 25 January, NSA published a baldly predictive report. Titled "Coordinated Vietnamese Communist Offensive Evidenced in South Vietnam," it began in unambiguous language: "During the past week, SIGINT has provided evidence of a coordinated attack to occur in the near future in several areas of South Vietnam. While the bulk of SIGINT evidence indicates the most critical areas to be in the northern half of the country, there is some additional evidence that Communist units in Nam Bo may also be involved. The major target areas of enemy offensive operations include the Western Highlands, the coastal provinces of Military Region (MR) 5, and the Khe Sanh and Hue areas."

Details were most profuse in the northern areas, while Nam Bo got relatively short shrift. This appears to have been because SIGINT was more voluminous in the north, rather than an attempt to steer the reader toward the idea that the north would be the major objective. American SIGINT attention had always been focused on the northern provinces, where the largest concentration of American troops was. Moreover, like the party organization itself, communist communications structures in the south had always been looser and less susceptible to intercept and analysis.

The report was succeeded by a series of follow-ups providing additional details as they unfolded. The reports grabbed a lot of attention at MACV, and by all accounts, deeply influenced Westmoreland's counterassault strategy. He continued to beef up American units in the north and the Central Highlands. He also cabled the White House to recommend cancellation of the Tet truce which was scheduled to take effect for the duration of the holidays. He got a reduction in the number of days, but the truce itself was in effect when the offensive began. According to political scientist James Wirtz, the failure of the Johnson administration to cancel the truce in the face of overwhelming evidence that a conflagration was imminent was one of the major miscalculations of the war.

SIGINT product reports began referring to "N-day" and "G-hour," never-before-seen terms which seemed to refer to attacks of unprecedented magnitude. On 28 January, an NSA product report detailed the N-day for the Central Highlands—it was 0300 (local) on 30 January. The commonality of terms throughout the country clearly pointed to massive, coordinated attacks. (This was the first of the NSA report series to be addressed to the White House.)

MACV was ready, but the ARVN were not. They took the Tet holidays quite seriously, and when the blow fell, were generally in a holiday mood and a holiday deployment. The White House, too, seemed unprepared for what was about to happen. There was no mood of crisis at 1600 Pennsylvania Avenue.

The Storm

The difficulty of coordinating such an unprecedented offensive proved insurmountable for the NVA. Some units in the Central Highlands attacked a day early, on 29 January. Pleiku and Kontum City, as well as smaller provincial towns, were assaulted in the early morning hours, and the attackers were not finally thrown back until four days had passed.

The blow fell on the rest of the country twenty-four hours later. The coastal areas were hammered with coordinated attacks on 30 January. The major provincial capital of Nha Trang was occupied by the NVA for several days before being ejected with heavy losses. Quang Tri City was also attacked, but the most devastating blow fell on Hue. On 30 January, ARDF showed major NVA units clustering outside the city, and the next day the forces stormed into the city. American Marines finally completed the retaking of Hue on 24 February after a bloody struggle that left more than 2,000 NVA dead. The North Vietnamese captured and executed many of the leading politicians in the city, a tactic which caused them so much ill will that they pointedly avoided it in 1975. More than 3,000 civilian corpses were exhumed after the battle. It was one of the sorriest episodes of the war.

In the III Corps area (including the Saigon environs), attacks opened on 31 January. The largest assaults were against Saigon and the Bien Hoa-Long Binh complex, but attacks also included Tay Ninh City, An Loc, and many others. Vietnamese Communist forces entered Cholon (the old Chinese quarter) from the west, and a sapper battalion assaulted the presidential palace and the American embassy. Though costly and unsuccessful, these attacks produced camera footage that horrified a nation and undoubtedly produced the turning point in American attitudes that Giap was after.

The Assesments

The postmortems began even before the last NVA troops were routed from Hue and Saigon. CIA put together a study group, at PFIAB request, which included representatives from NSA and all the other Washington area agencies. Maxwell Taylor, the new PFIAB chair, requested that the DCI "ascertain to what extent, if any, our intelligence services and those of our allies were at fault in failing to alert our military and political leaders of the impending large-scale attack on the cities and towns of South Vietnam."

The resulting study stated that "communications intelligence was able to provide clear warning that attacks, probably on a larger scale than ever before, were in the offing. Considerable numbers of [censored] enemy messages were read. These messages appeared in many areas of South Vietnam. They included references to impending attacks, more widespread and numerous than seen before. Moreover, they indicated a sense of urgency, along with an emphasis on thorough planning and secrecy not previously seen in such commimications. . . . The indicators, however, were not sufficient to predict the exact timing of the attack." Aside from the last statement (invalidated by the N-day, G-hour warning that NSA issued on 28 January), the DCI assessment seemed pretty accurate. COMINT did indeed serve as the main predictive element in the intelligence puzzle preceding

Tet. The sense of foreboding that cryptologists felt throughout January 1968 was transferred to MACV and Westmoreland's staff.

That was about as good a prediction as could have been advanced. There was no precedent for the scope and ferocity of Tet, because it was a unique event in the war. But the military authorities in Saigon were as ready as they could have been under the circumstances.

The sense of urgency did not appear to have penetrated the White House. This was unusual in Lyndon Johnson's administration. He and his staff were avid consumers of intelligence in general and SIGINT in particular. But they did not seem to have been ready.

What SIGINT was criticized for was not the fault of the cryptologists. Owing to the concentration of SIGINT resources on the central and northern parts of the country, and to the historical ineffectiveness of SIGINT in the south, the product reporting drew the customer toward the northern and border areas. There were fewer SIGINT indicators in the south, and SIGINT cannot report what it does not hear.

What occurred was a phenomenon that became famous after the Battle of the Bulge in World War II. SIGINT had only part of the picture, and intelligence analysts relied too heavily on the single source. In hindsight, it is clear that too little attempt was made to flesh out the rest of the picture through rallier interrogations, captured documents, and the like. SIGINT became the victim of its own success. The lesson was a moral in all-source analysis.

In a far greater sense, however, it did not really matter. Westmoreland was ready for the major attacks, and he successfully countered them. The NVA lost 30,000 dead, an immense military blow from which it recovered very slowly. The structure of the VC insurgency in the south was shattered forever.

The White House, however, had the job of countering the political blows. It did a poor job of it, and the sense of panic and disorganization was palpable.

The War Is Vietnamized

"In the previous administration, we Americanized the war; in this administration, we are Vietnamizing the search for peace. . . ." —Richard Nixon, 1969

The President Pulls Out

Following Tet, the Pentagon decided that the time to win the war was now or never. General Wheeler, chairman of the JCS, sent Johnson a request for 206,000 more troops. This demand created a crisis within the Johnson administration's inner circle. It would require the call-up of reserves and would place the American people on an all or nothing track in Southeast Asia.

Clark Clifford, the new secretary of defense, suggested that he form a group which had become known as the "Wise Men," long-time advisers to Democratic presidents. Reporting in March, ten out of the fourteen recommended against an increase in troop strength, and many felt it was time to begin a gradual disengagement.

The Wheeler troop demands, and the resulting debates within the Johnson administration, leaked to the press. The story played all through March, and toward the end of the month Robert Kennedy announced his candidacy for president. Johnson announced that he would go on television March 31 to make an amouncement.

In a historic speech delivered to television viewers from the Oval Office, Johnson announced a halt to the bombing above the 20th parallel and the beginning of formal negotiations with the North Vietnamese. Long-time Democratic stalwart Averell Harriman was named to head the negotiating team. And in a surprise announcement at the end of the speech, the president stated that he would not run again in 1968.

For Americans, the war was only half over from a chronological standpoint, and more American soldiers were killed after Tet than before it. But the 31 March speech began a new phase. The United States was beginning a military withdrawal and would henceforth rely on negotiations to reach a peace accord.

Vietnamization

Almost immediately, the JCS set to work on a plan to gradually turn over military operations to the ARVN. When President Nixon took over, with the avowed goal of Vietnamizing the war, the JCS was already moving in that direction.

A formal plan to support Nixon's version of Vietnamization was first drafted in late 1969, following his Vietnamization speech. Called JCSM 42-70, it contained a cryptologic tab written by NSA in collaboration with the SCAs. It was coordinated with the Vietnamese SIGINT service (then called the SSTB, or Special Security Technical Branch), but it was never offered for the approval or disapproval of the South Vietnamese government.

NSA planned to turn over much of the SIGINT mission to the SSTB. In order to do this, it would be necessary to both augment its numbers and increase its competence. It had a long-range goal: "The RVNAF eventually will be capable of providing COMINT in satisfaction of its military requirements generated by the ground war in RVN."

At the time, SSTB consisted of about 1,000 people, three fixed sites (Saigon, Can Tho, and Da N ang), a small ARDF effort using U-6s, and a four-station DF net. It had no ELINT mission. It had plans for a major expansion of its tactical capability, modeled after the ASA DSU concept, but as yet only one of the ten planned units was in existence.

In 1970, at the inception of the Vietnamization program, Admiral Gayler characterized the organization as "fairly effective" but in need of certain managerial and technical improvements. The ARDF effort was "considerably less than satisfactory" and the medium-range direction finding (MRDF) net was "not accurate". Still, he concluded that "it is considered feasible for RVNAF to be able within the next three years to cover all Vietnamese Communist communications..." Gayler felt the job was difficult but do-able.

The South Vietnamese SIGINT system had been headed by [censored] since 1963. [censored] was considered by CIA to be a strong point, especially in the area of security. He ran a "tight ship," according to a CIA evaluation, and as a result, the SIGINT organization was a bulwark of security, especially when compared with the porous South Vietnamese government. [censored] reported directly to the J7 element of the ARVN Joint General Staff. COMINT was considered to be highly sensitive, and SIGINT matters would sometimes wind up in President Thieu's office.

To support the Vietnamese military structure as NSA understood it in 1970, SSTB strength would have to climb from about 1,000 to approximately 1,500 bodies. It would add one fixed site at Pleiku, collocated with the ASA unit there. This would bring the SSTB fixed sites to a total of four: Saigon, Can Tho, Da Nang, and Pleiku. In places like Can Tho, SSTB operators would sit side by side with ASA operators in order to enhance training.

NSA maintained overall control of Vietnamization and established the training plan. NSA instructors taught some of the higher-level training courses, but the execution of the plan was decentralized. ASA and AFSS both got major training responsibilities.

ASA was given responsibility for training the SSTB ground COMINT effort, including the ten tactical units. A team of advisers was attached to each of the units, called DARR (Division) and CARR (Corps) Advisory Radio Research units. Regarding ARDF, NSA decided to turn over twenty EC-47 ARDF aircraft to the ARVN. Thus, to AFSS would fall the responsibility for ARDF training.

Vietnamese SIGINT communications security had to be improved. NSA initiated Project LACEBARK, which would upgrade crypto gear. The new COMINT network would internet the four fixed sites, EC-47 unit, and the tactical units.

This was part of a larger project to upgrade South Vietnamese military communications in general. NSA intended to get rid of the obsolete Python tape system. The KL-7 off-line crypto equipment would be provided to RVNAF crypto nets. M-209s, of World War II vintage, affording minimal security, would be provided to the National Military Police, while NESTOR secure voice equipment would be provided to selected RVNAF combat units.

Nixon did not wait to see the results of the Vietnamization program. In March 1970 he announced a phased withdrawal of 150,000 U.S. troops over the course of the next year, despite the anguished protests of General Abrams, who had succeeded Westmoreland at MACV. The next year the president ordered the removal of another 100,000, and this continued until, by the beginning of the 1972 Easter Offensive, there were only 95,000 American troops in Vietnam, of whom only 6,000 were combat troops.

This rapid withdrawal schedule was not reflected in the SIGINT plan. The 1970 cryptologic Vietnamization plan showed a phasedown from 8,500 cryptologic spaces in Vietnam in 1970, to 6,654 in 1973. The secretary of defense commented to the JCS that the cryptologic levels did not seem in concert with the president's ideas about the pace of Vietnamization. It became characteristic of the cryptologic posture that it trailed rather badly behind the removal of combat troops. This undoubtedly reflected the long lead time required to get SSTB up to speed, in people, equipment, expertise. Despite Admiral Gayle's initial guarded optimism, NSA and the SCA's all expressed ambivalence about the long-range capability of SSTB to do the job.

American Special Operations

The slowness of the cryptologists to depart was reflected in the continuing vitality of American SIGINT operations in the theater. One manifestation was SIGINT support for Task Force Alpha.

Task Force Alpha or TFA was organized by 7th AF in the spring of 1968 and positioned at [censored] Its mission was to gather NVA infiltration data from such sources as IGLOO WHITE (the electronic sensor system in Laos) and SIGINT. A primary source was infiltration communications collected by the RC-135 in the Gulf of Tonkin. This information was downlinked in near-real-time to a special USAFSS unit collocated with TFA. This unit also had available SIGINT collected by EC-47s from the ARDF unit, as well as information from USM-7 at Ramasun Station.

Task Force Alpha, with its unexcelled access to the key intelligence systems targetted on the Trail network, was very successful. In the summer of 1968 it even directed aerial bombardment of the Trail. Although this authority was pulled back to Tan Son Nhut at the end of the summer, the long-range effect on the cryptologic community in the theater was considerable. It began a shift of cryptologic operations into Thailand and an increased focus on using SIGINT to try to choke off infiltration, rather than on supporting American ground combat forces. It was in line with the direction that the war was going.

Another special operation was COLLEGE EYE, an EC-121 that flew out of [censored] COLLEGE EYE was an airborne radar station that was used to extend American radar coverage farther north. It was also used as a communications relay so that Monkey Mountain could still talk with its aircraft outside VHF communications range.

Aboard the COLLEGE EYE aircraft were four SIGINT positions, codenamed RIVET GYM. Manned by USAFSS, the positions were used for COMINT tactical voice intercept. SIGINT was passed directly to the on-board controller, who correlated it with the information that he got off his radar scope. Thus he knew not only where the North Vietnamese fighters were, but what they were saying to their ground controller.

In the Gulf, the Navy was going its own way on SIGINT. The larger vessels had small afloat detachments for direct SIGINT support. Among other things, they all copied North Vietnamese Air Defense nets, both radar tracking and VHF air/ground voice, to provide support to Task Force 77 air operations. At any given time there were four or five such detachments, each operating independently.

In 1969 the detachments were internetted under a project called CHARGER HORSE. Through the net they began exchanging information. This allowed them to divide up the responsibility for air defense monitoring so that they weren't all copying the same nets, and to intercept lower level NVA air defense communications to reduce the leg time by several minutes. The information, which included both air defense tracking (considered sanitizable) and VHF voice (not sanitizable), was exchanged over the Naval Tactical Data System.

A second naval operation was called FACTOR, which was an attempt to use SIGINT to stop North Vietnamese maritime infiltration. It had a long history behind it.

FACTOR's story stretched back to 1962. In November of that year NSG first isolated a communications net that supported NVN maritime infiltration. The North Vietnamese called it Group 125, and its mission was to load war material aboard steel-hulled trawlers and run them down the coast to South Vietnam. The trawlers would stand off in international waters until they felt they were not being watched, then dart into the coast to unload the goods.

At the time the cryptologic community was simply following the operation in SIGINT; no attempt was being made to tip off any counterinfiltration operations. But the longer they listened, the less activity they intercepted, and by July 1966 they had completely lost continuity on Group 125 communications. NSA suspected that the vessels had been diverted to other operations, particularly escorting combat vessels to and from China.

After the 1968 bombing halt, Group 125 went back to maritime infiltration, and by November 1968 NSA had again isolated communications from a net that eventually proved to be continuity of Group 125. By 1970 maritime infiltration represented a significant problem, and NSA decided to see what it could do about designing a SIGINT tip-off system. A special position was designed under a new project, called FACTOR. The equipment maximized intercept of ground waves from the frequency range used by the trawlers, the equipment was sent to Cam Ranh Bay, and from there it was loaded aboard two P-3s being used for "Market Time," an interdiction operation.

Success was immediate, and the P-3s intercepted trawler communications on their first mission. NSA designed a tip-off system to flash the intercepts to Market Time operations. A CIA assessment later in the year waxed poetic about the success that Market Time was having, at least partly a result of improved SIGINT support.

The Cambodian Incursion

In the long story of the Vietnam War, one military foray stands virtually alone in the extent and consequences of its failure. The Cambodian incursion was an unmitigated disaster.

The seeds of that failure were in the unstable political situation in Cambodia. The Cambodian leader, Prince Norodom Sihanouk, had lacked the political and military will to keep out NVA forces, which used the eastern section of his country virtually at will as a logistics and infiltration base. In March 1970, his chief lieutenant, General Lon Nol, and a coterie of his Army supporters overthrew him.

While all this was going on, Richard Nixon was considering what to do about NVA domination of sanctuary areas in Cambodia. In February 1970 he authorized a secret bombing campaign which would target NVA base areas in Cambodia. Although supposedly secret, the bombing became known to many American correspondents in Vietnam. In May a *New York Times* reporter, William Beecher, officially revealed it. Nixon's reaction was rage, and he directed that the source of the "leak" be discovered. He ordered wiretaps on suspected journalists and eventually on White House staff members. Thus began a pattern of White House paranoia which led eventually to Watergate. It started with Cambodia.

The pro-Western Lon Nol was no sooner in power than he launched his own campaign to evict the NVA and VC from Cambodian soil, and this was followed by a plea for aid from abroad. The White House responded almost immediately, announcing in late April that the U.S. would provide military supplies and advisers to the new Cambodian government.

On 30 April Nixon announced to a stunned American public that American troops had crossed the border into Cambodia in hot pursuit of NVA forces. The press denounced the move as a virtual renunciation of peace talks begun earlier by President Johnson. Demonstrations erupted, and on 4 May panicked National Guardsmen fired into a group of students at Kent State University.

The incursion took three directions: one in the Central Highlands (Binh Tay, Peace in the West), another in the central border area around the Fishhook and the Parrot's Beak (Toan Thong, Total Victory), and the third in the Delta area (Cuu Long, Mekong River). American forces were heavily involved in the first two, but the only support rendered to ARVN in the Delta was riverine.

The SIGINT capability against Cambodia was good. [censored] Collection was done from a disparate group of sites ranging from ASA sites at Ramasun Station and Pleiku to [censored] USM-7 at Ramasun was the principal in-theater processing site.

Unfortunately, the planning for the incursion excluded the SIGINT system, allegedly for security reasons. The first word came to ASA lieutenant colonel James Freeze, commander of ASA's 303rd RRB at Long Binh. Freeze was tipped off on 28 April, only two days before the operation began, by the G2 of II Field Force Vietnam (FFV).

This began a frantic few days of planning and assembling resources. Ultimately, an extensive network of ASA DSUs deployed, including sixteen intercept teams and various higher-level organizations. Low-level voice intercept was of greatest value, but Morse proved almost worthless [censored] ASA instituted a complicated courier service which included helicopters to get the traffic back to Quan Loi, where it could be forwarded electrically to Bien Hoa. In June, ASA deployed a team (with the interesting title RATRACE) to Quan Loi to process the take and return it to the units in Cambodia. This eliminated the requirement to get the material back to Bien Hoa.

The most famous (or infamous) event of the incursion was the attempt to "get COSVN." Long known as the Central Office, South Vietnam, COSVN served as the VC/NVA headquarters in the south. Situated just across the border from Tay Ninh province, its location was fixed daily by ARDF. It moved occasionally, usually to get out of the way of B-52 strikes (which, as we know, were predicted with great accuracy by the NVA intelligence people), and repeated air strikes over the years had never succeeded in doing any effective damage.

Creighton Abrams wanted to "get COSVN." He had the ARDF fixes, and now he had the authorization to invade Cambodia. The timing seemed right. Whether the attack on COSVN was a primary objective of the incursion or an afterthought is no longer clear. But the press got hold of the COSVN story, and it became common knowledge to the American people. At that point, pressure from MACV to locate and overrun (or at least bomb) COSVN became considerable.

SIGINT was mobilized. Ground positions placed COSVN communications on cast-iron coverage. ARDF flights over Tay Ninh and eastern Cambodia darkened the skies. But the military system moved too slowly. COSVN was able to evade every B-52 strike and every ground maneuver. Abrams complained that he could have gotten COSVN had he not been forced to use the slow-moving ARVN 5th Division instead of an American unit.

But the fact was that MACV still did not fully understand the vagaries of SIGINT. SIGINT advisors explained again and again that they were only fixing an antenna and that the transmitter, to say nothing of the headquarters itself, could be miles away. Moreover, the military targetting system seemed inflexible—SIGINT reports that COSVN had pulled up stakes from location A and was now at location B were not enough to get a strike cancelled or diverted. American bombs tore up miles of jungle, and ARVN troops floundered through a trackless quagmire of Cambodia in pursuit of COSVN. They never caught up with the headquarters, which moved safely to central Cambodia ahead of the advancing Allies.

The best they ever did was to capture supplies. In early May, an ARDF fix located a base area of COSVN known as "The City" because of the extensive logistics depot suspected to exist there. Acting on this intelligence, an ARVN unit struck the complex and captured a vast store of material. It was enough to set back NVA offensive plans for a definable period of time. But it wasn't COSVN.

The incursion was a limited military success. American and ARVN troops proved capable of capturing any territory that they really wanted. But the long-range results were disastrous. The U.S./ARVN forces drove the NVA deep into Cambodia, where the NVA set up shop. By mid-May the major Cambodian provincial capital (and choke point on the Mekong) of Stung Treng fell, and within a month the NVA held every province in northeast Cambodia. Using this as a base of operations, their Khmer Rouge communist allies began an offensive against the Lon Nol government which ultimately led to the fall of Phnom Penh in April 1975, and began the great Pol Pot reign of terror. Few operations in American military history had such dismal consequences.

Lam Son 719

By early 1971 Creighton Abrams was becoming concerned about evidence pointing to a major NVA offensive during the 1972 dry season. The administration, as well, was concerned about the political consequences of a possible ARVN defeat so close to the November 1972 elections. Thus originated Lam Son 719, an attempt to invade Laos and disrupt the NVA logistics system that was being used to funnel record numbers of troops and supplies into South Vietnam.

As the Americans had correctly judged NVA plans, so too the NVA intelligence system sniffed out the American and ARVN plan for a preemptive strike. As early as October 1971, NSA reported that NVA communications were showing a heightened concern for the area that the ARVN planned to invade. Through November and December, NSA reporting showed increased NVA defensive measures along the Trail. Moreover, SIGINT was showing increased infiltration into the areas targetted for invasion.

Lam Son 719 was another disaster. The ARVN troops fought through to their major objective of Tchepone in Laos, but the going had been very tough and the troops were exhausted. Moreover, there was nothing remaining in Tchepone for them to take possession of. In the end they simply retreated. The retreat became a rout as large-scale NVA forces (shown by SIGINT to be massing for a counterattack) descended on unprotected elements of the retreating army.

SIGINT showed once again how flexible the Trail system had become. As the NVA lost sections of the Trail, it simply diverted shipments to other sections not under ARVN control. In the end, Lam Son 719 scarcely interrupted the flow, and the NVA spring offensive of 1972 went off with hardly a hitch.

The Son Tay Raid

Son Tay, the infamous attempt to rescue American POWs, rescued no one. As a military operation, however, and as a way to set up SIGINT support, it was exemplary.

Planning for the 1970 raid began in April. The SIGINT system was brought into the picture in August, which gave it time to react (as opposed to the Cambodian incursion, which did not). As briefed to a handful of cryptologists who were initially cleared for the operation, it would involve a wave of helicopters flying at low level to the prison camp at Son Tay, twenty miles northwest of Hanoi. It would also involve the participation of a diversionary attack by a naval force in the Gulf, along with combat air patrols, fire suppression aircraft, and various logistics flights.

Brigadier General Manor, the overall operation commander, requested that SIGINT give him the best ingress and egress routes from Takhli AB, Thailand (whence the raiders came), and apprise him of all NVA capabilities to interfere with the operation. The NSA representative to Manor's staff was Lieutenant Colonel [censored] the chief of Pacific Air Defense Analysis Facility (PADAF) in Hawaii. PADAF's job was to do just that sort of analysis, and people wrote a series of reports detailing to Manor the precise route that should be followed. Working with NSA analysts, [censored] people concluded that if Manor used their suggested route and went in at night, the NVA would have no capability to interfere. [censored] and his people were right, and the raiders entered and exited virtually undetected.

[censored] put together a complex network for SIGINT support. Working with people he could not clear for the project, he assembled RC-135 collection, COLLEGE EYE assets, and monitoring support from units all over the Pacific theater. He took extraordinary OPSEC measures. His biggest problem was that the RC-135 mission would have to fly at night, at a time when SIGINT reconnaissance missions never flew in the Gulf. He solved that by scheduling several nighttime missions in the weeks before the raid so that the North Vietnamese would get used to seeing them there.

[censored] himself flew to Da Nang to watch the operation unfold. He had an Opscomm link that began at Da Nang and was routed through NSA and ultimately to the Pentagon. On the other end of the link was Milton Zaslow, the NSA representative who kept the JCS apprised of the raid's progress as reflected in SIGINT.

As the raid unfolded, it was being monitored by a select group in the National Military Command Center headed by the secretary of defense, chairman of JCS, and certain three- and four-star officers. As Zaslow was briefing the group on activity in support of the raid, an officer broke into the room and announced that General Manor had declared a MIG Alert.

Everyone turned to Zaslow, who had just stated that there was no threat from MIGS.

Zaslow stood his ground. "No MIGs," he said. He spent a very uncomfortable five minutes as the assembled Pentagon generals stared at him, wondering how he could be so sure. Zaslow knew that intensive SIGINT analysis had identified all North Vietnamese night-qualified MIG pilots and at what airfield they were spending the night. Moreover Zaslow's communications with [censored] were the fastest at the Pentagon, and [censored] was reporting no MIGs, based on continuous monitoring of those airfields. Zaslow stuck to his story. A few minutes later another courier burst into the room crying, "Cancel MIG alert." Zaslow had been vindicated, and everyone breathed easier.

NSA's assessment was confirmed completely, and the SIGINT system worked as well as it ever had. No one ever found out for sure why the prisoners had been moved before the raid, but one HUMINT report said that about a month before the raid a Caucasian journalist had visited the camp and stated that the prisoners were moved immediately alterwards. Perhaps the North Vietnamese were "spooked" by the visit.

The Easter Offensive

Lam Son 719 did little to slow down NVA plans for a great spring offensive in 1972. NSA infiltration figures from the Vinh Window showed an unprecedented flow of supplies and a massing of forces in the border areas such as had never before been seen. For the first time, intelligence showed NVA tank concentrations in the south, pointing to the employment of conventional forces in an attempt to overthrow the Thieu regime.

As the classic SIGINT indicators mounted, NSA reporting became more and more specific about the timing and objectives. When, at the end of March, the offensive finally broke, it had been more than seven months in the offing. This only increased its fury. The NVA concentrated on the areas thought vulnerable prior to Tet 1968—the Central Highlands, Quang Tri Province, and the border areas near Cambodia in MR3. There was no comparahle assault on the cities, no appeal for mass revolution. This was a conventional attack with tanks and artillery. The ARVN barely held, but in the end it looked like another Pyrrhic victory for the NVA. They lost 50,000 troops, almost as many as did the United States during the entire war. The attack failed all around.

Nonetheless, it appears to have fallen on an unprepared Nixon administration. Several knowledgeable historians claimed afterwards that it was an intelligence failure. George Herring was extreme, stating that "American intelligence completely misjudged the timing, magnitude, and location of the invasion." Seymour Hersh, who is usually right, wrote that the offensive was so long delayed that the White House was focused on other things, and that Nixon claimed that the Pentagon withheld information from them. There is no SIGINT evidence to support the "surprise" hypothesis—perhaps there is other evidence.

TEABALL

One result of the Easter Offensive was the resumption of the air war. In early May 1972, Nixon ordered the bombing of Hanoi and Haiphong in an operation the Pentagon called Linebacker. Immediately, waves of B-52s roared over the North. It was the most intensive air bombardment of the war.

But the operation proved costly. The North Vietnamese adopted a new defensive strategy. Eschewing SAMs (which had proved ineffective and fratricidal in the face of American countermeasures), they launched pairs of MIGs. The MIG pilots would home in on one of the flights of B-52s, would execute a single high-speed pass, launch missiles, and turn tail for home. By the first of July, the U.S. had already lost eighteen aircraft to such tactics, with "only" twenty-four MIGs destroyed. The virtually one-to-one kill ratio had General Vogt, commander of 7th Air Force, looking for new tactics.

It had long been the desire of the cryptologic community to pass MIG warnings directly to threatened pilots. The Air Force Security Service had set up a variety of operations over the years, but all the warnings had had to pass through the filter of TACC/NS, unless extraordinary circumstances intervened. Every request to pass warnings directly to operations people had encountered the implacability of the director of Air Force intelligence, General Keegan.

In 1967, Security Service had informally suggested a mechanism for passing warnings directly to operations, but Keegan would not hear of "raw SIGINT" going to a pilot. Two years later, the NSA representative to the Pentagon proposed a similar operation, only to have the idea die in staffing channels, once again a victim of turf protection. It appeared that direct warnings would never get through the bureaucratic thicket and that the Air Force would not get anything similar to what the Army already had from ARDF—tactical warnings passed directly to operations people.

The Linebacker losses proved the undoing of the intelligence empire. In early July, General Vogt appealed to General Ryan, the Air Force chief of staff, for a new approach to the intelligence warning system. Ryan called Admiral Gayler, who already had the solution in his pocket. (It was the same solution that had died in staffing a year earlier.) He sent a team of SIGINT experts to Saigon, headed by Delmar Lang, who had been instrumental in devising a solution to a similar problem during the Korean War.

Lang knew that Vietnamese voice communications revealed the takeoff of the MIGs and that the North Vietnamese controller revealed which B-52 sortie would be targetted (the so-called "Queen for a Day," after a 1950s radio quiz show of the same name). He also knew that the SIGINT U-2, called the [censored] was intercepting those communications and that the intercept operators were sitting at the [censored] He recommended that the takeoff and targetting information be passed to a collocated 7th Air Force controller, who would alert the Air Force defensive patrol in the Gulf. When the MIGs arrived, theoretically the F-4s would be waiting for them. He called the operation "TEABALL."

Vogt established a new Weapons Control Center (WCC) in a van at [censored] right next to the vans housing the downlink for the [censored] operations. Security Service operators had a hotline from their intercept van to the WCC, where the information would be melded with other sources. In practice, SIGINT was virtually the only source of information, and AFSS linguists populated the WCC, sometimes passing information to the pilots when weapons controllers were not available. It was the kind of direct involvement in the air war that the SIGINTers had wanted.

The TEABALL operation got off to a slow start because of communications problems and lack of manning on the 7th AF side. But on 28 August, eighteen days after being declared operational, TEABALL got its first MIG kill. By the time Linebacker was cancelled on 15 October, American pilots had shot down nineteen MIGs while losing only five of their own. TEABALL was given credit for helping to vector U.S. pilots on thirteen of those nineteen kills.

TEABALL became caught up in inter-service rivalry. The Navy had its own control operation in the Gulf, a ground-controlled intercept (GCI) ship known as Red Crown (for its VHF callsign). Red Crown was supported by NSG afloat detachments, which claimed to be able to intercept MIG voice tracking on a more timely basis. Some of the MIG CAP operations got tangled up in jurisdictional disputes between the WCC and Red Crown, and it was not clear which could provide the more timely warning information. The dispute was untangled in a joint 7th Air Force-TF 77 meeting in mid-September, at which a compromise over control of fighter CAP in the Gulf was worked out. The WCC/TEABALL operation relinquished control authority in certain situations, but not in others.

When, on 13 December 1972, Le Duc Tho, the North Vietnamese negotiator, walked out of the peace talks, Nixon turned to the B-52 operation again. This time the raids, under the name Linebacker II, were not confronted with MIGs, which had been chastened by the new American tactics. The North Vietnamese went back to using the less-than-effective SAMs. One B-52 was lost, but it has never been shown that it was a SAM kill. Lacking MIGs, TEABALL wasn't needed.

Linebacker II was the most intensive aerial bombardment of the war. More than 36,000 tons of bombs were dropped, and though American pilots went to extraordinary lengths to avoid population centers, as many as 1,600 civilians may have died. Nixon and Kissinger claimed that it forced Le Duc Tho to return to the negotiating table. Soon thereafter the truce agreement was signed.

The U.S. Moves out of Vietnam

The cryptologists were still very active in Vietnam. There had been some changing around of people and positions; as some cryptologic operations got bigger, others got smaller. One technique that prospered late in the war was remoting. After the early trials on Black Widow Mountain and others, NSA brought in permanent gear in a remoting system called EXPLORER. EXPLORER I, consisting of four VHF receivers, was placed on a hill near Phu Bai in June 1970. A year later it was destroyed to prevent capture and was succeeded by EXPLORER III, destroyed under similar circumstances. EXPLORER II was located on a remote hilltop [censored] It was controlled by USM-604 at Pleiku and was withdrawn when U.S. forces left Vietnam in December 1972.

The last such operation in Southeast Asia was called SARACEN. Established in late 1972, SARACEN provided unique VHF collection primarily on GDRS communications. The remote location, on a hill south of [censored] was almost inaccessible except by helicopter, and the security situation remained precarious throughout its existence, sitting as it did virtually overlooking the Ho Chi Minh Trail. Its collection station was the AFSS site at [censored] which also collected GDRS communications from the [censored] U-2, until U.S. cryptologists were withdrawn [censored]

As diplomatic negotiations proceeded, the Nixon administration stepped up the pace of troop withdrawal. Status reports on cryptologic Vietnamization indicated that the SSTB was not yet ready to take on the load. The organization lacked people, needed more training in processing and reporting, and was short on good communications. NSA hurried the provision of communications and stepped up the training pace. NSA offered ten more EC-47 ARDF aircraft to help SSTB cope with the burden of supporting ARVN operations.

In the fall of 1972, Nixon announced that American troops would be out of Vietnam by year's end. ASA operations were moved to Ramasun Station, while AFSS collection and processing were hastily removed from Da Nang to [censored] to be collocated, with 7th Air Force command and control facilities. AFSS ARDF operatioiis moved to [censored] while the Army flight section transferred to [censored] The Dancer Vietnamese linguist operation moved to [censored] to provide assistance to 6908th linguists at the downlink end of the [censored]

As with the negotiations in Korea prior to the 1953 armistice, NSA provided SIGINT support to the Kissinger-Le Duc Tho peace talks. [censored]

The cease-fire that took effect in February 1973 required that all U.S. military people be out of the country. The cryptologic withdrawal that had begun with the Vietnamization program proceeded very quickly, [censored]

The Summing Up

Vietnam was a rude education for the American military. It was also an education for cryptologists.

Cryptologists had forgotten how to do direct tactical support in an effective manner. It took the cryptologic system most of the war to relearn the lessons of World War II and the Korean War. The cryptologic community paid a high price for dismantling its tactical support system.

Meanwhile, a skeptical military, by then unlettered in cryptology, tried to pry the SIGINT system into pieces and fragment the effort. The struggle for control of cryptologic assets lasted the entire war, and the effects remained for years afterward. The SIGINT system was kept generally intact (with some significant exceptions), but it was not the same one that entered the war.

No one truly knowledgeable of U.S. intelligence could quarrel with the value of SIGINT. It became the number one source of targetting information. An Air Force historian estimated that SIGINT provided 55 percent of all targetting information in Vietnam.

It was the best method of predicting NVA offensives. Beginning with the VC offensive at Ap Bac in 1963 (made famous by Neil Sheehan's book A Bright Shining Lie, a biography of John Paul Venn), SIGINT tipped off virtually every VC or NVA offensive.

It was the predominant source of information on infiltration. Especially after the opening of the Vinh Window in 1967, SIGINT overwhelmed all other sources of intelligence on the subject.

Its use, however, was very spotty. Some commanders, never having been exposed to it, did not know how to use it and either ignored it or misinterpreted it. Others, like Westmoreland, understood the source and used it to good effect.

It was often misused, especially by intelligence people who did not understand it. ARDF fixes were especially prone to errant analysis. According to [censored] the last NSA chief in Saigon, "G2 and J2 briefings all over South Vietnam blossomed with graphs, charts, plotting systems, and mathematicians trying to find the magic relationship between message flow and the number of ARDF locations which, like the secret of the pyramids, could somehow shed divine light on the thinking of the Communists."

Generally, the higher the echelon, the greater the dominance of SIGINT in the intelligence picture. Sometimes, like just before Tet 1968, the SIGINT signals drowned out other sources. Sometimes, as in the Gulf of Tonkin crisis, it was flat wrong.

What came out of the war was a better SIGINT system; more attuned to the needs of field commanders, better able to render support. On their side, military people began to appreciate how the information would be best employed, how it fit in with their war.

The fifteen years following the war represented, for the American military, a long slow road back to respectability and, eventually, dominance. As the military system went, so went cryptology. The ultimate payoff,

Desert Shield and Desert Storm, was a model of what the new system was and how effective it had become.

The Turn of the Wheel

Though cryptologists did not know it at the time, the end of the first Nixon administration would mark the end of an era and the beginning of another. Behind them was a period of almost unbroken expansion. The cryptologic system peaked in 1969 and by 1972 had begun a retrenchment the outlines of which could he only dimly perceived.

The heyday of centralization, too, was over. The desperate in-fighting that marked the latter years of the war would contribute to a limited reversal of the engines of centralization. The wave was about to wash the other way.

Ahead was a period of "downsizing," intensified by the Watergate crisis. The scandal that led to the president's resignation in 1974 would tar the intelligence system. It would not begin to recover until the last days of the Carter administration in 1979.

Book III: Retrenchment and Reform, 1972-1980

Chapter 14 Cryptologic Retreat from Southeast Asia

Direct American involvement in Vietnam ended with the cease-fire of February 1973. The Vietnamese were left to struggle on alone. [censored]

The War Is Vietnamized

The cease-fire that took effect in February of 1973 required that all U.S. military people be out of the country. The cryptologic infrastructure was already safely in Thailand, but the NSA office in Saigon had to remain to provide support to the ambassador [censored] Moreover, NSA was committed to advising the South Vietnamese SIGINT service, renamed the DGTS (Directorate General of Technical Security). There were NSA advisors at each of the major DGTS field sites and as DoD people, they were technically illegal according to the peace accords [censored]

As soon as Americans were out of South Vietnam; support for the military budget was reduced. The 1974 cryptologic budget almost dropped off the edge of the table, as major field sites [censored] took huge decrements. The Air Force EC-47 operation was discontinued in May of

1974, replaced by the much smaller remnants of the ASA U-21 program. ACRP programs declined by 50 percent, as many programs were either canceled or reduced. [censored] was closed in April, and the huge ASA station at Ramasun was ratcheted down by about 40 percent.

The actual effect of the cryptologic drawdown varied by entity. It was most severe on North Vietnamese civil traffic, which could no longer be heard by reduced RC-135 operations forced to fly south of the 17th parallel. NSA also reported substantial reductions in its capability to monitor GDRS (General Directorate of Rear Services, and thus infiltration) traffic. On the other hand, the ability to report on North Vietnamese air defense traffic suffered little or no decline.

In Vietnam, South Vietnamese military capability did not toughen up as fast as the Nixon administration had hoped, but the picture was not entirely dark. With only partial U.S. support (mostly from the air), the 1972 Easter Offensive had been blunted. Once American troops had left Vietnam completely, American arms and supplies bolstered ARVN capabilities. Vast quantities of military hardware arrived at South Vietnamese ports. So many trucks and jeeps sat on the wharves at Cam Ranh and Vung Tau that one congressman wondered whether the objective of Vietnamization was to "put every South Vietnamese soldier behind the wheel." The ARVN became, by the end of 1974, one of the largest and best equipped armies in the world, and its air force was the world's fourth largest.

The SIGINT situation was very complex. Although confronted with major deficiencies in manpower and equipment, [censored] DGTS had developed at least the rudiments of what NSA had hoped for when the Vietnamization program began. lt did a good job of collecting[censored] Its perforrnance in traffic analysis was spotty, mainly because the DGTS often did not see the value. It had an outstanding ARDF capability on paper, although that program was hindered to some degree by the reluctance of Vietnamese pilots to fly in areas of hostile fire. The EC-47 fleet that NSA bequeathed to Vietnam was aging and prone to mechanical failure, which drove aircraft downtime to unacceptable levels. The DGTS used ARDF results primarily for order-of-battle rather than for tactical targeting.

[censored] had picked his SIGINTers carefully, and DGTS dedication was very high. It was hindered by a corrupt and inefficient government and by declining American financial support. Moreover, NSA had been very slow to recognize the need to give DGTS first-class SIGINT training. The philosophy in the early years had been to "buy off" the government in order to develop political support in Saigon for the build-up of American cryptologic capabilities. NSA never permitted a level of SIGINT exchange with the ARVN SIGINT organization that the wartime situation demanded, and its lack of technical expertise was consequently low. When the Americans left, DGTS had a long way to go.

The improvements in overall ARVN capabilities had resulted in at least a marginal improvement in the situation in the countryside. Village security was better in many areas, and the government, still corrupt and oppressive, had nonetheless announced a new land reform program. At year's end, a shaky stalemate existed between the ARVN (Army of the Republic of Vietnam] and the NVA (North Vietnamese Army). Little had changed in the government's ability to control geographical areas since the cease-fire.

But trouble was afoot. NSA reporting since the cease-fire documented huge NVA shipments to the South. Unhindered by American bombing, they brought in engineers and road-builders, and turned the Ho Chi Minh Trail into the "Ho Chi Minh Road," an all-weather highway suitable for heavy transport. By early 1975, NVA forces were better equipped than at any time in the past. They were obviously waiting for the opportunity to renew conventional warfare.

The Fall Of Saigon

Hanoi's Final Campaign

The final round of the Vietnam War was apparently planned by Hanoi as early as August of 1974. With American support for the government in South Vietnam beginning to weaken, victory appeared to be just a matter of time. But the timetable was not 1975—it was 1976. No one in Hanoi really envisioned the imminent collapse of the opposition.

Through the fall, NSA was reporting infiltration figures unheard of except prior to the 1972 Easter Offensive. The NVA launched the first attack shortly after the first of the year against Phuoc Long Province in MR 3. After the seizure of the province, Hanoi sat back to judge the American reaction. There was none, so the NVA renewed the offensive in MR 1 and 2 in March.

About the first of March, SIGINT indicators pointed to a strong NVA attack on Ban Me Thout in the Central Highlands. The NSA office in Saigon, however, believed that the real objective was Pleiku, and that Ban Me Thout was a diversion, albeit a significant one. [censored] the NSA representative, accompanied by [censored] the DGTS commander, briefed the ARVN MR 2 commander, who refused to believe them. The commander reinforced Ban Me Thout, but it wasn't enough, and he still lost it. Meanwhile, just as SIGINT had indicated, NVA forces fell on Pleiku.

On March 15, President Thieu made the "tactical" decision to abandon the Central Highlands. ARVN troops at Pleiku abruptly abandoned the city, and it was in NVA hands within two days.

This began one of the most awesome and tragic civilian evacuations in modern times. Spurred by the military abandonment and the advancing NVA forces, hundreds of thousands of refugees jammed the single road from Pleiku to the sea, Route 14. About a third of the way to their objective of Tuy Hoe, Route 14 met with Route 7B at a town called Chen Reo. There, streams of refugees from other towns intermixed, creating gridlock. In the vicinity of the town, NVA forces attacked retreating ARVN forces, creating a bloodbath in which thousands of refugees and soldiers were killed. NVA harassment continued the length of the road, but Chen Reo was the worst.

The DGTS center in Pleiku kept operating until the final day, and then the center's people joined the fleeing refugees. Of the 87 men and 120 dependents who took to Route 14, no more than half ever reached the coast. The rest remained unaccounted for.

NSA was picking up indications that the North Vietnamese were moving reserve divisions south. The 968th, which had remained in Laos for its entire existence, showed up in the Kontum-Pleiku area, and there were indicators that divisions in the Hanoi area, which had never done more than train men for combat in other organizations, might be moving out. Still, CIA predicted that the South would hold through the dry season.

But military analysts in the Pacific were not so optimistic. USSAG (United States Support Activities Group), which was really MACV in Thailand under a different name, pointed ominously to the movement of reserve divisions, and predicted an all-out effort to take Saigon during the dry season. IPAC (Intelligence Center Pacific) hinted on March 17 that the entire country could fall.

There was no let-up; Quang Tri City, defended with such high casualties in 1968, fell to the NVA on March 20. At the same time, NVA units were besieging Hue. On March 22 they severed the coastal road between Hue and Da Nang. The old imperial capital was a captive.

The Fall of Da Nang

With Hue cut off and withering, refugees poured into Da Nang, the last important city in MR 1 still held by the government. By March 25 the city was choked with pedestrian and cart traffic. ARVN units had turned into an armed mob and were commandeering any form of transportation available to get out of the city. Mobs swarmed across the airport runway, and each successive World Airways 727 landing there found it more difficult to take off.

On the 26th, [censored] the NSA advisor to the DGTS unit at Da Nang, received a call from the CIA station chief. It was time to get out. [censored] drove his jeep to the air strip, leaving his personal goods behind, and squeezed aboard a jammed 727. He rode the overloaded plane to Saigon with a Vietnamese child on his lap.

The next day the Shell Oil personnel departed, closing the airfield refueling operation. Mobs on the runway made it impossible to land, and that morning an American embassy cargo flight was completely stripped by the mob after it landed. At that point World Airways ceased service to Da Nang.

The next day the last Americans got out of Da Nang via ships in the harbor. On March 29 the owner of World Airways took three 727s from Saigon to Da Nang without authorization from either the Americans or Vietnamese. According to the CIA description: "At Da Nang one 727 landed and was immediately mobbed, surrounded by trucks and was forceably boarded by GVN military on the airstrip. The plane made emergency takeoff procedures and was rammed by a truck at the left wing or hit a truck on takeoff. The plane was unable to take off from the normal runway as the VN military had it completely blocked with trucks or other vehicles. Accordingly, the plane took off on a taxiway. The pilot stated that once airborne he was unable to retract the wheels and assumed he had major hydraulic casualty. However, one of the other planes that look off (from Saigon) after him came alongside and reported that he had a body in the left wheel well that was jamming the wheel doors." The World Airways flight (the only one of the three that was actually able to land) arrived in Saigon with 385 passengers (about the right complement for a 747), of whom four were women, three were children, and the rest were ARVN soldiers.

The Da Nang DGTS station, at 429 people, was one of the largest in the country. The DGTS managed to evacuate two planeloads of equipment and dependents before the city fell. The operators continued operating until the site was overrun. The day before the end, the Da Nang communications operator told Saigon: "Only workers are left at the signal center and we will not be able to get out. We are just waiting to die. We will wait for the VC to come in, hold our hands over our heads for them to cut. We will be here until the last, but the government doesn't think about the workers. Please say something to ease our final hours." Photos of Da Nang on March 30 (the day the NVA entered the city) showed only a smoking shell of a building where the Da Nang center had been. All the operators were reportedly either killed or captured.

The Fall of Phnom Penh

NVA forces raced pell mell down the coast, gobbling up city after city. The advance was dizzying to hunters and hunted alike. Within a week of the fall of Da Nang, all of MR 2 was in NVA hands except for Nha Trang, which was abandoned to the enemy on April 7, but not actually entered until the 9th.

Then a brief quiet descended on the land. NVA forces had outrun their supplies and their military plans. Hanoi began collecting assault forces for the final push to Saigon, and the Saigon government began steeling itself for what had clearly become inevitable.

At that point, American attention refocused on Cambodia. As the NVA advanced down the Vietnamese coast, the Khmer Rouge organization in Cambodia had quietly but effectiveiy squeezed the Lon Nol government into a trap. All that the govemment held by January of 1975 was a narrow water alley through the center of the country. The communist forces held all the countryside, and began pinching off the Mekong waterway through which the capital obtained almost gill its supplies. Each year the KC (Khmer Rouge) had done the same thing, but like a bulldog tightening its grip, each year they choked the river closer to the city.

The American mission there was very small, only 140 people. It was well organized under an experienced ambassador, John Gunther Dean. Moreover it had outstanding intelligence support, almost all of it SIGINT. [censored] Moreover, the small ASA ARDF effort out of Thailand showed the tightening of the vise as the various KC headquarters moved closer to the city. But without American commanders to act on the information, there was little the U.S. could do. [censored] But, as it was New Year's Eve, they were all at parties, and the army made no preparations whatever. Gas tanks weren't filled, guns weren't even loaded.

On April 11, the AFSS unit [censored] intercepted KC plans for an all-out assault on the city. Admiral Gayler, by then CINCPAC, called Ambassador Dean to say it was time to leave. Dean agreed with him, and Gayler implemented Eagle Pull, the dramatic rescue of embassy personnel by helicopter from a sport field in downtown Phnom Penh. By the end of the day on April 12 the entire operation was over, and Phnom Penh waited for the KC to march in. Most of the cabinet refused evacuation and waited for the doom that would befall them. They were all executed.

The Fall of Saigon

As the NVA repositioned and refurbished for the final assault, an air of unreality settled on the American embassy. Ambassador Graham Martin believed that the governrnent could somehow hold out until the rains began in June. SIGINT, both from the DGTS station in Saigon and from the U.S. SIGINT system, showed the NVA massing around the city. Thieu, who knew the end was near, resigned. In Washington, the White House understood what was happening. But Martin refused to heed the signs. He and his CIA chief of station, Thomas Polgar, believed that the SIGINT was NVA deception. A bill was pending in Congress to send an additional $700 million in military aid to the governrnent in Saigon, and they held out the hope that this would pass and that it would come in time. The regime in Hanoi, Martin thought, was really getting in position to impose a coalition government, not a military victory.

NSA station chief [censored] main concern was his people. When the country began falling apart, he had forty-three employees and twenty-two dependents. The dependents he began evacuating on civilian commercial flights, along with the thousands of Vietnamese fleeing the country. Ambassador Martin put the evacuation of the government employees on hold. He feared that the SIGINT system would not support him if they left, and that the DGTS would not work without NSA assistance.

The signs of collapse became more ominous, and [censored] made almost daily trips to the ambassador's office, pleading for permission to get people out of the country. The exchanges became angry, and [censored] went to the director of NSA, Lieutenant General Allen, for help. In mid-April, Allen sent a distressed cable to the DCI: "I am fully aware of the complex political issues involved in any withdrawal of US. Government personnel from the RVN. I wish to reiterate, however, that the safety of the cryptologic personnel in the RVN is my paramount concern." Not even this was sufficient to change minds in the embassy. [censored] "smuggled" people out of the country by buying them commercial tickets, and his staff gradually shrank to just a few. Those who remained spent almost all their time at work, often sleeping in the office rather than returning to the hotel where they were billeted.

The final assault began on April 26 with the attack and capture of Bien Hoa. On the 28th, [censored] made a final visit to Martin, with a message from Allen directing him to secure his communications and depart. Still, Martin refused. The next morning, the NVA began rocketing Tan Son Nhut, and the airfield was closed to even military aircraft. The embassy and its people were now caught in a trap, and the only escape possible was by helicopter.

The evacuation plan was called Talon Vise (later changed to Frequent Wind). It envisioned the evacuation of all Americans and almost 200,000 of their Vietnamese allies. Evacuees would be airlifted by fixed-wing transport from Tan Son Nhut or picked up at the port of Vung Tau on the coast. Helicopters would be employed to ferry pockets of people from exposed locations to Tan Son Nhut. Politically sensitive Vietnamese, such as those who had participated in the Phoenix program, or SIGINT transcribers (the Dancers), and their families would be afforded special evacuation priority.

But with the ambassador bewitched by clouds of intelligence opiates, there was no time left to implement such an orderly departure. All that was left was to use the helicopter option to try to get the Americans out. Martin, debilitated further by walking pneumonia, stood alone. With shells landing on Tan Son Nhut, the president gave the order, and Admiral Noel Gayler directed the evacuation. Martin was obdurate to the end.

Gayler had been assembling a vast armada in the South China Sea. It contained seventy-seven vessels, including five aircraft carriers. On the morning of the 29th, the principal carrier to be involved in the operation, the *Hancock*, downloaded fighters and uploaded choppers.

At NSA, Director Lew Allen had been putting together a SIGINT support effort since mid-April. Most important was the monitoring of North Vietnamese communications to provide warning to the evacuation aircraft, since the NVA had brought SAMs into the vicinity of Saigon. A special AFSS SIGINT support team was flown to Clark Air Base to brief MAC (Military Airlift Command) crews on warning measures, should they be targeted by NVA antiaircraft units. As it turned out, MAC aircraft were not used in Talon Vise, although they did continue to fly into Tan Son Nhut until the morning of the 19th.

The [censored] U-2 collection [censored] served as the primary monitoring system for NVA communications, and also monitored U.S. communications to keep tabs on the progress of the evacuation. This information was passed to Gayler and on to the White House. In addition, RC-135 missions were tasked with both NVA and U.S. communications.

When, on April 29, President Ford directed the implementation of the evacuation plan, military planes had already evacuated almost 40,000 Americans and South Vietnamese over the preceding eight days. But since the plan called for over 200,000 to be evacuated, this was just a start.

The helicopters began flying from the deck of the *Hancock* on the afternoon of April 29. All through the night, the heavy thump of chopper blades was heard above the embassy. The operators at [censored] monitored the voice frequencies used by the chopper pilots, and sent their reports to Gayler in Hawaii.

The remaining NSA contingent found itself marooned at their offices in the DAO compound at Tan Son Nhut. [censored] found that no provision had been made to get him and his people out. He contacted General Smith, the military attache, who arranged for cars to take [censored] and his people to the embassy. There they boarded helicopters late on the 29th for the ride to the waiting ships.

At about midnight, Pineapple 6-1, a chopper pilot in the embassy compound, reported that he was in contact with the ambassador, who still refused to leave until the last Americans were out. Four hours later, intercept operators heard chopper pilot Lady Ace 9 tell Martin that the president had directed Martin to leave forthwith. The chopper hovered above the embassy rooftop as smoke from fires in the building made his landing temporarily impossible. Six minutes later an RC-135 operator heard the pilot broadcast: "Lady Ace 9 this is Tiger Tiger Tiger." This was the codeword indicating that the ambassador was on board.

The choppers continued to pluck people off the roof of the burning embassy for another three hours. The last to leave was not the ambassador—it was the ground security force.

It had been the largest helicopter evacuation in history. Seventy Marine helicopters had airlifted more than 7,000 Americans and Vietnamese from the embassy and the DAO compound. Among those who did not get out, however, were the DGTS operators. Saigon Center operated to the end, and CIA evacuated only about a dozen high-ranking officers, including [censored] The Dancers, DGTS linguists on duty in Thailand, were evacuated from Thailand to the United States. Their families in Saigon had already left South Vietnam and were waiting for them on Guam.

The Summing Up

Not having time for an orderly departure, the Americans left behind vast stockpiles of military equipment. Along with the runways full of planes and parking lots full of trucks, there were large amounts of crypto gear. Deputy Director Benson Buffham estimated that it was the largest loss of COMSEC equipment ever. In practical terms, however, it was not as great a blow as the capture of the *Pueblo*. The crypto principles of most of the equipment had been compromised earlier, and very little actual key was known to be in Vietnamese hands. Spare parts would be almost unobtainable, and Buffham expected that the U.S. would intercept very few NVA transmissions.

The DGTS organization was captured virtually intact. At the time it consisted of more than 100 manual Morse positions, 2,700 people, and seventeen ARDF aircraft. Many of the South Vietnamese SIGINTers undoubtedly perished; others wound up in reeducation camps. In later years a few began trickling into the United States under the orderly departure program. Their story is yet untold.

Their leader, [censored] made his way to Washington, D.C., and was hired as a linguist by NSA. He lived a quiet life in suburban Washington until his retirement in 1994. He now lives with his family in rural Virginia.

The *Mayaguez*

As if Southeast Asia had not caused America enough heartache, one last chapter remained to be written. The seizure of the *Mayaguez* had a murky beginning and to the end remained unsatisfying. It also had a cryptologic component which remains confused to this day.

The Khmer Rouge regime which rolled into Phnom Penh in mid-March 1975 quickly turned vicious. By early May, the White House was receiving SIGINT reports of widespread executions, of forced exodus to grim countryside reeducation camps, of families separated and of retribution on an unbelievable scale. Secretary of State Henry Kissinger, commenting on one such [censored] KC message, wrote to President Ford, "The magnitude of the KC liquidation effort has heretofore been unclear. It would appear that if similar efforts are being carried out in other parts of the country, this would involve a slaughter of immense proportions."

The Cambodian government of Pol Pot took a very aggressive approach to foreign relations, too. Among the territories which KC forces invaded were several small offshore islands which Vietnam and Cambodia both claimed. Among those islands was one named Poulo Wai. SIGINT intercepts of KC communications revealed a determination to hold Poulo Wai and to spread out farther into the offshore waters.

Beginning on May 5, NSA began publishing reports of the KC seizure of Thai fishing vessels and attacks on Panamanian and Korean merchantmen plying the waters in the Gulf of Thailand. But the intelligence community focused not on these commercial depredations, but on communist attempts to intercept Vietnamese refugees escaping after the fall of Saigon. Moreover, the U.S. government organization charged with issuing notes to commercial shipping had no links to the intelligence community. No notes were issued.

Into this nest of small-time raiders steamed an American flag container ship, the *Mayaguez*, plying a regular route between Hong Kong, Thailand, and Singapore. The first maydays from the vessel, on May 12, indicated that they were being boarded by Cambodians, and later that they were being towed to an unknown Cambodian port. An exploration company based in Jakarta received the broadcasts and notified the American embassy. The embassy issued the initial critic at 0503 EDT on May 12.

The president was briefed on the seizure that morning. It was not a military challenge and was scarcely an impediment to commerce. But the *Mayaguez* seizure clearly represented a political challenge. The evacuation of Saigon had been a profound American defeat in Southeast Asia. Here was a chance to prevent the tiny Cambodian navy from tweaking America's nose. Coming only two weeks after the fall of Saigon, it was an event which found American military forces still in place in Southeast Asia. The president directed that a response force be assembled and the crew recovered. The discussions with the president harked back to the disastrous *Pueblo* seizure. Ford was determined to prevent that scenario at any cost.

Initial Navy aerial reconnaissance ordered by the Pentagon established that the *Mayaguez* itself was anchored a mile off Koh Tang Island, thirty miles off the coast of Cambodia. The central concern of the Ford administration became the location of the crew. If it remained on Koh Tang (where it was, presumably), one sort of rescue operation would be mounted. If the crew wastransferred to the mainland, a very different operation would be called for.

Here was where good intelligence was required. NSA still had in place virtually all its intelligence assets from the war in Vietnam, and the Agency directed a total focus on Cambodian communications, [censored] NSA declared a SIGINT alert. Meanwhile, aerial reconnaissance continued to blanket the area. In the early morning of May 14 (Cambodian time), an American patrol craft spotted a thirty-foot boat, accompanied by escort vessels, making a run for the mainland, with eight or nine Caucasians on the deck. Since the least desirable option was for a mainland rescue, a tactical air strike was called in, and the escort vessels were sunk. But the main vessel continued on, and the attacking A-7s held their fire.

An early intercepted message indicated that the crew was to be taken to Koh Tang. This caused the administration to focus on the island. But that was it. There were no subsequent messages about the location of the crew, their destination or the intentions of the Cambodian government, until the very end.

The fragmentary SIGINT, and the lack of anything more definitive, caused the administrationto focus on Koh Tang. A complex rescue operation was hastily arranged, and on the morning of May 14, only three days after the initial seizure, 200 Marines assaulted the island. They were met by heavy resistance. The 150 Cambodians on the island were armed with 75-mm recoilless rifles, claymore mines, and rockets, in addition to small arms. Marine helicopters were cut down on the beach, and eighteen Americans were killed. The Marines were pinned down on the island, and they themselves had to be rescued the next morning.

Meanwhile, Navy F-4s struck Ream Airfield inside Cambodia, based on SIGINT intercepted by the USAFSS unit at Ramasun Station that the KC planned to move Cambodian combat aircraft there. They destroyed seventeen aircraft on the ground. and put the airfield out of commission.

On May 14, as the Marine assault was going on, there was a flurry of messages from various KC entities referencing response to the American attacks. Early on the 15th (in Cambodia) a message (probably from Phnom Penh) ordered a KC operational authority to let the Americans "take the ship and leave" and to "let the Americans go." Soon thereafter a KC gunboat appeared near the north end of Koh Tang showing a white flag. Four minutes later the destroyer USS *Wilson* scooped up the entire crew, and *l'affaire Mayaguez* was over, except for the extraction of the Marines on the beach, which was difficult and dangerous to the end.

The Ford administration claimed credit for a win. The crew was back safe and sound, although at the cost of eighteen Marines dead. President Ford went on television to explain the American response, and a Gallup poll taken shortly after showed the approval rating for the operation at 51 percent. To an administration which had been badly battered by its handling of the pardon of President Nixon, this was good news.

A month later the Vietnamese completed what the Americans had started. Intercepts revealed that the Vietnamese had wiped out the Cambodian garrison on Poulo Wai.

Although the crew was recovered and the vessel released, the *Mayaguez* incident has been counted as an intelligence failure. DIA and IPAC intelligence estimates of KC strength on Koh Tang were accurate but did not reach the deployed forces. Although this deficiency was cited in report after report, no one seemed to know why the information did not reach the users. But since the only reliable information on Cambodia at the time was SIGINT, classification difficulties are readily suspect.

There were other problems relating to the affair. The response of intelligence agencies in Washington was slow, and the NOIWON system was not used. While SIGINT classification undoubtedly hampered the dissemination of critical intelligence, in the opposite direction tactical commanders refused to share details of the military operation with NSA—details which would have improved intelligence responsiveness.

Why didn't SIGINT reveal the location of the crew? Reviewing the action some weeks later, an NSA analyst came up with the answer. Simply put, the operation was carried out by a local commander, without checking with higher authority. Khmer Rouge local commanders had long exercised such authority, and it is reasonable to suppose that it did not halt simply because peace had broken out in Southeast Asia. The first high-level SIGINT came from Phnom Penh on the 15th and was passed to Ta Mok, the regional commander, directing that the crew be released. There was no prior direction from higher headquarters because headquarters had not directed the action in the first place, and it got involved only when the military consequences had become serious. In a radio broadcast the following September, Ieng Sary, the Cambodian deputy premier, admitted as much. So in the end SIGINT, the only good source on Cambodia, came up short.

Chapter 15 Downsizing

Cryptology had waxed fat during the war years. It did not seem so to those who struggled for dollars and manpower to help fight the war in Vietnam, nor to those in other parts of the cryptologic system who desperately tried to maintain their hold on resources that seemed inexorably to slip into the pit of Vietnam. But in fact, the peak of the cryptologic system was reached in the late war years. After that, there came the reckoning.

The peak years in overall field deployment came from 1967 to 1970. After that, it looked like the cryptologlc system was going off a ski jump. (See table 1.) [table 1 is censored] The downslide lasted for a decade—field site deployment did not finally level out until 1981—and the loss of field sites was matched by an overall decline in manpower. The cryptologic system began the 1970s at approximately 89,000 people; it ended at about 50,000, a drop of 44 percent. The funding profile, unlike that of personnel and field sites, remained fairly steady over the period and was actually higher in 1975 [censored] than it had been in 1969 [censored] But the decade was one of runaway inflation, so a steady stream of dollars did not equate to the same level of resources as before.

The Great RIF Scare

At NSA, the work force shrank from 19,290 in fiscal year 1970 to 16,542 in fiscal year 1979, a reduction of 14 percent. Looking back, this doesn't seem so drastic, but in 1971 no one knew how far the cutbacks would go, just that Congress had decreed a huge cutback in the federal work force, called the General Austerity in Government Expenditures Act, and that the Department of Defense would absorb the brunt. To maintain some sort of fairness, cuts would be across the board, and NSA would give up its "fair share" of manpower, regardless of mission or need.

Soon after Congress levied the cuts, in September of 1971 Admiral Gayler, the DIRNSA, issued a memorandum to the work force confronting the rumors swirling through the halls. Yes, a RIF (reduction in force] might be necessary, and it was certain that promotions would get scarce. But a RIF would be an absolute last-gasp measure. He hoped that retirements and attrition would turn the trick. This was suspect, however, because NSA's attrition was notoriously low—about one-third of the federal average. With a closed-loop personnel system and unique, nontransferrable skills, NSA employees could not go out and look for other federal jobs. (By the same token, employees of other agencies could not come looking for jobs at NSA.) What finally forestalled the RIF, however, was a device called "discontinued service retirements." NSA began offering these immediately, and they were hugely successful. In 1972 the retirement rate doubled that of the previous year. In June of 1973, moreover, the Civil Service Commission authorized DoD to offer immediate annuities to individuals with twenty-five years of experience, regardless of age, or who were at least fifty years old with twenty years of service. In addition, a 6.1 percent cost-of-living increase was offered to those retiring before July 1. This did it—retirements in 1973 increased by 45 percent over the already-high level of the previous year. In the end, the RIF was never necessary.

NSA's manpower bottomed out in 1975, as Table 2 shows, and remained steady through the remainder of the decade, except for the military component, which continued to shrink slightly. It began its upward swoop in 1981 and topped out in 1989, the nominal end of the Cold War.

~~(C)~~ Table 2 [4]
NSA's Manpower History, 1973-1993

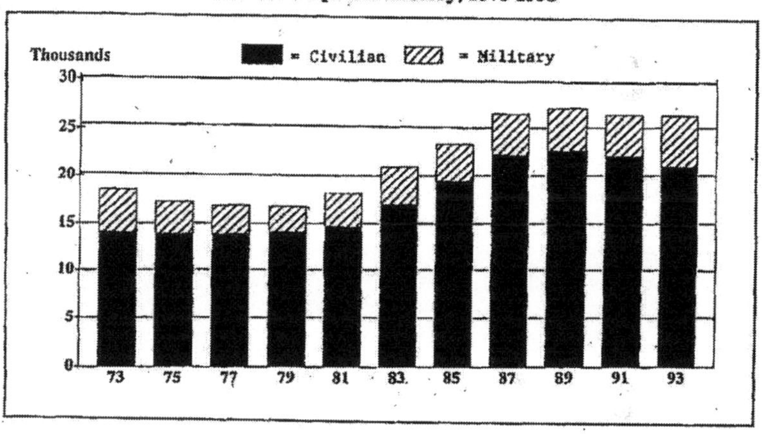

However, promotions were difficult to get throughout the decade. The problem was the grade structure. NSA's average grade had marched upward from 8.96 in 1965 to 10.2 in 1972 (see table 3). NSA was advancing faster than the federal averge. In 1965 its average tied for ninth place, while in 1972 it was in fourth. The grade problem led to a promotion freeze. Though it lasted only a few months, it damaged work force morale almost as much as the talk of RIFs.

While NSA experienced a modest downsizing, the Service Cryptologic Agencies (SCA) were devastated. Of the 39,000 cryptologic billets lost, almost 36,000 were military. Some [censored] military billets associated with direct support and training were transferred into non-CCP (Consolidated Cryptologic Program) areas, so the net loss to the cryptologic system was "only" [censored] The Army was hardest hit, losing [censored] billets from its CCP structure. Security Service lost [censored] percent of its billets, while NSG lost more than [censored] percent.

(U) Table 3 [6]
NSA's Average Grade, 1965-1972

Year	NSA's Average	All-Federal Average
1965	8.96	8.3
1966	8.67	8.3
1967	9.0	8.4
1968	9.2	8.5
1969	9.7	8.8
1970	9.9	8.9
1971	10.07	8.9
1972	10.2	8.9

The Clements Cuts

NSA was in the middle of a desperate downsizing effort when, in 1973, it was hit with a round of budget cuts which became known as the "Clements cuts." The real author of the directive was one James Vance, who worked for Dr. Albert Hall, assistant secretary of defense for intelligence and DIRNSA's immediate boss. Vance contended that cryptology was overfed and underworked, and he embarked on a detailed study of the cryptologic system. The upshot was a recommendation to Hall that cryptology be hit with an additional three percent cut. The Vance recommendation wound up in the office of Assistant Secretary of Defense William P. Clements. Clements imposed a total CCP billet reduction of 12,999 to be completed by fiscal year 1978. (Since the cryptologic budget already showed a large reduction during that period, the real additional manpower cut was "only" 5,110 jobs.)

Clements specified that reductions were to come from:

1. Management efficiencies. The crux of the problem, as viewed from the DoD level, was a bloated management system with overlapping authorities—basically, "too many" bureaucrats. The answer would be to squeeze out the fat, without cutting into bone.

2. Technological efficiencies. As will be seen later, NSAA was looking at a raft of modernization proposals, chief of which was remoting, that would reduce manpower without substantial mission reductions.

3. Mission reductions. This was a last option. At Clements's level, people felt that NSA could cut without reducing the mission.

Lieutenant General Sam Phillips, who would soon be leaving NSA, answered that NSA recognized the "bureaucracy problem" and had just completed an internal reorganization that cut 649 spaces. Phillips felt that further efficiencies could be accomplished, especially through technology, but he cautioned Clements not to be too hopeful that NSA could do it without any mission cuts. He convened a panel to work through the reductions and come up with a plan.

The study group had tough sledding. The first reaction was a decree from the production side of NSA that it would not take a reduction until all support billets worldwide had been cut, whereupon the support organizations replied that they could not cut support until they saw the operational reductions. The SCA representatives were similarly obdurate. It was enough to make a budgeteer tear his hair out.

They slugged away during the summer and fall of 1973. When, in October, the results were due to Clements, Lieutenant General Lew Allen had become director. By this time the committee had forged some numbers which sounded a little like a congressional budget-cutting exercise, but which were plausible on paper. Allen told Clements that:

1. Managerial efficiencies could absorb some of the needed reductions. The committee recommended cutting all deputy jobs below division level, consolidating some organizations that were split (such as A7 and A8), restricting hiring to one third of projections, virtually eliminating the analytic effort on Southeast Asia, reducing staff functions, and slimming down NSA overseas liaison offices. Overseas, support and managerial billets could be deleted by forcing closer integration of collocated SIGINT sites under the Single Service Executive Agent concept. A new concept in position tasking called COPES (Collection Operations Position Evaluation Standard) could theoretically reduce manual Morse positions by 25 percent. Since there were more than [censored] Morse positions worldwide, this would have amounted to a significant savings. The SIGINT system would have to rely more on Second and Third Parties. Worldwide logistics would be shaped into a more efficient mechanism, and some logistics operations would be contracted out. Some sites [censored] could be staffed by contractors. Army Security Agency and USAFSS had both built up theater-level administrative headquarters that could be eliminated without effect on the mission.

2. Technological innovations represented a higher risk option. The remoting program [censored] was still unproven, but Allen banked heavily on its success to save cryptology from the worst of the Clements cuts. Only the first site [censored] was far enough along to count on. Other new programs with interesting and obfuscatory names like[censored] offered potential savings, but their contributions remained to be seen.

3. Despite opposition from Vance, Hall, and Clements, Allen relied on mission reductions to make the mythical Clements's manpower ceilings. Some stations, like the Navy site at [censored] would be closed outright. The ASA trio of [censored] would be closed and the mission transfered [censored] The Air Force site at [censored] would be cut, the operators moved to [censored] and Single Service Executive Agent management would be applied to the new triservice station. [censored] Back at Fort Meade, NSA would stop doing [censored]

Some economies were logical yet unattainable. The creation of Central Security Service (CSS) the year before had created duplicate staffs at the NSA level. General Phillips had quietly scotched the operational effect of CSS, and the vestigial staffs had quietly taken on dual functions for the sake of economy, but the whole CSS exercise had made it more difficult to slim down because of the perceived need to keep up the appearance of a functioning CSS. The most far-reaching CSS proposal had been to bring the SCA headquarters to Fort Meade and collocate them with NSA, where, it was assumed, economies in the billet structure would be easier to effect. It had not happened and was not likely to happen in the future. The SCAs had successfully fended off collocation with "Mother NSA".

Lew Allen had replied with some well-thought-out planning options. Some, such as the [censored] Single Service Executive Agency, and heavier reliance on Third Parties, came to pass. The elaborate and expensive remoting option was implemented in later years, although not quite the way Allen envisioned it. But other options like major reductions in the Air Force's Rivet Joint airborne collection program fell to operational reality (and determined opposition within the parent services). Still others, like contractorization, simply transferred the cost to another budget category while yielding only minor savings.

While NSA struggled to protect its resources from the budget axe, its mission emphasis changed dramatically. [censored] The real cuts had come at the expense of other production elements. [censored] while G Group positions were down from 15 percent to only 8 percent.

The Field Sites

In 1970 the collection site system stood at its highest level ever. [censored] But the impending withdrawal from Southeast Asia, and the budgetary pressures that were moving DoD toward contraction, were about to hit.

The collection site posture went into sudden freefall, and by the end of the decade only [censored] sites remained. ASA was particularly hard hit, contracting from [censored] The Air Force lost [censored] while the Navy, with a small-site posture and emphasis on worldwide DF, lost [censored]

[censored] each service lost sites to a base consolidation movement. By 1975 all Southeast Asia sites were closed except for Clark Air Base in the Philippines. In Thailand, the closure of Ramasun Station resulted from a political forceout by the nervous Thai government. [censored] a massive base consolidation movement, which hit cryptogic and noncryptologic units with equal fervor, resulted in the closure of [censored]

The closures resulted from a complex of budgetary pressures from Congress and difficulties with the host countries. The period after the Vietnam War was one of exceptional instability in the Third World, and cryptologic sites, long held hostage to foreign aid by host governments, were battered about quite unmercifully. If they survived at all, it was usually in an altered, and less favorable, condition.

[censored]

[censored]

[censored]

Thailand

During the years of war in Southeast Asia, NSA had used Thailand as a principal base of cryptologic operations. The original ceiling of 1,000 cryptologists, while being a nice round number, soon ceased having any relationship to reality, and over the years NSA had brought more SIGINTers into Thailand, taking care of the increases with post-facto authorizations by the Thai government. After the 1973 Vietnam cease-fire, a large slug of displaced SIGINTers entered the country [censored]

With the fall of Saigon in April of 1975, the end of the American presence in Southeast Asia was only a matter of time. U.S. forces began leaving the country soon after, and the formidable base structure that had come into being during wartime quickly imploded. So where did that leave the cryptologists?

[censored]

[censored]

Negotiations with the Thais consumed the whole of 1975, but with no resolution. The Royal Thai Government would clearly have been relieved to see the last of American forces, which by late in the year was made up of the cryptologists and virtually no one else. The American embassy was on the side of the Thais, since the loss of the last American military forces would remove a thorn in the side of American-Thai relations.

[censored]

But in the end it wasn't enough. The Thai government was getting fierce diplomatic pressure from the PRC, with whom they were negotiating an improved relationship. Moreover, the Thai military-run government was being squeezed by an internal communist insurgency in the bush and an urban leftist student movement emanating from the universities. With the communists victorious all across Southeast Asia, everyone, it seemed, wanted to be on the winning side. America did not appear to be the winning side.

Udorn, the nearest large town to Ramasun Station, had a university, and it was full of restive students. In 1975 they got a cause, the infamous Leuchai incident. Leuchai, who managed the officer's club accounts, got into trouble with the base commander over the disposition of some monies and was summarily fired. But Leuchai had friends, and they brought out the students from the university. The base commander at Ramasun was confronted with daily demonstrations at the main gate. One day the military police, apparently thinking that the base area was sovereign American territory, arrested Leuchai, and the demonstrations got larger. In the end,

Leuchai was released, the American ambassador was upset, and the Thai government, with newly stiffened spine, was ready to order the Americans out of Ramasun.

[censored]

Closures and Consolidations

In [censored] base closures all resulted from budget cuts. The [censored] consolidation plan had actually originated from a study in 1967 which showed the economies that could be achieved by closing [censored] and moving the people and mission to a single location. ASA organized the original [censored] cadre in 1968, and the station was officially up and running in January 1972. Two years later the Security Service Site [censored] was closed, and the people and mission joined the triservice operation [censored]

[censored]

[censored]

The Airborne Communications Reconnaissance Program (ACRP) also slimmed down. In the 1960s it had consisted of a welter of strategic and tactical programs under various jurisdictions and controls. An Air Staff study in 1971 showed clearly that the program could be more economically managed if it were consolidated as a single program under a single manager. The outcome of the study was the RIVET JOINT program. Under it, the worldwide ACRP programs were consolidated into a single airframe, the RC-135. Twelve airframes were modified for both COMINT and ELINT collection by E-Systems in Greenville, Texas. The Air Staff recommended that the new Airborne SIGINT Collection Program—ASRP—be jointly managed by SAC and USAFSS. Moreover, the new program operated under the Air Force's MOB-FOB concept. That is, there would be a main operating base—in this case Offutt in Omaha, SAC headquarters—and forward operating bases in each theater. The crews and airframes would be based at Offutt and would deploy to the forward bases on TDY for missions. The new RIVET JOINT marked the first successful attempt to rationalize and centralize a large number of programs that had grown like weeds during the Cold War.

Tactical Systems

The war in Vietnam had displayed the inadequacies of the tactical SIGINT systems that had rusted away during the era of nuclear dominance. Vietnam produced a spate of development programs to fix the problem.

The Army came up with several entries. [censored] was an airborne communications intercept, DF, and jamming system aboard RU-21 dual-engine aircraft that had proved so useful to the ARDF program. [censored] supported tactical commanders at brigade, division, and corps levels. A second program, [censored] was a modernized version of the ARDF program [censored] The Army, being decentralized, fragmented its SIGINT effort.

The Air Force, being farthest behind the curve, had to develop a system from scratch. Their entry was [censored] a complete tactical SIGINT support system based in mobile shelters. The collection system, [censored] was mostly airborne—two mobile shelters stuffed into a slightly modified C-130. Processing and reporting were done in tents and shelters located well back of the combat zone. As with Air Force doctrine generally,this systen was highly centralized. [censored]

The Navy was least affected by the commotion in Vietnam. What was needed was simply an upgrading of shipboard SIGINT support that had existed since World War II. The new program was called [censored] an automated system designed to work against mobile naval emitters, [censored]

Even NSA came up with a "tactical" system. The [censored] program, an ELINT innovation, permitted NSA to deploy ELINT intercept equipmen [censored]

Remoting

The origins of cryptologic remoting were in 1962 and stemmed from an idea attributed to [censored] an NSA engineer. The first communications satellite, Telstar, had just been launched and, with it, a new era in communications. [censored] in a paper entitled "A Proposal for Utilization of Satellite Relays to Provide an Early Warning and Extended SIGINT Capability within the Z1", proposed that NSA look into the possibility of remoting signals intercepted in one location to another. The technology, he felt, could be developed to send large chunks of the RF spectrum from an overseas location to a location in the United States. [censored] justified the effort that would be required on the basis of improved timeliness, reduction of SIGINT people overseas, and cost-cutting.

The proposal generated interest, and in 1964 NSA conducted experiments to see if what [censored[proposed was really possible. [censored] It worked, and everyone was ecstatic. But for several years, that was it. The idea languished, awaiting sponsorship.

[censored] idea was revived in 1967 when K Group (which at that time dealt with collection and signals analysis) established a study group headed by [censored] Within a year [censored] had produced a preliminary concept for remoting [censored] back to a location at NSA. [censored] sites were small, and the [censored] study group simply discarded them from the study because the expense of installing the operational and communications equipment for such a small site would not be feasible. The group took it as a given that the technology was there—what was needed was practical application.

The [censored] idea did not have many sponsors in the early days. In particular, Dr. Albert Hall, assistant secretary of defense for intelligence, was known to oppose it as too expensive and technologically risky. But within NSA Dr. Robert Hermann adopted it as his own, and he set out to get sponsors. He created an "Industrial Advisory Board" to study the issue and enlisted important people from private industry to help him. His first ally outside of NSA was William Perry of ESD, who would later become secretary of defense. Within NSA, he had the support of Oliver Kirby, the assistant director for production. With this level of support, Hermann embarked on a major feasibility study.

The original [censored] study, publislied in 1969, proposed to remote [censored] to collection centers in the United States. Candidate locations were [censored] The follow-on system development plan produced the following year planned for an initial system, called [censored] in which [censored] in the US. The presumed success of the pilot would result in a wave of support, and by 1975 [censored] The savings would be staggering. Overall CCP economies would range [censored] could be eliminated. Some [censored] cryptologists overseas would come back. But the up-front costs were equally huge [censored] for the system through 1978 and [censored] to acquire dedicated communications satellites that were presumed to be required.

[censored] produced arguments galore. The biggest dispute was over the [censored] approaches. [censored] had originally envisioned remoting large portions of [censored] to the States, [censored]

The competing technology came to be called the long screwdriver approach. In this method, the operator sitting in the U.S. would remotely tune a receiver in an overseas location. [censored]

[censored] also produced arguments over management. Theoretically, every intercepted signal in the world could be collected into a single facility, if not a single room. Where would such a facility be? Was there enough room at Fort Meade? How would it be managed? What would the relationship be between collection and processing? Would operators accept being jerked out of their overseas bases and dumped in the high-cost Washington area? What kind of morale problems would result? Many elements of the Production organization lobbied for a [censored] simulation facility to test out all these problems—a fly-before buy approach. The engineering side naturally focused on the technical hurdles and ignored the management implications. A [censored] simulation center was planned but was never implemented. NSA bought the technology without testing the management problems first.

Ultimately, NSA succumbed to cost considerations and went for the long screwdriver technology. Even under the [censored] program, however, communications requirements were stupendous. For instance remoting the [censored] This was why NSA became the largest single user of DoD communications satellite capacity.

Dr. Hall continued to hold onto monies that NSA wanted [censored] Hermann's approach was radical—rather than scale back on the program to reduce the threat, he sent Hall a new proposal [censored] virtually wiping out the SCE component of the cryptologic system. All CONUS operator billets could be civilianized, less a 25 percent residual for tactical support. Financial savings from pulling people out of overseas locations and putting them in a single colleetion facility would be huge, both in direct operational costs and in logistics and overhead. Hermann's forceful approach finally got a tentative go-ahead from Hall.

[censored]

When the Clements cuts hit NSA in 1973, the [censored] concept seemed a heaven-sent solution to the budget crisis. Lew Allen became the director in August 1973, and he barely had time to put his hat down before confronting the issue. Remoting seemed to be the answer, and he promptly convened a panel to consider it. He called it the [censored] Task Force.

Allen came from the high-tech side of the Air Force, and he was well connected with private industry, which he considered an essential partner in solving big problems. The task force was composed of only four NSA people, plus representatives from fourteen companies, including such industry giants as Lockheed, Hughes, and IBM. Lew Allen understood that the cryptologic community could not work its way out of this jam without help.

He instructed the group to consider only [censored] They had two options: modernize [censored] or use remoting. (Standing pat was not an option.) The objective was clear—they were to devise a SIGINT system that was much less costly than the one that existed.

The task force cast aside casual tinkering and recommended radical surgery. Although they did consider modernizing the overseas sites, they ended up recommending that the whole lot be remoted. [censored] Task Force recommended that every site remaining be remoted to Fort Meade [censored]

Savings under the modernization option would be significant, but using the remoting concept they would far exceed the 3 percent cut mandated by Clements (see Table 5). Of course, DoD would have to wait a few years for the return. The entire remoting scheme would cost [censored] to be spread over a period of years from fiscal year 1976 to fiscal year 1981. Although each year's personnel savings would be significant, the procurement costs would not be completely amortized until fiscal year 1983—fully ten years down the road.

Full remoting would require that [censored] data would pass [censored] back to Fort Meade; [censored] To remote such huge volumes of data, the panel recommended that NSA purchase its own satellites rather than rent from the Defense Communications Satellite System (DCSS). Purchase would be more expensive, of course, but the amortization difference would only amount to less than a year.

~~(S-CCO)~~ Table 5[51]

The [redacted] Plan Costs

	Current	Remoting	[redacted] modernization
Number of [redacted] positions	[redacted]		
Personnel			
Annual CCP cost			
Estimated cost of remoting			

The organization at Fort Meade would be a nightmare. Here, the panel only hinted at solutions, but did originate the concept of the "problem center," which was to have a long life. At the Fort, signals would be shunted to areas that worked certain problems—for instance, all [censored] would go to one area. This would permit customized processing operations and would reduce duplication. For instance, the problem center [censored] would not require a timely reporting mechanism, while the problem center (or PC) [censored] would not need equipment [censored] for transfer to the computer complex in the basement.

Consolidaton at NSA would permit the introduction of many efficiencies that might be unaffordable in a dispersed system. The panel foresaw the automation of search through the employment of automated scan systems [censored]

[censored]

What emerged from the private sector's blue-sky planning was an implementation plan, [censored] It represented what the cryptologic community could get cranked into the CCP, and it was much different from the [censored] system. Under it, NSA scaled the system back to [censored] a far more realistic plan, more in line with the original [censored] planning (see table 6).

[table 6 is censored]

Out of the [censored] billets at the [censored] affected sites, [censored] would remain overseas to do tactical support, Peacetime Aerial Reconnaissance Program, and other operations that would be difficult (if not impossible) to perform from Fort Meade. Some [censored] people would be moved back to the collection operation center at NSA, and the billet savings would be only [censored] The plan allowed for some modernization at the residual overseas sites, but offered specifics in only one case—the Navy site [censored] which would stay largely untouched by remoting. At Fort Meade, the "problem center" organizational scheme was adopted from the [censored] plan.

While the [censored] plan remained through the end of the decade, harsh realities soon intruded. Remoting would incur very high initial costs, and the ever-present Dr. Hall was willing to proceed initially with only one site. [censored]

Not even [censored] survived intact. Pieces of it were eventually implemented, but they resulted from pressures and events not even anticipated when the plan was written. The name survived, but the eventual system could not have been recognized by the original planners.

[censored]

The first remoted site had nothing to do with the grandiose plans originating from the [censored] planning efforts [censored] Instead [censored] became the guinea pig for the whole system.

[censored]

[censored]

[censored]

Remoting the Small Sites

[censored] was never intended for the small sites [censored] It had become a truism early in the project that the cost of earth terminals and ancillary equipment would make such a proposition uneconomical. [censored] all presupposed that [censored] would become candidates for remoting.

The implementation of remoting stood this assumption on its head. As it turned out, the big payoff was in small-site remoting. Part of this resulted from the decline in earth terminal costs, but mostly it related to the importance of the mission. The small sites, with their [censored] highly selective focus [censored] became the high value items in the system.

The first step was data linking, in which operators at overseas sites intercepted signals and plugged the receiver outputs into communications channels.

[censored]

The advantage of data linking was speed—critical signals could be intercepted, forwarded and processed in something approaching near real time. It did not remove the operator at the distant end, nor did it reduce the number of people in the system. The operational payoff could be significant [censored] but these operations did not help with overseas visibility, international balance of payments, or CCP reductions.

The next system was a true remoting operation. [censored] an Army-sponsored project, sprang from the dismal budget-cutting days of the late 1960s, when ASA was strapped for cash and looking for a way to reduce expenses. The [censored] sites, although top producers, had been a financial drain for years. They were expensive to keep operating, [censored]

NSA recognized immediately that the potential payoff for [censored] remoting was far greater than ASA realized. [censored]

In a lengthy memo in late 1971, Major General John Morrison, NSA's ADP (assistant director for production, i.e., DDO) laid out the prospects. [censored] collection had to be fata linked back to NSA. ASA's [censored] was a good idea, but it got the material only part of the way home. NSA needed a data link to get [censored] to Fort Meade.

[censored]

NSA's engineers became involved [censored] from its inception, and in October of 1970 the ASA project manager, Colonel Vernon Robbins, formally invited NSA into the development process. ASA resources were strapped, and only NSA could provide the expertise to steer such a large project. NSA's Richard Bernard was named the deputy project manager.

The combined ASA/NSA project planning committee selected Radiation (later called Harris) Corporation as the prime contractor and let a contract for $25 million. The committee had to scale beck an early proposal [censored] Although NSA and Harris became ensnared in the almost inevitable cost overrun disputes, the system succeeded technically and operationally.

For NSA, the payoff was the data link. [censored]

Once remoting was available, everybody wanted it. The earliest field applications were in Southeast Asia, where NSA began remoting signals from isolated mountaintops during the later stages of the war in Vietnam. Called EXPLORER, this program got people out of danger zones and back into defensible base areas, while leaving the equipment (antennas, receivers, and communications) in exposed locations. The aptly named Black Widow Mountain along the Cambodian border was the most famous of the remoting operations.

Remoting was next employed to fix serious SIGINT support problems [censored] The problems [censored] arose from the disparity between tactical systerns available to field commanders and strategic systems tailored for national-level support. By the early 1970s, strategic SIGINT had far outrun what was available tactically. In September of 1970, [censored] complained to Admiral Gayler (then DIRNSA) that his SIGINT support assets were not what they should be. [censored] His mobile collection equipment was antiquated [censored] Moreover, the intercept vans [censored] were slow to get out of the way in case of attack [censored] Communications were clearly inadequate [censored]

[censored] knew about the systems that had been devised for Southeast Asia, and he wanted them [censored] He wanted airborne systems that did not have to retreat over roads that were vulnerable to interdiction. He wanted communications to get the intercept back to safe areas where they could be processed. And most of all, he wanted ARDF.

At NSA, Gayler instigated a planning whirlwind. He sent an NSA team [censored] to look at the situation. The team devised a radical solution—an airborne remoting operation similar in concept to the [censored] in Southeast Asia. When the matter came to a head in a JCS meeting in January of the following year, NSA was ready with the solution. The Agency called it GUARDRAIL.

GUARDRAIL would [censored] NSA, ASA, and USAFSS jointly put up the money to run the GUARDRAIL test.

The first test was only partly successful. [censored] GUARDRAIL II was a spectacular success. [censored]

Early GUARDRAIL was an Army-specific asset. Despite the fact that air-related intelligence dominated the collection "take," the Air Force participated reluctantly, and then only after considerable prodding at the JCS level. One Air Force problem was survivability. The U-21 was a propeller-driven utility aircraft [censored] The U-2 would be a far better platform. It may also have been that the Air Force feared Army dominance and wanted to use Air Force money to fund its own systems.

GUARDRAIL II became the final system. Even prior to its deployment, the Army, [censored] and NSA had all agreed that it would be left behind to provide tactical support. There were no plans to fund a production system.

While GUARDRAIL I was being tested [censored] a separate SIGINT operation was being deployed [censored]

This changed radically in 1972.Major General John Morrison proposed an [censored] to do the same work [censored] that GUARDRAIL was doing [censored] At a stroke, NSA would be satisfying the constant demands of American commanders [censored] to improve SIGINT support and add a DF capability.

The final system, called GUARDRAIL IV, looked a lot like GUARDRAIL [censored] but it did not solve the strategic-tactical interface problem. It used U-21s [censored] It remained an integral part of the strategic SIGINT system. Once again, the Air Force entered the system reluctantly. Its concerns probably related to a fear that GUARDRAIL IV threatened the continued viability of the RIVET JOINT fleet, rather than to any criticism of the way the program operated technically or conceptually.

Reorganization

The war in Vietnam produced wide dissatisfaction with the performance of intelligence. This was in some ways unwarranted. It had performed better than in Korea, and the problems that beset intelligence early in the war were on the way toward solution by the time Richard Nixon became president in 1969. But the perceptions persisted and led to demands for change.

The Fitzhugh Panel

When Nixon assumed office, he called for a reexamination of the total Defense effort, appointing a blue ribbon defense panel to recommend changes. The panel conducted the broadest review of the Defense Department since the Hoover Commission of the mid-1950s. Part of that effort was a Panel on Command Control and Defense Intelligence chaired by

Gilbert W. Fitzhugh. This committee consisted primarily of industry figures and lawyers and was clearly intended to represent a totally dispassionate view of Defense intelligence.

The committee discovered that management was fragmented (not the first time someone had discovered that salient fact), uncoordinated, and not well focused. There appeared to be no effective control of intelligence requirements, a great deal more information was collected than was required, and consumers were overwhelmed by a welter of disjointed reports from all corners of the intelligence structure. DoD had never developed a substantial corps of intelligence professionals. (The only exception appeared to be NSA, which had obtained special legislation.)

Fitzhugh recommended that the Office of the Secretary of Defense focus intelligence management under a single deputy, called the assistant secretary of defense for intelligence. (At the time, intelligence was loaded onto the assistant secretary of defense for administration as an additional duty.) Under him there would be a Defense Security Command (consciously modeled after the NSA structure), which would enjoy broad authority to supervise DIA, NSA, and all other Defense intelligence. Such changes might have been logical but politically fell very wide of the mark. The Fitzhugh Panel had little ultimate influence over the course of actual events.

The Schlesinger Study

The Fitzhugh Panel had no sooner submitted its report than the president commissioned another study. But there were differences. This new study, chaired by James Schlesinger, head of OMB, dealt exclusively with intelligence, while Fitzhugh had also looked at command and control. More important, Schlesinger examined all of intelligence, while Fitzhugh had looked only at the Defense Department.

Not surprisingly (considering what job he held), Schlesinger concluded that intelligence centralization could best be effected by giving the DCI broader budget authority. Nixon invested then-DCI Richard Helms with a broad grant of authority to review all governmental intelligence activities in order to rationalize programs and priorities within the budgetary structure. But Nixon and Helms did not get on, and the president never followed this up with specific authorities for his DCI. Helms was left to study, to coordinate, to cajole, but he was no closer to reigning in the disparate parts of intelligence, particularly those in Defense. He never did get what the Schlesinger study promised him.

Helms did accomplish one thing, however, that had long-range effects. He created a small staff, composed of a cross-section of the intelligence community, to look at the budgets of the respective (and disrespectful) agencies. This staff still existed at Langley in 1973 when Schlesinger became DCI. The new intelligence chiefs intentions went awry as he struggled to contain the damage from Watergate by reorganizing CIA, but he definitely intended to grant that staff more power. William Colby, his successor in the job, pushed the status and authority of Schlesinger's small staff, which had become known as the IC (Intelligence Community) Staff. At the time, President Ford issued a new executive order putting teeth in the IC Staff's authority to control the budgets of the warring intelligence agencies, and in 1978 President Carter issued the executive order which gave the DCI "full and exclusive authority for approval of the National Foreign Intelligence Program budget." By then the IC had moved into its own quarters in downtown Washington, and thus attained its own facility, with its own identity.

CSS

The cryptologic reorganization that occurred in the early 1970s was the culmination of two decades of conflict between NSA and the JCS over control of cryptologic assets and operations. As NSA gained more authority and as the cryptologic system became more centralized, Pentagon officials became less and less pleased. A decade of war in Vietnam had produced, among other things, an internal war over cryptology. NSA's attempts in the 1960s to further centralize the business were bitterly opposed within the JCS, which had embarked on efforts to fragment SIGINT by shaving off small areas that they could call by different names (electronic warfare-EW, electronic support measures-ESM, etc.) and rid itself of the codewords that controlled dissemination. By the time James Schlesinger looked at the organization of intelligence, the deep fissures between NSA and the armed services had become almost unbridgeable.

Schlesinger intended to solve the problem for all time, in NSA's favor. Clearly driven by budgetary concerns, be proposed to stamp out any JCS control over, and even involvement in, the SIGINT business. The dispute over the control of cryptology that had continued since the end of World War II would come to an abrupt end.

The "end of the war" came on November 5, 1971, when Richard Nixon announced the conclusions of the Schlesinger Study. Buried in the text of this "Nixon letter" was the announcement that, by the first day of the following year, there would be a "unified National Cryptologic Command" under the director, NSA, for the conduct of United States government communications intelligence and electronic intelligence activities.

And then controversy erupted. What was a National Cryptologic Command (NCO)? What did the president intend it to do, and what were its authorities? Was this really the end of SCA independence? What would the new organization control? What was meant by "command"?

Many, both within NSA and without, felt that it meant the death of the SCAs, and a new organization chart was even prepared showing all service collection activities directly under DIRNSA. One view was that the chief of the NCC would also serve as DIRNSA. In one role he would control the national cryptologic system as before; in the other, he would command the SCAs through the JCS chain of command. Most agreed that the SCA theater headquarters would expire and that their functions would be effectively assumed by existing NSA theater organizations. The opinion of Admiral Gayler counted the most, and Gayler viewed his role as akin to that of a Unified & Specified (U&S) commander, with total control over assets within his purview.

In the Pentagon, near panic ensued. Theoretically, the NCC would control all SIGINT collection. This could include the Navy's VQ squadrons, the Air Force's EC-47 and the Army's U-21 ARDF capability, [censored] the overhead mission ground stations, tactical ELINT (including the Third Party programs that the Air Force had guarded for so many years) [censored] Under its NCC hat, NSA might begin managing Army and Air Force tactical SIGINT programs rendering support to field commanders. At the very least, the struggle to control EW and ESM programs would be resolved in NSA's favor.

DIA predicted that NSA would swing hard toward satisfying national requirements and would cease paying any attention to the satisfaction of the SIGINT requirements of tactical commanders. The independence of the SCAs would end, and, worst of all, tactical ELINT units would find themselves answering to NSA through the NCC.

Within NSA a certain smugness settled in. The war was over, the battle was won, and to the victor belonged the spoils. The spoils consisted of those SIGINT assets that had formerly been controlled by rival factions: primarily the armed services and CIA. As November faded into December, plans were being laid to assume control of the outlying assets that NSA had never owned. This was a big win—a major revolution in the way cryptology was handled.

But things began to go awry even before the end of the year. On December 23, Secretary of Defense Melvin Laird informed Gayler that the new organization would not be a command—it would be called the Central Security Service. Implicit in the new name was a diminished world view. "Services," after all, could not exactly "command." Laird instructed Gayler to come up with an organizational plan and to create the new organization by February 1, 1972, a slippage of one month from Nixon's original deadline.

Concurrently, a new NSCID 6 was being written. Issued in February of 1972, it gave NSA significant new powers—and failed to give it others that, in the heady days of November 1971, folks at Fort Meade assumed they would get.

The directive officially established CSS, which would be collection oriented, and would "include SIGINT functions previously performed by various Military Departments and other United States governmental elements engaged in SIGINT activities." It did not define these functions, nor did it refer to CIA, which by omission managed to hang onto its SIGINT system. The mobile SIGINT system remained under military control, thus answering one of the biggest questions which had arisen from the Nixon Letter. But in NSA's favor, NSCID 6 resolved the EW issue by placing it under NSA control. And on the administrative front, NSCID 6 gave the director authority over tasking, logistics, research and development, security, and career management of personnel.

Following Laird's decision on December 23, Gayler created a series of internal panels to flesh out the CSS plan. Progress was uneven because no one seemed to agree what it should be or how it should function. Gayler gave the task of managing the disputatious committees to Paul Neff, a World War II cryptologic veteran who had held key positions in NSA's policy councils for many years. Neff's most vital assistants were Major General John Morrison for operations and Frank Austin for training. Much of the action fell into their bailiwicks.

Under severe time constraints (the plan was due to Laird by February 1), the committees solved the easy problems and left the tough ones for later. The new cryptologic system would be unitary, with centralized control and decentralized execution (hardly a new or controversial concept). It would be composed of NSA and the SCAs as they then existed, thus putting off the question of the system acquiring assets then controlled by the JCS and CIA. The SCAs would provide men, equipment, and facilities—CSS would operate the system.

CSS would be headed by DIRNSA in a dual-hat role, and it would be assisted by a staff of its own. Composed of some 205 billets (75 from operations), it looked just like the NSA staff (see Table 7). All the staff heads were dual-hatted with their respective NSA jobs—thus John Morrison was both head of NSA production and chief of CSS operations, while Frank Austin headed NSA's training school and CSS's training organization.

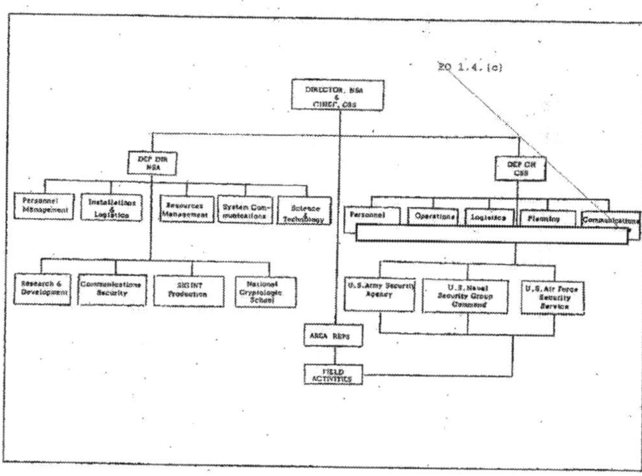

(U) Table 7
NSA/CSS Organizational Structure

The CSS plan produced serious fissures between Gayler and the SCA commanders, who viewed the new organization as the death knell of the independent SCAs. So they fought back, and the struggle spilled over into almost every aspect of cryptologic organization. They fought the training plan because the role of training and equipping servicemen for cryptologic duty had always been central to their being. They fought NSA's encroachment into R&D and logistics in direct proportion to the size of their respective staffs in those functions.

A struggle ensued over cryptologic organization in the theaters. Gayler wanted SCA theater offices to collocate with the senior NSA/CSS headquarters, but eventually agreed that they could collocate instead with the component command headquarters. The senior SCA commander would be responsible for the SCA and CSS functions, and most of his people would do the same. Gayler also wanted component command level CSGs to be NSA elements, and went toe to toe with Major General Carl Stapleton of USAFSS over this issue. Stapleton won, and all component command CSGs became part of their parent SCA. The chief was the senior SCA representative in the theater.

They enlisted U&S commanders to defend their interests. Admiral McCain, CINCPAC (which would soon become Admiral Gayler's own command), predicted the beginning of the end of responsive SIGINT support: "In summary, the proposed plan is viewed as placing in concrete the sterile, inherently unresponsive centralization philosophy to which field commanders have so long been opposed. The centralization of SIGINT has not been tested in a major conflict. The concentration of analytical functions at the national level will soon cause a decline in the ability of the uniformed cryptologic activities to function responsibly in a support role in combat operations especially when access to a national database is denied and integration with other intelligence data is vital. The proposal is a long step backward in the Armed Services quest for more responsive intelligence. . . ."

The most contentious issues related to resources, and it was here that NSA had eyes bigger than its stomach. In the first heady days of CSS planning, many in the Agency envisioned swallowing every SIGINT collection asset worldwide, the theater ELINT centers, and even scientific and technical centers like the Air Force's Foreign Technology Division.

In April of 1972, Admiral Gayler convened a panel (which he himself chaired) to survey the field. The most cursory study revealed a very wide field indeed. For instance, NSA discovered that [censored] had ELINT collection gear, [censored] The list of CIA sites was very long, and the theater ELINT centers were very well-entrenched tactical assets.

When the smoke cleared from the battlefield, NSA had won operational control over some of the assets under contention, most notably Air Force SIGINT platforms doing national jobs. But theater ELINT centers remained under theater control; programs designed for purely tactical jobs stayed with their parent services; the Navy held onto its entire fleet of airborne SIGINT reconnaissance aircraft; and the Army kept its electronic warfare companies. CIA assets were not even filtered into the mix, and NSA's relationship with Langley remained on hold. When confronted with determined service opposition, Gayle had elected to smooth the waters.

One of the key aspects of the CSS reorganization was to collocate the headquarters at Fort Meade, and a new DIRNSA, General Samuel Phillips, began looking at this in the fall of 1972. The move was superficially attractive because of the money that could be saved, and it would certainly permit further dual-hatting of SCA and NSA staffs. The idea did not begin to burn itself out until a study group quantified the amount of space needed: 550,000 square feet, to be exact, at a cost of $30 million. NSA, chronically short of space, was busy expanding into the Baltimore suburbs and could offer no space to the SCEs. It might be possible to get some office space on Fort Meade from 1st Army, but it was still inadequate, even if it could have been converted into cryptologic work space (a very doubtful proposition indeed). So the idea was virtually dead anyway when Major General Stapleton confronted Phillips with the most determined opposition that any aspect of CSS had faced. It was obvious that the Air Force would never agree, and the plan was dropped. As Phillips later said, rather laconically, in a message to the theater cryptologic chiefs, ". . . there is specific and determined opposition by the SCA chiefs to such collocation. It isthe expressed view of the SCA chiefs that proximity to their service headquarters is more important than collocation with NSA/CSS." It was the understatement of the year.

At the Defense Department, Dr. Albert Hall told his chief of resources management, Lieutenant General Phillip Davidson, to keep watch over the implementation of CSS. By January of 1973, Davidson's watchdog, Robert E. "Red" Morrison, was ready to throw in the towel. Morrison wrote to Hall that the CSS staff concept had not worked. Agency employees had not accepted the dual-hat idea and were not ready to relinquish their carefully garnered authority. According to Morrison, ". . . the 'dual-hat' concept has served mainly as a way to keep the status quo." NSA had never transferred authority over tactical SIGINT assets to CSS, and field commanders had reciprocatcd with suspicion and mistrust of the CSS mechanism. CSS had cost NSA over 200 billets and had produced nothing in return.

At NSA, Sam Phillips had seen enough. Lacking any semblance of DoD support, and unwilling to make the drastic changes in CSS authority that would be necessary to keep the concept functioning, Phillips killed it. The date of death was listed as April 16, 1973. On that date, Phillips eliminated the CSS staff, transferring authority instead to a new deputy director for field management and evaluation (DDF), who also became deputy chief, CSS. He dropped the idea of dual-hatting and instead transferred authority for CSS activities to existing NSA positions, elevating them at the same time to deputy director status. Thus assistant director for production became deputy director for operations, communications security became ruled by a deputy director, and Phillips created the post of deputy director for research and engineering, with authority over both NSA and SCA research efforts. Other staff chiefs were elevated to assistant directors; all had additional responsibilities for CSS management.

In 1976, when a new director, Lew Allen, went looking for CSS, he found only a paper organization. Associated with CSS, his resource people could find only General Allen himself (he was named on paper as chief of CSS); the DDF incumbent, who served as the deputy CSS; and a military staff of fewer than ten people.

The CSS exercise benefited the cryptologic system by further centralizing such functions as research and development, personnel administration, and certain aspects of logistics. In these areas, NSA's staff authority expanded into areas that were of common concern to NSA and the services. The biggest changes were in training, where Frank Austin, the dynamic leader of the National Cryptologic School, presided over a long-term centralization of training functions, and a rationalization of the system to the point where the individual SCAs served as executive agents to separate aspects of a now-joint training system. And, though the meetings were often stormy, the SCA chiefs were brought into closer contact with Gayler and his staff. Gayler institutionalized this into Wednesday morning breakfasts with his SCA chiefs, and thus brought a more direct and personal atmosphere into what had been a remote and long-distance relationship.

So in certain respects, the addition of "CSS" to the NSA logo marked a permanent change in the way business was done. But the larger changes that had been so keenly anticipated in the fall of 1971 would have required steamroller tactics worthy of Brownell at his best. The JCS had been bested by Brownell in 1952 because he had the backing of the president. Twenty years later the president was not engaged, and the JCS won.

The Murphy Commission

The period following the Vietnam War was extraordinarily fruitful with reorganization studies. Those which touched cryptology bent the process in a new direction. One such was the Murphy Commission.

The Murphy Commission was set up by Congress rather than by the president. Its main purpose was to examine the process by which American foreign policy was set. The chairman, former ambassador Robert D. Murphy (then chairman of Corning Glass), was to report back to Congress by June 1975. Murphy was looking at foreign policy at a time when Henry Kissinger occupied positions as both secretary of state and national security advisor, and perhaps this was the reason that Murphy concentrated on national security and intelligence issues. Of the four subcommittees, the one on national security and intelligence, chaired by Murphy himself, dealt with NSA.

It was hardly surprising that Murphy should echo the climate of the times. Following Schlesinger (and a host of others before him), he recommended splitting the job of DCI into two people—the political advisor to the president should work downtown, while the administrator of CIA, who would be his deputy, would manage the agency itself. He advocated giving the DCI further control over the intelligence budget (meaning, in essence, authority over the Defense component thereof. And he predictably proclaimed that the secretary of state and national security adviser roles should never again reside in the same person.

As for NSA, Murphy remarked rather quizzically that NSA was the only national ctyptologic agency in the West that reported through the defense rather than the foreign affairs institution. This tended to bias the satisfaction of requirements in favor of military needs. But, having examined the pros and cons of that arrangement, Murphy opted to leave cryptology within Defense. He recommended, however, that the Agency report to an executive committee composed of the DCI and the assistant secretary of defense for intelligence, to broaden its responsiveness. Moreover, he favored changing the rule by which the director be strictly a military officer. The rule, he felt, should be the same as at CIA—civilian or military did not matter as long as the director and his or her deputy were not both military officers.

The key thrust of the Murphy report, however, was in the direction of further centralization of the process. The SCAs should be abolished, and NSA should take on the job of cryptology unhindered and unassisted. This would at once simplify the process and eliminate the bickering that had characterized NSA-SCA relationships since the day NSA was established.

The Hermann Study

In the long run, the most influential study was one that was not even completed, let alone published and promulgated. In 1975 Dr. Robert Hermann asked Lew Allen for the opportunity to study SIGINT support to military commanders. Hermann formed a committee of just three people: himself, [censored] and William Black. Together, they formulated an elegant and timeless statement of the problem that confronted cryptologic organization.

To Hermann, the central dilemma emanated from the abortive establishment of CSS. NSA had been given theoretical control of the complete cryptologic process by which military commanders obtained cryptologic support, but the enforcement mechanism had never been implemented: "The most recent NSCID-6 . . . provided for very broad NSA responsibilities and authorities well beyond present practices. . . . the 1971 Presidential Memorandum from which the directive was written specifically includes 'tactical intelligence' within the scope of the national level responsibility. However, the Presidential memorandum and NSCID-8 are not being enforced and are probably not enforceable. . . . The political forces which generated NSCID-6 did not develop the near term enforcement means necessary to persuade an unwilling management structure. . . . This has been a major cause of stagnation in the development of adequate SIGINT support to military operations as well as inhibiting the general development of SIGINT support for other purposes.. . . "

Hermann pointed to a cascade of changes to the SIGINT system which had irreversibly altered the way business was done. He referred to an "electronic explosion" in the signals environment which tactical commanders were increasingly occupied with and were exploiting to their own advantage. Electronic warfare, electronic support measures, and other terms were being applied to signals in order to get them out from behind the codewords that restrained their dissemination and exploitation. According to Hermann, "The notion that all SIGINT activity is naturally a part of a coherent SIGINT system organized separately to support all national interests and organizations at every echelon is probably unsound. SIGINT is clearly not the most natural primary management dimension for an increasing number of activities." While NSA held to the rigid codeword protection mechanisms that had been built up since 1952, these barriers were becoming increasingly anachronistic. The SCAs, confronted with a two-way tug on their loyalties, increasingly opted for allegiance to their own services. They no longer hungered to expand the large field site system, no longer viewed their future as lying within a national cryptologic structure. According to the study, ". . . the traditional role of the SCA as the field collection arm of the national SIGINT system is eroding and is even now, not a viable mission."

To solve the dilemma, Hermann recommended a revolutionary strategy. The SCAs should cease being cryptologic agencies and should become what he called Service Signal Warfare Agencies (SSWAs). They should be integrated with the commands they supported, and their main job would be to provide signal warfare functions such as ECM, ECCM, tactical SIGINT/electronic support measures, MIJI (meaconing, intrusion, jamming, or interference), and radar surveillance. Except in unusual cases, they would no longer staff large fixed sites.

The existing classification system should be completely scrapped. According to Hermann, ". . . we now provide SI, TK, or EARPOP protection for sources that we no longer hold to be sufficiently sensitive to require these caveats. The reason for protection is historical not deliberate." Cryptologists had cast aside the fine gradations which had evolved during World War II to permit wider dissemination of less-sensitive SIGINT and more restrictive handling of the products of cryptanalysis. In effect, everything was handled at a minimum Category II level, and the advantages of the World War II Y Service system had been lost. He pointed to the handling of clear text speech intercept (then normally protected as Category II material) as an example of how not to protect information. Other sources [censored] were scarcely more sensitive. Signals externals should not be held in COMINT channels unless clear justification was provided.

Even more radical was his proposal for the handling of TK information. According to the study, "There is very little justification today for providing SI access without TK. There is no justification for providing TK SIGINT access without Byeman access." (The Byeman compartment was created to protect technical and contractual details of overhead systems.) The study proposed that overhead SIGINT should be completely removed from the TK compartment and should be handled as ordinary SIGINT information and that Byeman should be eliminated except as it related to the relationship with contractors.

Hermann recommended new initiatives for SIGINT support to NATO, long a cryptologic planning backwater. [censored]

The planning group was keenly aware of the developing gulf between SIGINT available in the field and that available at NSA [censored] Because of processing mechanisms and dissemination restrictions, information of vital concern to the field commander piled up at NSA. This was being compounded by the accelerating dominance of overhead SIGINT. Even large field sites were becoming increasingly irrelevant unless the information they produced was combined (at NSA) with overhead [censored] In most cases the tactical commander was not even aware of the existence of this information.

Though he had no solutions, Hermann did articulate the dilemma and recommended that a mechanism be established to provide field commanders with support from national systems. That mechanism would necessarily involve more direct NSA control of overhead SIGINT resources, and Hermann recommended that the director take full control of SIGINT satellites in order to facilitate support to field commanders. This was an issue of hot dispute, and Hermann himself opposed this proposal when NSA placed it on his desk in the 1980s, when he was then director of the National Reconnaissance Office.

According to Hermann, NSA should develop a strong planning office for support to military operations. Not only should it be centralized, but it should begin directing the entire process, rather than simply reviewing work already done by the SCAs.

Following the study, Hermann himself went off to NATO to serve as a special assistant to SACEUR for intelligence support planning. The rudiments of the existing system of SIGINT support to NATO owe much to his planning. Although he never returned to NSA, his ideas lived on, and most were eventually implemented. NSA soon had an office that did support military operation, as Hermann had recommended. The idea of establishing a planning function to improve national support to tactical commanders got off the ground the next year, officially initiated by a memo from George Bush (then the DCI) to the secretary of defense. It became known as TENCAP. The SCAs eventually evolved into organizations more akin to what Hermann had recommended—more attuned to tactical support in all modes of the signals spectrum, less inclined to staff large field sites at NSA's bidding. The boundaries between SI and TK crumbled, and eventually, though the TK compartment held up, everyone involved in national-level cryptology had the clearance. The SIGINT compartment system was not changed significantly. Though proposal followed proposal, especially relating to eliminating the codeword protection for reports based on plaintext voice intercept, the Cold War ended with the restrictions still in place.

The Ursano Study

Robert Hermann's thinking dovetailed nicely with the direction that the Army was moving. That direction came out in very stark terms in 1975 as a result of the Intelligence Organization and Stationing Study (IOSS).

IOSS resulted from a memo from the secretary of the army, Howard Callaway, to Army chief of staff Frederick Weyand in late 1974. Commenting about Army intelligence, Callaway said, "We maintain considerable information which is of questionable value and seldom used," a fact that "really makes me wonder about how much money we are wasting and raises serious questions as to the cost-effectiveness of our intelligence system." What was on Callaway's mind was apparently money. The Army was continuing to take monstrous post-Vietnam cuts, and Callaway was looking at intelligence as a place to save money.

The man Weyand appointed to study the issue, Major General James J. Ursano, was unencumbered by any experience with, or knowledge of, the intelligence function. At the time, he was Weyand's director for management, His study group was not very high powered, nor did it contain much expertise in the discipline. It was a completely outsider's look.

It did not take long for the Ursano group to find out how fragmented and overlapping Army intelligence really was. Intelligence production was being carried out by a vast welter of rival organizations with competing agendas. The Army expended much effort toward HUMINT and comparatively little on SIGINT, which was found to be isolated and neglected. ASA came under severe criticism. Since the creation of CSS, ASA amounted only to another bureaucratic layer. The elimination of its field headquarters in both the Pacific and Europe gave it an unmanageable span of control. It devoted too much of its effort to field station operations, too little to tactical support. It had monopolized electronic warfare and held everything under a cloak of secrecy which inhibited real tactical support. In the field, the Army G2 had to manage two separate intelligence systems, SIGINT and everything else, and staff to integrate the two sides was in short supply.

Ursano looked at the vertical cryptologic command line which had been instituted following World War II and which had been reinforced with every subsequent study of Army intelligence. For once, someone took the opposite tack. Verticality must end, and ASA must rejoin the Army.

Ursano's central and most important recommendation was to dismantle ASA. A new organization would be created, called INSCOM (Intelligence and Security Command), which would integrate all Army intelligence functions. Combining SIGINT and HUMINT, Ursano recommended the amalgamation of USAINTA (U.S. Army Intelligence Agency) with strategic

SIGINT. INSCOM would continue to manage [censored] field stations, to supply billets to NSA and other centralized cryptologic activities, and to provide SIGINT support to echelons above corps. Tactical assets (corps and below) would join the supported command echelon.

INSCOM would be an interesting mix of SIGINT, HUMINT, and counterintelligence organizations. Joining the new command would be the military intelligence groups [censored] and to this were added groups in CONUS (CONUS M1 Group) [censored] TAREX, which had existed as a SIGINT-related effort since the waning days of World War II, would join the intelligence groups. There would be a unified Intelligence and Threat Analysis Center (ITAC) for all-source analysis. But, in sum, the new organization would be considerably smaller than ASA had been, primarily because of the loss of the tactical units. Training functions would be absorbed by other commands, and the training school at Fort Devens would belong to the Army Intelligence Center and School at Fort Huachuca, Arizona.

To virtually no one's surprise, Major General George Godding, the incumbent ASA commander, opposed the dissolution of his agency. Godding's reasoning, however, should have sounded bells somewhere in the Army staff. ASA should be retained because of the unique cryptologic expertise which had been developed and nurtured over a period of many years. Ursano's solution ignored that aspect of the problem.

The proposals caught NSA seemingly by surprise. When routed for comments, the Ursano proposals elicited little reaction. Each staff element viewed the problem from its own very narrow perspective, and each concluded that the matter was an Army problem, not one which should interest NSA. At the Directorate level, Norman Boardman of the director's policy staff understood the implications: "It is our general feeling that the loading of all army intelligence, security, and EW functions onto ASA, with a new name, and the stripping of specialized support functions . . . can do nothing but downgrade the quality and timeliness of SIGINT support to the army and army tactical commanders. . . ." But NSA did not take a hard line, and its response to the Ursano proposals was less than warlike. And so INSCOM officially came into existence on January 1, 1977, without NSA having taken a strong stand one way or the other.

When Vice Admiral Bobby Inman became director in July of 1977, he hit the roof. Noting that the CSS concept assumed central control of cryptologic assets, and that ASA was the organization that was to control the Army's component to that structure, he pointed out acerbically that divestiture of cryptologic assets at corps and below abrogated that agreement and fragmented the system. Moreover, cryptologic training, considered an essential aspect of maintaining a skilled cryptologic work force, had been removed from INSCOM's authority. TAREX, formerly an exclusive cryptologic preserve, now appeared to be a SIGINT-HUMINT amalgam. "Throughout the plan SIGINT operational relationships and functions are described that impact directly on NSA/CSS. These relationships and functions have not been coordinated with this Agency." In fact, they had been coordinated—but with Lew Allen, not with Inman. And that train was much too far down the track for one angry admiral to turn it around.

The central problem of the INSCOM decision was one of expertise. The Army no longer had a unique cryptologic organization. It had been diluted by other disciplines and other interests. The cryptologic focus was lost and was replaced by a picture gone all dim and mushy. To participate in cryptology, the Army would have had to increase its emphasis on technical specialization. It chose to go the other direction.

The Creation of ESC

In its own way, the Air Force chose the same path, but at a slower rate. The Air Force Security Service had begun to lose its SIGINT focus in the late 1960s. When the Air Force Special Communications Center (AFSCC) SIGINT mission was moved to NSA in 1968, the organization survived by acquiring a new role. The mission, straight out of Vietnam, was to do electronic warfare analysis of tactical combat. Such analysis involved a variety of analytic skills, of which SIGINT was the largest component and was thus a natural for USAFSS. AFSCC could employ all the SIGINT and COMSEC skills of a seasoned work force in a new role of direct concern to Air Force commanders.

As the command shrank in size during the 1970s, the electronic warfare analysis being done in AFSCC grew proportionately larger. Like ASA, USAFSS slowly eased out of the business of providing manpower to large fixed sites. Security Service sites which survived became smaller, and the command began shedding its management of air bases around the world. In 1978, USAFSS gave away its last remaining bases to other Air Force commands: Goodfellow AFB went to Air Training Command, [censored] were turned over to USAFE, and PACAF began managing [censored] With its intermediate headquarters in Germany and Hawaii closed, the command ended the decade with just under 12,000 people, down from a peak size of over 28,000.

General Lew Allen, who had become Air Force chief of staff, was intensely unhappy with the Air Force approach to, and use of, electronic warfare. His experience as DIRNSA had taught him how SIGINT could affect the modern battlefield. He had an especially keen appreciation for TEABALL, the command and control facility that had operated so effectively in Southeast Asia based on SIGINT support, and he wanted the new organization to create other such mechanisms. So he formed a high-level steering group to look at the problem.

In April of 1978 the Air Force announced that it would disestablish Security Service and consolidate intelligence functions within a new intelligence center at Kelly Air Force Base. This would involve USAFSS, the Foreign Technology Division at Wright-Patterson Air Force Base in Ohio,

AFTAC (which monitored nuclear testing around the world), and Air Force Intelligence Service. The concept was clear, but the details were fuzzy; the affected organizations spent the summer thrashing out the implementation.

The grand Air Force Intelligence Center study became subsumed under two other high priority Air Force concerns: how to organize electronic warfare and what to do with a growing responsibility called C3CM (command, control, and communications countermeasures). All three functions were closely related, and Allen wanted an organization that combined all three. As it happened, USAFSS had the majority role in intelligence and C3CM and was a major player in electronic warfare. So whatever happened would surely center on the USAFSS complex at Kelly AFB.

In January of 1979 a general officers board recommended to Allen that, not surprisingly, a new electronic warfare command be created, and that it be composed of all three USAFSS missions. Like ASA, USAFSS would continue as a major command. Unlike ASA, however, it would not swallow the other intelligence disciplines, at least not yet. USAFSS reopened its doors in August of 1979 under a new name, Electronic Security Command. Its commander, Major General Doyle Larson, was known to be a Lew Allen confidant. When he appointed Larson, Allen told him not to emulate INSCOM, but to insure that all elements of electronic combat were integrated into a single structure. Together, they were moving the Air Force away from a major role in cryptology, toward a closer tie with Air Force tactical combat.

Chapter 16 Cryptology and the Watergate Era

Background To Scandal

The greatest political scandal in American history originated with an obscure note in the Metro section of the *Washington Post* on Sunday, June 18, 1972. In it, two Metro section reporters, Bob Woodward and Carl Bernstein, covered what appeared to be an amateurish break-in at the Democratic National Headquarters in the Watergate Hotel in downtown Washington.

The Nixon administration managed to cover over the political effects of the break-in until after the elections in November. But when Congress returned in January, it was ready to investigate. In February 1973, the Senate voted to establish a Select Committee, commonly referred to as the Ervin Committee after Senator Sam Ervin, Democratic senator from North Carolina, to hold hearings. At the time, no one associated with the committee knew where they would get information, since the administration was keeping a tight lip, and the Watergate burglars weren't talking. But on

March 23, one of the burglars, James McCord, turned state's evidence. The federal judge, John Sirica, had been pressuring the defendants by threatening lengthy prison terms if they did not cooperate. Now McCord was cooperating, and the entire thing began to unravel. The president, concerned with getting on with his second term, tried to shush the whole thing.

The scandal, of course, would not shush. Instead, it mushroomed, swallowing first Nixon's White House staff, than much of his cabinet, and finally the president himself. On August 8, 1974, Nixon resigned and Gerald Ford moved into the White House.

In a real sense, Watergate resulted from Vietnam. President Nixon was obsessed with the disorder and demonstrations that hurled the Johnson administration down and played a large role in the defeat of Hubert Humphrey in 1968. One of the central incidents of the disorderly 1960s was Daniel Ellsberg's decision to publish a collection of the Johnson administration's papers on the war, which came to be known as the Pentagon Papers. Nixon ordered an investigation of Ellsberg, and two of his White House confidants, Egil "Bud" Krogh and David Young, put together a clandestine unit, which they called the "Plumbers" because the objective was to plug leaks. The group obtained the assistance of White House Special Counsel Charles Colson, who brought in some experts in clandestine surveillance formerly from CIA and FBI, among them Howard Hunt and G. Gordon Liddy. The Plumbers broke into the office of Ellsberg's psychiatrist, Lewis Fielding. The unit itself was eventually disbanded, but the individuals were retained by the Committee to Re-Elect the President (CREEP), and they eventually bugged the office of Lawrence O'Brien, chairman of the Democratic National Committee, in the Watergate complex.

For a time, cryptology was a bystander in this turmoil, but the antiwar demonstrations eventually touched NSA's business. In 1966, Stanford University students picketed Stanford Electronic Laboratories, where Lockheed Missile and Space Corporation (LMSC) was designing [censored] satellite payloads. When students occupied the building, James DeBroekert of LMSC smuggled one of the payloads out of the building, through Moffet Naval Air Station and over to Building 190 where the rest of the Lockheed [censored] effort resided. This very close call [censored] had a happy ending only because the students never really knew what they were picketing.

Next year disorder hit the Princeton University campus. The radical group Students for a Democratic Society (SDS) discovered the existence on campus of the Communications Research Division of the Institutes for Defense Analyses (IDA/CRD), which had been set up in the late 1950s to help NSA with difficult cryptanalytic problems. Unclassified CRD publications appeared to link the organization with the Defense Department, and SDS set out to force a campus eviction. After several months of sporadic demonstrations, on May 4, 1970, students broke through police lines and vandalized the inside of the building. A few days later a student was arrested as he attempted to set the building on fire. CRD built an eight-foot-high fence around the building and occupied it in a permanent siege mode. But the students had already achieved their objective. The atmosphere was no longer good for defense contractors, and Princeton asked CRD to move. CRD found other quarters off campus and moved out in 1975.

In June 1971, amid the hysteria over the American invasion of Cambodia, the *New York Times* began publishing a series of documents relating to the war effort. The papers had originally been given to journalist Neil Sheehan of the *Times* by one Daniel Ellsberg, a former defense analyst during the Johnson administration. Two days later a federal judge issued a restraining order, but that did not stop the presses. Ellsberg sent copies to seventeen more newspapers, and the revelations continued. On June 30, the court lifted its restraining order, and the *Times* published the rest of the batch. Journalists quickly labeled them the Pentagon Papers.

Ellsberg had been hired into the Pentagon as one of Robert McNamara's "whiz kids." In 1967 Ellsberg was assigned to a project under Lawrence Gelb to undertake a study of U.S. involvement in Vietnam. Brilliant and dogmatic, Ellsberg turned against the war. He felt that the documents could be damaging to the war effort, so when he left the Pentagon to take a job with the Rand Corporation, he reproduced a copy and carried it with him.

It was a very large document indeed—over 7,000 pages—and Ellsberg spent thousands of dollars making copies. For several years he tried to use the papers to convince policy makers (Henry Kissinger and William Fullbright, among others) to change U.S. policy in Southeast Asia, but in vain. As a last resort, then, in 1971 he turned the documents over to the newspapers.

Ellsberg claimed that the Pentagon Papers, although officially classified, were actually unclassified. [censored] Newspapers did not release the information in 1971, but journalist Jack Anderson got the last four volumes and released them in 1972. [censored]

The Pentagon Papers and subsequent Anderson columns began a trend. The trend was to tell all. It started small, but became a tidal wave of revelations. [censored]

[censored]

The previous insider-tells-all account, Herbert Yardley's *The American Black Chamber*, had been written in a fit of greed (Yardley needed money). People like [censored] could apparently be bought by ideology. It echoed the climate of the 1930s, when the Soviets got their spies for free (or at the very least, for expense money).

Ideology-based public revelations became fashionable with the publication in 1975 of ex-CIA agent Phillip Agee's *Inside the Company—A CIA Diary*. [censored]

Using the indefatigable [censored] as a key source, the Canadian Broadcasting Corporation did a 1974 series entitled "The Fifth Estate—the

Espionage Establishment," which made a wide-ranging exposure of intelligence organizations in the United States and Canada. [censored]

NSA And Clandestine Activities

Over the years, cryptologists had participated in two activities whose legality was eventually called into question. One, codenamed Shamrock, was a way to intercept messages without setting up intercept sites. The other, Minaret, became enmeshed with an illegal use of information for domestic law enforcement.

Shamrock

The easiest way to get access to telegrams was to get them from the cable companies which transmitted them. This method actually dated back to World War I, when the federal government, using the implied war powers of the president, set up cable and postal censorship offices. A copy of every cable arriving and departing from the United States was routinely sent to MI-8, which thus had a steady flow of traffic to analyze. After the war, the Army closed all intercept stations. Yardley's Black Chamber continued to use messages provided by the obliging cable companies until 1927, when the Radio Act of 1927 appeared to make this illegal, and the Communications Act of 1934 reinforced this. Lack of traffic forced Friedman's SIS to set up intercept stations in the 1930s.

In 1938, the Army's chief signal officer, General Joseph Mauborgne, approached David Sarnoff, president of RCA, with a request from the secretary of war to renew the arrangement whereby the Army received drop copies of cable traffic. Sarnoff was willing, and during the war the major cable companies (RCA, AT&T, and Western Union) once again provided cables to the cryptologists. Signal Intelligence Service set up Radio Intelligence Companies to collect cables through censors installed at the cable company offices. Following the surrender of Japan, military officials approached the companies to request their continued cooperation, as they had after World War I. This time, however, they met considerable resistance. Cable company officials argued that the Federal Communications Act of 1934 appeared to make this illegal in peacetime. They wanted legislation.

What they got was a promise from the attorney general, Tom Clark, that they would be protected from lawsuits while the Justice Department sought authorizing legislation. (Opinions differ as to whether or not President Truman put this in writing.) But the legislation was not forthcoming, and in 1947 the company executives contacted Secretary of Defense James Forrestal, who had to renew Tom Clark's assurance that they would not be prosecuted, and that the operations would not be exposed. Two years later, still lacking legislation, they approached the new secretary of defense, Louis Johnson. He advised them again that Clark and Truman had been consulted, and had once again approved the practice. Somewhat mollified, they finally dropped the subject.

At NSA the cable drop operation was treated as a compartmented matter, and only a few employees knew where the traffic came from. Couriers carried cabled messages to NSA, but there was no direct contact with the cable companies themselves. NSA selected about 150,000 cables per month for further analysis—the rest were destroyed. Although not technically illegal, Lew Allen, who was director in the mid-1970s, said it did not pass the "smell test" very well. Stopping it was not a difficult decision for him.

Minaret

There is no stark line between "foreign intelligence" and domestic law enforcement. The phrases, which appear to be watertight, actually leak into each other at many points. But this never became an issue until the Watergate period.

In the collection of foreign intelligence, cryptologists often came across unrelated communications, which were routinely destroyed because of their irrelevance. But when items of importance to the FBI came available, they were normally passed on. This was done without much thought given to the boundaries between foreign intelligence and law enforcement, which were by law to be kept separate. The practice began in the 1930s and continued through the war years and into 'the 1950s.

In 1962, following the Cuban Missile Crisis, the White House wanted to know who was traveling to Cuba (which had been made illegal but for exceptional cases). This involved passing on American names and violated customary SIGINT rules by which information on American citizens was to be ignored. It was clearly related to law enforcement, however, and it was the origins of the so-called "Watch List" which became known as the Minaret program.

The idea proved to be irresistible. In 1965, as a result of the conclusions of the Warren Commission, the Secret Service asked NSA to be on the lookout for certain people who might be a threat to the president. The first list was composed almost entirely of Americans, but NSA complied because of the obvious implications of not providing such important information. In 1973 the Agency asked that the Americans be removed from the list and hung onto that position despite anguished protests from the Secret Service.

The Watch List expanded in the 1960s to include people suspected of narcotics trafficking, and at one point most of the names on the list were individuals suspected of narcotics-related activity. The list was formally documented by USIB in 1971. But by far the most controversial expansion of the list occurred in 1967, and it involved domestic terrorism.

In 1967 the country appeared to be going up in flames. Vietnam War protests were becoming common, and "ghetto riots" in America's urban centers had virtually destroyed sections of Detroit and Los Angeles. President Johnson wanted to know if the domestic antiwar movement was receiving help from abroad, and he commissioned Richard Helms at CIA to find out. CIA came up with very little, but in the process of mobilizing the intelligence community, the Army was tasked with monitoring communications for the purpose of answering Johnson's question. On October 20, Major General William P. Yarborough, the Army chief of staff for intelligence, informed NSA of the effort, in which ASA was involved, and asked for help.

With FBI as the prime source of names, NSA began expanding the watch list to include domestic terrorist and foreign radical suspects. The watch list eventually contained over 1600 names [censored]

The project, which became known officially as Minaret in 1969, employed unusual procedures. NSA distributed reports without the usual serialization. They were designed to look like HUMINT reports rather than SIGINT, and readers could find no originating agency. Years later the NSA lawyer who first looked at the procedural aspects stated that the people involved seemed to understand that the operation was disreputable if not outright illegal.

ASA's monitoring of domestic radical communications was almost certainly illegal, according to the legal opinions of two different groups of government lawyers. Even worse, it had come to public notice in 1970 when NBC aired a program alleging that ASA had monitored civilian radios during the Democratic Convention of 1968. ASA quickly closed it down and went out of the civil disturbance monitoring business.

Minaret was quite another matter, and it did not depend on ASA for its existence. Lew Allen had been director for less than two weeks when his chief lawyer, Roy Banner, informed him of Minaret—it was the first the new director had known of the program. Banner noted a recent court decision on wiretaps that might affect the Watch List. A federal judge had ruled in a case involving leading Weathermen (SDS radical wing) that all federal agencies, including NSA, must disclose any illegal wiretaps of the defendants. NSA's communications monitoring, although not technically a wiretap, could be construed as such by recent court decisions. Although the Weathermen in question might not be on the Watch List, the time was not far off when a court case would expose the list.

This operation did not pass the "smell test" either. According to Allen, it appeared to be a possible violation of constitutional guarantees. He promptly wrote to Attorney General Elliot Richardson to request that Richardson himself authorize the retention of all individuals by name on the list.

This was in September 1973. The Watergate hearings in Congress had just wrapped up, and the special prosecutor, Archibald Cox, had subpoenaed the presidential tapes. The executive department was in chaos. Richardson's predecessor, Richard Kleindeinst, had been forced out under pressure, and his predecessor, John Mitchell, was almost sure to go to jail. In that atmosphere, the attorney general was not going to permit the continuation of an operation of such doubtful legality. He requested that

NSA stop the operation until he had had a chance to review it. With that, Minaret came to a well-deserved end.

Clandestine Methods

If you can't break a code, the time-honored method is to steal it. Two of NSA's most cherished secrets, the black bag job and the wiretap, became public knowledge during the Watergate period.

Black bag jobs referred to the art of breaking, entering, and theft of codes and cipher equipment. The Office of Naval Intelligence (ONI), an unlikely leader in the field, became the first practitioner. In 1922 ONI picked the lock of the safe in the Japanese consulate in New York and filched a Japanese naval code. This theft led to the establishment of the first permanent American naval cryptologic effort, OP-20-G, in 1924.

ONI continued to be the main practitioner of the art. Prior to World War II the Navy pilfered a diplomatic code which was used at embassies which lacked a Purple machine. Joseph Mauborgne, the head of the Army Signal Corps, hit the overhead when he found out. Mauborgne reasoned that if the Japanese ever discovered the loss, they might change all their systems, including Purple, and extracted from the Navy an agreement that all such break-ins in the future would be coordinated with the Signal Corps.

[censored]

The Huston Plan

Richard Nixon had been president just over a year when he initiated a string of actions which ultimately brought down his presidency. The White House-ordered invasion of Cambodia, a militarily ineffective foray, unleashed a wave of domestic protests, culminating in the shootings at Kent State in May of 1970. Stung by the reaction, the president called the heads of the intelligence agencies, and on June 5 he told Richard Helms of CIA, J. Edgar Hoover of the FBI, Lieutenant General Donald Bennett of DIA, and Admiral Noel Gayler of NSA that he wanted to know what steps they and their agencies could take to get a better handle on domestic radicalism. According to journalist Theodore White, who later reconstructed the meeting: "He was dissatisfied with them all . . . they were overstaffed, they weren't getting the story, they were spending too much money, there was no production, they had to get together. In sum, he wanted a thorough coordination of all American intelligence agencies; he wanted to know what the links were between foreign groups—al-Fatah; the Arab terrorists; the Algerian subsidy center—and domestic street turbulence. They would form a committee, J. Edgar Hoover would be the chairman, Tom Huston of the White House would be the staff man."

Thomas Charles Huston, the evident object of the president's displeasure, was a young right-wing lawyer who had been hired as an assistant to White House speech writer Patrick Buchanan. His only qualifications were political—he had been president of the Young

Americans for Freedom, a conservative campus organization nationwide. And Huston wasn't even the key player. Hoover was named chair of the committee, in order to place him in a position in which the FBI would finally be forced to confront domestic radicalism."

The committee report confronted the issue, all right, and it laid out a number of "further steps," many of which were illegal. The report recommended increasing wiretapping and microphone surveillance of radicals; relaxing restrictions on mail covers and mail intercepts; carrying out selective break-ins against domestic radicals and organizations; lifting age restrictions on FBI campus informants; and broadening NSA's intercepts of the international communications of American citizens. But Hoover knew the score, and he attached footnotes to each of the techniques which he did not want the FBI involved in. When it went to the president, it was carefully qualified by the FBI, the one organization that would be the most involved.

The president sent word back to Huston, through Haldeman, of his approval, but did not initiate any paperwork. So when the committee was tasked to implement the recommendations, it was tasked by Tom Charles Huston, not the president. Hoover informed John Mitchell, the attorney general, that he would not participate without a written order from Mitchell. Mitchell discussed this with Nixon, and both agreed that it would be too dangerous. Ultimately, the president voided the plan, but not before NSA had become directly involved in the seamier side of life.

NSA was ambivalent. On the one hand, Gayler and his committee representative, Benson Buffham, viewed it as a way to get Hoover to relax his damaging restrictions on break-ins and wiretaps. Gayler had personally pleaded with Hoover, to no avail; now the committee mechanism might force the stubborn director into a corner. But that was a legal matter for the FBI to sort out. When asked about intercepting the communications of Americans involved in domestic radicalism, Gayler and Buffham became more pensive. They informed the committee that "NSA currently interprets its jurisdictional mandate as precluding the production and dissemination of intelligence from communications between U.S. citizens, and as precluding specific targeting against communications of U.S. nationals;" Of course American names occasionally appeared in intercepted traffic, but use of even this incidental intercept needed to be regularized by a change to NSCID 6. As with the FBI, NSA wanted a legal leg to stand on.

What stand did NSA take? Gayler genuinely wanted to be helpful, especially when the president so insisted on getting help. In meetings he seemed ready to turn NSA's legendary collection capability to the services of the Huston mandate. But his lawyers advised caution, and, according to Huston himself, NSA was more nervous than any of the other intelligence agencies. Gayler clearly wanted a legal mandate.

The White House Tapes

General Lew Allen, General Phillips's successor, came to the job with a strong admonition from his boss, Secretary of Defense James Schlesinger: stay as far away from Watergate as possible. He was aghast, then, when he learned on a Friday in January 1974 that a virtual army of lawyers was on its way to Fort Meade with the White House tapes. Howard Rosenblum, the director of research and engineering, had made it known that NSA might be able to analyze the infamous White House tapes which had been subpoenaed by the special prosecutor. They all arrived in staffcars on a Friday with boxes of tapes. NSA's experts went through the tapes for hours, then gave them back to the lawyers. They had found an eighteen-minute gap on one of the tapes. It appeared to be a deliberate erasure, as the tape had been gone over multiple times in a manner that did not support the president's contention that the erasure had been accidental.

The Allen Era At NSA

Occasionally a person's impact on events demands that the period be named after him or her. General Lew Allen was such a man. But the "Allen Era" did not actually begin with Allen.

In July 1972 Noel Gayler departed the Agency. He got a fourth star and became CINCPAC. Gayler, an upwardly mobile officer with high ambitions, was the first director to move up. NSA had always been a dead end, where mavericks could end their careers at an agency where mavericks were appreciated, even required. He was not to be the last—rather, Noel Gayler was the first of four officers in succession who gained their fourth star and moved on. The second was his successor, Air Force lieutenant general Sam Phillips.

Phillips came from a highly technical background. A fighter pilot in World War II, he came to NSA from the Apollo program, where he had been the director. The visibility of the program, and the accolades that had been heaped on his management of it, indicated that he was destined for bigger things. According to one source, he knew before he arrived that he would stay only one year, and would move on to command the Air Force Systems Command as a four-star general. However, his successor, Lew Allen, believed that Phillips became aware of NSA's vulnerability to the Watergate mess once he was ensconced and that this influenced his determination to move on.

Lew Allen came from the same sort of background; but more so. He had a doctorate in nuclear physics, had worked at Lawrence Livermore Laboratories, worked in the satellite collection business for the Air Force, and when nominated to be DIRNSA, was de facto director of the Intelligence Community (IC) Staff.

He had become a protégé of James Schlesinger, who had brought him onto the IC Staff. But owing to a temporary feud between Schlesinger and Congress over whether the job should be civilian or military, Allen had not been confirmed. So when Schlesinger became secretary of defense, he asked

Allen to become DIRNSA, a position that did not require congressional confirmation.

Lew Allen was easy to like. His quick mind was covered over by a kindly demeanor and a slowness to anger. Even Stansfield Turner, who feuded endlessly with Allen's successor, Bobby Inman, wrote that Allen "particularly impressed me with a firm statement that the NSA took its direction on what information to collect from the Director of Central Intelligence. All I needed, he said, was to tell him what I wanted."

Lew Allen once described candidly the baggage that he brought with him to NSA. Schlesinger was convinced that NSA was too large and too expensive, and he told Allen to look into the charge. (He found it to be unsubstantiated.) He had always been impressed with the technical competence resident at NSA, but he felt that "NSA, like many large bureaucracies, had a lot of turf. . . ." Having come from the NRO side of the satellite business, he knew firsthand of NSA's desire to control SIGINT satellites and ground stations, and he felt that NSA harbored "ambitions for responsibilities that somewhat exceeded the grasp." He had heard that NSA had enormous warehouses of undecipherable tapes. (This too he found to be exaggerated).

His focus on the technical side of life was perfect for NSA, a technical agency. Allen had no patience with bureaucratic turf battles, and he did not think that constant reorganizations were a good use of time. But he did bring over from the Air Force a penchant for systems design, and for that, one needed a designer. So one of his first acts was to appoint an architectural planning staff to design the various components of the cryptologic system. He had an architect for everything: [censored] Third Party, overhead, support to military operations, high-frequency systems, line-of-sight systems, signals search, and so on. One of Lew Allen's most important legacies was to institute a planning mentality where one had not existed.

In 1977, in the last year of his tenure, he confronted a congressional proposal to pull NSA out of the Defense Department. To a man as firmly grounded in the military as Allen, this was a nonstarter. Pointing out that 75 to 80 percent of NSA's material supported the military, he came down firmly on the side of staying in the Defense Department. As to the concurrent proposal to civilianize the director's job, the continued credibility with military commanders was too important a qualification to lose.

The Church Committee

When John Dean, the president's legal counsel, began unburdening himself to the Ervin Committee in the spring of 1973, the testimony implicated the CIA in aspects of the Watergate scandal. So William Colby, the deputy for operations, decided to do a survey.

The "Family Jewels" was a 693-page report of possibly illegal CIA activities through the years. Colby, who had become DCI by the time the report was finished, informed the four chairmen of the House and Senate committees which had oversight of the CIA and succeeded in convincing all of them that the matter was over with and that CIA would clean up its own house. But by then so many people within the CIAknew about the report that its eventual exposure became almost inevitable.

On December 22, 1974, journalist Seymour Hersh published a story in the New York Times based on the "Family Jewels," charging that the CIA had been involved in Chaos, an operation to monitor domestic radical groups during the Nixon administration. The next day, President Ford detailed Henry Kissinger to look into Hersh's allegations. (Although informing Congress, Colby had never told the White House about the report.) Colby confirmed the general outlines of the story to Kissinger, and the president knew that he would have to investigate. So on January 4, Ford appointed a President's Commission on CIA Activities Within the United States. It was headed by Vice President Rockefeller, and the press promptly dubbed it the Rockefeller Commission.

While the commission was deliberating, the president himself revealed, on January 16, that some of the allegations of wrongdoing included plots to assassinate foreign heads of state. As if enough controversy did not already surround the commission, this new charge served to scuttle its effectiveness. In the end it issued a very reasonable and workmanlike report which recommended certain structural reforms to guard against future transgressions, and it set forth specific prohibitions of certain activities like illegal wiretaps and participation in domestic intelligence operations. (It declined to rule on assassinations, pleading lack of time to get to the bottom of these allegations.) But by then no one was listening.

Senators were clamoring for an investigation, and on January 27 the Senate established the Senate Select Committee on Intelligence. Philip Hart of Michigan was originally approached to chair the committee, but he was gravely ill with cancer, and so the job was offered to Frank Church of Idaho. Unlike Hart, Church harbored presidential ambitions, and some feared that he would use the committee as a pulpit to advance his ambitions. Like the Rockefeller Commission before it, this investigative body came to be known after its chair and has gone down in history as the Church Committee.

Some, like Church himself, were suspicious of the intelligence community and sought to expose as much as possible. Into this camp fell Democrats Gary Hart of Colorado and Walter Mondale of Minnesota, along with Republicans Charles McMathias of Maryland and Richard Schweicker of Pennsylvania. Many were moderates (Warren Huddleston of Kentucky and Howard Baker of Tennessee being examples) while two senators, Barry Goldwater of Arizona and John Tower of Texas, did not believe in exposing intelligence secrets no matter what the provocation.

To begin with, NSA was not even on the target list. But in the course of preliminary investigation, two Senate staffers discovered in the National Archives files some Defense paperwork relating to domestic wiretaps which referred to NSA as the source of the request. The committee was not inclined to make use of this material, but the two staffers leaked the documents to Representative Bella Abzug of New York, who was starting her own investigation. Church terminated the two staffers, but the damage had been done, and the committee somewhat reluctantly broadened its investigation to include the National Security Agency.

What the committee had found was the new Shamrock operation. It had become easier to use wiretaps than to get traffic from cable companies, and NSA was using this technique with increasing frequency. But the Church staffers quickly uncovered the older Shamrock operation, and this became the focus of its early investigation of NSA. Knowing the ramifications, Allen terminated the portion of Shamrock that dealt with the cable companies on May 15, in the middle of the preliminary hearings.

NSA's official relationship with the Church Committee began on May 20 with a visit from the committee staff; five days later Church himself came to Fort Meade for briefings and tours. This began a close association which extended over the entire summer and through October 1975. In the beginning it was a rough road, with committee staffers trying to dig deep, while NSA officials tried to protect. But with a few choice words from Allen, NSA's responsiveness improved and, with it, the cooperation of the committee. By the time it was all over it had become a model of how an intelligence agency should relate to Congress, and it enhanced NSA's reputation on Capitol Hill. But it had been tough slogging.

In September, the committee decided to request open testimony by Allen. They discussed two operations, Shamrock and Minaret, and in the end decided to question him about only Minaret. The committee discussions on the question were among the most rancorous of all, and Goldwater and Tower openly dissented from the proposition of requiring anyone at NSA to testify on any subject. But they were outvoted, and Allen was subpoenaed, despite a phone call from President Ford to Frank Church.

Never had NSA been forced into such a position, and Lew Allen was very nervous. In a preliminary letter to Church he stated: "As we prepare for open hearings, I am struck even more forcibly by the risks involved in this method of reporting to the American people. . . . Despite the honest and painstaking efforts of your Committee and Staff to work with us to limit damage, I remain concerned that the open hearing presents significant and unnecessary risks." Allen pleaded that the cost of exposure of Minaret could be very high. The Watch List was a byproduct of NSA's operation to monitor ILC (international commercial) communications. [censored]

The Church Committee conducted its open hearing on NSA on October 29, after two days of meticulous closed-door rehearsals. The director began with a prepared statement describing NSA's mission in very general terms and used historical examples (the Battle of Midway and the decryption of the Japanese Purple machine being two) to depict the value of such operations. He detailed the Agency's legal authorities and defined what NSA thought was meant by "foreign intelligence" and "foreign communication." Conceding the murky nature of the definitions, he then launched into a discussion of the Watch List, placing it in historical context and discussing how NSA interpreted the tasking and executed the support to requesting agencies. He stated that he himself had closed down Minaret two years before.

Lew Allen's performance was a triumph. Future vice president Walter Mondale noted to the director that "the performance of your staff and yourself before the committee is perhaps the most impressive presentation that we have had. And I consider your agency and your work to be possibly the single most important source of intelligence for this nation." Despite the accolades, however, when the committee in closed session discussed how much to tell about NSA, the majority voted to include Shamrock, which Allen had opposed because of the embarrassment to the cable companies. Goldwater, Tower, and Howard Baker were set in bitter opposition, but Church contended that legislation would be necessary to insure that abuses would not be repeated, and both Shamrock and Minaret constituted important material to back up the request for legislation. When asked, Secretary of Defense James Schlesinger and the DCI, William Colby, viewed the release of these two projects to be affordable.

When the Church Committee issued its final report in February 1976, the discussion of NSA was brief. Focusing on what NSA could potentially do, rather than what it was doing, Church concluded: "The capabilities that NSA now possesses to intercept and analyze communications are awesome. Future breakthroughs in technology will undoubtedly increase that capability. As the technological barriers to the interception of all forms of communication are being eroded, there must also be a strengthening of the legal and operational safeguards that protect Americans." NSA's existence should be based on a congressional statute which established the limitations, rather than on an executive order then twenty-three years old. And so ended the discussion of NSA, just seven pages in a report comprising seven volumes of hearings.

The Pike Committee

The backwash of Hersh's Family Jewels article also infected the House of Representatives and produced the predictable clamor to investigate. So the House held its own investigation, under Representative Otis Pike of New York. Not surprisingly, it became known as the Pike Committee.

But it did not begin that way. The first chairman was to be Lucien Nedzi, who chaired the Intelligence Subcommittee of the Armed Services committee. But this effort dissolved in controversy when Democrats on the committee discovered that Colby had taken Nedzi into his confidence over the original Family Jewels report and had convinced him not to investigate. Fatally compromised, Nedzi resigned, and the task fell to Pike.

While the Church Committee focused on CIA, the Pike Committee had a much broader charter. It was to review the entire intelligence apparatus and to focus on operational effectiveness, coordination procedures, the protection of individual liberties, possible need for more congressional oversight, and on planning, programming, and budgeting. Pike promised to evaluate the performance of the intelligence community against its budget. But the membership was liberal (somewhat more so than that of the Church Committee) and the staff intrusive. The focus quickly swung to the topic of abuses of individual liberties, and stayed there.

NSA had already had one experience with Pike, when he had chaired a subcommittee investigating the *Pueblo* capture of 1968. It had not been a happy encounter. The committee had leaked in camera testimony of the director, Lieutenant General Carter, to the press, and Carter was furious. Once-burned, the NSA staff was wary.

The House charter gave the committee the power to determine its own rules concerning classification, handling, and release of executive department documents. Burned during the *Pueblo* investigation, NSA lawyers were anxious to nail down an agreed-upon set of procedures, but preliminary meetings yielded no agreement on the procedures for handling SIGINT documents. Lew Allen, who later characterized the Pike Committee staffers as "irresponsible," issued instructions to "limit our discussions with the full House committee and staff to administrative, fiscal and management matters.

Relationships quickly deteriorated. NSA officials described the committee staff as "hostile," the procedures for handling classified material as questionable, their willingness to learn about NSA as nonexistent. One NSA official noted that only one Pike staffer ever visited NSA, in contrast to the Church Committee, whose entire membership and staff visited Fort Meade in May 1975. Pike staffers objected to having NSA officials in the room when NSA employees were being questioned, and the staff interrogation of [censored] degenerated into a shoving match.

In August, the committee called Lew Allen to testify. The letter requesting his presence stated that the budget policies and procedures would be the topic, but questioning soon turned to supposed monitoring of Americans. Allen objected to covering this ground in open session, and after a long committee wrangle and Allen's adamant refusal to go further, the committee voted to go into executive session. Summarizing NSA's objections, he said: "I know of no way to preserve secrecy for an agency such as NSA other than to be as anonymous as possible, and to abide by the statutory restrictions which the Congress instructed us to, and those are that we do not discuss our operations; we do not discuss our organization; we do not discuss our budget in public." Throughout Allen's appearance, Pike and Congressman Ron Dellums of California seemed suspicious and disbelieving. At one point Pike interrupted the interrogation to say; "Now why don't you just tell us and be forthcoming, without my having to drag it out of you, or any other member having to drag it out of you, what sort of communications of American citizens you are intercepting, how you are intercepting them, what you are doing with them, and why you feel it is necessary to keep on doing it." The presumption of guilt was palpable.

[censored]

The final report criticized NSA's reporting policy, which amounted to fire-hosing the intelligence community. [censored] It noted that NSA frequently had the right answers, but that customers probably did not fully understand what NSA was really saying. [censored] Like Church, Pike recommended that NSA's existence be authorized through congressional legislation and that "further, it is recommended that such legislation specifically define the role of NSA with reference to the monitoring of communications of Americans."

The Pike Committee ended awash in controversy. On January 19, the committee distributed its final report. The Ford administration protested that it contained classified information, including several sections with codeword material. The committee voted, 8-4, not to delete the classified sections, and it sent the 340-page report to the House. Faced with anguished protests from the Ford administration, the House Rules Committee on January 29 voted 9-7 to reverse the Pike Committee decision. (Pike condemned this as "the biggest coverup since Watergate") But it was already too late. On January 22 the *New York Times* reported that it had knowledge of details of the report. On January 25, CBS correspondent Daniel Schorr stated triumphantly on national television, "I have the Pike Report." Four days later the House secured all copies of the report except the one in Schorr's possession. Fearing a Ford administration backlash and possible prosecution, CBS refused to publish. Schorr then contracted with the *Village Voice,* and the report appeared in entirety in that publication in February, an event which led CBS to terminate his employment.

Despite protestations by Pike that the executive department was doing all the leaking, his own committee appears to have been the source. The draft report was distributed to committee members the morning of January 19, and by four o'clock that afternoon a *New York Times* reporter was already on the phone with the staff director asking questions based on the report. Versions of the report would appear in the press, the committee would make wording changes, and the next day the new wording would be in the newspapers.

Pike apparently began the investigation determined to produce a fair and balanced evaluation of American intelligence. He focused at first on job performance measured against funds expended. But the committee was top-heavy with liberal Democrats, and things quickly got out of hand ideologically. The committee and its staff refused to agree to commonly accepted rules for handling classified material, and when the executive department thwarted its desire to release classified material, it leaked like a sieve. The dispute with the administration over the release of NSA material produced an impasse, and diverted the committee from its original task. The House committee that was appointed to investigate the investigators turned up a shabby performance by the Pike Committee. In the end, it did Pike and Congress more damage than it did the Ford administration. All in all, it was a poor start for congressional oversight.

The Abzug Committee

Serious (if ideologically polarized) inquiry descended into opéra bouffe with the charter of yet a third investigation. The leader was Bella Abzug, who had been elected to Congress in 1972 from a liberal district in New York City amid the early voter reactions to Watergate.

Abzug chaired the Government Information and Individual Rights Subcommittee of the Committee on Government Operations. In mid-1975, with the Church Committee holding preliminary investigations in executive session, Abzug got hold of some of the more sensational information relating to Shamrock and Minaret. (The information was apparently leaked by Church Committee staffers.) The climate for a full investigation of NSA was right. The press had picked up some of the themes resonating in the Church and Pike hearings. An article in the September 8 edition of *Newsweek* described the "vacuum cleaner" approach to ILC collection and referred to NSA as "Orwellian." This was counterbalanced by a statement that "the NSA intends nothing like tyranny—it is probably the most apolitical agency in Washington." But the fourth estate had clearly discovered the technological advances that permitted NSA to cast a very broad net, and characterized it as a potential threat to individual liberty.

NSA relationships with the Abzug Committee staff were poisonous. At their very first session, Abzug staffers refused to sign the normal indoctrination oath, and further discussions proceeded at the noncodeword level. Despite the refusal to accept executive department rules on clearances, the committee subpoenaed huge amounts of material. One subpoena, for instance, demanded every record, including tape recordings, of every scrap of information pertaining to the Agency's COMINT mission since 1947; (Tape recordings alone comprised in excess of a million reels.) Fearful of leaks that might dwarf those of the Pike Committee, the Ford administration decided to deny these requests.

In October, Abzug began maneuvering to get Lew Allen to testify in open session. The sparring sessions (Allen had no intention of complying) ended on October 29 when Allen appeared before the considerably less hostile Church Committee. Preempted, Abzug pressed for lower level NSA officials, and subpoenas began arriving at NSA. With the climate of mutual suspicion that existed, NSA resisted. Allen went to Jack Brooks, chairman of the full committee, to protest, and extracted a promise that Abzug could subpoena, but Brooks would refuse to enforce the subpoenas. In the end, Abzug got her hands on one unfortunate NSA official, Joseph Tomba, who appeared in open session and refused, at the request of DoD lawyers, to answer most questions put to him. The committee held Tomba in contempt, but Jack Brooks was good to his promise, and the citation was not enforced.

In the process of dealing with Abzug, Lew Allen and his staff were subjected to fearful browbeating, but they held fast, defended by not only the full executive department, but by Congressman Jack Brooks himself. Hearings dragged on into 1976, making Abzug the longest running of the investigative committees. Then, in September of 1976 they began to fade, as Abzug became involved in a campaign for the Senate, and hearings ceased. (She ultimately lost.) The committee eventually issued a draft report (February 1977) which predictably concluded that there were still loopholes which would allow NSA to intercept U.S. communications for foreign intelligence purposes and that these loopholes should be closed. But the importance was secondary. Church had already exposed the loopholes and had made the same recommendations. Moreover, by then President Ford had issued his new executive order, 11905, which forbade many of the "abuses" that Abzug had in mind. The committee faded into irrelevance.

With that, the investigative process had run its course. It had been a pretty thorough public housecleaning for all intelligence agencies. For CIA (and to a lesser extent FBI) it had been traumatic and damaging. For NSA, the trauma had been much less. The principal reason wasthe director. Lew Allen—kindly thoughtful, intellectual, and forthright—was just the right person at just the right time. He disarmed most of NSA's more reasoned critics with the way he directed his staff to respond to Congress. He headed off controversy before it got well started. Most of all, his five star performance before the Church Committee convinced many that NSA had not gone seriously off track and that it should be preserved at all cost. A glimpse under the cryptologic curtain convinced most senators and congressmen that NSA was the true gem of the intelligence world.

The Backwash

The Watergate era changed cryptology. The tell-all atmosphere resulted in a flood of revelations unprecedented then and now. It also resulted in restrictions on cryptologic operations and ushered in a new era of congressional oversight.

The Revelations

The investigations were conducted amid an absolute fury of press revelations, many apparently stemming from the committee staffs. [censored]

More serious still were articles on American cryptologic relationships with Second Parties. [censored] In New Zealand, members of Parliament demanded that the government confirm or deny the nation's membership in UKUSA.

[censored]

Glomar Explorer

[censored] In 1968 a Soviet Golf-class nuclear submarine on patrol in the Pacific mysteriously went to the bottom with all hands. The Soviets could not locate the wreck, but the U.S. Navy could, and the US began to study the feasibility of capturing it. [censored]

[censored]

Koreagate

[censored]

Newspapers were, of course, following the Fraser investigation, and rumors began appearing that the indictment was based on NSA information. On September 4, 1977, the *New York Times* published an article alleging that Henry Kissinger, Melvin Laird, and other top officials had been aware of the South Korean bribery ring at least as early as 1972. In discussing the source of this information, the *Times* said: "While the investigators did not identify the documents precisely, other sources said that the documents came from the Central Intelligence Agency, which was earlier to have agents in the presidential executive mansion in Seoul, and from the National Security Agency, which has been reported to have intercepted South Korean cable traffic between Seoul and Washington." [censored]

On September 6, two days after the *Times* story, a federal grand jury indicted Tong-Sun Park on thirty-six felony counts of bribery, conspiracy, mail fraud, illegal campaign contributions, and other charges. A California congressman and several former Korean intelligence officials were listed as "unindicted co-conspirators." This placed the issue in the realm of the courts.

But the Koreagate affair was hardly dead. In October 1977, the *New York Times* reported the bizarre case of Sohn Young Ho. Sohn, the top KCIA agent in New York City, was in the process of asking the United States for political asylum when Edward J. Derwinski, a member of the Fraser Committee, allegedly tipped off the KCIA, which went looking for Sohn, possibly intending to mailbag him back to Seoul for safekeeping. Fortunately, the FBI got to him first, but the source of the information about the Derwinski leak, according to the *Times*, was NSA.

[censored] Congressional oversight was fine as long it was kept within a narrow range and subjected to the greatest restrictions. As a test of providing SIGINT support to law enforcement, however, it had a much shorter influence. The Reagan administration began reversing that course in 1981, insisting that SIGINT be expanded to provide more, rather than less, support to domestic law enforcement.

Executive Order 11905

If the president did not act to restrict the intelligence community, it was clear that Congress would. So during the fall of 1975, with the Church hearings in full throttle, President Ford appointed an Intelligence Coordinating Group, chaired by White House counselor Jack Marsh, to draft a comprehensive order, at once organizing the intelligence community and placing checks on it. The result was Executive Order 11905.

Organizationally, the president gave the DCI more authorityto supervise the intelligence community, including the critical budget review "club" that Nixon had tentatively preferred to Richard Helms in 1971. The DCI became chairman of a new Council on Foreign Intelligence, which included the assistant secretary of defense for intelligence (a newly created position which would supervise NSA's director). Ford abolished the 40 Committee, which had ruled on all covert operations [censored] and replaced it with an Operations Advisory Group. He continued the President's Foreign Intelligence Advisory Board and directed that three of its members constitute a special Intelligence Oversight Board to keep track of possibly illegal activities by intelligence organizations. The executive order attempted to draw a clear line between "foreign intelligence" and "domestic law enforcement."

The organizational aspects were of less concern to NSA than were the specific prohibitions. The order prohibited the intercept of communications made from, or intended by the sender to be received in, the United States, or directed against U.S. persons abroad, except "under lawful electronic surveillance under procedures approved by the Attorney General."

The new executive order resulted in the termination of many NSA activities in support of law enforcement. [censored]

The crisp wording of the order obscured the resident subtleties. How did an analyst know if a person was an American citizen, a resident alien, or just a person with an American-sounding name? How would NSA segregate within its database those individuals against whom collection was legal, from those against whom collection was authorized only in specific instances? In fast moving crises such as the *Mayaguez* affair, how could NSA determine if collection was authorized? If it was not, but lives were in danger, who would rule on permissibility? And how much easier it was to Monday morning quarterback the situation than to operate during crisis in the dim, floating world of possible prosecutability. In mid-1976 the NSA DDO, Robert Drake, noted to the IC staff that "To the question of whether or not day-to-day SIGINT production can continue under the provisions of the Executive Order, the answer is yes. In other words, although the guidance is annoying, at times conflicting, and necessarily subject to interpretations at the desk level, I can cope with it . . . On Monday morning, of course, we all can judge that that incident [*Mayaguez*] was reportable but in cases such as this Monday may be too late." Despite such uncertainty, NSA drafted the general wording of the executive order into a new regulation, USSID 18, which stood the test of time for many years. As with the executive order, it was an attempt to preempt more restrictive congressional legislation. Lew Allen considered the matter to be extremely important and got White House approval.

One result of the Watergate period was to complicate NSA's life [censored] The matter of [censored] for law enforcement had been contentious since the first Supreme Court decision in 1927, which gave the federal government broad latitude to do electronic surveillance. Courts gradually narrowed this down, and by the 1970s the new climate of concern for individual liberties had basically made warrantless electronic surveillance inadmissible as evidence. But [censored] foreign intelligence did not fall within this rule, and in the early 1970s federal courts ruled that foreign intelligence [censored] were legal.

The "New Shamrock" operations involved [censored] Begun in the 1950s, those [censored] had continued for years despite periodic resistance by J. Edgar Hoover. Through the decade of the 1960s, the number of such [censored] fluctuated in the sixty to seventy range. But in December 1974 Attorney General Levi instituted new and cumbersome approval procedures which both lengthened the time needed for approval and broadened the exposure of specific operations from just a few people to a number spread around the intelligence and national security community. At the top of the heap, the attorney general maintained personal control and began disapproving requests that sported justifications that he regarded as weak. Lew Allen tried to divest Levi of control of domestic foreign intellience [censored] but was unsuccessful. But, though EO 11905 specifically stated [censored] foreign intelligence would be treated differently from [censored] domestic law enforcement, successive attorneys general continued to control foreign intelligence through the Carter administration. To NSA, it was a cost of doing business that had not existed before Watergate.

The last act in the play occurred in 1978 when Congress passed, and the president signed, the Foreign Intelligence Surveillance Act (FISA). This added another approval layer, consisting of a special court of seven judges which would rule on requests from the attorney general [censored] Although this lengthened further the process of instituting the [censored] it had no effect on their approval. [censored]

Congressional Oversight

Congressional oversight of the intelligence community sprang from the Watergate period. Prior to the Church and Pike committees, oversight was more or less nominal and was confined to just four committees: the Armed Services and Appropriations committees in both houses of Congress. Had Congress no budget to approve, oversight probably would have been even more sketchy than it actually was.

Each of the four committees set up special intelligence subcommittees, comprising the full committee chairman and three or four trusted members from both sides of the aisle. Their examination of funding requests was cursory, and they never asked embarrassing questions about operations. The president controlled the requests, and if someone's intelligence budget were to be shaved down, the executive department would have to do the shaving—congressmen did not get into those details. Thus, inclusion in the president's budget was tantamount to approval.

In the Senate, one man dominated oversight— Richard Russell of Georgia. Serving from 1933 to 1971, Russell, chaired both the Armed Services Committee and the Intelligence Subcommittee of the Appropriations Committee. In the House, a succession of chairmen, almost all from conservative southern states with strong national defense leanings, dominated the proceedings. Mendel Rivers, Carl Vinson, and F. Edward Hebern strongly supported intelligence projects and insured that the information was held as tightly as possible in Congress. Lawrence Houston, the CIA general counsel, once said that "Security was impeccable. We never had the slightest breach." Summing up the dealings with Congress, Clark Clifford said, "Congress chose not to be involved and preferred to be uninformed." This situation lasted as long as bipartisan consensus continued.

Special intelligence clearances remained mysterious and obscure. In 1968, at the time of the Tonkin Gulf hearings in the Senate Foreign Relations Committee, no committee members, not even the chairman, William Fulbright, had even heard of clearances above top secret. This problem tied the committee in knots during the testimony of Robert McNamara relating to the August 4, 1964, attack:

"Senator Gore: Mr. Chairman, could we know what particular classification that is? I had not heard of this particular classification.

"Senator Fulbright: The staff, Mr. Marcy, and Mr. Hold are cleared for top secret information. This is something I never heard of before either. It is something special with regard to intelligence information. However, Mr. Bader was cleared for that.

"Secretary McNamara: If the staff would wish to request clearance, I am sure the Government would do it.

"Mr. Marcy: All of the members who are here submitted renewal requests for top secret clearance recently and, so far as I know, all of those requests have been granted.

"Secretary McNamara: But that is not the issue. Clearance is above top secret for the particular information involved in this situation."

By the time the congressional hearings had ended in 1975, the culture had completely changed. Church had termed CIA a "rogue elephant," and closer congressional scrutiny was inevitable. The first thought of Congress was to set up a joint House-Senate committee, but the House fell behind and, unwilling to wait, the Senate established the Senate Select Committee on Intelligence (SSCI) on May 19, 1976. The tardy House, consumed with procedural wrangling over the release of the Pike Report, delayed until July 17, 1977, more than a year later, when it established the House Permanent Select Committee on Intelligence (HPSCI).

Ultimately, all members of Congress were to be presumed cleared, and all staff members from the two oversight committees had SI and other security clearances to allow them to do their job. Clearances were also granted to select staff members of certain other committees (like Appropriations) to permit them to do their jobs. Though there were some rough spots at first, NSA-congressional liaison came to be a more or less routine function bedeviled only occasionally by security problems. Certainly there were no repeats of the maverick Pike Committee performance. NSA senior Walter Deeley summed up the matter ten years later: ". . . I think one of the best things that ever happened to this country is the fact of the establishment of the House Committee on Intelligence and the Senate Committee on Intelligence, and they have total, absolute total, scrutiny over what NSA does."

The Enabling Legislation

The same Congress that decreed congressional oversight also wanted enabling legislation for the intelligence agencies that had not been established by law, as well as specific limiting legislation for CIA (which had already been established by the National Security Act of 1947). NSA was the most visible of the agencies that had come into being by executive order, and the Agency was one of the main targets of the draft legislation. All the drafts took the same basic form. NSA would have the same authorities as under the Truman Memorandum and would remain within the Department of Defense. The director and deputy director would be appointed by the president and confirmed by the Senate. As with the CIA, the director could be either civilian or military, but if military, the deputy must be a career civilian. What distinguished these drafts from the Truman Memorandum was the heavy emphasis on civil liberties, to be guaranteed through an overlay of oversight bodies—checkers and people to check the checkers. The driving force behind the legislation seemed to be the final report of the Church Committee, in which the committee promised to end the abuses of the past.

Initially the enabling legislation was pushed along by the strong breeze of reform dominating the Carter White House. But as the president settled into the business of governing, he found this focus on supposed abuses of previous administrations to be increasingly irrelevant, Moreover, the intelligence agencies, and especially NSA, yielded a cornucopia of information. He became less and less interested in pushing legislation that would remove NSA from his total control and give part of that control to Congress. The Carter White House allowed the breezes of reform to blow themselves out, and NSA remained firmly tied to the president's authorities. The Truman Memorandum stood.

The Enigma Revelations

In England, far away from Watergate's tumultuous effects on government, a storm was brewing that was to help NSA, even as it stripped away the gauze of anonymity that remained. It became known as the Enigma revelations.

The story of cryptology's role in World War II had been kept secret since 1945. Only the Americans, who had publicly investigated the surprise attack on Pearl Harbor, had uncapped that bottle, and even they had managed to confine the story to 1940 and 1941, and to limit the disclosures to the breaking of Japanese diplomatic codes and ciphers. The other 95 percent had remained hidden.

The story began to trickle out in 1972, with the publication of John Masterman's book *The Double Cross System*, which covered the capture and turning of German human agents in Britain during the war. How they were captured was another story and went to the heart of the Enigma story, but Masterman kept that a secret.

The first break to the Enigma story itself occurred in France in 1973, when Gustave Bertrand, then head of French intelligence before the war, published his memoirs revealing the Polish break into Enigma and the conference in 1939, just before the German Blitzkrieg swept over the country. Bertrand detailed his key role in obtaining information on Enigma for the Poles, and he described France's attack against Enigma in the final months preceding the German invasion of 1940. He also described what the British knew about the system.

For a time the British remained silent. But within the ranks of World War II veterans there was a movement to tell their own story, largely to set right what they felt were distortions in the Bertrand account. Leading this effort was Frederick Winterbotham, a former RAF lieutenant colonel who had devised the system for protecting SIGINT during World War II. Winterbotham began working on his own book, published in 1974 as *The Ultra Secret*. He did not speak with a grant of authority from his government and had in fact been warned not to publish. But since the publication of Bertrand's book a year earlier, references to the British attack on Enigma had appeared in nooks and crevices of articles and book reviews, many of them authored by people who had participated in the operation during the war. Winterbotham knew that it was only a matter of time, and he determined to beat the rush. His book laid out the entire story of Bletchley Park, albeit with certain inaccuracies which came with the fading of memory.

Following Winterbotham, many participants told their stories. For some, like Peter Calvocorresi, editor-in-chief of Penguin Books, revelation became eloquent literature. For others, like Gordon Welchman, it became a detailed technical description that caused the government to blanch (and NSA to pull his accesses).

But none exceeded in scope and detail Harry Hinsley's book on British intelligence during World War II, which was largely a detailed history of Bletchley and the Enigma project. Alone among the writers and historians,

Hinsley was given access to the still-classified documents, so that a well-documented story would emerge from among the welter of revelations and memoirs. Hinsley was given permission to use classified documents largely to correct misimpressions stemming from the memory-based accounts of Winterbotham, Calvocoressi, and others.

The story of American codebreaking successes was later in coming. Ronald Clark's *The Man Who Broke Purple,* a somewhat breathless (and not entirely accurate) biography of William Friedman, came out in 1977, and was followed by less memorable personal accounts by two Navy men, Edward Van Der Rhoer's *Deadly Magic* in 1978 and Jasper Holmes's *Double-Edged Secrets* in 1979. These could not compete in drama and readability with the stories churning out of the British press, and it took an Englishman, Ronald Lewin, to begin to tell the American story in his book *The American Magic*. The British story captured the moment, while accounts of similarly significant American COMINT successes bobbed unhappily in their wake.

Memoirs, biographies, and selective leaks of information would not, of course satisfy either the public or the historians. The only realistic alternative was to begin declassifying and releasing documents. Here, national security came to loggerheads with the public's right to know, and the issue was resolved only during the post-Watergate sorting out. The declassification effort resulted from two post-Watergate initiatives, FOIA and EO.

Congress passed a new Freedom of Information Act (FOIA) in 1974. In it the congressmen took an old law relating to government documents, which required the requester to prove the need for the documents, and reversed it, instead requiring the government to prove the need to maintain secrecy. Under this new law each government agency set up special arrangements to process FOIA requests. For several years NSA's FOIA team routinely denied every request based on national security. This worked under President Ford, but the new Carter administration in 1977 took the side of the plaintiffs on FOIA. Releasing significant numbers of documents became only a matter of time.

Executive Order 11652, issued in 1972, dealt with openness in government, and decreed that government documents be automatically declassified and released to the National Archives after thirty years. The order actually preceded FOIA, but it did not have a major effect on NSA until after the Church and Pike hearings. By then, Lew Allen had become director, and Winterbotham had begun the Enigma revelations. Seeing that it was only a matter of time, Allen's staff began negotiating with GCHQ for a coordinated bilateral policy on release. They agreed to concentrate on World War II records (those most in demand) and to restrict their declassification initially to the COMINT effort against German, Japanese, and Italian armed forces. In Britain, declassified records would go to the Public Records Office—in the United States to the National Archives in Washington. NSA would also look at selected Korean War and Vietnam era records, [censored]

NSA began the Herculean task of reviewing millions of pages of World War II (and prior) records in 1976, with four reemployed annuitants hired on a temporary, sixty-day basis. The program expanded as more and more files were discovered. Admiral Inman decided to set up a classified NSA archives to hold the records which had been saved but were not yet ready for declassification, and the new "Cryptologic Archival Holding Area" was set up in SAB-2, which had been built in the early 1970s as a warehouse to hold material being transported to a records destruction facility. (At the time NSA did not have its own facility.)

FOIA ran parallel to the systematic declassification effort, and the two threads became frequently intertwined. In 1978 a researcher named Earnest Bell, who had worked in the Army's wartime COMINT office in London, submitted a FOIA request for all German and Japanese COMINT material for the entire war. NSA's legal counsel, Roy Banner, advised Inman that NSA would likely lose a lawsuit, and the Bell FOIA request greatly expanded the volume of material that the reemployed annuitants had to review. Ultimately twenty-one REAs were hired under Inman to plow through the enormous pile of raw COMINT reports to satisfy Bell's request.

The Impact Of Watergate

The Watergate period resulted in a massive change in the way the cryptologic system related to the American public. Congressional oversight, which sprang from the Church and Pike Committees, fundamentally altered the way NSA related to the legislative branch of government. In a real sense, NSA had to answer to two masters, and the relatively simple life of prior decades became more complex. The new arrangements took some getting used to, but in many ways accountability worked to the advantage of an agency that worked within the law, and within a decade few could imagine going back to the old way of doing business.

If congressional oversight ultimately worked to NSA's benefit, the public exposures accompanying the Watergate period did not. Too many sensitive operations were exposed; too many exposés were splashed across the newspapers. The deleterious effects of the Watergate period stayed with the cryptologic community for many years to come.

Chapter 17 The New Targets and Techniques

The demise of the Southeast Asia problem caused a revolution in SIGINT targeting. In many ways, though, it was no revolution at all, because the new focus was simply an old problem—the Soviet Union. [censored]

Strategic Arms Limitation

History shows that many presidents who have been given credit for starting something actually did not. This was the case with the negotiation of strategic arms limitations with the Soviets. President Lyndon Johnson, rather than Richard Nixon, initiated negotiations in 1967. At the time, Secretary of State Dean Rusk predicted that it would become "history's longest permanent floating crap game." He was very nearly right.

The Warsaw Pact invasion of Czechoslovakia in 1968 brought the abortive Johnson negotiations to an early and abrupt end. But Richard Nixon, hoping for some real departures in the foreign affairs field, got them started again. His new foreign policy ombudsman, National Security Adviser Henry Kissinger, contacted the Soviet ambassador to Washington, Anatoly Dobrynin, and they agreed to meetings in Helsinki. The "crap game" than floated to Vienna and finally to Geneva, where it settled for the duration of the Cold War. Negotiations survived the bombing of Hanoi, the Watergate crisis, and the invasion of Afghanistan in 1979.

In May 1972 the protracted negotiations produced the first Strategic Arms Limitation Treaty, called SALT I The treaty had two parts.

a. Part 1 was defensive. The two sides agreed to limit their antiballistic missile forces to two locations. Each side was permitted to defend its capital city with defensive missiles, plus one other site, which would be a single cluster of silo-based launchers. This part of the treaty was of unlimited duration, to be reviewed every five years.

b. Part 2 was offensive. It froze the silo-based missiles and submarine-launched ballistic missiles at their current (1972) level for five years (until October 1977). Since the Soviets would not admit what total number they possessed, the treaty did not express any numerical figures. American intelligence estimated that they possessed about 2,400 launchers while the U.S. had only 1,700. This left the Soviets with a larger total missile force, but there were compensations. It did not cover strategic bombers and excluded MIRVs (multiple independently targettable reentry vehicles)—the U.S. was far ahead in both categories.

Congress ratified both parts of the treaty, but Senator Henry M. Jackson of Washington succeeded in passing an accompanying resolution requiring that future treaties embody the principle of numerical parity. This set the tone for treaty negotiations through the end of the decade.

With "numerical parity" being the goal, the two sides continued negotiating and set 1974 as a goal to hammer out a SALT II treaty. But Watergate turmoil set back the timetable, and when Gerald Ford moved into the White House in August of 1974 things were far from settled on the SALT front. But then chance intervened. Kissinger had arranged a "getting to know you" meeting between Ford and Brezhnev in the Russian city of Vladivostok, and the meeting produced an unexpected interim agreement, henceforth called the Vladivostok Accords. The two chiefs agreed on a numerical ceiling of 2,460 launchers (which just happened to be the approximate total of Soviet launchers) and a ceiling of 1,320 MIRVed warheads for each side. The Soviets had for the first time accepted the principle of numerical equivalence, and in return the U.S. had agreed to count strategic bombers. They dropped their insistence that future treaties include U.S. forces in Europe, which the American side regarded as strictly tactical and defensive.

The Vladivostok Accords left as many loose ends as they tied up. They did not define "strategic bomber," and future years saw endless wrangling over whether or not the new Soviet Backfire would be counted in SALT II. On the American side, the F-111 fighter-bomber would have a nuclear capability, but would it have any sort of strategic mission? These issues remained murky.

[censored]

[censored]

[censored]

[censored]

COMSAT/INTELSAT

The rapid growth of communications satellites spurred NSA in the 1960s to develop a whole new SIGINT program. The original idea had been to try to do all space-related collection from the same set of facilities [censored] But the idea, while seductive, soon fell to the ground. [censored]

[censored]

[censored]

[censored]

[censored]

Cryptologic Communications In The Post-Vietnam Era

The communications engineers who had devised ways to get raw traffic back to Fort Meade electrically in the 1960s were not permitted to rest. The new requirement for the 1970s was to bring back raw RF so that all intercept and processing could be done in the U.S. The new communications capabilities came just in time to solve the woeful budget problems of the early 1970s [censored] In a way, the communicators had become victims of their own success—remoting and data linking, now technically feasible, became the minimum essential requirement for a cryptologic system that was becoming increasingly centralized.

To understand the explosion of circuit requirements, one need only glance at Table 9. Cryptologic remoting brought the number of NSA circuits up to 1,755 by 1981, an increase of almost 1,100 percent in fifteen years. Cryptology had become the largest single user of DoD communications capability.

[censored]

The communications conflicts of the 1960s were not resolved by the end of the decade. The great move toward centralization was a creation called the Defense Special Security Communications System (DSSCS), which was to combine Criticomm (the NSA system) with Spintcom (the DIA system to support the SSOs). It involved new sponsorship (DCA, Defense Communications Agency), new technology, and lots of money. Within five years all was wreckage. DSSCS was grossly over budget and under capability, and DCA terminated it in 1969. So the decade ended with NSA still clinging tenaciously to its own unique communications network, with all its offshoots—Criticomm, Opscomm, Strawhat, and the like. NSA had designed the entire system to support unique cryptologic requirements, and DCA, despite promises, had been unable to meet them.

(U) Table 9 [71]
Growth of NSA Telecommunications Circuits (1966-1981)

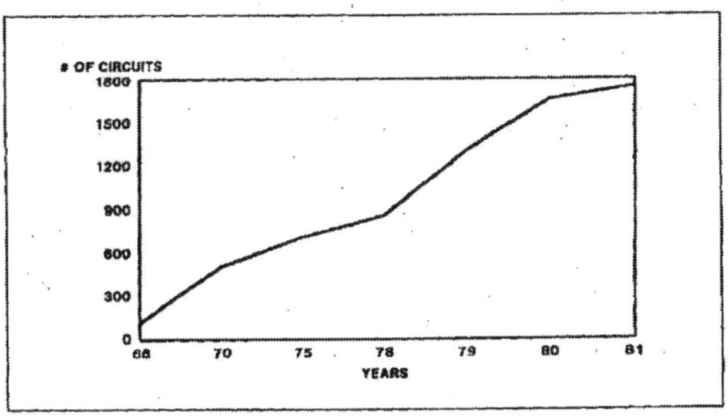

In 1970, the secretary of defense decided that the remnants of DSSCS would join its new Autodin communications system, which had been created to carry Genser traffic for the rest of the Department. Because Genser (general service, non-SI) communications centers operated on the basis of noncodeword traffic, all cryptologic traffic would have to enter the system already encrypted. To insure that a firewall existed between codeword and noncodeword messages, DCA introduced a special communications router system—Genser stations had R routers, while cryptologic stations had Y routers. NSA joined Autodin in 1972, phasing in over the ensuing three years.

DCA had great hopes for the Autodin system, and in this case they were (mostly) fulfilled. Manpower required to operate the system declined by almost 1,800 billets, while speed of service increased dramatically. But while record traffic melded into the Autodin system, NSA retained its "special" systems: IATS (which had replaced Strawhat), Opsoomm, and direction finding circuits. The General Accounting Office pointed out rather testily in 1973 that the IATS circuitry alone had a higher capacity than all the circuits NSA had integrated into Autodin. NSA admitted this and promised that it would work to achieve IATS/Autodin integration.

The Opscomm explosion of the 1960s had continued unabated into the 1970s. By 1973 there were 323 of them, being used for every conceivable purpose from passing analyst-to-analyst chatter to technical reports and diarized raw traffic. The largest single owners were NSOC, DEFSMAC and the COC [censored] These operators loved having their own communications system, but the communicators chafed. Chief NSA communicator Max Davidson wrote in that same year that "Production personnel consider the OPSCOMM complex as their 'own' communications, quite apart from the CRITICOMM, et al., systems. . . . It is unconventional, expensive, uses nonstandard procedures and requires dedicated circuits. Paradoxically, it either rigidly enforces specific formats or ignores formats and procedures entirely." Despite such protests by communications people, Opscomms survived because of their great versatility. They had been the bases for the revolution in timely reporting and no one in DDO could conceive of operations without Opscomms.

NSA continued its communications improvement program to speed message processing. After the activation of IDDF, the new communications center in 1972, the Agency matched the new technology with AMPS (Automated Message Processing System), which was a way to prepare outgoing messages in a format that could be read by an OCR (optical character reader) by typing it on an IBM Selectric typewriter with a special ball. Mating the AMPS message preparation system with the OCR devices in the communications center relieved communications operators from the drudgery of retyping messages for transmission. Initially activated in May 1970, AMPS technology spread slowly through the headquarters and out to the field.

After working with DCA for many years to come up with an automatic switch for comm center use, NSA turned to its own resources and finally developed a usable product in the early 1970s. The new system, called Streamliner, automated communications center functions like traffic routing. It was married to OCR technology and new Teletype Mod 40 terminals to replace the antiquated Mod 35s. Streamliner was developed at NSA, and the contract was awarded to General Telephone Electronics Information Systems in 1974. The first of thirty-three Streamliner systems was activated at Northwest, Virginia, in 1976.

COMSEC And The Secure Voice Problem

Operations security studies like Purple Dragon brought home the vulnerability of telephones and speech sent over unprotected tactical radios. Of all the various areas of OPSEC, the unsecure telephone was the greatest security threat. A DoD study in 1971 stated that "Voice communications are the most significant exploitable weakness in present-day military communications. The highest national COMSEC priority is assigned to research, develop, production and operational deployment of techniques and equipment to reach an acceptable level of voice security." It was estimated that voice security was required on five to ten percent of all the Department of Defense telephones."

Through prodigious effort, NSA had fielded families of equipment for use on the battlefields of Southeast Asia, some of which filled the need, and some of which were wanting. But voice security was costly and added considerably to the weight of equipment that had to be dragged along. Narrowband systems produced Donald Duck voice quality, while wideband systems, while producing good voice quality, were hardly small enough to be called "tactical." Keying was always a problem, and most potential users did not use voice security in any form. The enemy went right on exploiting voice communications. This was the most frustrating of all NSA's COMSEC concerns.

NSA's first program for DoD telephone protection had been Autosevocom, a cumbersome and expensive system that was available only for high-level users. Because of its inadequacies, the Defense Department capped it at 1,850 terminals, and in the late 1960s, hoping for something better, decided not to continue with the expansion of Autosevocom.

In order to produce a system that worked, NSA needed to solve two problems: voice quality and keying. The first was solved through a revolutionary system called "linear predictive coding," which permitted good voice quality in a narrowband system.

In 1967, because of the tremendous pressure to build a cheap, high-quality voice encryption system, Howard Rosenblum of NSA's R&D organization proposed a radical departure in key distribution. At the time, the limit of keyholders for a single secure telephone system was about 300. So Rosenblum proposed that each secure telephone should have its own unique key, and that secure telephones communicate with each other after using their unique keys to receive a common session key from a central key distribution center. When a user picked up his secure telephone and dialed a number, the transmission would go to a central key facility which would look up the key of both the sender and receiver and match them so they could talk. Neither end had the key of the other; only the central facility would hold both. He called the concept Bellfield, and through it, he hoped to be able to put a secure telephone on the desks of everyone in DoD.

NSA secured a secret patent on the concept and worked on Bellfield for several years, first designing a system called STU-I (Secure Telephone Unit I). STU-I would involve a narrowband, full-duplex voice security system using commercial telephone lines. Everything would be contained within the terminal device, so that no communications center would be needed to encrypt the voice. The goal was to develop a system that would cost, initially, about $5,000 per unit, but that cost would slide to $2,500 once contractors began full production. The key to it all was to deploy huge numbers of the devices so that unit production costs could go down to an affordable level.

STU-I did not measure up. It was as big as a two-drawer safe and cost $35,000 per copy. But it validated the Bellfield operational concept, and NSA gave no thought to not continuing. The COMSEC organization promptly embarked on its replacement, STU-II.

To tackle the tactical secure voice problem, NSA launched the Saville program in the late 1960s. The objective was inexpensive, small, lightweight, high-voice quality (i.e., wideband) tactical COMSEC appliques for the warfighter. The war in Vietnam drove this program almost completely. Vinson, designed to replace the far bulkier KY-8, was part of the Saville family and became virtually synonymous with Saville. Perhaps the most innovative area in Vinson design was the application of Seville Advanced Remote Keying, which permitted local users to generate cryptographic keys and distribute them over the Vinson protected net. Eventually over 250,000 Vinson tactical secure voice equipments were delivered to U.S. and Allied forces.

The Soviet Threat

During the 1960s U.S. counterintelligence officials got wind of Soviet SIGINT operations in the United States. In the early years, the information, primarily from HUMINT, was rather vague, but was sufficient to focus attention on the Soviet embassy on 16th Street in downtown Washington, only two blocks from the White House; the Soviet mission to the UN in Manhattan; and the Soviet residential centers at Oyster Bay, New York, and Glen Cove, Long Island. There were also reports of the Soviets using cars to conduct microwave surveys and of their using apartments in Arlington, Virginia, and New York. A defector reported that the Washington area intercept was the most valuable source of intelligence that the Soviets had in the U.S.

[censored]

In the early years the Soviets concentrated on U.S. government communications, including military commands like SAC and NORAD, military airborne command posts, and nonmilitary agencies, including the State Department, FBI, and NASA [censored] In 1968, 126 military command and control circuits were rerouted from microwave to cable in the Washington area, but these were the only countermeasures taken before the mid-1970s.

In the early 1970s Soviet interest began to shift to defense contractors. A 1971 KGB directive ordered that intercept work against scientific and technical work be strengthened. Grumman, Fairchild, GE, IBM, Sperry Rand, and General Dynamics were all named as targets by confidential sources. The Soviets reportedly obtained information on the most sophisticated new weapons systems, including the F-14 fighter, B-1 bomber, Trident submarine, and advanced nuclear weapons developments. If true, this would mean that the Soviets no longer needed spies as they had during the years of the Philby and Rosenberg rings. They could simply get the information from the airwaves. This brought a new factor into the equation. If telephones were such lucrative targets, the U.S. would have to start thinking about voice security for defense contractors, too.

[censored]

The Solutions

[censored] The initial result was a highly sensitive National Security Defense Memorandum 266, signed by Henry Kissinger, then the National Security Advisor, and addressed only to the secretary of defense, director of OMB, DCI, and the director of Telecommunications Policy. This memorandum directed that Washington area microwave communications be buried to the extent possible. This would be a near-term measure. Longer term solutions would include expanding secure-voice communications throughout the government and private industry. The Office of Telecommunications Policy would work on the long-term solutions.

[censored]

The issue remained under study, and President Ford reviewed the options in the waning days of his administration. By that time [censored] it became obvious that securing only Washington area communications would not do. Some circuits had been secured, but many had not. The major corporations were cooperating with the government program, but other, smaller companies just entering the market did not have the capital base to pay for a large program of rerouting their circuits to underground cables. Forcing them to bury their circuits could put them at a competitive disadvantage with AT&T. Ford's advisors outlined a wide-ranging and complex program which would include burying more microwave circuits, developing and distributing more and better secure telephones, close interworking between government and private industry, and federally mandated programs directing implementation of approved protection techniques throughout the national microwave net. Securing the nation's vital national defense-related communications would cost in the neighborhood of $1 to $2 billion.

Ford approved a program to proceed with protection of both government and private sector communications. He also approved the establishment of a joint National Security Council/Domestic Council Committee on Telecommunications Security to oversee the effort. But he did not approve making a public announcement about the problem.

Just prior to the November elections in 1976, President Ford signed PD-24, a presidential directive so sensitive that only fifteen copies were made. Expressing the administration's concern over the Soviet exploitation program, the directive brought contractors into partnership with the government to evaluate the potential damage. Five companies—Vitro Laboratories Division of Automation Industry, Newport News Shipbuilding and Drydock Company, General Electric, IBM, and Lockheed—were named to work with the federal government on the issue. Only a matter of days later Ford lost the election, and the whole issue became Jimmy Carter's problem.

Ford and his vice president, Nelson Rockefeller, had been strong supporters of NSA's efforts. Carter's administration brought a new look. New White House officials were not so inclined to view this solely as a national security issue, but as related also to the protection of individual liberty and privacy. Carter directed a complete review of the Ford administration program. Carter was concerned about countermeasures, including the legality of the program to secure wirelines in the Washington, New York, and San Francisco areas under Project [censored] He questioned the effect of proposed countermeasures, including denial of Soviet requests to purchase more property in the Washington area. He also wanted to know what effect the [censored] project, which involved close interworking with AT&T, would have on the ongoing Justice Department antitrust suit against that same corporation. He suggested that countermeasures could lead to Soviet retaliation, especially the possible increase in microwave bombardment of the US. embassy in Moscow. In short, he wanted a new program that would have the stamp of the Carter administration. And he wanted the entire thing kept absolutely secret.

The joint government-contractor study initiated by Ford concluded that the Soviets were getting very valuable national security data from defense contractor communications. The CEOs of the participating companies were shocked at the degree to which their telephone conversations were being exploited. With this report in hand, in June 1977 the deputy secretary of defense told Lew Allen to alert certain other defense contractors and bring into the problem. Ultimately, NSA contacted seventeen contractors and briefed them about their vulnerabilities.

Meanwhile, Carter's national security adviser, Zbigniew Brzezinski, directed that [censored] the wireline security project, be rushed through to completion. He also requested that government-developed wireline and circuit security technology be made available immediately, but here the competing Defense and Commerce authorities slowed things. The Carter administration, initially suspicious of Defense influence in the private sector, wanted Commerce to take the lead in dealing with private industry on the issue. A presidential directive in 1979 divided responsibility between Defense (with NSA as the executive agent) for the protection of government communications, and Commerce for the protection of private and industry communications. This was to be the first of many conflicts between Defense and Commerce over cryptographic and telecommunications technology policy.

As part of the Carter strategy, the White House directed the DCI to assess the state of vulnerability. [censored]

Brzezinski, who was turning out to be a hawk's hawk in a generally dovish White House, actually considered employing active measures such as jamming the Soviet interception program. But his DCI, Stansfield Turner, pointed out that the U.S. could lose much more than it might gain by this, and headed off further consideration.

Another diversion which proved not at all helpful at solving the problem was Vice President Mondale's concern for the protection of individual privacy. The vice president viewed the matter in the context of civil liberties, and he kept wanting to know how we were going to stop the

Soviets from reading the mail of individual Americans. This frequently diverted cabinet-level discussions into fruitless pursuits, until Brzezinski succeeded in relegating it to a low priority at meeting agendas. As the national security advisor told Mondale at one point, "An effective program in this area would cost several billion dollars and we need to know much more about the actual threat before recommending an expenditure of this magnitude. . . ." Budgetary realities do have a way of killing off diversionary issues.

The whole matter became a key input into the "battle of the embassies" that was so important during the Reagan administration. In 1966 the U.S. and the Soviet Union began negotiating for new space in Moscow and Washington for the construction of new, modern embassies to replace the cramped and aging buildings than in use. State notified Defense [censored]

[censored] The protest did not crest until after Ronald Reagan had been elected, but the Carter administration was concerned about it, even though determined to keep the whole matter quiet.

The long-range solution was to develop the elusive universal telephone encryption device. STU-I, with its $35,000 price tag, had not been the answer. The follow-on, STU-II, came in at half the cost, but still required that all contacts run through a central key facility. This made call set-up awkward and time consuming and meant that even people having the instruments would use them only when they had plenty of time or were certain that they would get into classified material during the call. Moreover, the instrument itself rested on a fifty-pound box that resembled the aged KY-3. It just wasn't user friendly, and only 15,000 of them were produced before the program ended. It began in 1979 and ended in 1987 when it was overtaken by the "real deal," the STU-III.

[censored]

Record communications were easier to protect than were voice systems, and the U.S. government had secured just about all the circuits that it needed to protect long before. But the redoubtable KW-26, which had been the standard since the mid-1950s, was showing its age. NSA had known about the KW-26's drawbacks since its first deployment. A point-to-point circuit encryption device, its numbers had to be multiplied by the number of circuits arriving in a comm center. In the mid-1960s NSA began working on a replacement under Project [censored] was designed under the premise that the only thing unique to an individual circuit was the key generator. All other equipment, including modems and amplifiers, could be used by all circuits in common.

What emerged from [censored] was the KG-84, the next generation of key generator. It was a key generator only, and a very fast one which could be used on the high-speed circuits that had evolved since the early days of the KW-26. NSA awarded the contract to Bendix in 1979, with delivery scheduled to begin in December of 1981.

NSA Computers Enter The 1970s

By the 1970s NSA was no longer making computer history. Industry development was more diffuse, and many of the ideas that spawned corporate computer development were originating in other places. Important as it was, cryptology did not drive technology to the extent that it had earlier. Internally, concerns were shifting to organizational issues.

The Era of Mainframes

Beginning with Harvest in 1962, NSA was dominated by general-purpose mainframes. These were "nested" in centralized complexes consisting of many computers, and each complex was dedicated to a particular purpose. A 1973 study of NSA computers done by a panel chaired by Dr. Willis Ware of the Rand Corporation identified six large complexes.

At the front end of the process was the communications complex. This complex consisted primarily of Univac and Honeywell products, which were especially adaptable to receiving streams of data typical of those originating from communications centers (Honeywell, in fact, provided the IATS computers at field sites.) IDDF, the main communications center, used Sigma computers which processed record traffic from the Criticomm system. On the operations side, the complex of Univacs and Honeywells sucked up the deluge of intercept files being forwarded from field sites via the IATS system. It entered NSA through the Daysend program, and from there it was sent to [censored] which split out the intercept files for various applications programs according to the target signals (A Group, B Group, and G Group, primarily).

The next stop was [censored] These fourth generation computers were the most advanced on the market, but IBM products were notoriously difficult to mate with those of other companies, and material from the [censored] system had to be reformatted and spun off onto magnetic tapes, which were then hand-carried to the [censored] complex and processed in job batches according to their priority. Batch jobs tended to be run at night so that the material would be ready for the analyst in the morning. [censored] ran the applications programs that were specific to each analytic organization. This was almost entirely a traffic analytic process.

The Rye complex began in the late 1960s supporting NSOC's predecessor, the Current SIGINT Operations Center (CSOC), which served as a timely operations center on the Soviet problem. Klieglights were the grist for the mill—short, highly formatted information fragments which often became formal product reports. The technology had been put together by [censored] and a team of traffic analysts and computer systems people. Like his boss, Walter Deeley, [censored] was abrasive and iconoclastic. But he got things done, and Deeley liked that.

The Rye complex ran several different software systems, most important of which was called Tide, which processed incoming Klieglights. Rye became the central nervous system for NSOC, and it internetted over

100 Opscomm circuits. By this time the Opscomm traffic (primarily Klieglights) flowed directly into two Univac 494s, which distributed it via CRTs to analysts on the NSOC floor. But by the mid-1970s Tide had become overburdened. [censored] The end was near, and programmers and systems analysts hurried a new system, called Preface, into being. Preface operated on a Univac 1100. Although it began handling its first job in 1978, it took several years to move all the processing off the 494s and onto the new system.

Cryptanalytic processing was still the biggest computer processing effort. [censored] In addition, cryptanalysis was still the home of the special-purpose device (SPD). [censored] Two other complexes made up the NSA computer mainframes. [censored] The CDC 6600, considered by many to be the first supercomputer, was built by the successor to ERA, which had done so much contracting in support of NSG in the days following World War II.

In fact, the CDC 6600 represented the dawning of the supercomputer business in NSA. It was succeeded by the CDC 7700, four times as fast and more capable in every respect. Seymour Cray, who started at CDC, formed his own company, Cray Research Incorporated, in 1972, and NSA purchased the first machine, the Cray 1, in 1976. (Table 10 contains a brief history of supercomputer purchases by NSA.) [Table 10 is censored]

In 1973 a full-scale debate erupted within NSA over closed versus open-shop programming. Under the closed-shop system, naturally favored by C Group, all programming and systems design people would be concentrated in a central organization (i.e., C Group), which would take care of all requests for support. In the open-shop concept, most computer people would be distributed to customer organizations where they could write applications programs while in daily contact with the people who needed the support. Needless to say, DDO favored this approach and even pushed the idea that the best applications programmer would be a person who came from the supported organization and did programming on the side. Dr. Willis Ware, a Rand Corporation executive who served on NSASAB, sponsored a compromise, wherein large systems would be centralized in C Group, but applications programming would be done, in the main, in the customer organization. After a long and bitter argument, this approach prevailed, to the relief of many who believed that this was the inevitable outcome.

A year earlier another simmering organizational feud had resulted in a special study. The debate, which had begun at least as early as 1970, involved the possible merger of computer and telecommunications functions into the same organization. The two had become so inextricable that the technology drove the issue. In 1972 Paul Neff, the chief of the policy staff, suggested that a full study be made, and this spawned the Carson Committee, chaired by Neil Carson of PI. Carson recommended that the computer organization should be pulled out of DDO and merged with telecommunications, the so- called "take T and C" approach. DDO strongly opposed the divestiture of resources, and the issue remained an irritant for four more years, when Lew Allen took a new look and finally directed the merger.

Platform

The great weakness of the disconnected mainframes was interaction. As systems became more interdependent and SIGINT requirements became more time-sensitive, the need to send information across computer boundaries affected NSA more and more seriously. Under Walter Deeley's direction (Deeley was then chief of V, the organization that ran NSOC), William Saadi wrote a requirements paper for the internetting of Agency computers. [censored]

Kermit Speierman, the chief of C, asked his deputy, Cecil Phillips, to put together a seminar of NSA and non-Agency people to look at the problem. A young systems engineer named [censored] was urging NSA to look at some technology that had been developed by the Defense Advanced Research Projects Agency (DARPA). In 1969 DARPA had developed a computer internetting system called ARPANET. At the seminar called by Phillips, the DARPA representative explained ARPANET, and NSA quickly adopted the DARPA solution. The project was called Platform.

The schema for Platform was worked out for NSA by Bolt, Beranek and Newman, Incorporated, which released its report to NSA in 1974. The original plan allowed for four host complexes, which could be expanded as the system got bigger. The core process was to be run on a Honeywell 316, which would be the Interface Message Processor (IMP). Platform soon expanded to the field [censored] was the first field site brought into the system.

The 1970s was a period of accelerated development of software and database systems. The volumes of data flowing into the Agency every day demanded very sophisticated databases, and in this NSA pioneered relational systems. Some, like M-204, were developed specifically for NSA. One database, called COINS (Community On-line Information System), began in the mid-1960s under NSA executive agency. Initially a joint NSA/DIA project, it became a community-wide database at the SI/TK level. COINS became a substitute for various product reports, and customers were simply given direct access to massaged SIGINT data rather than having NSA take the data and manufacture a product report of mind-numbing length and detail. Still another database, then called SOLIS, was created in 1972 to hold all NSA electrical product reports.

NSA's Foreign Collaboration

Scarce resources meant reliance on outside help. And as the budgets got slimmer, NSA turned increasingly to the help that foreigners could provide. This trend accelerated in the 1970s to a greater degree than at any time in U.S. post-World War II cryptologic history.

There were dramatic differences in reliance on foreign partners depending on the target. [censored]

[censored]

Great Britain

With the British, collaboration remained almost total. The key decisions that kept the two countries closely tied related generally to advances in new technological realms. At each bend of the road, NSA made a conscious decision to remain engaged.

[censored]

[censored]

Each country lived with the foibles of the other. The American tendency to leak everything significant to the press was counterbalanced in England by the Official Secrets Act, by which the government tried, often unsuccessfully, to stop publication of material regarded as "sensitive." GCHQ employees were unionized from an early date, and this introduced some interesting twists to the relationship with the Americans, who were not unionized. Politically, the Left in England was stronger than in the U.S., and they employed some novel techniques to attempt to wreck the intelligence business. One such was the device of "public foot paths," a Medieval concept by which, under British common law, paths that had been used by walkers in previous centuries were required to be kept open. Careful research into public records almost always yielded one or more such ancient walking routes through military installations. Thus diligent British researchers discovered foot paths across both [censored] and would endeavor, at least once a year, to walk them to maintain the concept. [censored]

Australia

American intelligence had enjoyed a long and close relationship with Australia from the time of the election of Robert Menzies (of the Liberal Party) in 1949 through the end of his very long term of office (1961). His successors were also inclined to be pro-American, and the sunny situation continued through the end of the decade. But in 1972 the Australian Labor Party (ALP), headed by one Gough Whitlam, assumed the reins, and relations turned stormy. While conservative Australians generally supported the bilateral relationship with the U.S., the ALP had developed a leftist and decidedly anti-American stance.

Whitlam was opposed to Australian participation in the war in Vietnam, and he pulled Australian troops out of the combat zone. He also announced that he would see to it that Australian forces came home no matter where they were; this included a small contingent in the island nation of Singapore.

[censored]

Cryptology and Whitlam were not done, even after he departed for private life. Soon after he was sacked, the press revealed that Whitlam planned to accept a hefty financial donation to the ALP from the Ba'ath Party in Iraq. [censored] Even in 1975 the regime of Saddam Hussein was so odious that Whitlam could not survive the besmirchment. His political career was effectively over. The new prime minister, Malcolm Fraser, was decidedly pro-American, and U.S.-Australian relations returned to something approaching an even keel.

During his days in power, Whitlam subjected his entire intelligence establishment to a searching evaluation. To take charge of the investigation, he appointed Mr. Justice R. M. Hope, whom everyone in Labor regarded as a dedicated civil libertarian. The Hope Commission continued to investigate and deliberate for almost three years, releasing its final report in 1977, long after Whitlam was at home growing roses. But instead of destroying the intelligence mechanism that Whitlam so detested, Hope proposed to strengthen it. His greatest praise was reserved for DSD, which he and his committee members regarded as the best source of intelligence available.

DSD resided in the Defence establishment, but rather than remove it, Hope proposed to give it more autonomy, more people, and more money. In many ways Hope's recommendations paralleled events in the United States in 1952, when NSA was created within Defense, but autonomous from the JCS. DSD's mission was a national one, Hope wrote, and should be strengthened in all its aspects, especially in economic and diplomatic intelligence important to non-Defence organizations. The commission also praised the relationships with NSA and GCHQ.

[censored]

[censored]

Third Party Programs

Until 1974, NSA's Third Party programs had been run by the deputy director, Louis Tordella. This highly centralized management arrangement worked as long as Third Parties remained relatively unimportant. By the time Tordella retired in 1974, this was no longer the case, and the new deputy, Benson Buffham, promptly changed the arrangement, naming a separate Third Party program manager (originally Robert Drake, the DDO, who wore it as a second hat). This effectively decentralized Third Party management outside of the deputy director's office and got more people involved in decision-making. It was a long-overdue reform.

[censored]

[censored]

Chapter 18 The Middle East and the Yom Kippur War

[censored]

Background To War

The Middle East War of 1967 ended as World War I had ended—that is, in a most unsatisfactory way. Arab nations were humbled and bitter, while triumphant Israel had finally gained the additional territory it needed to make its precarious borders "defensible". Palestinian refugees invaded neighboring countries and became a thorn in the side of all who wished to forget about the Arab-Israeli problem. In short, nothing had been solved, and the situation was made to order for another war.

In the aftermath of 1967 the United Nations Security Council passed resolution 242, which served thereafter as the formal basis for peace. Its basic premise was the "inadmissibility of acquiring territory by war," and it established an important quid pro quo. If the states of the Mideast agreed to recognize Israel's right to exist and its territorial integrity, Israel would in turn withdraw from the occupied territories. This was coupled with the principle of navigation through international waterways (including, of course, the Suez Canal and Straits of Tiran) and the repatriation of refugees.

As a general proposition this was recognized by most contending parties (Syria being the noted exception). But all parties interpreted the seemingly solid prose to fit their own cases. Arab states, for instance, assumed that the resolution required total withdrawal, while Israel contended that it only meant withdrawal to "defensible borders." This would not, in the Israeli view, include withdrawal from the West Bank (and certainly not Jerusalem). On the Arab side the most divisive issue was the refugee problem, which beset all the states bordering Israel to some degree. Israel felt that the Arab states should accept all refugees within their borders; the Arab states wanted to return them all.

In the years following the war, political developments changed the face of the dispute. In one year, 1969, revolutions resulted in the overthrow of three moderately pro-Western governments: Libya, Sudan, and Somalia. Of these the most significant was the advent of Muhammar Gaddhafi in Libya. Gaddhafi became the first sponsor of "state-sponsored terrorism," that most unwelcome development of the Mideast situation. Gaddhafi was only twenty-seven at the time—clearly the Middle East would contend with him for a long time to come.

In the same year, Egypt's Gamel Abdel Nasser, unrepentant of his disastrous sojourn to war in 1967, announced that he would begin a "war of attrition" which would include shelling the Israeli positions on the Bar Lev Line in the Sinai. This elicited a predictable Israeli response, and for several years artillery duels raged in the desert.

But the most difficult problem remained the refugees. The two largest groups were in Lebanon and Jordan, and in the Jordanian camps, the Palestinian political and military organization advanced to the point where it had become an independent power within the state of Jordan. In 1970,

George Habash's Popular Front for the Liberation of Palestine (PFLP) hijacked four commercial airplanes filled with tourists to a remote air strip near Amman, demanding a massive release of Arabs imprisoned in various capitals. His harsh treatment of the hostages brought worldwide condemnation, and the obstreperous behavior of his minions within the camps in Jordan brought clashes between his forces and the Jordanian Army. Nasser stepped in to negotiate a cease-fire, but the strain was too much, and he died suddenly of a heart attack. Ultimately the PFLP blew up the planes, European governments freed seven Arab prisoners, and the guerrillas released 300 hostages and dispersed the rest to refugee camps in and around Amman.

British trained, the Jordanian army of King Hussein was small but effective. On September 17 it moved against the Palestinian camps, and the U.S. responded with an intensified military buildup in the eastern Mediterranean to insure that Hussein kept his hold on his throne. Syria attacked Jordan from the north, but withdrew before U.S. intervention was necessary. The refugees were driven out, and decamped for Lebanon, thus transferring the central refugee problem to that country. The embittered Palestinians formed the Black September terrorist movement (after the September date of their ouster from Jordan).

In Egypt, the completely unexpected rise of Anwar Sadat, one of the original group that ejected the ruling monarchy in 1956, injected new dimensions to the Mideast situation. Sadat was at once more democratic, more intelligent and more skilled in military matters, than Nasser had been. Thought to be a temporary figurehead, he quickly maneuvered politically to put down his rivals. He also maneuvered his forces toward the inevitable future clash with Israel, but in new and unpredictable ways, and with less fanfare and rhetoric. Once he had secured his power base in Egypt, he ejected the Soviet advisors on whom Nasser had relied and began negotiating with the West for military aid. It was shaping up as a diplomatic revolution in the Middle East.

The early 1970s were the heyday of international Mideast terrorism. The PLO, the PFLP, and various other warring factions contended for press attention. In 1972 the PLO attacked the Olympic Village in Munich. They also targeted a trainload of emigrants from the USSR entering Austria and helped assassinate the U.S. ambassador in Khartoum.

[censored]

The Preparations

Sadat and his allies in Syria and Jordan decided on a preemptive war at a meeting in Cairo in September of 1973. They agreed to launch simultaneous attacks on Israeli forces in the Sinai and Golan Heights, while Jordan, lacking a missile defense capability, would hang back in a defensive posture in the early stages. They did not at the time set a precise date, but agreed that they would launch their initial attack during the Yom Kippur observances in early October.

[censored]

[censored]

The Attack

Unlike previous offensives by Arab states, this one was well coordinated. Egyptian troops sprang against the Bar Lev Line in the Sinai, throwing back the 600 Israeli troops and sweeping into the desert beyond with two armies. They came armed with SAMs, and Israel did not enjoy its customary air superiority in the early going. Soon the Egyptians had advanced ten kilometers into the Sinai, but then they slowed, apparently not anticipating such a rapid advance. It appeared that they had made no follow-up plans for such a breakthrough. To the north, meanwhile, Syria charged the Golan Heights with tanks and threw the surprised Israelis back.

The Israeli mobilization had only just begun that morning, but it was made swifter by the fact that it was Yom Kippur, and everyone who was needed for defense could be found in the synagogues. Israel concentrated its initial defense on the Golan Heights, fearful of the consequences of failure so close to population and industrial centers. The northern front was soon stabilized; then Israel turned its attention to the Sinai. Intelligence located a weak point in the center of the peninsula, at the point where the two Egyptian armies joined, and Israel launched a thrust through the center which dominated the second week of the war. At the end of the week, Israeli troops had reached the Suez Canal and, amid heavy casualties, crossed it.

At the beginning of the second week the United States, fearful of an Israeli defeat, began a huge arms resupply, flying in planeload after planeload. At the same time, the Soviet Union signaled its continued support for the Arab cause with its own resupply operation. In retaliation for the U.S. position, OPEC, at the urging of Sadat, imphsed an oil embargo on the United States and any European country that appeared excessively pro-Israel. (Only the Netherlands was singled out.) The Yom Kippur War thus launched the first great oil crisis in American history.

[censored]

Week three was the crunch point. Israel had exploited its penetration of Egyptian lines, and the week began with both Egyptian and Syrian forces in serious trouble. Both the U.S. and the USSR, fearing a major superpower conflict, groped desperately for a cease-fire. The Nixon administration was in complete chaos—Vice President Agnew had just resigned in disgrace, and Nixon had fired special Watergate prosecutor Archibald Cox, throwing the entire government into constitutional crisis. In the midst of this, National Security Advisor Henry Kissinger flew to Moscow and hammered out a temporary fix with Brezhnev, including a cease-fire in place, reaffirmation of UN Resolution 242, and immediate diplomatic negotiations among the contending parties.

[censored]

Ultimately the Egyptians got to keep some of their gains in the Sinai, the Israelis were pressured into pulling their troops from the western side of the Canal, and they also had to give up portions of Syria captured from the Assad government. Israel came out of the experience convinced that they had been jobbed, but Sadat was so pleased with it that he helped Kissinger persuade Faysal of Saudi Arabia to drop the oil embargo. The compromise outcome of the Yom Kippur War also got the peace process started at long last, and Egypt eventually won the entire Sinai through negotiation. Sadat finished the process of converting from a Soviet to an American alliance, thus completing a diplomatic revolution in the Middle East in which Washington, rather than Moscow, became Egypt's closest ally.

The Postmortems

[censored]

Self-delusion was a strong factor in the 1973 debacle. U.S. intelligence had concluded that Arab military armies possessed questionable prowess."There was . . . a fairly widespread notion based largely (though perhaps not entirely) on past performances that many Arabs, as Arabs, simply weren't up to the demands of modern warfare. . . ." It was supposed that the Arabs themselves understood this and would thus never think of attacking impregnable Israeli forces. Then there was the problem of reinforced consensus. The Israelis were confident that war was not imminent. Their followers within the U.S. intelligence community, wanting to look smart, parroted the Israeli view, and as one agency after another weighed in with its conclusion that war was unlikely, those assessments themselves became the footnotes for new assessments. Moreover, each agency assembled its own microscopic piece, in the manner of assembling a Chevrolet, without stepping back to look at the whole.

[censored]

[censored]

Chapter 19 The Rebirth of Intelligence during the Carter Administration

The return of the Democrats to power in 1977 had ominous implications for intelligence. After eight years lost in the wilderness, the Democratic politicians were eager to get into the White House and fix the "Watergate mess." This would include a thorough housecleaning of a supposedly out of control intelligence establishment. And indeed Jimmy Carter started down that road. But as so often happens, things did not work out that way, and the decade ended with a very different fate for the intelligence community and for NSA.

The Inman Era

The first event that changed the fate of NSA was the appointment of a new director. General Lew Allen departed in July 1977 as a hero to those in NSA who understood what he had achieved in dealing with Congress in 1975. He was rewarded with a fourth star and command of Air Force Systems Command. He would soon become the Air Force chief of staff, the first NSA director to be so honored. His replacement was an unknown admiral named Bobby Inman.

Inman came from the obscurity of an east Texas town, the son of a gas station owner. He went to school at the University of Texas in Austin, majored in history, and did not quite know what to do when he graduated. He tried law school, but dropped out, then taught grammar school for a year. In the course of events he joined the Naval Reserve and during the Korean War left schoolteaching to enter the Navy as an ensign. He never returned.

Bobby Inman was one of life's outsiders. He competed for promotions in a system that rewarded Annapolis school ties, which he did not have. He was a restricted line officer when it was well known that only seagoing line officers could gain a star. He spent his entire career in intelligence, a kiss of death at promotion time.

His early career carried him through a variety of intelligence duties, including a three-year stint as a SIGINT analyst at NSA [censored] In the early 1970s he became executive assistant to the vice chief of Naval Operations, Admiral Bruce Holloway. The vice-CNO recognized Inman's talents, and in 1974 rewarded him with his first star, as director of the Office of Naval Intelligence.

Inman came to this position just prior to the Church and Pike Committee hearings in 1975. The poisonous atmosphere could, and did, destroy careers, but in the cases of both Allen and Inman, it enhanced their standing. Inman worked very closely with Congress and first established his close ties with the legislative branch. His exceptional performance also came to the attention of the White House and President Ford. Thus in 1976, when the Defense Department needed a new lineup at DIA, Inman was picked as vice-director. This earned him a quick promotion from rear admiral to vice admiral. The objections of the naval establishment could be heard in the halls but did not hold up against Inman's connections and his acknowledged brilliance. To Inman, though, even this extraordinary accomplishment was not quite what he wanted. He had always wanted to be director of NSA, which he regarded as the most powerful military job in the intelligence community.

As he sat "languishing" at DIA, a revolution was about to send him to the job he coveted. The 1976 changeover at DIA had sent the director,

Lieutenant General Eugene Tighe, packing. (He was reduced in rank and sent to be the director of intelligence at SAC, a subordinate position that clearly indicated loss of favor.) A new administration wanted to rehabilitate Tighe. In the maneuverings that saved Tighe's career, it became necessary to put Inman somewhere else. That "somewhere else" became DIRNSA.

Inman brought to the job some extraordinary talents. He was known as a brilliant workaholic with a photographic memory. *Washington Post* investigative journalist Bob Woodward once said of him: "Inman's reviews are extraordinary, almost hyperbolic. Nearly everyone who knows him mentions a piercing intellect, honesty, unusual memory for details and prodigious capacity for work. In his Washington years Inman rose each day but Sunday at 4 a.m., his first hours absorbed in reading and private thoughts." Another writer, Joseph Persico, wrote that "If Inman had a hearing at nine o'clock in the morning, he'd be up at four prepping for it. He'd read the answers to maybe a hundred hypothetical questions. He'd essentially memorize the answers. Then he'd go before the committee and take whatever they threw at him, without referring to a note."

His brilliance enabled him to take on things that no other DIRNSA had been capable of. His staff had trouble keeping up with him, and missteps or misinformation was feared because Inman would remember the facts that his staff so laboriously collected. Being in the some room with him was an experience that no one would ever forget. He appeared perpetually calm, but in reality was about as stable as high voltage across an air gap.

Inman's management style was unique. Rather than simply representing the Agency to the outside world as previous directors (even Ralph Canine) had chosen to do, Inman got involved in the technical details of the business. He was the first and only director to become so schooled in the minutiae of cryptology.

One of his first actions was to take hold of the personnel system. He understood that NSA was actually managed by a collection of powerful civilian czars under the long-serving deputy director Louis Tordella (who had been replaced by Benson Buffham in 1974, on his retirement). This smacked to Inman of a certain collegiality which reduced the real authority of the director. Being an outsider his entire career, he determined to change the system. So one of his first acts was to create a career development panel which was to identify the next generation of top NSA managers to replace the World War II generation that was still in power. The panel named for Inman a collection of GS 13-15 "fast burners" whom they expected to take the reins of senior management in the future. Inman then decreed that this group of up-and-coming leaders would be rotated from job to job. One benefit would be to give them wide experience; the other, unsaid, was to remove them from their own bases of power. If continued over a period of years, this would change the flavor of NSA and would centralize power within the directorate.

Inman also made the crucial decision to create a revolving deputy directorate. He felt that a long-serving deputy diluted the authority of the director, and he was determined to have no more Tordellas. Thus he sent Buffham off to SUSLO in 1978 and brought in Robert Drake. Only two years later he again changed deputies, naming Ann Caracristi the first woman deputy director. Both were acknowledged products of World War II—the postwar generation would get its chance, but not quite yet.

Bobby Inman's views were strongly reinforced by a management study which he commissioned in 1978. A consulting firm, the Arthur H. Little Company, looked at NSA management from top to bottom and issued a scathing report. Calling the management style "paranoid," "untrustworthy," and "uncooperative," the company lit into the entrenched bureaucracies, each a sealed unit driven by the personality of its dominant "baron." In a cover letter to Inman, the authors wrote: "A second important concern involves the attitudinal outlook of much of the staff of the Agency. A pervasive defense mechanism seems to be a driving (as well as a cohesive) force. . . . Our concern is that the siege mentality affects not only the Agency as a whole, but also each of the subunits which must compete for visibility, resources, and control of programs and assets and even the individual who must compete for the few promotions and for the really good jobs."

The company also identified much managerial layering which it contended produced many levels of staffing, slowing decisions and diffusing responsibility; NSA also created many positions that had come to be regarded as "parking lots" for managers who no longer fit into the Agency's plans.

Inman also intervened in a personnel case that he regarded as one of his most difficult decisions. A young NSA linguist, who had just graduated from the Foreign Service Institute with a very high score in an exotic language, announced that he was homosexual. He also hired a lawyer, signaling that he would not go quietly despite the well-known prohibition against homosexuals at NSA. Inman's general counsel, Daniel Schwartz, advised him that they could lose the case in court and with such a loss would go much of the director's authority in personnel decisions. It was a tough call because homosexuality was often an avenue for entrapment by hostile foreign intelligence agents. The possibility of blackmail was always considered to be very high.

Inman's decision was to let the young man stay on, but under stringent rules. He would have to admit his homosexuality to his entire family, personally (not in writing), so that there would be little likelihood of blackmail. He would have to avoid public lewdness and must refrain from violating state and local laws on the subject. He could not participate in public demonstrations relating to homosexuality in which he could be identified as an NSA employee. And, finally, he would have to submit to an annual polygraph. He accepted all four stipulations and was kept on.

With his strong background in intelligence in general and SIGINT in particular, Inman was inclined to jump into the technical details of managing the system. As soon as he became director, he took control of the CCP, informing his program manager that he wanted to review all CCP change requests. He became personally involved in the planning mechanism that Lew Allen had set up to staff major initiatives, taking on such projects as Banded Signals Upgrade, the remoting program, and overhead collection, among many others. These tasks had formerly been reserved for the deputy director; under Inman they became the province of the director himself.

The net result was a serious weakening of the upper level staff at NSA. Many senior managers chose to resign rather than compete with Inman for authority. But it was temporary—no other director could continue down that road.

One more of Inman's eccentricities deserves mention—his profound distaste for human intelligence and covert actions and his discomfort with economic intelligence. He trusted technical intelligence—SIGINT and photography—and disliked the spy business, which he regarded as somehow "unclean." While director of ONI, Inman had closed a Navy HUMINT outfit called Task Force 157. While at NSA, he became involved in a dispute with Commerce Secretary Juanita Kreps over the provision of economic intelligence. The problem with this was similar to HUMINT and covert actions—the possibility of misuse. Inman leaned strongly toward "clean" methods and uses of intelligence. It was an attitude that had endeared him to Congress, which also viewed these things askance.

The Carter White House

Inman's term as director overlapped almost perfectly the administration of Jimmy Carter. Carter brought to the White House an almost paranoid distrust of the intelligence establishment. DCI George Bush later commented on his transition briefings with the incoming president that "beneath his surface cool, he harbored a deep antipathy to the CIA." The consensus was summed up by intelligence historian John Ranelagh: "Carter had run against the CIA and Washington; he was an outsider, suspicious of Washington sophistication, and so he stood fast against the corrupting compromises that informed people have to make. . . . He did not understand the need for secret intelligence—a failing that contributed to the Iranian crisis. . . . He saw no real use for the CIA. He had a view of intelligence as order of battle—about detail."

His transition team peered unapprovingly at NSA, the home of vacuum cleaner collection and the suspected invader of individual privacy. They initially proposed a reorganization that would have placed the attorney general directly in NSA's chain of command. The "short leash" approach was soon abandoned, but the latent hostility remained. As a new president, Carter granted the attorney general interim authority to continue electronic surveillance of Americans who might be acting for a foreign power in the course of doing foreign intelligence work. But he also got a special coordinating committee working on draft legislation relating to NSA and the intelligence community.

Carter brought with him a new DCI, Admiral Stansfield Turner, whose suspicions of secret intelligence mirrored Carter's. They shared a proclivity toward an open society that was fundamentally antithetical to many intelligence operations and changed this view only under the press of events. But Turner was not a Carter administration insider. They had been Naval Academy classmates, but had barely known each other, and Turner was only Carter's third choice for DCI. As events unfolded, Turner was to have less influence than might have been imagined for such a key official.

The White House national security structure was dominated by Zbigniew Brzezinski, a strong national security advisor who picked up where Henry Kissinger had left off. Brzezinski proceeded to reduce Stansfield Turner's access to the president. Brzezinski would not permit a CIA briefer into the Oval Office, and when the president's Daily Brief was delivered from Langley, Brzezinski always put his own spin on the items that went to the president. As a result, Brzezinski and Turner did not enjoy a close relationship.

One thing that all three—Carter, Turner, and Brzezinski—had in common, however, was an afinity for "technical" intelligence. In his account of his own term as DCI, Turner stated that "Today, [technical intelligence] all but eclipses traditional, human methods of collecting intelligence. . . . technical systems had opened vast new opportunities for us to collect information regularly with a precision that no human spy network could ever offer. . . ." He created strident ill will within CIA by gutting the power of the DO and getting rid of 802 covert operations people. Turner's dictum was ". . . never send a spy when you can get the information you want by technical means."

In the technicial field, two systems competed for favor. SIGINT, unchallenged since the days of Lyndon Johnson for its speed and accuracy, finally got a competitor. At Carter's first National Security Council meeting on January 22, 1977, Henry Knoche, the acting DCI, brought in the first downlinked photos from the KH-11. Only hours old, the pictures spread out on the cabinet room table made a tremendous impression on this group of outsiders who had had no close association with intelligence. It was a very impressive performance for the new overhead photography system.

NSA was well situated to compete with PHOTINT. As Carter arrived in the White House his new Situation Room chief was [censored] from NSA; [censored] named [censored] of NSA as his deputy. Although there was no formal link with NSA (each employee in the Situation Room responded to the White House rather than his or her home agency) the task of interpreting SIGINT was greatly simplified for NSA.

[censored] commenting on his tenure in the White House, said: "I found that Carter and Brzezinski in particular were very much attuned to SIGINT.

He [Brzezinski] used it and asked for it, and very much understood what he was seeing. . ." The Situation Room authored a separate series of intelligence reports that trickled into the Oval Office during the day. Heavily laced with SIGINT, they contributed Brzezinski's unique spin to national security topics. At times, [censored] these reports were almost entirely from NSA.

Carter responded with frequent, handwritten comments on the reports themselves. Like Inman, he was a details man, and he asked detailed questions [censored] One day the president called Inman directly to request that two names be deleted from a by-name product distribution list. He sometimes invaded the Situation Room to look at reports or just to talk. His interest in intelligence was, like Lyndon Johnson's, apparently insatiable and very much at odds with the public perception of an antiestablishment outsider determined to reduce the intelligence structure. He was definitely NSA's number one customer.

The War Between The Admirals

Below Carter and Brzezinski, a virtual war erupted between NSA and CIA. Turner began his tenure determined to reduce NSA's independence. One of his first actions as DCI was to ask Carter for control of NSA. The White House turned the matter over to the attorney general, Griffin Bell, for a recommendation. In the course of his investigation, Bell first encountered Bobby Inman, who gave him a disquisition on why NSA must remain in the Defense Department. According to Inman, when Turner showed up to brief Bell on why NSA should be resubordinated, Bell said, "Well, Stan, that's all very well, but Admiral Bobby Ray Inman convinced me this morning that he should work for Defense." Turner ascribed his defeat to a curious president. "Presidents want to have multiple sources of information, and the NSA is a particularly intriguing one."

"Distant" would not adequately describe the relationship between Inman and Turner. At about the same time as Turner's play to capture NSA, the two clashed about NSA's budget. The Carter administration proposed deep cuts in the intelligence budget in its first year, and Inman felt that Turner "rolled over" too easily on the issue. Subsequently, Inman dealt mostly with Turner's supporting cast, finding an especially sunny relationship with the deputy DCI, Frank Carlucci. The Carter years also marked the peak of conflict between NSA and CIA over control of cryptologic assets, a conflict which resulted ultimately in the "Peace Treaty" of 1977). The personal animus between the two admirals was exacerbated by their different Navy upbringing—Turner was an exclusive member of the "Annapolis club," while Inman, ever the outsider, owed no favors to this group of kingmakers.

[censored]

President Carter was so concerned about this that he sent a delegation headed by Inman to tell the publisher of the *Times*, Arthur Sulzberger, what had happened. The upshot of this was an agreement between the Carter administration and the *Times* to have an administration point of contact on such matters whom journalists could check with if they suspected that national security issues were involved. The president named Inman as the contact man—this included all forms of intelligence, not just SIGINT.

The system continued through the remainder of the Carter administration, and in general it worked well. The word got out to other publications; and soon all the leading newspapers and weekly news magazines had Inman's name and number. But news of the system also leaked to Turner, who felt that this should have been his role. It did not help the relationship between the two admirals.

[censored]

[censored]

APEX

In 1978 a bizarre struggle arose over a Turner proposal to rationalize and simplify the various intelligence compartments. The plan, called Apex, resulted from a study group headed by John Vogt, a retired Air Force general who had not been a close friend of SIGINT. It was good in theory. All the various intelligence compartments would be subsumed under a single system, with all subcompartments controlled and managed by a central authority. The logic of the new system carried the day, and Turner got the president's concurrence, documented in a new directive, PD/NSC-22, dated January 7, 1980.

Turner proposed that the DCI be the single manager, and that was where the battle lines formed. He liked that idea—it would give him more power. None of the other intelligence chiefs did, but only Inman was willing to confront Turner head-on. NSA, of course, had the most to lose. And the Inman-Turner rift was already in the open, so Inman himself would not be losing ground by confrontation.

Apex was particularly vulnerable on budgetary grounds, and there was where Inman took his stand. ". . . It is unrealistic to believe that supplemental resources will be provided in FY 81 for Apex," he wrote, noting that the cost would be $26 million to fix NSA's computers to accommodate the new system. [censored]

Apex inched toward implementation, but time was not on its side. Turner had named January 1, 1981, as the official implementation date, but in November 1980 Carter lost the election to Ronald Reagan. A few days later NFIB informed Turner that Apex should be abandoned. Turner knew when he was beaten, and in his memoirs he ascribed the defeat mostly to Inman. Apex was put on hold and remained a work unfinished when Reagan became president. It was officially killed as soon as Stansfield Turner was safely out of Langley.

The New Executive Order

Carter's people got right to work on a new directive for the intelligence community. What emerged was Executive Order 12036, the successor to Ford's directive (EO 11905). The new order retained much of the mechanism set up by Ford, including centralization of collection tasking within the DCI, and retention of the Intelligence Oversight Board. USIB was renamed NFIB, but little was changed beyond the name. The DCI was given tighter control of the intelligence budget, and new mechanisms were set up to effect that control. But the tone of the executive order was more punitive, and much of its language dealt with specific restrictions on the intelligence community. Reflecting the prevailing suspicion about secrecy and overclassification, the order reduced the length of time that a document could remain classified from thirty to twenty years. (NSA managed to slip an exception into the order for "foreign government information," thus exempting material provided by the UKUSA partners. This materiel continued under the old thirty-year rule.)

As for the draft legislation for the intelligence community (which included a congressional charter for NSA), Jimmy Carter's ardor soon cooled. What had looked good from Atlanta did not look so good to a sitting president. In a memo to a White House staffer, the president commented: "Be sure not to approve Charter provisions which are excessively detailed, specific or an intrusion into my duties and responsibilities. JC" Congress continued to tinker with the drafts throughout the Carter years, but it had lost the sponsorship of the head of the Democratic party, and the proposed legislation ultimately went nowhere.

Panama

Jimmy Carter arrived at the White House determined to negotiate a permanent resolution to the mess in Panama. The issue did not resonate with the intelligence community. [censored] But they were, fortunately, quite wrong.

The Panama problem began with the terms under which the United States constructed and operated the canal, the highly one-sided Hay-Bunau-Varilla Treaty of 1903. This document granted the United States virtually unimpeded occupation of the Panama Canal Zone in perpetuity. This was an arrangement fit for a dominant colonial power, but there was an achilles heel. The American public was well known to have a conscience, and the Panamanians played to it.

Trouble began under Lyndon Johnson in the 1960s. Panamanian nationalists began agitating for a better deal, and in 1967 mobs entered the Zone and precipitated bloody riots that the U.S. had to suppress with force. Following this fiasco, the Johnson administration agreed to negotiations to change the provisions of the treaty. But Johnson was preoccupied with the war in Vietnam, and Panama lacked the power to press its case.

In 1968, a messianic officer of the Guardia Nacional named Omar Torrijos overthrew the left-leaning civilian government of Arnulfo Arias.

Torrijos immediately took up the struggling negotiations with the United States as a personal call, and he guided his nation through relations with four American presidents (Johnson, Nixon, Ford, and Carter). Employing secret threats, bald intimidation, and diplomatic maneuvering that would make Machiavelli blush, Torrijos had, by 1977, placed the United States in a most uncomfortable position. Carter arrived in Washington determined to rid the United States of the festering sore of Panama.

[censored]

[censored]

SALT II

The SALT I treaty of 1971, coupled with the Vladivostok Accords of 1974, helped turn NSA's sources back onto the Soviet problem. But SALT I was just a beginning. Both sides specifically averred that a more comprehensive treaty would be negotiated.

The Carter administration brought a completely new look to strategic arms negotiations. Carter placed the issue in the context of his dovish views on the arms race and human rights, and he began his administration with the declaration that he would scrap the Vladivostok Accords and go for deep cuts in overall levels. Given the charge, his negotiators fashioned a proposal that would bring the overall level of launchers from 2,400 apiece to something between 1,800 and 2,100. Rather than the 1,320 MIRVed launchers permitted by the accords, Carter would try for a limit of between 1,100 and 1,200. The original Carter proposals contained myriad details relating to strategic bombers, shorter range missiles, and mobile missile development, all of which leaned toward a smaller strategic force.

The proposals fell flat initially, owing to Carter's use of open diplomacy. When Secretary of State Cyrus Vance went to Moscow in the spring of 1977 to begin negotiations, he announced the American position in advance to the press. Given Carter's known position on strategic arms, the Soviets might not have been surprised by the position, but they viewed the new administration's propensity to conduct diplomacy through the press with incomprehension. The negotiations broke down.

More progress was made later in the year, and, under the cloak of a less public negotiating system, the two sides neared agreement on a comprehensive treaty. But the process of placing limits on specific strategic arms resulted in a much more detailed draft treaty. As the two sides grew closer to agreement, they found it necessary to spell out everything, and the result was a thirty-one-page document resembling a legal agreement. It became a nightmare for the intelligence agencies expected to verify its terms.

How, for instance, would verification determine how many warheads a MIRVed missile carried? Photography could not see into the missile silo [censored] When the Soviets began deploying unMIRVed missiles to missile fields near Derazhnya and Pervomaysk, the U.S. contended that all missiles in the field should count as MIRVs. When the Soviets countered that the

MIRVed missiles could be distinguished by a unique domed antenna distinguishable from a photographic satellite, [censored]

There were similar rules defining types of missiles, depending largely on range and payload, and these depended on SIGINT for verification. Telemetry from missile tests was vital to determine both facts and, on occasion, indicated that new missile capability might exceed the limits in the draft treaty. The same pertained to defining whether a missile was a new type (prohibited in the draft treaty) or simply a modidifcation of an older type (permitted). [censored]

The arguments were not confined to missiles but also pervaded bombers, submarines, and cruise missiles. Would the Backfire bomber, employed in a theater role by the Soviets, be counted in the strategic mix? [censored]

Telemetry was critical to verification. The US first began intercepting evidence of Soviet telemetry encryption ability as early as 1974. The USSR always employed this selectively, encrypting telemetry on certain missile testing programs, but not others. The [censored] for instance, was most heavily covered by telemetry encryption, and this encryption hindered SALT verification.

In 1978 the Soviets first began encrypting reentry telemetry on the [censored] This was a direct threat to verification, and it raised the temperature. In Washington, NSA was concerned about telemetry encryption but opposed permitting the negotiators to discuss specifics on the grounds that this would reveal US SIGINT capabilities. But the urgency of the [censored] encryption problem forced American negotiators to bring this to the table, and it was eventually resolved. The two sides agreed to language that would bar "the encryption or encoding of crucial missile test information. . . .' " as long as such a practice would hinder verification."

The issue of mobile missiles was a hot SALT II topic. The U.S. pushed for a ban on them, even as the Soviets were testing their SS-X-20 mobile missile system. The first SS-20 site became operational in 1977 [censored] The missile did not appear in the treaty because its range kept it out of the ICBM category. An SS-16 program, which would have converted the SS-20 into an ICBM by adding a third stage, was scrapped in 1977, thus ending a potentially contentious issue. [censored]

SALT II was signed and ready for ratification in May 1979. It was one of the most complex treaties the U.S. ever negotiated, and many of the clauses required verification. [censored]

[censored]

HF Modernization

With the increasing focus on the collection of exotic signals using high-tech means, high frequency collection was threatened with irrelevance. Every budget cycle became a time for reappraisal of the SIGINT system, and the Cassandras predicted the "demise of HF." A 1978 study articulated the perception: "The very term 'HF' seems to carry with it a connotation of antiquity and of old age, of something not very much used anymore and not of much importance. . . . Newer systems are available, and they are used extensively [censored]

The HF Studies

NSA did four major studies of the HF system in the 1970s, and each came to the same conclusion. [censored]

[censored]

When Inman arrived in 1977, he was confronted with a system in a state of partial change. Pushed by the Clements cuts, NSA had thrown its lot in with HF remoting as a principal solution to the money problem. But the grand system envisioned during the early years of Lew Allen had been contorted by events and further budget cuts till it scarcely resembled the design of its creators.

[censored]

The whole problem was made worse by strict DoD accounting requirements that demanded that costs be amortized within a rigid time schedule. This meant, in practice, that the proposal had to show quick manpower reductions. Remoting was a very expensive proposition, and NSA found many options foreclosed by the need to recoup costs in a short period of time.

Inman Comes In

On arriving at NSA in July 1977, one of the new director's first actions was to get involved in HF planning. Writing to the ongoing [censored] study group, he turned all the rules on their heads. Henceforth, the main objectives would not be to save money, but to improve timeliness and maximize target coverage. "In this regard," Inman wrote, "manpower is not our principal concern. We will not justify programs solely on people savings." In one sentence, he had revolutionized the process and redirected the committee.

Inman viewed the exercise with new eyes. He understood the planning options as a modernization of the system to improve the product. Modernization could come in many forms, remoting being only one of them (and the most expensive option in the shortrun). Planning would consider people factors, including the desirability of the location selected for the people who would have to staff the systems. The study group would have to consider the military and civilian mix, recruitment, career progression, cost of living, and other factors that had not before been part of the equation. Site selection and staffing would not be a function of SCA-proprietary aims.

[censored]

[censored] The authors still wrote breathlessly about constructing a single grand Central Collection Operations Facility, with major target centers, centralized systems management, and problem centers. It produced little original thinking.

By 1978, under the influence of Inman, this had all changed. The director told the group to begin a station-by-station evaluation of options, all the way from no change through site modernization, partial remoting, or full remoting. For each station the group must develop three options: preferred, practical, and minimally acceptable. Target improvement would be the driving force, while manpower requirements would be just one of several considerations. The panel must consider support to military operations and would have to complete a ranking of site tenure based on geopolitical factors. The SCAs would be pulled into the process so that NSA would have their inputs up front.

[censored]

When the panel looked at individual sites, the obsolescence became palpable. The R-390 was still the workhorse receiver, but it had become so old (the first models went to the field in the late 1950s) that the internal parts had become worn, and it could no longer be accurately frequency calibrated. Its vacuum tubes caused heat buildup, causing instability and receiver drift (not to mention air conditioning problems in tropical climes).

Operators were still using what amounted to electronic typewriters (in an IATS configuration), despite the increasing prevalence of personal computers that could reduce the workload and increase the accuracy of the copy. They were still searching for targets manually, even while automated frequency scanning and signal recognition equipment was available. Operations in an HF collection site closely resembled those of thirty years before. The committee concluded that "the operator positions are the key to the collection/field processing problem area. . . . To obtain any degree of improvement to both quality and timeliness, the operator positions must be modernized first."

Other equipment was in a similar state. Tape recorders, though possessing new labels, were still products of post-World War II technology. Reporting was a manpower-intensive exercise with a long paper trail and little automation. Much of the equipment on the operations floors was tube technology, and even much of the semiconductor equipment had germanium transistors which were impossible to repair or replace. In the communications area, NSA was still using versions of the Teletype Corporation Model 28, an ancient, clattering, wheezing machine that reminded one of World War II IBM card equipment. Teletype had stopped producing them, and cannibalization was the only solution to repair problems.

Outside the operations building, many sites were still surrounded by rhombic antenna fields. Highly accurate in their day, they had long been outmoded by CDAA technology, and the group concluded that every rhombic antenna field should be pulled down.

The committee decided that the R-390 must be replaced with a solid state, digitally tuned receiver. Field sites must have automated signals acquisition systems and be upgraded with banded signals processors being planned under the BSU project. There was a need for improved reports generation and transmission systems. Collection positions must have the capability to automatically extract and log data in machine format.

[censored]

[censored] Following Inman's guidance, the program was not justified on the basis of manpower savings, and it did not contain the complex amortization schedules of previous plans. The justification, simply, was a more effective cryptologic system.

Kunia

One of Inman's planning guidelines was to consider personnel factors in shaping the system. He was concerned about the prospect of moving large numbers of military people to the high-cost Washington area. His thinkin may have been influenced by clamorous SCA protests over the looming centralization at Fort Meade. Only weeks before Inman became director, USAFSS had proposed that NSA consider alternative locations for the remote operation facility (ROF). Perhaps two locations would be better—a primary ROF and an alternate (ALTROF), to enhance survivability (and incidentally to answer fears of a tour in the Washington area).

The modernization panel estimated that about 3,000 people would be needed for the ROF under Alternative 2. Before they recommended a location, they surveyed both the military and civilian populations. The idea of actually assessing the reaction of the work force before acting reversed the selection process used in 1951 to decide on the Fort Meade location. Then, a virtual revolt by the civilian component doomed the original selection, Fort Knox.

Military attitudes toward duty at Fort Meade were unambiguous. They opposed it. The panel summarized in a single sentence the prevailing mood: "Many SCA enlisted members, who find job satisfaction high and Service life to their liking in the field, reflect a marked apprehension toward life at NSA/CSS." Topping the list of negatives was the cost of living, which was significant for enlisted members who would be dragged home from overseas. But this was by no means the sum of it. They objected to being submerged in a civilian-dominant organization offering lower status and fewer managerial opportunities. Many SCA officers feared that closeness to NSA would mean loss of service associations. And a tour at Fort Meade was not regarded as good for anyone's career. It was too far off the path to military advancement, and for enlisted collectors, analysts, and linguists, it represented a loss of skill proficiency. Not doing their primary job much of the time (that is, field site-peculiar jobs) would mean slipping down the proficiency ladder and, ultimately, slower promotions. The study revealed that of the 300 people certified in the collection field from 1967 to 1978, only twenty-nine had been military.

As if this were not enough, a severe space crunch at Fort Meade virtually sealed the fate of NSA as the location for most of the 3,000 people who would have to be added to the population. Alternative 2 would require 161,000 more square feet, and the committee noted the reluctance of Congress to approve military construction money for the National Capital Area.

The USAFSS study of the previous year had turned up an interesting proposal. When NSA had tasked USAFSS with identifying locations for an ALTROF, PACOM had suggested that NSA look at Kunia, an underground command and control facility that had fallen into disuse. The Navy proposed to get rid of it, and PACOM hoped to find a buyer. Perhaps the NSA ALTROF would be just the thing. Inman liked the idea, and requested that the panel consider establishing a major collection and analysis facility [censored] at Kunia.

The committee considered three options for an ALTROF: Kunia; Goodfellow AFB, Texas; and Fort Monmouth, New Jersey. Of the three, Fort Monmouth was quickly discarded as a possibility. It received only about a one-third approval rating from both civilian and military survey participants, while its negatives were commensurately high. The post was shabby, military housing and barracks would need-significant upgrades to meet NSA's more exacting standards, and its civilian facilities were regarded as entirely too close to the high crime New York-New Jersey megalopolis. In cost it ranked below Fort Meade and Hawaii, but above Texas. More than $20 million in military construction would be required.

Goodfellow ranked lowest in cost of living and was well liked by the military. But civilians did not want to move to West Texas—this was almost the Fort Knox option replayed. Moreover, military construction costs would be the highest of the three options: over $22 million.

Despite being in the highest cost area, Kunia proved the most popular choice by far—almost three-quarters of the survey participants wanted that option. For the military, available base housing would insulate them against financial crises, and for the civilians, the Hawaiian lifestyle was viewed as worth the cost. It had the lowest negatives in the survey—only 10 percent. For NSA, Kunia represented by far the cheapest alternative—only [censored] million to convert what were almost ready-made facilities. In sum Kunia offered:

International gold flow avoidance

A U.S. rotational base

Proximity to CINCPAC

[censored]

[censored]

[censored] This would involve a large shift of NSA civilians, as well as SCA military bodies. Kunia would be a triservice operation, with Army as host (since it was on Army land). It was a visionary restructuring of the [censored] collection problem.

Kunia was an enormous three-story bunker of 248,000 square feet, located under a thirty-four-acre pineapple field in central Oahu. It was at historic Schofield Barracks, which was a setting for James Jones's novel From Here to Eternity. Its construction was almost an accident of history. In the days following the Japanese attack on Pearl Harbor, the War Department, fearing a second attack, set out to build a hardened underground facility on Oahu for the construction of folded-wing fighter aircraft. The Army Corps of Engineers designed and built a large factory with four-foot-thick reinforced concrete walls and ceiling, covered with, and hidden by, the pineapple field. There were no interior walls; the ceiling was supported by load-bearing columns. But facilities such as that take time in the building, and it was not finished until 1944. By then the Japanese carrier fleet was virtually destroyed, and an air attack was no longer feared. Fighters were being built at Ford's Island, and the facility at Kunia was never used for the purpose intended.

At the end of the war, the Army Air Corps owned the underground white elephant. Kunia was kept in reserve status until 1953, when it was turned over to the Navy, which turned it into a warehouse for the storage of ammunition and torpedoes. Finally, in the late 1950s the Navy converted it into an underground command and control facility for the Pacific Fleet. It was hardened for CBR (chemical, biological, and radiological) attack, including strengthening the already-formidable walls and constructing decontamination centers. It was during this period of Kunia's existence that the interior walls went up.

In 1976 the operations center was moved to another location, and Kunia was again up for bids. The General Services Administration requested that the Navy maintain the facility while they looked for a new occupant. It had been "on the market" for only a year when NSA first expressed interest.

[censored]

Kunia would consist of all three SCAs, each operating a completely separate field site. This would preserve service-unique command and control, and it represented a compromise in how to get the services to work together in close quarters.

Kunia also incorporated some unique operational concepts. From the beginning it was regarded as an extension of B2 [censored] For the first time, a field site would have on-line access to the B [censored] database, through remote terminals. Kunia would also have an interlocking relationship with [censored]

[censored]

Approval for a quick reaction program was announced in January 1980. An initial station would be up and running by the end of the year. In the QRC phase the Air Force agreed to rehab the third floor for triservice use. [censored] The people came partly from pipeline diversions from the now-shuttered BROF operation. Kunia was opened on schedule in December 1980.

Conventional Signals Upgrade

By 1980, "HF modernization" had become "conventional signals upgrade (CSU)." R6 designed a complete field site overhaul, based on the problems that had been surfaced in the HF modernization study groups. The bedrock of the new system would be personal computers on position. According to the R6 design, "Modernization of site SIGINT systems is virtually synonymous with computerization of them." And modernization was not restricted to HF field sites—all existing conventional sites were included in the upgrades.

The revamping would begin with the microprocessor to be integrated into each position. Recognizing that it took at least five years to field a system, but that microprocessors had a half-life of months, R6 decided, logically enough, to specify computer standards—actual system selection would take place at the time of the buy, which would be off-the-shelf commercial products.

As for HF receivers, the R390 was out, and the Racal 6790 digital receiver was in. Automated signals acquisition equipment would be integrated into the collection systems. Everything would be modernized based on microprocessor technology—mission management, special identification techniques, signal recording, processing and reporting. As for Morse collection, NSA continued to pursue the holy grail of an automatic Morse translator, without much success.

Conventional signals upgrade quietly integrated a parallel project into its design. Bauded signals subsystems [censored] appeared as part of the new equipment mix. It was a logical marriage of the conventional signals system with a decidedly unconventional project.

Bauded Signals Upgrade

[censored]

[censored]

The Perry Study

In 1976, NSA brought together the highest powered group ever to study the cryptanalytic process. Chaired by future Secretary of Defense Dr. William Perry, it included many of the finest minds in post-World War II cryptology (see Table 16). After a thorough assessment of the state of the art, the Perry Committee issued a report that was a shocker, even considering the prevailing optimism of the time.

"During World War II, the U.S. and the U.K. achieved spectacular success in cryptanalysis which had a profound impact on the execution of the war. We stand today on the threshold of a cryptanalytic success of comparable magnitude. . . . No one can guarantee that we will 'break' any specific machine of the new generation, but we do not see the problem as being more difficult—relatively speaking—than the one posed [censored] thirty-seven years ago by ENIGMA."

[censored]

(U) Table 16
The Perry Committee [60]

Dr. William Perry, Chairman	President, ESL Incorporated
Mr. Edward L. Glaser	Systems Development Corporation
Mr. Arthur H. Hausman	President, Ampex Corporation
Mr. Oliver R. Kirby	Vice President for Operations, E Systems
Mr. Arthur J. Levenson	Retired Chief of A Group
Dr. John Martin	Acting Assistant to Secretary of the Air Force for Research and Development
Dr. Lloyd R. Welch	Department of Electrical Engineering, University of Southern California

Cryptanalytic resources had not kept pace with these developments. [censored] The solution, of course, was more resources. Perry recommended the NSA stoke the resource box up to the level that had preceded the Vietnam War. He also requested more collection, more computers, and the purchase of a Cray I for long-term cryptanalysis. [censored]

[censored]

The Wagner Study

The homework on the [censored] problem culminated in 1978 in a report issued by a panel chaired by Marlin Wagner, an R Group engineer. By this time yet a new prospect loomed. [censored]

[censored]

Bauded Signals Upgrade—the Project

The Wagner study drove NSA into a revolutionary development program, which became known simply as Bauded Signals Upgrade (BSU). The principle, as articulated by James Boone, NSA's deputy director for research, was "plan for success." Rather than await a breakthrough and then be faced with the time-consuming planning, design, and acquisition process [censored] assume success and begin development immediately. Boone briefed the idea to Inman, who bought it.

Inman decided to place the project outside the regular chain of command, and he created a project management office. However, to retain operational security, it looked like just another division, R84. The new chief, John P (Jack) Devine, did not report to the chief of R8 [censored] he answered to James Boone, chief of R, and, on many matters, directly to Inman.

The new office started very small—with just three people—but it got bigger, [censored] Devine brought in strong DDO representation—his deputy was [censored] from the cryptanalysis world, and the next person hired was [censored] from DDO. Devine established a close link with CSU, which was headed by [censored] in R6. The interplay between the two was an important aspect of the entire program.

BSU had more push behind it than any program in NSA's history. Inman concluded that the project could not be funded within the existing budget—what was needed was a supplemental allocation. He secured the funding [censored] dollars by going to see Secretary of Defense Harold Brown and explaining the potential. Brown got the money and spread it out through the DoD budget so that it did not appear in the CCP. He informed the president and the DCI.

Inman's personal involvement was critical to its success. He personally chaired the formative meetings and approved all resources requests himself. At one point he asked Devine how he would spend [censored]

Security was a nightmare for such a large project. BSU grew so big that Devine eventually had to bring some of the staff members of the two intelligence committees into the picture, [censored] The SCAs needed to be brought in, and Devine suggested that each provide a representative to the PMO. (ESC and NSG did; INSCOM did not). But the SCA command structure was not told the whole story, to minimize the number of people who knew the core secret.

[censored]

So was it money down the drain? Devine himself estimated that only 5 percent of the total, that which was used to purchase certain special-purpose processors, was wasted. The rest was used to modernize a system that was turned to other collection and exploitation tasks, now fully modernized to attack the most modern communications. The digitization, the remoting, the diagnostic systems, all proved a lifesaver for the cryptologic system and served it well through the end of the Cold War and beyond. As for management, most observers felt that BSU was the best-managed project in NSA's history. Still, it was technically true that, in the words of one NSA senior official, "The operation was successful, but the patient died."

The Third World Situation

In 1979 Inman appointed a panel to assess G Group cryptanalysis. Chaired by Arthur Housman, president of Ampex Corporation, it contained many of the same people who had comprised the Perry Committee. Their conclusion: G Group cryptanalysis was at an all-time peak.

[censored]

Hausman's panel saw troubling trends that threatened this remarkable record. Overall cryptanalytic resources had declined over the years, and many important cryptanalysts had retired without effective replacement. [censored] and an infusion of cash would be needed to move into the next decade. [censored] Public cryptography was already producing technology that had been available only to the specialist in past decades. [censored]

NSA relied too heavily on commercial organizations for the acquisition of sensitive cryptanalytic machines.

But help was on the way, in a project called [censored] The idea was to develop a special-purpose device [censored] Its application would be so wide that it would be a quasi-general-purpose machine. [censored]

The Peace Treaty With CIA

When Admiral Inman became the director in 1977, NSA and CIA had operated parallel, and in some cases rival, SIGINT systems for a quarter of a century. Jurisdictional disputes had been acrimonious at times, the most serious occurring in the late 1950s between Canine (NSA) and Dulles (CIA). After that, a period of relative peace settled in. Major disputes, [censored] were resolved by uneasy compromises and activities nosed over into partial quiescence. In large measure this "era of good feeling" was a product of the diplomatic skill of Louis Tordella, whose term as deputy director spanned the entire time (1958-1974). Veterans of battles with CIA seemed content to let the relationship stabilize, but a generation of "young turks" at NSA was determined to renew the battles and gain more ground for NSA.

[censored]

[censored]

An outsider looking at the jury-rigged SIGINT system of the federal government might have suspected insanity. Rather, it appears to have been a product of opportunity. As one CIA wag observed, it resulted from the "first agency" rule—that is, "the first agency to get there gets the mission." House Appropriations Committee investigators also noted a cultural gulf between the urbane and worldly-wise CIA and the technologically focused NSA. CIA had been established to be small and flexible and relied heavily on covert funds for which they owed no effective accounting. Thus Langley could react very quickly to developing events, moving into hot spots with covert collection and expanding intelligence relationships with the countries affected. NSA was encumbered by restrictions laid down by Congress on all DoD activities. The cultural differences had a profound effect on the way things operated. Noted a HAC staffer in 1976, "While NSA is bureaucratic . . ., CIA is very autocratic. It has not felt a need to explain to outsiders what it is doing." This attitude did not stand CIA in good stead when, in 1976, it had to explain why it was operating a parallel SIGINT system.

[censored]

The HAC Investigation and the Negotiation of a Peace Treaty

The matter of cryptologic integration had bumped along for years with patched together compromises—an issue here, an issue there. It appeared doomed to more of the same over a longer period of time until, in the spring of 1976, it was brought to a head and, in a single swift stroke, resolved in favor of NSA. This happened in the unlikely forum of the House Appropriations Committee.

The HAC had been looking at the intelligence budget where, it appeared, major economies could be achieved by consolidating NSA and CIA SIGINT operations. The staff chief, Charles Snodgrass, had little experience in intelligence—his expertise was agriculture. Butin 1976 he was taking great interest in intelligence, and he seemed to harbor a visceral distrust of CIA.

In the very early spring of 1976, Snodgrass interrogated both agencies and at the end of the process issued a report that was devastating to CIA interests. Contending that money could be saved by placing NSA in charge of both SIGINT organizations, he rejected every explanation and contention to the contrary that Langley advanced. [censored] "In regard to the overall question as to whether the CIA SIGINT activities should be transferred to NSA, the Investigative Staff is not impressed with the answers given by the DCI. . . ." Regarding NSA as a perceived military organization, Snodgrass pointed to [censored] places where NSA civilians were doing the job.

[censored]

The HAC report, issued in April, demanded consolidation of SIGINT programs into a single entity within NSA's national SIGINT program. Only a few exceptions appeared to Snodgrass to be worthy of consideration, [censored] The two agencies answered the report separately, implying serious disagreement. For NSA, Lew Allen was willing to accept most CIA SIGINT operations under the NSA umbrella, but he suggested that certain ones, [censored] remain under Langley control (but under the national SIGINT system). On the extremely contentious [censored] issues, he proposed leaving them under CIA supervision but increasing NSA representation and operational control.

At Langley they stalled, hoping somehow that Snodgrass would go away. George Bush was the DCI, and his instructions to his staff were vague and vacillating—clearly CIA thought that they could muddle out a compromise, as in years past. Allen's boss, Deputy Secretary of Defense Robert Ellsworth, sensed a kill, and pressed home the point. At Defense, they were not going to let the moment slip away.

The result was the Knoche-Allen letter of January 17, 1977. (Henry Knoche, Bush's deputy, was effectively running CIA, as the Carter people had made it known that they regarded Bush as too political and did not intend to let him stay on.) This short, seven-page document set up the basis for a resolution. It drew CIA SIGINT assets firmly into the national SIGINT system run by NSA. [censored] Much of the funding would roll over to the CCP.

But the Knoche-Allen letter did not bring all the issues to closure. [censored] And in each instance where the two sides could not agree, the DCI would decide. The DCI was hardly passive on these issues. And that was where the matter stood when Admiral Bobby Inman became DIRNSA in July of 1977.

[censored]

The Peace Treaty

The "Peace Treaty, [censored] was signed by the two agencies on August 26, 1977. Much of the language related to rather dull aspects of how programs were to be managed and funding to be apportioned, but the central principle was that all SIGINT assets would, with rare exceptions, be centrally managed by NSA. Third Party programs were meticulously worked out country by country [censored]

The formulation of the Peace Treaty resulted from a unique set of circumstances. But for the advent of Charles Snodgrass in the House Appropriations Committee investigative staff, it could hardly have gotten started. And even then, it could have run aground but for the timely ascension of Admiral Bobby Inman at NSA. The Peace Treaty owed much to his negotiating savvy and political connections. He cultivated Snodgrass, other key congressional figures, and contacts within the National Security Council. His connections were unassailable, and behind his negotiating strategy was always the mailed fist of White House or congressional intervention—once again, on the side of NSA.

The Peace Treaty brought an end to much of the sniping that had been going on between the two agencies since their birth. In NSA's view it was vindication; from CIA's standpoint it was surrender on the SIGINT front. A memo from two NSC staffers to Brzezinski called it a good working arrangement whose effects would be beneficial only if the two agencies cooperated on its implementation. The transition to the new arrangement was in fact painful and bumpy. [censored] The working out depended on the good will of both sides, rather than on a piece of paper. As the years moved, the long-term benefits became clearer, but even in 1977 the light could be seen at the end of the tunnel.

Public Cryptography

Modern cryptography has, since its earliest days, been associated with governments. Amateurs there were, like Edgar Allan Poe, who dabbled in the art, and it has held a certain public fascination from the earliest days. But the discipline requires resources, and only governments could marshal the resources necessary to do the job seriously. By the end of World War II, American cryptology had become inextricably intertwined with the Army and Navy's codebreaking efforts at Arlington Hall and Nebraska Avenue. But this picture would begin changing soon after the war.

Modern public cryptography originated with a Bell Laboratories scientist, Claude Shannon, whose mathematics research led him to develop a new branch of mathematics called information theory. A 1948 paper by Shannon brought the new discipline into the public domain, and from that time on, cryptography became a recognized academic pursuit.

Public cryptography had no market in those days. So when IBM researcher Horst Feistel developed a line of key generators to be embedded in IBM computers, called Lucifer, there was no immediate use for it. But in

1971 Lloyd's Bank of London contacted IBM to ask about the possibility of securing transactions from a cash dispensing terminal. Feistal sent Lucifer to Lloyd's. IBM then formed a group, headed by Walter Tuchman, to develop the idea of encrypting banking transactions.

While IBM was developing a market for public cryptography, computers were becoming more common within the government. The 1965 Brooks Act gave the National Bureau of Standards (NBS) authority to establish standards for the purchase and use of computers by the federal government. Three years later, Dr. Ruth Davis at NBS began to look into the issue of encrypting government computer transactions and concluded that it was necessary to develop a government-wide encryption standard. She went to NSA for help. NBS, it was decided, would use the Federal Register to solicit the commercial sector for an encryption algorithm. NSA would evaluate the quality, and if nothing acceptable appeared, would devise one itself.

In 1973 NBS solicited private industry for a data encryption standard (DES). The first offerings were disappointing, so NSA began working on its own algorithm. Then Howard Rosenblum, deputy director for research and engineering, discovered that Walter Tuchman of IBM was working on a modification to Lucifer for general use. NSA gave Tuchman a clearance and brought him in to work jointly with the Agency on his Lucifer modification.

The decision to get involved with NBS was hardly unanimous. [censored] This argued the opposite case—that, as Frank Rowlett had contended since World War II, in the long run it was more important to secure one's own communications than to exploit those of the enemy.

Once that decision had been made, the debate turned to the issue of minimizing the damage. Narrowing the encryption problem to a single, influential algorithm might drive out competitors, and that would reduce the field that NSA had to be concerned about. [censored] they compromised on a 56-bit key.

The relationship between NSA and NBS was very close. NSA scientists working the problem crossed back and forth between the two agencies, and NSA unquestionably exercised an influential role in the algorithm. Thus, when DES became official in July 1977, a debate erupted in the academic community over the security of the standard. Scientists charged that NSA had secretly pressured NBS into adopting a nonsecure algorithm. Not only did they contend that the key length was to NSA's liking, they also alleged that the Agency had built a "trap door" into the system that would allow cryptographers at Fort Meade to read it at will. In 1976 David Kahn, the leading non-governmental authority on cryptography, lent academic support to this view. Kahn's allegations were repeated by writers and scientists worldwide. The issue became so charged that a Senate committee in 1977 looked into the allegations. The hearings resulted in a "clean bill of health" for NSA, but it hardly quieted the academic uproar.

To calm the waters, NBS called a conference in August 1976. It solved nothing. Leading academic figures contended that the DES algorithm was so weak that it could be solved with fairly modest resources (on the order of $9 million), while defenders pronounced it secure against virtually any attack feasible at the time. National Bureau of Standards ultimately promised that the DES algorithm would be reevaluated every five years.

The problem was, in large part, one of timing. During the Church and Pike Committee hearings, NSA had been tarred with the same brush that smeared CIA and FBI, and the exculpatory conclusions of the Church Committee were lost in a sea of fine print. What the public remembered were the sensational allegations of journalist Tad Szulch [censored] Whether NSA was an apolitical collector of foreign intelligence information or truly a governmental "Big Brother" had not yet been adjudicated in the public mind. The concern for individual privacy, largely an outgrowth of the Watergate period, exercised an important sway on the American public, and even Walter Mondale, with years of experience watching over intelligence agencies from his Senate perch, was consumed by this issue when he was Carter's vice president. Any endeavor that would make NSA out as an inspector of private American communications would play negatively. The DES controversy was one of those issues.

In 1976 a related chain of events began which was to flow together with the DES controversy. In that year Martin Hellman of Stanford, one of the world's leading practitioners of the cryptographic arts, and his graduate student, Whitfield Diffie, published "New Directions in Cryptography" in the November issue of *IEEE Transactions on Information Theory*. It contained the first public exposition of what was to become known as public key cryptography. In the Hellman-Diffie scheme, it would be possible for individual communicants to have their own private key and to communicate securely with others without a preset key. All that was necessary was to possess a publicly available key and a private key which could be unlocked only with permission. This revolutionary concept freed cryptography from the burdensome periodic exchange of key with a set list of correspondents and permitted anyone with the same equipment to communicate with complete privacy.

This was the public face of the issue. But like public key cryptography itself, it contained a private story that was much more complex. Hellman, it turned out, had been one of the leading opponents of DES, for the very reason that he distrusted NSA's hand in the algorithm. He had obtained a National Science Foundation (NSF) grant to work on the project. It turned out that there was no legal prohibition against a governmental entity funding private research into cryptography, despite the possibility that such research would break the governmental monopoly on leading edge techniques. And in fact, Hellman and Diffie [censored].

In April 1977 David Boak and Cecil Corry of NSA visited Dr. John Pasta, director of NSF's division of mathematical and computer research, to discuss the issue. Since the early 1970s there had been sporadic contact between NSA and NSF, and NSF had agreed to permit a certain amount of NSA "assistance" on these types of projects, but only to examine grant proposals on their technical merits rather than to institute a formal coordination process. Pasta, believing that academic freedom was at stake, held fast to the NSF position and refused to permit NSA to exercise any sort of control over future grants.

The difficulties with NSF did not end with the Hellman imbroglio. In 1977 Ronald Rivest of MIT published an NSF-funded paper expanding the public key cryptography idea. He postulated a method of exchanging public and private keys, protecting the private key based on the known fact that large integers are extremely difficult to factor. The new RSA technique (named after its inventors, Rivest, Shamir, and Adleman) depended on finding very large prime numbers, upwards of 100 digits long, a technique that was later adopted for STU-III key exchange. [censored] Since the technique had been jointly funded by NSF and the Office of Naval Research, NSA's new director, Admiral Bobby Inman, visited the director of ONR to secure a commitment that ONR would get NSA's coordination on all such future grant proposals.

[censored]

[censored]

NSA hunted diligently for a way to stop cryptography from going public. One proposal was to use the International Traffic in Arms Regulation (ITAR) to put a stop to the publication of cryptographic material. ITAR, a regulation based on the 1954 Mutual Security Act, was intended to control the export of items that might affect U.S. security by establishing a Munitions List, including SIGINT and COMSEC equipment and cryptographic devices. Companies desiring to export items on the list would have to secure licenses. Within NSA the controversy centered on the academic use of cryptography, absent a specific intention to export the techniques. The legislation granted general exemptions in cases where the information was published and publicly available, but skirted First Amendment issues and focusing on commercial motivations.

This idea was pushed internally by one Joseph A. Meyer, but was just one of several techniques being considered. In July 1977, Meyer took matters into his own hands. The Institute of Electrical and Electronics Engineers would be holding a symposium on cryptography in Ithaca, New York. Concerned about the potential hemorrhage of cryptographic information, Meyer sent a letter to E. K. Gannet, staff secretary of the IEEE publications board, pointing out that cryptographic systems were covered by ITAR and contending that prior government approval would be necessary for the publication of many of the papers. The letter raised considerable commotion within IEEE, with scholars racing to secure legal opinions and wondering if the federal government might arrest them and impound the information.

The issue did not stop with IEEE. Someone notified the press, and journalist Deborah Shapley published the entire controversy in an issue of *Science* magezine. Although Meyer wrote the letter on plain bond paper, Shapley quickly discovered his association, and she claimed that NSA was harassing scientists and impeding research into public cryptography. In her view, the lack of direct traceability constituted smuggling NSA's official view covertly to academia, with plausible deniability. Congressional reaction was swift, and the Senate decided to hold hearings on the issues.

The Meyer letter was dispatched, recalled Inman ruefully, on virtually the same date that he became director. It presented him with his first public controversy, only days into his new administration.

Inman began cautiously enough with that all-purpose bureaucratic solution, the study committee. That fall and winter he had two groups, NSASAB and a committee of NSA seniors, looking at public cryptography and proposing options. To this extremely complex issue the board of seniors proposed three alternatives:

a. Do nothing. This school of thought, championed by G Group, held that any public discussion would heighten awareness of cryptographic problems and could lead to nations buying more secure crypto devices. This threat was especially acute in the Third World.

b. Seek new legislation to impose additional government controls.

c. Try nonlegislative means such as voluntary commercial and academic compliance.

[censored]

Inman first chose the legislative solution. Daniel Silver, the head of NSA's legal team, circulated a draft of a new Cryptologic Information Protection Act. This proposed creating a new entity, the U.S. Cryptologic Board, which could restrict dissemination of sensitive cryptologic material for up to five years and would impose severe penalties (five years in prison, a $10,000 fine) for violation.

But Inman himself recognized the unlikelihood of getting Congress to act. NSA's proposed legislation would run against a strong movement in the opposite direction in both Congress and the White House, where the desire was to unshackle U.S. commerce from any sort of Pentagon-imposed restriction on trade. Even as the NSA seniors were recommending strengthening NSA's control over cryptography, President Carter was signing PD-24. This presidential directive divided cryptography in half. "National security cryptography," that which pertained to the protection of classified and unclassified information relating to national defense, would remain with NSA. But the directive also defined another sort of issue, "national interest" cryptography, which pertained to unclassified information which it was desirable to protect for other reasons (international currency exchange information, for instance). Protecting this type of information and dealing with the private sector on such protection (for instance, on DES), would become part of the domain of the Commerce

Department. The National Telecommunications and Information Administration (NTIA), within Commerce, would be responsible for dealing with the public; NTIA moved promptly to assert its authority in the area of cryptographic export policy and to deal with academia over cryptography. NSA mounted strong opposition to both moves.

Daniel Silver's draft legislation was basically dead on arrival, and there is no evidence that it was ever seriously considered. But the war between NSA and Commerce was only beginning. Congressman L. Richardson Preyer, who had taken over Bella Abzug's House Subcommittee on Government Information and Individual Rights, led a series of hearings on NSA's "interference" in academia. Preyer worked under the direction of Congressman Jack Brooks, chairman of the full House Government Operations Committee, who was the most vocal sponsor of Commerce's encroachment on NSA's COMSEC turf. Bolstered by the testimony of David Kahn and George Davida, he was predictably critical of NSA's role in public cryptography. Inman, upset with the draft subcommittee report, went to Congressman Edward Boland, who chaired the HPSCI. Boland, agreeing with Inman's complaint, told Brooks that future matters of this sort, which affected national security and intelligence operations, should be coordinated in advance with his committee. This did not end the sniping between NSA and Brooks, but did give the Agency a powerful ally.

Within the administration it was guerrilla warfare. The Carter people came to town temperamentally allied with Brooks and Preyer. Their bent was to loosen Pentagon control of anything, especially anything that might affect individual rights and academic freedom. But Inman was a tough infighter and got the Department of Defense to line up behind NSA's position in opposition to NTIA. Through four years of Carter, the matter dogged the White House and frustrated compromise between the Commerce position and the Pentagon determination to gain back its authority. By the time Dr. Frank Press, Carter's adviser on technology policy, was ready to adjudicate the dispute, the 1980 elections were upon the administration, and the solution was deferred to the incoming Reagan people. In the meantime, Inman had succeeded in dividing Congress and securing allies in the fight.

Inman was convinced from the start that the legislative approach, even if successful, would have to be supplemented by some sort of jawboning with academia. Early in his administration, he decided to visit Berkeley, a center of opposition to any sort of government intervention, and a hotbed of raw suspicion since the early days of the Vietnam War. He found himself in a room with antiestablishment faculty members, and "for an hour it was a dialogue of the deaf." Then the vice chancellor of the University of California, Michael Heyman, spoke up. Just suppose, he said, the admiral is telling the truth and that national security is being jeopardized. How would you address the issue? Instantly the atmosphere changed, and the two sides (Inman on one side, the entire faculty on the other) began a rational discussion of compromises. This convinced him that he was on the right track, and he pursued this opening to the public.

Inman followed this with a visit to Richard Atkinson, head of the National Science Foundation, to discuss the ideas that had emerged at Berkeley. The faculty had expressed a desire to get an "honest broker," one that both sides trusted, to sort through the issues and get to a compromise. Atkinson suggested that they approach the American Council on Education (ACE), and agreed that if ACE would agree to sponsor the effort, the National Science Foundation would fund it.

This presented NSA with a historic opportunity to engage in a rational debate with the private sector, and it drove Inman to bring the issue to the attention of the American public. His forum was the annual meeting of the Armed Forces Communications Electronics Association in January 1979. It was the first public speech by an NSA director, and as Inman said at the outset, it was "a significant break with NSA tradition and policy." He then laid out the conflicting interests—academic freedom versus national security. He advocated a problem-solving dialogue, but also acknowledged that the government might on occasion have to impose restrictions on extremely sensitive technology to protect national security. "I believe that there are serious dangers to our broad national interests associated with uncontrolled dissemination of cryptologic information within the United States. It should be obvious that the National Security Agency would not continue to be in the signals intelligence business if it did not at least occasionally enjoy some cryptanalytic successes." On the other hand, the govemment might have to permit the free exchange of technology, taking action in only the most difficult cases. The important thing, he stressed, was to talk through these issues so that both sides understood what was at stake and could appreciate the position of the other side. And he articulated the long-range importance of the problem: "Ultimately these concerns are not those merely of a single government agency, NSA. They are of vital interest to every citizen of the United States, since they bear vitally on our national defense and the successful conduct of our foreign policy."

The public opening was followed by a series of meetings, sponsored by ACE, to devise a forum to begin the dialogue. Some members (most notedly George Davida) held out for a complete absence of any controls on academia, but the majority concluded that controls would be necessary when national security was involved. What emerged was a procedure for prior restraint, involving a board of five members, a minority of whom would be from NSA, to review publication proposals. Submissions would be voluntary, and the area of examination would be very limited. The proposal passed with the unlikely Yes vote of Martin Hellman, who had earlier been subjected to some private jawboning by Inman. He, along with others in academia, had come to believe that there was, indeed, a legitimate national security interest in what they were doing.

Prepublication review turned out to be less of a real than an imagined threat to First Amendment freedoms. The committee requested very few changes to proposals, and most of those were easily accomplished. In one case, NSA actually aided in lifting a secrecy order placed on a patent application. The submitter, Shamir of RSA fame, thanked NSA for its intervention. At the same time, NSA established its own program to fund research proposals into cryptography. Martin Hellman was one of the first applicants.

As for DES, the controversy quieted for a period of years. DES chips were being manufactured by several firms and had become a profitable business. In 1987, NSA proposed a more sophisticated algorithm, but the banking community, the prime user of DES, had a good deal of money invested in it and asked that no modifications be made for the time. By the early 1990s it had become the most widely used encryption algorithm in the world. Though its export was restricted, it was known to be widely used outside the United States. According to a March 1994 study, there were some 1,952 products developed and distributed in thirty-three countries.

Chapter 20 The Foreign Policy Crises of the Carter Years

Late in his administration, Jimmy Carter was dogged by a series of foreign policy crises that ultimately led to his defeat in 1980. In all of those crises there was a cryptologic component.

The Iranian Revolution

[censored]

[censored]

At the beginning of the Carter presidency, White House advisor Samuel Huntington predicted that Iran was the most likely trouble spot for Americans. It was a lonely prediction, because there was little direct indication that the shah was in trouble or that Iran would descend from a developing Third World country with substantial oil resources into a medieval swamp.

The trouble began in mid-1978 and developed with frightening speed. By November a previously obscure radical cleric named Khomeini, in exile in Iraq, seemed to hold all the cards. By then, CIA, DIA, and the State Department were pessimistic about the shah's prospects for holding onto his throne. Indeed, the shah departed in January of 1979, and Khomeini swept into power. It was a breathtaking defeat for CIA, which had invested so much stock in the shah personally and in Iran as the pedestal of American presence in the Persian Gulf region.

[censored]

[censored]

The Carter presidency became hammerlocked over the hostage crisis and remained so until the very hour that Carter turned the White House over to Ronald Reagan. Brzezinksi, always a hardliner on foreign affairs, began planning for a hostage rescue attempt the day after the second embassy takeover. He received little encouragement from Carter, who didn't believe in force to settle matters, but continued to direct a Pentagon response which envisioned some sort of forcible recapture operation. The DCI, Admiral Turner, participated in the early planning, but security was very tight, and neither NSA nor DIA was informed.

[censored]

Carter remained committed to diplomatic efforts through February 1980. Through intermediaries the State Department was in touch with Iranian president Bani-Sadr, who agreed to work a face-saving compromise that would get the hostages out. This fell through when Khomeini discovered the scheme, and the president felt the last hope was gone. He turned to the Pentagon, which had been refining its scheme for three months. The JCS plan was to fly eight helicopters from the USS *Nimitz,* anchored in the Gulf of Oman, to a secret staging base in southern Iran, where they would meet six C-130 transports carrying ninety members of the rescue team plus fuel and supplies. The transports would return [censored] while the choppers would continue on to another secret base outside Tehran. The next night trucks purchased by an American agent in Tehran would carry the team into the city. Once they got the hostages, they would all be retrieved by the helicopters, which would ferry them back to the secret base, where they would be met and placed aboard C-141 transports for the trip out of Iran.

[censored]

Admiral Turner at CIA had setup the intelligence support to the White House, a flow which excluded NSA from direct participation. [censored] This state of affairs produced the by-then inevitable sword play between the two admirals and contributed yet another stone to the wall being built between Turner and Inman.

[censored]

[censored]

The Soviet Invasion Of Afghanistan

The takeover of the U.S. embassy in Tehran in November 1979 set the Middle East ablaze. Inspired by the radical Islamic movement in Iran, radicals stormed the Grand Mosque in Mecca, only to be put down with great violence by the conservative Saudi regime. Reacting to rumors that it was really the "wicked Americans" who were behind the troubles in Saudi Arabia, American facilities in Pakistan, including the U.S. embassy in Islamabad, were mobbed. A few weeks later, following more troubles for the United States elsewhere in the Middle East, the American embassy in Libya was attacked. For a time it seemed that the entire region would come apart.

The Carter administration, already immobilized by the hostage drama in Tehran, feared that the destruction of the political status quo could be an opening wedge for Soviet ambitions, which seemed boundless at the time. The Persian Gulf, now lacking the stabilizing pro-American force of the shah, could succumb. This fear was heightened by a series of Soviet military exercises which had as their objective a postulated invasion of Iran and a march to the Gulf.

The president responded with a State of the Union Address in January of 1979 that did not sound like the old Jimmy Carter. "Let our position be absolutely clear. . . . An attempt by any outside force to gain control of the Persian Gulf region will be regarded as an assault on the vital interests of the United States of America, and such an assault will be repelled by any means necessary, including military force." He followed this Carter Doctrine with a request for a 5 percent increase in military spending and a proposal that all men eighteen to twenty-six be required to register for a future draft. He began an expansion of U.S. military presence in the Gulf, and announced that the U.S. would not participate the next year in the Moscow Olympic Games.

Afghanistan did not become important on the world stage until, in the latter half of the nineteenth century, Russian expansion into Central Asia ran into British expansion in the Indian subcontinent. Following a series of small wars in which the British were spectacularly unsuccessful, Afghanistan became a buffer between the two larger powers. The British continued to muddle unhappily in Afghanistan's affairs through World War I, when the tables turned and the independent-minded Afghans began cozying up to the new Soviet government under Lenin. Had the Soviet Union fully understood how much trouble the British had had in Afghanistan, they might not have gotten involved.

As the United States moved into the area to try to replace British influence after World War II, the Soviet Union continued a more successful penetration from the north. In the 1960s a communist movement under Nur Mohammad Taraki and Babrak Karmal, sponsored by the Soviets, began to challenge the constitutional monarchy. In April 1978 a group of army officers carried out a well-planned, if bloody, coup in Kabul. The president, Mohammad Daoud, and his entire family were summarily executed, and Taraki became prime minister. His foreign minister, Hafizullah Amin, had played a key role in the military operation.

With influence built up through many years of aid to the Afghan government, the Soviets were in a strong position. In May they established a military assistance group, and by mid-year 2,700 Soviet military advisers were in country. Afghan air bases at Bagram, Shindand, and Kabul came under direct Soviet supervision. The Soviet Union announced that, in the event of a crisis (even an internal crisis), they would intervene. This was not an entirely hypothetical possibility. The Afghan regime under Taraki was absolutely riven by tribal-based factions, the most important of which were the Khalkist group under Taraki and the Parchemi faction under Babrak Karmal. Taraki had ousted Karmal, who was living in the Soviet Union and waiting for his turn. The Parchemis longed for power.

[censored] Internecine warfare between Khalkists and Parchemis grew worse through 1978. Early in 1979 anti-Taraki forces kidnapped ambassador Adolph Dubs, and in the ensuing ill-advised rescue attempt (supervised by the Soviets) Dubs was killed. In retaliation, President Carter reduced the American diplomatic presence and halted all U.S. aid.

Soviet contingency planning for an invasion probably began as early as 1978, but by March 1979 the urgency of the situation pushed them into hasty preparations. Soviet exercises in the spring took on the look of an invasion scenario. Top KGB officials met with Marshal Sergey Sokolov, first deputy minister of defense, on May 25 to discuss the route of march for an invasion.[censored]

[censored]

Soviet frustration with the Taraki government was growing. His deputy, Hafizullah Amin, was becoming increasingly autocratic, and Taraki was no longer in full control of the situation. Soviet concern was tipped off in June with a press announcement that General Pavlovskij, commander in chief of the Soviet Army, would visit Afghanistan in August. His visit lasted until October: As one journalist commented, "Pavlovskij stayed on in Afghanistan far longer than he had needed eleven years earlier to plan the invasion of Czechoslovakia."

The first crisis came on September 14, while Pavlovskij was still in country. At a meeting in Kabul arranged by the Soviets, at which Taraki supporters were to have ended the Amin threat, the opposite happened. There was a shootout between Amin and Taraki supporters. Amin's people came out on top; Amin arrested Taraki, and two days later Taraki's resignation was announced "for health reasons."

The White House was well aware of Soviet concern over the situation. Beginning on September 10, intelligence reports to the president, [censored] began to discuss the possibility that the Soviet Union might be forced to act. On September 15, the day after the shootout, CIA made its first prediction of Soviet intervention. This was, in fact, probably earlier than the Soviets themselves decided. Most probably they waited for the return of Pavlovskij to Moscow. In any case, the decision was probably made sometime in October.

Then the issue began to fade in Washington. The Iranian hostage crisis of early November pushed Afghanistan off center stage, and there appeared to be nothing especially dramatic happening in Kabul. But early December saw accelerated activity, [censored]

During the week prior to Christmas, Soviet forces continued to pour into staging bases in southern USSR, [censored] At this point, the CIA made a strong push at the White House for Presidential attention to Afghanistan. [censored]

[censored]

This time there was no "intelligence failure." The postmortems, which began at the White House level only days after the invasion, were unanimous in describing it as an intelligence success. Generalized warnings had begun in September, and specific warnings preceded the operation by at least ten days. The Soviets followed their own doctrine, and intelligence followed the Soviets every step of the way. [censored] There were no pictures of the invasion as it was happening—it was dark, and satellites could not photograph in darkness.

December of 1979 marked a high-water mark of sorts [censored] After years of struggle, it was now possible to predict with some clarity and speed the intentions of the major antagonist. It had been a long walk from Pearl Harbor.

The Sino-Vietnamese Dispute

With the United States out of Southeast Asia, the inhabitants of that area took to internecine disputes. Every country, it seemed, had a border dispute with its neighbors. One of the most serious was between Vietnam and Cambodia. Years of low-level conflict broke out in full-scale battle in December 1977. It did not take Vietnam long to decide that the only solution was to take over Cambodia and install a puppet government, and they accomplished this by ejecting the blood-stained forces of Pol Pot from the capital and placing their own man, Hun Sen, in power.

Vietnam was still supported economically and militarily by the Soviet Union, to neighboring China's great concern. The expansion of Vietnamese influence in Southeast Asia was thus a matter of considerable nervousness to the Chinese, and they openly supported Pol Pot, partly to insure a balance in the country. But there were other, peripheral, issues that went into the mix. The two countries were involved in a dispute over the ownership of some potentially oil-bearing islands in the South China Sea, and the Sino-Vietnamese border was still in dispute in places. Vietnam had a large ethnic Chinese population, whose treatment China regarded as falling within its area of concern. During 1978 Vietnam moved many Chinese out of population centers and into "new economic zones" to ease an economy in crisis, but China considered this to be discrimination.

China opened up a diplomatic war on Vietnam in the spring of 1978, portraying Vietnam as a Soviet Cuba in Southeast Asia. But diplomacy was getting them nowhere, and in the late summer they began planning for punitive military action. The movement of troops, begun in a very small way in late spring, moved forward in earnest in October. [censored] Chinese ground forces began moving from their garrisons in Kunming and were joined by other units from the central provinces of Wuhan and Chengdu, the Chinese Army's base area. By February 1979 the Chinese enioyed a numerical superiority of more than four to one over Vietnamese forces along the Sino-Vietnamese border.

The air defense posture, too, underwent considerable augmentation. The Chinese bolstered their tactical air strength along the border, the main increase coming after the first of the year. In all, they moved nearly 500 aircraft into the area, bringing their military aircraft total to about a four-to-one advantage. They coupled this with large-scale air exercise activity. The naval changes were slower and less dramatic, but had the same effect and, in the end, increased Chinese naval forces in the Gulf of Tonkin to record levels.

None of this was a secret, nor was it designed to be. Unlike the Soviets, the Chinese relied on well-publicized moves as part of their negotiating posture. [censored]

Just to insure that there was no mistake, Chinese premier Deng Tsao Ping, in his state visit to Washington in January 1979, told President Carter that they intended to "teach Vietnam a lesson." Carter's main concern, aside from wanting to resolve all international disputes peacefully, was about possible Soviet reactions. [censored]

The assault began early in the morning of February 17, and within a few days the Chinese had achieved their military objectives, which consisted of capturing several small border towns. But it was a much tougher fight than they had bargained for. Against the outmanned Vietnamese they took heavy casualties, and when Deng announced on March 5 that they would begin to withdraw, it was in the manner of declaring victory and going home. Their ground forces had taken a pounding, and they never even tried to match their air force against the more capable Vietnamese. [censored]

[censored] And every diplomatic tiff between the two countries was accompanied by Chinese threats to teach Vietnam a "second lesson." But the lesson never came—the Chinese were apparently not anxious to display further military weakness.

The Soviet Brigade In Cuba

Near the end of the Carter administration, one of the most bizarre episodes in American [censored] history occurred. It related to Soviet forces in Cuba and began with the Cuban Missile Crisis of 1962.

During the crisis the intelligence community believed that a Soviet ground combat unit was present near Santiago de las Vegas in Cuba. The matter came up in the context of the removal of the offensive missiles, and in early 1963 President Kennedy admitted publicly that some 17,000 Soviet troops were still on the island. Included in the number were four combat units totaling about 6,000 men. The Kennedy administration dropped the subject with the Soviets, and in February of 1964 CIA concluded, on the basis of photography, that most of the combat troops were gone and the bases transferred to Cubans. This seemed to end the issue.

But the issue refused to die. In the early 1970s intelligence (what type we are not informed) indicated that the Soviets still had about 2,000 troops in Cuba: 1,500 at the Lourdes SIGINT site and the rest at the MAG (military advisory group). [censored]

In November 1978 the Cuban issue suddenly got a boost. In that month intelligence discovered new MiG-23 aircraft in Cuba with a possible ground attack role. While the Community stewed about the possible meaning of this new information, it hit the press. The Carter administration was already becoming sensitized to the Cuban issue, as Cuban soldiers began appearing in Ethiopia and Angola. Journalists and amateur fanciers of international intrigue worked the issue to a frenzy, and in the spring of the following year the White House, at the instigation of an NSC staffer, Colonel William Odom, decided to do a full-scale study of the Cuban threat. Odom, a Brzezinski protege, frequently took a hard line on Soviet issues.

[censored]

The intelligence community might have continued to mull the issue for months, but time ran out. On July 11 Senator Richard Stone of Florida made a public announcement referring to a Soviet combat unit in Cuba. Stone evidently had inside information, [censored] Just a week later Stone sent a letter to the president stating that it appeared that "the Soviet Union was setting up a high-ranking command structure in Cuba."

[censored]

The matter made the rounds of the press corps, but it was the August recess, and not much could jar Washington during the summer doldrums. But then Senator Frank Church, who was engaged in a tough (and ultimately unsuccessful) reelection campaign, was briefed on the issue by a White House aide, and asked Secretary of State Cyrus Vance if he could go public with it. Vance realized that it would come out anyway and authorized Church to go with it.

Church's sensational press releases brought the argument to a boil in the Senate, and hardliners proclaimed that ratification of SALT II (which had been on the senatorial plate for the fall session) would be placed on hold. The administration, not wanting to seem less hardline than the Senate, bungled the issue by demanding withdrawal of the unit or a revision of its mission. Alarmed at the problems that the issue was causing for SALT ratification, Carter called a team of foreign policy experts dubbed the Wise Men.

The administration had been scrambling to review the history of the unit and by mid-September had concluded that it was probably a lineal descendant of the unit that had been at Santiago since the Missile Crisis. Somehow the intelligence community had lost track of it, and when it again appeared [censored] in 1976 it seemed to be a new thing. There was still some question concerning whether or not it had taken on a new and more aggressive-looking role, but the Wise Men advised Carter to simply ignore this and smooth the issue over. Otherwise it wouldjeopardize other, more important, foreign policy objectives.

Unfortunately, Carter could not leave well enough alone. His speech on October 1, while intended to return things to the status quo, did nothing of the kind. In it he announced that he was increasing surveillance of Cuba and strengthening American presence in the Caribbean. The disbelieving Soviets told the White House that the unit had always been there, that the issue was a phony one, and that they would make no changes. So the bellicose speeches of Carter and Vance achieved nothing.

A month was lost on SALT ratification, and the matter was still perking in the Senate when, on Christmas day 1979, the Soviets invaded Afghanistan. The ratification process came to an outraged halt and was never resumed. So this tempest in a teapot had real and undesirable consequences.

Admiral Turner predictably blamed NSA for the fiasco. He accused the Agency of grandstanding on the issue, by coming out with a product report declaring that there was a Soviet combat brigade in Cuba without previously sharing its secret with the rest of the intelligence community. NSA, he claimed, acted on SIGINT, with a little HUMINT and IMINT thrown in, when in fact the Agency was not supposed to draw such analytical conclusions. "When readers saw the designation 'combat', they imagined a unit preparing to move out of Cuba and go to war in Central America. . . . Because intelligence had never before reported a Soviet combat unit in Cuba, people assumed that the brigade had just arrived."

Turner's post-CIA autobiography took NSA seriously to task: "The NSA is mandated to collect intelligence, not to analyse it. . . . Processing is regularly stretched by the NSA into full-scale analysis. In this instance, the abuse of processing was flagrant. . . . The NSA's analysis is bound to be biased in the direction of what signals intercepts tell, and is less likely to take account of photographic or human intelligence. . . . A dangerous side effect of the NSA's regular transgression from processing into analysis is that it leads to deliberate withholding of raw information from the true analytic agencies. The NSA wants to get credit for the scoop. Even when the NSA does release information promptly, it is so digested that other analysts can't use it. . . . There is a fine line to be drawn here, but there is no question in my mind that the NSA regularly and deliberately draws that line to make itself look good rather than to protect secrets."

[censored]

The basic fault, aside from that of forgetting history, was in the political handling of an intelligence event. As with the Gulf of Tonkin crisis of 1964 and the Tet Offensive of 1968, the issue seems to have been mishandled at the top.

The Final Days

[censored]

The scene in the Oval Office that morning was best described by Zbigniew Brzezinski in his autobiography: "I found in the Oval Office a large group of people. The President, sitting behind the desk with the red phone in his hand [it was actually a STU-II] listening to direct intelligence reports pertaining to the two Algerian aircraft parked on the runways at Tehran airport, said to me, 'They have been ready to take off since 8:35'. Everybody is standing around or sitting. The Vice President on the sofa, Rosalynn coming in and out and looking consumed, (Presidential assistant Jack) Watson, Gary Sick, Muskie, Jordan, Phil Wise, Pat Caddell, Jody in and out, Cutler, Kirbo. . . . At 9:55 the President talked to the operator monitoring Tehran. No flight plan has been filed yet. Moreover, the Iranians apparently have asked the Algerians not to announce any departure until the plane is outside of Iranian airspace. . . . Until the very last minute the transfer of power and departure of the President is dominated by the Iranian affair. I went down to the Sit Room before leaving my office to monitor the latest developments from Iran. The plane as of 11:30 was still on the ground. It became clear that the Iranians were deliberately holding it up so that the transfer of the hostages would not occur while Jimmy Carter [was] President of the United States."

Chapter 21 The Reagan Revolution

Background

Nineteen-eighty marked more than just a change of decade. It was a change of mood. Some have called it the Reagan Revolution. Reagan, a forever optimistic actor from California, came to office with a world view in complete contrast with that of the 1970s. He was tired of talk about limitations, wanted none of the gloom that had settled over the White House in the late Carter years. He would restore America's power in the world. He would start by spending the nation back into prosperity.

When Gerald Ford left office, the national debt was $644 billion. When Jimmy Carter departed, it was $909 billion. When Ronald Reagan left office, it was more than 2 and one half trillion dollars. The severe gap between income and expenditures had a long-term impact on many areas of national life, not the least on the funding of defense programs.

It was Reagan's dual approach that created the problem. He would generate demand by cutting taxes, but, paradoxically, he would increase spending on national defense. This would leave a gap between revenues and expenditures that would be made up by cutting domestic programs. But domestic programs could not be cut that much, and a considerable portion of the national debt came from the funding of defense programs.

At the core of Reagan's defense revival was intelligence. It meant getting good information on adversaries, and it meant employing that information in active ways—a strong covert action program. The new DCI was a long-time Reagan friend, the manager of his successful presidential campaign in 1980—William Casey. Casey's intelligence background was

OSS in World War II. OSS had been excluded from COMINT during the war, and so to them intelligence meant HUMINT, i.e., agents. He had no experience with SIGINT, but he was a fast learner.

When Casey became DCI, "technical intelligence" had just about taken over. The Carter administration believed in it, and most of the money went toward it. Despite the well-known Reaganesque proclivity toward agents and covert actions, this did not really change during his administration. His transition team wanted more money dumped into satellite programs, and the Reagan administration cut its sails in that direction from the first day. Casey himself quickly came to understand the value of SIGINT, and did not share the institutional view of NSA that so dominated the thinking of his own staff. His own deputy, Bobby Inman, said later that "For all of my difficulties with Bill Casey on so many other issues, on this one I would give him a clean bill of health....While he set out to rebuild and revitalize the DDO, he recognized the value of Signals Intelligence and the role it played....He did not bring an instinctively parochial view to the issue. Was it relevant? Was it timely? Was it useful? Did you need more money? These were the sorts of basic attitudes he brought."

The Reagan administration marked the height of the Cold War. The president referred to the Soviet Union as the Evil Empire, and was determined to spend it into the ground. The Politburo reciprocated, and the rhetoric on both sides, especially during the first Reagan administration, drove the hysteria. Sorne called it the Second Cold War. The period 1982-1984 marked the most dangerous Soviet-American confrontation since the Cuban Missile Crisis.

Despite the president's support of intelligence programs, NSA was wary. The White House viewed intelligence as a foreign policy tool, and used it to advance larger foreign policy interests, regardless of security implications. Three instances make the case.

[censored]

The best known exposure of SIGINT since the Pearl Harbor hearings of 1945 had actually come in 1983, when the Reagan administration played the intercepted cockpit conversations of the Soviet pilot as he shot down KAL-007. The SIGINT gave the administration a tremendous foreign policy coup [censored]

There were numerous other instances. British historian Christopher Andrew cites just one—the 1988 exposure of the decrypt of Iraqi military communications relating to the Iraqi use of poison gas on their Kurdish population. It came from an atmosphere in which the loss of sources and methods was deemed less important than the foreign policy gains.

Counterbalancing the Reagan administration's penchant for misuse of intelligence was the president's strong support of his intelligence agencies. In 1986 he became the first American president to visit NSA, as he gave the official dedication speech for NSA's two new buildings, Ops 2A and Ops 2B. He wanted to loosen the legal reins governing intelligence, and signed a new executive order, 12333, which gave NSA latitude in SIGINT collection that it had not had during the Carter years. Reagan revived the President's Foreign Intelligence Advisory Board (PFIAB), moribund under Carter. The new chair, Anne Armstrong, was a strong and effective advocate for the intelligence community.

The National Security Mechanism Under Reagan

The Inman Appointment

Casey needed a deputy, and he was not inclined to go to the existing CIA structure. Thus the search turned outside CIA, and eventually settled on NSA director Admiral Bobby Inman. The way that Inman was selected became a Washington legend. His prime sponsor was Senator Barry Goldwater, who had urged that Reagan make Inman the DCI. As DIRNSA, Inman's reputation had become so special that he was regarded as essentially untouchable. Bob Woodward, in his book *Veil*, described Inman in the adulatory tone of the times: "Inman knew the intelligence business cold. He was the best source on everything from the latest spy satellite to the bureaucratic maneuvering required to get intelligence programs going. He had a fabulous memory. With his boyish, toothy smile, large head, thick glasses, Inman looked like a grown-up whiz kid. He was one of the few intelligence officials who would talk to reporters and get them to hold off on stories that compromised intelligence. He had nurtured all the important relationships in the Congress. Goldwater could not recall an instance in which Inman had failed to return a phone call or to track down an answer on the rare occasion when he didn't know it."

Others in the news media had similar comments. According to the *Washington Star*, "It is reassuring both to those who want to see U.S. intelligence operations strengthened and to those who don't want to see the CIA crashing through the forest in its previous 'rogue elephant' role.... 'There is not a mark on him,' says a former admiral who worked with Inman in naval intelligence." At the Senate confirmation hearing, Senator Goldwater opened by saying: "You have my vote even before I hear your testimony...." Inman became the first superstar to emerge from NSA. Most expected him to maximize the role of SIGINT and to turn up his nose at covert operations and other messy programs.

General Faurer Becomes NSA's Director

Inman's successor as DIRNSA was Air Force Lieutenant General Lincoln D. Faurer. Faurer had a strong flying background (he piloted both B29s and RB-47s) and experience in missile and space operations. Although he had no direct experience in cryptology, he had served two tours at DIA and three others in intelligence-related jobs. He came to NSA from Europe, where he had been both J2 USEUCOM, and deputy chairman of the NATO Military Committee. He thoroughly understood the intelligence needs of theater commanders, and he made support to military operations a central theme of his tenure at NSA.

If Inman could be described as "brilliant and brittle," "Linc" Faurer might have been accurately depicted as avuncular but determined. He valued accommodation and collegiality, and he tried to reconstruct NSA's management system based on new management principles emphasizing cooperation and corporate decision-making. It was difficult to redirect NSA's staff system in such a radical way. Under Inman, management had been top down, and Inman neither needed nor wanted a staff system. Faurer was just the opposite.

Much of Faurer's energy was directed toward sharpening support to military operations. As the former deputy chairman of NATO's Military Committee, he focused on SIGINT support to NATO [censored] Multilateralism was the only feasible approach in the NATO environment.

Much of his effort along this line was doomed to frustration. During the Grenada operation, NSA was shut out of operational details, bringing the dispute over this long-running problem to a boil. After the bombing of the Marine barracks in Lebanon in 1983, the Navy insisted that SIGINT support to the remaining Marines be routed through Sixth Fleet. Faurer, experienced in the ways of military operations, rejected that approach. "We fought that battle and it got more heated after the bombing than it did before and it's dead wrong. I mean, you just can't live with it that way." He cultivated his relationships with the J3 (chief of the JCS operations staff) throughout his tenure, trying to educate each successive occupant of the chair, and he got understanding nods but no results. "And it went on the entire time. We never solved the problem."

Faurer developed a high regard for both his bosses, Casey and Weinberger. As for Casey, once Faurer got over the difficulty of understanding what he was saying (a problem that followed Casey his whole life—unintelligible speech), he acquired great respect for the DCI. "I happen to think Bill Casey is as fine a DCI as we've had in the time I've been associated with intelligence, and I go back to Jim Schlesinger." But Faurer read his own charter literally, and believed that in DoD, his direct supervisor was Weinberger. He never accepted the delegation of NSA to the deputy secretary of defense, William Taft. Faurer fought Taft constantly to insure that NSA's national role remained an independent responsibility. They had disputes over NSA's national role in policy issues and over budget issues that transcended the Defense Department. They were never resolved, and Faurer was actually fired at Taft's behest over a now obscure budget issue several weeks prior to the agreed-upon retirement date. General Faurer, a bulldog to the end, went down fighting for what he believed in.

The Odom Administration

Faurer's replacement in 1985 was a former armor officer who had become one of the Army's top Sovietologists. William Odom had had a tour at the Potsdam mission in the mid-1960s. The Potsdam mission was one of the best training grounds for attaché work, and it was followed six years later by a tour as assistant Army attache in Moscow. Odom was exposed to SIGINT, especially in Moscow, and over the years he developed a keen appreciation for the interplay of intelligence disciplines.

When Zbigniew Brzezinski became Jimmy Carter's national security advisor, he plucked his former student, William Odom, out of the Army to serve on his staff. Said Brzezinski, "I knew him from an earlier association with me at the Research Institute on International Change at Columbia, I respected his views on Soviet military affairs and strategy, and I considered him to be an innovative strategic thinker."

After four years in the White House, Odom had gone on to serve as the deputy assistant chief of staff for intelligence in the Pentagon, and soon took over as the ACSI. His broad exposure to Army intelligence made him a prime candidate to succeed Faurer. And the Army had not had a director since Marshall Carter departed in 1969.

Odom brought a unique personality to the job. According to his deputy, Robert Rich, he was a good listener and a reasonable person to work for, who could examine the intellectual facets of a decision and come up with the right answer. But he did not project this image. What most NSAers remember was a different Odom: "...ready, fire, aim; loud, boisterous, ranging over all kinds of intellectual territory, strategy of the nation, strategic concepts, tactical concepts." Many felt that he suffered from the typical disease of ivory tower intellectuals—hearing one voice only: his own.

Odom had a different perspective on NSA. He likened the job to that of commanding a specified command. It had, he liked to point out, operational control over three service components, a worldwide scope of operation, its own logistics system, its own training school, a unique research and development organization, its own procurement system, and so forth. Next to the DCI, it was the most powerful job in American intelligence.

For a specified command, though, it lacked certain essentials. Most prominently, NSA had no staff system analogous to that of a military command. Without a staff, the director simply had to accept the judgments of his deputy directors, and had no independent means of managing actions or verifying information. It was a consequence of historical evolution at NSA, and it fitted NSA's unique way of doing business. Odom battled the system his entire time at NSA, but felt that he never changed the way NSA operated.

What NSAers remembered most distinctly from the Odom era were the Ten Thrusts:

Table 18 General Odom's Ten Thrusts

1. Modernize the SIGINT collection and processing systems to cope with the changing target communications technology.

2. Integrate tactical and national SIGINT capabilities to satisfy more effectively military requirements in peace, crisis, and war.

3. Maintain and improve our capabilities to support diplomatic, economic, and other nonmilitary requirements for SIGINT support.

4. Maintain a large U.S. lead in cryptanalytic capabilities (both computer capability and personnel).

5. Design a framework for a survivable SIGINT system, under all conditions, including general war, which we acquire incrementally and through astute dual-use applications over the next decade.

6. Provide easily attainable, inexpensive, user-friendly Information Systems Security features.

7. Speed up research for major breakthroughs in the technology of computer security; at the same time, help industry manufacture more "trustworthy " computer products for defense and other government needs.

8. Establish a program to reduce significantly the HUMINT threat to Information Security Systems.

9. Provide modern, secure, user-friendly key management systems.

10. Remove the COMSEC block obsolescence condition by the end of 1991 and establish a program to protect against this condition in the future.

Originally written by Odom himself, these began as six thrusts relating to SIGINT, and focused primarily on maintaining NSA's edge in various technical disciplines such as cryptomath and in sharpening the focus of customer support. Harry Daniels, the DDI, took immediate exception to a list of thrusts which excluded INFOSEC issues, and submitted his own. Odom struck one of the original six from the list and added Daniel's five, to come up with a nice round number. It was a good list, just right for the mid-1980s. Odom did seem to understand the business.

The most controversial thrust was to insure a survivable system. Fashioned during the Second Cold War, it made a lot of sense at the time. [censored] According to his successor, Rear Admiral William Studeman, there was a tendency at NSA to try to wait out the Odom directorship in hopes that [censored] would simply go away.

Like Faurer, Odom worked for two bosses, Weinberger and Casey, but he managed the trick with aplomb. Within DoD he generally reported directly to the secretary of defense but, aware of the Faurer-Taft confrontations, carefully kept William Taft in the loop with occasional briefings. His real affinity, however, was clearly for Casey. The two got on well together, and Odom held Casey in high respect for his substantive knowledge of intelligence issues and his ability to deal with them off the cuff. They formed a united team in 1986 to try to stop the press from publishing leaks that damaged intelligence sources and methods.

At the White House

NSA still enjoyed a special relationship with the White House. After a brief and fitful flirtation with the idea of bringing someone from State Department in to run the Situation Room, Richard Allen, the first of a long line of Reagan's national security advisors, chose NSAer [censored] as his

Situation Room chief. [censored] stayed during the first Reagan administration, long enough to get a clear picture of how intelligence issues were handled.

Under Carter, intelligence and national security topics got a highly organized, if somewhat egocentric, direction from Brzezinski. But this process never got started under Reagan. The leaks, the employment of SIGINT to push a foreign policy agenda, the disjointed way in which intelligence in general was treated (culminating in the Iran-Contra imbroglio) was a true bill of the process. For in fact, there never was a process under Reagan.

Reagan modeled his White House administrative procedures after Nixon, with a strong staff chief, Edwin Meese. Everything was routed through Meese, and even Richard Allen contacted the president through him. This cut off the president from direct access to intelligence, and when Allen departed he had never been able to establish a relationship with Reagan. His successor, Judge William Clark, accepted the job only on condition that he enjoy access to the president, but the damage had been done, and during the first Reagan administration the White House never had a strong national security advisor, nor did it ever have a system in which tailored, focused intelligence arrived in the Oval Office. The job became a revolving door, with first Allen, then Clark, then Robert McFarlane, John Poindexter, and finally Frank Carlucci, cycling through. According to [censored] the process, if there was a process, lacked substance, and difficult intelligence issues were dealt with in a superficial way.

SIGINT Resources In The Reagan Years

Ronald Reagan inherited a cryptologic system in parlous shape. Manpower over the previous decade had dropped from 88,600 to about 41,000 (see Table 19). At first glance, money appeared to be on the increase, but that was before inflation was factored in. The 1970s was a decade of high inflation, and the gap between current and constant dollars had widened progressively through the ten years (see Tables 19 and 20).

The Reagan administration began pumping money back into intelligence programs. From the 1980 through 1986 fiscal years, the overall cryptologic budget rose [censored]

[censored]

Along with money came people—lots of them. NSA's total population rose by 40 percent during the 1980s. Beginning with 19,018 in 1983, the Agency's population peaked in 1990, just before the collapse of the Soviet Union, at a total of 26,679. The dramatic rise was across the board, civilian and military, but was most pronounced on the civilian side (see Table 22). While the military component rose 24 percent, the civilian side increased by 46 percent.

(C) Table 19
Cryptologic Manpower, FY 1970-FY 1979 [22]

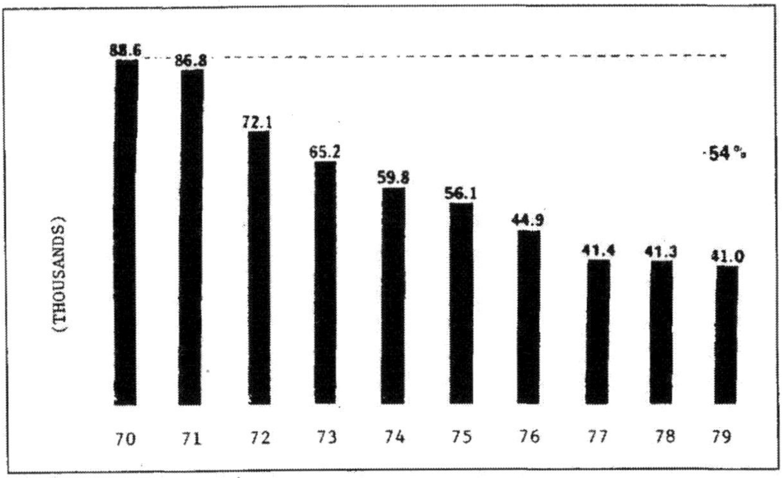

(C) Table 22
NSA's Full-Time Civilian Strength, 1982-1989 [27]

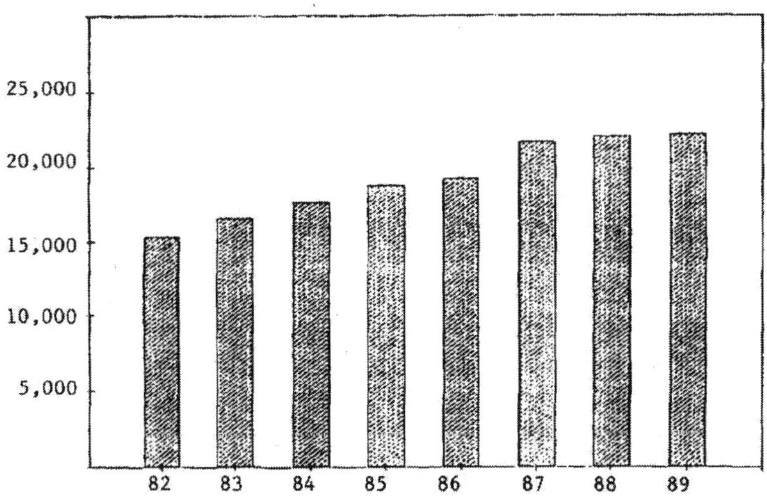

Almost a thousand billets came to NSA in 1986 as the result of a decision by the General Services Administration to turn over support operations. Part of a broader plan to relinquish maintenance to single-tenant government-owned facilities, the GSA plan for NSA involved both maintenance (542 billets) and security guards (381 people). In October of 1985 Terence Golden, administrator of GSA, met with General Odom, and in April of 1986 Odom formally accepted the plan.

The hiring glut took place mostly at the lower grades, but NSA's average grade level stayed in the range of GG-10, substantially higher than the government-wide average. What took place to level it out was rapid promotions. The 1980s saw a major surge in promotions, with a dramatic spike in fiscal year 1985. But the downside was the slide in average experience level, as new hires replaced old hands.

In the light of the rapid civilian hiring program, the military contribution to cryptology became a source of concern. As the percentage of the military population declined, its influence would also inevitably decrease, along with military cryptologic experience levels. This could unfavorably impact support to military operations. Moreover, rapid civilian hiring was taking place primarily out of colleges, and military conversions, once a dominant source of civilian manpower, had declined by 1982 to 6.7 percent of all hiring actions. In 1988 Dr. James Donnelly headed a panel that looked at military manpower in the cryptologic system. Donnelly's main concern was the increasing congregation of military billets at the front end of the system, leaving very few at NSA, where much of the "technology transfer" had to take place.

The fastest-growing segment of NSA's population during the 1980s was actually the part-time work force. A product of the Carter administration, the part-time segment grew [censored] This explosive growth outstripped all other hiring areas, and a significant percentage of hiring actions (8.7 percent in fiscal year 1982) came from part-time to full-time conversions. One major reason for the increases in part-time employees was that NSA management discovered that they did not count against the Agency's official strength. It was thus a way to increase personnel without appearing to do so.

As the work force grew, so did the percentage of women and minorities on the rolls. From 1977 to 1993, for instance, the percentage of women at NSA grew from about 26 percent to 39 percent (see Table 23). But the percentage of women by grade declined dramatically as grade rose, even though the decade opened with NSA's first female deputy director, Ann Caracristi. Women constituted a majority up through grade eight, but at that point the chart dipped dramatically, and women made up less than five percent of the grade fifteens. This compared closely with the overall government statistics, as Table 24 shows.

The concentration on college-level hiring increasingly tipped the scales toward a more highly educated workforce. In the ten fiscal years from 1972 to 1982, for instance, the percentage of employees with college degrees increased 24 percent, while those with advanced degrees increased 125 percent. Those with less than two years of college actually declined by 22 percent.

More people required more space. And as personal computers became more common (during the decade 70 percent of the workforce was provided with a PC), people tended to require larger offices. So NSA launched an unprecedented building boom which resulted in the addition of 240,000 square feet per year during the decade. Much of it was leased space. The International Tower Building came under an NSA lease in 1980. The following year the Agency began leasing the new Airport Square buildings, which were replacing woods and fields in the vicinity of the FANX complex at BWI.

~~(C)~~ **Table 23**

NSA's Population by Gender, 1977-1993 [32]

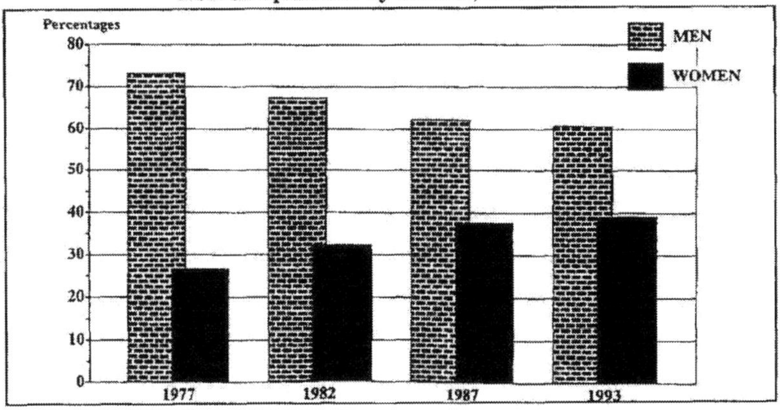

(U) Table 24

Percentage of Women by Grade at NSA, DoD and Federal Workforce [33]

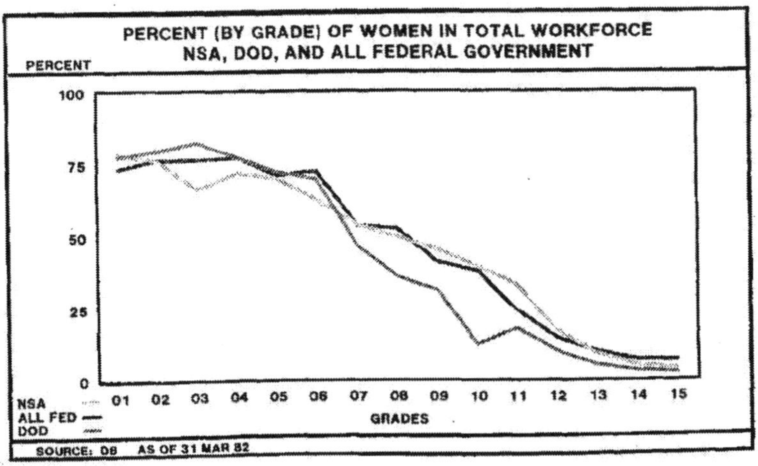

That same year General Faurer broke ground on Ops 2A and Ops 2B, which were dedicated by President Reagan five years later. In 1990 the new Research and Engineering building was dedicated, to add to the Special Processing Lab (opened in 1988) and numerous leased facilities in the general Fort Meade vicinity. (see Table 25)

One solution to the space problem was to go upward. In 1983 NSA awarded a contract to American Seating Company to provide and install systems furniture, which would permit the workforce to add personal computers and other office aids without increasing floor space per person. The original contract provided for some 8,000 workstations at a price of about $5 million. But it was only the beginning, and by 1993 approximately

20,000 workstations had been installed at a cost of $60 million. This improvement came in the late stages of an earlier movement to provide raised flooring. Begun in the basement of Ops-1 in the 1960s, raised flooring was originally installed only in rooms with computer mainframes. As smaller computers took over the Agency, people got tired of tripping over cables strung across tile floors from one machine to another. Slowly, workspaces were vacated and raised flooring installed. By 1993 some five million square feet of raised flooring had been installed in NSA buildings at Fort Meade. It not only got unsightly and potentially dangerous electrical cables off floors; it had the attendant benefit of providing carpet tiles, which reduced noise (and looked nicer).

(U) Table 25
Growth of NSA Space from 1973 to 1994

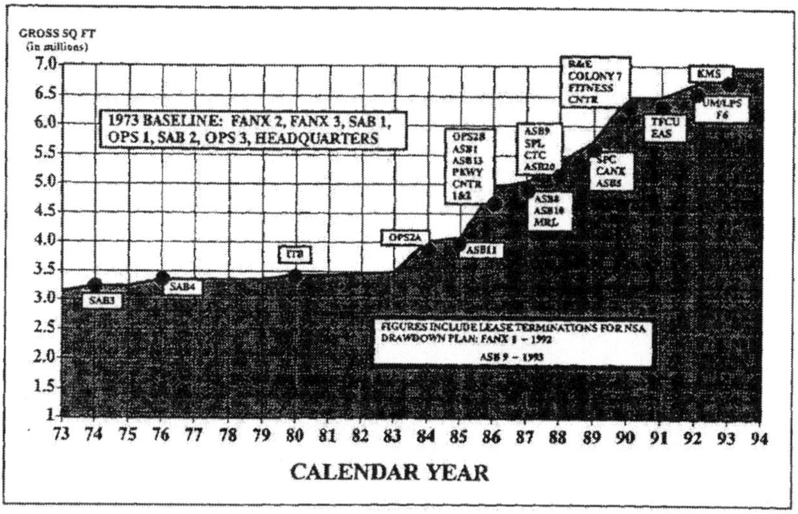

In the early days Fort Meade had been serviced (excepting only the Baltimore-Washington Parkway) by narrow, winding roads going east and west to bedroom suburbs of Severna Park, Glen Burnie, Laurel and Columbia. The drive to either Severna Park or Columbia commonly took half an hour or more, much of it spent waiting in a long snake of cars twisting through the Maryland countryside. With NSA population projections going virtually through the roof, NSA began looking at an environmental overhaul. In the early 1980s the State of Maryland began widening Route 32 both toward the east and west. It was called the Patuxent Freeway project, and as sections became functional in the late 1980s and early 1990s, traffic congestion around Fort Meade declined (but didn't go away).

The Cryptologic System In The 1980s

[censored]

[censored]

The FSCS Study

In 1983 NSA began a study of the increasing cost of the system [censored] its conclusions caught the attention of the DCI and Congress, and in December of that year Vice Admiral Burkhalter, director of the Intelligence Community Staff, established the Future SIGINT Capabilities Study (FSCS). Burkhalter broadened the study to the entire SIGINT system. The objective was to match existing and programmed systems against assumed target changes and to identify the gaps. Phases I and II would look at everything [censored]

The resulting documents highlighted the increasing technological sophistication of the targets, and they marked a watershed of sorts. It was no longer possible to think of the SIGINT system in the same terms as professional cryptologists had thought of it since World War I. [censored]

The study focused on target changes that would affect collection and processing. [censored]

[censored]

Though FSCS concentrated on hardware and software, it did stray into manpower implications. [censored] Moreover, the skill mix would move rapidly into high-tech areas, and the people hired would be engineers, cryptomathematicians, and computer systems designers. The armed services did not produce people like that—NSA would have to hire increasingly from colleges or private industry to find the kinds of people it needed. Retention would be more difficult as NSA would have to compete with private industry for college-trained technical people. The federal salary structure simply could not compete in these areas—job satisfaction would have to be the carrot.

To a workforce of the late 1990s grown accustomed to the new communications challenges, this sounds very familiar. In the mid-1980s, it was visionary. The FSCS study spawned a plethora of committees looking at various aspects of the problem. [censored]

Battlestar Galactica

The plan for an overall SIGINT system was dependent on the resolution of an ongoing donnybrook over overhead resources. [censored]

[censored] The proposed system was so grandiose that it was referred to by Admiral Inman as "Battlestar Galactica."

The outlines of the new system were revolutionary. [censored]

[censored]

[censored]

NSA, being the signal processing organization, participated in all the system discussions and studies. The Agency generally kept its political opinions to itself, confining its advice to technical assessments of the feasibility of various approaches. Robert Hermann, director of NRO in the early 1980s, once said "NSA didn't care, shouldn't have cared." But under the surface there was growing concern at the Agency about costs. An NSA advisory board wrote to General Odom in July of 1985 that SIGINT satellite costs in the National Reconnaissance Program were growing so fast that they could squeeze out some favored programs in the CCP. It would be a good idea to get a handle on satellite program costs, and soon.

In fact, NSA's role in the overhead system was not so sterile as it appeared from the outside. Within the vortex was a fierce bureaucratic battle to control the SIGINT satellite business. Part of this undoubtedly stemmed from the philosophy of SIGINT management that NSA had always lived by. In the United States, SIGINT was monolithic, and control was vested in a national manager. But the overhead business was controlled by the NRO, and when NSA tried to intervene, either to manage the satellite planning and programming, or to exercise day-to-day direction over satellite operations, it was on NRO's turf.

But viewed from NSA's perspective, the issue revolved around a management system that was inefficient from a cost standpoint. NSA managers believed that NRO was paying far too much to its favored contractors for satellite system design, launch and operation, and that this was impacting on money that should have been available for other SIGINT programs. [censored]

Despite disagreements at the top, NSA and NRO managed to cooperate in the creation of a new system tasking center, the Overhead Collection Management Center (OCMC). It resulted from a July 1983 conference between [censored] (chairman of the SIGINT Committee), Robert Rich (deputy director of NSA) and Jimmy Hill (deputy director of NRO). [censored] could not secure agreement even in such a small group, so he wrote a memo to John McMahon (deputy DCI) proposing a new joint tasking center on the DEFSMAC model. (Attached to the memo was a two and a half page nonconcurrence from Hill.) [censored] presented McMahon with three options, and McMahon selected one which created an OCMC at NSA headquarters, and permitted DIRNSA to name the director, the director of NRO to name the deputy, and the DCI to name the chief of requirements. This permitted conflict resolution at a technical level, and resulted in a joint organization that soon proved its worth.

Disputes over satellite system control continued into the program. [censored]

[censored]

In the fall of 1987, after a war of paper between NSA and the intelligence community staff, General William Odom took NSA's case to Congress. He had several complaints. [censored] And he did not like the vast sums required. "I thought [the new system] was sheer robbery of the public purse," he said later.

Much of NSA's dislike came down to system control. Odom felt that NSA's views had not been taken into account by NRO. He viewed NRO as a vast bureaucracy in which two programs, A and B, warred with each other, to the detriment of the national SIGINT manager. NRO tended to view the issue as a simple competition between a new program on the one hand, [censored] on the other. NSA looked at it in the context of the entire SIGINT system, and from that perspective a decision that seemed right to NRO looked wrong to NSA.

In January of 1988 the new DCI, Judge William Webster, cancelled the new system. In a letter to Senator David Boren of the SSCI, he explained that recent budget cuts put too much of a squeeze on the program. The NRO could save [censored] by not deploying it, and intended to do so. What he did not say was that NSA, the chief operator of the SIGINT system, was now in active opposition. But this was not news to Boren, owing to Odom's testimony on Capitol Hill.

Comsat

[censored]

[censored]

[censored]

Cryptologic Communications

No area of cryptologic operations was expanding faster than communications. A chart of communications capacity from 1973 to 1993 (Table 28), [censored] Yet the system was being operated by about the same number of people as it had required twenty years earlier.

~~(S//SI)~~ Table 28

Cryptologic Communications, 1973-1993

Worldwide capacity	
Number of circuits	
Messages annually	
Secure phone systems	
Instruments	
Cost of communications	
Manpower	

NSA had become the largest single user of the DSSCS system, and by the early 1980s had outrun the ability of the DoD system to support it. The only answer was to lease large numbers of commercial circuits, from landline and microwave to satellite.

Internally, NSA replaced its communications terminal system under a new project called EMBROIDERY; Under EMBROIDERY every communications terminal became a computer, just as field site collection positions were being computerized. Using off-the-shelf IBM equipment, NSA outfitted its [censored] IDDF/[censored] TIDEWAY, and DAYSEND communications systems with new equipment and new methodology. [censored] replaced STREAMLINER, which had been deployed in the mid-1970s.

NSA's impressive communications design capability was sometimes employed in the service of other organizations. This was the case with a system called Umstead, a commercial design originally adapted for government use by an NSA engineer named [censored] to transmit voice and data via satellite. It was light, mobile and inexpensive, and looked like the answer to an Army tactical communications problem. The Army's problem came into rather stark relief during a large 1981 exercise called Crested Eagle. Army tactical forces simply lacked enough communications channels to carry what they needed, and intelligence got such a low priority that little of it got to the customers. Sixty percent of the signals intelligence traffic had to be couriered, and much of it was still in courier two weeks after the exercise had ended.

Through mid-decade, top Army field commanders insisted that Umstead would solve the problem. But it was opposed by Signal Corps generals on somewhat obscure grounds, and was never purchased. Umstead was used on a few occasions by NSA, but never achieved its true potential, and wound up sitting on the shelf.

Cryptologic Computers

If the 1960s and 1970s were the era of mainframe computers, the 1980s were an era of small systems. By the late 1970s the mainframes at Fort Meade were becoming so congested that they looked like the Beltway at rush hour. As access time increased, a movement away from mainframes accelerated. In the early 1980s computer companies were beginning to produce personal computers in large quantities at low prices, and NSA managers began defecting to these systems. Kermit Speierman and Walter Deeley were early proponents of personal computers and off-the-shelf software.

The improved efficiency and cost effectiveness of the computer-on-every desk approach was counterbalanced by a strong trend toward nonstandard equipment and software. With so many products available in stores, it was difficult for NSA's computer people to keep up. The driver was maintenance: when hardware and software malfunctioned, it was impossible to keep everything running. Moreover, central control over formats, file access, etc., the basis of the cryptologic system's effectiveness, could be lost. Chaos could be the result.

To save the situation, NSA tried to standardize PC hardware. In 1984 it issued a request for proposal for an Agency Standard Terminal Workstation (ASTW). The IBM PC XT, a relatively new entry in the world of personal computers, won the award. It was a big win: the contract was ultimately valued at $199 million, and NSA bought 21,000 units. The next year the Agency awarded a contract for an Agency Standard Host (ASH), which would interconnect the ASTWs. American Telephone and Telegraph won the contract, valued at $150 million. Seven hundred twenty systems were finally sold to NSA.

In the early days, most personal computers ran on the DOS operating system, but it was not suitable for internetted systems. Kermit Speierman of NSA discovered that Bell Laboratories had devised an operating system called UNIX, which was at the time the only system that operated in a multi-user, internetted environment. UNIX became the dominant operating system in the 1980s.

Computer power was the essential ingredient in cryptanalysis. In the 1970s NSA had forged ahead with the help of supercomputers, first from Control Data Corporation (CDC) and later from Cray. But the early 1980s were a period of tension in the supercomputer business. The Japanese were rumored to be about to enter the business, and in view of their devastating impact on the commercial VCR business, there was a potential threat to national security if American supercomputer companies were to be bested or even driven out of business. These problems were part of the background noise of 1982, when NSA's Kermit Speierman was doing some work at Los Alamos and talking to scientists there about NSA's computer power problems. The outgrowth of those discussions was a decision to jointly host a conference at NSA in 1983 on supercomputer problems. Called "Frontiers in Supercomputing," the week-long conference focused on how to design and build faster supercomputers. It was clear that serial processing would not be fast enough—the industry needed massively parallel processing to have a chance of staying ahead.

General Faurer, who gave the closing speech, had become convinced that a permanent institute was needed, and asked Speierman to create one. Working through an NSA committee, Speierman put together a concept for a Supercomputer Research Center. Faurer needed $16 million and a lot of executive push, so he briefed the outlines of the research center around Washington. He was able to muster support from every quarter but the JCS and the Office of the Secretary of Defense, where his boss, William Taft, was staunchly opposed. But Taft was ultimately outflanked, and NSA began looking for a home for the center. Although Boston and North Carolina were considered, NSA finally selected the nearby Bowie area, and on November 27, 1984, Maryland governor Harry Hughes announced from the steps of the State House in Annapolis the creation of the Supercomputer Research Center. The center would not have survived without Faurer's forceful intervention at the DoD level. Said Speierman several years later, "...he was completely convinced. I think that's a real tribute to him. And he never flinched from that conviction. Without that 100 percent conviction on his part...I don't think any of this would have happened." It was one of the disputes with Taft that resulted in Faurer's early departure from NSA.

Computer Security

In 1965 a small computer science firm called SDC of Santa Monica, California, became concerned about security of their computer products. With computer networking in the offing, computer files could become vulnerable to unauthorized users, almost as if a safe had been jimmied. SDC hosted a conference attended by several computer companies and by the head of the Rand Corporation computer sciences division, Dr. Willis Ware. Ware quickly took the lead on the issue.

Ware, as it happened, sat on NSA's Scientific Advisory Board, and called General Carter to tell him that he was about to get a hot new issue on his plate. Contending that NSA was the only agency in the federal government that had the technical expertise, Ware plugged for the Agency's direct involvement. The issue bubbled slowly for two years, but in 1967 the Defense Supply Agency (DSA) at Cameron Station, Virginia, made a formal request to the secretary of defense that NSA be named the computer security authority. This was followed in short order by requests from several other federal agencies. NSA first became involved with these requests on a voluntary basis—it had no charter to do this unless cryptographic equipment was involved, and in this case it wasn't. Nor did NSA have an organization officially tasked with the job. The DSA request to the secretary was still pending and had generated a lot of controversy within NSA. Many felt that NSA should avoid the task.

Having dodged responsibility for the new COMPUSEC mission for several years, NSA finally made a partial step in 1969 with the issuance of a memorandum by the deputy director, Louis Tordella. Noting that NSA possessed no official responsibility, Tordella nonetheless acknowledged that a moral responsibility was involved. Thenceforth, NSA would provide assistance to other intelligence community (IC) organizations based on experiences that NSA had had with its own systems. NSA would not assist non-IC organizations.

In 1972, the consequences of continued inaction were starkly illustrated by an incident involving DIA. The Defense Intelligence Agency had created several intelligence community databases designed for multilevel security access, and DIA contacted USIB about running a security check of the system so that they could get their systems accredited for SI and TK information. NSA and other members of the intelligence community, with participation from defense contractors, obliged. By the time the attacks terminated, the penetration was so thorough that a penetrator at a distant remote terminal had actually seized control of the system. DIA never got its accreditation, and the results of the exercise made many at NSA skeptical that multilevel security could ever be achieved.

NSA's role in computer security expanded in 1973. Needing a focus for research on the subject, Tordella named the ADC (assistant director for COMSEC) as the responsible official, and ADC established a small center for technical information on the subject, specifically to support federal agencies. Despite Tordella's decision, however, little happened through the end of the decade. Lew Allen requested sixty-seven billets for the fiscal year 1975 program, but was turned down, in part because NSA's role was still controversial.

Late in the decade an OSD staffer and former NSA employee, Stephen Walker, approached Bobby Inman about the computer security mess. Walker explained that in OSD there was a strong feeling that NSA should expand its effort and become the office of primary responsibility for computer security in the federal government. However, Walker personally opposed locating the organization within COMSEC. Inman agreed and asked George Cotter, the assistant director for telecommunications, to take on the task. Working closely with Walker, Cotter set up the Computer Security Center as a separate organization. It was formally created on the first of January, 1981, as the Department of Defense Computer Security Center, with a small staff working directly for Cotter. Originally it was to have a separate building, to be located in the parking lot outside Ops-3 on the main Fort Meade campus. But, as often happens with money, the line item was diverted, and went into construction of the Special Processing Laboratory. In the end, the center never got its own building, and it continued to operate out of borrowed spaces.

NSA's role in computer security remained a lightning rod for dissent both within NSA and in the outside world. That role waxed and waned depending on the political winds. Under Reagan, it expanded, and under NSDD 145 the DoD Computer Security Center became the National Computer Security Center, with an expanded mission to bring computer security products to non-national security organizations. At the same time, Walter Deeley and Harry Daniels, who were running the COMSEC organization, convinced General Odom that COMPUSEC should be part of their organization, and so the Center was resubordinated to the (now called) DDI, responsible for INFOSEC, which included both COMSEC and COMPUSEC.

But NSDD 145 encountered congressional opposition, and it was overturned in 1987 by the Computer Security Act. This legislation split the mission between NSA and the National Bureau of Standards (NBS, which soon changed its named to NIST, National Institute of Standards and Technology). NSA retained its role within the national security community, but NBS got the mission to deal with all others. It was clear from the legislation, however, that NSA would retain a strong technical advisory role with NBS, which lacked the expertise on the subject.

Operations Security

The experience in Vietnam had generated an operations security program called Purple Dragon. NSA had been the core of the effort, and it became the institutional memory for OPSEC. But as Vietnam faded from mind, memories of OPSEC programs grew dim. So in the early 1980s NSA began holding OPSEC seminars around the Pacific Rim for military organizations. The program quickly expanded to the Coast Guard, the White House, GSA, Customs, and NASA. This nascent effort became a full-blown OPSEC training program at the National Cryptologic School. The National OPSEC Course was open to all federal agencies, and 80 percent of the attendees were non-NSA.

In 1983 Caspar Weinberger directed that all DoD organizations have OPSEC programs, and NSA became responsible for OPSEC education. But while NSA spread the word about effective OPSEC programs, it had none itself. The "Year of the Spy" brought on a thorough internal examination of security practices. The panel, headed by David Boak, concluded in 1986 that NSA had effectively flunked its own OPSEC exam. This led to the establishment of a DDI OPSEC working group to bring NSA into compliance with its own established standards.

In 1988, President Reagan signed NSDD 298, which established the OPSEC program of the federal government. Every agency with "classified or sensitive activities" would establish a formal OPSEC program. The order gave NSA the training and technical support mission for all federal programs. It also established an Interagency OPSEC Support Staff, with representatives from NSA, FBI, CIA, DOE, and GSA. A SIGINT professional, [censored] was named to head the NSA effort.

INFOSEC and the New Way of Doing Business

In 1983 the Communications Security organization got a new boss. Walter Deeley, who had revolutionized SIGINT timely reporting, was sent by General Faurer to do the same thing to the COMSEC business. Deeley took stock of American COMSEC, and did not like what he saw. As he later said to a congressional committee, "I was appalled. Within weeks I told Faurer that I would rank the United States in the top half of the Third World countries when it comes to protecting its communications. What I found was a secluded organization with fewer than 2,000 people, including all the printers of our codes and ciphers, no charter to effect change, no money except to engage in research and development, and customers who really didn't want our products. Two years later he said to another committee: "The United States is in jeopardy because it does poorly protecting its vital communications....As a nation so far, we have not made this commitment... "

The New Way of Doing Business, as the Deeley revolution was termed, was based on embeddable COMSEC products, or "COMSEC on a chip." Instead of protecting point-to-point circuits, NSA would go for bulk encryption. The Agency would get into a partnership with commercial manufacturers to produce encryption technology. The revolution did not just happen; it was carefully planned and executed.

One of the first battles of the Deeley era was over national policy. The struggles of the Carter administration over what federal agency was to control national COMSEC policy continued into the Reagan years. Admiral Bobby Inman had been sure that Carter would lean toward expanded authorities by the Department of Commerce, and he successfully stalled the Carter White House on the issue, hoping for a more favorable decision from the incoming Reagan people. The new administration was temperamentally inclined to give the problem to DoD. This was strongly reinforced by the problems in Soviet exploitation of U.S. domestic communications, the problems with Moscow embassy security, exposure of the Walker ring, and concern over potential penetration of American computer systems. A coterie of NSC staffers, headed by Kenneth deGraffenreid, pushed hard for NSA involvement. The result was a new National Security Decision Directive, NSDD 145. Issued in 1984, it established COMSEC as a high-priority national objective, and named the secretary of defense as the executive agent for the security of government communications related to national security. NSA was designated the "National Manager for Telecommunications Security and Automated Information Systems Security," a longish title which placed the Agency directly in the center of the COMSEC business. Moreover, NSDD 145 did away with the old United States Communications Security Board, which had accomplished so little over the years. Instead, the directive replaced it with a new Systems Security Working Group (SSSC) and, under it, the National Telecommunications Information Systems Security Committee (NTISSC, pronounced "entissic"). NBS had separate responsibility for the private sector, but even there, NSA had a technical and advisory role. NTISSC, the real player in this game, was dominated by NSA, and its secretariat was located in NSA spaces.

The ink on NSDD 145 was hardly dry when it was attacked in Congress. The issue turned on a congressional distrust of DoD involvement in computer security. The Department of Commerce, which had been involved in COMPUSEC by the Carter order (PD 24), was anxious to reverse the course of NSDD 145, and a behind-the-scenes brawl developed between NSA and Commerce over the COMPUSEC authority. The fight was ultimately settled by Congress, which in 1987 passed Public Law 200435, legislation which was promoted by Congressman Jack Brooks of Texas. This gave Commerce control over COMPUSEC in all cases except those involving classified government contracts, in which NSA was still the prime actor. Although the new law was supposed to affect only computer security, NIST was expected to establish crypto standards and policy for computer security, a domain in which NSA had formerly operated with complete freedom. The hearings which led to the legislation revealed the huge technological lead that NSA enjoyed in the field of computer security, but the demons of congressional distrust could not be overcome.

The secure voice revolution that had begun in the 1970s accelerated under Deeley. He brought with him the perspective of a SIGINTer who knew how to exploit other countries' communications. [censored]

[censored] In 1980 Deputy Secretary of Defense Graham Claytor endorsed the STU-II program and recommended large-scale procurement. In 1982, his successor, Frank Carlucci, decided to buy 5,000 STU-II sets and allocated $120 million for the program. The STU-II was strongly endorsed by Alexander Haig, Carlucci and President Reagan himself.

But STU-II was just a waystation. The revolution in voice security was wrought by a new product, the STU-III. The basis for the STU-III was a public key algorithm called [censored] designed by engineers from NSA's R1. When Deeley came to the COMSEC organization, he "captured" R1 and created a special projects office to develop the STU-III. Deeley made the decision to have the STU-III built by private industry, and three contractors—RCA, AT&T, and Motorola—each developed a unique STU-III device, all three of which sold competitively. It was a low-cost (about $2,000 per copy) terminal that would sit on a desk. There would be unique plastic key for each device, but the device would not work without another key, developed on demand from a central key management center. [censored]

The key management facility was originally collocated with a contractor in Waltham, Massachusetts. In 1988 NSA moved the facility to an old 1950s-era bomb shelter in the Maryland countryside owned by AT&T, near Finksburg.

The crypto gear that NSA had designed for the new communications era had, by the early 1980s, come to the end of the rope. The KW-26, a marvel of its day, could only secure 100-word-per-minute circuits. The KG-13 and KW-7 were out of production and becoming more difficult to maintain every day. The replacement device, developed under a project named [censored] would be the KG-84. Small, lightweight (20 lbs), cheap (base price of about $5,100), it was designed to operate at speeds up to 9600 bps. Cost of maintenance was also a big selling point: while the KW-26 mean time between failure (MBTF) was 1,840 hours, the worst-case MBTF for the KG-84 was 17,000 hours. The KG-84 began appearing in comm centers in the mid-1980s.

One of the COMSEC improvements of the 1980s was OTAR (over-the-air re-keying). NSA had long wanted to dispense with paper tape re-keying, with its attendant courier problems and possibility of loss or pilferage. The Agency had incorporated OTAR into the Vinson tactical voice system of the late 1970s, but the rationale was combat. If an American unit with a Vinson were overrun, the field commander would need a way to quickly re-key all other Vinson equipments. Vinson was an OTAR device by exception only; it was normally keyed just like any other COMSEC device. The KG-84 was designed with an optional OTAR capability, but DCA thought so little about it that at one time it directed that all KG-84s be rewired to disable the OTAR feature.

But two events in the 1980s spurred a reversal of fortunes for the OTAR concept. One was the invasion of Grenada, which conclusively demonstrated that the services could not easily talk to each other, and drove the JCS to reform the concept of jointness and to direct the services to marry their communications system. This led, ultimately, to a new COMSEC key distribution doctrine which would permit U.S. forces to communicate with each other on almost all tactical crypto devices using electronically distributed key.

The second was the arrest of John Walker in May of 1985. Walker had been stealing crypto key since 1968 and selling it to the Soviets. The massive hemorrhage of classified information was directly attributable to the wide and easy availability of crypto key, and sparked a complete re-look at COMSEC keying doctrine.

What resulted was a JCS decision in 1988 to implement OTAR on every KG-84 device in the world. Vice Admiral Jerry Tuttle, the JCS J6 in 1988, forced the issue after being told that NSA was having a hard time keeping up with the demand for paper keying tape and that the KG-84 had been designed with an OTAR capability that was not being used. Tuttle made the historic decision to require OTAR on KG-84 circuits, and by the early 1990s the KG-84 had been completely converted to the new method of operation.

Until NSA came up with an effective OTAR strategy in the 1980s, the best it could do was to protect the crypto keys from tampering. The Agency always had a small group working on protective packaging, but the big breakthrough came with the hiring of a chemist name [censored] in the 1960s. [censored] a Harvard Ph.D. in chemistry, had specialized in the detection of poison gasses during World War II. [censored]

[censored]

[censored]

The Second Parties—The United Kingdom

[censored]

[censored]

[censored]

Australia

[censored]

Australia's parliament had been controlled by Conservatives since the sacking of Gough Whitlam in 1975. But in 1983 the Australian Labor Party (ALP) regained control. The left wing of the party had been critical of Prime Minister Malcolm Fraser's close relationship with the United States. There were threats to close Aussie ports to American warships and strident declarations of brotherhood with the government of Vietnam. But when party leader Bob Hawke took the premiership, he excluded the left wing of the party and repudiated the anti-U.S. planks of the party platform. In foreign affairs he formed a close bond with Ronald Reagan. Soon after his election he publicly declared that the U.S. would continue to enjoy access to defence facilities in Australia, including Alice Springs (also known as Pine Gap). His public statement in support of the facility revealed the base's purpose: "...provision of early warning by receiving from space satellites information about missile launches—and the occurrence of nuclear explosions." It was more than the U.S. wanted him to say, but was received with relatively good graces in view of his strong support for the joint effort.

[censored]

[censored]

New Zealand

[censored]

The new relationship occurred just in time for controversy. In the summer of 1984 the Labor Party under David Lange assumed power in New Zealand. The party had long had a nuclear-free plank, and left-wing members were pressing for withdrawal from ANZUS. Lange, being a centrist by persuasion, tried to ignore the anti-U.S. tide, continuing to push a decision into the future. The Reagan administration also tried to ride out the storm, believing that Lange would be a New Zealand Bob Hawke on the issue. But it did not understand the depth of Lange's difficulties. Lange's problem turned on the nuclear-free issue and the determination of his left wing that no American nuclear vessels would be permitted in New Zealand ports. The U.S. delayed port visits in hopes that Lange could solve the political problem. Finally, in March of 1985 the U.S. requested permission for a non-nuclear vessel, the USS *Buchanan,* to visit Auckland in connection with a scheduled naval exercise. This was done under a tacit agreement with the Lange government that the first port visit would be by an obviously non-nuclear vessel, following which Lange could announce that he had determined that it was not a nuclear vessel and could enter. But the deal broke down because Lange could not push it through his party caucus, and he announced that the *Buchanan* would not be permitted to enter port. The outraged Reagan administration cancelled the joint exercise and suspended all military cooperation with New Zealand, including the flow of intelligence information.

[censored]

Third Parties

[censored]

[censored]

[censored]

All the Rest

[censored]

[censored]

Chapter 22 The Second Cold War

The SIGINT System And The Soviet Problem

By the end of the 1970s, the SIGINT system was optimized for its principal target, the Soviet Union. [censored]

What distiniguished the system, however, was the way that it all knitted together. Analysis of Soviet force posture was a complex weave [censored] Exploitation of the best source, [censored] was prioritized for processing based on an assessment of all the other indicators.

This system had been employed in an analysis of Soviet and Warsaw Pact [censored]

[censored]

[censored]

[censored]

The Second Cold War

The most distinguishable characteristic of American foreign policy during the Reagan administration was hard-line anticommunism. Reagan's views were so well-known that they apparently induced great consternation in Moscow. The Soviet view of Reagan was confirmed when, barely two months into his first term, Reagan referred to the USSR as the "focus of evil," and seized every opportunity to brand the Soviet Union as an international outlaw. The Soviets reciprocated by launching a propaganda blitz, at one point comparing Reagan to Hitler. This was not in the spirit of detente.

Militarily, the Reagan administration opened a campaign of psychological military warfare. American aircraft, especially from the Strategic Air Command, probed East Bloc borders in increasingly provocative flights. SAC sent B-52 flights over the North Pole to see what the Soviet reaction would be. The Navy was by all odds the most daring, however. Two huge naval exercises—one near the Murmansk coast in 1981, the other in the Sea of Okhotsk in April of 1983—served notice that Allied naval forces would intrude into what the Soviets had come to regard as their own private lakes. The Navy also delighted in using sophisticated evasion techniques to elude the USSR's ocean reconnaissance systems. These techniques would frequently be turned against the Soviets in high-tech sub-shadowing exercises.

These actions were calculated to induce paranoia, and they did. In early 1981, KGB chief Yuri Andropov, who had apparently come to believe that the U.S. had decided to launch a first nuclear strike, launched Operation Ryan. Ryan was an attempt to get as much information as possible about this supposed attack. The scare peaked in 1983. In February of that year the U.S. began the deployment of nuclear-armed Pershing missiles. In March, Reagan made his famous "evil empire" speech, and only two weeks later he announced the inauguration of his Strategic Defense Initiative, later dubbed "Star Wars."

Cold War hysteria reached a peak in the autumn of the year with two events: the Soviet shootdown of KAL-007 and the NATO exercise Able Archer. The latter was an annual NATO command post exercise of a distinctly nonthreatening nature. But in 1983 the scenario was changed to involve the secretary of defense, the chairman of the JCS, the president, and the vice president. Moreover, Able Archer 1983 added a practice drill that took NATO forces from the use of conventional forces through nuclear release. This, says Gordievsky, was interpreted in Moscow as the possible initiation of a preemptive strike, and this extremely dangerous postulation was used as a spur to intensify intelligence collection. It also, according to the same source, resulted in a very high state of KGB alert.

A last bit of melodrama was provided by the "Bogus War Message" of 1984. This bizarre episode had its origins in Reagan's penchant to ham for the microphones. Just prior to his weekly radio address on August 11, 1984, he was asked to do a voice check. Not content to do a routine countdown, he said "My fellow Americans. I'm pleased to tell you today that I've signed legislation that will outlaw Russia forever. We begin bombing in five minutes." Although this was supposedly off the record, it was overheard by all three networks and was broadcast over NBC and ABC. The Soviets took a very dim view of the incident, calling it "unprecedentedly hostile toward the USSR and dangerous to the cause of peace."

[censored]

[censored]

[censored]

KAL-007

[censored]

But it was a real aircraft. Early on September 1, Korean Airlines flight 007 had taken off from Anchorage, Alaska, on its way to Seoul. It was programmed to fly commercial track R20, which skirted Soviet airspace along Kamchatka. It was obviously off course.

[censored]

While the SU-15 maneuvered, the airline pilot was engaged in routine conversations with the tower at Narita airport, outside Tokyo. At 0320 the tower controller gave KAL-007 permission for an altitude change, and three minutes later the pilot reported that he had climbed to the new altitude and had leveled off. At 0327 the controller tried to contact KAL-007, but the answer was lost in a haze of static. Tokyo tower never heard from KAL-007 again.

[censored]

[censored]

[censored] was making the call at the request of Major General James O'Donnell, commander of 5th AF.) The analyst at [censored] began reading a just-published UPI dispatch: "A Korean Air Lines jumbojet flying from New York to Seoul Wednesday with 269 people aboard, including a U5. congressman, was forced to land on Sakhalin, a Soviev-occupied island north of Japan. The congressman was identified as Larry MacDonald, Democratic representative of Georgia..."

[censored]

[censored]

Washington

[censored]

[censored]

Saturday afternoon an outraged secretary of state, George Shultz, who was the ranking administration official in Washington that day, accused the Soviets of shooting the aircraft down in cold blood. He stated that the the Soviets had tracked KAL-007 for 2 1/2 hours, [censored]

[censored] arrived at the White House just before 1700 that Saturday. They met in the Situation Room with NSC officials John Poindexter, Ken deGraffenreid. Bob Kimmel, and Oliver North and [censored] The NSC people informed them that they would be briefing President Reagan the next morning.

[censored] returned to the White House at 0800 Sunday, and were ushered into the Cabinet Room, where they briefed the president. [censored] The briefing lasted only ten minutes, but the questions that followed went on for almost forty. Following that, the president conducted a highly unusual Sunday morning press conference to condemn the Soviets and demand an admission of guilt.

On Monday evening Reagan went on television again to repeat his charges and outline a program of sanctions against the USSR. To back up his charges, he played part of the tape. At the same time, administration officials were appearing on TV talk shows to condemn the Soviet shootdown. The State department frantically rounded up support for sanctions from friendly capitals. It was a full-scale propaganda blitz.

Moscow

The Soviets went into public denial. In the first official press release from Moscow, almost twelve hours after the shootdown and some nine hours after debris was confirmed floating on the ocean, Tass reported an encounter with an unidentified plane, which, it was alleged, failed to respond to queries and continued on its way. The next day Tass still denied any knowledge of the fate of the aircraft, but began hinting that it might have been some sort of "spy flight." It was not until Sunday, September 3, that Soviet official sources admitted that it might have been the missing KAL flight; but they reiterated that it was undoubtedly on an espionage mission.

The spy scenario was one that the Soviets repeated and embellished. A writer in the Moscow *Literaturnaya Gazeta* for September 7 alleged that KAL-

007 was "...a provocation hatched a long time ago and carefully prepared by the US CIA." He went on: "It is universally known that Boeing passenger aircraft are equipped with modern control instruments and also that they can be fitted with the most advanced intelligence gathering intruments to carry out highly secret assignments."

The Soviets did not finally admit that they had shot the aircraft down until September 6, three days after President Reagan had played the incriminating tapes. They expressed regret that it had proved to be a civilian aircraft, but held the U.S. "fully responsible," in line with their contention that its flight course had been charted by the CIA.

On September 9, with worldwide criticism mounting, the Soviets took the unprecedented action of putting the chief of their general staff on television to explain the Soviet side of the story. Nikolay Ogarkov proved to be an articulate spokesman for the Soviet story, gesticulating at the flight route on the map and hammering away at the spy theme: It has been proved irrefutably that the intrusion of the South Korean airlines plane into Soviet airspace was a deliberately, thoroughly planned intelligence operation. It was directed from certain centers in the territory of the United States and Japan. A civilian plane was chosen for the mission, deliberately disregarding or, possibly, counting on the loss of human life. American radars, he asserted, tracked the flight (ignoring the laws of physics which prevented that) and would have warned the plane had it not been a spy flight. He contended that it flew in tandem with the RC-135, in a pattern designed to confuse Soviet air defense, then broke off into Soviet territory, deliberately evading pursuit.

A by-product of the press conference was Ogarkov's assertion that the Sukhoi pilot fired cannon bursts at the airliner. [censored]

[censored]

Soviet reactions to KAL-007 were a product of history. The insular nature of the regime had produced over years an obsessive concern with safety and secrecy, [censored] The 1983 shootdown was, in fact, preceded by a similar incident involving a Korean Airlines commercial flight five and a half years earlier. On April 20, 1978, a KAL 707 flying from Paris to Seoul by way of Anchorage strayed into Soviet airspace over the Kola Peninsula. [censored]

[censored]

The Soviet concern for border security had escalated to paranoid intensity by August of 1983. The Reagan administration's campaign of psychological warfare and border probing had been bringing up the temperature for two years. Soviet tempers boiled over in April of 1983 as a result of the U.S. naval exercise in the Sea of Okhotsk. [censored]

New York

U.S. ambassador Jeane Kirkpatrick represented the United States at the UN. The Reagan administration intended to lay the wood to the Soviet

Union, and she was well equipped to do this. Acerbic even in calm seas, she could be ferocious in a fight.

After listening to denials from the Soviet ambassador, she launched an attack reminiscent of Adlai Stevenson's charge during the Cuban Missile Crisis in 1962. She played the tape [censored] following which she made a point-by-point refutation of Soviet denials and evasions: Contrary to Soviet statements, there is no indication whatsoever that the interceptor pilot made any attempt either to communicate with the airliner or to signal it to land....at no point did the pilots raise the question of the identity of the target aircraft...At a distance of two kilometers, under the conditions prevailing at the that time, it was easily possible to identify a 747 passenger airliner. Either the Soviet pilot did not know the Korean plane was a commercial airliner, or he did not know what he was firing at [sic]. Her interpretation of what had happened was near perfect, and her language was supported by the voice transcript. Her more general charge later in the speech about historic Soviet brutality and disregard of international law had much less to do with the evidence, and was part of the Reagan administration's diplomatic offensive against the USSR. KAL-007 simply opened the door of opportunity.

The Postmortems

When it was all over, the intelligence community, as well as the journalistic world, had some reassessing to do. What did the Soviets know, and when did they know it? What did the intelligence community know, and how did they use it? And what contributions did the White House make to the situation?

To answer the last question first, the White House pounced on the shootdown and squeezed it dry of propaganda value. It was one of those opportunities that comes but once in a lifetime. There is no question that the Reagan administration made the very, very most of it. In years following the collapse of the Soviet Union, a Russian journalist assessed it as the single most disastrous propaganda defeat they ever suffered.

[censored]

[censored] It was an example of how quickly a large and far-flung bureaucracy could move once pricked. It is hard to see how anyone could have done better. Seymour Hersh, one journalist [censored] singled out NSA for excellence and for a non-political approach. (He did not, however, have kind words for the Reagan people.)

[censored]

[censored] William Casey decreed on September 21, 1983, that "...it is now time to circle the wagons and stop talking." But the Reagan administration, in some ways the most porous in memory, could not seem to stop talking.

And, finally, how culpable were the Soviets in the incident? [censored] Given the paranoia that had existed since April, it was unthinkable that such a penetration could be permitted without action. A scenario like that would place everyone's jobs at stake.

The Soviet SU-15 pilot claimed that he did not recognize it to be a civilian airliner. Flying in the dim light of an early dawn, with the cabin blacked out so passengers could sleep, it could have looked like a military aircraft from a distance. The size of the silhouette, the rotating beacon, argue the opposite case. But far more egregious errors of visual identification are made every day, and were made during the attack on the *Liberty* in 1967, to name just one case.

[censored]

It was the Reagan people who insisted that the Soviets could not have mistaken a 747 for a 707. That was their value judgment. It was wrong, but not so wide of the mark that one can inpute anything more sinister than righteous wrath. It was the height of the Second Cold War.

Verification

SALT II was never ratified by the Senate, thus leaving a huge question mark about the fate of strategic arms limitation. In the absence of a ratified treaty, however, both sides decided independently to abide by the provisions of the draft. When Reagan became president, that was how matters stood.

Reagan, too, continued the informal arrangements that the Carter administration had left him. But under Reagan there was much less trust. The issue of a "Soviet strategic breakout" from the treaty was never far from anyone's mind, and the intelligence work to discover such a "breakout" was intense. In late 1982 intercepted telemetry from a Soviet missile test showed 95 percent encryption, the first time Soviet telemetry encryption had ever hit that level. The intelligence community assessed that above 70 percent amounted to denial of capability to monitor treaty compliance. The next year, as the debate of telemetry encryption continued to rage, an advisory committee reported to the president on a long history of Soviet arms control treaties, including SALT I. The report reinforced Reagan's natural tendency to distrust the Soviets anyway.

[censored]

In 1983, the Reagan administration decided that all future U.S. ICBMs would have encrypted telemetry, partly in retaliation for the earlier Soviet decision to encrypt theirs. [censored] In this case the defense won, and U.S. telemetry became unreadable.

The Relocatable Targets Problem

Monitoring the Soviet operational force was the key to SALT verification. [censored]

[censored]

The Soviets introduced the SS-20 in 1977. The SS-20 was an IRBM with a range of 5,000 kilometers, [censored] This made it a threat to NATO forces.

But the real news about it was its mobility. The SS-20 was the first relocatable strategic missile in the inventory.

SS-20 units moved into former SS-4 and SS-5 sites in the western USSR, and in the Far East they occupied former SS-7 complexes. By the mid-1980s the Soviet SRF had ten SS-20 divisions composed of 48 regiments and [censored] Units in garrison were not fully operational—to achieve that, the unit had to go to the field.

[censored]

[censored]

Following on the heels of the SS-20 was a new threat—the SS-25 ICBM. With a range of 10,500 kilometers and a deployment MO similar to the SS-20, the SS-25 soon became the highest priority in the intelligence community. The first units became operational in 1985.

[censored]

The relocatable target problem continued to be a research effort until 1985. Then, in July of that year, the intelligence community got its marching orders, in the form of NSDD-178. The directive was specific and unambiguous. It directed the Department of Defense "to develop a program to provide a capability to attack relocatable targets with U.S. strategic forces..." Soviet relocatable targets would be placed at risk and kept that way beyond the year 2000. "At risk" was defined as having the ability to destroy at least 50-75 percent of the force.

NSDD-178 generated money and priority. Essentially, the intelligence community was to remove all stops to find relocatable targets. The effort was headed by the Mobile Missile Task Force, a multi-agency committee set up within DoD to direct the effort.

[censored]

Chapter 23 The Rise of Terrorism and Unconventional Targets in the 1980s

The U.S. SIGINT system had developed a modus operandi in dealing with military targets which drove the functioning of the system for many years. When faced with other types of targets, however, the system tended to become unstuck and dysfunctional. Paradoxically, the Reagan period, with its focus on Soviet strategic forces, became the time when the system was first wrenched into a response to unconventional targets.

They had been there all the time, of course. One of the earliest targets of the post-World War I period were the rumrunners, a target that virtually defined the successful Coast Guard SIGINT effort in the interwar period. The establishment of NSA was due partly to CIA's insistence [censored] But resources were hard to come by, and most of the money went to watching the Soviets and fighting the Vietnam War.

In the late 1960s, as SIGINT budgets began to slide, some of NSA's prime contractors, [censored] attempted to sell their wares on the international market. [censored]

Terrorism

The single biggest factor in nonmilitary targeting, however, was the rise of international terrorism. Originating in the Middle East as an Arab reaction to successive military defeats at the hands of Israel, the disease spread to Northern Ireland in 1969, to the Basque country of northern Spain in the 1970s, and elsewhere. From 1968 to 1970 terrorist incidents worldwide increased 113 percent each year, and 24 percent from 1970 to 1972. The infamous Palestinian assault at the 1972 Munich Olympics was followed by a brief decline in incidents, but in 1976 they began to rise again—41 percent each year from 1975 to 1978. Moreover, terrorists shifted their attention from property to people. In 1970 half the incidents were directed against people, but in 1981, 80 percent were.

NSA's response was delayed by organization and methodology. From the latter standpoint, international terrorism [censored]

[censored]

The other problem was organizational. It was not until after the Munich Olympics that NSA created an organization whose task was, specifically, international terrorism. [censored]

[censored]

In 1981, following the conclusion of the Iranian hostage crisis, Dick Lord, who was then chief of G, commissioned a study to see if NSA could do better than it had been doing on the terrorist problem. At about the same time the fledgling Reagan administration directed that all intelligence agencies devote more resources to counter-terrorism. [censored]

[censored]

[censored]

[censored]

Airline Hijackings

Terrorism in the 1980s was dominated by a series of high-profile hijackings. Most, though not all, were orchestrated by Middle Eastern political organizations like Amal and Hezbollah. President Reagan, like President Carter before him, was seized by these incidents, and each in turn claimed the total attention of his NSC staff until it was resolved. Likewise, most of the intelligence available to the NSC during the course of hijacking operations [censored]

Typical of these support operations was the reporting series on TWA 847. Hijacked by Islamic terrorists on a flight from Athens to Rome on June 14, 1985, the flight was diverted to Beirut. Over the ensuing three days it played hopscotch across the Mediterranean between Algiers and Beirut. At one of its Beirut stops the terrorists executed an American naval enlisted man, Robert Stethem, and threw his body on the tarmac beside the plane. They threatened to execute many more. On June 16 the plane departed Algiers for the last time and came to rest in Beirut. There ensued two weeks of diplomatic negotiations among the United States, Israel, Syria and the Amal organization under Nabih Barri. Ultimately, Syrian president Hafez al-Assad of Syria obtained the release of the American hostages from TWA 847, in return for the Israeli release of several hundred Lebanese Shiite captives being held illegally in Israeli jails after an Israeli army raid into southern Lebanon. The hijackers never succeeded in their primary aim—the release of seventeen terrorists being held in Kuwaiti jails.

[censored]

[censored]

[censored]

[censored]

The War On Drugs

Although the federal government had always been concerned about drug trafficking, the first significant effort did not occur until 1972, with Nixon's "War on Drugs." This campaign was mostly words and was soon drowned out by the Watergate affair. President Ford created the Drug Enforcement Administration, and under Jimmy Carter the State Department got involved through the creation of the Bureau for International Narcotics Matters. But it did not receive much push until the administration of Ronald Reagan. Although the Reagan approach came to be symbolized by Nancy Reagan's "Just Say No" advice on the use of drugs, Reagan's thrust was to stop drugs before they arrived in the country. The idea was that, eventually, there would be nothing to say No to.

Faced with rising complaints about the burgeoning drug trade in Florida, in 1982 Reagan created the South Florida Task Force, an unfunded consortium of federal and state agencies involved in combatting drugs and the drug trade. In order to give it prestige, Reagan named his vice president, George Bush, to head the task force.

Growing out of this was the National Narcotics Border Interdiction System, or NNBIS, an attempt to combat drug smugglers at U.S borders. Under NNBIS, the federal government organized six regional centers in New York, Chicago, Long Beach, El Paso, New Orleans and Miami. Each center was staffed by representatives from participating agencies—fourteen on the federal side, including DEA, FBI, Customs, Coast Guard, Bureau of Alcohol, Tobacco and Firearms (BATF), Immigration and Naturalization Service, and the Border Patrol. Associated with it were more than 14,000 state and local law enforcement agencies.

Intelligence support for the effort was critical, and NSA was called in almost immediately. In 1983 NSA sent a representative [censored] in response to a specific request from the vice president's office. Later, the Agency sent representatives [censored]

[censored]

From the first, legal issues drove much of the effort. The Posse Comitatus Act prohibited defense organizations from participating in law enforcement except in certain very narrowly defined circumstances relating to the information having been collected as incidental to the foreign intelligence mission. In May of 1983 NSA, under pressure to assume a more proactive stance, requested clarification of the rules of engagement. The Department of Justice reply was not an especially useful restatement of the rule that the information could be disseminated to the Coast Guard and Customs Service as a by-product of NSA's foreign intelligence mission. But the next year the attorney general issued a new set of guidelines which loosened the rules. [censored]

When SIGINT support began, law enforcement agencies were enthusiastic, and all kinds of partners turned up in NSA's antechamber. One of the closest working relationships was with the Coast Guard [censored]

Other partnerships were more difficult. The Drug Enforcement Administration had no experience with foreign intelligence organizations, working instead with the law enforcement authorities in various countries. Unlike the FBI, DEA had no experience in using SIGINT leads to help an investigation, and chafed under any restrictions regarding the use of evidence in court. If SIGINT could not be introduced at trial, many in DEA did not understand its value. In the late years of the decade, relations with DEA cooled.

Once involved in counternarcotics, NSA discovered a big wide world of SIGINT efforts beyond the confines of NSCID 6. [censored]

The Asian drug problem, though far less visible to the administration, was of much longer standing, At least 90 percent of the world's opium came from Burma, Iran, Afghanistan and Lebanon, and the Golden Triangle (a point where the borders of Burma, Laos and Thailand meet) was the single most productive area. In Burma, the Shan United Army (SUA), a nation unto itself, managed the reduction of raw opium into #4 heroin (a process that reduced its volume by a factor of ten) and transportation, often by pack animals, over the border into Thailand for onward shipment. Owing to the complete lack of cooperation of the Burmese and Laotian governments, opium production rose dramatically in the 1970s.

[censored] The push came from the US Army. In 1971 it was estimated that between ten and fifteen percent of U.S. troops in Southeast Asia were addicted. In the United States, the dramatic rise in drug addiction prompted President Nixon's War on Drugs campaign.

[censored]

[censored]

SIGINT And Counterintelligence

[censored] Project VENONA had resided in that office. As productive as VENONA had been, it represented [censored]

CIA, too, had fallen on parlous times. The counterintelligence division headed by James Angleton had acquired a lurid reputation (made famous by David Martin's book *A Wilderness of Mirrors*). CIA director William Colby had fired Angleton in 1974, and in the ensuing commotion the counterintelligence mission had been virtually shut down.

The resurrection began in 1981 with the Casey regime at CIA. In response to increasing intelligence community calls for more emphasis, NSA in 1983 created G14, the counterintelligence division.

[censored]

[censored]

[censored] This and Vienna had emerged in the 1980s as the key international cities for KGB operations. (Pelton and Walker, for instance were both summoned to Vienna for meetings.) [censored]

NSA's participation in counterterrorist, counternarcotics, and counter-intelligence problems gave Agency people valuable experience in these nontraditional areas. The pessimism of the late 1970s turned into optimism within ten years. Yes, SIGINT could make a real difference, and NSA did not have to cede the field to HUMINT efforts. [censored] In the White House and the NSC staff, where it really counted, SIGINT had become an integral part of the national security apparatus. It was to give the cryptologists a big jump on the SIGINT problems that were to confront the nation in the post-Cold War World.

Chapter 24 Military Crises and SIGINT Support during the Reagan Administration

The effects of Vietnam lingered on in NSA's relationship with military commanders. Through the late 1970s the JCS and NSA continued to squabble over the ownership and employment of SIGINT assets, and a new JCS directive, "Concept of SIGINT Support to Military Commanders," issued in 1982, failed to completely set things to rest. Within NSA, however, there were new efforts to satisfy requests for SIGINT support throughout the period. One of the key issues, which was rapidly being resolved by 1980, was that of making available information [censored] through rapid sanitized reporting.

General Faurer probably struck the best balance between strategic SIGINT managementand military support mechanisms. It was paradoxical, then, that the biggest disaster in the military support arena occurred during his administration. It was the invasion of Grenada.

Urgent Fury

Grenada, a microscopic speck in the far eastern Caribbean Sea, had virtually no name recognition for Americans before October of 1983. A British colony since 1763, it had gained improbable autonomy in 1967 and complete independence seven years later. Widespread dissatisfaction with its prime minister led to a coup and a new leader, Maurice Bishop, a charismatic Marxist. Bishop appeared to fall under the influence of Fidel Castro's Cuba. Cubans began showing up in waves to "assist" the Marxist regime, and the government began construction of a 9,000-foot runway near the capital which, [censored] would be ideal for Soviet Bloc military aircraft. Then, just when the U.S. intelligence community was becoming concerned, the Bishop government was supplanted on October 13 by a more radical movement under the finance minister, Bernard Coard. Six days later Bishop and three other cabinet ministers were executed under the direction of the army commander, Hudson Austin.

Amid the civil disturbances that spread throughout the island during the coup, the Reagan administration became concerned about the fate of approximately 1,000 American and other foreign nationals, and began considering a rescue mission. But the postulated influence of Cubans in the situation undoubtedly weighed more heavily on their minds than the fate of innocents. On October 14 the JCS was told to whip up an invasion plan in very short order. General Vessey, the chairman of the Joint Chiefs of Staff, requested an implementation date of 25 October, less than two weeks away.

Owing to an extremely compressed time schedule, the plan was not a model of coordination. Vessey decided at the outset to exclude a number of peripheral organizations, including the Strategic Air Command, Defense Management Agency, NSA, and four parts of the JCS staff, J4, J5, the Deputy Directorate for Political-Military Affairs, and the Public Affairs Office. Vessey chose to rely entirely on DIA for intelligence. This was done partly for secrecy, partly because of the short time schedule.

The JCS decision to exclude NSA and the Public Affairs Office turned into a major fiasco. The exclusion of NSA had been tried before, [censored]

[censored]

The operation succeeded, in the sense that the JCS got 8,000 U.S. troops onto the island, rescued nearly 600 Americans and 120 foreign nationals trapped by the political chaos, restored popular government, and eliminated the potential threat to U.S. lines of communications in the Caribbean. All this was accomplished with only nineteen Americans killed and 116 wounded. The main antagonists turned out to be the Cuban soldiers on Grenada, who had established a much more secure foothold than American intelligence had suspected.

But it was recognized by everyone involved as a "learning experience" for a military machine gone rusty since Vietnam. The post-operation critiques named intelligence as one of the areas of failure, but did not come to the obvious conclusion that intelligence was hamstrung by the JCS refusal to involve any agency but DIA in the preparation. It also identified communications as an abysmal failure. In their haste, units deployed without compatible CEOI (communications equipment operating instructions). Secure voice equipments (i.e., Vinson-equipped radios) supplied by NSA could not talk to each other because they did not have compatible key. On several occasions Army units on the ground could not call the Navy vessels anchored just offshore for air and artillery support, and twice the Navy began bombing Army units, but the Army could not reach the Navy to tell them to stop firing. In one well-publicized incident, an officer of the 82nd Airborne Division had to use a pay phone on the island to call Fort Bragg to ask authorities there to call the Navy.

After the invasion a dispute erupted between NSA and the Pentagon about the exclusion from planning. This resulted in a commitment by the director of DIA, Lieutenant General Williams, to routinely involve NSA in the planning, but this commitment lasted for only a few days—NSA was not even invited to the JCS critique sessions. In reviewing the situation, General Faurer blamed the top man: "So General Vessey undoubtedly had his reasons and I applaud them for everybody but us. I recognize the advantage of secrecy in what he did. I also recognize the difficulty of having secrecy in our government, but I have no sympathy for secrecy being used as an excuse for not finding a way to get NSA involved...."

[censored]

[censored]

[censored]

Just Cause

The American military invasion of Panama in 1989 was as smooth as Urgent Fury had been rocky. The crisis in American-Panamanian relations had been in slow-motion evolution for several years, and this allowed the JCS to do long-range planning. Many of the units involved in Grenada also participated in Just Cause and learned from the earlier experience. [censored]

Following his successful Panama Canal Treaty negotiations, Panamanian strongman Omar Torrijos enjoyed almost messianic popularity in his home country. But Torrijos was killed in a plane crash in 1981, and the country was temporarily rudderless. This did not last long, however. A new strongman, Manuel Noriega, soon grabbed the tiller.

Noriega had joined the Torrijos entourage soon after the ousting of the Arias government in 1968. His specialty was intelligence, and he worked closely with American military intelligence people over the years, attending special training at Fort Bragg in 1967. When Torrijos died, Noriega emerged as one of three powerful army officers heading the Guardia Nacional. But Noriega was the smartest of the three, and soon eased the other two into early retirement. He gained control of the Guardia and, through a succession of figurehead presidents, the governmental machinery.

His relationships with the U.S. were convoluted. Of all the Guardia figures, U.S. intelligence regarded him as the least appetizing, and the State Department viewed his rise as a scarcely mitigated disaster. But he proved a useful partner in many respects, [censored] US. military authorities at SOUTHCOM were forced to work closely with him, but they did not enjoy the experience. His sexual escapades were legendary, and it was rumored that he was involved with drug trafficking.

Noriega's reputation, already vile among knowledgeable Americans, took a turn for the worse when he "stole" the Panamanian elections in 1984. With his own man in the presidency, the way appeared clear for him, but the next year a Noriega opponent, Dr. Hugo Spadafora, was brutally murdered, and it was widely rumored that Noriega had ordered the execution because Spadafora had exposed Noriega's drug dealings. In the midst of the Spadafora crisis, Noriega replaced the mostly compliant president, Nicolas Ardito Barletta, with an even more compliant operative, Arturo Delvalle. Alarmed, the State Department sent its Latin American troubleshooter, Elliott Abrams, with National Security Advisor John Poindexter, to warn Noriega to back off, The warning had little effect, partly because Noriega was deeply involved in supporting the Reagan administration's undeclared war against the Sandinistas, and thus considered himself invulnerable.

With the onset of the Iran-Contra scandal in 1986, Noriega's usefulness came to an end, and the Reagan administration began exerting considerable pressure on him to reform. In June of that year, journalist Seymour Hersh published a *New York Times* article exposing Noriega's drug trafficking, and Senator Jesse Helms opened a Senate investigation into the matter. In February of 1988, two Florida grand juries simultaneously indicted him for drug trafficking, and he became a fugitive from the American judicial system. While all this was going on, Panamanians were rioting in the streets, and the Guardia, which had been renamed the Panamanian Defense Force (PDF) by Noriega, initiated brutal repression. The economy was in collapse, and under intense pressure, Noriega agreed to "democratic" elections for May of 1989. Although the elections occurred as scheduled, the opposition appeared headed for victory. Noriega then annulled the elections and appointed his own man.

JCS planning for intervention in Panama had begun in 1988, following the Florida indictments, in an operation code-named Blue Spoon. The operation envisioned a quick military strike composed of SOUTHCOM troops on the ground, considerably augmented by airborne troops from Fort Bragg. [censored]

[censored]

On December 16, Panamanian forces shot and killed a Marine officer. On the same date, they detained and interrogated a Navy lieutenant and his wife. These two incidents culminated months of calculated harassment by the PDF, and the next day President Bush directed a military invasion, to begin in the early morning hours of December 20. [censored]

[censored]

Airborne forces hit the country so quickly, in so many places, that the Panamanian military quickly disintegrated. [censored]

[censored]

Noriega disappeared from view at the outset of operation Just Cause, and he was never located [censored] until he took refuge in the Papal Nunciature on December 24. His last known location, during the evening of December 19, [censored] By the time troops were on the ground, he had disappeared.

The mystery was eventually cleared up by one of his bodyguards who surrendered and was debriefed by U.S. intelligence. [censored] Partway to Panama City, however, he split from his convoy and headed for a recreation area outside the Torrijos-Tocumen Airport, where he had planned to spend the night with a prostitute. This dalliance was interrupted at about 10 that evening by a phone call from the minister of health, who reported that the Americans were planning to invade. According to the bodyguard, Noriega ignored the warning until he heard explosions at the airport. (It was the XVIII Airborne Corps paradropping into the area.) In panic, he got into his car and drove around in circles for the rest of the night, not daring to stop anywhere for longer than a few minutes. The next day he went to the house of his secretary's husband's sister and stayed there until December 24, when he sought Papal asylum.

Meanwhile, [censored] HUMINT sent US Special Forces charging first in one direction, then in another, presumably hot on his trail. At one point they invaded Farallon, finding hot coffee and still-smoking cigarettes, but no Noriega. Everyone believed that they were only minutes behind their quarry, but if the bodyguard is to be believed, these forays were all blind alleys. He was never at Farallon, or, for that matter, at any of the other hideouts the Army was monitoring. In all, Special Forces conducted more than forty attempted snatch operations.

[censored]

[censored]

There were other problems, too. [censored]

All in all, however, Just Cause did much to restore relationships between SIGINTers and the supported forces. This relationship became critical during Desert Storm two years later.

Chapter 25 Iran-Contra

The Iran-Contra scandal dominated the newspapers during the second Reagan administration. The affair hit the newsstands in October of 1986 when the Sandinistas shot down an aircraft making arms deliveries to the Contras, and captured an American, Eugene Hasenfus, who had been kicking pallets of material out the back end of the aircraft for the Contras waiting on the ground. Almost simultaneously, a Lebanese newspaper broke the story of attempts by the Reagan administration to free American hostages in Lebanon with sales of arms. From that time on, it was never out of the press.

Contra

[censored]

Ronald Reagan's Republican Party had generally opposed an accommodation with Panama, and when Reagan was elected president there was some talk about trying to reverse the treaty. But it was never a serious threat, and Congress chose to let the issue ride, in hopes that arrangements with Torrijos would work out. Reagan's Latin American focus was decidedly elsewhere—toward Nicaragua.

The Nicaraguan Revolution and the Concern about Communist Subversion

Nicaragua, in company with most Central American principalities, was a country wracked by periodic revolution, military coups, tyranny and subversion. The situation had gotten so bad that in 1912 President Taft had sent in the Marines. They stayed until 1933. In 1927, Henry Stimson was sent to the country to negotiate a political settlement He succeeded in obtaining the agreement of all but one general, Augusto Cesar Sandino. Sandino fled to the hills with a few followers and tried to disrupt the American-sponsored elections of 1928. He and his followers continued fighting a guerrilla war for seven years, but in 1934 National Guard troops under an emerging strongman, Anastasio Somoza, collared the obstreperous revolutionary and summarily executed him. Later that year Somoza ousted the government and inaugurated forty-five years of dictatorship.

Sandino remained the hero of the dispossessed, and the movement, which came to be named after him, took onvan anti-American hue. Somoza and his greedy family stayed in power, imposing one of Latin America's least enlightened regimes on the defenseless country.

By the early 1970s Somoza's son, Anastasio Somoza Debayle, was in power. Less politically adept than his father, he fought off the growing Sandinista guerrilla movement through brute force. His resort to force attracted the attention of Amnesty International, as well as the liberal wing of the American Democratic Party, which demanded that foreign aid to the Nicaraguan government be cut off. The issue resonated with President Carter, but Carter had his hands full with other matters and tried to let the Nicaraguan situation ride. Omar Torrijos, no stranger himself to strongman rule, once said, "...the crisis in Nicaragua can be described as a simple problem: a mentally deranged man with an army of criminals is attacking a defenseless population....This is not a problem for the OAS; what we need is a psychiatrist."

On August 22, 1978, the Nicaraguan scene was permanently disrupted. On that date an obscure Sandinista general, Eden Pastora, captured the National Palace while congress was in session and extorted from Somoza a list of concessions, including releasing various Sandinista figures from jail. Nicaragua went into a state of long-term turmoil, with mob rioting, looting, government retaliation, executions, and the like. For almost a year the country descended into chaos, a descent that was finally interrupted on July 17, 1979, when Somoza and his family finally left the country. The Sandinistas took over.

The triumph of a viscerally anti-American revolutionary group in Nicaragua presented the Carter administration with a square dilemma. Carter, always predisposed toward such popular movements, on the one hand welcomed the overthrow of the odious Somoza regime, while on the other tried to convince the Sandinistas not to throw in their lot with Cuba and the Soviet Union. The U.S. promptly shipped $39 million in food aid to Nicaragua.

It didn't work. The Sandinistas turned slowly but surely toward Moscow. In March of 1980 they signed a comprehensive economic, scientific and cultural agreement with the USSR. In July, on the anniversary of the revolution, Fidel Castro was the most prominent speaker. Cuban advisors moved into Managua. In the meantime, the Sandinista leader, Daniel Ortega, announced that democratic elections were to be postponed until 1985, and forced the moderate element, led by newspaper publisher Violetta Chamorro and Alfonso Robelo, into opposition.

The problem for Carter was not Nicaragua, but the tinderbox satrapies to the north—El Salvador, Honduras and Guatemala. Following the treaty with Moscow, the [censored] Nicaraguan support for similar guerrilla movements, especially in El Salvador. Carter tried to play the issue both ways. In order to continue foreign aid to Nicaragua (the carrot approach to Ortega and company), he publicly certified that the Sandinistas were not supplying arms to neighboring guerrilla movements. [censored] Carter privately signed a finding to support democratic elements (read Contras) in Nicaragua. Just before the elections that would result in Ronald Reagan becoming president, the Sandinistas began flooding El Salvador with arms in hopes of overthrowing the government outright. An outraged Carter sent his ambassador, Anthony Pezzullo, to deliver a stinging rebuke to Ortega. Rejected, Carter continued arms deliveries to the repressive right-wing government of El Salvador.

While Carter smoldered with pent-up fury at Sandinista perfidy, Reagan was completely out front with it. The Republican platform for the election of 1980 called for the overthrow of the Nicaraguan government. As soon as Reagan became president, he suspended the final $15 million of a $75-million aid package for the country, and in March [censored] that Carter had begun. A finding of December 1981 stated that the American objective was to interdict the flow of arms to neighboring countries, rather than to overthrow the Nicaraguan government. [censored]

The Contra movement in Nicaragua had begun in 1980 as an inchoate agrarian protest against government policies. As the Sandinistas swung to the left, the Contras got stronger. There were small Contra groups in the south, unorganized at first, but led later by the very same Eden Pastora who had begun his public life as a prominent Sandinista general. In the north the groups were larger and better organized; they came to be dominated by a unified organization under a former National Guard officer, Enrique Bermudez. Pastora and Bermudez did not get along (for obvious ideological reasons, if nothing else). Forced to choose, [censored]

It is essential to understand the U.S. political conditions under which the guerrilla war was being fought. A 1974 amendment to the annual Foreign Assistance Act, called the Hughes-Ryan Amendment, required the president to "find" that each covert activity was "important to the national security of the United States," and that the president report such operations to Congress "in a timely fashion."

It had become customary to report such "findings" to the HPSCI and SSCI—that constituted "notification." Thus Congress was aware of, and had acquiesced in, the Contra operation. But in November of 1982 the "covert" effort was publicly exposed in the nation's leading newspapers. This produced a great deal of congressional agitation for an end to the effort, and resulted in a compromise, called the Boland Amendment, after Edward Boland of Massachusetts, the Democratic chairman of HPSCI. According to the amendment, no appropriations could be spent "for the purpose of overthrowing the government of Nicaragua or provoking an exchange between Nicaragua and Honduras." Although somewhat restrictive, the amendment dealt with intent, not activities. Support to the Contras remained legal as long as its overt objective was not overthrow, just interdiction of arms. But the next year, following the harbor mining episode, a second Boland Amendment (called "Boland Two") prohibited the expenditure of funds for the purpose of Contra support, whatever the motivation. This meant that, at least for fiscal year 1985, the flow of aid would run dry.

[censored]

[censored] It was clear, long before Eugene Hasenfus was shot down, that the Nicaraguans had a good handle on [censored] resupply flights and that the Sandinistas had shoulder-launched missiles that could bring them clown. (This was how the Hasenfus aircraft was grounded.)

[censored]

The Reagan administration's effort to stop Sandinista subversion in Central American ran into all sorts of political problems. It had only a hair-thin majority in Congress when, in April of 1984, The Wall Street Journal released a story claiming that CIA was helping mine Nicaraguan harbors, thus endangering commercial shipping. (Several ships, including a Soviet tanker, had been damaged.) The story created chaos in Congress, where administration allies were delicately trying to steer the 1985 Contra aid package to approval. Barry Goldwater broke openly with William Casey, alleging that he had not been informed of the operation (not that he did not approve, however). Other congressmen opposed a direct CIA presence in the operation. Aid was voted down, and the administration was confronted with its first outright break in the funding cycle for its Contra guerrilla groups. Aid was not restored in any fashion until the 1987 budget year. But no sooner was aid reestablished than a Contra resupply flight was shot down in late 1986 with a CIA contractor, Eugene Hasenfus, aboard. Chaos again roiled the Contra program.

The Reagan effort against the Sandinistas was smart because it was broad-based. Not putting its eggs in one basket, the administration funneled military aid to El Salvador and Honduras, increased intelligence surveillance, and mounted a public information program to build domestic support. Despite missteps like the harbor mining, they could rely on Sandinista administrative incompetence and heavy-handed domestic repression. Slowly, the tide began to turn.

[censored]

[censored] The problem was not just CIA's dealings with its clients; it also related to the legality of applying money to a problem whose spending authorization was constantly in question. Sometimes money had been appropriated; sometimes it hadn't. Sometimes CIA was trying an end run around congressional restrictions by trying to use defense money. [censored] actions required a legal ruling. Should an employee inadvertently step over a line, would he or she be liable? And who would pay legal fees if the matter ever went to court? It was not a moot question, as the Iran-Contra scandal would soon demonstrate.

Iran

In the summer of 1985, Oliver North, an obscure Marine lieutenant colonel on the NSC staff, was running a covert operation to try to get Western hostages out of Lebanon. His primary contacts were with Iranians, who were presumably backing the Lebanese terrorists holding the hostages. It involved covert dealings with Israeli intelligence, trips to Iran, and direct dealings with an Iranian businessman named Ghorbanifar. The operation suffered from leaky security.

[censored] The matter remained strictly a White House affair until, on September 12, 1985, [censored] Charlie Allen, the NIO for counter-terrorism and the designated CIA contact point for Oliver North's hostage release project, [censored]

[censored]

In November of 1985, Ken deGraffenreid, the NSC staffer in charge of intelligence issues, discovered that North was devising hand codes for use in the operation. DeGraffenreid, who fully appreciated the insecurity inherent in such a bootleg code, called NSA's [censored] Harry Daniels, the assistant deputy director for information security (DDI). [censored] went to the White House that afternoon and discussed the matter with deGraffenreid, and they decided that [censored] should give North a threat briefing. North understood the problem and asked about COMSEC equipment.

The problem was tangled. North would need COMSEC equipment to secure his own communications, but he did not tell [censored] who else might be involved in the communications. The relationship with North broadened as [censored] continued to work with him to protect the operation. In December, North told him that he was involved in an effort to free the hostages in Lebanon, and was dealing with Iranians. Thus, [censored] understood from an early date that North was engaged in trying to extricate the hostages from Lebanon.

[censored] had limited choices. If only US. government officials were involved, [censored]

[censored] first gave North [censored] advising him that if he were not satisfied, to come back. North soon called to say that the [censored] equipment was not doing the job. [censored] then provided a certain number (the precise number is unclear) [censored] and demonstrated their use to North in the White House on at least one occasion.

On several occasions North's Iranian contacts requested encryption support, and in February of 1986 North called [censored] to ask for some encryption equipment that "might fall into Iranian hands". [censored] delivered [censored] equipment to North for this purpose, but the equipment was never actually handed over to the Ilranians.

Unknown to NSA and [censored] North had, in early 1986, decided to mix the Iran and Contra operations. He needed money to support the Contras, and could get it by overcharging the Iranians for the missiles that they so badly wanted. But the two operations got intertwined in other areas too. North used some of [censored] to secure communications in Latin America in order to cover the drop zones where arms were being supplied to the Contras. Some of this equipment might have been used by non-Americans. [censored] on the other hand, were used to secure hostage-related communications, and some of them might have been made available to Israelis.

There was no "standard operating procedure" for support to the White House. [censored] did things on the fly and did not keep good track of receipts much less monitor exactly how, and by whom, the equipment was being used. Because of the sensitivity of the mission, he had little or no staff support. He kept the DDI, Walter Deeley, and his deputy, Harry Daniels, informed, and also touched base with the DDO, Dick Lord (who was primarily concerned about Oliver North's method of operation) and Robert Rich, the deputy director. He received general guidance to press ahead and give the White House whatever it wanted; but to make sure that North understood [censored] He followed those instructions.

One of the consequences of the press exposure of Iran-Contra was exposure of NSA's dealings with North on encryption gear. General Odom was outraged. He had tried his best to keep NSA out of the scandal, and believed that he had done so, but the North-[censored] connection dragged NSA into the investigations. This produced an investigation within NSA itself to determine if procedures had been followed. The NSA inspector general discovered numerous procedural violations and concluded that some of [censored] were still not accounted for. The hindsight report also concluded that both [censored] had been "loaned" to foreign nationals. But it was more difficult to sort out the "What would I have done in his shoes" issue. The investigation came up with clear contradiction between [censored] version of what happened and Odom's. According to [censored] he briefed Odom on the whole matter in March of 1986 and got the approval to continue; according to Odom, this meeting never happened.

There was no resolving the differing accounts, but because there were procedural violations, Odom decided to discipline [censored] suspending him without pay for fifteen days. [censored] hired a lawyer and fought the charges. He apealed, and a review panel ruled that the disciplinary action should be dropped and [censored] legal fees (at that point amounting to about $40,000) be paid by the government. Odom was reportedly furious at the board action and decided to lower the recompense of legal fees to less than $10,000. [censored] appealed to Secretary of Defense Frank Carlucci. The appeal dragged on until 1988, when a new director, Admiral William Studeman, ruled in [censored] favor.

Outside of NSA, the [censored] affair" was a very minor blip on the public radar. It never had the potential to rock the Agency the way Watergate had. But inside NSA, it was one of the most divisive personnel issues in Agency history. It pitted a director determined to keep NSA out of public scandal against virtually the entire civilian hierarchy, determined to protect one of its own from retaliation that they perceived as scapegoatism. The puzzling gaps in chronology and differing recollections of what had happened were never resolved. But the bottom line was a verdict in favor of [censored] by the investigative board, by one former director (Bobby Inman, a member of the board) and by General Odom's successor, Admiral William Studeman.

But that was not the end of the affair. North had overcharged the Iranians for the weapons, and had siphoned the profits (which amounted to several million dollars) into special bank accounts to fund the Contra operations during periods when congressional funds were either not appropriated or outright prohibited. A special prosecutor, Lawrence Walsh, was called in to investigate the possible illegal diversion of funds to the Contras.

[censored]

[censored] This approach had worked within the Pelton investigation in 1985 and during the Church Committee hearings a decade earlier.

It did not work with Walsh's team. The prosecutors, failing to appreciate the sensitivity of the information, structured an indictment of North that made [censored] central to the issue, thus virtually guaranteeing that North's attorney, Brendan Sullivan, would request their use in court. The inevitable Sullivan request was a classic case of "grey mail"—a demand to introduce documents in court, the sensitivity of which guaranteed that prosecutors would not use them. Sullivan alleged that the reports would show that North's superiors in the NSC were being kept informed of the operation at every step. Walsh wanted to use them for the opposite purpose—to depict in considerable detail how the arms-for-hostages operation functioned.

Sullivan's request [censored] touched off a fierce dispute between NSA and the Walsh team. Walsh simply could not understand NSA's concerns about [censored] and contended that, since aspects of NSA's mission had already been discussed in the press, revealing [censored] would do no further damage. In December of 1988 NSA and the Walsh team tried to patch together a compromise position, but could not arrive at an agreement that the federal judge, Gerhard Gesell, would accept. In a climactic meeting on December 21, Walsh confronted NSA's general counsel, Elizabeth Rindskopf, who refused to back down. The matter was referred to the attorney general, Richard Thornburg, who backed Rindskopf. Walsh, in frustration, moved to dismiss the conspiracy counts which were the centerpiece of the indictment against Oliver North.

Although the principals in the Iran-Contra investigation were ultimately pardoned, the decisive moment had actually been reached on December 21, 1988. It was a constitutional crisis nearly as significant as that which nearly brought an end to Executive Department cooperation with the Pike Committee in 1975. Once again, the sensitivity of NSA materials was the centerpiece of the dispute, and once again, the administration came down on the side of NSA.

Like Otis Pike, Walsh never forgave the intelligence community, and specifically NSA. He viewed the Agency's conduct as part of a Reagan administration conspiracy to thwart the Iran-Contra investigation and free North, Poindexter, McFarlane and others involved in the operation. In his account of the investigation he discussed the forces arrayed against him: "If I had overlooked the invisible forces on Capitol Hill, I had also underestimated the power of the formidable departments and agencies responsible for national security. The national security community comprised the largest and most protected government entities, each with its own legal staff....We had not begun to address our greatest vulnerability, which derived from the national security community's power to overclassify information to prevent the full exposure of its misconduct." He never seemed to consider the inherent sensitivity of the source—to Walsh, it was all a smokescreen intended to hide malfeasance.

Chapter 26 The Year of the Spy

The Cold War topped off with a series of bizarre counterespionage incidents in the mid-1980s which served to increase mutual U.S.-Soviet paranoia. More newspaper ink was expended on these incidents than almost anything since Watergate. They came to be lumped into a convenient moniker, like Watergate: the "Year of the Spy." Like Black Friday, the term was not quite accurate in a technical sense—far more than just 1985 was involved, and far more than just agents were in question. But like Black Friday, the term stuck as a convenient shorthand. In most of these incidents, NSA was heavily involved.

Gunman

Of all the problems, the troubles with the new embassy building (termed the NOB, New Office Building) in Moscow appeared to be the least likely venue for NSA involvement. But appearances sometimes deceive, and embassy security was one of those cases. In fact, NSA had developed a certain technological expertise by virtue of its oversight of the Tempest emanations control program. This, combined with NSA's charter to establish standards for the protection of all COMSEC equipments, [censored] got NSA into the act.

NSA representatives began serving on a committee in the mid-1950s that dealt with this problem and began to assert both its expertise and authority in the area. [censored]

When, in the 1960s, the U.S. and the USSR arranged to build new chanceries, NSA was one of the first agencies to express reservations about the security of the U.S. building in Moscow. It had become well known in the early 1950s that the Soviets were inclined to bug anything in the U.S. embassy that they could get their hands on. The infamous bugging of the Great Seal (exposed in 1952) showed that they possessed sophistication beyond what would normally have been expected. In 1966, in commenting on the plans for the NOB in Moscow [censored] of NSA wrote to U.S. Ambassador to Moscow Malcolm Toon that "In past Soviet building activity concerning embassies it could be predicted that every attempt would be made to 'fix' the materials and the construction. Experience has shown that some of the fixes can only be found by extensive destruction. In the case of the Moscow site every attempt should be made to use U.S. building materials and construction personnel."

State did not follow the NSA advice. When construction of the NOB began in Moscow in 1979, the state-owned Soviet company was permitted to prefabricate concrete columns and other components off site, without American inspection. Meanwhile, the Soviets insisted that all components for their embassy in Washington be fabricated under the watchful eye of their own inspectors. Once on-site construction began, the Soviets used thirty security people to monitor an American work force of about 100 people, while in Moscow twenty to thirty Navy Seabees tried to watch six hundred to eight hundred Soviet laborers.

In the early 1980s people on Reagan's National Security Council became concerned about the hostile foreign intelligence threat in general and about the security of the Moscow embassy in particular. So in 1982 NSA sent a team of people to look at technical penetrations in the Moscow embassy. They found the chancery honeycombed with insecurities, [censored] NSA alerted the FBI, which did its own survey and confirmed the problems that NSA had found, plus others. [censored] teamed up with an FBI representative to brief President Reagan on the matter. The State Department, already suspicious of NSA "meddling" in embassy affairs, was reportedly unamused.

[censored]

The project, called Gunman, involved the removal of eleven tons of electronic equipment from the Moscow embassy—teletypes, printers, computers, crypto devices, copiers—almost anything that plugged into a wall socket. Every piece of equipment had to be replaced with the same or an upgraded model on a one-for-one swap-out. NSA's cover story was that the equipment was being shipped back to the States for an OSHA inspection.

NSA procured the replacement equipment from sources in the U.S. and Europe and packaged it for shipment in specially constructed boxes to Frankfurt, Germany, where it would be staged for shipment to Moscow. The boxes were equipped with special sensing devices that could detect any attempt at tampering. (At the Moscow end no such tampering was detected.) NSA logisticians loaded all eleven tons onto two chartered Lufthansa Airbuses. They were flown directly from Frankfurt to Moscow, where they were trucked on flatbeds to the embassy. They were then winched manually to the attic, which was the only area large enough to stage that much equipment. Then, as equipment was pulled from working spaces and trucked to the attic, new equipment was carted down the stairs to the working spaces.

The last items crammed into the boxes at NSA were fifty IBM Selectric typewriters. The typewriters were an afterthought. They were electric, and some of them did process classified or sensitive information, but this had been overlooked in the initial evaluation. A hurried inventory revealed about 250 of them in use in the embassy, but the IBM plant at Lexington, Kentucky, could spare only fifty, and NSA took them all. Said the NSA official in charge of the swap-out, "I had no targeting against typewriters....Had those typewriters not come [in time] from Lexington... I would have shipped without them without a wink..."

Back at NSA, a team of about twenty-five technicians worked around the clock to try to find bugs in the equipment taken from the embassy. Everyone was aware that the operation involved huge sums of money and had required presidential approval. NSA's reputation was literally on the line. Walter Deeley, the DDI, had personally pushed Gunman through to the

White House and in turn pushed his own people to lay out a maximum effort. But for two desperate months, nothing turned up.

Then they turned to the typewriters, a lower priority than the equipment that had come from the communications center. One evening in July Michael Arneson, a technician analyzing one of the typewriters, found a "ghostly gray" image on his x-ray film coming from the power cord. Immediately suspicious, he x-rayed the set from the top down. The x-ray images coming from the center of the set were cluttered and definitely nonstandard.

What Arneson had found was a sophisticated bug implanted in a structural metal bar that ran the length of the machine undercarriage. It consisted of sensing devices that picked up tiny fluctuations in current caused by the typewriter ball rotating as it selected the next letter to be typed. It drew its power by bleeding the power line (that was the "ghostly gray image" that Arneson first noticed) and stored the information for periodic burst transmissions to KGB receivers waiting in locations outside the embassy. The bug was undetectable using current technical survey equipment, and the modifications to the metal bar were imperceptible to routine examination. It could be found only by x-ray devices.

Technicians discovered ten bugged Selectrics in that first shipment. NSA immediately retrieved the Selectrics that still resided in Moscow (and in the consulate in Leningrad). Ultimately they found sixteen implants—but only in typewriters. They had been installed somewhere in transit (perhaps Poland or Moscow itself) as they awaited customs inspection. There was a rule that equipment to be used for processing classified information was to be shipped only in courier channels, but a small percentage had "escaped" and were shipped in regular shipping channels with office furniture. The KGB could easily identify candidate typewriters by finding those with Tempest modifications.

Bugged typewriters had been used in [censored] Others were in less sensitive areas, like the office of the [censored] but paradoxically it was that typewriter that yielded some of the best information. [censored]

NSA had additional information on the Soviet project. [censored] The entire thing amounted to a major penetration of the embassy.

Back in Washington [censored] backed up by an FBI representative, briefed President Reagan about the Moscow embassy situation. [censored] Although the President was supportive, NSA received little cooperation from State Department below the Shultz-Eagleburger level. The ambassador was reluctant to accept the Gunman discovery, and actions at the State Department end proceeded very slowly until the matter came to the attention of the press. In 1985, Walter Deeley was asked about State Department cooperation. In a statement uncharacteristically low-key, Deeley replied: "I guess I can tell you the bureaucracy was opposed to any operation in there." This visit began the eventual unraveling of the State Department defense of its own security practices, and it led eventually to the decision not to accept the new embassy building in downtown Moscow, an imbroglio with the Soviets that stretched well beyond the time frame of the Cold War.

[censored]

Probably no diplomatic problem was ever subjected to as many high-level investigative panels as the Moscow embassy. In 1985 the Reagan administration halted construction of the NOB and barred Soviet workers from the site. A panel headed by former NSA director Bobby Inman looked at embassy security worldwide, with special reference to the problems in Moscow. Inman was especially critical of the way State handled technical security issues. Two years later former Secretary of Defense Melvin Laird specifically examined the situation in Moscow. [censored] Finally, the PFIAB subjected the much-examined Moscow embassy to its own microscope and made recommendations concerning the improvement of the administrative arrangements for embassy security.

NSA recommended a "tiger team" approach to fixing the problems. The NSA plan would have established an interagency Protective Security Engineering and Evaluation Center that would monitor the situation and devise new solutions. It would need seventy-six people and just over $28 million per year. The proposal got active NSC support but opposition from State Department. After a long bureaucratic wrangle, it died. In the process, however, NSA's technical expertise in the detection of bugs had become generally recognized within and outside of government, and it was considered essential that expertise be employed in diplomatic protection. NSA's insistence on employing only Americans received full support. When the federal government set up new administrative arrangements for embassy security, NSA was asked to send representatives to virtually every organization. It was a mission that was a natural outgrowth of the Agency's expertise.

The technical penetration of the embassy had long-term effects on the way Americans did business in Moscow. Buildings were considered penetrated until proven otherwise. According to historian Michael Beschloss, in the late 1980s Ambassador Jack Matlock refused to type out messages on electric typewriters, assuming that the impulses would go straight to the KGB. He wrote his drafts in longhand.

Prime

From January of 1984 to the spring of 1987, twenty-eight people, almost all of them Americans, were accused of espionage against the United States. One slipped out of the grasp of the FBI, but the rest were arrested. Twenty-one pleaded guilty, and almost all received lengthy prison sentences. Of the seven remaining, all went to trial, and six were convicted. There were probably others who were never caught.

The first spy was not an American. He was Geoffrey Prime, a British linguist who worked for GCHQ from 1964 to 1977. Prime's case was of major importance to cryptology.

[censored]

[censored] But amazingly enough, he was at the time out of touch with the KGB, and apparently did not report to them again until 1980. Even then the KGB seemed slow to recognize what they had, and it was not until the following year, 1981, that they got a knowledgeable interrogator to debrief Prime on the operations.

But by that time Geoffrey Prime was no longer "in the know." He had resigned from GCHQ in 1977 without informing his Russian handlers. Prime seems to have become uninterested in both GCHQ and espionage and simply drifted away from the work. His official reason for leaving was a a dislike of lecturing, but that was a comparatively small part of his job. He did not like to supervise, and he did not get along with computers. The KGB did little to keep him engaged. GCHQ speculated in later years that Prime may have become tired of the mental stress of spying, and his private life was in a state of turmoil during the later 1970s. But no one really knew why he quit.

Prime was finally uncovered as a result of an investigation into allegations of a bizarre sex life, including pederasty. But the sex allegations eventually spread into espionage, and Prime pleaded guilty to both. In January of 1982 he was sentenced to three years on sex charges and thirty-six years for espionage.

[censored]

Pelton

On January 14, 1980, FBI surveillance recorded the following telephone call made to the Soviet embassy in Washington:

"First person: May I know who is calling?

Caller: I would not like to use my name if it's all right for the moment.

First person: Hold on, please. Sir?

Caller: Yes, um.

First person: Hold the line, please.

Caller: All right.

Second person: Hello, sir.

Caller: Ah, yes. I would—-

Second person: Ah, Vladimir Sorokin speaking. My name is Vladimir.

Caller: Vladimir. Yes. Ah, I have, ah, I don't like to talk on the telephone.

Sorokin: I see.

Caller: Ah, I have something I would like to discuss with you I think that would be very interesting to you.

Sorokin: Uh-huh, uh-huh.

Caller: Is there any way to do so, in, ah, confidence or in privacy?

Sorokin: I see...

Caller: I come from—I, I, I am in, with the United States government.

Sorokin: Ah, huh, United States government....Maybe you can visit."

A meeting was set up for the next evening, when it would be dark. But at 2:32 the next afternoon the caller phoned the embassy and said he would be there in two minutes, and abruptly entered the embassy. FBI surveillance was caught off guard, and managed only to get a picture of the mystery caller's back as he darted into the embassy grounds." (U) When the caller walked in, he was interviewed by the duty officer, who also happened to be a KGB colonel, Vitaly Yurchenko. Yurchenko did not know who he was dealing with, and the interview proceeded gingerly, until the caller pulled out an NSA Personel Summary and began discussing highly sensitive operations [censored] The mood changed abruptly. Yurchenko did not know enough about the technical aspects of NSA's work to proceed further, but he knew that he had a very valuable potential defector. He made elaborate arrangements to get the caller out of the embassy disguised as a Soviet workman, gave him $500 and instructions on how to establish the next contact. Yurchenko never saw him again.

Five years later, the same Vitaly Yurchenko appeared in Washington once again, but this time as a KGB defector. During the initial interrogations Yurchenko recalled the conversation with the mystery caller, whom he (Yurchenko) identified as a former NSA employee. [censored]

[censored]

Ron Pelton, then forty-five years old, had come into the cryptologic business in June of 1960, as a USAFSS Russian language intercept operator. After four years in the Air Force, he converted to an NSA civilian billet. Through his years with NSA, Pelton had become identified with collection technology and collection management. He had participated in some of NSA's most sensitive collection projects, but gradually drifted into jobs associated with cryptanalysis. By 1979 he was a very highly regarded staff officer Pelton had, in fact, written the manual describing those systems. He had served as a staff member on the Wagner Committee, which had worked on plans for Bauded Signals Upgrade. Given his grade level (GS-12), it was hard to imagine a more damaging defector.

Pelton possessed a nearly photographic memory and a gift of gab which marked him as a rising star in A5. But unknown to his management chain, he had also been operating on the margins of financial ruin. In the early 1970s he decided to house his family [censored] Without proper funding, he began building a large house on a five-acre tract in rural Howard County, Maryland, doing the work himself as he could scrounge the materials. Meanwhile, his family lived in squalor, [censored] But Pelton soon ran into financial difficulty, and in April of 1979 he filed for bankruptcy. He resigned from NSA the following July, evidently to improve his financial condition. Outside of NSA, Pelton failed at everything he tried, and without a regular paycheck his condition sank further. He tried marketing a product that was supposed to improve automobile gas mileage, but it didn't work, and he drifted from job to job in retail sales.

On October 23, 1985, just three days [censored] the FBI found Pelton living in an apartment in downtown Washington and working as a boat and RV salesman for Safford Yacht Sales in Annapolis. Previously religious and abstemious, he had undergone a complete personality change. He and his wife since 1961 were divorced, and Pelton was living with another woman. Financially, Pelton was doing better than at any time since his resignation from NSA, but the FBI quickly discovered that the two drank heavily and were deeply into drugs. They could be observed on frequent drug buys. The FBI initiated twenty-four-hour surveillance.

Yurchenko's information was old, and no one was sure if Pelton was still passing information to the Soviets. Then on November 4 Yurchenko redefected to the Soviet Union, and the FBI lost its only witness, were they to arrest Pelton and bring him to trial. Not only had they lost Yurchenko, but they had recently let former CIA agent and Soviet spy Edward Lee Howard slip through surveillance to escape to the USSR. With Yurchenko and Howard gone, could Pelton be far behind? The FBI threw a virtual blanket over Pelton—at one point over 200 agents were involved in the surveillance.

David Faulkner, the FBI agent in charge of the case, was afraid Pelton would flee the country, but had no evidence to hold him, unless Pelton himself gave it to them. Wiretaps (authorized by the Foreign Intelligence Surveillance Court) showed that Pelton and his girlfriend, Ann Barry, were into alcohol and drugs, [censored] But there was no evidence of contact with the USSR. So Faulkner, after a thorough workup on Pelton's character and personality, decided on a risky strategy. He rented rooms at the Annapolis Hilton and set one of them up as an interrogation room for him, Pelton, and a second agent Dudley "Butch" Hodgson. Then, at 0930 on Sunday, November 24, Faulkner called Pelton, who was at the yacht company office, identified himself, and asked Pelton to come to the hotel to talk to him on a matter of "extreme urgency" involving sensitive national security.

Once Pelton was in the room, Faulkner proceeded to detail the life of a hypothetical person, who clearly was Pelton himself. The two FBI agents also played the tape of the phone calls to the Soviet embassy in 1980. Pelton immediately understood that the FBI knew all about his espionage, but seemed to think that they wanted him to become a double agent. So, declining the offer to have a lawyer present, he proceeded to try to talk his way out of it, admitting obliquely that the person that Faulkner and Hodgson sketched was really himself. He admitted a lot—contacts with Soviets, trips to Vienna, payments of $35,000 plus expense money, all to secure the FBI's "cooperation.

By the end of the interview, Pelton so trusted the two agents that he gave up his passport to them and was permitted to go back to his apartment in Washington. But that evening Faulkner again called Pelton, who was by this time at his apartment, an asked him to come back for more questions.

During this second interrogation in Annapolis, Pelton placed an X on a map [censored] (His mark was off by a considerable distance.) Once Pelton admitted that what he had done would damage the United States (a key element in the evidentiary chain), Faulkner and Hodgson gave Pelton a waiver of rights, which he signed. Once they had his signature, they arrested him.

Pelton's "confession" told the FBI that he had several contacts with the Soviets in Washington and had met KGB interrogators at the Soviet embassy in Vienna, Austria, twice: once in 1980 and once in 1983. A third trip was planned in October of 1985, but Pelton missed his contact in Virginia in September, and made no further contact with the Soviets. In fact, by the time of his arrest he was trying to avoid them.

His first Vienna meeting had been very thorough, consisting of some forty-four hours of debriefing, but it was conducted by people who had no expertise in cryptology and was less productive. The 1983 meeting was conducted by a KGB handler who, although not an expert in cryptology, was highly skilled at interrogation. This time there was very little that Pelton did not tell them about his job. [censored]

Throughout, Pelton had been unhappy with the amount of his KGB payments, and he tried to drop contact following each meeting. He initially demanded $400,000, but in the end settled for $35,000 spread over five years. For him, spying was not very lucrative.

Ronald Pelton was the first spy that NSA took to court. In pretrial negotiations NSA worked gingerly toward a plea bargain, which was how all previous espionage cases had been resolved. But Pelton's defense lawyer, Fred Warren Bennett (who had also defended John Walker earlier in the year) advised Pelton to hang tough and go to trial. Bennett expected that the "confession," consisting of unrecordeds admissions to two FBI agents in a hotel room, would be thrown out. Without it, the government didn't have a case.

The trial was scheduled to begin on May 27, 1986. Preparations were lengthy and elaborate. The government had to establish the sensitivity and fragility of SIGINT, and had to reveal in open court SIGINT of value that Pelton had revealed to the Soviets. The Agency decided to put William Crowell, the chief of A Group, on the stand to tell the jury about SIGINT. [censored]

[censored]

The strategy worked. The judge allowed FBI agents to testify about Pelton's admissions in the hotel room, even though they did not amount to a signed confession. Crowell's testimony and cross-examination did not result in damaging revelations beyond those already agreed upon. In the end, the jury convicted Pelton on four of the six counts. Sentencing was left to the judge.

The trial was followed by a long interval before sentencing, agreed to in order to debrief Pelton on what he had told the Soviets. The carrot was the sentence: if he cooperated, the government would ask for a lighter sentence. The debriefing was done in a [censored] It lasted from July to December, and was excruciating. Without documents, it was a matter of dredging through Pelton's memory. [censored] NSA came away with information that it would never have thought to ask Pelton. One of the most jolting was the revelation that, before going to the Soviets, Pelton had tried to sell his wares to muckraking journalist Jack Anderson. Anderson took the information and published it, but never paid Pelton. Desperate for cash, Pelton then decided to contact the Soviets.

At the sentencing, the FBI indicated that Pelton had cooperated. But it wasn't sufficient. An outraged judge gave him the maximum sentence on all counts—three consecutive life terms plus ten years. He was remanded to Lewisburg Penitentiary in Pennsylvania.

Ronald Pelton was the most damaging cryptologic spy since William Weisband in the 1940s. [censored] It was a devastating blow, far exceeding anything that other, more famous spies like Aldrich Ames later gave to the Soviets.

But to the public Pelton was a minor spy, and today few Americans even remember who he was. This curious twist resulted partly from Pelton's own personality. He came across as a buffoon—haggard, stubbly chin, hang-dog expression. The press constantly referred to him as a minor functionary at a relatively low salary level, as if this somehow separated him from truly sensitive information. [censored]

The Pelton trial eventually became notorious for a sideshow—the Ivy Bells incident. This bizarre story overshadowed the trial itself, and became a cause célebre on the issue of First Amendment rights.

It began in December of 1985, soon after Pelton was arraigned in federal court in Baltimore. An alert newspaper reporter heard the name "Ivy Bells" being introduced by the defense lawyer, and it appeared in the newspapers the next day. An even more alert *Washington Post* reporter, Bob Woodward, picked up the reference and went to his editor, Benjamin Bradlee, with a proposal that the *Post* publish a story on Ivy Bells, an operation that Woodward had been tracking for years through his collection of various bits of journalistic exposé. But instead of approving the article for publication, Bradlee called the federal government.

The first meeting took place in the offices of the intelligence community staff on F Street in downtown Washington, on December 5. Bradlee attended, in company with Len Downie (the managing editor) and his lawyers. The principal for the government was General Odom, along with his own lawyer, Elizabeth Rindskopf, and the director of naval intelligence, Admiral Richard Haver. Bradlee outlined the story that Woodward had put together, and said that, since Pelton had told the Soviets all about the [censored] he could see no damage to national security. Odom replied that [censored] that publication could result in severe damage to national security. Bradlee scoffed at this and gave to the government team a synopsis of previous publications [censored] beginning with a *New York Times* article by Seymour Hersh in 1975, during the Church and Pike Committee hearings. Admiral Haver later summarized Bradlee's charge: "All of this indicates that the security of very sensitive information with the U.S. government is very poor, a fact that Mr. Bradlee finds most disturbing." But Rindskopf assured the *Post* that NSA did not intend to use Ivy Bells at trial except in a very general sense, and Bradlee agreed to withhold publication, at least until he could examine the trial transcript to see how much information the government revealed. Odom remarked later about Bradlee that "I found his behavior in that situation beyond reproach." And so the immediate threat receded.

But the story "had legs," as journalists like to say. The next April, with trial about to begin, Woodward put together a story on the Ivy Bells operation that would run concurrent with the trial. Scheduled to run on May 4, its publication was once again delayed after William Casey called Bradlee to protest. On the tenth, Ronald Reagan called *Post* publisher Katharine Graham, urging that portions of the article be deleted in the interest of national security. But he added ominously that, if the *Post* did not police itself, the Department of Justice might initiate prosecution under Section 798 of the criminal statute.

The issue remained secret until later in May, when NBC released a rather general story on Ivy Bells. Casey stated publicly that he was considering recommending prosecution of NBC under Section 798. But with the story already out, the *Post* decided the time was ripe for its own story. A newspaper that had published The Pentagon Papers and the Watergate story, both under threat of retaliation by the Nixon administration, was not likely to back down in this case, but Bradlee ultimately agreed to delete details of the story. He later said that fear of prosecution did not faze him, but national security did. "In my heart, I think the Russians already know what we kept out of the story. But I'm not absolutely sure of that."

Once again, Casey went to Justice with a request to prosecute and issued a public warning to news organizations not to publish "speculation" on sensitive national security issues. The warning related to material that was being revealed in the Pelton trial. But the DCI was out on his own limb. Justice Department lawyers were notoriously reluctant to prosecute news organizations in situations where first amendment rights could be at issue. In this case, they openly scoffed at the idea of prosecuting for "speculation."

The Pelton trial occurred at the tail end of military operations against Libya resulting from the La Belle Discoteque bombing. Government leaks in that case led to threats by Casey [censored] to prosecute news organizations that published the leaks. It also led the Reagan administration to threaten to polygraph everyone with access to "sensitive intelligence" (read primarily SIGINT), a threat that was derailed when Secretary of State George Shultz threatened to resign if anyone from his department were confronted with a demand to be polygraphed. Senator David Durenburger of the SSCI examined the issue from both sides and cast a pox on both houses. The Reagan administration had been a notedly leaky ship and had to tighten up if it were to have any credibility in the courtroom when prosecuting news organizations. But, on the other hand, news media seemed to have taken the wraps off. "...For whatever reason, there is a growing sense that there is nothing which is not fair game."

Walker

In the late 1960s, the KGB created a new organization. Called the Sixteenth Department of the First Chief Directorate (foreign intelligence), it was set up specifically to recruit and handle foreign code clerks who could provide cryptographic information. [censored]

[censored]

[censored] They still didn't know about John Walker.

In November of 1984, one Barbara Walker, then living in Maine, contacted the FBI about her ex-husband, John A. Walker, who was living in Virginia. John, she alleged, was a spy. Barbara Walker was an admitted alcoholic, and the FBI initially did nothing about her charges. But agents in the Norfolk office took her charges more seriously, and retrieved Walker's personnel file from the Navy. It was written in almost unintelligible Navy personnel language, and they needed an interpreter. The agent in charge of counterintelligence investigations in Norfolk had recently collaborated with a threat analysis office in NSA's COMSEC organization. He called his contacts at NSA and asked them to look at the Walker file. NSA's conclusion was that, if Walker were a spy, the United States had a big problem. John Walker had had access to a huge number of cryptographic keys and equipments.

The Bureau opened a full field investigation and got a court order to tap his phones. For some weeks it seemed that they were running aground, but then he began talking about an important meeting in the Washington suburbs. On the assumption that he would be going to a dead drop, the FBI deployed a huge tracking team.

On May 19, Walker drove north on I-95 to the Maryland suburbs of Washington. Once there, he proceeded along a serpentine route that had him driving to and fro for hours (the FBI estimated that the full route would have taken four hours) to the drop location on a country road outside of Poolesville, Maryland. There, just after 8:30 in the evening, by a telephone pole with a "No Hunting" sign on it, he deposited a package containing classified material. The FBI swooped down and picked it up as soon as he was out of sight. But when he proceeded to the Soviet drop location, there was no package there (which would have contained the Soviet payments for Walker's previous drop material). Puzzled, he drove back to his own drop location, which was the alternate location for the Soviet material. He found neither the Soviet payment nor the package he had so recently deposited there. He drove back and forth between the two locations several times, checking and rechecking. Then, puzzled and suspicious, he returned to his motel, a Ramada Inn in Rockville, Maryland, which he reached just before midnight.

At 3:30 A.M., an FBI agent posing as a motel desk clerk phoned Walker's room to tell him that his car had been hit and damaged and that he was needed downstairs. As Walker left the room he was confronted by two FBI agents, In the confrontation, all three drew their weapons—Walker dropped his first. The Bureau had just bagged the most damaging spy in American history.

Walker became Walkers, with Whitworth thrown in. It was not just a spy—it was an entire ring. Walker, a comm center operator and crypto technician when he had been in the Navy, had been supplying crypto key to the Soviets since 1968. Walker had recruited Jerry Whitworth, another Navy man in the same line of work, and when John Walker retired from the Navy in 1976, Whitworth continued to provide crypto material to Walker, who passed it on to the Soviets. He had recruited his brother, Arthur, and his son, Michael, and when arrested, John Walker was attempting to pass documents stolen from the Navy by Michael. The Walker ring had passed operational and technical documents to the Soviets. But more important, they had supplied crypto key for the KW-7, as well as several other devices, including the KW-37, KL-47, and KG-13.

The Walker operation was built around supplying used KW-7 key. Once a key had expired, the crypto security person (i.e., Walker) had seventy-two hours to destroy it. Walker (or Whitworth as the case may be) simply copied the key cards before destroying. Periodically (generally a matter of months), Walker would give the copied key cards to a Soviet agent using the dead drop procedure.

[censored]

The Soviet operation of the Walker ring was a textbook in how to handle an espionage ring, They assigned only their very best KGB agents to the case. These agents went to unprecedented lengths to keep the operation from exposure, and the instructions that Walker received to dead drop operations were breathtakingly detailed and precise. The FBI believed that at any given time, only three people in the Soviet embassy in Washington were cleared for the operation. In Moscow, only the agents supervising the operation and a few top KGB officials were in on the secret.

[censored]

Processing the take that was potentially available would have strained the resources of the best espionage organization. Vitaly Yurchenko claimed that the KGB had "thousands" of people exploiting the material, and decrypted over a million messages, but this has never been confirmed. [censored] He knew nothing of any other exploitation group. It is possible that only a fraction of the available material was exploited because of the inefficiencies inherent in the Soviet bureaucracy.

[censored]

These reforms were uncontroversial and relatively speedily accomplished. More divisive was the demand that the use of the polygraph be broadened. This reform was already being implemented within the military population at NSA when the Walker ring was exposed. But it undoubtedly reduced opposition to the polygraph in the wider armed services. NSA's Walter Deeley, the chief of Communications Security at NSA, informed the SSCI that he was reinstituting the crypto clearance, with its requirement for a non-lifestyle polygraph. His determination to force this despite doubt about his authority to do it on his own drew chuckles of admiration from the senators.

John Walker, the principal villain in the story, was paid over a million dollars by the Soviets. Jerry Whitworth received about $400,000, while the others received considerably lesser amounts. It is thus paradoxical that John Walker himself did not receive the longest prison sentence. In the days before his trial was to begin, he plea bargained to two concurrent life sentences plus ten years. Under the impenetrable mysteries of the federal sentencing guidelines, this means that he could theoretically get out of jail by age 75. His son pleaded guilty at the same time and received a twenty-five year sentence. Both agreed to cooperate with federal prosecutors.

John Walker's cooperation was most unhelpful to his former friend and compatriot Jerry Whitworth. Whitworth, receiving decidedly bad advice from a coterie of San Francisco lawyers, chose to go to court. Walker testified at Whitworth's trial and was a key factor in Whitworth's sentence of 365 years in prison and a $410,000 fine. Jerry Whitworth will die in prison.

Pollard

In September of 1979 the Navy hired a young Stanford graduate named Jonathan Jay Pollard to be an intelligence research specialist. Pollard was assigned to the Naval Intelligence Support Center (NISC) in Suitland, Maryland, where he was given a set of special clearances that would permit him to go to work. Included was access to SIGINT material.

In 1984 Pollard made contact with Israeli intelligence. He showed them samples of what he could provide, and they were interested. A flurry of meetings ensued, including trips to Paris and Israel. One of his contacts was Rafael Eitan, a legendary Mossad agent who had masterminded the capture of Adolf Eichmann and had headed the vengeance squad that tracked down and killed Palestinians who had participated in the 1972 Munich Olympics affair. Clearly, Pollard was regarded as a potential star in the espionage world.

Pollard was assigned to the antiterrorism alert center at NISC. His routine duties would thus give him access to information that Israel was interested in. But Pollard didn't stop at passive collection. He took a "shopping list" of desired information from his handlers and scanned DIA's computer databases for "hits." When he found something that looked interesting, he simply asked the relevant office for the document. He was rarely refused.

He accumulated documents quickly, and three times a week he put them into a briefcase and, using his courier pass, simply walked out with them. He batched the documents and once a week delivered them to a handler in a safe house in downtown Washington, D.C., not far from where Ronald Pelton lived. (They lived so close, in fact, that Pelton's girl friend noted surveillance, but decided that it was unrelated. It was FBI surveillance of Pollard.) There, the accountable documents would be copied so that Pollard could return the original; the rest they would not bother to copy. Once a month, Pollard made contact with his main handler, Joseph Yagur, who would evaluate the month's take and pay Pollard.

In September of 1985, Pollard's commanding officer at NISC, Commander Jerry Agee, learned that Pollard's computer searches had included excursions into some material unrelated to his job. Agee directed that a close watch be placed on Pollard. On October 25, a coworker reported to Agee that Pollard had apparently walked out of the building with classified documents. Surveillance of his activities became intense. A computer check showed that Pollard had acquired a huge number of documents on the Middle East, and a surreptitious search of his work spaces turned up none of them. At this point Agee called in Naval Investigative Service and the FBI.

The net closed on Monday, November 18. Pollard was arrested trying to leave NISC in his Mustang with a satchel full of classified documents. Interrogation continued off and on all week, as Pollard gradually admitted more and more facts about his espionage. On Thursday he tried to flee to the Israeli embassy but was refused admittance. The FBI finally arrested him outside the embassy. Pollard and his wife Anne, who was deeply involved in the espionage, were out of options. His handlers had fled the country, and Israel was disowning him. Naval and FBI agents had recovered large numbers of documents in his apartment. A full confession was in order.

The Pollard arrest on November 21 came only three days before the arrest of Pelton and overlapped the exposure of the Walker ring. It heightened the sense of betrayal during the "Year of the Spy."

[censored]

The Department of Justice legal team wanted to try Pollard, but State pleaded that the diplomatic embarrassment would be too great. Ultimately DOJ fashioned a plea bargain that worked. Jay Pollard pleaded guilty and was sentenced to life in prison. (But the terms of a life sentence have already allowed him to petition for parole, which has been denied.) In return, Anne Pollard was given only two concurrent five-year terms and is already out of jail. All along the Pollards maintained that their motivation was ideology. But they received $2,500 in cash monthly, had $30,000 per year going into a "retirement account," and were treated to lavish all-expense paid trips to Europe and flashy jewelry by their Israeli handlers. [censored]

Hall

James Hall, a young Army enlisted man, was assigned to INSCOM [censored] in 1983. Hall liked money, and in 1983 he contacted Soviet intelligence in Berlin. By this time he had become [censored] and he offered to share with the Soviets everything that he knew [censored] From February of 1983 to his reassignment to the US. in 1985, Hall did just that, in thirteen face-to-face meetings with his Soviet handlers, along with dead drops in various locations around Berlin.

Prior to his reassignment, Hall had contacted an East German intelligence agent, Hussein Yildirim, who headed the post auto shop. In order to supplement his already substantial income, Hall agreed to provide East Germany the same information that he was giving the Soviets.

During his year in the States, Hall continued to provide information to Yildirim, although the value was down because he was no longer associated with INSCOM. The Soviets also set up procedures for receiving Hall's information, but they were complex and difficult, and Hall chose to drop the association. Then, just a year later, he was back in Germany with 5th Corps and renewed his contacts with East Bloc intelligence. When he PCSed to Fort Stewart, Georgia, in 1988, he maintained contact with Yildirim, who moved to Florida to continue to work his contact with Hall. But by then the rigidities of the Cold War were beginning to crack, and an East German source identified Hall as one of their agents.

The FBI got Hall on a sting, in which one of their employees posed as a Soviet agent wanting to know what Hall had been providing to the East Germans. In a [censored] Hall essentially confessed to espionage. He was arrested and is serving a forty-year sentence at Fort Leavenworth. Yildirim, arrested the day after Hall, is serving life without parole.

Hall provided the Soviets and East Germans with "tradecraft" information. [censored] In return, Hall took away somewhere between $200,000 and $400,000. He was definitely in it for the money.

Carney

In the spring of 1990, [censored] that he had information [censored] It was an old lead; the spy had been active in the mid-1980s, but was no longer in the business. [censored] The information was fragmentary and conflicting, and it became bogged down. Then a second source identified the spy as one "Yens Carney." The FBI traced Yens Carney to one Jeffrey Martin Carney, a former Air Force German linguist then living in the Soviet sector of East Berlin.

Carney came from a difficult family background. He had dropped out of high school and had enlisted in the Air Force at seventeen. But he was extremely bright, and had been sent to German school, where he had gotten awards as the best German linguist in his class. [censored] This began a downward spiral in his Air Force work relationship. Carney became argumentative and difficult on the job. He also realized that he was homosexual, which led to an identity crisis. In the midst of this turmoil, the immature Carney, then only nineteen, made a sudden decision to defect to East Germany, and went to Checkpoint Charlie, where he made contact with the other side. They, however, convinced him to spy, and he remained on the job.

Carney began carrying a hidden camera in a Lipton Tea can. He collected miscellaneous documents while on burn detail and smuggled them out of the operations building. He met with his East German handlers every three weeks. In 1985 he PCSed to Goodfellow Air Force Base, where he continued to photograph documents. These he passed to his handlers during meetings in Berlin, Rio and Mexico City. But he became increasingly unstable and finally got his clearance pulled after an incident of uncontrolled rage with his supervisors. At that point Carney defected to East Germany through Mexico City and Cuba (the same route that Martin and Mitchell had taken in 1961).

He became a driver on the U-Bahn (Berlin's subway system) while continuing to work for East German intelligence. But he was in the wrong country. After the fall of the Berlin Wall it was not impossible to arrest spies, and Carney was arrested in April of 1991 outside his apartment. Brought back to the U.S. to stand espionage charges, he plea bargained for a twenty-five year sentence in exchange for his cooperation. He was debriefed, and NSA got a good picture of the damage. Fortunately, it was much less than it would have been had Carney worked within NSA.

[censored] They were both active in Berlin at the same time, one working in ASA, the other in ESC. They also worked for East German intelligence, although Hall passed information to the Soviets, too. Although neither had high-level information, [censored]

The Puzzle Palace

The 1982 publication of a book about NSA, *The Puzzle Palace,* by James Bamford, brought a new focus to the efforts of journalists and independent writers to break down the Agency's vaunted anonymity. *The Puzzle Palace* became the most significant breach in NSA's anonymity since David Kahn's *The Codebreakers* in 1967.

As a former NSG enlisted man, Bamford had participated directly in the cryptologic process. While still in the Navy he had volunteered to help the Church Committee during its 1975 investigations. The late 1970s found him out of the Navy and working in Boston as a part-time private detective. He had gone to law school, but had not taken (or had not passed) the bar exam. In 1979 he approached publisher Houghton-Mifflin with a proposal to do a book on NSA. The publisher accepted and gave him a $7,500 advance.

Bamford proposed a comprehensive description and history of the Agency, a task that had never been attempted. Public Law 86-36 had served as a useful barrier against this type of research, but Bamford proved to be cleverer than others. He began with a barrage of requests for information under the Freedom of Information Act (FOIA). Through this and a lot of poking through publicly available information, he accumulated a small but useful stack of documents. Then he hit the Mother Lode—a collection of documents that William Friedman had deposited at the George Marshall Library at Virginia Military Institute in Lexington, Virginia. Among the scattered remains of Friedman's lifetime accumulations were copies of the NSA Newsletter, addressed to "NSA Employees and their families." Bamford then submitted a FOIA for the entire collection, using as his rationale the offending phrase indicating that the information had been intended for dissemination to uncleared people. NSA succeeded in redacting portions using PL 86-36, but a disgruntled former NSA employee gave Bamford an almost complete collection which permitted him to fill in the redacted blanks.

During the Church Committee hearings of 1975, the attorney general had asked his staff to investigate the legal culpability of the various intelligence agencies. Bamford FOIA'ed the resulting document, and he got most of it from the Justice Department. (Justice did not inform NSA because, they reasoned, the investigation was still on-going, and they could not inform a possible target of the investigation.) The document, with some Justice redactions, contained a good deal of information about the NSA-GCHQ relationship, and served as the basis for Bamford's information on Second Party issues. During the ensuing negotiations between NSA and Bamford's lawyer, the government claimed that the documents had been improperly released and should be returned under threat of prosecution. The lawyer, veteran civil rights attorney Mark Lynch, invited Justice to do just that, but no case was ever brought.

Bamford knew how to get information. He drove through the NSA parking lot jotting down diplomatic license plates and checking known lists to see which countries maintained representatives at Fort Meade. He badgered retired NSA senior officials, including famed cryptanalyst Frank Raven, former head of NSA research and development Ray Tate, and former director Marshall Carter, for information, using as a wedge the information that he had already gotten from unclassified sources. Some pushed him aside, but others agreed to talk at length about NSA operations. Carter, for instance, talked with him for a day and a half at his retirement residence in Colorado Springs. All was technically unclassified, but it helped Bamford complete his mosaic. [censored]

James Bamford broke new ground in intelligence agency research, and his techniques were adopted by others seeking to investigate reclusive federal agencies. He did it all within the limits of the law—through attributable interviews, FOIA'ed documents, and meticulous research in public libraries and newspapers, not with classified documents provided by unnamed accomplices under cover of darkness. He "wrote the book" on how to put together a comprehensive picture of an organization that wanted no such comprehensive picture. [censored]

The single exception was the exposure of the relationship with the British. This was properly classified, and GCHQ was not amused. Bamford's lawyers turned out to be tough and determined, and the information stayed in the public domain. The release of classified material by, of all organizations, the U.S. Justice Department, left NSA non-plussed.

Bamford produced a book that was [censored] and a preoccupation with a lack of statutory controls on NSA. Like Jack Anderson's columns, the book—[censored]

The American Library Association Suit

Following publication of *The Puzzle Palace,* General Faurer sent NSA's [censored] to the Marshall Library to see where Bamford had gotten so much of his information [censored] discovered that an archivist had given Bamford access to sequestered portions of the Friedman collection. NSA re-sequestered the documents, and was challenged in court by Bamford's lawyer, Mark Lynch of the American Civil Liberties Union, acting on behalf of the American Library Association.

This time the law was on NSA's side. Since the early negotiations with Lynch over the FOIA'ed Justice Department records, President Reagan had signed a new executive order, 12033, which permitted publicly available documents to be withdrawn if it could be shown that they had been improperly declassified. NSA's argument was supported by the U.S. District Court of Appeals in 1987, which dismissed the case against NSA and ruled that the plaintiff, the American Library Association, lacked standing.

Epilogue

On November 9, 1989, the East German government announced that its citizens could leave the country without special permission. Within hours, jubilant crowds were surging through the formerly impenetrable Berlin Wall, to be greeted by their West German countrymen. The crowds sang and danced that night. They hacked at chunks of the infamous Wall, and swirled through the Brandenburg Gate. It was liberation day.

November 9 was the culmination of both long- and short-term events. Such imponderables as the inherent weaknesses of Marxism and the latent inefficiencies of the Soviet state moved glacially, but they eventually produced Gorbachev, a man who recognized the situation and tried to reform it. *Glasnost* and *perestroika* (openness and economic restructuring) were the pillars of his reform program.

But short-term events overtook socialist reform. It was not necessary for the Soviet government to invent a new form of socialism—a dandy economic model glittered just across the Iron Curtain in Western Europe. Encouraged to devise their own socialist economic models, Hungary and Poland moved quickly. In East Germany, Eric Honecker, the long-time Communist Party boss, thumbed his nose at reform, and got in return unrest and agitation. Agitation turned into street demonstrations in August.

Gorbachev withdrew Soviet support for more repression, and without this guarantee the East German authorities could no longer contain the population. In October, Gorbachev personally told Honecker that the Soviet forces in his country would not come to his rescue. Honecker, sick with gall bladder cancer, knew the end was near.

So the end of the Cold War swept in like a sudden storm, leaving prognosticators dazed. It happened so fast and went so far that it would take a breathless world some considerable time to assess the event.

For the cryptologic community, it was a new beginning. Nothing like it had happened since the end of World War II. Major target countries disappeared literally overnight. Foreign relationships changed, and former enemies became new Third Parties with scarcely an intervening day.

But from a historical perspective, it was also an ending, a milepost in the course of history. The bipolar world had defined American cryptology for forty-four years. It was now over, and it was time to write the history.

15248583R00268

Printed in Great Britain
by Amazon